Readings in
Psychology
for the
Teacher

DENNIS CHILD is Professor of Education at the University of Newcastle upon Tyne. A Fellow of the British Psychological Society and a university representative on the Executive of the University Council for the Education of Teachers, he holds degrees from London, Leeds and Bradford Universities. He is the author of many articles, research papers and the widely acclaimed book *THE ESSENTIALS OF FACTOR ANALYSIS*, and he was active in the preparation of the ATCDE report *FACILITATING RESEARCH IN COLLEGES OF EDUCATION*. With Professor R.B. Cattell of the University of Illinois he has collaborated to produce the book entitled *MOTIVATION AND DYNAMIC STRUCTURE*. His current research interests include organization and achievement in junior schools, thinking styles, motivation and personality.

Readings in Psychology for the Teacher

Dennis Child

Professor of Education
University of Newcastle upon Tyne

Holt, Rinehart and Winston
London · New York · Sydney · Toronto

Preface

This Reader was put together at the request of students and teachers who wanted a companion text for *Psychology and the Teacher*, a third edition of which, revised and updated with new material, is now available. Many of the references in *Psychology and the Teacher* are popular and so much sought-after that they are often difficult to obtain. It seemed entirely justified, therefore, to gather crucial articles together under one cover in order to give students and teachers an opportunity to see the range of primary sources and specialist writings which supplement the generalizations inevitable in a textbook.

Highly technical papers have been avoided although a few of the papers included contain simple statistics. In some cases a paper has been written especially for the Reader (the article on self concept and academic achievement by Dr R. Burns, for example). Where the discourse is contentious, opposing points of view have been juxtaposed, as in the chapter on examinations and in the Chomsky–Skinner debate on the origins of language behaviour.

The readings are organized in such a way that those references designated in the core text by a bold **R** (for Reader) may be found here under the relevant subject heading. For example, reference 22**R** in chapter 2, John McFie, 'Factors of the brain', is included in the Reader under Part 2, 'The nervous system'.

In view of the number of topics that must be included, only a selection of references for each has been possible, and in some cases only those parts of a paper germane to the core text have been reproduced. Three centred asterisks indicate that a portion of the original material has been omitted, and references given in omitted material, unless they appear elsewhere in the text, have been deleted from the references list at the end of these articles.

Whilst the first intention was to compile a companion Reader for a particular textbook, it is hoped that the diversity and adequacy of the selections will satisfy the needs of students in other, similar disciplines; those studying education principles with an element of psychology for the Diploma in Higher Education, for example, or social science students requiring introductory material for a psychology course or, indeed, beginning psychology students.

The Reader's specialist papers may be seen as a starting point for discussion, in-depth study or small-scale projects and one of its most attractive features in these days of ever-growing syllabuses and financial restraints must surely be that it constitutes the cheapest way, in terms of time, effort and money, of assembling relevant literature and using it at leisure.

I am indebted to all the contributors and their publishers for permission to reproduce their work. Acknowledgements are given at the end of each article in the text.

School of Education   *Dennis Child*
University of Newcastle upon Tyne
September 1976

Contents

Contents

PART 1

Psychology and education

INTRODUCTION

The possibility of studying human behaviour scientifically has concerned psychologists from the earliest days of the discipline. Richer, whilst not attempting to resolve the problem, points to a distinction in the way we might view human experience and consequently the way in which we might observe it. He talks of D-type (Demonstration) and N-type (Negotiation) agreements between people giving rise to two types of psychology. The *public* life of each individual is possible because there are phenomena about which some degree of concordance can be recognized. The features of agreement can be publicly demonstrated and this kind of agreement is critical to the sciences. But the human sciences have an additional burden to contend with; that is the private and emotional life – 'feelings' and 'intentions' – which can only be shared at second hand. Agreement can be reached by negotiating and trying to share the experience.

Two broad traditions stem from the distinction drawn above. One is the behaviourist tradition, interested essentially in the scientifically explorable D-type phenomena. The other is the realm of the introspectionist, psychoanalyst or humanist interested more in N-type phenomena.

When it comes to putting psychological findings of either the D or N variety to the test as an aid to educationists, the contemporary literature is abundant with doubts and misgivings. Glaser comes down strongly in believing that the conventional wisdom and findings of psychology have a role to play and he chooses examples to demonstrate his point – but

1

contrast this with the writing of Ausubel, a theme taken up again in Part 16. Glaser recognizes the flaws in attempting to relate theoretical and laboratory findings to practical situations. In concentrating on individual differences in the social sciences we have tended to undervalue the multitude of settings within which these differences can be expressed. Glaser illustrates his points using several areas covered in the core text such as curriculum processes, human abilities, testing and evaluation.

1   Two types of agreement – two types of psychology [*]

JOHN RICHER

I want to advance the thesis that there are, from a logical point of view, two types of psychology. One lies within the broad tradition of science, the other does not but can be a valid and useful exercise if there is a proper awareness of its nature. I believe that the distinctions I shall make are not new, and that they have echoes in the writings of many psychologists and philosophers. However, I hope to clarify these distinctions, say why they must exist, and precisely how they divide psychology into two.

One of the many reasons why psychology has made so little progress and is not held in high regard either by other scientists or by lay people is that psychologists have failed to comprehend fully this essential dualism in their subject and so have not acted accordingly. Yet this low opinion is not totally deserved, since psychology (and related 'human sciences') are faced with a dilemma not encountered by the other sciences. The dilemma is that the psychologist is faced with two worlds, two realities – the public and the private. The subject matter of physics, chemistry, biology and so on is unmistakably public phenomena. This is not to say that the *search* for knowledge in these fields is objective (how could it be?); it is intuitive and imaginative. But the subject matter and final arbiter of disagreements are public phenomena – things which two or more people can observe. The vital *agreements* in these fields take the basic form, 'Yes, that is the case'.

Psychology is not in this happy position, for there is another type of reality which is very relevant to our study of man – the reality of private states. It seems necessary to describe thoughts, intentions, feelings, etc., to get at a complete description of human beings. That this might not be a hopeless exercise is reinforced by (i) the accuracy and ease with which we seem able to infer the intentions, feelings, etc., of others, and (ii) the way these private states seem embodied in the language and other artifacts of the group so that they almost seem

---

[*] This was the slightly revised second part of a discussion paper presented to the Developmental Section meeting at Birmingham University in September 1974. The title of the discussion was 'Ethology or Observation?', which I took, not very confidently, to mean: what is the difference between ethology and psychology? Although I dislike the demarcation disputes which such questions might engender, I attempted to unravel a few of the basic differences of logic and approach between the two disciplines.

public property. The study of man, some might argue, must include the study of feelings, intentions, etc., as well as behaviour and when and where it occurs.

Yet can we come to the *same sort of agreement* about private states as we can about public phenomena? Some, for instance Sullivan (1974), imply we can, since our experience of public events is unique like our experience of private events. Each of us has thoughts just as each of us sees behaviour, and we can communicate the nature of these thoughts, just as we can communicate the nature of behaviour – by the use of language.

I would argue that the *agreement* we can come to over private states is not the same as the agreement we come to over public phenomena – is not of the basic form 'Yes that is the case'. I would argue that its basic form is something like 'Yes we shall do that with this'. The first sort I shall call *D-type agreements* since it is possible to agree after a *Demonstration* of the phenomenon; the second I shall call *N-type agreements* since they come after a *Negotiation* (Fig. 1.1).

```
Agreement:           D-type         N-type
Arrived at after: Demonstration     Negotiation
Basic form:          Yes, that is the   Yes we shall do
                     case.              that with this.
Basic tense:         Present/past.      Future.
```

Figure 1.1.   Two types of agreement.

In science there are, of course, many N-type agreements; people agree to classify certain things together, agree that certain ideas imply certain things, and, of course, agree that the words of ordinary language mean certain things. However, scientists feel that if they cannot come, at some point, to a D-type agreement, then they are not doing science or rather, and more importantly, they are not on their way to finding out useful and interesting things about the (public) world. Even if two scientists disagree how to explain, say, the different patterns produced when light of different colours shines through a diffraction grating, they will not differ, given comparable precision of their experiments, about the patterns themselves; at least they can come to D-type agreements about the patterns.

On the other hand, let us suppose that two people, A and O, are discussing the feelings of one of them, A, the agent. An important aspect of the discussion will be A's introspected state. This is not available to O, the onlooker, who only has what A says and does to go on. If A's private states are taken into account, then it is impossible, in principle, for A and O to come to a D-type agreement on A's feelings, since part of the evidence is denied to O. This is *not* to say that O cannot say what A is feeling and A agree with him, or even that O cannot persuade A that, far from feeling what he (A) thought he felt, he was in fact feeling something else.

This dualism is embodied in the words we use to describe feelings, intentions, etc. Implicit in the meaning of the word fear, for instance, is not only how it feels to be afraid, but how it looks. There is both the agent's and the onlooker's view, both private and public phenomena. [In the meaning there must of course be public phenomena if the word is to have any (shared) meaning.]

Private states are the other reality confronting psychology. They have not bothered the other sciences, only the 'human sciences' They have not even seriously impinged upon subjects like ethology where the animals and phenomena studied overlap considerably with psychology. Ethology started, of course, by studying geese, gulls, sticklebacks, bees and so on. Now whilst bees talk to each other, they do not talk to us. We are not under much pressure to acknowledge and study their private states, so ethologists have operated within the broad scientific tradition and their basic data, behaviour and when and where it occurs, can be agreed upon in a D-type way.

Psychologists have not been so lucky since they started out studying man. This is not to say that there is anything intrinsically different between men and other animals except that we, you and I, are men (and women), so we have the 'inside view'. Nor does this imply that we do not ascribe feelings, intentions, etc., to dogs, cats, horses and budgerigars; we do. But as scientists we do not feel under much pressure to study them, whereas we do in the case of man. Why we do is partly that animals do not talk back to us, and partly again that we are, in everyday life, very good at ascribing private mental states to others; we seem to be very accurate, it is very useful and we do it naturally. We often say we know another person's mind. Trevarthen (1974) and others have called this 'intersubjectivity'. Since we are so good at this, and since it seems so useful, why should we not study private states scientifically?

The answer, I suggest, is that although they can be studied we shall, in such studies, be stepping outside the scientific tradition since there will be vital areas where D-type agreements would be necessary but impossible (since they would concern private states).

How then do we come, as we do, to agreements about private states? It has been suggested that these agreements are negotiated, they are N-type agreements. The meanings of words, and other symbols are, as Harré and Secord (1972), Newson (1974) and Shotter (1974) have asserted, negotiated. We negotiate shared meanings. Harré and Secord (1972) assert that the major phenomenon in social psychology is meanings and these are generated by the agency of people – by agents.

N-type agreements are fundamental in one of the two types of psychology. This type treats people as free agents who negotiate shared meanings with each other, and who, being capable of free choice, are essentially, in these terms, unpredictable. A meaning is what people make it, and as such exists only as long as people continue to agree to its existence. But an agreement can be broken at any time, by individuals (Humpty Dumptys) or the group merely deciding to. D-type agreements cannot be broken like this.

The study of meanings is, as Shotter (1974) rightly says, a Moral and not a Natural science. It studies people as free moral agents and not as biological phenomena. This is a consistent logical position to adopt, I believe, but it is not within the broad scientific tradition, and it is necessarily a never ending study, since it contains built-in unpredictability. People, as free moral agents, can change meanings at any time. This is not to say that human behaviour is essentially unpredictable, but if we allow private states as proper 'objects' of study, if we allow meanings in the sense of what something means to an individual himself (as opposed to asking what some piece of behaviour means), if we study people in these terms, then we build in unpredictability, because we can never come to D-type agreements about crucial aspects in our investigations, namely meanings.

The psychologist studying private states and meanings in this sense is a little like a fashion reporter. He is constantly trying to catch up with the latest fashion – the latest meanings. In addition, just as the fashion writer can influence fashion, so the psychologist's results, new ideas, new meanings, may well influence what he is studying. (This applies to more scientific psychology too, but to a lesser extent in practice since its terms are usually less accessible to lay people.)

Although this endeavour is not science in its traditional sense, it is a valid exercise. It is after all what writers, artists and philosophers have been doing for a long time – reinterpreting people to themselves (they do other things too, of course).

So I am suggesting there are two types of psychology. One is within the broad scientific tradition which studies behaviour and when and where it occurs, and which is not clearly demarcated from physiology. The other is within the tradition of the humanities and studies private states, mental phenomena, verbal reports, agency, meanings, feelings, intentions and the like. This dualism, and perhaps the recognition of it, is as old as psychology, with, for instance, the introspectionists and psychoanalysts on one side and the behaviourists on the other. But problems have arisen and progress has been retarded because the divisions have not been clearly drawn. So psychologists on the one hand try and measure the people's answers to questions about their private states (all right for market research on soap-flakes or voting intentions, but no good for more permanent and fundamental research). On the other hand, behaviourists study things like emotions whose identification in everyday life is a matter of negotiation, and because of the way they do it they end up with one of two absurdities. Either (i) they say such and such a behaviour is a 'measure' of the emotion, without, of course, being able separately to identify the emotion, or (ii) they operationally define the emotion in terms of a very narrow range of behaviours and situations and this way lose all relevance and generality, but they craftily slip back into talking about the emotion in general when all they have observed is a change in rate of bar-pressing, so the behaviour just becomes a 'measure' of the emotion again.*

These problems, especially the lack of relevance, are also partly an outcome of the so-called experimental method. This is the method of having a theory first and *then* trying to find phenomena to fit it. Failing to have an explanation for something is an everyday problem, but failing to have something to explain, yet having an explanation all the same (of what?) is a bizarre state of affairs. The whole enterprise fails because psychologists, as many have said (e.g. Tinbergen, 1963), have not observed people in their everyday environments to any appreciable extent, and so have no ('real' or 'natural') phenomena to explain. It is no wonder that a lot of psychology has been derided as astonishingly irrelevant to ordinary human behaviour.

Yet this lack of direct observation is understandable, I think, for are we not, after all, surrounded by people every day? Do we not have an intimate knowledge of what people do, feel and think? Are we not extremely skilled at getting on with our fellow human beings and predicting and adapting to them? Yes, of course. Yet this knowledge is not the sort of knowledge we need, and get, from direct observation of behaviour, and here I return to my dualism. We ordinarily observe people in terms of their feelings, intentions, etc.; this is how we see them. It produces a practical, 'technical', knowledge used in getting on with people, it embodies the logic of the agent, the person who *does* things. We do not ordinarily observe people in terms of limb movements, facial expressions, spatial orientation and so on – in the terms of the onlooker who does not react. Yet it is precisely this latter sort of data that we

---

* Ethologists admittedly use terms like aggression, fear, etc., but these are 'defined' in terms of all or most of the relevant behaviours seen in everyday (natural) situations, i.e. the 'definition' is both relevant and in terms of observable behaviour and situations.

need for a scientific study of man. This type of psychology, which, if given an evolutionary perspective, would be the same as the ethological study of man, is still in its infancy. The other type of psychology, the study of meanings, etc., is well advanced. We are all, lay people as well, to a greater or lesser extent psychologists in this sense. Some of us, including professional psychologists, get paid for it and we should be better at it than lay people. I hope we are, but I doubt it.

ACKNOWLEDGEMENT

This article first appeared in *Bull. Br. Psychol. Soc.* (1975), **28**, 342–345, and is published here with the kind permission of author and editor.

REFERENCES

Harré, R. & Secord, P. F. (1972) *The Explanation of Social Behaviour*. Oxford: Blackwell.
Newson, J. (1974) Towards a theory of infant understanding. *Bull. Br. Psychol. Soc.*, **23**, 251–257.
Shotter, J. (1974) The development of personal powers. In M. P. M. Richards (Ed.), *The Integration of a Child into a Social World*. London: Cambridge Univ. Press.
Sullivan, L. (1974) Behaviourism re-viewed. *Bull. Br. Psychol. Soc.*, **27**, 352–364.
Tinbergen, N. (1963) On the aims and methods of ethology. *Z. Tierpsychol.*, **20**, 410–433.
Trevarthen, C. (1974) Intersubjectivity and imitation in infants. (Paper read at BPS Annual Conference.)

2   Educational psychology and education*

ROBERT GLASER

Psychologists, particularly educational psychologists, are being asked more frequently than ever before what their discipline can offer to education. They have, in the past, responded in either of two ways. One answer has been that psychology is a young science; that we psychologists need more time to work at discovering facts and building theory; and that, at the moment, we are not able to be very helpful to education. A second answer has been that psychologists have identified certain principles that can be applied to practical settings for in-

*This article was the presidential address to the Division of Educational Psychology, presented at the annual meeting of the American Psychological Association, Honolulu, Hawaii, September 1972. Preparation of this article was carried out under the auspices of the Learning Research and Development Center at the University of Pittsburgh, supported in part by funds from the Office of Education, U.S. Department of Health, Education and Welfare. The opinions expressed in this article do not necessarily reflect the position or policy of the Office of Education and no official endorsement should be inferred.

dividual and public good, and that our need is to train practitioners who can use these principles properly. These two answers were prevalent modes of response some years ago, but it is now apparent that they are no longer the most appropriate responses for either building theory or improving education. Basic researchers are recognizing the need for investigating problems of real-world complexity, and those interested in the application of knowledge now perceive the need for assessing the effective range of the phenomena that can be encompassed by present principles and the necessity for feedback from applications to research.

Many sciences have shown tremendous progress as a result of attempts at application, and a stance for the application of psychology to education seems quite clear at this time. The behavioral and social sciences are at a point in their development where they absolutely require the direction and disciplining effects that come from contact with real-world problems. Fortunately, this is more possible than ever in the light of the growing openness of society toward innovation and experimentation. What knowledge and theory have been accumulated now need the elaboration and correction that can result from such engagement. The sequence from basic research, to applied research, to development, to practice and application on which most of us were weaned is no longer applicable if, in fact, it ever was. A stance that seems required for scientific and social progress in our field has been described by E. E. David (1972) as follows:

It is essential that the impact of science on society be viewed not as a linear progression from the discovery of knowledge to technology, leading to innovation and new products and services, but as a complex set of mutually dependent matters. The linear progression is a simplistic one. It should be axiomatic that technology feeds on science, but it has never been made fully clear that science, in turn, feeds on technology and is often invigorated by goal-oriented enterprises. In fact, the coupling between these two once-disparate elements is far closer than many of us ever realized in the past. This close coupling of science and technology, and the feedback system it implies, carries with it a self-correcting mechanism. Failures in technology often encourage fundamental science [p. 13].

It is this interactive mode of operation between application, technology, and basic science which I would like to encourage for educational psychology. It is certainly not the only mode by which we may care to do our work. I cannot for a moment deny the importance of undirected basic research. Nor can I deny the importance of the intuitive design of educational practices by outstanding teachers. Good practice has an artistry and intuition which must not be restricted and which may far outrun any momentary attempts at definitive understanding and analysis. Ideally, our job as educational psychologists is to work within these two extremes, contributing to knowledge and practice and trying to understand both without inhibiting either.

There is a growing number of individual researchers and research and development groups beginning to work in this interactive mode. I have been engaged in one of these enterprises for some years now. Our main concern, in addition to conducting specific research and development tasks, has been to discover how the interactive mode best works in educational and psychological research: how a research and development organization should relate to schools and school systems, how it should relate to research in the sciences and disciplines relevant to education, what kinds of problems appear to be most valuable to work on, and what kind of developments to pursue that might influence school practices. Influenced by this experience, I propose in this article to sample some areas in elementary school education to which educational psychology can offer its services and through which the requirements of educational practice can press for improvements in educational psychology. As a sampling, I will mention four areas: subject-matter learning, the teaching of basic abilities and aptitudes, adaptation to individual differences and testing and measurement.

SUBJECT-MATTER LEARNING

One educational objective central to the elementary school is subject-matter learning. Basic literacy is an obvious goal, and it is a priority of an educational system to insure that all of its children acquire fluency in the skills that dominate their lives. In subject-matter learning, the design of teaching methods and analysis of curriculum content have been continuing educational tasks. Large curriculum projects have been launched in order to make the content of school materials as coordinate as possible with the latest organizations of knowledge by leading individuals in a subject-matter field. This work has been eminently successful in assuring that schools do not continue to live with outdated knowledge. However, from the experience of these projects, it is quite clear that another dimension is necessary if this work is to have the significant impact that it can have on the effective transmission of the knowledge and intellectual skills that comprise subject-matter literacy. This dimension involves study of the psychological processes that underlie the learning, retention and skillful, creative performance of what is learned. For example, while there has been much analysis of the content of the mathematics curriculum, there has been much less investigation of the fundamental nature of mathematical thinking, the acquisition of mathematical concepts and the conditions of practice required for the retention and effective use of mathematical skills. Forced by this concern, there is much useful work currently being reported on the learning of quantitative concepts in children, the analysis of problem solving in mathematics and the conditions of drill and practice in computational skills. This work needs to be joined together with curriculum design so that effective instructional strategies can be developed and studied.

Task structure in a curriculum

In this regard, I would like to consider briefly one aspect of the relationships among subject-matter structure, curriculum content and instructional design. The relationship I wish to mention can be seen by making a distinction between the structure of a subject-matter domain as it is organized by scholars studying that domain and the structure that is devised for teaching the knowledge or skills that comprise it. The structure of a subject-matter discipline, as employed for the purpose of advanced scholarship, consists of theories, concepts and definitions that serve to make the domain manipulable for the work of subject-matter experts. However, the structures employed for this purpose are not necessarily the most useful for facilitating the learning of an individual at a less advanced level of development or subject-matter sophistication. Good theory for the scholar may not be good pedagogical theory; what is epistemic, that is, what leads to knowledge, for the expert, may not lead to knowledge for the novice or help him to develop competence. It follows that a significant consideration for instructional design is the organization of curriculum sequences that provide knowledge structures optimally organized for moving the novice toward expertise.

Bruner (1966) made the point some years ago when he wrote that 'a theory of instruction must specify the ways in which a body of knowledge should be structured so that it can be most readily grasped by the learner [p. 41].' The merit of a structure depends on the extent to which it facilitates instruction by optimizing such criteria as speed of learning, the extent to which the learner generates new propositions and manages subsequent learning, the extent to which information is simplified for comprehension and memory and the extent to which it is related to the talents and background of the learner.

Appropriately designed structures for learning can reduce the amount of information that must be held in mind to comprehend the subject matter, for example, a verbal label, a conceptual formulation, or a formula or a principle which helps to organize and summarize a large number of observations. Some ways of remembering may permit better memory retrieval than other ways and, as a result, the capacities of the learner can be extended by facilitating retention, thus allowing easier access to and manipulation of information for thinking and problem solving. Good pedagogical structures also can facilitate the learner's capacity to generate new information or learn new things on the basis of what he has already learned. Consider, for example, a student learning to spell or to draw without being taught any spelling rules or rules of perspective. The student learns, but says 'I can do it, but I don't understand what I'm doing.' The student's uneasiness in the matter arises because he has not learned the theory or rule that will enable him to generalize his skills to other tasks of the same kind. Knowledge of the rules and concepts involved (perhaps not always verbalized) would allow him to transfer to new variations and remember better what he has mastered, since the general rule codes and prompts the act of spelling and drawing. The rule can be thought of as a structure or representation by which an individual is directed or directs himself to look at the relevant features of what might otherwise be an unorganized task situation. As a consequence, a student can generalize across the superficial details of the limited set of experiences encountered in instruction (Gilbert, 1962).

The organization of subject-matter content can do for the learner what advanced theory does for the expert. It can facilitate remembering and supply generative power. Such theories, however, are not readily available, but are devised by ingenious teachers and built by them into instructional procedures. The nature and design of these theories or pedagogical structures are a unique province of study for educational psychology. The general point is that while we have usually thought in terms of fitting learning to how knowledge is organized, we need also to think in terms of organizing knowledge to fit learning (Bruner, 1968). Analysis of the structure and sequence of school subject matters has been a continuing concern of educators and now should become of increasing concern to those interested in the psychological analysis of instruction.

BASIC APTITUDES AND ABILITIES

Another component of the elementary school curriculum that demands study is what has been called readiness skills, that is, the perceptual and cognitive processes and concepts that are basic to subject-matter learning and fundamental to subsequent effective learning and performance. Examination of many programs of early education which attempt to teach reading, arithmetic and related subjects at earlier ages than usual indicates that there is a whole series of preparatory skills and concepts that may need to be taught in order to make subject-matter learning successful and efficient. In fact, it may make little difference exactly what subject matters comprise the content of early instruction; the basic objective may be to employ that subject matter or those materials and environmental settings that are most suitable for teaching basic cognitive abilities (Rohwer, 1971).

An obvious rationale for teaching these basic aptitudes evolves from observation of the differential sets of talents with which children from different backgrounds enter pre-school and the first grade. Children from certain kinds of family backgrounds have a learning history that results in capabilities well matched to the typical school environment even if the parents have made no conscious effort to teach them. Children from other kinds of backgrounds appear not to have had the opportunity to learn these capabilities. This repertoire of abilities includes such performances as the following: perceptual discriminations that allow children efficiently to scan and categorize new visual and auditory stimuli, spatial and temporal concepts that permit orientation to objects and events in time and space, the ability to recognize and focus attention on relevant aspects of a learning situation, a linguistic competence that facilitates learning from verbal exposure, the ability to use examples as a way of learning new concepts and the ability to ask questions to gather new information (Resnick, 1967). A six-year-old who has these skills and concepts is said to be ready to begin school, and the problem of early education is how to create an educational environment that will maximize this readiness to begin school for children from all kinds of home backgrounds. From a research and development point of view, the implementation of such a program can be an application of current theories that view intelligence and aptitude as learned and responsive to experience.

A basic question is how theory and knowledge of learning and of developmental processes can be used to design procedures for optimizing this early learning. In regard to this task, certain polarities exist with respect to underlying theoretical conceptions and the instructional practices that they indicate.* A key question is whether education should be concerned with the design of total learning environments or with the development of specific teaching components. Most work concerned with optimizing learning has focused on strategies of lesson design, that is, on determining efficient ways of teaching specific learning objectives such as instructional sequences, stimulus conditions and feedback conditions. In contrast, many developmental psychologists have focused attention on the design of total environments that would foster learning of the various kinds considered appropriate to the pre-school and early primary years. For example, earliest compensatory education efforts focused on providing an environment for the disadvantaged child that would replicate key features of the middle-class home. The differences between environmental design and direct instruction have centered largely around two points: (i) whether instructional exchanges should be primarily child or primarily teacher initiated and (ii) whether instructional intervention should take place throughout the child's time in school or only during specified (and relatively brief) periods.

It has been argued, largely on the basis of Piagetian stage theory, that a critical aspect of instructional design is finding a way of matching new cognitive demands to the child's current level of competence. The implication is that, in the absence of detailed scientific knowledge concerning optimal matches of instruction to development, permitting children to choose their own tasks from among a variety available to them may be the most effective

---

* For detailed references relevant to this section, see Glaser and Resnick (1972).

procedure. The Montessori program is pointed to as an example of a workable model of such free choice by children. A number of early education models have also stressed free choice of tasks and, concomitantly, intrinsic motivation for performing these tasks. One of the effects of the emphasis on free choice and intrinsic motivation is a concern with designing a total environment in which the tasks available and environmental responses to the child are those that will optimally foster learning. To date, no comparisons of free choice versus presciption by the teacher for the same set of tasks have been made.

Other programs have represented the direct instruction point of view. Bereiter and Engelmann (1966), for example, in accord with their emphasis on the teaching of specific cognitive skills which have been identified as missing in the repertoire of disadvantaged children, have argued that the instructional designer's concern should not be with total environment but with a limited period of time each day in which intensive and carefully sequenced direct instruction is given. These programs have paid primary attention to developing the lesson materials and teacher-training materials for implementing a direct instructional approach. Underlying these programs is a theory of intellectual development that can best be described as cumulative and hierarchical. The assumption is that cognitive competence is acquired through the combination of simple behaviors into successively more complex performance; attainment of a new level of cognitive development depends on the prior or simultaneous acquisition of specific simpler competencies.

Curriculum hierarchies (sequencing)

Consider the instructional design implications of these two points of view. If we work in terms of the theory that the acquisition of complex behavior is cumulative and hierarchical, then a program of education is effectively implemented by delineation of the component behaviors that lead to advanced attainments. As a consequence of this, a statement of the outcomes of elementary school education should describe a sequence of intermediate objectives that lead to more complex performance; this involves analysis of hierarchical learning prerequisites which provide sequences of objectives that guide the design and evaluation of instruction. Insofar as possible, these instructional hierarchies should reflect an understanding of developmental stages, underlying learning processes and related individual differences. School programs that do not take account of such acquisition sequences will produce discouraging results because they can lead to less than optimal attainment for many children and because they introduce certain kinds of instruction at times in a sequence of learning when transfer and generalization are not likely to occur. Learning hierarchies have been carefully analysed in both scientific and practical aspects by Robert Gagné (1966, 1970) and need not be elaborated here. In a more recent paper, William Rohwer (1972) has suggested a rule of thumb for the timing and sequencing of instruction in which he recommends that instruction designed to foster certain educational aims should begin after prerequisite skills have been mastered and when the developmental curve for the skill to be taught is in a period of transition. A job for educational psychologists is to identify the knowledge required for this purpose in relation to school tasks.

By analysing component objectives, curriculum sequences can be prepared so that students can be rapidly advanced to or immediately started at a level of work challenging to their performance capabilities, thus minimizing the necessity for small-step learning for every student. In the development of these sequences, special attention can be paid to possibilities for multiple options for progress. Careful hierarchy validation can determine competencies that do not necessarily need to be learned one before the other so that options are available at any time for different student interests or for different tries at success. Given these options, a child can move from one task to another, experiencing success where he or she finds it, and then return with additional experience to tasks previously found difficult. Tests or observational procedures can be designed for each objective in the sequence, and teaching materials can be prepared for them. Designed in this way, a carefully analysed curriculum sequence can actually permit a greater degree of individualization than is possible without the detailed statement of objectives. The sequence tells the teacher what observations to make in assessing children's learning and what constraints or freedoms to apply in permitting or encouraging the child to progress. The detailed curriculum sequence need not be evident to the learner as a constraint and should permit the possibility of a best 'match' between the child's present conceptual structure and the kinds of lesson materials that are available to him. Thus, formal curriculum sequences can be an effective means of translating the results of psychological analysis into a form that is readily usable by teachers and by the designers of teaching materials. A task for educational psychologists is to provide behavior analysis techniques and ways of deriving teaching sequences from them. (See, e.g., Resnick, Wang and Kaplan, 1970; Beck and Mitroff, 1972; Rosner, 1972.)

Exploratory learning

In addition to the prescriptive requirements of cumulative hierarchical theory, theory recommending the design of general learning environments suggests another instructional mode that usually takes the form of exploratory activities which provide significant opportunities for children to define and structure tasks for themselves. In the sequential, prescriptive instructional mode, much of the burden of matching the developing capabilities of the child to the sequence of possible tasks falls upon the diagnostic ability of the teacher, assisted by tools provided by the curriculum designer. In contrast, the exploratory mode makes the assumption that, given available options and the opportunity to initiate exploration of these options, children will determine the match between their capabilities and task requirements. Put another way, children, left alone, are good at finding the right match of materials for their own abilities and learning style. Assuming that many children are good at making this match and that this can facilitate the objectives of adaptive education, then the instructional problem is to design adequate displays of options and alternatives and to design conditions for guiding learners among them so that their choices maximize the likelihood of meeting their own goals.

My colleague, Lauren Resnick, has recently suggested that the difficulties encountered in displaying alternatives for exploration vary with the degree of literacy of the learner and to some extent with the nature of instructional options and materials (Resnick, 1972). For those who can read, options can be displayed in the form of written descriptions. The task then lies in collating, cross-referencing and adequately characterizing the alternatives and in making these alternatives easily accessible. At sophisticated levels, this involves the use of libraries and information retrieval systems and perhaps the exploratory capabilities of a laboratory. With young children who cannot read or interpret lists of choices and have a limited range of prior learning experience on which to base judgments of the alternatives being offered, what is required is the opportunity to sample various learning options directly. This suggests an open stack or browsing model for available options rather than an information retrieval setup where various alternatives need to be identified and retrieved. Resnick has pointed out that

free-choice early education programs have attempted to solve the problem of display by combining physical display of the learning materials with modeling of their use. The open display permits browsing and sampling. Modeling is accomplished largely by permitting children to watch each other at work, and thus to learn what activities are available for future activities of their own. The heavy reliance on modeling probably accounts for the interest in both Montessori and informal classrooms in vertical age grouping (children of several ages together in a single classroom); older children in such classrooms provide natural models for younger ones [p. 73].

With respect to exploratory activities that rely on learner control of instruction, it is fashionable today to go to the extreme of insisting that no one can be a better judge of what is best for the student than the student himself. However, evidence on the effectiveness of learner control is not clear, and experimentation is called for (Atkinson, 1972). The best stance to take at the moment is that the learner's judgment is one of several items of information to be used in making instructional decisions.

To summarize this section on the teaching of basic abilities, it should be stressed that educators are more aware than ever of the tractability of early development and that psychologists have the obligation to assess the extent and the limits of this tractability. At the moment, new knowledge is accumulating rapidly, theoretical debates abound, and educational experiments are controversial. An interactive mode of research and application imposed on this scene by educational psychologists would, I believe, contribute to the improved design of educational efforts and the generation of useful knowledge on which these efforts can be based.

INDIVIDUAL DIFFERENCES

I turn now to another critical dimension of elementary school education: adaptation to individual differences. It seems more apparent than ever that new educational methods that are insensitive to individual differences can account for only a small part of the variance in instructional effects; and it is likely that strong instructional strategies will necessarily be adaptive to a learner's background and educational history. For example, based on his recent work in teaching initial reading, Richard Atkinson (1972) stated:

Method variables like the modified teaching alphabet, oral reading, the linguistic approach and others undoubtedly have beneficial effects. However, these effects are minimal in comparison to the impact that is possible when instruction is adaptive to the individual learner [p. 20].

In a previous paper (Glaser, 1972), I attempted to call attention to psychological processes other than the usually measured aptitudes that offer possibilities for adapting to individual differences and that could result in profound changes in the nature of the elementary school. These individual differences are related to the basic abilities that I have just discussed, and they refer to learning processes and developmental capabilities that influence the activity of the learner as an active processor of information. For example, it has been pointed out (Rohwer, 1972) that as a result of their cultural backgrounds, children develop different habits of recoding and mentally transforming materials presented to them for study and memorization. Developmental psychologists have pointed out various processes of thought that are available to children at different stages of their growth. The extent to which the nature of instructional tasks, the timing of instruction and the content of the elementary school can be related to these cognitive processes is currently a matter of investigation (Glaser, 1972; Rohwer, 1972). Their implications for the individualization of instruction need to be analysed and eventually built into attempts to redesign educational practice. Along with these processes, more obvious characteristics also can be attended to in school environments designed for individual adaptation. Consider the following examples which come out of observations of individualized classrooms.

In subject-matter instruction, one major mode of adaptation involves learning achievement. Based on a student's attainment of certain performances, decisions can be made about subsequent instruction. The emphasis on the achievement of competence should be quite deliberate and different from what it has been in the past. The assumption now is that ways can be found to insure that most children will master the literacy objectives of elementary school, and the explicit tactic is to place the burden on the instruction to maximize the ways in which the child can progress rather than necessarily assuming that the child lacks a particular capability or aptitude. The implications of this emphasis are important. The school environment should convey to students that they are differentiated on the basis of their performance and that the school is oriented toward assisting them in maximizing their attainment regardless of their particular background or labels they have obtained on other bases such as I.Q. tests, etc. What is emphasized is not the discrepancy between potential and accomplishment; rather, accomplishment, not potential, is viewed and valued in its own right. For this purpose, techniques need to be developed for analysing the properties of individual performance frequently enough and in enough detail for individualized instructional decisions. Recent studies of computer-assisted instruction and testing are of interest in this respect.

Another obvious kind of individual difference is the rate, pace and rhythm of learning. It is fashionable to say that adaptation on the basis of mere learning rate is not very important since there are deeper concerns with process and style. However, rate has some interesting ramifications. If it is not limited by a teacher's concern for a child moving beyond the amount of subject matter approved of for that grade, self-pacing does give the student the option of moving ahead if he or she so desires. It permits the student to exercise some sense of his own rhythm of work. There are individual differences in this respect: some students like to spend a concentrated amount of time on their work, complete it, and then get more work to do. Others like to work for shorter periods of time, enjoy their distractions, and come back to their work. Some like to engage in some exploratory activity to test and display newly learned skills, and then get on with new work. Others like to reward themselves with some playful activity upon the completion of their successful performance. These tempos of work are very obvious, and the relationships between rhythm and pace of work and learning, retention, and transfer are interesting matters for research investigation and have been studied to some extent in the work on reflective and impulsive styles in children.

A third obvious source of individual differences in the classroom relates to the outcomes and consequences of a child's activity. There are individual differences in needs for feedback: some children need more questions answered than others; some need more careful explanation of directions; some need frequent praise for their accomplishments; others need very frequent attention for small accomplishments. This mechanism of adaptation can be facilitated by designing classroom procedures in such a way that a teacher can organize activities in order to pay some attention to all students in a circumscribed period of time. For example, keeping the principles of reinforcement in mind, the teacher can constantly scan the activity of the children and comment to those who appear to be working, and spend little time with those who for some reason or other are not attending to their work when it is appropriate for them to do so. Teacher attention is important and children will shift their activities to obtain it, as they observe the activities for which the teacher provides attention and conversation. A teacher can also become aware of children who have initial needs for much contact and then systematically withdraw support as the child becomes more self-sustained. This continuous 'feedback role' of the teacher is one important way in which individual differences can be adapted to, and training a teacher for this role is to be particularly emphasized in educational settings adaptive to individual differences. The presently very active field of behavior modification is designing and analysing such school practices, and among the many interesting questions for study, one of the most interesting is the issue of the relationship between reinforcement contingencies used in the classroom and the 'natural community of reinforcers' present in later learning situations both in and out of school (Bandura, 1969; Resnick, 1971; Wolf and Risley, 1971).

Another aspect of individual differences is the degree to which children can manage their own enterprises – the extent to which they can set up and conduct their own lessons and assess their own performance. Self-management skills involve such things as following directions, identifying current assignments, deciding on and selecting appropriate materials, setting up the task, completing the task, obtaining an evaluation of it and being able to identify the available options for new work. Children vary in this respect, and appropriate classroom management can adapt to these differences. However, skill at self-management is both an individual difference to which the instructional environment adapts and which the environment can influence and change. Self-management skills can be actively taught, and many of us have been amazed at the extent to which very young children can conduct their own enterprises in a classroom setting. An area of psychological study related to these skills is investigation of the process of self-reinforcement, whereby individuals exercise control over the rewards and punishments consequent to their own actions (Bandura, 1971). Study of such self-regulation is a new area of research that seems very relevant to school learning. Such questions as the following are involved: How do children develop self-prescribed standards of behavior for evaluating the adequacy of their performance? What are the effects of social comparison and modeling on the use and maintenance of these standards? How are reinforcing events made available so that students can serve as their own reinforcing agents? Under what conditions do children in the classroom acquire self-rewarding and self-punishing behavior? And what is the effectiveness of these self-administered consequences in influencing learning?

TESTING AND EVALUATION

Finally, in this sampling of areas in which educational psychology can offer its services to education and in which educational requirements can press for improvements in educational psychology, I must mention the problem of testing and evaluation. Of all the technological fields related to education, educational measurement has been the most fully developed by psychologists, and the field has had a powerful influence on the nature of schooling. The influence of testing has been so strong that in the deluge of recent writings on educational reform, testing is frequently seen as a central evil to be challenged and exorcised. However, if our prevalent educational model shifts from its present, primarily selective mode to an adaptive mode where it is possible to provide wider varieties of instructional methods and opportunities for successful school attainment, then new kinds of tests will be required. These tests will be criterion referenced in addition to being norm referenced and will assess performance attainments and capabilities which can be matched to available educational options in more detailed ways than can be carried out with currently used aptitude and achievement tests (Glaser and Nitko, 1971; Glaser, 1972).

The nature of testing is changing. In the near future, testing will not stand out as an extrinsic, external adjunct of instruction; it will become an integral part of the educational process itself. For instructional purposes, tests will be interpreted in terms of performance criteria so that student and teacher are informed about the student's progress relative to standards of competence, and, in this way, provide information for deciding on an appropriate course of instruction. Tests of this kind will have an intrinsic character of openness as compared with most currently used tests. In general, they would be examined in advance by the students who would eventually use them and in this way serve as a display of the competencies to be acquired. The tests would be easy to understand once they are inspected, since the behaviors measured would not be masked by incidental demands designed to increase the difficulty and 'discrimination power' of the individual items (Resnick, 1972). The task for psychologists is the development of a performance test theory to parallel their success in prediction test theory.

Educational measurement is also an integral part of 'evaluation' – today's heady catchword and panacea for restraining the onslaught of untempered, wasteful, expensive educational innovation. Evaluation is a serious concern and needs equally serious examination. As the alliance between educational psychology and educational practice has become more viable, there has been an increased demand for objective, analytical evaluation. This increased demand has also come from societal pressures that arise from the necessity to make competing social investments. Basic questions are being raised in the field of evaluation; the problems involved are complex, and simple solutions do not seem to be possible. This is certainly attested to in fields other than education, such as the evaluation of new medicines and drugs, the effects of new welfare programs and economic reforms, etc.

The state of the field is in disarray, and as a result, many outstanding individuals have turned their attention to an analysis of its practices and methodological requirements. My colleague, William Cooley (1971), wrote:

The field does not have a significant literature. There is an abundance of papers about evaluation models and strategies, and 'how-to-do-it recipes.' There are many attempts at developing a taxonomy of evaluation-type activities. But there is a great scarcity of publicly available publications which report the procedures and results of actual evaluation studies [p. 1].

In our work at the University of Pittsburgh, we have been conducting evaluation studies on the effectiveness of new instructional systems while searching for appropriate models of evaluation (e.g., Lindvall and Cox, 1970; Wang, Resnick and Schuetz, 1970; Cooley, 1971; Lohnes, 1972; Popp, 1972). When the work in pilot experimental programs appears encouraging enough, the next step is to move from the 'hot house' version into the field. The central problem that arises relates to the different ways in which a particular instructional model is implemented in different classrooms in the field; changes occur as one moves away from the artificial bolstering of the initial experimental situation. What is needed is a procedure for determining the way in which and the extent to which each classroom or school actually implements the instructional model that they have adopted, and then to relate these data on the degree of implementation of the model to the performance of children in the school (Cooley, 1971).

Certain fundamental requirements for evaluation research in the elementary school are apparent. One is the need to assess the outcomes of elementary school education in terms of both literacy attainment and intellectual processes. This means two things: first, the development of accepted measures of student literacy and of methods to show the effective transfer of this attained competence to the immediate requirements of further schooling and everyday life; and, second, the development of accepted measures of intelligence in terms of cognitive processes, since, as I have indicated, elementary school education should give evidence of increased intellectual and cognitive skills in youngsters. A further requirement for evaluative research is the need to dimensionalize the components of an instructional model so that as an instructional innovation is disseminated, the variation in degree of implementation of the model along its various components can be related to characteristics of the student population before and after instruction in a particular educational environment. Data analysis conventions are needed that are appropriate to accounting for the multivariate nature of these three domains of variables: student characteristics, instructional model variables and student attainments (Lohnes, 1972).

CONCLUSION

I want to call attention to the strong possibility that educational psychologists, by working in what I have called the interactive mode of application, development and research, can help create and preserve an experimental mood in education whereby scientists, educators, curriculum designers, teachers, parents and students feel that they have a direct part in decisions to improve their schools. There is the need to encourage the notion of the experimenting society described so well by Donald Campbell (1971). Campbell suggested that the experimenting society is one that vigorously tries out proposed solutions to recurrent problems, that makes hardheaded and multidimensional evaluations of outcomes, and that moves on to try other alternatives when evaluation shows a reform to have been ineffective. The experimenting society prefers exploratory innovation to inaction or continued study of the problem and is committed to action as research rather than research as a postponement of action. An experimenting society is accountable and challengeable and provides for informed change by supplying reasonable alternatives and varied solutions for the community to consider and from which to choose.

In summary, I have suggested that psychological research and theory related to education are now in a position to move into the interactive relationships among application, development and research that are characteristic of strong sciences. In fact, I believe that such a move is fundamental to the growth and maturation of the behavioral and social sciences and educational psychology in particular. I have indicated areas where interaction would be fruitful: subject-matter learning; the teaching of basic aptitudes and abilities; the analysis of instructional strategies; the structure of the content of learning as it influences curriculum design; individual differences relating to adaptive, individualized models for education; and new requirements for measurement and evaluation. In brief, I recommend the enjoyable and stimulating schizophrenia that is induced by having one foot in the laboratory and one foot in the field.

ACKNOWLEDGEMENT

This article first appeared in *Am. Psychol.* (1973), **28**, 557–566, and is published here with the kind permission of author and editor.

REFERENCES

Atkinson, R. C. (1972) *Ingredients for a Theory of Instruction* (Tech. Rep. No. 187). Stanford: Institute for Mathematical Studies in the Social Sciences, Stanford University.

Bandura, A. (1969) *Principles of Behavior Modification*. New York: Holt, Rinehart & Winston.

Bandura, A. (1971). Vicarious and self-reinforcement processes. In R. Glaser (Ed.), *The Nature of Reinforcement*. New York: Academic Press.

Beck, I. L. & Mitroff, D. D. (1972) *The Rationale and Design of a Primary Grades Reading System for an Individualized Classroom*. Pittsburgh: Learning Research and Development Center, University of Pittsburgh.

Bereiter, C. & Englemann, S. (1966) *Teaching Disadvantaged Children in the Preschool*. Englewood Cliffs, N.J.: Prentice-Hall.

Bruner, J. S. (1966) *Toward a Theory of Instruction*. Cambridge: Harvard University Press.

Bruner, J. S. (1968) Culture, politics and pedagogy. *Sat. Rev.*, **51**, 69–90.

Campbell, D. T. (1971) Methods for the experimenting society. Paper presented at the annual meeting of the American Psychological Association, Washington, D.C.

Cooley, W. W. (1971) Methods of evaluating school innovations. Invited address presented at the annual meeting of the American Psychological Association, Washington, D.C.

David, E. E., Jr (1972) The relation of science and technology. *Science*, **175**(4017), 13.

Gagné, R. M. (1966) Elementary science: a new scheme of instruction. *Science*, **151**, 49–53.

Gagné, R. M. (1970) *The Conditions of Learning* (2nd ed.). New York: Holt, Rinehart & Winston.

Gilbert, T. F. (1962) Mathetics: the technology of education. *J. Mathetics*, **1**, 7–73.

Glaser, R. (1972) Individuals and learning: the new aptitudes. *Educational Researcher,* **1**(6), 5–13.

Glaser, R. & Nitko, A. J. (1971) Measurement in learning and instruction. In R. L. Thorndike (Ed.), *Educational Measurement* (2nd ed.). Washington, D.C.: American Council on Education.

Glaser, R. & Resnick, L. B. (1972) Instructional psychology. In P. H. Mussen & M. R. Rosenzweig (Eds.), *Annual Review of Psychology*, Vol. 23. Palo Alto, Calif.: Annual Reviews.

Lindvall, C. M. & Cox, R. C. (1970) *Evaluation as a Tool in Curriculum Development: The IPI Evaluation Program* (AERA Monograph Series on Curriculum Evaluation 5). Chicago: Rand McNally.

Lohnes, P. R. (1972) *Planning for Evaluation of the LRDC Instructional Model*. Pittsburgh: Learning Research and Development Center, University of Pittsburgh.

Popp, H. M. (1972) *Test Project for the LRDC Beginning Reading Program 'Stepping Stones to Reading'*. Pittsburgh: Learning Research and Development Center, University of Pittsburgh.

Resnick, L. B. (1967) *Design of an Early Learning Curriculum*. Pittsburgh: Learning Research and Development Center, University of Pittsburgh.

Resnick, L. B. (1971) Applying applied reinforcement. In R. Glaser (Ed.), *The Nature of Reinforcement*. New York: Academic Press.

Resnick, L. B. (1972) Open education: some tasks for technology. *Educ. Tech.*, **12**(1), 70–76.

Resnick, L. B., Wang, M. C. & Kaplan, J. (1970) *Behavior Analysis in Curriculum Design: A Hierarchically Sequenced Introductory Mathematics Curriculum*. Pittsburgh: Learning Research and Development Center, University of Pittsburgh.

Rohwer, W. D., Jr (1971) Prime time for education: early childhood or adolescence? *Harvard Educ. Rev.*, **41**, 316–341.

Rohwer, W. D., Jr (1972) Decisive research: a means for answering fundamental questions about instruction. *Educ. Res.*, **1**(7), 5–11.

Rosner, J. (1972) *The Development and Validation of an Individualized Perceptual Skills Curriculum*. Pittsburgh: Learning Research and Development Center, University of Pittsburgh.

Wang, M. C., Resnick, L. B. & Schuetz, P. A. (1970) *PEP in the Frick Elementary School: Interim Evaluation Report of the Primary Education Project, 1968–1969*. Pittsburgh: Learning Research and Development Center, University of Pittsburgh.

Wolf, M. M. & Risley, T. R. (1971) Reinforcement: applied research. In R. Glaser (Ed.), *The Nature of Reinforcement*. New York: Academic Press.

PART 2

The nervous system

INTRODUCTION

Following on from the theme developed in Part 1 on the division between subjective and objective methods, it seems appropriate to include two papers which give opposing views on the nature of physiological mechanisms in the body and the bearing these have on psychological functioning. Joynson, for example, argues that if we look for all the answers to human behaviour in the workings of the nervous system we are no longer concerned with psychological but with physiological explanations. Therefore, a plea is made for a return to greater use of introspection in the study of mental conscious processes in the belief that man's actions are more than the sum of his physiological functions.

Hebb underlines the statement 'psychology is a biological science' and goes on to denounce the humanist approach as strictly for literature and not as part of the science of behaviour. For Hebb, 'the central concern must be man's mind and thought' and without compromise he claims that the study of physiology of the brain is a crucial way of meeting this concern.

McFie's article carries Hebb's theoretical paper into some interesting practical findings about the location of special cognitive functions for particular parts of the brain. The powerful case made by Hebb against the dual theory using the bilaterality of the brain is supported by McFie.

3   The return of mind

R. B. JOYNSON

In an article called 'The Breakdown of Modern Psychology' (Joynson, 1970), the writer made a critical examination of what Broadbent (1961) has termed the 'generally accepted doctrine' of objective experiment. The article concluded by hoping that broader and more appropriate ideals would prevail, but it did not attempt to specify those ideals. It concentrated upon the negative case against the accepted doctrine. Since then, a number of comments has been made. One writer has denied that there is a breakdown (Zangwill, 1971). Two writers, however, have made proposals for radical reform (Harré, 1971; Taylor, 1971). In my view, the upshot of these comments is to lend further strong support to my criticisms of the accepted doctrine. The object of this paper is to substantiate this assertion, and to indicate the direction in which I think we should look for a positive alternative to objective experiment.

In general terms, the alternative is familiar enough. The method of objective experiment defines the subject matter of psychology as behaviour rather than mental life; it rejects the view that psychology investigates conscious experience through introspection. If this method is found wanting, there must follow a disenchantment with the behaviourist outlook, a renewed emphasis on mental life and introspection and a growing interest in a psychology concerned with 'persons' rather than 'organisms'. But this general alternative may, of course, be interpreted in various ways, and my aim will be to indicate the particular interpretation which seems preferable to me. Many writers have discussed this theme in recent years, and to some of these we shall return. First, it may be advised to recall the wider historical context in which the problem arises.

THE HISTORICAL CONTEXT

At the end of the 19th century the traditional conception of psychology was still universally accepted. It was the study of mind or mental life. This was the conception which had governed its long connection with philosophy; which had guided its many important developments during the 19th century; and which still prevailed when James declared in 1890 that 'Introspective Observation is what we have to rely on first and foremost and always' (James, 1890). And in those days it must have seemed highly improbable that a tradition which had been established so long, and which contained so many illustrious names, would ever be successfully challenged.

But there were already signs of change. James himself remarked: 'I have heard a most intelligent biologist say: "It is high time for scientific men to protest against the recognition of any such thing as consciousness in a scientific investigation" ' (James, 1890). The biologist expressed the spirit of a 'new' or 'modern' psychology, as it was often called, which was then gathering support. Its adherents, wishing to approach psychology from the strict standpoint of natural science, were inclined to the view that consciousness was an epiphenomenon and that its explanation was to be sought in physiology. This movement was strongly resisted by leading exponents of the traditional psychology. Ward (1893) set out his objections in an article entitled ' "Modern" Psychology: a Reflexion'; and Stout attacked the belief of 'certain physiologists that the only way of explaining the phenomena of consciousness is by connecting them with the physical phenomena of the brain and nervous system' (Stout, 1896). The disagreement was never resolved, and was soon followed by a revolutionary upheaval.

The protest for which James' biologist had called came with Watson's objective behaviourism and its dictum that 'psychology must discard all reference to consciousness' (Watson, 1914). Ward's reaction was intense: 'As a *method* in the hands of psychologists it has done some good; as a pretended *science* in the hands of tyros whose psychological training has not even begun, it has done infinite harm' (Ward, 1918). The introspective tradition retained considerable influence, especially in British psychology, where it may be traced in the writings of Spearman and McDougall, of Burt and Mace. But, in general, introspection was increasingly dismissed as an armchair exercise; and among the numerous developments of the 20th century it has been the behaviourist outlook which, in one form or another, has dominated psychology. Even in British psychology many leading exponents seem now to have abandoned finally the original conception of their subject. Zangwill (1950), in his *Introduction to Modern Psychology*, finds no place for Ward and Stout even in the historical background, and looks to experimental and physiological psychology for the foundations of a science of behaviour. Broadbent traces the origins of this science to Watson, and claims the method of objective experiment as the 'generally accepted doctrine' (Broadbent, 1961). In short, although there would be many differences of detail, it seems now to be widely assumed that the objective standpoint is the only reputable position, and that, after a long pre-scientific period in which psychology was regarded as the study of mind, it is now firmly founded as the science of behaviour. James' biologist, it might seem, has won the day.

But once again there are signs of change. During the past ten years powerful objections have been raised on both sides of the Atlantic to the tenets of behaviourism (Burt, 1962; Koch, 1964). Burt regretted that: 'Today, apart from a few minor reservations, the vast majority of psychologists, both in this country and in America, still follow [Watson's] lead' (Burt, 1962). As a basis for a general theory, behaviourism was 'hopelessly inadequate', and 'the need to reintroduce the concept of consciousness seems inescapable' (Burt, 1962). A little later, Mace (1965) remarked: 'Behaviourism, it would seem, is on the way out. Psychology is regaining consciousness'. Since then, there has been increasing evidence, I believe, that such views are gathering support (Smail, 1971).

•   •   •

It is notoriously difficult to assess the significance of contemporary trends. To some people these signs may seem unimportant; to others they may be important but capable of being incorporated within an expanded behaviourism; to still others they may have a revolutionary import. And further interpretations may also be possible. The writer's previous article (Joynson, 1970) has elicited some representative reactions to the present situation. I hope that a brief examination of this exchange of views, though inevitably coloured by my own convictions, will help to clarify the issues.

AN EXCHANGE OF VIEWS

I must first recapitulate my criticism of the accepted doctrine, stressing certain features which may not have been sufficiently evident. The form to be taken by the argument was stated at the outset: 'The reader is asked to consider what is supposed to be involved in the practical application of the doctrine, according to the recommendations of its supporters' (Joynson, 1970). That is, I proposed to follow out the procedures recommended in order to determine the consequences. The argument then started from the conventional distinction between external or stimulus (S) variables, and internal or organic (O) variables. Many experimenters, notably the early behaviourists, have restricted themselves mainly to S-variables. This neglect of O-variables, I argued, is due at least in part to the admitted difficulty of identifying and controlling them, and must always prove inadequate. But attempts to include O-variables by various *indirect* means have also proved inadequate, so it becomes necessary to consider *direct* means, namely the methods of introspection and of physiology. Introspection, however, is rejected by adherents of the objective standpoint; hence I wrote: 'Introspection may be set aside' (Joynson, 1970). (This was not an indication that I personally rejected introspection. It was only an indication that it was permissible for me, in the context of this argument, to set introspection aside, since I was only following the recommendations of the adherents of the objective method.) Having rejected introspection, the method of objective experiment is thus finally driven to the conclusion that the explanation of behaviour is to be sought in physiological mechanisms. Two conclusions followed. First, the difficulty which objective experiment has experienced in identifying and controlling O-variables, combined with the limitations of current knowledge of the neural mechanisms relevant to behaviour, substantiates the warning of Gibson (1967) that scientific psychology is 'ill-founded' and its gains 'puny'. Second, even if the recommended neurological knowledge were available, it would not help psychology, for finding physiological explanations is primarily the task of physiology, and leaves psychology with no distinctive role. Thus the method of objective experiment leads to an impasse.

Harré formulates this argument as follows: 'the only possible theoretical basis for the explanation of human behaviour is to be found in the physiology of the brain and central nervous system, and the adoption of this basis necessarily leads to the disappearance of psychology as an independent science' (Harré, 1971). This provides a useful summary of the central difficulty to which, in my view, the objective method leads. Harré calls it 'Joynson's Dilemma'. We shall later return to the origins of this argument. Here some clarification is required of my own position in relation to the dilemma.

Since my previous article concentrated upon the negative case against the accepted doctrine, my positive position needs to be brought out more clearly. The reader will note that, if the above argument is valid, the only escape lies through the rejected method of introspection. My object, then, was simply to help clear the ground for the familiar alternative to the objective standpoint.

•   •   •

We should first consider a short communication by Zangwill (1971), for he concludes with the reassurance that 'Breakdown, fortunately, may lie in the eye of the beholder'. If his comments are studied with care, however, I think it will be found that they in fact go some considerable way towards confirming my criticisms. His discussion of the status of experiment makes it clear that he has become less confident of its potential, for he writes that he 'no doubt came into psychology with too exalted an idea of the role of experiment', and also that 'we in experimental psychology may well have displayed arrogant over-confidence in our scientific pretensions'. Some reasons for this increased caution are given – that 'its uncritical adoption has led in some fields to total failure to progress', and that its clarification 'has as yet by no means been fully achieved' (Zangwill, 1971). But having admitted so much, he then reasserts his belief in the value of the method without specifically examining a major difficulty raised by my article, of how internal variables are to be identified and controlled. This is a serious obstacle in the path of experimental psychology, and while it remains it is not unreasonable to hold that breakdown does not lie wholly in the eye of the beholder.

But further, it is difficult to avoid seeing a connection between Zangwill's omission of any specific discussion of this problem, and the views which he expresses concerning the relation of psychology and neurology. He writes: '. . . one may hope that as understanding of the brain conceived as the instrument of behaviour advances, both psychology and neurology will become increasingly integrated into a single scientific discipline' (Zangwill, 1971). But is it not largely because neurology appears as the only, or the most effective, way of investigating internal variables, that this single scientific discipline is proposed? However this may be, this proposal leads to the further question of whether it avoids 'Joynson's Dilemma'. It seems to endorse the first half of the dilemma – that the only possible theoretical basis for the explanation of human behaviour lies in the physiology of the brain . . .' (Harré, 1971); for advance in the understanding of the brain is seen as the main, if not the sole, factor leading to integration. But then the proposal encounters the second half of the dilemma – 'that the adoption of this basis necessarily leads to the disappearance of psychology as an independent science' (Harré, 1971). Certainly Zangwill envisages a change in respect of the present independence of psychology, but he denies that this view implies a 'takeover' by neurology, 'or that psychology as we know it today will simply cease to exist' (Zangwill, 1971). I am far from wishing to deny that there should be a very close association between psychology and neurology; but it seems essential to provide a clear and positive indication of the role of psychology in any such alliance. In particular, does Zangwill have any workable conception of a psychological explanation as something in any way distinguishable from a physiological explanation? Unless he does, the conception of a single scientific discipline remains in danger of appearing no more than a means of concealing the disappearance of psychology. Although it is clearly Zangwill's intention to affirm that accepted procedures are working satisfactorily, it can hardly be without significance that he has now abandoned his earlier attempts to distinguish psychology and neurology; but the conception of a single discipline remains to be formulated in sufficient detail to permit proper assessment.

●　　　●　　　●

Harré (1971) adopts a still more radical position. He accepts that 'Joynson's Dilemma' is insoluble from the behaviourist standpoint, and states that its resolution 'may be painful in that a good many cherished preconceptions must be abandoned, both as to the methods of empirical study and of theoretical explanation'. Thus his starting point is to agree with me that behaviourist science has broken down, placing this in the wider context of the collapse of positivism. He writes: 'The situation described by Joynson is not just a consequence of the breakdown of paradigms of psychological science derived ultimately from behaviourism, but follows from the wider collapse of the more general positivist point of view . . .' He then makes a persuasive plea for the conception of psychology as the study of 'persons', and advocates 'introspection' as one means of investigating performances which take place 'in the mind'. Thus Harré's position continues a sequence: Zangwill denied a breakdown, and naturally found no occasion to urge that consciousness should be reintroduced; Taylor (1971) argues forcefully for the restoration of conscious experience, but still within a behaviourist framework; Harré is in no doubt that conventional approaches are outworn, and proposes to replace the physiological picture of human beings with the concept of the person.

So far Harré's position is very close to my own, but from this point onwards I must dis-agree with him, for his way of developing the theme seems to me open to grave objections. Unless I have misunderstood him, he considers that his approach falls demonstrably within the framework of the natural sciences, and that the steps which have already been taken in this direction are to be regarded as marking at last that Copernican Revolution which scien-tific psychologists have so long and so vainly sought. Psychology, he concludes, 'has only just begun'. One might agree that, if psychologists in general placed as much weight on people's accounts of their behaviour as Harré advocates, this would constitute a revolutionary change for many psychologists in their approach to their subject, and a most desirable change too. But to speak of this as a Copernican Revolution implies the possession of a radical scientific theory of wide general significance. Such claims have been made in psychology before, and psychologists may well view them with caution, especially with the fate of behaviourism still fresh in mind.

Harré appeals both to empirical work and to theoretical argument. His references to empirical work are slender. He mentions Goffman, Argyle and J. J. Gibson as introducing the concept of the person, but this is a limited view. With respect to the accounts which people give of their performances, he refers to a study by himself and Secord of 'some im-portant steps which have already been taken'. At the time of writing, this is not available from his publisher. Nowhere in his article does he indicate how his procedures are to be related to the experimental method, though this would need to be clarified if Harré wishes to persuade experimental psychologists that he can offer a workable scientific psychology.

Harré is mainly concerned with theoretical analysis. His starting point is 'Joynson's Dilemma'. He takes it for granted, as mentioned above, that this dilemma is insoluble from the behaviourist–positivist standpoint, and offers to resolve it along lines which would enable psychology to remain a natural science – or rather, in his view, to become a natural science for the first time. His attempt is ultimately unsuccessful; but since he places so much emphasis upon this dilemma, its origins should first be traced.

The argument expressed in this dilemma is in fact an old one, and in my previous article I referred to the earliest use of it which I had encountered – in Stout's *Analytic Psychology* of 1896. The relevance of Stout's discussion will be immediately appreciated, for he there dis-cusses the view that psychology may be treated as a physical science, and in particular the opinion of 'certain physiologists that the only way of explaining the phenomena of consciousness is by connecting them with the physical phenomena of the brain and nervous system' (Stout, 1896). This is the belief of the 'new' psychology of the late 19th century, referred to above; and as against this belief, Stout argued that 'the distinctive aim of the psychologist is to investigate mental events themselves, not their mechanical accompaniments or antecedents. If the course of mental events is not regulated by discoverable uniformities capable of being interconnected so as to form a coherent system, the psychologist has nothing to do. It is incorrect to say that on this assumption his science becomes absorbed in physiology. It does not become absorbed; it simply ceases to exist in any form whatever' (Stout, 1896). This argument, it will be seen, confronted the 'new' psychology with 'Joynson's Dilemma'. In repeating this argument in my article, I quoted the last two sentences reproduced above. Thus Harré, in failing to note that I gave the source of the argument, and in attaching my name to it, gives me an altogether undeserved credit.

For Stout, this argument was one way of defending the introspective study of mental process. When the behaviourists rejected this tradition, they faced a difficulty which I described as follows: 'Watson, wanting to make psychology a natural science, faced a dilemma. He must avoid the Scylla of "mentalism" – introspection is not a scientific method; but he must also avoid the Charybdis of physiology – psychology must not be defined in terms which make it indistinguishable from another science. Watson thought that the conception of a science of behaviour – establishing the laws connecting stimulus and response – provided an escape . . . But this assumption has broken down. The stimulus–determination position has failed, and the modern behaviourist himself now asserts that the next step is the construction of theories about the events within the skull' (Joynson, 1970). But this development, so it seems to me, essentially returns us to the position as it was before the behaviourist revolution. Once again there are those who can see no way of explaining psychological phenomena other than by connecting them with the physical phenomena of the brain, and once again one must object that on this assumption psychology simply ceases to exist. Stout's argument seemed to me as relevant as when he first formulated it; so I repeated it, quoting his own words.

•   •   •

STUDENTS OF MENTAL LIFE

It would be absurd to propose that psychologists should restore conscious experience, use introspection, study what goes on 'in the mind' and so on, without recalling that many others have already undertaken these tasks over a long period. Their contribution will need to be reconsidered if psychology is not to embark upon a laborious rediscovery of old truths. We have already noted that the tradition of Ward and Stout exerted a strong influence in British psychology for many years. There are, of course, many other familiar sources offering alternatives to behaviourism.

Although it seems true that a majority of experimentalists have tended to regard the subject's report as at best a secondary source, there have always been those in the broad field of 'general experimental psychology' who have resisted this narrow view. Sometimes they have maintained an independent standpoint, like Woodworth who always included introspection in his experimental programme, or like Bartlett whose theory of the schema gave to consciousness a definite function. At other times they have allied themselves to a systematic position, as when Gestalt psychologists advocated phenomenological observation. Nor is there a lack of contemporary studies in which central importance is attached to the practical problems and theoretical implications of self-observation (e.g. McKellar, 1962; Babington Smith, 1965; Bakan, 1967). Such contributions demonstrate that the exclusively objective approach has never been found wholly satisfactory even in the tough-minded experimental field, and today they offer valuable guidance for those tackling the immensely difficult problems which are raised by the use of introspection. In another direction, psychoanalysis and its derivatives have confronted the academic psychologist with a broader conception of his subject, however controversial. Though Freud's emphasis on the unconscious initially reduced the significance of the conscious, the subsequent tendency of psychoanalytic thought has redressed the balance. The therapeutic method seeks to deepen self-understanding, and the conscious ego has gradually acquired a more central role in theory. At the same time, Freud's original insights stand as a permanent reminder of the deceptions of self-report. Although behaviour therapy has attempted to oust this profound contribution, there is currently strong support for concepts of the person and conscious experience in both theory and therapy (e.g. Smail, 1968; Mair et al, 1970). Again, there is the long-standing 'personalistic' tradition, going back through Kelly, Allport, Murphy and many others, to Spranger and Stern, and continued today by such writers as Bannister, Laing and Smedslund (1969). It is to these writers that we are primarily indebted for the conception of psychology as the study of persons; their frequent neglect by the behaviourist illustrates the remark of Sprott (1938): 'the most significant difference between psychologists concerns the direction of their interests to people or behaviour'.

To assert the value of these traditions is to accept the plea of Koch (1961) and Hudson (1970) that greater attention should be paid to humanist approaches to psychology. Such a list could indeed be continued indefinitely. But it might be said that, if the writer sees so much to support in 20th-century psychology, it was unreasonable to speak of the 'breakdown' of modern psychology. Nevertheless, the phrase seems justified. It is appropriate in part because behaviourism has claimed with wide support to be the distinctively modern science of psychology, and its departure must radically alter the outlook of psychologists in general. It is appropriate also because these alternative traditions do not provide a coherent and agreed position to replace behaviourism. Taken individually they comprise many of the most significant developments of psychological thought; and taken collectively they provide a powerful counter-weight to the behaviourist dominance. But they offer a climate of opinion favourable to conscious experience, personal values, and the subjective world, rather than precise and systematic principles. It seems to the writer, therefore, that this eminently desirable trend needs to take on a sharper and more decisive direction.

In a witty commentary on technical sophistry in psychological experiments, Phillips (1969) advises a 'great leap backwards' to simpler and more sensible methods. His advice may be generalized. The return of consciousness brings with it the recollection that psychology was originally conceived as the study of mental life: and the decline of behaviourism recalls the psychology which behaviourism rejected – the psychology for which man was first and foremost a selfconscious and rational agent. There have been many indications that psychology was preparing for this leap, and disillusionment with the lack of genuine progress will give the final impetus. In a review of current work on memory, Tulving and Madigan

(1970) state plainly that 'the broad picture we have of human memory in 1970 does not differ from that in 1870'; and they ask, what is the solution to 'the problem of lack of genuine progress in understanding memory'? Their answer is this: '. . . why not start looking for ways of experimentally studying . . . one of the unique characteristics of human memory: its knowledge of its own knowledge'. In this, as in so many other ways, the contemporary psychologist is finding that the way ahead lies through the original conception of his subject.

The psychology of mental life, as it existed in the late 19th century before the rise of behaviourism, already possessed a remarkable diversity of approaches, exemplified in the varied work of Ebbinghaus, Lloyd Morgan, Ehrenfels, Galton, Janet, Cattell, Preyer, Binet, Titchener and many others who contributed to the growth of fresh empirical inquiries. But the most important element was that which possessed the longest history then, and has been most neglected since – the philosophical tradition of introspective psychology which reached its greatest expression in the writings of James, Ward and Stout. Its essential function may be seen most clearly perhaps in Stout's *Analytic Psychology*. We have already demonstrated the contemporary relevance of this work in one respect; its full significance is very much wider.

Stout did not regard his way of doing psychology as the only legitimate way. It was one way among many; and he expressly states that the subject may also be approached from the point of view of physiology, of mental pathology, of ethnology and of psychophysical method – from the various points of view, that is, of the new empirical inquiries to which we have just referred. But in addition to these inquiries, what Stout called 'the traditional English method' still had its distinctive value. Its aim was 'to bring systematic order into the crowd of facts concerning our mental life revealed by analysis of ordinary experience . . . to ascertain and define the processes of the developed consciousness as we now find them' (Stout, 1896). The *Analytic Psychology* provides an analysis of the main forms of mental life, and the relations among these. In Stout's view this 'time-honoured procedure' became more important, not less, when fresh lines of inquiry arose; for it could now be useful not only within its own limits, but also as a help to these inquiries: 'its utility to other branches of psychological investigation is comparable to the guidance which an inland explorer of a large island may receive from a chart of the coast' (Stout, 1896). It is entirely mistaken, then, to suppose that the traditional psychology was in principle opposed to the newer lines of investigation; on the contrary, one of the principal factors encouraging the growth of fresh empirical inquiries lay in the circumstance that older procedures (not necessarily in the form proposed by Stout) had brought their contribution to the point where new possibilities were shown to be both feasible and necessary. When the chart of the coast is prepared, the exploration of the interior becomes imperative.

But James' biologist was declaring it high time to protest against the recognition of consciousness. Behaviourism completed the process; and the new empirical inquiries, deprived of the essential tradition which might have guided their steps, fell into conflict and confusion. The need for that tradition is becoming increasingly evident today. When Taylor, a leading behaviourist theoretician, asserts that 'it is high time for psychologists to get rid of their ridiculous prejudice against the armchair', and that psychologists 'must restore conscious experience to its rightful place as a legitimate area of research' (Taylor, 1971), that need has become undeniable.

Shotter has suggested that psychology today needs to construct 'a new perspective, an integrated conceptual landscape upon which the many aspects of human modes of knowing could be placed in an intelligible order' (Shotter, 1970). This was the task which Stout's *Analytic Psychology* undertook for the late 19th century. No doubt the 20th-century version, when it comes, will differ in many important respects. But its success will be measured by the extent to which it carries us further along the same road, and it may well take its inspiration from the earlier tradition. 'There are no doubt dangers in interpreting the past anachronistically,' writes Hearnshaw, 'but Stout's theories often seem to anticipate views current one or two generations later. In his emphasis on "wholes"; in his doctrines of conative activity and the spontaneity of the mind; in his references to the striving for equilibrium (which has since become known as homeostasis); in his doctrine of "relative suggestion"; and in his frequent allusions to the role of the social factor in the development of human mentality; in all these ways Stout tunes in with a good deal that contemporary psychologists have become interested in after long wanderings' (Hearnshaw, 1964). It is the combination of so many significant concepts in a coherent whole which is so striking a feature of Stout's work. Those who study it will find, I believe, that Passmore's judgement is sound: 'far from being antiquated Stout is much more revolutionary than exponents of such "modern" doctrines as the conditioned reflex' (Hearnshaw, 1964).

After suggesting that the current belief in objective experiment needs radical revision, Shotter continues: 'Only by once again merging empirical with philosophical activity can such a revision be carried out. And this time there must be no subsequent divorce of the two activities . . .' (Shotter, 1970). This is the bitter lesson of modern psychology; and the best hope for the future.

ACKNOWLEDGEMENT

This paper first appeared in *Bull. Br. Psychol. Soc.* (1972), **25**, 1–10. Extracts are published here with the kind permission of author and editor.

REFERENCES

Babington Smith, B. (1965) *Laboratory Experience in Psychology.* Oxford: Pergamon Press.

Bakan, D. (1967) *On Method: Toward a Reconstruction of Psychological Investigation.* San Francisco: Jossey-Bass.

Broadbent, D. E. (1961) *Behaviour.* London: Eyre & Spottiswoode.

Burt, C. (1962) The concept of consciousness. *Br. J. Psychol.*, **53**, 229–242.

Burt, C. (1968) Brain and consciousness. *Br. J. Psychol.*, **59**, 55–69.

Gibson, J. J. (1967) In E. G. Boring & G. Lindzey (Eds.), *A History of Psychology in Autobiography*, vol. 5. New York: Appleton-Century-Crofts.

Harré, R. (1971) Joynson's dilemma. *Bull. Br. Psychol. Soc.*, **24**, 115–119.

Hearnshaw, L. S. (1964) *A Short History of British Psychology.* London: Methuen.

Hudson, L. (1970) The choice of Hercules. *Bull. Br. Psychol. Soc.*, **23**, 287–292.

James, W. (1890) *The Principles of Psychology*, vol. 1. New York: Holt.

Joynson, R. B. (1970) The breakdown of modern psychology. *Bull. Br. Psychol. Soc.*, **23**, 261–269.

Koch, S. (1961) Psychological science versus the science–humanism antinomy: intimations of a significant science of man. *Am. Psychol.*, **16**, 629–639.

Koch, S. (1964) Psychology and emerging conceptions of knowledge as unitary. In T. W. Wann (Ed.), *Behaviourism and Phenomenology*. Univ. of Chicago Press.

McKellar, P. (1962) The method of introspection. In J. Scher (Ed.), *Theories of the Mind*. New York: Free Press of Glencoe.

Mace, C. A. (1965) Causal explanations in psychology. In *Stephanos: Studies in Psychology: Essays presented to Sir Cyril Burt,* edited by C. Banks & P. L. Broadhurst. London: Univ. of London Press.

Mair, J. M. M. et al (1970) Symposium on the person in psychology and psychotherapy. *Br. J. Med. Psychol.*, **43**, 197–256.

Phillips, R. (1969) Psychological psychology: a new science? *Bull. Br. Psychol. Soc.*, **22**, 83–87.

Shotter, J. (1970) The philosophy of psychology: the psychological foundations of psychology. *Bull. Br. Psychol. Soc.*, **23**, 207–212.

Smail, D. J. (1968) The place of conscious experience in clinical and medical psychology. *Br. J. Med. Psychol.*, **41**, 169–176.

Smail, D. J. (1971) Statistical prediction and 'cookbooks': a technological confidence trick. *Br. J. Med. Psychol.*, **44**, 173–178.

Smedslund, J. (1969) Meanings, implications and universals: towards a psychology of man. *Scand. J. Psychol.*, **10**, 1–15.

Sprott, W. J. H. (1938) *General Psychology*. London: Longmans.

Stout, G. F. (1896) *Analytic Psychology*, vol. 1. London: Sonnenschein.

Taylor, J. G. (1971) A system built upon noise. *Bull. Br. Psychol. Soc.*, **24**, 121–125.

Tulving, E. & Madigan, S. A. (1970) Memory and verbal learning. *Ann. Rev. Psychol.*, **21**, 437–484.

Ward, J. (1893) 'Modern' psychology: a reflexion. *Mind*, **2** (n.s.), 54.

Ward, J. (1918) *Psychological Principles*. Cambridge Univ. Press.

Watson, J. B. (1914) *Behaviour: An Introduction to Comparative Psychology*. New York: Holt, Rinehart & Winston.

Zangwill, O. L. (1950) *An Introduction to Modern Psychology*. London: Methuen.

Zangwill, O. L. (1971) Correspondence. *Bull. Br. Psychol. Soc.*, **24**, 88–89.

4   What psychology is about *

D. O. HEBB

For a quarter century or more, ever since the end of the Second World War, psychology has been growing fast in ideas, methods, knowledge – data all over the place. To maintain perspective is difficult enough, but the difficulty is increased by our publications. It is bad

* This article was the APA Invited Address presented at the annual meeting of the American Psychological Association, Montreal, Canada, August 29, 1973.

The critical advice of Dalbir Bindra and Virginia Douglas is gratefully acknowledged.

not to see the wood for the trees, but worse not even to get to see a real tree because you're lost in the bushes, the undergrowth of insignificant detail and so-called replications, the trivial, the transient, the papers that haven't an idea anywhere about them. This one must find his way through also. There is a useful maxim that I owe to my colleague Reg Bromiley: What's not worth doing is not worth doing well. The journals are full of papers that are very well done and will not be heard of again. One well-known journal almost makes them its specialty. For all these reasons or in one or another of these ways it is easy to lose sight of the fundamentals of psychology as it stands today.

•   •   •

The current flood of papers, that deluge of data, leads us to forget fundamentals. I meet graduate students in seminar each year. They come from good schools and they've had as good teaching as there is. And most of them have no clear ideas about the relation of mind to body, or about consciousness, or what thought is, or free will. I didn't say good ideas (those are the ones I agree with); I only said clear ideas. They seem not to have been led to think about such problems. In seminar they hope the problems will go away if they just keep quiet about them. A majority, I would say, have no clarity even about the heredity–environment question; and this, ladies and gentlemen, I am inclined to give *you* the discredit for, since the literature suggests that some of you don't either.

•   •   •

The questions of mind, free will, thought – these are not unimportant matters, not insignificant. That book of Fred Skinner's (1971) *Beyond Freedom and Dignity* has demonstrated that they have real practical meaning. Skinner thinks the questions are important, and so do I. You no doubt realize that my answers differ from his, but I applaud his concern with fundamentals. And some of the criticism of *Beyond Freedom and Dignity* shows (like some of the criticism of Arthur Jensen) that there are questions on which some human psychologists – you know, the ones who don't work with animals – feel no need to think. They have ready-made answers.

One of those ready-made positions goes back to Thomas Jefferson, who swore 'eternal hostility' to any form of 'tyranny over the mind of man.' Skinner proposed to make people want to be good – and caught hell for it. He was told it is wicked to 'manipulate' the minds of others, and wicked to do anything to interfere with full freedom of choice. This is evil; this is something that no good humanistic, democratic, libertarian would ever do? Such statements are pure unthinking nonsense.

For what is a moral education? The very psychologists and philosophers who talk most about freedom are the ones who tolerate no nonsense from their children or their students, in moral and political questions. A liberal, democratic, moral education sets out, rightly, to *remove* freedom of choice from a child's mind in moral questions. The tyranny Jefferson objected to was imposing ideas *he* didn't agree with (and *we* don't agree with today, either). Imposing ideas we agree with is O.K., and necessary too. Education is in a bad way if a boy on reaching maturity has to sit down and argue out the question before deciding whether race prejudice is a good thing, or cruelty to animals, or fascist governments, or 'Watergating'

– or if a girl leaving home has still to figure out whether a career in shoplifting or prostitution would be a good idea. Impose ideas? Try to limit freedom of choice? Of course we do, all of us. Skinner's critics will say at once that this isn't at all what they were talking about. Maybe so, but it's clear they didn't stop to think before giving out the word, and I still don't see what's wrong about making people *want* to be good – if we could only make it work!

I am gradually getting around to an answer to the question, What is psychology about? by first telling you some things it is not or should not do. I have said that psychology is not one of the many narrow specialties that, between us, we cultivate. It is more than any one of them. It is important for the welfare of psychology to keep reminding oneself about fundamentals and to *think* about some of those issues. Now, what psychology *is*.

Psychology is a biological science. I think anyone will agree – including the monkey trainer, the rat-brain plumber and those who write down baby talk – that the urgent psychological problems are *social* and *clinical*. These are the big ones on which more light is needed to promote human welfare. These are the problems of prejudice and social conflict – at the worst, war – and the problems of mental disorder, neurosis and psychosis. Knowing more about the rat and pigeon is – I personally am sure – a step toward understanding man; maybe for practical purposes it's a necessary step; but it's peripheral; it's a means, not an end. Memory, however studied, is an essential component of behavior – but one component only. There is a larger picture to take account of, and its social and clinical implications are vital.

*   *   *

There are many people who are unhappy about the course of modern psychology and, I regret to say, this includes some psychologists. The objectors do not want an objective science, but a sort of self-contemplation. Not the hard-shell introspection of Titchener, Külpe and Wundt, but something sloppier. They tend to be dualists at heart, and they dislike what they think of as the materialism of experimental psychology; and they consider that psychology's true business is not with cats or monkeys, not brain lesions, not the use of tachistoscope or the analysis of variance. The more profound human experiences are what we should be working on. They want us to deal directly with the mystery of existence *now*. Some of this is simply antiscience – antiscience of any kind – which we needn't bother with here. But when someone thinks a science can be run that way, there *is* much to be said.

Subjective science? There isn't such a thing. Introspectionism is a dead duck. It is theoretically impossible: See Charles S. Peirce, America's greatest philosopher, 100 years ago; Gilbert Ryle, Oxford philosopher; Garry Boring, *Mr Psychology*; and George Humphrey, American-trained Oxford Professor of Psychology – a pretty distinguished lot for you to disprove if you think introspection is still in business. And then, if you do disprove them (nobody has tried so far), you still have to explain how come, if that subjective approach is the true path to a knowledge of man, it has achieved so little. What can you point to that either Wundt or Titchener left behind him, what light on the problem of mind and thought and feeling? Külpe, in a way, did better, for his work pointed straight to the proposition that psychology is objective, not subjective. William James is not an argument for subjective psychology; he took introspection for granted, but search his pages and you'll find precious little introspective data. Introspecting was *not* what James did.

And Freud – you realize of course that Freud's method with the unconscious was, by definition, objective – the study of that part of mental activity that the patient *cannot* report.

Piaget – objective method; Lashley on serial order and thought – objective method; Köhler on insight; Lewin on leadership; Harlow on love – all objective. What is there to cite as a contribution from subjective method that can be put beside their work?

And the same question must be asked about humanistic psychology. What is the payoff? What is its contribution to knowledge? I sympathize with the feeling that scientific psychology, as far as it has gone today, leaves much to be desired in the understanding of man and has little to tell us about how to live wisely and well. I am inclined to think that scientific psychology will always be incomplete in that sense. But the remedy is not to try to remake a science into one of the humanities. Humanistic psychology, I think, confuses two very different ways of knowing human beings and knowing how to live with self-respect. One is science; the other is literature. A science imposes limits on itself and makes its progress by attacking only those problems that it is fitted to attack by existing knowledge and methods. Psychology has made much progress in this century, and the rate of progress is accelerating, but it is limited and must be limited if it is to continue its progress – limited in the questions it can ask, but sure in its results.

The other way of knowing about human beings is the intuitive artistic insight of the poet, novelist, historian, dramatist and biographer. This alternative to psychology is a valid and a deeply penetrating source of light on man, going directly to the heart of the matter. If you refer to literature as a source of knowledge to a scientific type, he'll laugh at you. How can a novelist or a poet – a poet for god's sake – make discoveries? How can *he* have a knowledge of man that science hasn't? Science is the up-to-date thing; the paraphernalia of experiment and controlled observation and analysis of variance are the ways to find things out. Pick and shovel are out of date, now that we have bulldozers? But you can do things with a pick and shovel that you can't with a bulldozer; a man on foot can make observations that you can't make from a limousine. I challenge anyone to cite a scientific psychological analysis of character to match Conrad's study of Lord Jim, or Boswell's study of Johnson, or Johnson's of Savage.

It is to the literary world, not to psychological science, that you go to learn how to live with people, how to make love, how not to make enemies; to find out what grief does to people, or the stoicism that is possible in the endurance of pain, or how if you're lucky you may die with dignity; to see how corrosive the effects of jealousy can be, or how power corrupts or does not corrupt. For such knowledge and such understanding of the human species, don't look in my *Textbook of Psychology* (or anyone else's), try *Lear* and *Othello* and *Hamlet*. As a supplement to William James, read Henry James and Jane Austen and Mark Twain. These people are telling us things that are not on science's program. Trying to make over science to be simultaneously scientific and humanistic (in the true sense of that word) falls between two stools. Science is the servant of humanism, not part of it. Combining the two ruins both.

So, then, finally, what is psychology about? And the answer I give you is one I got from K. S. Lashley: psychology is about the mind; the central issue, the great mystery, the toughest problem of all. I grant that psychology is concerned with other matters, subsidiary questions; in fact, I have just been saying that a science must move slowly and can't hope to go right to the heart of things. There are many subsidiary questions to be clarified before we will have final answers to the central question, before we understand the operations of mind – if we ever do really understand them. Nevertheless, there are some answers possible that were not possible when Lashley first saw a set of Golgi slides of the frog brain and thought it might be possible to find out how the frog works. We still do not know how the frog works, let alone man. In fact, the problem looks tougher now than it did to Lashley in 1910, but we have made some advances, and there are some things one can say – that a biological science should say – about the human mind.

It is hardly necessary to say that the mind, for Lashley, was not a spirit held in the body. Biological science long ago got rid of vitalism. The idea of an immaterial mind controlling the body is vitalism, no more, no less; it has no place in science. I know that many of you are dualists and *do* believe that the mind is something other than brain activity. Indeed, it is conceivable that you are right. There is no way of proving the null hypothesis, no conceivable way of proving the nonexistence of something as slippery as the soul. But I put it to you that the null hypothesis can be disproved. If you believe in the existence of a spirit that guides man, the scientific and logical procedure for you is to assume its nonexistence, with the expectation that some day it will be found that this 'null hypothesis' is insufficient. That is, if you will take as a working assumption that there is no soul, you may one day show that there *is* one. This means that believers and unbelievers can avail themselves today of the same working assumption, of monism instead of dualism. Anything else, today, is not science.

Mind then is the capacity for thought, and thought is the integrative activity of the brain – that activity up in the control tower that, during waking hours, overrides reflex response and frees behavior from sense dominance. I do not propose here to refute, once more, the Watsonian notion that thought is muscular activity, mainly of the vocal organs. Walter B. Hunter, a tough, behavioristically minded scientist, showed how to refute it in 1913. The delayed-response method shows that response is not controlled by sensation alone. There are other demonstrations of the same thing, and the learning theorist who does not recognize it is simply refusing to face reality.

The fact of thought as a semi-independent factor in behavior is something that anyone working with mammals is familiar with. It is summed up in the third law. (The first law is, If anything can go wrong in the experiment, it will; the second law, Training takes time, whether or not anything is learned; and the third law, Any well-trained experimental animal, in a controlled environment and subject to controlled stimulation, will do as he damned well pleases.)

That's an old joke and you may be bored by hearing it again. But it has a significance that may not have struck you. What the third law is talking about is the fact of free will in animals – higher animals, at least – and what it says is that free will is not some fancy philosophical abstraction or something J. B. Rhine thought up, but an ordinary, familiar, biological phenomenon, a product of evolution. Free will is not a violation of scientific law; it doesn't mean indeterminism; it's not mystical. What it is, simply, is a control of behavior by the thought process. Not all behavior is so controlled, even in the higher animal, reflexive response being excluded. But most behavior of man or monkey or ape is under a joint guidance by sense input and the immediately prior pattern of cortical activity; and the cortical component in that control is free will. The idea that free will means indeterminism is simply a misunderstanding.

Let me take a minute more on this, because it's important. I am a determinist. I assume that what I am and how I think are entirely the products of my heredity and my environmental history. I have no freedom about what I *am*. But that is not what free will is about. The question is whether my behavior is entirely controlled by present circumstances. Heredity and environment shaped me, largely while I was growing up. That shaping, including how I think about things, may incline me to act in opposition to the shaping that the *present* environment would be likely to induce: and so I may decide to be polite to others, or sit down to write this article when I'd rather not, or, on the other hand, decide to goof off when I should be working. If my past has shaped me to goof off, and I do goof off despite my secretary's urging, that's free will. But it's not indeterminism.

Free will thus has a physiological basis, in the relative autonomy of the activity of the cerebrum. Here again is evidence of the way in which physiological and biological conceptions can be clarifying, as we think about the evolution of that equipment up in the control tower – between the ears – and how it works. One would think consequently that physiological psychologists should be first among those who see man as a whole, those who keep us reminded of the main objective: an understanding of that integrative function of the cerebral cortex that makes man what he is. And are they?

Mostly, no. Mostly they are afraid of theory. Mostly they are even worse at keeping an eye on the ball than the paired-associate learners and the analysis of variance experts. Mostly. But some exception must be made for those whose work takes them into the neurological clinic and exposes them to the real problems of real people. A couple of Montreal examples are Brenda Milner, on the devastating effects of total loss of capacity to form new memories, and Ronald Melzack on pain – pain being pretty good at bringing out man's humanity, in one way or another. But the outstanding example for my present purposes is the work of Sperry and Gazzaniga on split-brain patients. For any one of you who is concerned about the mind–body question, for anyone who proposes to philosophize about the fundamental nature of consciousness, that work is essential. Read that if you never read anything else about the brain. I speak to the dualist especially, the one who considers that consciousness can't be something produced by the brain. Sperry (1968) made a case for his conclusion that longitudinal sectioning of the human brain into left and right halves has the result that the patient has two minds: a left-hand mind and a right-hand mind, each with its own separate purposes, thoughts and perceptions. The surgeon's knife can cut brain tissue, no problem there: can it also cut an immaterial mind in two, make a longitudinal section of the ghost in the machine? Today, no one, psychologist, philosopher, neurologist or humanist, is entitled to an opinion on the mind–body question if he is unfamiliar with the split-brain procedure and its results in human patients.

•   •   •

I may have missed someone in these unprovoked aggressions, in this catalog of gripes, but it's time for me to wind it up. I have argued that psychology is a biological science, including its social and clinical wings; that a science is self-limiting, holding more or less strictly to its own narrow modes of procedure; and consequently that mixing psychology up with other ways of knowing human beings – the literary and artistic way – is to the detriment of both. We must honor the humanities, but a science cannot imitate them. I have answered the implied question, What is psychology about? by saying that its central concern must be man's mind and thought. Each of us has his own avenue of approach to that understanding, which we must approach by degrees. It is a far prospect, and in the meantime we have to keep on with the study of memory, perception, psycholinguistics, fear, and so on and so forth; but it may be disastrous in the long run for psychology when the specialist digging his own path deeper and deeper loses sight of what others are doing in other fields and so loses an invaluable perspective.

ACKNOWLEDGEMENT

This paper first appeared in *Am. Psychol.* (1974), **29**, 71–79. Extracts are published here with the kind permission of author and editor.

REFERENCES

Skinner, B. F. (1971) *Beyond Freedom and Dignity.* New York: Knopf.
Sperry, R. W. (1968) Hemisphere deconnection and unity in conscious awareness. *Am. Psychol.*, **23**, 723–733.

5   Factors of the brain *

JOHN McFIE

An attempt to relate activity of different regions of the brain to specific cognitive functions will not, of course, interest information theorists – to whom the shape of the black box is irrelevant – and among others may arouse the suspicion of being no more than a new brand of phrenology. The historic study by Lashley (1929) has left an almost indelible impression on current psychological thinking, to the extent that Vernon (1950), in his review of the structure of intellectual abilities, explicitly rejected the possibility of a correlation with the structure of the brain: 'We know now that traits and abilities are not located in particular parts of the brain.' Later (1965), he proposed that it is environmental factors which largely determine the nature of intelligence: 'that intelligence is no one thing, but rather a name for a group of overlapping mental skills whose content depends considerably on what a particular culture values, or on what psychologists who belong to that culture like to include within their concept'. Though less emphatic, the same point of view is implicit in Bruner's (1964): 'We move, perceive and think in a fashion that depends upon techniques rather than upon wired-in arrangements in our nervous system.'

It is worth recalling, however, that Lashley himself admitted that his study was essentially one of learning ability and that if a distinction were to be established between learning and intelligence, his conclusion might be 'irrelevant to the problem of intelligence'.

---

* In both form and content, this paper was intended to be a compliment, and perhaps a complement, to the work of Sir Cyril Burt, and I had hoped that he would be able to read it as such. Under the circumstances, it becomes a kind of tribute; and I should have wished it to approach his own level of clarity and erudition. These, however, I cannot hope to emulate, and I therefore offer it as a token of respect.

Moreover, as the number of clinical studies of localized brain injury in man accumulated, Lashley himself (1938) modified his point of view, at least with regard to the human brain, to allow for regional subdivisions serving particular abilities.

In his review of factorial theories of mental function, Burt (1940) noted that the hierarchical classification of intellectual factors followed the predicables of medieval logic as to *genus*, *species*, *proprium* and *accidens*. If we follow the same principles of classification in neuropsychology, we start with the brain. Here we may note not only the obvious relationship of mental function to the contents of the skull but also the clear relationship shown by Wechsler (1958) between brain weight and uncorrected total test scores at different ages, the curves running parallel to each other from childhood to old age.

Turning to specific differences within the brain, the obvious distinction is between the left and right hemispheres; and these correspond functionally to the broad subdivision of cognitive abilities into verbal and non-verbal. Until recently the only evidence of this functional relationship derived from studies of intellectual impairment in patients with cerebral lesions, but in a series of studies comparing the relative efficiency of perception of the two half-fields of vision and of the two ears, Kimura (1966, 1967) has shown that these hemispheric differences may be demonstrated in normal subjects. To this extent, the old objection that the site of a lesion which impaired a function did not necessarily indicate the localization of that function loses much of its force. In the days when large parts of the cerebrum were dismissed as 'silent areas' it might have seemed possible to suppose that a function was mediated by a region other than that in which a lesion impaired it; but today, with much of the cortex demonstrably occupied with psychological functions, there is little place for this argument.

Under the predicable *proprium* the appropriate functions of the greater part of these formerly uncharted areas have now been elucidated and correspond not surprisingly to higher levels – what Rylander (1939) has termed 'intellectual antecedents' – of disorders known to the neurologist as aphasia, apraxia, agnosia and the rest, and associated with specifically localized lesions. Expressive or motor aphasia is associated with lesions of the left frontal lobe, and Milner (1964) has shown that excisions in this part of the brain result in lower scores on a test of verbal fluency. Receptive or sensory aphasia is associated with left temporal or temporo-parietal lesions and in a study of a series of more than 200 adult patients with localized lesions, McFie (1960) demonstrated a specific association between impairment on the Similarities, and to a lesser extent on the Vocabulary, subtests of the Wechsler Scales and lesions in the left temporal lobe.

Acalculia and constructional apraxia are features of damage to the posterior part of the left parietal lobe and McFie (1960) found that patients with left parietal lesions (not clinically acalculic or apraxic) showed significant impairment on the Arithmetic and Block Design subtests of the Wechsler Scales. The posterior part of the left temporo-parietal region is characteristically associated with alexia and agraphia – disturbance of reading and writing – and although these are skills rather than intellectual (in the sense of problem-solving) functions, they must be included in the psychological chart of the left hemisphere (see figure 5.1).

To judge from current textbooks of physiology and psychology, the right hemisphere remains (except for its sensory and motor functions) uncharted; nor, to judge by the blank expressions of many graduates on being asked its functions, are most lectures any more up to date than textbooks in this respect. Yet it is in this country that the work of Zangwill and

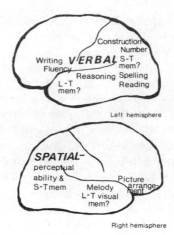

Left hemisphere

Right hemisphere

Figure 5.1   Abilities impaired by localized cerebral lesions. L-T, S-T mem = long-term, short-term memory.

his colleagues, first with cases of missile wounds of the head and later with patients with naturally occurring lesions, elucidated the primary importance of the right parieto-temporo-occipital area in spatial perception. These patients were significantly more impaired on the Block Designs Test (McFie, 1960) and were therefore viewed as having visual–constructional disabilities, not dissimilar from constructional apraxia.

However, a qualitative comparison with the type of impairment shown by patients with similar lesions in the left hemisphere by McFie and Zangwill (1960) lent support to the impression that the disorder in the left hemisphere patients was one of manipulation, whereas in the right hemisphere cases it was of perception. Subsequently, experimental studies of patients with localized lesions (e.g. Warrington and James, 1967a) have confirmed the right hemisphere deficit as a perceptual one. Moreover, studies of impairment of proprioceptive function (Lenz, 1944) and of vestibular function (Hécaen, de Ajuriaguerra and Massonet, 1951) suggest that it is within this large cortical area that visual, auditory, vestibular and proprioceptive information is integrated to form the basis of spatial perception.

More anteriorly in the right hemisphere there are, admittedly, large areas of 'terra incognita' but Milner (1962) has shown that there is impairment of appreciation of tone patterns with lesions of the right temporal lobe. An interesting study of Warrington and James (1967b) suggests that whereas memory for new visual material (in this case, photographs of unfamiliar faces) is impaired with right parietal lesions, recognition of 'old' visual material (well-known faces) is more disturbed by right temporal lesions. Another perceptual deficit associated with right hemisphere lesion involves the interpretation of pictorial material; Milner (1968) has found impairment on the McGill Picture Anomalies Test and on the Mooney Figures Test with right temporal lesions, while McFie (1960) found significantly greater impairment on the Picture Arrangement subtest of the Wechsler Scales with right frontal and temporal lesions.

It will not have escaped the informed reader that many of the functions described as impairment of localized cerebral lesions correspond to the principal factors of intellectual ability derived by factor analysis of test scores of normal subjects. Indeed, the impairment noted by Milner in cases of left frontal lesion was on Thurstone's test of verbal fluency; and Similarities and Vocabulary load highest among the Wechsler subtests on the verbal reasoning factor (Wechsler, 1958). Performance on the Arithmetic subtest may likewise be identified with the numerical factor, though this loading in factor analysis is complicated by the memory and verbal content of the test material – in partially hearing subjects, Hine (1970) has shown that a numerical factor emerges from analysis of the Wechsler subtests; Constructional ability is paralleled by Alexander's (1935) F factor.

The spatial abilities related to right hemisphere function may similarly be identified on the intellectual level with the spatial factor. It is true that no accepted test of this factor has been used in the study of patients with cerebral lesion: an attempt by the writer to test a patient with a right parietal lesion on Thurstone's Primary Mental Abilities tests was frustrated by the fact that the patient's spatial disorientation led him to mark the answers incorrectly even on the verbal tests. Nevertheless, it seems unreasonable – even unparsimonious – to insist that the evidence for cerebral localization of psychological functions does not apply also to group factors of ability. The reason for their emergence as factors from the intercorrelations of test scores of normal subjects may be due to the relative proximity, or profuseness, of neural connections between the relevant cerebral areas. In this view, the correlations would be due, as Thomson (1939) suggested, to the interaction of the neurones involved; but not in the kind of brain which Thomson had in mind – 'a rich, comparatively undifferentiated complex of innumerable influences' – but in a heterogeneous structure.

The position of memory in this classification is an uncertain one. Spearman (1927) found relatively low correlations between memory tests and tests of intellectual ability and held that 'retentivity' was a process different from 'intellection'. Vernon (1950) also reported conflicting evidence on the association of mnemonic and intellectual ability. To this extent, memory may be a *genus* of its own; and recent studies of its subdivision into short-term and long-term components suggest that it bears little relation to the intellectual abilities. Memory must, however, be of material of one kind or another, and to this extent it may be divided into memory for verbal and for non-verbal (visual) material; and here the same neurological associations apply as to intellectual material. McFie (1960) found that whereas Digit Span was impaired by left hemisphere lesions, Memory for Designs was impaired by lesions on the right; more recently Shallice and Warrington (1970) reported a case of profound impairment of short-term auditory–verbal memory associated with a left parietal lesion which may be contrasted with the demonstration of impaired memory for visual material in right parietal lesions (Warrington and James, 1967a).

Impairment of long-term memory is the classical sign of organic dementia (though neurologists would call it 'memory for recent events'). Long-term memory has been demonstrated in a number of studies, reviewed by Milner (1970), to be dependent upon the integrity of the hippocampus and mamillary bodies and their connections, deep in the medial parts of the brain. Here again, the evidence suggests that these structures on the left side are concerned with retention of verbal material, and on the right with non-verbal.

We are left with the predicable *accidens*, and here we may include departures from the conventional pattern of organization described in the above paragraphs. Approximately 1% of right-handed individuals may suffer a speech disorder as a consequence of a right hemisphere lesion, and in left-handed subjects the chances of speech disorder are approximately twice as likely with right- as with left-sided lesions (Piercy, 1964). In some left-handed patients, however, further anomalies of organization have been reported, such as coexistence of disturbances of writing and of spatial perception with right hemisphere lesions (Ettlinger, Jackson and Zangwill, 1956).

These incidental differences need not, however, detract from the burden of our argument: that intellectual abilities are organized in specific regions of the brain. Nor, of course, need the evident difference in intellectual level attained by different individuals diminish its force. Indeed, the fact that each individual tends to reach a similar level in all his intellectual abilities is not only an argument for the overall unitary nature of intelligence but also provides an opportunity for using psychological tests in neurological diagnosis.

What, the reader may ask, is the consequence (apart from its clinical utility) of this point of view? What does it matter if one can 'localize' all these abilities, when it is obvious that the brain normally works as a whole? First, I think, it gives one a new viewpoint from which to consider cognitive abilities. We may note, for instance, that although impairment of arithmetical ability is characteristically associated with the left parietal lesions, some studies (e.g. Weisenburg and McBride, 1936; McFie, 1960) have reported impairment of calculation with right-sided lesions. We find in this strong support for the view that calculation in some way involves spatial abilities.

Further, we avoid erroneous associations, such as thinking of 'abstraction' as a non-verbal ability (de Renzi et al, 1966, showed that its impairment was related to impairment of verbal comprehension), or of reading as involving spatial ability (the two functions are organized in opposite hemispheres).

Thirdly, studies of the effect of localized cerebral lesions may suggest the existence of specific abilities not hitherto revealed by analysis of test results of normal subjects. Thus a particular kind of reasoning may be involved in the aspect of Picture Arrangement which is sensitive to right fronto-temporal lesions; or the distinction between visual recognition and spatial perception suggested by Newcombe and Russell (1969) and Warrington and Rabin (1970) may be confirmed by appropriate experiments.

Finally, the demonstration that the main factors of intellectual ability have a neuro-anatomical reality places them in a rather stronger position than Vernon's (1965) culturally determined theory would suggest. To this extent, it is appropriate that new tests of intelligence, in whatever culture, should be designed to sample the intellectual abilities whose existence has been confirmed by neuro-psychological methods.

ACKNOWLEDGEMENT

This article first appeared in *Bull. Br. Psychol. Soc.* (1972), **25**, 11–14, and is published here with the kind permission of author and editor.

REFERENCES

Alexander, W. P. (1935) Intelligence, concrete and abstract. *Br. J. Psychol. Monogr. Suppl.* 19.
Bruner, J. S. (1964) The course of cognitive growth. *Am. Psychol.*, **19**, 1–15.
Burt, C. (1940) *Factors of the Mind.* London: Univ. of London Press.
de Renzi, E., Faglioni, P., Savoiardo, M. & Vignolo, L. A. (1966) The influence of aphasia

and of the hemispheric side of the cerebral lesion on abstract thinking. *Cortex*, **2**, 399–420.

Ettlinger, G., Jackson, C. V. & Zangwill, O. L. (1956) Cerebral dominance in sinistrals. *Brain*, **79**, 569–588.

Hécaen, H., de Ajuriaguerra, J. & Massonet, J. (1951) Troubles visuo-constructifs par lésion pariéto-occipitale droite. *Encéphale*, **40**, 122–179.

Hine, W. D. (1970) The abilities of partially hearing children. *Br. J. Educ. Psychol.*, **40**, 171–178.

Kimura, D. (1966) Dual functional asymmetry of the brain in visual perception. *Neuropsychologia*, **4**, 275–285.

Kimura, D. (1967) Functional asymmetry of the brain in dichotic listening. *Cortex*, **3**, 163–178.

Lashley, K. S. (1929) *Brain Mechanisms and Intelligence*. Chicago: Univ. of Chicago Press.

Lashley, K. S. (1938) Factors limiting recovery after central nervous lesions. *J. Nerv. Ment. Dis.*, **88**, 733–755.

Lenz, H. (1944) Raumsinnstörungen bei Hirnverletzungen. *Dtsch. Z. Nervenheilk.*, **157**, 22–64.

McFie, J. (1960) Psychological testing in clinical neurology. *J. Nerv. Ment. Dis.*, **131**, 383–393.

McFie, J. & Zangwill, O. L. (1960) Visual–constructive disabilities associated with lesions of the left cerebral hemisphere. *Brain*, **83**, 243–260.

Milner, B. (1962) Laterality effects in audition. In V. B. Mountcastle (Ed.), *Interhemispheric Relations and Cerebral Dominance*. Baltimore: Johns Hopkins Press.

Milner, B. (1964) Some effects of frontal lobectomy in man. In J. M. Warren & K. Akert (Eds.), *The Frontal Granular Cortex and Behavior*. New York: McGraw-Hill.

Milner, B. (1968) Visual recognition and recall after right temporal-lobe excision in man. *Neuropsychologia*, **6**, 191–209.

Milner, B. (1970) Memory and the medial temporal regions of the brain. In K. H. Pribram & D. E. Broadbent (Eds.), *Biology of Memory*. New York: Academic Press.

Newcombe, F. & Russell, W. R. (1969) Dissociated visual perceptual and spatial deficits in focal lesions of the right hemisphere. *J. Neurol. Neurosurg. Psychiat.*, **32**, 73–81.

Piercy, M. F. (1964) The effects of cerebral lesions on intellectual function. *Br. J. Psychiat.*, **110**, 310–352.

Rylander, G. (1939) Personality changes after operations on the frontal lobes. *Acta Psychiat. Neurol.* suppl. 20.

Shallice, T. & Warrington, E. K. (1970) Independent functioning of verbal memory stores. *Q. J. Exp. Psychol.*, **22**, 261–273.

Spearman, C. (1927) *The Abilities of Man*. London: Macmillan.

Thomson, G. H. (1939) *The Factorial Analysis of Human Ability*. London: Univ. of London Press.

Vernon, P. E. (1950) *The Structure of Human Abilities*. London: Methuen.

Vernon, P. E. (1965) Environmental handicaps and intellectual development. *Br. J. Educ. Psychol.*, **35**, 9–20.

Warrington, E. K. & James, M. (1967a) Disorders of visual perception in patients with localized cerebral lesions. *Neuropsychologia*, **5**, 253–266.

Warrington, E. K. & James, M. (1967b) An experimental investigation of facial recognition in patients with unilateral cerebral lesions. *Cortex*, **3**, 317–326.

Warrington, E. K. & Rabin, P. (1970) Perceptual matching in patients with cerebral lesions. *Neuropsychologia*, **8**, 475–487.

Wechsler, D. (1958) *The Measurement and Appraisal of Adult Intelligence*. Baltimore: Williams & Wilkins.

Weisenburg, T. H. & McBride, K. E. (1936) *Aphasia*. New York: Commonwealth Fund.

PART 3

Human motivation

INTRODUCTION

One omission from the first edition of *Psychology and the Teacher* was recognition of the contribution made by Cattell and McClelland to the study of motivation. This has now been rectified both in the core text and here. I had the privilege of working with Ray Cattell in America and it was during this period that I learnt sufficient of his theory and practical contributions to motivation. The paper on Cattell's theory of dynamic structure was intended to simplify a difficult area and it tells only a small portion of the story, attempting to quantify and apply motivational measures to educational settings. McClelland's work, which overlaps with Cattell's, uses a quite different approach to measurement. Whereas Cattell employs almost exclusively psychometric techniques, McClelland uses projection techniques (Thematic Apperception tests and interpretation) in order to tap achievement motivation. The paper used here gives some evidence in support of specially designed courses for improving achievement motivation. It is important to note the age (14–15 year olds), and the subjects showing improvement (science and mathematics). This latter finding has significance for those taking ROSLA groups.

The now famous and much criticized work of Rosenthal and Jacobson has been included so that students can read and evaluate the work for themselves. There is a logic about the self-fulfilling prophecy in classroom performance, although its influence may well have been exaggerated. Notice in their work that *I.Q.* was used and not classroom performance; some I.Q. values were interpolated (did not appear in the conversion tables and had to be calculated by assuming the scales extended beyond the age ranges given); only two grades (the youngest ones at six to seven years) out of six gave significant results.

Mention is made of the Yerkes–Dodson Law in the main text. Broadhurst attempted to show the multiple relationship between motivation, level of anxiety, level of difficulty and performance in animals. If the findings can be transferred to human subjects they have important implications for all manner of classroom performance and practices.

6   Motivation and dynamic structure – Cattell's theory of motivation and its application in education *

DENNIS CHILD

A number of serious explanations of human motivation has arisen during this century. Many of them have taken us no further than theoretical appraisals having some face validity, that is a certain common-sense feel about them without any corresponding experimental evidence to substantiate the claims made.

In some ways, the experimental psychologists have come closer to firmer foundations by fixing their attention on animal motivation research. This has the advantage that powerful manipulation can be used, and physiological alterations arranged, including vivisection. However, though general laws of animal motivation might arise, their transfer to human affairs is by analogy only because the tremendous investment of human motivation in cultural domains has scarcely any counterpart.

It was at this point that Raymond Cattell entered the scene in the mid 1930s. As a matter of fact, he is an Englishman by birth but has lived in America since the 1930s. He is, perhaps, better known for his researches into personality (chiefly in the form of the 16PF) and intelligence (his theory of fluid and crystallized intelligence). But his contribution to the study of motivation, whilst it has not received anything like the same amount of publicity and praise as his other work, has nevertheless been very substantial and the first part of this paper

---

*Extracts from papers given to a conference of B.Ed. students in the University of Birmingham Institute of Education area, February 1974.

is devoted to an elaboration of the theoretical model. The latter part looks at the application of the theory to educational problems. We shall also see in this theory a subtle blending of the biogenic/sociogenic spectrum.

The most significant element running through Cattell's work is his use of the mathematical procedure known as factor analysis. This is a technique for exploring a large number of related variables (using a statistic known as a correlation coefficient) in order to discover the factors which are responsible for their interrelationship. In other words, we start with a large number of interrelated variables and by using factor analysis we end up with a small number of independent (or almost independent) factors – some would go as far as to say 'causes' – which account for the relationships. But the important point to notice about the technique is that it depends upon the existence of multivariate happenings and *not*, as in the case of much research in psychology, on bivariate, controlled experiment. The reason why this is important rests on the obvious observation that man is a multivariate creature living in a multivariate environment, and the only feasible way of studying him *in situ* is to employ multivariate analysis. Bivariate methods – taking dependent and independent variables and manipulating the latter whilst observing corresponding change in the former – have only a limited use in the very complex network of human actions. Multivariate designs, on the other hand, have the marked advantage that we can let nature do its own powerful experiments with human emotional learning whilst we tease out by a superior statistical device the connections we cannot establish directly.

WHAT IS THE BASIC S–R UNIT USED BY CATTELL IN THE DYNAMIC STUDY OF MOTIVATION?

It was with this powerful technique that Cattell explored the very tricky realm of human motivation. The first important question was 'what fundamental concept could be used in order to assess the quantity and quality of motivated behaviour?' Other workers in this field, especially in the behaviourist tradition, have used the 'reflex' or even operantly conditionable 'bits' of behaviour as in the work of Skinner and his associates. However, Cattell preferred to use a larger unit which represented a more substantial course of action. Thus he entered the hierarchy of complex stimulus–response behaviour at the level of the *attitude* which comes as close as any other to defining an element, the strength of which in a given situation foreshadows a given course of action. The situation may be that my boss refuses to raise my salary and my attitude to this stimulus can become manifest in a variety of ways: I may slacken my effort at work; I may try to impress my boss in words and deeds so that he may reverse his decision; I may start a campaign amongst fellow workers or appeal to a union representative; or I may just move to another job. All of these courses of action – i.e. responses to a given situation – are of a reasonable and manageable 'size' in the totality of behaviour. The basic questions which Cattell asks and which he hopes the measurement of attitude and interest will answer include such considerations as: are there unitary structures or uniformities in the pattern of response which reflect basic human drives? How are new interests and motives acquired? Do patterns of interest show any order in a given culture? Notice, by the way, that the terms 'attitude' and 'interest' are used interchangeably by Cattell.

Let us look more closely at the term 'strength of an attitude' as used in this context and how it might lead to the exposure of unitary traits. The term 'strength of an attitude' is used in a highly specific sense as a measure of *the strength of a course of action, or tendency to a course of action, in response to a stimulus*. It is not to be confused with the popular 'ballot box' questionnaire meaning which has become associated with the concept. Thus for some social scientists an attitude represents a static opinion or inclination for or against an object, idea or institution without there necessarily being a corresponding course of action. On the contrary, attitudes as defined in the present context *always* proceed to a course of action including the course of action requiring a verbal response which has a physical correlate.

As indicated elsewhere (Cattell and Child, 1975) one problem in this popular use is that 'the investigators have generally been prepared to accept the individual's purely verbal behavior as evidence of his attitude (giving yes/no answers to a set of statements). This naïve, verbal, conscious method of response represents only one of many ways by which we can tap the domain of human attitudes. There can be a world of difference between what a person thinks he might do or say in a given situation and what that person *actually* does. If a child is asked how many ice-cream cornets he would enjoy, he might say a dozen. In practice, he might enjoy the first six, but once he becomes satisfied he may begin to experience aversion to eating more.' As we shall see presently, there are many devices available for measuring the strength of attitudes drawn from such diverse psychological fields as memory, perception, selective attention, retroactive inhibition, animal research, neurophysiology and psychodynamics. The important point to notice is that the strength of action or tendency to action is not only (or necessarily) verbal, but physiological, emotional and intellectual.

Clearly, as we have noted, there is a hierarchy of stimulus–response relationships which vary within each situation. The problem is to break into this hierarchy at a point where we can make a meaningful measure and Cattell has taken the attitude to be the point of entry. Obviously, an attitude is reflected in many stimulus–response activities because the tendency to respond to a situation involves a number of motor responses connected with 'sub-situations'. Where the reactions to sub-situations compound to give a consistent response pattern, we have an attitude. In turn, higher order patterns combining attitudes to form habits, generalized attitudes and sentiments also exist.

Cattell (1957) has suggested a paradigm in the following form:

In these circumstances	*I*	*want so much*	*to do this*	*with that*
(stimulus situation)	(organism)	(interest–need of a certain intensity)	(specific goal, course of action, response)	(object concerned in the action)

Examples of attitude statements might be: 'I want to become a proficient teacher', 'I want to know more mathematics', or 'I want to see my political party maintain or increase its influence'.

Thus, for a particular person in a particular situation, the parts are (a) the nature of the course of action, (b) the intensity of the interest in the course of action and (c) the object involved in the action. The paradigm contains rather more than the traditional stimulus–organism–response model (S–O–R) of many learning theorists, because there are two qualifying terms, 'want so much' and 'to do this', which require a consideration of both the *magnitude* and the *direction*, respectively, of the attitude.

MEASURING THE STRENGTH OF AN ATTITUDE-INTEREST

How have psychologists in the past tried to measure the strength of an interest or motive? In fact, the psychological literature is rich in measures of interest from physiological, clinical and learning theory researches. At least seventy principally psychological methods have been devised (Horn, 1966). A few are given below:

Preferences – greater interest in an object or idea would tend to motivate an individual more readily. Therefore, given two courses of action as possible solutions to a behavioural problem, a person is most likely to choose that course which appeals to him most.

Autism – (a) That is misperception or distorted perception of objects, noises, etc., in accordance with the direction of interests (e.g. the Bruner coin perception study where children were shown coins at a distance. Children from homes where little money was available overestimated the size and value of the coins as compared with children from rich homes.

(b) misbelief or distortion of beliefs such as to make the facts favour a course of action.

Utilities choice – willingness to use one's capital or labour for the sake of an interest (Unions give money to the Socialists, some industries give money to the Conservatives).

Fantasy rumination – tendency to spend one's time ruminating on interest-related material (most interesting college subjects tend to steal the most time).

Rationalisation – a tendency to interpret information in a way which makes one's interest appear more significant than it is.

Threat reactivity – psychogalvanic resistance drop and increase in cardiovascular output when interest is threatened.

Selective perception – ease of finding interest-related material embedded in complex field (e.g. the 'cocktail party effect').

Learning speed – speed of learning is increased with interest-related material.

Information – tendency to accumulate more information with interest-related events.

These are just a few of the ways in which we respond to interest-provoking situations and each of these can be measured. To illustrate briefly a few response patterns which accompany heightened interest, consider a young man studying a subject of his own choice to 'A' level. He would tend to recall and reminisce (and even dream) about aspects of the subject; whenever the subject is mentioned (on TV, in the press or by others) it is likely to attract his attention; he is more likely to get involved in discussion and debate, to learn the material more rapidly and to accumulate more information; more time and money (buying books, visiting libraries, plays, museums, etc.) will be invested in the objects and places of interest associated with the subject; new discoveries, concepts mastered, problems unresolved may be accompanied by physiological arousal. All these legitimate signs of motivation-strength become, for Cattell, the *devices* for measuring attitude strength. Notice that the devices come from diverse psychological fields such as perception, clinical psychology, physiology.

THE ANALYSIS OF DEVICES

We have defined, therefore, a variable in motivation, which is the *attitude*, and a collection of *devices* for measuring the strength of an attitude-interest. Cattell next factor-analysed the information obtained from large samples of adults using many devices for many attitudes. Figure 6.1 in the shape of a box demonstrates the three modes of analysis possible from the three sources of variation. We have, in addition to attitudes and devices, the variation amongst those people involved in the experiment. The 'slices' of the data box obtained give rise to factors as follows:

(i)   many devices completed by a large sample of people using one attitude at a time give rise to *Primary Motivational Components*;

(ii) many attitudes completed by a large sample of people using one device at a time give rise to *ergs* and *sentiments*;

(iii) many devices and attitudes completed by one person (on several occasions or analysed one person at a time) and this gives rise to the components suggested in (i) and (ii) above.

We need say little about the motivational components (seven substantial factors) at this point except that they favour, in some respects, the Freudian concepts of Id, Superego and Ego. Whilst to some extent this may seem to validate the theoretical Freudian structure, I must point out that the motivational components bear only a superficial resemblance to this structure (see Cattell and Child, *op. cit.*).

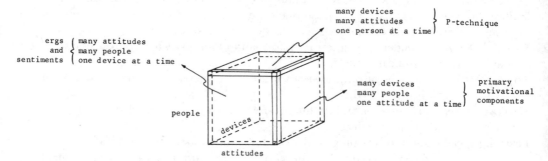

Figure 6.1   The data box for the analysis of motivational factors.

Because of the way in which the original data were analysed, it is possible to carry out a second order analysis on these components, i.e. to take the seven factors and treat them as variables in another factor analysis. Intriguingly, two major factors emerge which Cattell has called the *Integrated* (I) and *Unintegrated* (U) components. Briefly, the Integrated component brings together those devices which show relatively firm, cognitively invested, experience and consciously integrated and controlled interest. The Unintegrated component, on the other hand, reflects spontaneity – that is a susceptibility to momentary stimulation and is, in part, unconscious or pre-conscious. It is possible to obtain a measure of conflict by subtracting the integrated from the unintegrated score (U − I). The larger this figure, the greater the conflict likely.

THE ANALYSIS OF ATTITUDES

Turning now to the results obtained when the second slice of the data box is factor analysed, in order to explore the attitude realm, a very careful selection of devices was made in the light of the pattern of components just mentioned above. A Motivation Analysis Test battery (MAT) was designed using the four devices of Autism, Utilities, Information and Association (paired words). In selecting these particular devices, Cattell had made sure that the four most significant motivational components were present *and* at the second order level; Autism and Utilities were U (unintegrated) components whilst Information and Association were I (integrated) components. Thus we have four major components represented and of these two are Integrated and two Unintegrated second order factors. Using an extensive item bank for these four devices, Cattell looked at the underlying structure of attitudes towards a wide variety of human activities concerning work, play, friends, political parties, church, etc. The level of the attitude would of course be specific, such as 'I want more free time', 'I want to resist adverts and save my money', 'I want to support my local church', etc.

Now we come to one of the most fascinating discoveries from the analysis. Cattell found two kinds of factor. He referred to these as *sentiments* and *ergs*.

Sentiments   These are clusters, or collections of acquired attitudes centred on persons, objects or particular social institutions whereby an individual can attempt to satisfy his basic *human needs* (I stress human because there is as yet little evidence to suggest that sentiments are to be found in animals). The *human needs*, as we shall see, relate to the ergs. We do not go directly to the satisfaction of biological goals such as satisfying hunger, thirst or being assertive, escaping to security, mating, etc. In the complexities of civilization, we use certain subgoals, employing, where appropriate, the pathways provided by our culture in order to achieve these goals. If you look at figure 6.2 you will see a lattice – the *dynamic lattice* – showing how the attitudes subsidiate to certain sentiments such as hobbies, one's country, God, one's occupation, etc. Note that these attitude aggregates in the form of sentiments become learned through membership of a home, school, society, etc. They are acquired. There are naturally many sentiments, and I will mention just five substantial ones which have figured in Cattell's researches: career; sweetheart or spouse; home (parental); superego – which is concerned with a person's attitudes towards social obligations and is often expressed in terms of conscience and fundamental moral values; and self-sentiment, i.e. a set of attitudes which grow up around the self-concept and has to do with the individual's interests in maintaining self-respect, good social reputation, high level of self-control, being good at his job and so on.

Ergs   We mentioned *basic human needs* in the previous section on sentiments and as it transpired the other major factors obtained by Cattell were similar in appearance to the hypothesized instincts of McDougall and the drives of Hull. A glance at the dynamic lattice will reveal several ergs at the right-hand side of the chain. There are more, but in Cattell's researches five have been prominent. They are: mating; assertiveness; pugnacity (or aggressiveness); narcism (short for narcissism – which is the tendency to seek comfort and, if present in excess, will lead to self-indulgence, avoidance of work which is in any way uncomfortable, etc.); and the fifth erg frequently used is fear.

These ergs are thought to be innate, but the dynamic lattice shows how distorted the satisfaction of these urges can become. If we look at the dynamic lattice as a whole, it is evident that the ergic goals such as eating food, mating, and responding more readily with fear to thunder and the dark, are largely inborn, relatively unlearned responses – or at least they are responses that are learned far more readily than any random behaviour would be. But in the history of the culture, direct routes to satisfaction have been hedged in or blocked by rituals and taboos in various ways. Also one must realize that the spread of the dynamic lattice grows from right to left, and by the time we get to the extreme left, we are dealing with whole series of attitudes and courses of action that are learned as a means of satisfying the goals on the right of the lattice.

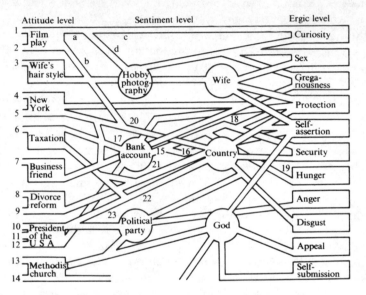

Figure 6.2   Fragment of a dynamic lattice showing attitude subsidiation, sentiment structure and ergic goals. (Source: Cattell, 1965.)

By means of a rigorous, quantitative approach, Cattell has given substance to some of the speculations which have accumulated over the years from the theoretical workers in this field. His findings have justified *some* of the common-sense views of human motivation but, most importantly, he has given us, for the first time in the history of the subject, a substantial empirical foundation for the measurement of motivation.

In his recent book on morality, Cattell (1972) crisply summarizes the position as he sees it:

From the plastic, potential ergic structure of the inborn drives, roughly adapted to the primitive existence of the last million years, there emerges, by social rewards and punishments, a very different structure which we can map factor-analytically as a system of subsidiated attitudes, to church, to hobbies, to occupation, to country, and finally to the vital image which each individual forms of himself – the self-sentiment.

P-TECHNIQUE AND VALIDATION RESEARCH

Looking now at the third face of the data box, let us suppose that one person was tested on many successive occasions (say 100 consecutive days) using many devices across several attitudes. This is called P-technique to distinguish it from conventional sample testing or R-technique. The fact that the test will be familiar after a number of retestings is not too important because this will not affect the score in the same way as retesting in something which has a right or wrong answer (e.g. an I.Q. test or an achievement test) because the responses will vary according to mood.

Provided the factors we are isolating, that is the ergs and sentiments, are *state-like* (fluctuate within a person) as well as *trait-like* (fluctuate between people) we should find that the enduring factors will emerge. Let me explore this in a little more detail. Taking the erg of fear, we might suppose that the response to fearful events will vary in intensity from one person to another *in the same situation*. A dark and windy night does not have the same effect on everyone. Thus, whilst everyone possesses fear in varying degrees – that is the *trait* of fear, the presence of individual differences in a tested sample will enable us to locate the factor. We rely on systematic variation to provide a means of identifying factors. The fact that everyone possesses the erg of fear as a stable, enduring quality makes it a trait. On the other hand, we know from day-to-day experience that within one individual there are variations in the amount of fear provoked by different situations. Consequently, if we retest someone on several occasions, the variations in his fear response will emerge as a factor of fear. A similar argument applies to all the other motivational factors. Thus fear is also a *state*-like quality, i.e. it varies with circumstances.

In short, if we use several devices across several attitudes with one individual on several occasions we should obtain precisely the same factors as with the trait analyses using a sample of people. Researches (Cross and Hurley)* involving retesting over 100 days with many individuals have confirmed the major ergs and sentiments.

There is a second question which can be answered using P-technique. How does the overt or expressed mood of a person tie in with fluctuations (modulation, as it is known technically) in the ergic tension levels? The question was investigated quite recently by Kline and Grindley.* One subject, a woman, completed the MAT every day for a period of one month. Additionally, a diary was kept by the subject in which she was encouraged to record any event, even trivial thoughts, which occurred during the day. Fluctuations in the erg and sentiment scores were compared with these recorded events. The correspondence between the MAT scores and the diary make extremely convincing reading as a validation study.

APPLICATION IN EDUCATION – ACHIEVEMENT CHARACTERISTICS

Let us now turn to some important applications of motivation variables to education. One of the crucial considerations in formal educational settings is the assessment of achievement both from the point of view of present capacity and the prediction of potential. But how often do these assessments take account of significant aspects such as personality and motivation? Many have given lip-service to the relevance of these – there cannot be a teacher

---

* Summarized in Cattell and Child (1975).

in the country who has not at one time or another recognized the place of motivation in scholastic performance. The main problem has been to find valid and reliable sources of information about these variables.

Only as an outcome of Cattell's quantitative approach to the study of motivation has research been successfully directed to answering this question as to how much variation in performance is ascribable to intelligence, personality and motivation. Cattell, Barton and Dielman in the United States have conducted very careful independent experiments in this field and I want to summarize their findings. But before doing so, I need to explain, in simple terms, the idea of a *specification equation* because it is important both to an understanding of the present research and to an explanation of profiles to be discussed later.

Using the results of factor analysis, it is possible to discover the relative importance of particular factors to a given criterion. For example, if our criterion was achievement, an equation could be drawn up which expresses the relative contribution of each factor. A simple equation might be:

$$P = b_a A + \ldots b_t T + \ldots + b_d D + \ldots$$

Where P = achievement score (expressed in standard score form), b is a weighting measure to be applied to each of the actual scores (expressed in standard score form) obtained by an individual in A = ability tests, T = temperament tests (personality) and D = dynamic tests (motivation). The expression $b_a A + \ldots$ represents the sum of a series of ability scores each with its own weighting, and similarly for $b_t T + \ldots$ and $b_d D + \ldots$

Strikingly, the relative contributions (variance, we call it technically) of A, T and D work out to be approximately 25 per cent apiece. In words, the most reliable measures of ability account for about 25 per cent of the variation in academic performance, personality accounts for another 25 per cent and motivation a further 25 per cent. These figures are only approximate and await further verification. Our day-to-day observations have taught us that ability is not enough. Adequate performance also depends on the degree of interest and the attitudes of people as well as the temperamental characteristics which might favour or impinge on performance. The remaining 25 per cent is most probably accounted for by social variables and, of course, error variance inherent in the test. Apart from the obvious consequences of socioeconomic background, there is ample ground for believing that role relationships, both inside and outside school or college, can affect students' achievement.

In Barton's work achievement in at least ten school subjects formed the base-line for his 'sizing up' of the relative contributions of ability, personality and motivation. Minor fluctuations did occur; for example, motivation was a more substantial predictor in mathematics and English than in most other subjects (science, social science, art, religion, etc.). Nevertheless, the overall sum of contributions was most consistent at 75 per cent. If anything, the sum of motivation and personality was slightly more than 50 per cent, whilst I.Q. was less than 25 per cent in mathematics and English. In summary, the prediction of achievement is enhanced by a knowledge of motivation and personality as well as intelligence.

MOTIVATION AND SCHOOL ACHIEVEMENT

To this point we have been concerned with the overall contribution of motivation alongside the other possible domains. But we must now examine some hypotheses about achievement for a person in terms of particular ergs and sentiments.

The extensive study of Cattell, Barton and Dielman (1972) is worth repeating here because it shows just how important a number of the ergs and sentiments are to achievement in particular school subjects. One thing to notice in table 6.1 is the consistency of magnitude and direction for the correlations between achievement and the various motivational factors for most school subjects. Two particularly significant motivation factors are self-sentiment and superego. Interestingly, these two correlate very highly with McClelland's 'achievement motive' or n'Ach scores. Also sentiment to school is an obviously important dynamic. Educational systems, certainly in Western cultures and probably to an increasing extent in the East, are geared more and more to a meritocratic model which rewards those who attain well in conventional school and university systems. It is not surprising, therefore, to find that those who are high on self-sentiment, i.e. those who are well disposed to socially acceptable behaviour, bent on maintaining self-respect and social status, tend to have elevated achievement scores when we control for differences in intelligence. It also stands to reason that those high on superego will tend to perform better at school, other things being equal. As superego has its roots in societal influences, parents and school have the important role of establishing the non-conscious motives of service and high moral standards. Pleasing others in the reference group (parents, other relations, close friends) spills over into school achievement. The much quoted work of sociologists in the field of social class and educational opportunity repeatedly shows the crucial impact of the home in which little encouragement (often outright antagonism) is offered to continuation into higher education. Both self-sentiment and superego stand to suffer by this subsidiation to parental attitudes towards further education.

Table 6.1 shows a correlation profile for achievers and offers some preliminary approximations to a specification of the qualities which assist in scholastic achievement. The positive influence of the conscious integrated aspects (I) of the motivation factors stands out.

Amongst the total scores (T), in addition to self-sentiment, superego and school sentiment already mentioned, the influence of fear (or in reverse, security seeking) reminds us of the 'fear of failure' effect in our schools and the children's striving to avoid the embarrassment of being at the bottom of the pile.

In another study by Cattell dealing just with high and low achievers' profiles (figure 6.3), some interesting, if obvious, differences were found. The positive influence of curiosity is self-evident and should come as no surprise. There is common sense in the idea that a child who explores and pays attention to his environment, manipulates those things around him – sometimes referred to as the 'attention needs' – will tend to appreciate and recall his surroundings more accurately than the child who is not so concerned.

The negative correlation between gregariousness and achievement is not quite so obvious at first. But there is some correlation between gregariousness on the motivation scale and exvia–invia (or extraversion–introversion) on the personality scales. It would seem from this that the reserved, sober, less social child would tend towards solitary pursuits such as study, reading and writing. This finding is now commonplace in the research on personality and attainment in secondary and higher education.

The negative effect of pugnacity is a little more difficult to explain. It may be that we have a hen–egg problem of whether pugnacity is a quality which leads to low achievement or

Table 6.1   Correlations between motivation variables and achievement

Grade 6 ($N = 169$)

ETS Achievement tests	Assertiveness			Sex			Fear			Narcism			Pugnacity		
	U	I	T	U	I	T	U	I	T	U	I	T	U	I	T
Social studies	02	19[a]	13	15	16[a]	13	03	20[b]	14	−01	07	04	−05	36[b]	20[b]
Science	00	07	14	00	20[b]	13	15	17[a]	22[b]	08	11	12	−09	22[a]	07
Mathematics	−03	09	03	00	20[b]	13	06	14	14	−14	13	−02	−14	34[b]	12
Reading	−03	19[a]	09	10	19[a]	20	15	29[b]	30[b]	14	23[b]	23[b]	−18[a]	36[b]	09

	Protectiveness			Self-sentiment			Superego			School sentiment			Home sentiment		
	U	I	T	U	I	T	U	I	T	U	I	T	U	I	T
Social studies	00	08	04	−10	30[b]	12	02	40[b]	26[b]	−07	23[b]	08	08	13	14
Science	−07	14	02	00	37[b]	24[b]	−02	31[b]	18[a]	−02	27[b]	15	−05	12	02
Mathematics	06	17[a]	15	−07	29[b]	13	−04	32[b]	17[a]	−01	24[b]	13	−13	21[b]	01
Reading	10	15	17[a]	−09	49[b]	26[b]	−01	43[b]	26[b]	05	33[b]	24[b]	−08	17[a]	03

Grade 7 ($N = 142$)

ETS Achievement tests	Assertiveness			Sex			Fear			Narcism			Pugnacity		
	U	I	T	U	I	T	U	I	T	U	I	T	U	I	T
Social studies	04	19[a]	15	−07	23[b]	12	21[b]	05	20[b]	01	25[b]	17[a]	−02	25[b]	15
Science	00	23[b]	15	01	27[b]	20[b]	19[a]	15	24[b]	04	17[a]	14	−11	28[b]	10
Mathematics	08	27[b]	23[b]	00	42[b]	30[b]	19[a]	13	22[b]	04	24[b]	18[a]	00	28[b]	19[a]
Reading	−03	27[b]	15	−13	43[b]	22[b]	29[b]	16	32[b]	02	31[b]	22[b]	−24[b]	28[b]	00

	Protectiveness			Self-sentiment			Superego			School sentiment			Home sentiment		
	U	I	T	U	I	T	U	I	T	U	I	T	U	I	T
Social studies	08	20[b]	18[a]	03	33[b]	24[b]	−06	32[b]	17[a]	08	30[b]	24[b]	−15	25[b]	−00
Science	12	31[b]	28[b]	−01	31[b]	19[a]	−02	34[b]	20[b]	13	32[b]	29[b]	−18[a]	24[b]	−03
Mathematics	19[a]	20[b]	28[b]	04	32[b]	24[b]	−15	23[b]	04	11	32[b]	28[b]	−22[b]	25[b]	−06
Reading	21[b]	20[b]	30[b]	−63[b]	41[b]	24[b]	−02	42[b]	25[b]	15	39[b]	35[b]	−23[b]	34[b]	−03

Source: Cattell, Barton and Dielman (1972).
[a] $P < 0.05$.
[b] $P < 0.01$.
Note: Decimals omitted.

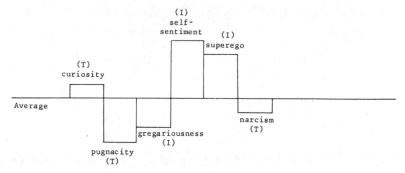

Figure 6.3   Profile showing relationship of dynamic structures to achievement.

whether low achievement generates frustration and thence pugnacity and aggression. The latter is far more probable in the light of our knowledge of the state-like nature of motivation dynamics, but some people are more susceptible than others. Finally, the appearance of narcism is relatively clear when we remember that the broad interpretation of narcism is of a factor displaying self-indulgence, avoidance of work, selfishness and rejection of moral standards. The implicit distractions from achievement towards self-love are suggested as the source of the negative correlation.

Amongst the sentiments, the sentiment to school and to teachers deserve our attention. They have not, as yet, been scrutinized as they should by psychologists. Yet the research prospects in this area are tremendous. For example, we have not determined with any degree of accuracy the clusters of attitudes most frequently involved in these sentiments, let alone speculated on the way in which these attitudes can be influenced by the school. A dynamic lattice for a child's sentiment to school might reveal the subsidiation of several ergs, presumably such basic ones as gregariousness, exploration, self-assertion, pugnacity and acquisitiveness. At least, the school permits of these ergs to be gratified, but we have no idea of the extent or direction which the dissipation takes.

The researches reported above are rudimentary and clearly there is much more to be done. However, even the casual and untutored observer cannot help but notice the advance which quantification of the kind shown here can offer. The chief value of the findings is that of counselling and guidance, for once we know the extent of trait-like characteristics and can specify which particular traits are likely to influence school achievement, we are in a strong position to give help to the needy. It may be that the adaptability (variability in state-like qualities) of the individual is sufficient for the teacher or counsellor to provide a compensatory programme. However, we must not be blind to the fact that in certain kinds of activity, be it at school or work, some people are, and possibly always will be, dynamically and temperamentally ill at ease.

REFERENCES

Cattell, R. B. (1972) *A New Morality from Science: Beyondism.* New York: Pergamon.
Cattell, R. B. & Child, D. (1975) *Motivation and Dynamic Structure.* London: Holt, Rinehart and Winston.

Cattell, R. B., Barton, K. & Dielman, T. E. (1972) Prediction of school achievement from ability, personality, and motivation measures (sixth and seventh grade). *Psychol. Rev.*, **30**, 35–43.

Horn, J. L. (1966) Paper in R. B. Cattell (Ed.), *Handbook of Multivariate Experimental Psychology*. Chicago: Rand McNally.

7   What is the effect of achievement motivation training in the schools? *

DAVID C. McCLELLAND

A number of attempts have been made to develop achievement motivation in school children and to observe the effect of such training on their behavior in and out of school. What conclusions can be drawn from these studies? Previous work with adults has demonstrated that brief intensive training courses in achievement motivation for businessmen increase their entrepreneurial activity for some years after the training (McClelland and Winter, 1969). If achievement motivation can be developed in adults, why not try to develop it in children? The question seemed eminently worth trying to answer, if only because teachers so often complain that many children are 'unmotivated.' If psychologists have invented a technique for increasing motivation, it might well be applied to school children in such a way as to make them want to work harder and learn more.

Though such an argument seems simple and straightforward, it glosses over a theoretical difficulty. The achievement motivation measure (*n* Achievement Score) used in previous studies – based on content analysis of fantasy – has never been shown to be consistently related to academic performance – to grades in school, or to scores on tests of academic talent. Why, then, should increasing achievement motivation improve school performance? Despite this obvious problem, the studies were undertaken because achievement motivation training *might* work and because it ought certainly to help children to think more seriously about their work habits and career planning, even if it does not directly affect their grades. Furthermore, it might well improve grades a little for those most likely to drop out of school by helping them to see the importance of at least minimal school success for attaining longer range vocational goals. Finally, direct attempts to increase motivation in school children have been so few and far between that it seemed likely much might be learned just from making the attempt.

By now dozens of achievement motivation courses have been given for hundreds of pupils in Boston, St Louis and California. A full description of how they were carried out has been published by Alschuler, Tabor and McIntyre (1970). In general, they involved teaching

* The research described in this article was conducted under Office of Education Project No. 7–1231, Grant No. OE–0–8–071231–1747.

children directly how to think, talk and act like a person with high *n* achievement and then examining carefully the extent to which they wanted to plan their lives in the immediate future according to this model. Extensive materials have been published for teaching achievement motivation (by Educational Ventures, Inc., Middletown, Conn.). Many teachers have been instructed in how to use the material. Pupils who have been trained have been followed up one and two years later to see whether their in-school or out-of-school performance has changed in any way as compared to control groups of students who have not been trained in achievement motivation.

Most of these studies have been conducted under the aegis of two independent though allied groups of researchers. Beginning in 1965 the Office of Education granted funds to Harvard University, to be used under the general direction of David McClelland, to explore the effects of achievement motivation in the schools. In the first year of this project, Richard deCharms visited Harvard University and participated fully in the early planning of the research. When he returned to Washington University in St Louis, he started his own project, eventually receiving separate funding for it, and he is reporting his work separately. However, his findings are very much a part of the total enterprise, and many of the most important ones will therefore be summarized here. The projects at Harvard University and Washington University started out with quite similar training ideologies, and then pursued different but complementary research strategies. Manohar S. Nadkarni, who had conducted achievement motivation training courses for businessmen in India, trained those who later gave motivation courses both at Harvard and in St Louis. The Harvard group then decided to continue the tradition of giving short intensive courses for school children to be offered by a trained project staff. They followed this strategy because in the early days the main thrust of the project was in the direction of trying to find out how best to introduce achievement motivation into schools so as to maximize its impact. Thus it was desirable to try out many different types of short courses. Furthermore, the Harvard group focused especially on the effects of motivation training outside school, since it was considered likely on theoretical grounds that increasing achievement motivation would have slight effects on academic performance.

The St Louis group under deCharms, on the other hand, concentrated primarily on studying the effects of achievement motivation training on school work.[*] Partly for this reason, they trained the teachers themselves to introduce achievement motivation training into the classrooms in whatever way they found most convenient. Thus, so far as most of the pupils in the St Louis experiments were concerned, they experienced achievement motivation training inputs throughout an entire school year more or less as a part of other things that they were studying. In contrast, in the Harvard studies, the pupils were exposed to brief intensive courses given by outsiders which were separate and distinct from the rest of what was going on in class and usually concentrated into something like 20 to 40 hours of work spread out over three to ten days, or at most three to four weeks. These contrasting strategies have tended to increase the variety of information obtained about the effects of motivation training on junior high and high school pupils.

---

[*] Later this developed into a form which deCharms has labelled 'origin training' to distinguish it from what is described in Alschuler, Tabor and McIntyre (1970).

THE EFFECTS ON SCHOOL PERFORMANCE

No very convincing evidence is provided by the Harvard studies to show that achievement motivation training improves grades or test scores. In the first study of potential drop-outs from Arlington High School, the boys who completed the residential training in a rural setting did show a slight improvement in grades (from D+ to C− on the average), but it was not large and selection was confounded with treatment. Perhaps those who stuck the program out were made of sterner stuff and did better for that reason rather than because of the training. In later studies at Arlington High School, grades did improve more in the tenth grade for the boys who received the complete motivation training course, as contrasted with the control group, but the girls did not show an improvement, and even for the boys the gain had disappeared by the eleventh grade. In short, the findings from these studies as far as academic performance is concerned are inconsistent, small, and not impressive (Alschuler, 1971).

On the other hand, the St Louis group has reported quite dramatically different results. Consider the findings reported by Ryals, for example, as summarized briefly in table 7.1 (Ryals, 1969).

He had arranged for achievement motivation courses to be given for eighth graders on four different weekends, either on the school grounds ('campus') or in a camp up in the mountains. He corrected test scores and grades for differences before the testing and found that while there were no effects of training on grade point average or social studies test scores, training did seem to improve science and math performance quite significantly in the year after the training. Furthermore, the gains on the average were larger for pupils coming from a high school containing a high proportion of minority groups (blacks, Chicanos) than for students coming from a middle-class white high school. The chief difference between these brief training courses and those sponsored by the Harvard group was that the students were taught by their own teachers who had received achievement motivation training from Mr Nadkarni.

Table 7.1 Effects of achievement motivation training on residualized gain scores[a] (San Mateo County, eighth and tenth grades combined)

Training group	N	GPA[b]	N	Social studies test	N	Science test	N	Science test	N	Math grades
							Students attending 3 or 4 weekends			
Campus	68	48.6	55	49.2	56	50.1	42	50.8	45	52.3
Camp	68	50.9	49	49.0	49	50.5	44	51.3	47	59.6
Control	75	51.7	49	49.3	49	46.9	49	46.9	69	47.0
Significance of training effect		NS		NS		P<0.05		P<0.01		P<0.05

[a] Actual score obtained one year after training subtracted from predicted score based on pretesting plus 50. Thus scores over 50 represent greater than predicted gains.
[b] Grade point average, English, social studies and math grades combined.

Training by teachers from the schools concerned is even more effective when it is spread out over the entire year, as illustrated by the findings summarized in figure 7.1 (deCharms et al, 1969). These charts present average scores on parts of the Iowa Test of Basic Skills which is standardized by grade level so that any average class should score, for example, 7.0 at the end of the seventh grade. The children involved here are all from ghetto schools in a largely black area of the city of St Louis. Those who did not receive achievement motivation training from their teachers in general fall more and more behind expected grade levels on various

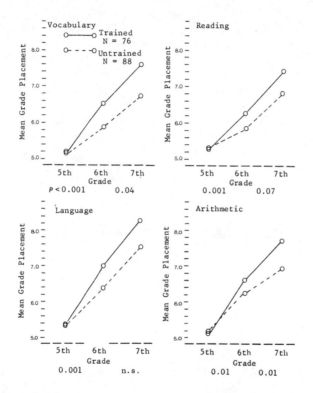

Figure 7.1   Mean grade placement on Iowa test of basic skills for students trained and untrained in achievement motivation self-contained classrooms.

test scores as they get older. However, if they received motivation training throughout the sixth and seventh grades, they ended up with scores which are at or a little above grade norms for the test, as figure 7.1 makes clear. Results such as these which have been reported by the deCharms project leave little doubt that achievement motivation training can have fairly dramatic effects on school performance if it is properly understood by teachers and integrated throughout the year with their regular classroom work.

•   •   •

ACKNOWLEDGEMENT

This article first appeared in *Teachers College Record* (1972), **74**, 129–145. Extracts from it are published here with the kind permission of author and editor.

REFERENCES

Alschuler, A. S. (1971) Four experiments in maximizing the yields of achievement motivation training for adolescents. In *Achievement Motivation Development Project, Final Report* (chapter 7). Office of Education, Bureau of Research.

Alschuler, A. S., Tabor, D. & McIntyre, J. (1970) *Teaching Achievement Motivation*. Middletown, Conn.: Education Ventures, Inc.

deCharms et al (1969) *Can Motives of Low Income Black Children be Changed?* St Louis. Mo.: Washington University.

McClelland, D. C. & Winter, D. G. (1969) *Motivating Economic Achievement*. New York: The Free Press.

Ryals, K. R. (1969) An experimental study of achievement motivation training as a function of the moral maturity of trainees. Doctoral dissertation, Washington University, St Louis, Mo.

8   Teachers' expectancies: determinants of pupils' I.Q. gains *

ROBERT ROSENTHAL and LENORE JACOBSON

Within each of 18 classrooms, an average of 20 per cent of the children were reported to classroom teachers as showing unusual potential for intellectual gains. Eight months later these 'unusual' children (who had actually been selected at random) showed significantly greater gains in I.Q. than did the remaining children in the control group. These effects of teachers' expectancies operated primarily among the younger children.

Experiments have shown that in behavioural research employing human or animal Ss, E's expectancy can be a significant determinant of S's response (Rosenthal, 1964; 1966). In studies employing animals, for example, Es led to believe that their rat Ss had been bred for superior learning ability obtained performance superior to that obtained by Es led to believe their rat had been bred for inferior learning ability (Rosenthal and Fode, 1963; Rosenthal

* This research was supported by Research Grants GS–177 and GS–714 from Division of Social Sciences of the National Science Foundation. The authors thank Dr Paul Nielsen, Superintendent, South San Francisco Unified School District, for making this study possible; Dr David Marlowe for his valuable advice; and Mae Evans, Nancy Johnson, John Laszlo, Susan Novick and George Smiltens for their assistance.

and Lawson, 1964). The present study was designed to extend the generality of this finding from Es to teachers and from animal Ss to school children.

Flanagan (1960) has developed a nonverbal intelligence test (*Tests of General Ability* or *TOGA*) which is not explicitly dependent on such school-learned skills as reading, writing and arithmetic. The test is composed of two types of items, 'verbal' and 'reasoning'. The 'verbal' items measure the child's level of information, vocabulary and concepts. The 'reasoning' items measure the child's concept formation ability by employing abstract line drawings. Flanagan's purpose in developing the TOGA was 'to provide a relatively fair measure of intelligence for all individuals, even those who have had atypical opportunities to learn' (Flanagan, 1960, p. 6).

Flanagan's test was administered to all children in an elementary school, disguised as a test designed to predict academic 'blooming' or intellectual gain. Within each of the six grades in the school were three classrooms, one each of children performing at above average, average and below average levels of scholastic achievement. In each of the 18 classes an average of 20 per cent of the children were assigned to the experimental condition. The names of these children were given to each teacher who was told that their scores on the 'test for intellectual blooming' indicated that they would show unusual intellectual gains during the academic year. Actually, the children had been assigned to the experimental condition by means of a table of random numbers. The experimental treatment for these children, then, consisted of nothing more than being identified to their teachers as children who would show unusual intellectual gains.

Eight months after the experimental conditions were instituted all children were retested with the same I.Q. test and a change score was computed for each child. Table 8.1 shows the mean gain in I.Q. points among experimental and control Ss in each of the six grades.* For the school as a whole those children from whom the teachers had been led to expect greater intellectual gain showed a significantly greater gain in I.Q. score than did the control children ($p = 0.02$, one-tail). Inspection of table 8.1 shows that the effects of teachers' expectancies were not uniform across the six grade levels. The lower the grade level, the greater was the effect ($rho = -0.94$; $p = 0.02$, two-tail). It was in the first and second grades that the effects were most dramatic. The largest gain among the three first grade classrooms occurred for experimental Ss who gained 24.8 I.Q. points *in excess* of the gain (+16.2) shown by the controls. The largest gain among the three second grade classrooms was obtained by experimental Ss who gained 18.2 I.Q. points in excess of the gain (+4.3) shown by the controls.

An additionally useful way of showing the effects of teachers' expectancies on their pupils' gains in I.Q. is to show the percentage of experimental and control Ss achieving various magnitudes of gains. Table 8.2 shows such percentages for the first and second grades only. Half again as many experimental as control Ss gained at least 10 I.Q. points; more than twice as many gained at least 20 I.Q. points; and more than four times as many gained at least 30 points.

An important question was whether the gains of the experimental Ss were made at the

---

* There were no differences in the effects of teachers' expectancies as a function of S's initial level of educational achievement; therefore, the three classrooms at each grade level were combined for table 8.1. In one of the three classrooms at the fifth grade level, a portion of the I.Q. test was inadvertently not re-administered so that data of table 8.1 are based on 17 instead of 18 classrooms.

Table 8.1   Mean gains in I.Q.

Grade	Controls M	σ	Experimentals M	σ	Difference	t	P[c]
1	12.0	16.6	27.4	12.5	15.4	2.97	0.002
2	7.0	10.0	16.5	18.6	9.5	2.28	0.02
3	5.0	11.9	5.0	9.3	0.0		
4	2.2	13.4	5.6	11.0	3.4		
5	17.5	13.1	17.4	17.8	−0.1		
6	10.7	10.0	10.0	6.5	−0.7		
Weighted M	8.4[a]	13.5	12.2[b]	15.0	3.8	2.15	0.02

[a] Mean number of children per grade = 42.5.
[b] Mean number of children per grade = 10.8.
[c] P one-tailed.

expense of the control Ss. Tables 8.1 and 8.2 show that control Ss made substantial gains in I.Q. though they were smaller than the gains made by experimental Ss. Better evidence for the proposition that gains by experimental Ss were not made at the expense of control Ss comes from the positive correlation between gains made by experimental and control Ss. Over the 17 classrooms in which the comparison was possible, those in which experimental Ss made greater gains tended also to be the ones where control Ss made greater gains (rho = 0.57; p = 0.02, two-tail).

Retesting of the children's I.Q. had been done in classroom groups by the children's own teacher.* The question arose, therefore, whether the greater gain in I.Q. of the experimental children might have been due to the teacher's differential behaviour towards them during the retesting. To help answer this question three of the classes were retested by a school administrator not attached to the particular school. She did not know which children were in the experimental condition. Results based on her retesting of the children were not significantly different from the results based on the children's own teachers' retesting. In fact, there was a tendency for the results of her retesting to yield even larger effects of teachers' expectancies. It appears unlikely, then, that the greater I.Q. gains made by children

Table 8.2   Percentages of experimental and control Ss gaining 10, 20 or 30 I.Q. points (first and second grade children)

I.Q. Gain	Control Ss[a]	Experimental Ss[b]	χ^2	P[c]
10 points	49	79	4.75	0.02
20 points	19	47	5.59	0.01
30 points	5	21	3.47	0.04

[a] Total number of children = 95.
[b] Total number of children = 19.
[c] P one-tailed.

* Scoring of the tests was done by the investigators, not by the teachers.

from whom greater gains were expected could be attributed to the effect of the behaviour of the teacher while she served as an examiner.

There is a number of possible explanations of the finding that teachers' expectancy effects operated primarily at the lower grade levels, including: (a) younger children have less well-established reputations so that the creation of expectations about their performance would be more credible; (b) younger children may be more susceptible to the unintended social influence exerted by the expectation of their teacher; (c) younger children may be more recent arrivals in the school's neighbourhood and may differ from the older children in characteristics other than age; (d) teachers of lower grades may differ from teachers of higher grades on a variety of dimensions which are correlated with the effectiveness of the unintentional communication of expectancies.

The most important question which remains is that which asks how a teacher's expectation becomes translated into behaviour in such a way as to elicit the expected pupil behaviour. Prior research on the unintentional communication of expectancies in experimentally more carefully controlled interactions suggests that this question will not be easily answered (Rosenthal, 1966).

But, regardless of the mechanism involved, there are important substantive and methodological implications of these findings which will be discussed in detail elsewhere. For now, one example, in question form, will do: how much of the improvement in intellectual performance attributed to the contemporary educational programmes is due to the content and methods of the programmes and how much is due to the favourable expectancies of the teachers and administrators involved? Experimental designs to answer such questions are available (Rosenthal, 1966) and in view of the psychological, social and economic importance of these programmes the use of such designs seems strongly indicated.

ACKNOWLEDGEMENT

This article appeared in *Psychol. Rep.* (1966), **19**, 115–118, and is published here with the kind permission of the authors and editor.

REFERENCES

Flanagan, J. C. (1960) *Tests of General Ability: Technical Report.* Chicago: Science Research Associates.

Rosenthal, R. (1964) The effect of the experimenter on the results of psychological research. In Maher, A. B. (Ed.), *Progress in Experimental Personality Research*, Vol. I, pp. 79–114. New York: Academic Press.

Rosenthal, R. (1966) *Experimenter Effects in Behavioral Research.* New York: Appleton-Century-Crofts.

Rosenthal, R. & Fode, K. L. (1963) The effect of experimenter bias on the performance of the albino rat. *Behav. Sci.*, **8**, 83–89.

Rosenthal, R. & Lawson, R. (1964) A longitudinal study of the effects of experimenter bias on the operant learning of laboratory rats. *J. Psych. Res.*, **2**, 61–72.

9   Emotionality and the Yerkes–Dodson Law

P. L. BROADHURST

The Yerkes–Dodson Law (1908) which states that the optimum motivation for a learning task decreases with increasing difficulty has been shown to hold for several species (see Young, 1936). It is the purpose of the present experiment to extend the range to include the rat. However, individual differences in drive strength are clearly important here, as may be seen from the current work showing the differential effect of anxiety on human learning (Taylor, 1956). Recent evidence (Eysenck, 1956) supporting the identification of neuroticism as an autonomic drive (Eysenck, 1955) suggests that emotionality, as defined by defecation scores in Hall's open-field test (Hall, 1934), may be a relevant variable, since the lability of the autonomic nervous system probably underlies both neuroticism in humans and emotionality in rats (Hall, 1934; Eysenck, 1953). Emotional rats will therefore be expected to show greater drive than non-emotionals in a situation in which the motivation used (air deprivation) is intense and of a kind likely to give rise to fear responses, and consequently to learn faster when the task is easy, but more slowly when it is hard. That is to say, the optimum drive level in the Yerkes–Dodson situation should be lower for the emotionals than for the non-emotionals. We may therefore predict an interaction between emotionality and the two variables of motivation and difficulty level which should themselves interact in the manner suggested by the Yerkes–Dodson Law.

METHOD

Apparatus   The **Y**-shaped discrimination apparatus designed by Jonckheere (1956) for surface swimming was adapted for underwater use. This is a conventional **Y** unit with metal walls 2 ft high and alleys 4 in. wide. The stem of the **Y** is 7 in. long and the arms make an angle of 52° to the center line. Vertical partitions across each arm, 7 in. beyond the bifurcation, extend from top to bottom of the alley and contain the discrimination panels. The *S*s were forced to swim through the unit completely underwater by roofing in the alleys before the partitions with stainless steel hardware cloth just below the water level (9 in.). The discrimination panels were hung vertically and hinged below the surface of the water. They were made of frosted Perspex and each presented an illuminated area, $3\frac{1}{2}$ in. square, at right angles to the line of sight from the bifurcation. Either could be locked into place, or left free, to be opened underwater by *S* to allow escape to the part of the alleys beyond the partitions which were not roofed in below the surface. From here, hardware cloth ramps gave access to a platform above water level.

The illumination was provided by two lamps in parallel in a 24-v. circuit. One lamp was located above water level behind each discrimination panel with its filament parallel to the panel. A fixed portion of a wire resistor could be switched into the circuit of either lamp in order to dim the intensity of the light shining through the adjacent panel, the other lamp being undimmed. The *S* was thus presented with a choice between a well lit and a less well lit avenue of escape from underwater. Three amounts of resistance were used; the greater the resistance the dimmer the light, yielding a greater difference between the illumination of the alleys, and an easier discrimination. Measurements with a light meter (Avo No. 2) indicated that this difference in illumination could be represented, in ascending order of difficulty, by the ratios 1:300, 1:60 and 1:15. These constitute the three levels of difficulty and are designated easy, moderate and difficult.

A submersible cage, measuring $9 \times 6 \times 4\frac{1}{2}$ in. wide, also made of stainless steel hardware cloth, was fitted with a sliding guillotine door which could be released from above the surface, thus allowing escape through the discrimination apparatus. Following a suggestion by Mason and Stone (1953), the intensity of the air deprivation used as motivation was manipulated by detaining the Ss for different lengths of time submerged underwater before releasing them to make the discrimination on which the promptness of their escape depended. Preliminary work, using 20 female rats as Ss, gave the results shown in figure 9.1.

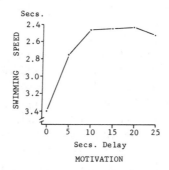

Figure 9.1   The relationship between speed of swimming a 4-ft straightaway underwater and intensity of imposed motivation (air deprivation) measured by the number of seconds' delay underwater before release. Each point represents the mean time for 20 Ss; the data were collected on successive days.

There is clearly no advantage in using delays longer than about 10 sec., since performance is not thereby improved. Indeed, delays longer than 20 sec. result in decreased swimming speed, presumably because of the effects of anoxia. Delays were therefore kept short, and delays of 0, 2, 4 and 8 sec. before release were selected, which represent approximately equal increments in swimming speed (see figure 9.1). These constitute the four levels of motivation.

Subjects   Five replications of the $3 \times 2 \times 4$ factorial design (24 treatments) were used – that is, a total of 120 Ss was required. These 120 Ss were male albino rats which formed part of the second and third generations in a selective breeding study of emotionality being conducted in this laboratory (Broadhurst, 1957b). When Ss averaged 105.5 days of age ($SE \pm 0.25$), they were given the modified and standardized open-field test described in detail elsewhere (Broadhurst, 1957a). Briefly, Ss were exposed for 2 min. per day for four successive days in a circular arena $32\frac{3}{4}$ in. in diameter with white plywood walls $12\frac{1}{2}$ in. high. A battery of loudspeakers and of photographic lamps above the arena provided sound ('white' noise) and light fields whose intensity at floor level in the arena averaged 78 db (ref. 0.002 dynes/sq. cm) and 165 cp., respectively. The average number of fecal boluses deposited per day constitute the emotional reactivity score, and only Ss scoring 3.3 or more were assigned to the emotional group (mean = 4.1, ±0.15), and only Ss scoring 1.3 or less were assigned to the non-emotional group (mean = 0.8, ±0.17). These two groups constitute the two levels of treatment in the emotionality variable; the difference between them is significant beyond the 0.1 per cent level by *t* test.

The populations from which Ss were selected by virtue of their emotional elimination scores had been bred by brother × sister mating from a heterogeneous Wistar stock. They had been reared under standard conditions which are described fully elsewhere (Broadhurst, 1957b). In brief, these conditions featured controlled temperature and light/dark cycle in standard living quarters, standard conditions of husbandry – diet, routine care, number of animals per cage, etc. – and the minimum of handling. Some of them had been used for breeding purposes in the interval between testing in the open field and in the underwater discrimination unit, which interval itself varied with Ss' generation, but there is evidence (Broadhurst, in press) to suggest that neither the sexual experience, nor age differences of the order encountered, are likely to affect Ss' emotionality as measured. The mean age when experimentation began of the 45 Ss belonging to the second generation was 322.0 days (±6.09), and the mean age of the 75 Ss belonging to the third generation 213.4 days (±3.31). This difference is highly significant ($P < 0.001$ by *t* test); accordingly, the possible effect of this age difference upon the scores analysed was investigated. There was no significant difference by *t* test between the over-all means of the two groups for the learning score used (discussed later), but, as might be expected, the older Ss swam significantly more slowly ($P < 0.01$, by *t* test). It need not, however, be anticipated that any systematic bias is thereby introduced into the analysis of the speed score since Ss had been assigned to treatments randomly. As a check, a χ^2 test of the proportions of Ss of the two age groups assigned to each treatment combination showed no significant difference from that existing in the total group (45:75).

Procedure   The random assignments of Ss to the 24 treatment combinations was made by forming the 60 emotional Ss into 12 groups of five each, equated as far as possible with respect to defecation scores, and the 60 non-emotional Ss into a further 12 groups of five each, similarly equated. The groups thus formed were then randomly assigned, within the emotionality dichotomy, to the various treatment combinations. The Ss were tested in groups of 24 (one complete replication) on 15 successive days. The first five days were devoted to preliminary training during which Ss were successively given surface and underwater swimming practice in a 3-ft straightaway, at which time the appropriate detention periods for the different Ss were established, then practice in the underwater discrimination unit to familiarize them with the operation of opening the doors formed by the discrimination panels. During this time the doors were unlit, and one side of the Y unit was blocked at the bifurcation by a solid partition, thus forcing the rat to one side or the other, in order to avoid the development of position habits. The side by which escape was thus permitted was varied randomly by use of a Gellerman series (Gellerman, 1933). At the end of this training all Ss were leaving the starting cage promptly on release, and opening the escape doors without difficulty.

On the next 10 days, 10 trials per day – a total of 100 trials – were given in the apparatus with a choice of alleys permitted and differences in illumination between the panels. No other illumination was present in the darkened room containing the water tank except for a small recording lamp and a radiant heat lamp above the self-draining metal boxes in which Ss were kept in the intertrial intervals. This interval was maintained relatively constant for all Ss despite the variation in delay ranging from 0 to 8 sec. by running them in larger or smaller groups, respectively. The brighter side of the unit was designated correct and kept open; an S choosing the darker side where the panel was locked was thereby forced to retrace its way to the brighter side in order to escape. That is, the correction method was used. The bright side was selected since it was constant for each of the three levels of difficulty, and because there was no tendency for Ss to prefer one side over the other. Thus, on the first trial upon which a choice was permitted, 56.7 per cent went to the right-hand or bright side, and 43.3 per cent to the dimmer one on the left. The difference from chance expectation yields a nonsignificant χ^2. The 'correct' side was randomly varied from trial to trial by use of a selection of 10 Gellerman series, the same ones being used in the same order for all Ss. The water temperature was maintained at 20° C, the air temperature during testing averaged 19.5° C (± 0.21).

The time from the moment when the door of the starting cage was released until S's snout broke the surface of the water beyond the illuminated panel through which it had passed was recorded to the nearest $\frac{1}{10}$ sec. by stop watch, and errors, defined as any entry into the 'incorrect' alley of S's head and shoulders or more, noted. These constitute the time and error scores, respectively.

The five replications of the experiment were tested at intervals over 4 mo. and were followed by a partial replication which supplied substitutes for the three Ss which died during experimentation and the seven whose results were excluded because they developed position habits. A position habit was defined for this purpose as the choice on two days (20 trials) or more during the last five days of testing of one side – left or right – exclusively.

RESULTS

The number of errorless trials out of the 100 trials given was counted for each S and the data subjected to a three-way analysis of variance after Pearson and Hartley's test (Pearson and Hartley, 1956) had disclosed no significant inhomogeneity of variance. The results are presented in table 9.1. The F ratios for the difficulty and motivation main effects were calculated by using the Difficulty × Motivation interaction variance estimate, in view of the significance of the interaction between these two variables. The nature of this interaction is indicated in figure 9.2. Table 9.2 shows the mean scores and SD's for the various levels of the two treatments having significant main effects. These data indicate the efficacy of the experimental manipulation of these two independent variables. Thus, each increase in the difficulty of the discrimination yields a significantly lower learning score, reaching the 0.01 level (by 1-tail t test) in the case of the easy v. moderate difference, and the 0.001 level in the case of the moderate v. difficult one. Increasing the time of air deprivation first increased the mean learning score significantly (0- v. 2-sec. delay); then caused a significant decline from the peak value (2- v. 8-sec. delay; $P < 0.05$ in both cases by t test). This latter finding is com-

Table 9.1   Analyses of variance of learning and speed scores

Source	df	No. of correct trials		Average time to swim 21 in.	
		MS	F	MS^c	F
Difficulty (D)	2	2260.2	23.5[b]	2.17	1.8
Motivation (M)	3	143.7	1.5	4.73	4.0[b]
Emotionality (E)	1	114.1	3.0	7.21	6.1[a]
D × M	6	96.1	2.5[a]	1.05	0.9
D × E	2	48.9	1.3	0.73	0.6
M × E	3	77.8	2.1	2.48	2.1
D × M × E	6	54.9	1.4	1.21	1.0
Ss	96	38.0		1.18	
Total	119				

[a] $P = 0.025$.
[b] $P = 0.01$.
[c] Units 1/10 sec.

parable with that of many workers reporting a curvilinear relationship between motivation and performance when increasingly intense motivation is employed (see also figure 9.1).

It is clear from these results that the Yerkes–Dodson Law may be taken as confirmed. The optimum motivation for a discrimination task demonstrably decreases with increasing difficulty of the task. This effect, represented by the first-order interaction between the difficulty and motivational treatments, is significant at a satisfactory level, and part of the prediction is thus verified. It is equally clear that the prediction, as made above, relating to the effects of emotional reactivity on this complex relationship is not fulfilled. The trend of the results is partly in the predicted direction. Thus emotionals learn the easy discrimination faster than non-emotionals, and are about equal on the moderately difficult one, and similarly learn faster under low motivation, and are about equal at medium levels. But on the difficult discrimination or under the most intense motivation used they again show a

Table 9.2   Breakdown of learning scores

Motivation level (air depriva- tion	Difficulty of discrimination							
	Easy		Moderate		Difficult		All	
	Mean	SD	Mean	SD	Mean	SD	Mean	SD
0 sec.	84.8	6.6	81.3	6.3	71.1	9.0	79.1	9.4
2 sec.	86.4	4.7	84.7	5.9	79.5	4.8	83.5	6.0
4 sec.	87.7	3.9	83.0	7.1	71.6	6.2	80.8	9.0
8 sec.	86.8	3.9	83.2	5.9	66.1	6.5	78.7	10.6
All	86.4	5.0	83.1	6.5	72.1	8.3	80.5	9.1

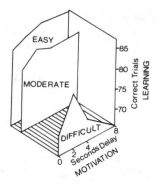

Figure 9.2   A three-dimensional surface showing the relationship between learning scores in a discrimination task and (a) the intensity of the imposed motivation (air deprivation) measured by the number of seconds' delay underwater before release and (b) the level of difficulty of the task. The lamina are spaced to represent the over-all mean score for the appropriate difficulty level (see table 9.2). Each point represents the mean score for 10 Ss.

slight superiority. Consequently, the emotional Ss show an over-all superiority in learning, which, however, does not reach significance, and this is reflected in the failure of the one second-order and the two remaining first-order interactions, all of which involve the emotionality variable, to reach significance.

If it is conceded that the curvilinear relation involved makes such a procedure permissible, the partial success of the prediction relating to drive level and emotionality can readily be demonstrated. An analysis of variance based on the first two lowest levels of motivation only – that is, before the decline in learning associated with motivation greater than the optimum begins (see figure 9.2) – shows two significant effects. The first is the expected and highly significant one associated with level of difficulty, the second is the first-order interaction between Motivation and Emotionality ($P < 0.05$). This effect may be summarized by saying that the emotional Ss show superior learning under the minimal motivation used, but that this advantage disappears with the increase of motivation from 0 to 2 sec. delay before release.

Another way to investigate the relation of emotionality to drive level is to consider the *speed* of the response made to the motivational stimulus, irrespective of whether or not it resulted in improved learning. In order to derive a speed score for each S, and one which reflects its speed of swimming independent of the degree of learning attained, the time scores for the first day upon which all 10 trials were recorded as correct were averaged. In this way the individual Ss' speeds may be compared at exactly comparable points on their respective learning curves. Since the distance swum in the apparatus is essentially the same for each S making a 'correct' choice (21 in.), the time scores can be used directly for the purpose, as was done in preparing figure 9.1, thus avoiding the difficulty relating to averaging time over distance scores discussed by Crespi (1942). For the 13 Ss assigned to the difficult discrimination who never learned it to perfection, the average of the last day's trials was calculated, omitting times for those trials when incorrect choices were made. An analysis of variance performed on these data after no significant inhomogeneity of variance had been demonstrated gave results which are also shown in table 9.1. From this analysis it will be seen that the superiority of the emotional Ss over the non-emotional Ss in speed of swimming reaches satisfactory significance. The mean time scores are 1.80 and 1.96 sec., respectively. Inserting these values on a plot of swimming speed against motivational delays (like figure 9.1) shows that the difference of 0.16 sec. is equivalent to the effect on over-all speed scores of an increase in motivational delay of about 4 sec. Moreover, this effect is not significantly associated with any of the other variables in the analysis, from which it can be concluded that the emotionally reactive rats display a characteristically higher level of drive, which, within the limits of the present experiment, is not affected by the intensity of the motivation imposed. It may also be noted from this analysis that the absence of a significant effect for Difficulty shows that the speed score selected was in fact independent of the degree of learning, and that the significance of Motivation confirms the efficacy of the experimental manipulation of the air deprivation variable. Thus, the mean time taken to swim 21 in. underwater decreased progressively from 1.98 sec. for 0 sec. delay to 1.97 for 2 sec., to 1.85 (4 sec.), and finally to 1.71 (8 sec.). The SD's are 0.48, 0.33, 0.31 and 0.25 sec. respectively. Only the differences between each of the first three levels (0, 2 and 4 sec.) and the last one (8 sec.) reach significance (0.05 level or beyond by 1-tail t test).

DISCUSSION

The confirmation of the Yerkes–Dodson Law reported here gains in interest because it employed a different species from those hitherto used in demonstrating the principle, and because it occurred under rather different experimental conditions. The motivation in particular was very different from that used in any of the other studies of the Yerkes–Dodson Law; the electric shock previously employed as an aversive stimulus was eschewed because of the difficulty of controlling it, and because of its disruptive effect, especially when strong, upon early learning. Air deprivation as used shares with shock the quality of being a rather intense stimulus, and the advantage of being manipulable within the testing situation. It has, in addition, been shown in practice to be easily varied in intensity.

It is true that in both this and the original study a visual brightness discrimination was used as the method of varying the degree of difficulty of the learning tasks. The resemblance hardly goes beyond the semantic, however. The similarity between the actual pieces of apparatus used is slight. The Yerkes box has been described as 'spectacularly inefficient', (McClearn and Harlow, 1954), whereas the underwater discrimination technique as used in this study gave rapid learning without undue preliminary training.

The results obtained from the original study and the present one are surprisingly similar. A comparison of figure 9.2 with that given by Yerkes and Dodson (1908, p. 479) shows that the optimum motivation is in general slightly lower in the scale used than that encountered by them, and that there is no level of difficulty for which an optimum was never reached as was the case with their easiest discrimination. An increasing sharpness of the optimum peak with increasing difficulty is characteristic of both graphs. The dissimilarities mentioned can all be ascribed to differences in the levels of motivation selected. The relation of motivation to degree of learning is typically curvilinear, a decrease in learning following motivation more intense than the optimum, so it is not always easy to select suitable levels of motivation to reveal the optimum learning, especially if it is required to include different optima associated with different levels of difficulty, and more especially with a novel motivation like air deprivation about which little is so far known.

The confirmation of the Law is the more striking because of this difference in motivation. The needs arising from electric shock and from air deprivation are different physiologically, though they both give rise to drives mediated, in part, by fear. The further generalization of the Law must await experimentation using other situations and other drives, but the outlook is promising in view of the analogies in the human field already existing.

The possible role of anoxia must not be overlooked in connection with the use of air deprivation, since it is known (Hayes, 1953) that it can cause learning defects comparable to those caused by electroconvulsive shock. It seems unlikely, however, that air deprivation of the duration used here can have led to anoxic damage to the nervous system sufficient to account for the curvilinear relation with learning. To the arguments which lead Mason and Stone (1953) to reject this explanation of their comparable findings, we may add the following germane considerations from this experiment. Firstly, if anoxia were important in this connection, it would be reasonable to anticipate that all the groups subjected to the greatest air deprivation would show a decrement in learning. A glance at figure 9.2 shows that this is not the case. Secondly, the analysis of the speed of swimming showed no significant difference between the difficulty levels (see table 9.1). Now, the Ss assigned to the difficult discrimination had, at the time when the speed scores were selected, experienced much more air deprivation than had the other groups. They had made many more errors obliging them to hold their breath longer before escape, and they had also undergone many more trials. Neither of these circumstances, likely to increase any deficit ascribable to anoxia, depressed swimming speed, however.

The drive characteristics of emotionality as defined by open-field defecation scores are only partly elucidated by this experiment. Emotionally reactive Ss have a significantly higher speed of swimming – that is, they respond more vigorously to the same degree of imposed motivation. To this extent, they may be regarded either as having a higher drive level in general or as more susceptible to drive arousal. Further work to investigate the speed of swimming of these Ss, and employing a situation designed to demonstrate the Crespi effect (Crespi, 1942) consequent upon changes in drive level, confirms the superior speed of the emotionals and the presence of the 'elation' effect but indicates that they do not respond more to a sudden increase in drive than do the non-emotionals (Broadhurst, 1957d). It thus seems that drive level rather than drive arousal is involved.

Yet this higher drive level did not in general effect learning in this experiment in the manner expected. It seems unfruitful to enter into detailed speculations about the reasons for this seeming paradox – suffice it to say that it is probable that the situation used here is too complex to expect that any definitive solution may be found in the present data. Nevertheless the general finding relating to drive level does have some bearing on the postulated relation between emotionality in rats and neuroticism in humans. This cross-species identification is not directly verifiable, but it can be cautiously said that the present results, at the very least, do nothing to render it improbable.

Summary   The experiment was designed to test the validity of the Yerkes–Dodson Law and to investigate some of the drive characteristics of emotionality of rats. In a 3 × 4 × 2 factorial design having five replications, 120 male albino rats were used as Ss. Three levels of difficulty of an underwater brightness discrimination, four levels of motivation deriving from different degrees of air deprivation, and two levels of emotionality defined in terms of defecation scores on the open-field test were used. Time and error scores from 100 trials were secured.

Analysis of variance of the results shows that the Yerkes–Dodson Law, as demonstrated by an appropriate interaction between difficulty and motivation, is confirmed at an acceptable level of significance. The prediction relating to the effects of emotionality on motivation is only fulfilled in part; a significantly higher drive level of emotionals as shown by their swimming speed is shown.

ACKNOWLEDGEMENT

This article first appeared in *J. Exp. Psychol.* (1957), **54**, 345–352, and is published here with the kind permission of the author and editor.

REFERENCES

Broadhurst, P. L. (1957a) Determinants of emotionality in the rat: I. Situational factors. *Brit. J. Psychol.*, **48**, 1–12.

Broadhurst, P. L. (1957b) Emotionality in the rat: a study of its determinants, inheritance and relation to some aspects of motivation. Unpublished doctor's dissertation, Univer. London.

Broadhurst, P. L. (in press) Determinants of emotionality in the rat: II. Antecedent factors. *Brit. J. Psychol.*

Broadhurst, P. L. (in press) A note on a 'Crespi effect' in the analysis of emotionality as a drive in rats. *Br. J. Psychol.*

Crespi, L. P. (1942) Quantitative variation of incentive and performance in the white rat. *Amer. J. Psychol.*, **55**, 467–517.

Eysenck, H. J. (1953) *The Structure of Human Personality*. London: Methuen.

Eysenck, H. J. (1955) A dynamic theory of anxiety and hysteria. *J. Ment. Sci.*, **101**, 28–51.

Eysenck, H. J. (1956) Reminiscence, drive and personality theory. *J. Abnorm. Soc. Psychol.*, **53**, 328–333.

Gellerman, L. W. (1933) Chance orders of alternating stimuli in visual discrimination experiments. *J. Genet. Psychol.*, **42**, 206–208.

Hall, C. S. (1934) Emotional behavior in the rat. I. Defecation and urination as measures of individual differences in emotionality. *J. Comp. Psychol.*, **18**, 385–403.

Hayes, K. J. (1953) Anoxic and convulsive amnesia in rats. *J. Comp. Physiol. Psychol.*, **46**, 216–217.

Jonckheere, A. R. (1956) A study of 'fixation' behaviour in the rat. Unpublished doctor's dissertation, Univer. London.

McClearn, G. E. & Harlow, H. F. (1954) The effect of spatial contiguity on discrimination learning by Rhesus monkeys. *J. Comp. Physiol. Psychol.*, **47**, 391–394.

Mason, W. A. & Stone, C. P. (1953) Maze performance of rats under conditions of surface and underwater swimming. *J. Comp. Physiol. Psychol.*, **46**, 159–165.

Pearson, E. S. & Hartley, H. O. (1956) *Biometrika tables for statisticians*. Vol. 1. Cambridge, Eng.: Cambridge Univer. Press.

Taylor, J. A. (1956) Drive theory and manifest anxiety. *Psychol. Bull.*, **53**, 303–320.

Yerkes, R. M. & Dodson, J. D. (1908) The relation of strength of stimulus to rapidity of habit-formation. *J. Comp. Neurol. Psychol.*, **18**, 459–482.

Young, P. T. (1936) *Motivation of behavior*. New York: Wiley.

PART 4

Attention and perception

INTRODUCTION

One of the most important contemporary contributions in the field of memory is that of Broadbent. His filter theory and its possible message for education is well illustrated in the paper 'Cognitive psychology and education'.

Remembering and forgetting are so prominent in our work that it would be unthinkable to omit a paper on the problems as seen by teachers. Dale's contribution attempts this by considering the practical issues of long- and short-term memory. He admits that a lot of research so far has dealt with simpler 'messages' that we deal with in everyday life, and is frequently performed in laboratory conditions. However, there is some indication (see for instance Broadbent's paper) of the generalizability of the findings.

A short note by Morton which I came across recently raises a tricky question about methods of teaching – how much can we rely on incidental learning in our classes? To what extent is it necessary to bring material to the overt attention of pupils in a direct and purposeful way rather than relying on incidental learning? The almost total lack of motivation needed by anyone who uses a telephone to learn the order of the letters and digits may provide one reason for the poor performance in trying to recall them. Perhaps the lesson to learn here is that repetition of a sequence without conscious and purposeful effort to memorize it does not readily lead to learning – incidental or otherwise.

10   Cognitive psychology and education

D. E. BROADBENT

INTRODUCTION

Each of the areas mentioned in this title is a large one, and obviously we shall consider only some aspects of each. The broad field covered by 'Education' is already familiar: it can stretch from the primary school to the university, with forays beyond the frontier in either direction, and it can take in an enormous range of attitudes amongst educators. One could caricature the position at one extreme as that of the teacher as behaviour modifier, manipulating each shade of the pupil's behaviour with appropriate schedules of reinforcement: while the opposite extreme, and perhaps the more popular nowadays, would be the teacher who does not so much instil knowledge as make it available. If his pupils should choose to want it they can find it. As may be suspected, one purpose of this paper is to suggest some rationale for rejecting these extremes.

The rationale is to be found in 'Cognitive Psychology', which is itself almost as vague a term as 'Education'. Taking our start from the classic textbook of Neisser (1967), we can say that it includes all those parts of experimental psychology which have to do with complex perception, the organization of memory, language, thinking, and in general the complicated processes which underlie the intellectual side of human life. Investigators working in this area tend to express their theoretical findings in one of two ways. First, they may draw a *block diagram* consisting of a series of boxes, each representing a function or process going on within the nervous system, and any particular item of information is supposed to find its way from block to block as it is processed. A typical example is shown in figure 10.1, which represents a simple outline of some of the views of Broadbent (1958; 1971). In this diagram, information is supposed first of all to enter a short-term storage system which will hold a number of items of information simultaneously: some of these items are selected from this short-term store by a filter, and pass through a system for categorizing or encoding the item, so that the same central event will occur whether the man sees the word 'two' or '2' or 'II' or hears a male or female voice saying the word 'two'. From the categorizing system, the information is supposed to go to long-term memory. Thus, a particular item of information moves from one place to another within the system.

The other kind of diagram drawn by cognitive psychologists is a *flow chart* like that in figure 10.2. Here we are dealing no longer with information moving from place to place, but with events at one place at successive moments in time. In this example we see the successive events which might go on when a man is deciding on his future course of action at some time in the early evening. He might decide successively that he wished to eat his dinner, that he had no food in his larder, but that he did have money and would therefore go to a restaurant, or he might take a different decision at any point and go through a different set of actions. Indeed, he might get into an endless loop which can only be broken by his deciding that he does not wish to eat dinner after all! Notice that rather different kinds of behaviour would be produced by a man who thought about imposing on his friends before

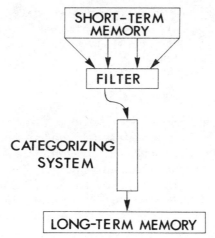

Figure 10.1   A typical 'block diagram' theory of cognitive processes. (Based on Broadbent, 1958.)

he considered the state of his own larder, rather than the opposite sequence, and one could, therefore, examine the actual behaviour to see whether it agrees with the theoretical model. The diagram does, however, represent a series of events in the same place at successive times, rather than a series of places in which the same information can be located: it involves time rather than space. An example of a flow chart for a more complicated piece of human behaviour is given by Winograd (1972, p. 64) for the case of a computer analysing a sentence and deciding on the tense of the verb.

Both kinds of diagram are extremely useful in representing what happens inside people.

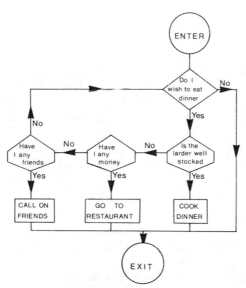

Figure 10.2   A typical 'flow chart' theory of cognitive processes.

However, they very rapidly become extremely complicated, and another purpose of the present paper is to point out another way in which psychological events can be described.

With these background points in mind let us consider three fields in which cognitive psychology can be related to education.

THE MICROSTRUCTURE OF TEACHING

If we think of a particular child in one school at one time, he or she is surrounded by a vast array of incoming signals, perhaps especially so in a modern open classroom. In general terms, however, figure 10.1 represents a genuine limitation on his performance: he cannot process simultaneously everything that reaches his senses, and has to select from what is present. If something is not noticed at the time it happens, it has hardly any chance of affecting long-term memory (Moray, 1959; Turvey, 1967). Yet it is by no means automatic that the particular stimulus which interests the teacher will be the one which gets access to the processing centres of the child. Even an adult, when faced by strange visual patterns differing in a number of features, tends to classify them by the features which vary most conspicuously (Imai and Garner, 1965); and similarly it would be optimistic to expect the child to notice inconspicuous features of visually presented letters, when there are large bright objects also in the visual scene, or to listen to a quiet and monotonous voice explaining a problem, when there are loud and suddenly changing bursts of laughter or traffic noise occurring at intervals. The extreme view of education described earlier, in which information is made available for the inquiring mind to discover, can only be a caricature because the information has to be presented in some physical form. That form and the background of stimulation which surrounds it will, in fact, decide whether the child attends to this item of information or to something else in the surroundings. No matter how apparently undirective a school or a home may appear to be, biases of this kind exist, and should be handled deliberately rather than left to chance.

Indeed, the doubt which many of us would have about a traditional 'chalk-and-talk' classroom would be that it violates some of the principles of control of attention; the use of low intensity stimulation continuing for a prolonged period from a single direction, the lack of link to any existing interest of the child (see Moray, 1959, again) and so on. The danger to be avoided is that, in changing such a situation, one might still fail to present information in such a way that is noticed. Audio-visual aids, for example, can indeed replace the traditional classroom by intense, changing and interesting stimuli, yet laboratory studies of attention would lead us to expect that there is still a limit to the amount of information which can be presented in a certain length of time, and merely by adding stimulation of the ears to that of the eyes we cannot expect twice as much to be assimilated. If what is being heard is truly independent of what is being seen, then we can take in either but not both (see for example Mowbray, 1953). The proper use of sound and vision together is rather to provide variety of stimulation by changing at intervals from one channel to the other, or else to present to eye and ear signals which are already closely related to each other in the child's experience, such as words being spoken by a face which is seen or words which pick out one part of the visual scene for special attention.

Most of the experiments which make these points have been performed with adults, yet the work of Maccoby and Konrad (1967) shows that similar principles apply with quite young children, and indeed, that younger children are less helped in attention by the occurrence of a sequence of probable events. As yet they do not know that a word dealing with a particular topic is likely to be followed by another word on that same topic, and the task of holding attention on a single problem may, therefore, be harder for them than uninstructed adults will realize. Experienced teachers already understand the importance of the physical facts underlying attention; perhaps they too may forget that their inexperienced colleagues do not know these things! The laboratory experiments of cognitive psychologists, therefore, can help us to design the detailed environment in which learning takes place, with a slightly better chance that the child will notice and react to the information that is being presented.

Even when a child has noticed something about a situation, the way it has been noticed is important. Morton (1967) has a light-hearted demonstration of the importance of this factor, in a study which involved asking regular telephone users to reproduce on the telephone dial the positions of the letters and digits. Although they have seen and reacted to these stimuli many times, most of them have not learned which holes in the dial contained which letters. They had, of course, no need to do so: their response to the letter when dialling it was merely to put a finger in the appropriate hole, and not to organize the information in some form appropriate to long-term memory. Here again, one can see the reasons for discontent with the traditional classroom. Suppose a child is presented with a list of the kings of England and merely processes this information in such a way as to pass a classroom test at the end of the week, it does not follow that his behaviour has been affected in any other situation. Yet, equally, one might deduce from Morton's experiments that some modern alternatives to drill are ineffective. A child who repeatedly discovers the results of multiplications by using rods or repeated addition will not therefore acquire a long-term store of information sufficient to check change in the supermarket.

There are many laboratory examples of a similar kind. For example, you can be made much less efficient at recognizing that the word 'jam' has been presented to you on a previous occasion, if last time it appeared it was accompanied by the word 'traffic' while on the test it was accompanied by the word 'raspberry' (Light and Carter-Sobell, 1970). Cognitive psychology not only warns us that information we present may fail to get into the nervous system at all, but also makes it clear that the future effects of what is seen or heard depend very much on the categories or codes into which the information is placed. Although we started by looking at an individual child in a particular classroom at a particular time, these categories and operations go well beyond a particular situation. We ought to turn, therefore, to the longer term problems of the organization of memory.

THE STRUCTURING OF LONG-TERM EXPERIENCE

Most of us are familiar with the situation of failing to remember something which on some later occasion we can recall quite easily – or which we can recognize as soon as somebody suggests it to us. In some sense the information is stored in memory, but it is not accessible. This everyday experience might mean merely that some memories were weaker than others and that, although detectable by sensitive means, they require some extra push to bring them above the threshold of recall. Laboratory experiments, however, confirm the everyday experience, and show that it is not to be explained away in such a simple fashion. To take just one example, an experiment by Broadbent and Broadbent (1975) measured performance for recognition of words drawn from a previously presented list. This was compared with another condition in which the experimental subjects first tried to recall the words from the list. As might be expected they forgot some words. Performance at recognizing these 'forgotten' words was, however, just as good as performance in the other condition. The forgetting of a word, therefore, does not mean that it is weakly stored within the nervous system: it must be that the stored trace is difficult to find under the conditions of the test of recall.

In terms of an analogy, suppose you lend a book to a friend: there may then be two quite different reasons why he does not return it. The first reason is that you may not have written your name in it, so that when he happens to come across the book on his shelves there is nothing to tell him who is the owner. The other possible difficulty is, however, that he has a lot of books in his house, that they are arranged in random order, and that consequently he cannot find your book although he knows that it is yours. The first of these is analogous to a test of recognition, in which the item is presented but the problem is to decide whether it has occurred previously. The second situation is analogous to the test of recall, in which the problem is to find the item which occurred on (belongs to) a particular occasion. One advantage of this analogy is that it makes clear that the storage of information is much less likely to cause trouble if certain steps are taken at the time of storage: if your friend thinks he is likely to meet the book and wonder whose it is, he should write your name in it. If on the other hand he thinks he is more likely to meet you and to be asked for the book, then he should keep his books in an organized fashion, such as alphabetically by authors or with borrowed books in a special place or with books on a certain topic in a certain place, or something of that sort. If we return to the case of human learning, the ability to make later use of one's experience depends on the encoding or organization of material at the time it arrives, and this has been the topic of many recent experiments.

One common theme, for example, has been the advantage for memory of subdividing experience into a number of related clusters or groups. Thus, if one presents lists of words in which several words belong to one category such as being parts of the body, while others belong to other categories such as being names of animals, types of transport, etc., it has been known for some time that the words in the same category tend to be recalled together rather than separately (Bousfield, 1953). Tulving and Pearlstone (1966) showed that recall in such a situation was helped by providing the experimental subject with the names of the categories to which the words belonged. It is important that the categories in which the material is divided are genuinely imposed by the learner rather than merely being present in the material. Mandler and Pearlstone (1966) showed that words arranged according to the subject's own organization were more readily learnt than words in a scheme devised by the experimenter. Nevertheless, the way the material is presented may make it much easier or much harder for the learner to structure it in useful ways: one of the most dramatic examples is a study by Bower et al (1969). In this case, lists of words were given which could objectively be divided into a number of sub-categories, and these in turn could be grouped together into larger categories, making a tree or hierarchy. For example, living things could be divided into plants and animals, the latter into vertebrates and invertebrates, and so on. It was much easier for learners to reproduce the material if they had had the classificatory scheme available at the time of the presentation, even though it was not given at recall.

This hierarchical classification of the material is very much the sort of system used in many libraries and can send us back to our analogy of somebody finding a book. It would seem that somebody who learns new material with a tree-like classification in mind has the same kind of advantage as the book-borrower who places the book on a shelf reserved for the modern English subsection of the bookcase devoted to poetry, which is in the room in which he keeps non-technical books. From the educational point of view, the point is once again that routine learning by drill is unlikely to give satisfactory performance later, but that equally it will not be useful to leave information about in a haphazard way for learners who have no strategy of analysis for classification of that which is being presented to them. As the experiment of Bower and his colleagues shows, such a procedure does not arise by the light of nature: it has to be implicit in the presentation, or possibly trained as habitual sets of operations to be performed on anything presented for learning.

Useful though it is, the hierarchical method of organization is not the only possible one. Much of the mental furniture of Western man consists of tree-like structures of subsets and supersets. Collins and Quillian (1969) even suggested that such a method of organization could be revealed in the time taken to check the truth or falsehood of certain statements. For example, it takes much less time to accept the statement that 'canaries are yellow' than 'canaries breathe', where the former is a specific property of canaries but not of all birds, while the latter is a property not merely of birds but of other kinds of animal as well. This is the sort of effect one might find if knowledge was stored inside the brain in a branching tree, so that it took less time to check the properties of a canary than it would take to go upwards by even one step and check the properties of all birds. However, this striking conjecture does not seem to be generally true, and probably applies only to particular kinds of material (Landauer and Meyer, 1972). Hierarchical organization is only one of the possible methods: the property of being yellow is not specific to a small subset of birds, but is shared with bananas which are not animals at all, or with gold which is not even living. There is, therefore, a different possible classification in terms of primary colours, exact shades and degrees of saturation and so on, cutting altogether across the kind of classification we mentioned earlier. A true representation of everything that is said or remembered about the world would be a network rather than a tree, so that all the yellow objects would be connected to a common point in the network, as well as all the birds connected to a different point. Furthermore, if the model of the world inside our heads is accurate, it would need to contain the nature of association in each case: it is not enough to know that 'man' and 'dog' are both associated with 'bites', because it is also very important to know whether the man is the agent or the patient of the verb, the biter or the bit. As a result, a complete network of properties and relationships will become very complex indeed. Examples are given by Lindsay and Norman (1972), and it can be seen that a network representing the information contained in a single sentence may spread over a whole page. In practice, the classifications used by human memory have to be rather simpler than this: they may be hierarchical, or cross-classified by, for example, colour and species in the example given above; or they may be by a single dominant link from each item to one other without the nature of the link being the same in each case (canary–sing–opera–conductor–bus). Each of these takes one set of paths out of the full possible network which represents the world, and uses it as a way of linking parts together – just as our book-borrowing friend is free to arrange his books in a number of different possible ways. As we have already said, he could have a hierarchical arrangement in which modern English poets were a subset of poets in general, and poets a subset of non-fiction as a whole; or he could have a cross-classified system in which poems were on one shelf and novels on another but modern English books were on the left-hand end of the shelf in each case and eighteenth-century French at the right-hand end of the shelf. He could even, as many of our friends do, put each book next to another which seems to him relevant, although the whole shelf may then have a very bizarre look.

As yet, we know little of the relevant advantages and disadvantages of organizing memory – nor indeed of organizing one's own books! Almost certainly, there is no single best method and the particular circumstances of a person will determine the approach he would be best advised to use. From the point of view of an educationalist, however, the main fact which should be borne in mind already is that fresh knowledge will always be entered into an organizational system which already exists, even though it may be primitive. If one presents material for learning in a fairly free situation and notices the manner in which people set about learning it, extreme cases can be found in which an individual works always on the basis of a single property at a time, so that he analyses what he is learning in a piece-by-piece way similar to that involved in a hierarchical system. Others on the other hand work with combinations of properties, as if they were using a criss-crossing method of organization. Most important of all, each kind of individual learns better with material designed on his own principles than he does on material arranged in accordance with the opposite principle (Pask, 1972; see also chapter 6 in Broadbent, 1973). Different teaching methods are appropriate for different people: it is particularly important to realize this, because each of us finds it intuitively unreasonable that a method of presentation he himself finds hard to understand may be positively easier for somebody else. At the level of anecdote, I can well recall a child taught history in terms of striking human incidents and personal drama, on the grounds presumably of adding interest, who complained bitterly that nobody had ever told her whether Nelson put his telescope to the blind eye before or after King Charles hid in the oak tree.

To summarize thus far, information of value must receive attention if it is to be stored: and it must also be categorized or processed so as to place it in an organized structure of knowledge. Because that structure already exists at least in part, different teaching methods will be appropriate for different individuals. All that we have said thus far, however, seems to refer to the knowledge which the child acquires, rather than to the development of the powers of the individual. It could well be argued that it is the latter rather than the former which is the chief business of education, and that development consists of fresh expansion of abilities rather than dead storage of facts. This would, however, be a false antithesis, and one of the best ways of seeing this is to consider some of the recent theoretical approaches to a popular problem in development, the attainment of the ability to perform tasks of the kind designed by Piaget.

•   •   •

GENERAL CONCLUSIONS

To summarize again, the message of cognitive psychology is:

(a) Only some of the information presented will receive attention, and if this is not decided deliberately it will certainly be decided by chance factors.

(b) When something is noticed in the environment, it can be processed or encoded in a number of ways, and the particular processing which takes place will decide whether the effects are long lasting or transitory.

(c) If the effects are to be enduring, then the information must be organized at the time it is stored, in such a way that a clear path leads to it from the likely situations in which it may be needed.

(d) Possible methods of organization range from the clear (but rigid) system of hierarchical subdivision to the flexible (but confusing) network of private association.

(e) By the time a teacher meets any child, some system of organization will probably already exist, and it is likely that fresh information will be best assimilated through the system which is already tentatively established.

(f) The achievement of formal intellectual skills probably depends on the availability of a set of general procedures or rules, each of which comes into play as the momentary external and internal circumstances make it appropriate. Because of the complex interplay of the various factors involved, the absence of one link in the chain will not be obvious, but will make certain formal processes of thought extremely difficult, and it is, therefore, necessary to look for such links. Particularly crucial ones will involve the organizational and selective factors already mentioned.

The study of cognition was, of course, a classic interest of psychology, and in some ways current concerns are taking up again older problems with new sophistication. It is perhaps appropriate, therefore, to remember the classic doctrines of 'faculty psychology' long derided in modern texts. It was indeed an error to suppose that the study of Latin and Greek would develop intellectual ability regardless of the way in which it was taught, or of the specific field to which the intellect was to be applied in later life. This does not mean, however, that the school environment is merely a cafeteria in which an autonomously developing intellect picks whatever suits its needs, nor that learning consists purely of elementary associations of stimuli and responses. Rather, the lesson of cognitive psychology is that each of us acquires during life certain strategies of encoding the outside world, of organizing memory and of proceeding from one step in an operation to the next, and that these may be highly general in their later use. The successful teacher, of course, has always known this, but in standing out for the middle ground between mechanical drill on the one hand, and the abandonment of all positive teaching on the other, he can now claim the support of contemporary cognitive psychology.

ACKNOWLEDGEMENT

This article first appeared in *Br. J. Educ. Psychol.* (1975), **45**, 162–176. Extracts from it are published here with the kind permission of the author and editor.

REFERENCES

Bousfield, W. A. (1953) The occurrence of clustering in recall of randomly arranged associates. *J. Gen. Psychol.*, **49**, 269–273.

Bower, G. H., Clark, M. C., Lesgold, A. M. & Winzenz, D. (1969) Hierarchical retrieval schemes in recall of categorised word lists. *J. Verb. Learn. Verb. Behav.*, **8**, 323–343.

Broadbent, D. E. (1958) *Perception and Communication*. London: Pergamon.

Broadbent, D. E. (1971) *Decision and Stress*. London: Academic.

Broadbent, D. E. (1973) *In Defence of Empirical Psychology*. London: Methuen.

Broadbent, D. E. & Broadbent, M. H. P. (1975) The recognition of words which cannot be recalled. In Dornic, S. & Rabbitt, P. (Eds.), *Attention and Performance V*. London: Academic.

Collins, A. M. & Quillian, M. R. (1969) Retrieval time from semantic memory. *J. Verb. Learn. Verb. Behav.*, **8**, 240–247.

Imai, S. & Garner, W. R. (1965) Discriminability and preference for attributes in free and constrained classification. *J. Exp. Psychol.*, **69**, 596–608.

Klahr, D. & Wallace, J. G. (1972) Class inclusion processes. In Farnham-Diggory, S. (Ed.), *Information Processing in Children*. London: Academic.

Landauer, T. K. & Meyer, D. (1972) Category size and semantic memory retrieval. *J. Verb. Learn. Verb. Behav.*, **11**, 539–549.

Light, L. L. & Carter-Sobell, L. (1970) The effect of changed semantic context in recognition memory. *J. Verb. Learn. Verb. Behav.*, **9**, 1–11.

Lindsay, P. H. & Norman, D. A. (1972) *Human Information Processing*. New York: Academic.

Maccoby, E. E. & Konrad, K. W. (1967) The effect of preparatory set on selective listening: developmental trends. *Monog. Soc. Res. Child Develop.*, Vol. 32, No. 112.

Mandler, G. & Pearlstone, Z. (1966) Free and constrained concept learning and subsequent recall. *J. Verb. Learn. Verb. Behav.*, **5**, 126–131.

Moray, N. (1959) Attention in dichotic listening: affective cues and the influence of instructions. *Q. J. Exp. Psychol.*, **11**, 56–60.

Morton, J. (1967) A singular lack of incidental learning. *Nature*, **215**, 203–204.

Mowbray, G. H. (1953) Simultaneous vision and audition: the comprehension of prose passages with varying levels of difficulty. *J. Exp. Psychol.*, **46**, 365–372.

Neisser, U. (1967) *Cognitive Psychology*. New York: Appleton-Century-Crofts.

Pask, G. (1972) Learning strategies and individual competence. *Int. J. Man-Machine Studies*, **4**, 217–253.

Tulving, E. & Pearlstone, Z. (1966) Availability *versus* accessibility of information in memory for words. *J. Verb. Learn. Verb. Behav.*, **5**, 381–391.

Turvey, M. T. (1967) Repetition and the preperceptual information store. *J. Exp. Psychol.*, **74**, 289–293.

Winograd, T. (1972) *Understanding Natural Language*. Edinburgh: University Press.

11 Memory and effective instruction

H. C. A. DALE

During the past decade there has been a spate of experimental research on memory, much of it on what has been called short-term memory (STM). The purpose of this paper is to review research on STM and discuss its relevance to effective instruction. Effective instruction, of course, leads to the establishment of permanent, or long-term, memory (LTM). The topic can therefore be restated as the relation between STM and LTM.

Research in STM flourished rather suddenly during the 1950s, when interest arose independently in laboratories on both sides of the Atlantic. The techniques which were developed differed markedly and led to emphases upon different aspects of memory. For this reason the techniques will be described separately.

In America, the beginning of this new wave of interest in STM was marked by the now classical experiments of Peterson (1959). In a typical task the subject was presented with a CCC trigram (three consonants such as KTL) followed by a three digit number. The subject was required to repeat the number and then count backwards from it by threes, keeping time with a metronome at 1 sec. rate, until stopped by the experimenter at a predetermined time, whereupon he was required to repeat the trigram. The period of retention varied from three to eighteen seconds, and the typical result expressed as the percentage correct trigrams taken from many tests at each retention period is: 90, 60, 36, 24, 12, 10, for periods of 3, 6, 9, 12, 15, 18 secs. respectively. The essence of Peterson's technique is that small amounts of material have to be remembered for short intervals during which rehearsal is prevented. The most striking feature of its application is that it reveals a memory system in miniature. Peterson's curve of retention over a period of 18 seconds shows a striking resemblance to Ebbinghaus' curve of forgetting over periods of days.

Subsequent experiments using this technique revealed further similarities between STM and LTM. Thus the rate of forgetting was shown to vary directly with the amount of material presented, and inversely with the amount of learning. It was also shown that STM was susceptible to interference in an analogous way to LTM.

To explain this, reference must be made to the relatively recent demonstration that the rates of forgetting obtained by Ebbinghaus and the comparable results obtained by many other early workers are to some extent artifactual. These typically show a loss of 75 per cent over 24 hours. But this substantial loss is only found when the same subject is used repeatedly in a succession of experiments. If subjects are fresh they will show little forgetting of their *very* first list. After a period of 24 hours their loss is only 25 per cent. When they learn their second and subsequent lists forgetting will be more rapid. In verbal learning terminology this decrement caused by prior learning is called pro-active inhibition (PI).

It been shown that PI also has an analogous but stronger effect upon STM. Using the Peterson technique it has been revealed that on his *very* first trial a subject's retention is nearly perfect throughout the retention period. Thus the result of experimentation using Peterson's procedure has been to reveal an STM system which is like a miniature LTM system.

The focal point of experimentation on STM in this country has been the Applied Psychology Research Unit of the Medical Research Council at Cambridge. It is significant that this unit was established by Sir Frederick Bartlett and that much of the work I shall describe is by one of his students, R. Conrad (Conrad and Hille, 1957). Conrad's interest in STM arose in response to a problem in applied psychology and his researches on this and on related questions provide an excellent example of the way in which attention to applied problems can stimulate fruitful fundamental research.

Conrad's problem was posed by the GPO. It was known that with the 4- and 5-digit telephone numbers which were in use at that time, substantial numbers of calls went astray because the subscriber made errors in dialling. With the advent of STD and the longer telephone numbers which this would necessitate, it was feared that even more dialling errors would result. The GPO engineers had some advance suggestions to make, namely that the dialling process itself might be speeded up and this is relevant to the research.

As a starting point Conrad checked the accuracy with which experienced telephonists can repeat back numbers of varying length. This was rather like a protracted immediate memory or 'span of apprehension' test of the kind used in the Stanford–Binet intelligence test. The results were rather startling. Fifty operators were tested. With 8-digit numbers, only 17 managed to repeat every number correctly, the average score being 77 per cent. With 9-digit numbers, the average was 41 per cent; only two gave perfect performances. With 10-digit numbers the average score was 32 per cent and none repeated all numbers correctly.

This confirmed that immediate memory is extremely limited, but of course this has been known for a long time and was well known to Binet. What had not been emphasized previously was the fact that the span is not absolute. If a given person's span is assessed as 8 digits he will occasionally make errors when repeating shorter numbers and will sometimes repeat longer ones correctly. Most of the work which is to be discussed here involves memory for lists of 6 digits or letters, and although generally within the span of apprehension for the normal adult subjects employed, substantial numbers of errors were recorded. The more interesting results came from these subsequent investigations.

The first examined the advantages of using admixtures of letters and digits, a telephone numbering practice already established in large cities. Conrad explored the possible advantages of various mixtures which might be employed (Conrad and Hille, 1957; Conrad, 1964). He looked at their relative ease of retention but in addition he looked at the patterns of errors which arose. This is important when choosing codes for numbering systems, largely because all possible codes will not be needed and if some can be omitted it is possible by judicious selection to avoid mutually confusable codes.

The error patterns he found for digits were nearly random. By contrast, the errors for letters showed systematic patterns. If B were correct, D P C or V would commonly be given in its place, but L X or S were rarely substituted. In general, the intrusion errors showed a striking resemblance to listening errors. When the message to be remembered was presented auditorially, this pattern could be attributed to mishearing, but the same result was obtained when the letters were presented visually. It appeared that in immediate memory the subject remembered the sound of the letters rather than any of their other characteristics such as their shape or their position in the alphabet.

Further experiments revealed the generality and the significance of this discovery. Thus it was found that messages consisting of letters with similar sounds, e.g. B C P T V or M F N X S were much less likely to be remembered accurately than messages consisting of letters with dissimilar sounds such as B M H Z J (Conrad, 1964).

The other practical question examined by Conrad was the effect of pacing the response. If we look up a telephone number and then dial it, the actual physical operation of dialling takes a substantial number of seconds, especially if the digits in the number are large. The GPO engineers were displeased with this feature of dialling because a line is effectively out of action during the period of operation. They therefore considered replacing dials by keyset devices, like the keyboards of cash registers, which can be operated more rapidly. To see whether a keyset was likely to reduce memory errors, Conrad examined the effect of pacing recall (Conrad, 1958). Telephonists were again used as subjects. This time, after hearing each message from a tape recording, they had to write it out digit by digit keeping pace with a timing device which clicked loudly at either a rate of 30 or 90 clicks a minute. The significant result was that performance was worse at the slow rate. Even at the fast rate it was substantially worse than under unpaced conditions. These tests were carried out at different rates of presentation, a rate of 90 items per minute being easier than one of 30 a minute. The general conclusion drawn from these results was that performance depended upon the total time the material had to be remembered. This was supported by additional experiments using a direct comparison between dial and keyset devices in which the effect of a prefix digit was examined (Conrad, 1958). With the prefix digit the operator had to dial 0 before the number being remembered. This had a negligible effect with the keyset where the extra delay introduced was very small. It had a large deleterious effect with the conventional dial, however, where the extra delay introduced was roughly $2\frac{1}{4}$ seconds.

The interpretation Conrad has placed upon this effect of pacing responses is that forgetting in STM can be attributed to a decaying trace. The effects of acoustic similarity can also be fitted into the same picture if we assume that the trace is coded acoustically and that partly decayed traces of acoustically similar letters cannot be distinguished from each other. Thus the partly decayed traces of the letters B C P T V are equivalent but can be distinguished from all other letters. This hypothesis has been supported by the recent finding that when the retention period is increased from 6 to 18 seconds errors become increasingly random (Conrad, 1967).

Conrad's results imply that STM is qualitatively different from LTM. There has been little support in recent years for a theory of LTM based upon trace decay. All the indications are that the rate of forgetting depends not upon the length of the retention period but upon the activities undertaken by the subject prior to learning or during the retention period, which create interference. The Gestalt school of psychology had proposed that there were autonomous changes in the 'trace' and claimed support for this from studies of memory for visual form. Recent work, however, has shown that these studies were poorly controlled. When adequate controls are introduced evidence of autonomous change is no longer forthcoming.

We have, then, a picture of an ephemeral STM which has the two distinctive features of (i) employing acoustic coding, and (ii) being susceptible to a rapid decay of the trace. These dual characteristics have been succinctly expressed in the idea that STM is an echo-box.

Clear distinctions can rarely be maintained for long in empirical endeavours. It is true that Conrad in his recent work (Conrad, 1967) has presented data which can be readily interpreted by a trace decay theory while being seemingly incompatible with interference theory. When, however, suitable interfering activities are inserted between learning and recall, performance can be markedly affected. Thus the present writer has shown that if messages like B T P have to be remembered while six other letters are read aloud, about 60 per cent of the messages are correct when the distracting letters differ acoustically from the message, e.g. F L M L M F, whereas only 30 per cent are correct if the distractors are similar to the message, e.g. V G D V D G (Dale, 1964). Results of this kind are readily explained by interference theory but present difficulties for decay theory. They eliminate any grounds for regarding STM as distinctive because it is susceptible only to decay.

The other criterion of distinction was the relative prominence of acoustic coding in

STM. Although Conrad himself regarded acoustic coding as a feature common to LTM, experimental evidence of this is very weak. Conrad quoted Woodworth's anecdotal reports that when trying to remember a name, an acoustically similar name might come to mind. This has been substantiated to some extent by investigation of the 'tip of the tongue' phenomenon (Brown and McNeill, 1966). In this, subjects are given a vocabulary test. Whenever they feel that the right word in answer to any particular test-word is on the 'tip of their tongue' but just cannot be recalled, they are asked to write down all the words that come to mind. With this technique it is found that a substantial proportion of the alternative words that come to mind are acoustically, rather than semantically, similar to the intended response-word.

Recent comparative studies of coding in STM and LTM, however, show that it is difficult to make a general distinction on these grounds. Thus, although acoustic coding is prominent in STM, the present writer has demonstrated effects which imply that there is also semantic coding (Dale and Gregory, 1966). In this experiment one message had to be remembered while another was read aloud. Both messages consisted of short words, thus in the first part of the experiment the message to be remembered could have been BLOWS NOSE ROSE. When the message to be read aloud was acoustically similar, e.g. SHOWS FLOWS GROWS FLOWS GROWS SHOWS, retention was impaired in comparison with control conditions in which the message to be read, although consisting of mutually similar words, e.g. FLOUT ROUT POUT FLOUT POUT ROUT was acoustically distinct from the message to be remembered. This part of the experiment demonstrated again the importance of acoustic similarity. The significant feature of the experiment was that when the same technique was applied to semantic similarity, the same kinds of effects were obtained but these were not as large as with acoustic similarity. In the semantic case the message to be remembered could have been : LOOK STARE SEE, and the semantically similar distracting message: VIEW SIGHT WATCH WATCH VIEW SIGHT. In the light of these results it would be wrong to assert that STM involves acoustic coding exclusively. STM therefore is not just an acoustic echo-box.

As stated earlier, the basic problem of effective instruction is to ensure that the required material enters LTM. This raises interesting questions of the kind: is STM the door to LTM?

The echo-box theory of STM which has been mentioned belongs to a class of model which proposes that an STM buffer storage system operates while material is entered into LTM. The implication of this is that if material survives the STM period immediately after presentation, it will enter the LTM system and will survive for much longer periods.

It has already been noted that messages consisting of acoustically different items are much easier to remember in immediate memory tasks than messages consisting of acoustically similar items. This indicates that they survive STM storage better. In a study of the way LTM for serial lists is established over a number of trials Baddeley (1966) has shown how STM and LTM interact in just this way. With a list of acoustically dissimilar items which was presented for a number of successive trials, learning as assessed by immediate retention was rapid. A recall test given ten minutes later, however, showed a considerable degree of forgetting. When the same procedure was followed using a list of acoustically similar items the immediate retention scores were relatively poor, but nothing was lost over a 10-minute period. Subsequent investigation revealed that if retention were tested after 30 seconds, during which the subject was prevented from rehearsing by being given a secondary task much like Peterson's, the scores on similar and dissimilar lists were the same. Furthermore, retention after 10 minutes showed no additional loss. Baddeley's experiment demonstrates neatly that material which survives the 30-second period also survives the 10-minute period. The question of whether it would survive much longer periods remains open at the present.

At this point the conditions which determine the chances of survival in STM will be reviewed. If it is assumed that material enters LTM via STM – and it must be stressed that this is only an assumption despite the supporting evidence just cited – then LTM can only be established if STM storage is successful. The main factors known to influence STM have already been mentioned and can now be elaborated upon. These are (i) the length of the message, (ii) the constitution of the message, (iii) the opportunity for initial learning and (iv) the interaction between successive messages.

Long messages are unlikely to survive even in immediate memory as we have seen with the example of the telephone operators. No absolute limit to message length can be given, however, since there is no sharp cut-off point beyond which no messages are correct; rather there is a gradually reduced probability of success. But there are other complications. The effect of length of message will depend upon the items in the message and the subject's prior experience with them. We saw how rapidly a CCC trigram was forgotten when rehearsal was prevented. It might be expected that a message consisting of three four-letter words would be forgotten more rapidly since its total content is twelve letters. But in fact the rate of forgetting is strictly comparable to that of the trigram. Words as elements are no more difficult than letters.

An important feature of messages which has not been previously mentioned is their sequential structure. Sequences of words such as: 'good books were examined and failed' are easier to remember than: 'examined failed good books and were'. The first of these examples approximates more closely to English syntax than the second in that the order of successive triples of words corresponds more closely with sequences found in English usage. There are therefore associative links between successive words which have already been learned outside the laboratory. This feature of word sequences has been known for some time. What has been discovered more recently is that a similar phenomenon works with letter sequences. Letter-messages such as *WISTON* in which the trigram structure corresponds with that commonly found in English words are easier to remember than unusual sequences like *TOSNIW*.

A special feature of the STM experiments which have been described is that the message to be remembered has been presented just once and no opportunity for rehearsal has been allowed – either memory has been tested immediately, or else rehearsal has been prevented by a distracting task such as counting backwards. These conditions minimize initial learning. They can be relaxed in a number of ways, by multiple presentation, by reduced rates of presentation which permit rehearsal between items, and by allowing a rehearsal period before the distracting task is begun. These all enhance retention. In addition, some attempts have been made to control the activity of the subject when rehearsing.

Under certain circumstances a period of silent rehearsal enables subjects to store messages so that they are relatively immune from the effects of subsequent distraction. Despite its obvious importance this topic has not been investigated very adequately and some observations are rather contradictory. In a study of Sanders (1961), however, it has been shown that for messages of eight digits, a 40-second period of rehearsal provides complete immunity from periods of distraction as long as 120 seconds. Shorter rehearsal periods provide less complete immunity for messages of this length, but it is likely that they would be sufficient for shorter messages.

The implication of these findings is, of course, that during rehearsal the material is transferred to a permanent long-term store. Subsequent tests of LTM, that is tests after a period of 24 hours or more, have never been conducted in these experiments, however, so this is no more than speculation at present. Conclusive evidence would in fact be difficult to obtain because LTM is seriously affected by interference when similar messages have to be learnt. Poor LTM under these conditions therefore would be expected even when each message had been initially entered into long-term storage so that it would survive if it were isolated. There are, however, some data which show that when a person is permitted to rehearse until satisfied he has learned an item, extremely reliable memory is established. The main data comes from a study by Wallace (Wallace, Turner and Perkins, 1957), in which pairs of words had to be learned so that the second could be given when cued by the first. This is the standard paired-associate learning task. But instead of being rigidly paced by the presentation apparatus, Wallace's subjects were allowed to take their own time. In addition, subjects were instructed to form an image which would link the words so that if given the pair BUG-HOLE they might construct an image of ants streaming from a hole in the base of a tree. In contrast with the results of the standard laboratory paired-associate learning procedure in which learning is slow and ephemeral, Wallace's subjects established strong and permanent memory for these pairs after a single presentation, and after three days could remember 95 per cent of a total list of 700 pairs. At the beginning of the task the subjects required about 25 seconds to form each association. When they had become practised, however, they took only five seconds.

One striking observation is that a brief distraction at the beginning of the rehearsal period can be disastrous. This was shown in yet another study by Conrad (1960). Eight-digit messages were used and a 10-second rehearsal period was inserted between presentation and test. Under these conditions 70 per cent of the messages were remembered correctly. When the subjects were required to say 'nought' immediately after the presentation, however, only 44 per cent of the messages were given correctly. Similar though less marked effects have been obtained by requiring subjects to rehearse aloud just once during a period of otherwise silent rehearsal.

When presentation is visual, vocalization by the subject enhances immediate memory. In general, full vocalization produces better results than whispering while whispering is better than 'mouthing'. If vocalization is prevented by obliging the subject to say something else at the time of presentation, an even poorer level of performance results. For instance, Murray (1967), using seven-letter messages, found the effects are considerable, with scores of 65 per cent correct when voiced as against scores of less than 30 per cent when vocalization is suppressed.

These findings and related observations have a bearing on the significance of acoustic confusions in STM. Conrad had originally suggested that the effect arises because the subject vocalizes and remembers the sounds he produced. Thus when vocalization is suppressed, messages consisting of acoustically confusing the letters are no more difficult than control messages. Furthermore, if the subject is instructed to vocalize by making similar sounds for every letter as when they are pronounced as small letters, e.g. *buh, duh, fuh*, instead of *bee, dee, eff*, retention is impaired. This strongly supports Conrad's contention.

Interaction between successive messages builds up extremely rapidly in laboratory experiments like those described. As we have seen, it is only the very first message a subject is given to remember which is free from the effects of pro-active inhibition (PI). The usual laboratory session is extremely intensive, one trial following another with minimum delay until the experiment has been completed. Two modifications of this procedure have been tried by Loess and his collaborators, both with beneficial effects on retention (Loess, 1967). In one modification a rest period is deliberately inserted between trials. This is not effective with short rests, but does work if the rest period is two minutes or more (Loess and Waugh, 1967). In the other, the rest period is filled with trials using different material (Murray, 1967). This is the more effective since it is found that PI does not build up when successive messages consist of different kinds of items. This is true even when all messages consist of triplets of nouns with the categories mixed so that, for instance, the first triplet might name three animals, the second three vehicles, and so on.

We can now question what relevance, if any, this research in STM has to the problem of effective instruction.

A summary statement of the experimental findings might run like this: for material to enter long-term storage it has to survive an initial period during which retention loss can be extremely rapid. In order to survive, the amount of material should be small; it should be as free as possible from inter-item acoustic confusions; it should be varied so that interference between successive messages is minimized; also an opportunity for a brief period of silent rehearsal should be provided after each component message is presented.

But before accepting this advice uncritically, and since it is not surprising advice it is readily acceptable, we should perhaps question the generality of the findings.

The experimental situations described have been extremely restricted. For instance, it is rare outside the psychological laboratory for a person to be required to remember strings of digits or letters while counting backwards. Admittedly some special real life tasks such as that of the telephone operator or an air traffic controller do resemble these artificial situations, but these are rare and are far removed from the classroom or lecture-room. There are, however, some other experimental procedures recently introduced in laboratory experimentation, which have more direct relevance to questions of generality. It has been shown, for instance, that when a long message, well beyond the immediate memory span, has to be remembered, the effect of the later items in preventing rehearsal is comparable to the effect of a distracting task such as counting backwards (Waugh and Norman, 1965). This alternative method which is now generally used in preference to Peterson's technique, more closely resembles the classroom or lecture-room situation in which retention is impeded because the lecturer continues rapidly and without pause. The procedures used in the studies described would not, therefore, appear to be without relevance for teaching.

The contents of most lectures or lessons consist of verbal statements rather than messages made up of strings of letters or digits. Verbal statements are relatively inconvenient in the laboratory and most of the work quoted in the present paper has been based upon experimentation with simpler material. But there is some indication that the limitations of STM do play an important role in learning meaningful verbal material. We have seen how approximation to English influences the ease of retention. This in one way shows how prior learning helps in the acquisition of new material. In a similar manner, Zangwill (1956) has shown how unreliable immediate memory for short prose passages can be and how it is influenced by prior expectations. All the phenomena demonstrated by Bartlett in his classical study of LTM for verbal material have been shown to be present in these immediate memory studies. At a more molecular level it can be shown that STM influences the comprehension of the sentence (Miller, 1962). Writers and speakers who wish to be clearly understood avoid long and complex sentences for this reason. If they are wise, they also avoid a certain form of sentence structure known as 'embedding'. This can be illustrated by reference to a familiar complex sentence:

'This is the cow with the crumpled horn that tossed the dog that worried the cat that killed the rat that ate the malt that lay in the house that Jack built.'

In this form the sentence is long but not unduly difficult to understand and remember. The alternative embedded form which is grammatically just as acceptable, can be built up as follows:

'The rat ate the malt
The rat that the cat killed ate the malt
The rat that the cat that the dog worried killed ate the malt
The rat that the cat that the dog that the cow tossed worried killed ate the malt, etc.'

The difficulty created by this form of construction is obvious.

The indications are, then, that the phenomena of STM being explored in the laboratory of the experimental psychologist do have some relevance to the problems of ensuring that instruction is effective in real-life training and teaching situations. Whether they have resulted in any new insights is for you, the reader, to judge. A problem frequently arising in psychology is that careful, protracted, laboratory experimentation serves only to underline what is already well known to practitioners, in education for instance, through experience and from informal observation. On the other hand, the informal study of memory has a long history, and while it has contributed to the development of teaching methods it cannot be denied that room for improvement still exists. Perhaps laboratory studies of the kind described in the present paper will eventually lead to increased effectiveness of instruction.

ACKNOWLEDGEMENT

This article first appeared in *Aspects of Educ.* (1968), **7**, 8–21, and is published here with the kind permission of the author and editor.

REFERENCES

Baddeley, A. D. (1966) The influence of acoustic and semantic similarity on long-term memory for word sequences. *Q. J. Exp. Psychol.*, **18**, 302–309.

Brown, R. & McNeill, D. (1966) The 'tip of the tongue' phenomenon. *J. Verb. Learn. Verbal. Behav.*, **5**, 325–327.

Conrad, R. (1958) Accuracy of recall using keyset and telephone dial, and the effect of a prefix digit. *J. Appl. Psychol.*, **42**, 285–288.

Conrad, R. (1960) Very brief delay of immediate recall. *Q. J. Exp. Psychol.*, **12**, 45–47.

Conrad, R. (1964) Acoustic confusions in immediate memory. *Br. J. Psychol.*, **55**, 75–84.

Conrad, R. (1967) Interference or decay over short retention intervals. *J. Verb. Learn. Verb. Behav.*, **6**, 49–64.

Conrad, R. & Hille, B. A. (1957) Memory for long telephone numbers. *P.O. Tele. J.*, **10**, 37–39.

Dale, H. C. A. (1964) Retroactive interference in short-term memory. *Nature*, **203**, 1408.

Dale, H. C. A. & Gregory, M. (1966) Evidence of semantic coding in short-term memory. *Psychon. Sc.*, **5**, 75–76.

Loess, H. (1967) Short-term memory, word class and sequence of items. *J. Exp. Psychol.*, **74**, 556–561.

Loess, H. & Waugh, N. C. (1967) Short-term memory and inter-trial interval. *J. Verb. Learn. Verb. Behav.*, **6**, 455–460.

Miller, G. A. (1962) Some psychological studies of grammar. *Am. Psychol.*, **17**, 748–762.

Murray, D. J. (1967) The role of speech responses in short-term memory. *Can. J. Psychol.*, **21**, 263–276.

Peterson, L. R. & Peterson, M. J. (1959) Short term retention of individual verbal items. *J. Exp. Psychol.*, **58**, 193–198.

Sanders, A. F. (1961) Rehearsal and recall in immediate memory. *Ergonomics*, **4**, 25–34.

Wallace, W. H., Turner, S. H. & Perkins, C. C. (1957) *Preliminary Studies of Human Information Storage, Signal Corps. Project No. 132C.* Institute for Co-operative Research, University of Pennsylvania.

Waugh, N. C. & Norman, D. A. (1965) Primary memory. *Psychol. Rev.*, **72**, 89–104.

Zangwill, O. L. (1957) A note on immediate memory. *Q. J. Exp. Psychol.*, **8**, 140–143.

12 A singular lack of incidental learning

J. MORTON

More than 200 people have been asked to recall the positions of the letters on a telephone dial, including all the staff of the Applied Psychology Research Unit (APRU), and not one has succeeded in performing the task. 151 of these people were tested formally and will accordingly be termed 'subjects'. The subjects were first given a sheet of paper on which were inscribed 10 circles arranged in the pattern of the telephone dial and were requested to fill in the digits. Following this they were given a sheet with a further dial with the digits correctly inscribed. On this they were requested to fill in the letters. If, as many subjects claimed, they had no idea at all where the letters were, they were requested to guess, or, in the extreme, to design their own telephone dial. Finally, a recognition test was given comprising 12 dials which had either been popular responses in preliminary tests or seemed plausible. All but one of these were required to be eliminated. The subjects, mostly members of the APRU Subject Panel, were divided into two groups, the smaller group consisting of people who had recently lived in London or had employment as switchboard operators. This sub-group was supplemented by a group from Birmingham and constituted a sample of 45 'experienced' subjects who frequently use the letters when making local or trunk calls. The 'normal' group contained 106 subjects, 47 of whom had no telephone in their homes.

Thirty-five of the normal group (30 per cent) and five of the experienced group (11 per cent) reproduced the digits incorrectly. Twenty-two of these began with 0 in place of 1 and moved all the digits up, and 18 put the digits clockwise, 11 with 0 in the correct place. A slightly higher proportion of those without telephones in the normal group mistook the digits.

No one succeeded in correctly recalling the letters. Partial learning was estimated by considering the following features of the letters on a dial:

(a) they are ordered and run anti-clockwise, largely in threes (termed hereafter 'admissible'); (b) O goes with 0 – (O); (c) 1 has no letters with it – (1); (d) Q goes with O (on some dials it is absent) – (Q); (e) Z is absent – (Z).

Seven of the experienced group (15.5 per cent) and 41 of the normal group (38.6 per cent) did not fulfil condition (a) and were excluded from the further analysis. They included three subjects who wrote:

1   ATU;   2   BSV;   3   CRW;   4   DQX;   5   EPY;

6   FOZ;   7   GN;   8   HM;   9   IL;   0   JK;

which has a pleasant if unusual pattern, and nine subjects who had the letters running clockwise but otherwise ordered. Of the remainder the number who correctly recalled the features are given in table 12.1.

As expected, the experienced group produced a higher proportion of admissible dials, and had a higher proportion of the features correct.

Table 12.1

	Total no. of subjects	Admissible	No. with feature correct				Total no. of features correct
			0	1	Q	Z	
Normal	106	65	12	4	5	10	31
Experienced	45	38	16	6	4	10	36

In the recognition test two of the 12 examples were termed 'correct', one with and one without the Q. Only ten of the normal group selected one of the correct responses, compared with nine of the experienced group. Neither of these figures differs significantly from chance. Half the recognition dials had no letters in the digit 1 position, but only 33 of the normal group selected one of these. This is significantly less than chance ($P < 0.001$). Twenty of the experienced group recognized this feature. Eight of the 12 dials had O with 0, but only 44 of the normal group selected one of these dials compared with 31 of the experienced group. The normal group again performed worse than chance ($P < 0.001$). It would seem, then, that despite any residual memory the Post Office dials are not as the population would expect.

Subjects were asked to indicate their confidence in their responses to the recognition and recall tests by writing a digit from 1 for complete confidence to 5 for certainty that the response was incorrect with three intermediate categories of variable uncertainty. Sixty-three of the normal group were certain that their responses in the recall task were incorrect; no subject wrote 1. In this group only two subjects were confident they had recognized the correct dial (both unjustifiably); 17 were certain they were incorrect. Seven of the experienced group were confident they were correct, of whom three in fact were.

One of the observations for which proponents of reinforcement theories of animal learning have difficulty in accounting is that animals appear to learn without motivation (Broadbent, 1961). Another observation which old-fashioned behaviourists find unreasonable is that monkeys will perform complex tasks merely to be allowed to look out of a window – to satisfy their general curiosity (Butler, 1953). It is thus of some considerable theoretical interest that so many people are incapable of recalling the layout of the digits of a telephone dial and that an almost negligible proportion of those tested were able to recall even individual features of the letter distribution or to recognize these features. It is clear that memory for the letters is better among those who, as a group, most frequently use them, but even this group performs badly in view of the amount of experience they must have had. For reasons of incidental learning or curiosity, better performance might have been expected. One possible explanation of these results may lie in the amount of time it takes for the dial to return to the resting position. In this time one can search for the next letter or digit and anticipation may in fact be a hindrance.

ACKNOWLEDGEMENT

This article first appeared in *Nature* (1967), **215,** 203–204, and is published here with the kind permission of the author and editor.

REFERENCES

Broadbent, D. E. (1961) Behaviour, p. 61. London.
Butler, R. A. (1953) in *J. Comp. Physiol. Psychol,* **46,** 95.

PART 5

Learning theory and practice

INTRODUCTION

Learning covers such a vast and diffuse area of research, development and application that a short collection of papers cannot really do justice to the subject. In choosing the following, I have tried to sample an extremely bountiful harvest of work.

Skemp's research was an early attempt to relate a theory of learning to teaching. He developed a schematic theory and conducted several researches using it. His paper highlights the difference between 'schematic' and 'rote' learning when meaningful material is used (rather than nonsense material so familiar in laboratory studies). A significant finding is the supremacy of schematic over rote learning both immediately and several weeks after the learning episode. An important supplement to Skemp's work is that of Rowell, Simon and Wiseman using very similar symbolic systems. They came up with the observation that explicit direction by teachers produced better performance than the guided discovery method – using both immediate and long-term recall sessions.

These two results put together with the suggestion from Morton's work in Part 4 are most instructive. It appears, within the limits of the material chosen and the age and ability of the pupils, that the structural presentation of work to motivated children in a systematic fashion is more likely to lead to better performance than non-schematic guided discovery. *But*, it is most important to read the tentative conclusions in both these papers. The generalizations above require a lot more hard evidence yet.

Behaviour modification techniques using the principles enunciated by Skinner have become widespread in the United States. A little research has taken place in Britain. The article by Whitman and Whitman is included because it stands as a good introduction to the application of behaviour modification as well as providing a source of further reading about the American research.

The extracts from a programmed guide on programmed learning kill two birds with one stone – they exemplify both the principles and practice of programming.

13   The need for a schematic learning theory

RICHARD R. SKEMP

Summary   Current learning theories have little direct application to problems of teaching and learning school subjects. The development of a schematic learning theory will, it is hoped, help to remedy this deficiency. Such a theory will also have wider applications.

INTRODUCTION

Among the branches of psychology applicable in the field of educational research, one would expect learning theory to be the most prominent of all. Learning is a child's chief task throughout his school days, and beyond: and the teacher's main concern is the extent and quality of this activity. How much help in these tasks have psychologists been able to offer, and teachers to use?

A search of the three main journals in the field of educational psychology and research, over the 21 years from 1940 to the year of writing (1961), has revealed a total of only five papers on application of learning theory.

*   *   *

The purpose of the present paper is to put forward the view that only by developing further a theory along the lines which Piaget (1950) has begun can learning theory be made fully relevant for educational psychology (particularly since it offers a hope of relating certain kinds of learning to intelligence); and to describe an experiment which both supports this view and indicates the kind of way in which a beginning can be made with the practical application of the theory in the classroom.

EXPERIMENT

The chief object of this experiment was to demonstrate the crucial importance of a schema even for a relatively straightforward learning task, less difficult than most of those required of pupils in the usual school subjects.

To isolate the schema as the experimental variable, two different artificial schemata were devised, each based on sixteen basic symbols with associated meanings. These symbols were combined into pairs and threes, and then into successively larger groups; symbolizing new meanings which were not arbitrary, but based on the meanings of the sub-groups, which, in turn, were based on those of the individual symbols. This can best be understood by reference to figure 13.1, which shows part of schema 1.

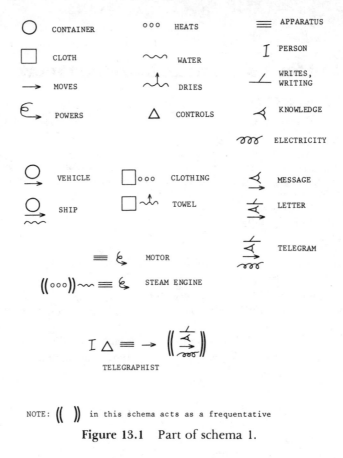

Figure 13.1   Part of schema 1.

For experimental control of the other variables a second schema was prepared, similar in principle to the first. Twelve of the same sixteen basic symbols were used but with new meanings, together with four new ones. An extract from this second schema is shown in figure 13.2. From considerations of space, it has only been possible to show a few of the more complex groups in these two figures. Apart from their content, however, it is hoped

Figure 13.2   Part of schema 2.

that they will help to clarify the concept by showing two examples of how schemata can be progressively built up.

The subjects were two parallel first forms at a boys' grammar school, numbering 23, 24, respectively, after excluding boys who were absent for any part of the experiment. In the preliminary part, each form learnt one of these schemata: that is, they were asked to memorize first the basic word and symbol pairs, and then the successively larger groups which symbolized new words. Pencil and paper were given to them, and they were advised that the best way to learn was by attempted recall with self-testing and correction of errors. This extended over three school periods on consecutive days, and the subjects were then ready for the final part of the experiment: which involved learning with, and without, the aid of the respective schemata which they had learnt.

For each schema a set of 10 multi-symbol groups was prepared, these groups ranging from 8 to 14 symbols in size, and each set totalling exactly 100 symbols together. (One example from each final set has been included in figures 13.1 and 13.2, being in each case the last one shown.) Both forms were asked to learn both of these final sets: the task being, as before, to learn the group of symbols associated with each word. For one set, they had learnt a schema into which the new symbols and their meanings could be assimilated; for the other, their own particular schema was no use. The aid given by the schemata could thus be quantified, by combining the scores which represented schematic learning for each group, and comparing these results with the combined scores on non-schematic learning (hereafter called rote learning). Both groups of subjects were learning the same total material, the two halves of which were of approximately equal objective difficulty. There was, of course, a considerable subjective difference; but this, the effect of the previously learnt schemata, is just what the experiment was concerned with.

The experimental design is summarized in table 13.1. It took care of any slight difference between the abilities of the two forms, and also of whatever differences there may have been between the two final tasks. The number of presentations of the individual symbols previous to the final tasks were equal for the two schemata. It should further be

Table 13.1   Summary of experimental design

Subjects	Preliminary stage	Final tasks and their nature for the subjects			
Group I	Learn schema I	Learn material assimilable to schema I	Schematic learning	Learn material assimilable to schema II	Rote learning
Group II	Learn schema II		Rote learning		Schematic learning

Composition of scores

Schematic learning: Group I, recall of material fitting schema I, combined with
Group II, recall of material fitting schema II.

Rote learning: Group I, recall of material fitting schema II, combined with
Group II, recall of material fitting schema I.

emphasized that, in the final test, all the subjects were learning to associate new groups of symbols with new meanings. There was no question of learning different meanings for any of the basic symbols, or earlier groups of symbols, which they had already learnt.

RESULTS

In table 13.2 are shown the percentages of symbols correctly recalled by all subjects immediately after learning, the following day, and 28 days later (i.e., 29 days after the original learning). By 'total scores' is meant percentage recall of all the symbols in the final learning

Table 13.2   Percentage recall by all subjects (N = 47)

	Immediate	1 day	28/29 days
Total Scores:			
Schematic learning	70	68	51
Rote learning	35	26	7
Controlled Scores:			
Schematic learning	69	69	58
Rote learning	32	23	8

task. The 'controlled scores' are calculated only for those symbols which occurred in both schemata, and which for each group constituted 12 of the 16 originally learnt by them.

In both cases, the difference between schematic and rote learning is striking. Schematic learning resulted in twice the number of symbols being recalled immediately after learning, and seven times as many after four weeks. It gave both faster learning and better retention.

The rates of forgetting, expressed in percentages of what was originally learnt (as shown by immediate recall), are shown in table 13.3. It can be seen that the subjects forgot more of the rote-learnt material in a day than of the schematically learnt material in four weeks.

Table 13.3   Amount forgotten (as percentage of amount originally learnt)

	First day	Following 28 days
Controlled Scores:		
Schematic learning	0	16
Rote learning	28	47

IMPLICATIONS FOR TEACHING

(a) *Schematic presentation of material*   The obvious consequence of these results is that, so far as possible, the subject matter of lessons should be arranged in such a form that pupils can use schematic learning rather than rote learning. What this means in its detailed application to the many subjects taught in schools and colleges has yet to be worked out. The main part of this task must, of course, be the concern of the teachers who are specialists in various subjects: but further psychological research is needed to establish more clearly what are the basic principles of schematic presentation. Probably the best teachers have always tended intuitively toward this method: but only by detailed investigation of the underlying processes can it be used most effectively.

(b) *Triple advantage of schematic learning*   The most obvious point established by the present experiment is the superiority of schematic learning over rote learning for both immediate recall and long-term retention. But two further advantages appear when the method is considered in the wider setting of school and college learning, and also in many of the learning situations of childhood and everyday life. In schematic learning, not only the material is learnt, but *the schema itself*: which is thus available to provide the same advantages for future learning (provided that this can be assimilated to the schema). Moreover, this subsequent learning, to the extent that it makes use of the schema, is also practising it: thereby providing, without extra work, revision of the earlier material. To give a simple example from algebra: a pupil who learns to factorize is also helping to prepare a schema for learning to solve many kinds of equation. When afterwards he is solving equations by this means, he is also revising factorization. These advantages are absent from rote learning, in which successive tasks remain unrelated.

The same is true for some of the most basic schemata, such as speaking, reading and writing one's own language. Not only is later learning made possible (and also structured) by them, but they are constantly being practised and developed during the learning and exercise of more advanced topics. These basic schemata are, therefore, never forgotten, though not practised as such after the initial learning.

Schematic learning thus has a triple effect: more efficient learning, preparation for future learning, and automatic revision of past learning.

(c) *The basic schemata*   Another point arises in connection with these. When a child first enters an entirely new field of learning, elementary schemata have first to be built up *ab initio*. What other forms of learning may enter into this process is a matter for further investigation, but two points of importance for teaching seem clear. First: learning will be much slower at the stage when a new schema is being formed than later when it has become available for use as a tool of further learning. The teacher must, therefore, know at which of these stages his pupils are, and adjust his pace accordingly. Second: the experiment has shown how little is retained of material which cannot be assimilated to a schema; and the discussion of the previous section has indicated how self-perpetuating a schema tends to be. It therefore follows that whatever schemata are formed in the early stages of a child's education are of crucial importance for his future learning; and that any major changes of teaching method, beyond the powers of accommodation of existing schemata, could bring progress almost to a standstill. One might well adapt William James' famous utterance about habit, and say that 'we must guard against the development of schemata that are likely to be inappropriate for future learning as we should guard against the plague.' Since the basic schemata are formed by children at an age before they are able to direct their own learning activities, it is parents and teachers who must guard them in this respect.

SOME OTHER CONSIDERATIONS

To consider all the implications for psychology in general of the concepts which have here been introduced, and the leads for further research which need to be followed to develop a useful body of knowledge about the processes of schematic learning, would be beyond the scope of this paper. Here I would like to mention two.

(a) *Learning theory and intelligence*   One of the criticisms here made of existing theories of learning, so far as they applied to educational psychology, has been their exclusion of the factor of intelligence. There may well be, even in adult humans, many learning processes into which intelligence does not enter. But where it is a factor at all, it is one which, to put it mildly, ought not to be ignored!

Piaget's concept of intelligence is a difficult one. 'To define intelligence in terms of the progressive reversibility of the mobile structures which it forms is therefore to repeat, in different words, that intelligence constitutes the state of equilibrium towards which tend all the successive adaptations of a sensori-motor and cognitive nature, as well as all assimilatory and accommodatory interactions between the organism and the environment.' (*Op. cit.*, p. 11.) It is hard to see immediately how this relates to the concepts of intelligence in the tradition of Binet, Spearman, Terman, Moray House, Wechsler, etc., which are familiar to British and American psychologists. Nor have we yet a Piagetian intelligence test, based on the above definitions.

Nevertheless, it is possible to see in the concept of a learning schema at least the possibility of a reciprocal assimilation (to use another concept from the same author) between theories of learning and of intelligence. This follows from the intrinsic properties of concepts in classifying knowledge and interrelating it in other ways also, thereby providing a ready means of schematization. The formation and application of concepts have always been an important feature of traditional intelligence tests. Thus, the development of certain kinds of schemata can be regarded also as the functioning of intelligence. Further development of our understanding along these lines would enable us not only to estimate the extent to which an individual is possessed of intelligence, but also to indicate how this intelligence might most effectively be used for various learning tasks. We could then, perhaps, teach children to use their intelligence intelligently.

(b) *Meaningful* v. *non-meaningful learning*   Much work has already been done relating to this, by the Gestalt school and others. A major contribution has been that of Katona (1940), who showed with an abundance of experiment that meaningful learning was better retained than rote learning, and also gave better transfer. The reader might, therefore, reasonably ask what is new about the present study.

The crucial difference lies in the introduction of the schema, itself the result of learning, as that which gives meaning. Hitherto the emphasis has been on meaning as a property present or absent in the material itself. 'We defined meaningful learning as learning which proceeds by organisation appropriate to *the inherent structure of the material*.' (Katona, *op. cit.*, my italics.) Where the meaning is not at once apparent, it is considered as resulting from a sudden perceptual re-structuring described as 'insight'. This gives an all-or-nothing character to the Gestalt approach. Insight either happens, or it does not, and the part played by learning in the process of organization is not considered. An unfortunate result is that conversely, the part played by organization in the process of learning has also been too little considered: in spite of its highly relevant subject matter, Katona's work is not mentioned by any of three books of Educational Psychology already cited.

The view here put forward is that meaning results from the existence *in the mind of the subject* of a suitable schema which, though it may be based on innate organizations, is chiefly the result of learning. Meaning is thus synonymous with the process of assimilation to an existing schema: and by the development of an appropriate schema, meaning can be given to a set of hitherto unrelated data. Scientific theories are advanced schemata of this kind: and it is a far cry from this lengthy, systematic and deliberate building up of meaning to the spontaneous perceptual restructuring of the Gestalt approach. Nevertheless, when the experiments of the latter are reconsidered in the light of the present approach, I think that they will be found to offer a useful contribution to a schematic theory of learning.

CONCLUSION

In this paper an attempt has been made to clarify and develop the concept of a schema in the context of educational psychology; and to point out its central importance for school and college learning. Before concluding, however, it must be remembered that there are many other kinds of schemata besides the examples here given: for as here used, the concept includes all mental organizations which integrate existing knowledge and behaviour, determine its use in new situations, and form the basis for further learning. They certainly need not be conscious – the ability to reflect on one's schemata is a highly sophisticated one. They can be predominantly sensori-motor, such as driving a car; predominantly cognitive, such as mathematics; or have important elements of both, as in a surgical operation. Even the simplest trial and error learning Piaget believes to be not random, but directed by an existing and more basic schema: while, as already argued, complex cognitive skills such as mathematics and systems of science are also examples of schemata. Their varieties, development, internal organization, transfer effects, and also their interaction with other factors of learning such as reinforcement and intelligence, are subjects for future research: having in every case applications within and beyond the field of educational psychology.

ACKNOWLEDGEMENTS

The author is most grateful to Mr F. H. Philpot, Headmaster of Stockport Grammar School, to Mr J. G. Gosling, and to the boys concerned, for their help in the experiment. Two student assistants, Mr M. C. Kilcross and Mr D. Castell, have also given valuable help in the preparation and scoring of the experimental material.

This article appeared in *Br. J. Educ. Psychol.* (1962), **32,** 133–142. Extracts from it are published here with the kind permission of the author and editor.

REFERENCES

Katona, G. (1940) *Organising and memorising.* New York: Columbia University Press.
Piaget, J. (1950) *The Psychology of Intelligence* (English edition). London: Routledge and Kegan Paul.

14   Verbal reception, guided discovery and the learning of schemata

J. A. ROWELL, J. SIMON and R. WISEMAN

Summary   Verbal reception and guided discovery techniques of teaching are compared in a classroom situation for effectiveness in promoting the formation of stable, usable, cognitive schemata in comparable groups of university students. The results indicate that explicit direction can produce performances superior to those resulting from a guided discovery approach for immediate recall, delayed retention and transfer. Tentative explanations of these findings are discussed.

INTRODUCTION

Two related topics of interest to educational psychologists are those of meaningful *versus* rote learning, and discovery *versus* reception techniques of teaching.

Skemp (1962) and Ausubel (1963) provide and discuss experimental evidence on the greater efficiency of meaningful learning for initial learning, retention and transfer. They also elaborate the characteristic 'cognitivist' view that, by definition, for new learning to be potentially meaningful, it must be capable of being related in a non-arbitrary manner to an existing cognitive schema or structure.

The deliberate attempt to assist the development of these schemata is a large part of the function of teaching but, as yet, there appears to be little or no agreement on the most effective techniques to use. Whether it is better for an individual to work things out entirely by himself (pure discovery), with prompts and cues (guided or intermediate discovery) or be presented with the whole structure ready made (pure reception) is a matter of continuing empirical inquiry. Available data are limited (Craig, 1956; Corman, 1957; Kittell, 1957; Kersh, 1958; Haselrud and Meyers, 1958; Wittrock, 1963; Guthrie, 1967) and the issue is confused by the champions of discovery methods (especially for teaching science) claiming that for a child to find out something by himself is 'obviously', even axiomatically, preferable, e.g., '. . . if man's intellectual excellence is the most his own among his perfections, it is also the case that the most uniquely personal of all that he knows is that which he had discovered for himself' (Bruner, 1961).

Ausubel (1963), in a book including an exhaustive summary of the available evidence, censures the uncritical acceptance of discovery and denigration of verbal reception methods, and urges a more balanced assessment of the situation. 'Careful examination of what research supposedly "shows" in this instance yields these three disheartening conclusions: (a) that most of the articles most commonly cited in the literature as reporting results supportive of discovery techniques actually report no research findings whatsoever, consisting mainly of theoretical discussion, assertion and conjecture; descriptions of existing programs utilizing discovery methods; and enthusiastic but wholly subjective testimonials regarding the efficacy of discovery approaches; (b) that most of the reasonably well-controlled studies report negative findings; and (c) that most studies reporting positive findings either fail to control other significant variables or employ questionable techniques of statistical analysis' (p. 165).

EXPERIMENTAL

(a) General

This experiment is an attempt to provide further information on the relative effectiveness of verbal reception and discovery techniques, in this case guided discovery, as methods of bringing about the formation of stable, usable, cognitive schemata in students who are assumed to have reached the stage of formal operations in Piaget's scheme of mental development.

However, the magnitude of the task clearly indicates that a single exploratory experiment such as this must be limited both in design and application, and these limitations are outlined below.

(i) All subjects taking part in the experiment were post-graduate, full-time students, studying for the Diploma in Education in the Department of Education of the University of Adelaide.

The nature of the sample imposes limitations on the applicability of the results of the experiment. It must be remembered that these are students who, because of the methods of teaching prevalent in many schools and, perhaps even more pronouncedly, in universities, probably already have had considerable practice, and success, at the method of verbal reception learning. The results, strictly, are applicable only to other groups of students at a similar stage of learning, and with a similar learning history, to those in the sample. Any extrapolation to other groups of students and other situations is liable to involve errors.

(ii) The same amount of time was used for teaching by each method.

This limitation was imposed because it was considered a more realistic situation than one in which the task is learnt to some initial criterion level of excellence.

(b) The sample

It is the policy of the Department to assign students to tutorial groups at the beginning of the year, and it was these tutorial groups who were used for the experiment.

In 1968, six tutorial groups were arranged, each containing a maximum of 12 students and a fairly similar number of specialists in the different subjects (historians, mathematicians, chemists, musicians, etc.). However, only the scores of the 59 students present throughout the entire experiment were used in the analyses of the results. Thirty-two of these were in the three tutorial groups, containing 12, 12 and 8 students respectively, taught by the method of guided discovery; 27 were in the three groups, containing 10, 9 and 8 students respectively, taught by the verbal reception method.

(c) The learning task

Following the idea of Skemp (1962), it was decided that the best method of obtaining a learning task equally unfamiliar to all students probably was by the invention of a purely artificial schema. The basic elements of the schema were 17 symbols each associated with a separate meaning carefully chosen to allow the production of new meanings by combination of the different symbols two, three, or more at a time, according to specific but simple rules. The elements of the schema and the rules of combination of symbols are given in figure 14.1.

Even in a situation such as this, however, the possibility still exists that the basis of the schema will be known better by some students than others because of the difference in their experimental backgrounds. For example, the presence of symbols and their required manipulation in the schema used in this experiment might be thought advantageous to students of science. For this reason, and also because it was considered that the two groups (science and non-science) might respond differently to the two methods of instruction, test scores were classified by degree course (science, B.Sc. *versus* non-science, B.A. and B.Mus.) as well as by methods of instruction for the purpose of analysis.

(d) Methods of presentation of the schema

(i) Verbal reception method   The verbal reception technique was relatively easy to standardize for the three groups.

A large sheet of white paper on which the 17 basic elements of the schema were clearly printed in black texta-colour was taped, without comment, on to a blackboard in front of

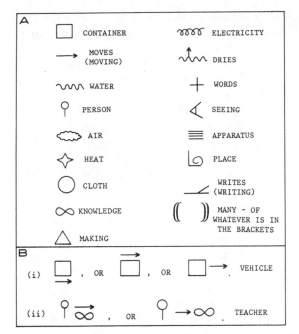

Figure 14.1   Basic elements of the schema (A) and rules of combination of the symbols (B). Rule (i): no distinction is made between the three forms of representation shown when, as in this case, no ambiguity of meaning is introduced. Rule (ii): there are two methods of connecting two or more symbols meaning a single thing, in this case teaching, when they form part of a larger symbol group, in this case meaning teacher.

the appropriate tutorial group. A carefully prepared lecture was then read to the students briefly explaining the schema and the method of building up new meanings by combining the basic elements in certain ways. This was illustrated on the blackboard by 14 examples of simple symbol combinations and their meanings (see Appendix).

At the end of the 14-minute lecture the students, who had been provided with paper, were allowed a further 15 minutes in which to learn the basic elements of the schema, the 14 examples of meaningful symbol groups, and to practise the building of more complex groups. When the 15 minutes had elapsed the schema and examples were removed from the board, and the practice notes of the students collected. This was their only contact with the original material, apart from subsequent tests.

(ii) Guided discovery method   Although the general technique of question and answer used for guiding discovery of each of the three groups was the same, it cannot be claimed the method was standardized in the same way as the verbal reception method in which each group received precisely the same set of words.*

---

* Even in the case of the verbal reception groups, of course, it would be untrue to say that each group, or even each member of one group, received precisely the same stimuli, even if they heard the same words.

Each student in the appropriate tutorial group was given a sheet of paper on which were printed the 14 combinations of basic elements of the schema, and their associated meanings, which were given to the verbal reception groups as examples of how new meanings could be built up by symbol combination. These included the possible variations in method of presentation, allowed by the rules of combination given in figure 14.1, which symbolized the same meaning.

When the sheets had been given out, the group were told that their task, initially, was to discover the meanings of the 17 basic elements of the schema, and the rules for building up new meanings by combining any number of these elements. They were told also that when they had discovered these things they would have to learn them, to learn the 14 examples of symbol combinations which they had been given, and to practise writing new symbol combinations and associated meanings.

The group were then asked for any ideas on how and where to start the task of discovery. All groups started by commenting on the element $\longrightarrow$, which was common to many of the symbol combinations given, and which they readily associated with the meaning 'moves' or 'moving'. After that point the course taken by each group differed, but each followed a typical technique of interaction of ideas through question and answer – question stimulating answer, which provoked a further question, until the group eventually converged on to the desired general meaning of the element under discussion. Each student made a record of the basic elements and their associated meanings as these were discovered. In each case the experimenter was able to complete the task on, or very close to (within $\pm\frac{1}{4}$ minute) the allotted time of 14 minutes.

As in the case of the verbal reception groups, at the end of the period of teaching the students were allowed a further 15 minutes in which to learn the schema and examples, and to practise the writing of new symbol combinations. When the 15 minutes had elapsed all papers were collected, and the students not allowed further contact with the original material, other than in tests of course.

To ensure, in so far as this was possible, that no group gave any indication of the task to be learnt to any other group, the co-operation of all students was enlisted not to discuss the experiment with anyone, even members of their own group. Fortunately, because of the maturity and professional nature of the groups involved, this was a relatively easy undertaking, and, it is believed, a successful one.

(e) Testing

To investigate the possible differences in effect of method of presentation of material on its learning by students three tests were used, each containing two related subsections examining, respectively, recall and application, i.e., ability to extend the schema in an internally consistent manner. Test 1 was given immediately after the initial half-hour of learning and practice, Test 2 one week later, and Test 3 ten weeks after the initial learning period. No attempt was made to measure any possible difference between the verbal reception and guided discovery groups in their subsequent ability to impose structure on tasks of a similar nature.

Recall was examined by requiring the students to write down the associated meaning or symbol(s) when cued by the other member of the symbol(s)–meaning pair for each of the 17 basic elements of the schema and 14 examples of simple symbol combinations. Five minutes were allowed for the 31 answers.

The application section of each test was divided into two parts. In the first part, the students were required, in three minutes, to make up symbolic representations of five meanings which were given to them, e.g., evaporation, ship, mobile library, electric fan, water pump, tourists and aircraft factory were a few of the meanings used. In the second part, five symbol combinations were presented and, again in three minutes, the students were required to work out appropriate meanings. A few examples of this latter group are given in figure 14.2.

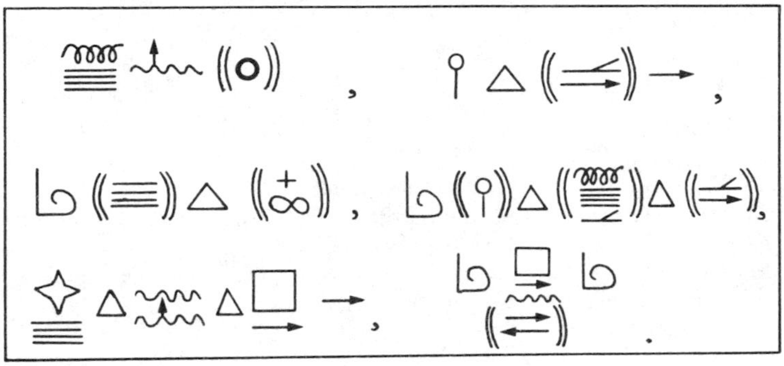

Figure 14.2   Examples of symbol combinations used in the tests of application.

An attempt was made to construct three tests of equal objective standard of difficulty (table 14.1). This was an easy matter in the examination of recall, only requiring alteration of which symbols and which meanings should be given as cues, but, unfortunately, whether this was achieved for the application questions cannot be known with certainty – a difficulty having implications discussed later in the paper.

Students were given no indication of how many tests they would receive, and the question, therefore, arose of possible differences in conscious practice of the scheme by the verbal reception and guided discovery groups. Replies given anonymously to a short questionnaire revealed no difference in amount of practice, but differences consistently favouring the guided discovery method were found in the degree of involvement of the groups. Perhaps, as proposed by Kagan (1966), deeper involvement is a product of the extra intellectual effort required by attempted discovery.

RESULTS

A two-way analysis of variance was carried out on the scores obtained from each test. Raw scores were used except for the recall scores of Tests 1 and 2 where normality of the distributions and stability of the variances were achieved by transforming the error +1 scores to logarithms. The addition of one error to each error score was necessary to avoid the impossibility of transforming an error score of zero to a logarithm. The results of the analyses are presented in table 14.2.

Table 14.1   Mean scores and standard deviations (groups combined) on recall and application tests: verbal reception method and guided discovery method

		Verbal reception		Guided discovery	
		Recall[a]	Application	Recall[a]	Application
Test 1	Mean	0.8292	6.72	1.2361	5.67
	Standard deviation	0.5924	1.29	0.6299	1.51
Test 2	Mean	1.2136	6.22	1.8028	3.91
	Standard deviation	0.9271	2.10	0.9332	2.37
Test 3	Mean	23.52	5.80	20.33	4.55
	Standard deviation	5.15	2.23	5.80	2.63

[a] Four places of decimals have been used for reporting the results of all calculations involving the logarithmically transformed recall scores from tests 1 and 2.

Note that the means and standard deviations reported for the recall scores of tests 1 and 2 are for the logarithmic transformations of error + 1 scores, not actual scores.

Table 14.2   Results of the two-way classification analyses of variance

Test 1(i)	Recall				
	Sums of squares	df.	Mean squares	F values	Signif. level
Method: V.R. v. G.D.	2.4245	1	2.4245	8.49	$P < 0.01$
Degree (method eliminated): science v. non-science	1.8146	1	1.8146	6.36	$P < 0.05$
Interaction: degree × method	0.4823	1	0.4823	1.69	N.S.
Subgroups[a]	5.7091	8	0.7136	2.50	$P < 0.05$
Residual	13.4164	47	0.2855		

[a] The subgroups referred to are the 12 science and non-science subsections of the six tutorial groups. The F values reported test the significance of the differences between the means of the three subgroups in each of the four sets of subgroups formed by the two-way classification by degree course and by method.

Test 1(ii)	Application				
	Sums of squares	df.	Mean squares	F values	Signif. level
Method: V.R. *v.* G.D.	16.16	1	16.16	8.18	P < 0.01
Degree (method eliminated): science *v.* non-science	2.80	1	2.80	1.42	N.S.
Interaction: degree × method	0.71	1	0.71	0.36	N.S.
Subgroups	17.64	8	2.21	1.12	N.S.
Residual	98.82	47	1.97		

Test 2(i)	Recall				
	Sums of squares	df.	Mean squares	F values	Signif. level
Method	5.0832	1	5.0832	6.55	P < 0.05
Degree (method eliminated)	0.6200	1	0.6200	0.80	N.S.
Interaction: degree × method	4.9180	1	4.9180	6.31	P < 0.05
Subgroups	7.2064	8	0.9008	1.16	N.S.
Residual	36.6017	47	0.7788		

Test 2(ii)	Application				
	Sums of squares	df.	Mean squares	F values	Signif. level
Method	78.55	1	78.55	17.00	P < 0.001
Degree (method eliminated)	16.10	1	16.10	3.48	N.S.
Interaction: degree × method	5.98	1	5.98	1.30	N.S.
Subgroups	49.16	8	6.15	1.33	N.S.
Residual	217.14	47	4.62		

Table 14.2   continued

Test 3(i)	Recall				
	Sums of squares	df.	Mean squares	F values	Signif. level
Method	149.06	1	149.06	5.37	P < 0.05
Degree (method eliminated)	50.43	1	50.43	1.82	N.S.
Interaction degree × method	55.02	1	55.02	1.98	N.S.
Subgroups	323.36	8	40.42	1.46	N.S.
Residual	1304.73	47	27.76		

Test 3(ii)	Application				
	Sums of squares	df.	Mean squares	F values	Signif. level
Method	22.86	1	22.86	4.11	P < 0.05
Degree (method eliminated)	17.36	1	17.36	3.12	N.S.
Interaction degree × method	0.68	1	0.68	0.12	N.S.
Subgroups	65.60	8	8.20	1.47	N.S.
Residual	261.17	47	5.56		

From table 14.2 it can be seen that significant differences ($P = 0.05$ or less) in favour of the verbal reception method exist both for recall and application on all three tests. The implications, and possible explanation, of these major findings are discussed in Discussion and Conclusions.

Analyses of the results classified by degree course (Science v. Non-science), with the effects of method eliminated, indicate the approximate equality of difficulty of the task for scientists and non-scientists – a significant difference between the groups ($0.01 < P < 0.05$) is evident only for immediate recall [Test 1 (i) and (ii)].

A significant interaction effect ($0.01 < P < 0.05$) is present only for recall in Test 2 (i) and (ii). The non-significance of all other interaction effects indicates that scientists and non-scientists were affected similarly by the two methods of instruction.

From table 14.2 it can be seen also that there is very little evidence for differences between the subgroups – a significant difference $(0.01 < P < 0.05)$ occurs only in the analysis of scores for immediate recall [Test 1 (i) and (ii)]. The non-significance of all other subgroup tests indicates constancy of the teaching methods in their replication and homogeneity of the tutorial groups, apart from any possible differences due to degree course.

DISCUSSION AND CONCLUSIONS

Subject to the several limitations acknowledged previously, the results of this study, when taken as a whole, suggest that instruction techniques of an expository or verbal reception nature can have greater pedagogic merit than has sometimes been assumed. This, of course, is no longer a unique conclusion; a number of writers have expressed basically similar views (see, for example, Ausubel, 1963).

But what does seem of importance in the present study is the extent and the degree of superiority of the verbal reception approach relative to the discovery approach. While the non-comparability of various studies raises obvious difficulties, it would appear that few, if any, previous research findings have produced quite such support for a detailed and explicit verbal reception approach. In the case of initial learning or immediate recall [as measured by recall in Test 1 (i) and (ii)], the results of this study – that explicit direction produces performances superior to those resulting from a guided discovery approach – are in general agreement with recent findings; but similar findings for delayed retention and, more particularly, for transfer, were rather less expected on the basis of the relevant literature (Ausubel, 1963; Wittrock, 1963).

Within the framework of a schematic view of learning, it could be argued that during the initial learning period, subjects in the verbal reception group acquired a better organized and more comprehensive schema than did discovery subjects; and that the superior performances of the verbal reception group in both delayed recall and application tests were due to this. The relatively slow, but steady, decline in performance on successive tests for this group could then be explained in terms of forgetting of some detail (for example, individual symbols or fragments of them), the overall structure still remaining so that, even after 10 weeks, sufficient of the basic schema remained for the group to have maintained their superiority over the guided discovery group. The poorer performances of the latter group can be interpreted within the same frame of reference: inadequate initial learning of the schema, possibly combined with some higher degree of rote learning, together resulting in more rapid forgetting and inferior ability to transfer the new learning.

But even if this rather speculative interpretation is accepted, the question could be asked: what enabled the verbal reception subjects initially to develop a better schema?

At least two factors, both of which have already been mentioned in a different context, may contribute to a possible explanation – the imposed time limit on the experiment, and the learning history of the subjects.

Discovery learning, even guided discovery, requires that the student first discover and organize any new subject matter before internalization in schematic form is possible. For verbal reception learning, however, the student has only a minimum of re-organization of the material before he can internalize the schema, provided that the material has been carefully structured to meet his requirements. There is another aspect to this situation too. Even in small interested groups, such as those used in this experiment, relatively few of the students voluntarily participate verbally in the discovery process. Finding out how many have followed the thought sequence leading to any particular discovery is a time-consuming process, the time required, and the difficulty of the task, increasing considerably as the number in the group increases. In a limited time situation the possibility exists, and is magnified by large classes, that an unknown number of students do not understand the basis of a discovery and, therefore, are in the worst possible type of verbal reception situation. Without understanding, if they learn at all, these students can learn only by rote.

Earlier it was hypothesized that most subjects in both groups probably had histories of school and university learning based largely on verbal reception techniques. If this hypothesis is justified, it seems probable that, it, too, contributes to any explanation of why the verbal reception group proved superior to their colleagues instructed by the guided discovery method. However, this in no way detracts from the observation that the verbal reception technique can be a very efficient method of instruction, at least for those who can be assumed to have reached the stage of formal operations in Piaget's scheme of mental development.

There is one further result which requires special mention. This is the recovery of the guided discovery group relative to the verbal reception group on Application Test 3 (i) and (ii). In terms of absolute scores on this test, the guided discovery group actually improved. To suggest that the test was objectively easier than the first two tests could account for this absolute improvement; but it would not explain the *relative* improvement in comparison with verbal reception scores, which continued to decline absolutely. A possible explanation, following the above theoretical approach, is that the guided discovery group's improvement on Application Test 3 (i) and (ii) was due to a largely unconscious organization of hitherto inadequately and inefficiently structured material into a more meaningful and integrated schema.

This organization, it would follow, took place in the time period between Tests 2 and 3. To speculate further, it could be argued that Test 2 [(i) and (ii)] was of greater long-term significance for the guided discovery group than for the verbal reception group, in that for the former group it possibly 'triggered' the new, better structuring of the material, leading to improved performance on Test 3. The verbal reception group, it was suggested above, had already acquired a relatively meaningful schema as a result of its initial exposure to the material, so that its lower application score on Test 3 relative to Test 2 was due to the steady and continued forgetting of detail.

APPENDIX: LECTURE EXPLAINING THE SCHEMA AND SIMPLE SYMBOL COMBINATIONS

For learning to be meaningful to a person it is essential that what is to be learnt should be relateable to what is already known by that person. For example, it would be no use talking to you about the effects of reinforcement schedules on the permanence of learning if you did not already know the meaning of the terms reinforcement, schedule and learning as they are used by psychologists.

I am now going to show you the basic elements of a very artificial schema. It is a set of 17 symbols to which meanings have been attached. I want you to look through these now, and later, I want you to learn them, and learn how to use them to build up meaningful groups of symbols.

(At this stage one minute was allowed for the students to look at the basic elements of the schema.)

Now let me show you how to build up groups of symbols which are meaningful in terms of our basic schema. As in other languages, of course, precise translations are not possible. What you must do is to think of getting as close as possible in terms of the available symbols.

(The symbol groups and associated meanings were written on the blackboard as they were mentioned. In the examples below, the symbol group has not been reproduced: instead, an asterisk indicates that the appropriate symbol group was written on the blackboard.)

1 In our schema a vehicle can be symbolized by * (square), it is a moving container. Note that no distinction is made in our language between * and * and * (arrow below, above and after the square: see example B (i) in figure 14.1), when, as in this case, no ambiguity is introduced.
2 An aeroplane is a container which moves through the air.*
3 A river is moving water.*
4 Teaching is moving knowledge.*
5 A teacher is a man who moves knowledge.* Another way of connecting two or more symbols meaning a single thing, when they form part of a larger meaning, is by single brackets, e.g., teaching, *, in the concept of teacher, could be written * (see example B (ii) in figure 14.1).
6 A towel is a cloth which dries.*
7 A tent is a cloth container.*
8 A loom is an apparatus for making cloth.*
9 Speech is moving words.*
10 A letter is moving writing.*
11 A book is words of knowledge.*
12 A library is a place where there are many books.*
13 An electric fire is electrical apparatus for making heat.*
14 An aeroplane spotter is a man who sees aeroplanes.*

ACKNOWLEDGEMENTS

This article first appeared in *Br. J. Educ. Psychol.* (1969), **39**, 235–244, and is published here with the kind permission of authors and editor.

The authors wish to express their thanks to Mrs M. Vaughton for statistical assistance.

REFERENCES

Ausubel, D. P. (1963) *The Psychology of Meaningful Verbal Learning.* London: Grune and Stratton.

Bruner, J. S. (1961) The act of discovery. *Harv. Educ. Rev.*, **31**, 21–32.

Corman, B. R. (1957) The effect of varying amounts and kinds of information as guidance in problem solving. *Psychol. Monogr.*, **71** (whole No. 431).

Craig, R. C. (1956) Directed *versus* independent discovery of established relations. *J. Educ. Psychol.*, **47**, 223–234.

Guthrie, J. T. (1967) Expository instruction *versus* a discovery method. *J. Educ. Psychol.*, **58**, 45–49.

Haselrud, G. M. & Meyers, S. (1958) The transfer value of given and individually derived principles. *J. Educ. Psychol.*, **49**, 293–298.

Kagan, J. (1966) In *Learning by Discovery.* Shulman, L. S. & Keislar, E. R. (Eds.). Chicago: Rand McNally.

Kersh, B. Y. (1958) The adequacy of 'meaning' as an explanation for the superiority of learning by independent discovery. *J. Educ. Psychol.*, **49**, 282–292.

Kittell, J. E. (1957) An experimental study of the effect of external direction during learning on transfer and retention of principles. *J. Educ. Psychol.*, **48**, 391–405.

Skemp, R. R. (1962) A schematic learning theory. *Brit. J. Educ. Psychol.*, **32**, 133–142.

Wittrock, M. C. (1963) Verbal stimuli in concept formation: learning by discovery. *J. Educ. Psychol.*, **54**, 183–190.

15   Behavior modification in the classroom

MYRON WHITMAN and JOAN WHITMAN

The transmission of knowledge has been an integral part of all human societies. Ancient man learned hunting skills just as modern man learns the fundamentals of reading and arithmetic. As societies have become increasingly more complex and differentiated, two types of professional people have become involved in the formal educational process: those who do it (teachers) and those who say how it should be done (philosophers, religious leaders, administrators, educational theorists and psychologists). In twentieth-century America, and in many other modern societies, the second professional group often has failed to meet the needs and demands of education. This becomes quite apparent when one observes student teachers or new teachers, who frequently are ill-equipped to teach. What they learned about the educational process in college is not particularly relevant to everyday situations that occur in their own classrooms. Concepts found in most educational theory or educational philosophy textbooks concerned with the child's personal growth, intellectual curiosity or motivation to learn do not help the teacher decide how to treat the student who continually wants to help pass out or collect materials or the student who flushes and stammers when he is asked to recite in class. Hopefully, the teacher's common sense will assist him in these situations, because it is unlikely that his training will. Teacher training leaves new teachers far short of being able to manage all aspects of the total classroom environment. It usually is not directly translatable into everyday classroom practice and to this extent is irrelevant.

Psychology is one of the disciplines that has attempted to influence the educational process. The data and theory generated by this discipline have had some impact upon all realms of the educational process, including specific materials, teaching modes and techniques, classroom organization and management, and administrative functioning. Although a distinction between the actual educational materials, tools and teaching modes and the classroom learning environment or milieu is not always easy to make, it does serve as a useful dichotomy. It is most frequently the learning environment variables – behavior management, classroom 'structure' and organization – that are the most difficult to translate from general psychological theory to specific classroom application with groups and individual students.

While teachers usually are required to take numerous psychology courses, most of these deal with broad principles, theoretical constructs and rather general statements about children, learning and teaching. The teacher is left with the burden of fitting this information into the scheme of his specific class. This usually is not only difficult, but also can lead to misinterpretation and imprecision. Few branches of psychology have made attempts to bridge this gap, but with the recent inception of behavior modification techniques the attempt has begun. Behavior modification may be defined as the use of learning theory principles to alter maladaptive behavior. These principles have evolved out of many years of research with humans and animals; the systematic application of these principles to maladaptive behavior patterns is behavior modification.

The first major application of behavior modification techniques was in the psychotherapeutic relationship, as psychologists used these techniques with clients. It is now used in many other situations, one of which is the application by the teacher in his own classroom. The results have been very encouraging (Ullmann and Krasner, 1965). This article presents the theoretical rationale for behavior modification, principally through its comparison with traditional psychotherapies, and suggests some behavior modification techniques for the classroom management of maladaptive behavior.

*   •   •

CLASSROOM APPLICATIONS OF BEHAVIOR MODIFICATION

While learning theory principles can be used both to promote academic learning and skill building and to modify maladaptive and promote adaptive classroom behaviors, only the latter is behavior modification. The focus of this discussion will not be upon academic learning and skill building, except to note their facilitation through the use of programmed instruction and teaching machines, both of which systematically incorporate learning theory principles (Birnbrauer et al, 1965; Brown and L'Abate, 1969). Reinforcement of correct responses, immediate feedback, minimization of incorrect responses, enlistment of the learner's active participation, and allowance for individual differences in learning are some of the basic principles utilized. These same principles often are used by teachers in classroom instruction, although not always systematically.

Experimenters have identified many principles of learning. A thorough coverage of these principles will not be presented; rather a few of the basic principles will be discussed in some depth and with the aid of some actual classroom examples. Reinforcement probably is considered by many behavior therapists to be the most important principle of learning. Reinforcement is used to shape and build desired goal behaviors. A reinforcer in the operant conditioning model refers to something that follows a response and increases the likelihood of occurrence of that response. (For a further discussion of the operant and classical conditioning models of learning see Skinner, 1953 or Bijou and Baer, 1961.) For example, a teacher desires to promote 'hand-raising' in a boy who frequently talks in class without raising his hand. If, the few times he did raise his hand, his teacher praised him, it is quite likely that he would begin to raise his hand more frequently. In this example, the teacher's praise reinforced the boy's hand-raising response.

It has been demonstrated in experimental studies that a large number of physical and social stimuli may serve as reinforcers. Several of the more common of these are praise, attention, food, water, sex and relief from pain. Reinforcers commonly used in schools include praise, attention, good grades, toys, candy and the granting of extra privileges and special activities. Most learning theorists believe that the systematic application of reinforcers is utilized too infrequently in behavior management, while punishments are utilized too frequently. For instance, when a child is sitting quietly and doing his school work he is usually ignored by the teacher (i.e., she doesn't praise him), but if he starts to create a disturbance, it is likely that the teacher will reprimand him.

Extinction occurs when reinforcement is withheld from a response. The ultimate result of such a process is the weakening of the probability of the occurrence of that response. Extinction and reinforcement are, therefore, opposite phenomena. Reinforcement leads to an increase in response strength; extinction, which involves the withholding of reinforcement, leads to a decrease in response strength. Teachers continually use extinction in their classrooms as a means to manage the behavior of their students. Some teachers apply extinction principles systematically; they seldom reprimand their students or call attention to deviant or inappropriate behaviors, yet may have very orderly classes. One of their primary behavior management techniques is likely to be the ignoring of inappropriate behaviors, which leads to a decrease in those behaviors.

Extinction is not to be confused with punishment. Whereas extinction consists of the withholding of a reinforcer after the occurrence of a response, punishment involves the application of negative consequences for that response. Thus, instead of ignoring a student's inappropriate behavior, the teacher might punish him by hitting the child or removing one of his privileges or desired activities. While all behavior therapists use reinforcement and extinction when attempting to establish or eliminate certain behaviors, not all use punishment. The use of punishment sometimes involves unwanted negative consequences, such as a fear of the punisher, and its effects are understood less thoroughly than are those of reinforcement and extinction (Skinner, 1953).

APPLICATIONS

The following studies reported all involve systematic application of behavior modification principles, including positive reinforcement of desired, correct or appropriate behavior and the extinction of inappropriate or incorrect behavior.

Zimmerman and Zimmerman (1962) report the classroom modification of the deviant behaviors of two 11-year-old boys. Both these boys attended the senior author's English class daily for one hour as part of an educational therapy program in a residential treatment center. The boys were of normal intelligence with no apparent organic disorder. When called upon to spell, the first boy would pause for several seconds, screw up his face, and mutter letters unrelated to the word. In addition, he would not spell words correctly on written tests or on the blackboard. Although he was always given help and encouragement by his teacher, his spelling behavior was deteriorating. A behavior modification program then was instituted. When the boy was asked to spell words on the board the teacher ignored him (extinction) until he was correct and then would offer praise for this correct response (reinforcement). After the quiz he received an 'A', more praise, and was allowed to help the teacher color some Easter baskets. Additional reinforcers used for appropriate spelling behaviors were smiling, chatting and physical proximity. Within a month the boy's bizarre spelling and other undesirable behaviors declined to a level close to zero per class hour. He was working more efficiently and making adequate academic progress.

The second boy had temper tantrums, spoke baby talk, and incessantly made irrelevant comments or posed irrelevant questions. His tantrums often resulted in his being in the middle of a crowd of staff. The senior author began to ignore his tantrums and made it clear to the boy that she was ready to work when he was. Conversation, physical proximity and appealing activities were used as reinforcers for appropriate classroom behaviors. The boy displayed a marked reduction in deviant classroom behaviors. It was noted, however, that he still had tantrums outside the classroom, probably because the consequence of tantrum behavior had not altered in these situations (i.e., he was still getting attentional reinforcement for these behaviors).

Patterson (1965) discusses the case of a nine-year-old, second-grade boy who was of borderline intelligence and diagnosed as minimally brain injured. Earl was extremely hyperactive and distractible and often aggressive. In the classroom he was in almost continuous motion and impossible to control unless he was in the immediate presence of his teacher.

After the frequency of occurrence of various inappropriate behaviors was ascertained, a behavior modification program was instituted. Although there were several aspects of this program, probably the most important was a simple reinforcement procedure. This procedure required the use of a small box, 6 x 8 x 5 inches. A small flashlight bulb was mounted on top of the box; the dial of an electric counter also was visible in the top of the box. The light and counter were controlled by the experimenter, who sat across the room from Earl.

At the beginning of the first conditioning trial and in Earl's presence the following instructions were given to the class:

'Earl has some trouble in learning things here at school because he is always moving around. This is a magic teaching machine that is going to teach Earl to sit still so that he can learn like other children. Each time that the light flashes on it means that Earl has been sitting still. It also means that he has earned one piece of candy (penny). The counter here will keep score. At the end of the lesson we will take the candy (pennies) and divide it up among all of you. If you want to help Earl earn the candy you can do so by not paying attention to him when he is "working" [Patterson, 1965, p. 372].'

Fifteen conditioning trials that lasted from five to 30 minutes each were conducted over a four-week period. During this time Earl's inappropriate behavior decreased markedly. His teacher reported that he was not as hyperactive or destructive on the playground. He began to play with other children rather than to hurtle himself at them. A telephone call to his parents four months after the study indicated continued improvement. For the first time other children were coming to his home to play, and he was making progress in a remedial reading program.

Some of the behavior modification programs instituted in classrooms include many or all of the students. For example, O'Leary and Becker (1967) report a study that took place in an adjustment class of 17 emotionally disturbed nine-year-old children. Deviant behaviors of the eight most disruptive children were recorded over a four-week period. Such behaviors as pushing, answering without raising one's hand, chewing gum, eating, name calling, making disruptive noises and talking were noted.

A token reinforcement program then was put into effect. A token reinforcer has no intrinsic reinforcing properties; it obtains its value because it can be exchanged for intrinsically reinforcing items. Money is perhaps the most common token reinforcer now in existence. In this specific classroom the tokens were ratings from one to ten that were placed in small booklets on each child's desk. The number of points a child received depended on his behavior and his ability to follow instructions. These points were exchanged later for prizes. The teacher was also instructed to give frequent verbal praise. In addition, she was to ignore instances of deviant behavior and simultaneously to reinforce the appropriate behavior of another child. The average amount of deviant behavior among the eight most disruptive children decreased from 76 per cent during the initial observation period to 10 per cent during the token reinforcement period. Moreover, the children's behavior improved in classes in which the reinforcement program had not been instituted, such as in music and library.

Although most behavior modification studies in classrooms have been conducted with deviant subgroups such as the emotionally disturbed or mentally retarded, Brown and Elliot (1965) describe an instance in which these techniques were used to modify the aggressive behaviors of 27 'normal' three- and four-year-old nursery school boys. Various indices of these children's physical and verbal aggressive behavior were rated by two college students. Then the teachers were instructed to ignore aggression and attend to acts incompatible with aggression. A large reduction in both physical and verbal aggression resulted. The authors state that the teachers, although skeptical of the success of the method when it was first proposed, ultimately became convinced of its utility.

One of the most comprehensive classroom applications of behavior modification has been instituted in the 'Programmed Learning Classroom' at Ranier School (Birnbrauer et al, 1965). This classroom was established for two purposes: (1) to develop programmed instruction materials in primary academic subjects for the educable mentally handicapped; (2) to develop procedures, based upon reinforcement principles, that would promote and strengthen motivation, good study habits, cooperation, perseverance and concentration.

Eight boys were selected as members of the 'Programmed Learning Classroom'. Their chronological ages ranged from nine to 13 years, mental ages between five years, five months, and seven years, three months, and they had extremely low academic achievement scores. The teachers were instructed to ignore instances of inappropriate behavior and to reinforce desired behavior or approximations of desired behavior. Praise and token stars were used to reinforce good school work. The stars were saved in booklets and exchanged for various items or privileges. The authors felt that within five months, seven of the eight boys could have been described as good students. They learned to study independently, for longer periods, and accomplished more work. In addition, disruptive behaviors virtually were eliminated.

Another principle of learning that is employed to establish appropriate behavior and to modify deviant behavior is modeling. The modeling phenomenon occurs when the probability that an individual will perform a behavior increases as a function of his observing another individual (the model) perform that behavior or a similar behavior. The powerful influence that modeling may have on children has been recognized and documented (Bandura and Walters, 1963). The fear that children (and adults) might model the violent behavior they see on television has been instrumental in the movement to reduce or eliminate violence in this medium.

Modeling techniques have not been used as prevalently or systematically in the classroom as have reinforcement and extinction, but several classroom uses of modeling have been reported in the literature. Quay et al (1966) in their discussion of the conduct problem child in the special classroom mention some interesting uses of modeling. The conduct problem child exhibits much aggressive behavior, which the authors state is of such an obvious nature that it has a high potential for modeling. They therefore suggest that it is important to increase class size slowly; the teacher brings a new child into the class only when he feels that the existing students are exhibiting appropriate behavior. In this manner examples of acceptable rather than deviant behavior are available for modeling by the new class member.

The conduct problem child usually is deficient in social skills and consequently is rejected by his peer group. In the special class reported on by Quay et al, 1966 a recreational specialist attempted to teach the child social skills through a combination of modeling and reinforcement techniques. In this program there were four phases in the teaching of these skills, of which modeling was a crucial component of the first phases. The adult model first demonstrated the behavior to be learned; when the child imitated it successfully (modeling), he was rewarded with a token that could be exchanged subsequently for candy (reinforcement).

ADDITIONAL EFFECTS OF BEHAVIOR MODIFICATION PROGRAMS

Although behavior modification techniques are used in the classroom for the purpose of behavior management, their application may involve many indirect effects. For example, the use of these techniques encourages objectivity and preciseness. Teachers must identify explicitly those behaviors that they wish to encourage and promote and those that they wish to modify. They also will want to note the specific situations in which these behaviors occur and their consequences. Additionally, when the teacher initiates a program to alter various classroom behaviors, he must observe carefully the effects of the program on these behaviors. In the studies reported in this article exact measures usually were taken of behaviors and their consequences. The classroom teacher might not find it necessary to go to this extreme, but when applying behavior modification techniques he is likely to find himself becoming a more objective and precise observer of human behavior.

A properly administered behavior modification program requires consistent application of consequences for students' behavior. Teachers often apply inconsistent consequences to their students' behavior – whispering in a reading class might be punished, ignored or even inadvertently rewarded through the teacher's attention. Such inconsistency usually interferes with classroom management. For instance, if a deviant behavior occasionally gets reinforced, it will be extremely difficult to extinguish. When applying behavior modification techniques the teacher has a stable framework from which to view behaviors and the consequences that may be applied to them. The presence of such a framework increases the probability that the teacher will be able to respond consistently to his students.

Teachers skilled in behavior modification are likely to identify deviant student behaviors and to institute programs designed to foster alternative and more desirable behaviors; both these processes are intrinsic aspects of behavior modification programs. In many school systems, children who exhibit deviant behaviors that interfere with their own learning or the learning of other students often proceed through their schooling without encountering a teacher who makes serious or consistent attempts to modify these maladaptive behaviors. The identification of these behaviors and the effort to replace them with desirable goal behaviors is a practice that might help to increase the total educational impact of most schools.

Some critics of behavior modification have stated that these techniques may be cold and impersonal, while in fact they have been used to foster warm, affectionate and positive means of interacting with students. Since the importance of reinforcement is stressed in behavior modification, it is incumbent upon the teacher to find behavior worthy of praise or recognition in all of his students. Thus, in a sense, all children have a chance to be 'good'. Behavior modification programs have provided many emotionally disturbed and mentally retarded children with their first opportunity to receive consistent reinforcement.

Other critics of behavior modification have objected to the supposedly coercive and arbitrary nature of the modifier's influence. However, it should be noted that people always influence one another when they interact, and teachers in particular exert a considerable amount of influence over their students whether they do so consciously or inadvertently. Regardless of his didactic techniques, methods of behavior management, or personal qualities, the teacher's role *per se* enhances these influential powers. Those who apply behavior modification techniques accept the fact that this influence exists and attempt to maximize it and to use it systematically and for clearly identified purposes. Of course, these techniques can be used ineffectively or for undesirable purposes, as can all techniques of behavior management. This should make the teacher cautious in his application of these techniques, but not discourage him from using them altogether. It seems only appropriate that behavior modification techniques, which are based on principles of learning, be used by those most invested in the learning process.

When behavior modification programs have been instituted systematically in classrooms, they usually have been instrumental in creating a more pleasant atmosphere for both teacher and students. Many of the studies in this article have alluded indirectly to these atmospheric changes; and perhaps this reinforcing aspect of behavior modification programs best explains their rapid increase in school classrooms.

ACKNOWLEDGEMENT

This article first appeared in *Psychology in the Schools*, **8,** 176–186, and is published here with the kind permission of authors and editor.

REFERENCES

Bandura, A. & Walters, R. W. (1963) *Social Learning and Personality Development*. New York: Holt, Rinehart & Winston.

Bijou, S. W. & Baer, D. M. (1961) *Child Development*, Vol. 1. New York: Appleton-Century-Crofts.

Birnbrauer, J. S., Bijou, S. W., Wolf, M. W. & Kidder, J. D. (1965) Programed instruction in the classroom. In Ullmann, L. P. & Krasner, L. (Eds.), *Case Studies in Behavior Modification*. New York: Holt, Rinehart & Winston.

Brown, E. C. & L'Abate, L. (1969) An appraisal of teaching machines and programmed instruction with special reference to the modification of deviant behavior. In Franks, C. M. (Ed.), *Behavior Therapy: Appraisal and Status*. New York: McGraw-Hill.

Brown, P. & Elliot, R. (1965) Control of aggression in a nursery school class. *J. Exper. Ch. Psychol.*, **2**, 103–107.

Lang, P. J. (1969) The mechanics of desensitization and the laboratory study of human fear. In Franks, C. M. (Ed.) *Behavior therapy: Appraisal and Status*. New York: McGraw-Hill.

O'Leary, K. D. & Becker, W. C. (1967) Behavior modification of an adjustment class: a token reinforcement program. *Except. Child.*, **33**, 637–642.

Patterson, G. R. (1965) An application of conditioning techniques to the control of a hyperactive child. In Ullmann, L. P. & Krasner, L. (Eds.), *Case Studies in Behavior Modification*. New York: Holt, Rinehart & Winston.

Quay, H. C., Werry, J. S., McQueen, M. & Sprague, R. L. (1966) Remediation of the conduct problem child in the special class setting. *Except. Child.*, **32**, 509–515.

Skinner, B. F. (1953) *Science and Human Behavior*. New York: Macmillan.

Ullmann, L. P. & Krasner, L. (1965) *Case Studies in Behavior Modification*. New York: Holt, Rinehart & Winston.

Zimmerman, E. H. & Zimmerman, J. (1962) The alteration of behavior in a special classroom situation. *J. Exper. Anal. Behav.*, **5**, 59–60.

16   A programed guide to writing auto-instructional programs

J. L. BECKER

THE DYNAMICS OF A FRAME

This chapter is presented in a vertical format. Use a blank sheet of paper to cover the answer to each frame until you have completed your response. Then, uncover the answer by moving the paper lower down the page and check your response.

1   If learning is defined as a change in behavior, teaching is an *interaction* with the student that effects this _____.

---

change in behavior

2   Teaching generally entails an _____ with the student.

---

interaction

3   In order for a program to teach effectively, it must _____ with the student.

_____
interact

4   The basic unit of a program is a frame. The f_____ teaches by interacting with the student.

_____
frame

5   A program is composed of chapters which are composed of sets which are composed of frames. The basic unit of a program is the _____.

_____
frame

6   Interaction in a frame means that activity is required of the _____ as well as from the program.

_____
student

7   A frame consists of a stimulus, a response and feedback. A frame is the _____ of the program.

_____
basic unit

8   The frame acts by providing a stimulus and feedback. The student acts by r _____ to the stimulus.

_____
responding

9   A set is a group of related f_____.

_____
frames

10   The three principal parts of a frame are s_____ , r_____ , and f_____.

_____
stimulus, response, feedback

11   After the student makes a response to the stimulus, the program provides_____.

_____
feedback

12   A group of related frames is called a_____.

_____
set

(Extract from pp. 49–51)

BRANCHING

1 Branching can be considered a separate idiom of programing or merely a technique. This branching idiom, called intrinsic programing by Dr Norman Crowder, differs radically from linear programing. It is based on the belief that a person can learn effectively even from his mistakes provided they are quickly followed-up by proper guidance. A high error rate is unhealthy in a linear program but not necessarily unhealthy in an intrinsic program.

In intrinsic programing much emphasis is placed on the student's covert reorganization of material. Thus, it is important to point out why the student is right and why he is wrong. To a linear programer, however, branching is not so much a way of teaching as it is a means of providing for individual differences.

The linear idiom considers branching as:

(a) an opportunity for guidance (see frame 7);
(b) a method of teaching (see frame 3);
(c) a means of providing for individual differences (see frame 5).

2 Why are you reading this frame? You were given the number of the frame you should go to after each response in frame 1. Go back to frame 1 and follow the directions.

3 Your answer to frame 1 was (b): the linear idiom considers branching as a method of teaching.
You are not correct.
Perhaps you are confusing the linear with the branching idiom. The linear idiom is based on the belief that the student learns best when he is making correct responses that are reinforced. With the branching (intrinsic) idiom it is believed that the student will learn regardless of the valence of his response, provided that the reason for his response is properly explained.
Do you see now that intrinsic programs use branching as a means of teaching? But branching is only incidental to the method of teaching in an intrinsic program. Go back to frame 1.

4 Since this text is largely practical, it is concerned from here on with techniques of branching. These techniques can be used in either the linear or the intrinsic idioms. Some of you may, however, be interested in the author's personal views concerning the linear and the intrinsic idioms. Those who are interested see frame 6; those who would rather get directly to the discussion of techniques see frame 8.

5 Your answer to frame 1 was (c): the linear idiom considers branching as a means of providing for individual differences.
You are correct.
Teaching is accomplished in a linear program chiefly by reinforcing correct responses; branching then is employed only for the important job of providing for individual differences, differences in intelligence, in interests, level of accomplishment or previous achievement.

The intrinsic idiom also uses branching to provide for individual differences but branching is used chiefly to point out the reason for errors and to guide the student in organizing the material for himself.

Go to frame 4.

6   Judeo-Christian culture is based on two commandments: love God; love thy neighbor. But these two commandments were defined by ten more, each prefaced by 'Thou shalt not'. Linear programing uses a purely positive approach, eloquent, but not always effective. A skill, like a virtue, is often beneficially described by pointing out what it is not. Intrinsic programing guides the student at the most opportune time. It is not just a sanction. But as the mother who, taking a knife from a child, says 'don't play with knives, you might hurt yourself,' the intrinsic program seeks to use the opportunity of an error to help the student gain insight. My own preference is for a combination approach where a basic linear program is supported by an optimum number of intrinsic nets. Go to frame 8.

7   Your answer to frame 1 was (a): an opportunity for guidance. You are probably answering from what you think should be the case but notice that we asked 'what the linear idiom considers to be the purpose of branching' and we have already told you that.

Reread page 1 carefully and select another response.

8   A branch consists of three parts: a *trigger*, the mechanism in a program which provides for the entrance upon alternate sequences, a *track*, or path, which is a frame or frames that occur in the alternate sequence, and a *re-entry*, the place in the program where the track merges with the basic program. All branches start with a:

    (a) trigger   (see frame 11);
    (b) track   (see frame 14).

9   If you wound up here, you've jumped the track and got lost, or maybe you just wandered down here from frame 8 while you were thinking it's time for lunch.

(Extract from pp. 149–151)

ACKNOWLEDGEMENT

These extracts from Becker, J. L. (1963) *A Programed Guide to Writing Auto-Instructional Programs*, pp. 49–51 and 149–151, were first published by R.C.A. Corporation, New Jersey, and are reproduced here with the kind permission of author and publisher.

PART 6

Concept formation and attainment

INTRODUCTION

The work of Piaget has so dominated our thinking on concept formation and cognitive development that criticism of his work was (and still is with some people) a heresy. But there are criticisms and suggestions for alternative interpretations of his work as seen in two papers included here. Both attempt to break clear of the somewhat rigid scheme of development laid down in Piaget's 'ages and stages' view. Povey and Hill find that even pre-school children (said to be in the 'pre-conceptual' stage) are capable of forming generic as well as specific concepts. The paper also gives a handy summary of concept theory. Bryant and Trabasso are more concerned with transitive inferences in young children. According to Piaget, very young children cannot deduce that A > C from the knowledge that A > B and B > C (> means 'is greater than'). Provided children can remember the exemplars of a particular transition problem, they should be capable of carrying it through, according to Bryant and Trabasso. For them, the young child's inabilities in concept manipulation are more a matter of poor memory than inferential deficits.

Bruner's concept of focusing and scanning has attracted much attention. In fact, problem-solving strategies are all the rage at present (convergent–divergent thinking, field dependence–independence, holist–serialist, etc.). But one important question raised by Wetherick, which could equally well be asked of any of the theories of thinking strategies, is do we use strategies according to circumstances rather than consistently irrespective of circumstances? Wetherick argues quite convincingly that problem-solving must be as much a matter of *how* a person sees the task as upon his intelligence, habitual and preferred methods of solution, and so on.

17   Can pre-school children form concepts?

ROBERT POVEY and ERIC HILL*

Summary   Fifty-six children between the ages of two years four months and four years ten months were given tests relating to the acquisition of both 'specific' and 'generic' concepts. Several tests of concept acquisition (HAPCAT)† were devised by the authors utilizing pictures drawn on card. A number of the children (N = 29) were also given some 'Piagetian questions' concerning class inclusion.

The results conflict with the widely held view (following the writing of Jean Piaget) that pre-school children cannot form generic concepts. Nearly all the children were able to identify the specific concepts as presented in the HAPCAT items and about half the group responded appropriately to the HAPCAT items involving an understanding of generic concepts. There was a clear and statistically significant relationship between the number of correct answers given to the HAPCAT items and the age and ability levels of the children. This was not the case, however, with the Piagetian test questions which showed no discriminatory power in these respects. It is argued that the Piagetian questions do not represent a sensitive or meaningful measure of concept acquisition at this age level whereas the HAPCAT items do appear to present pre-school children with intelligible tasks which allow many of them to demonstrate an understanding of generic concepts involving class inclusion.

BACKGROUND

According to various Piagetian interpreters (e.g. Stones, 1966; Beard, 1969) children are not capable of forming 'true concepts' during the pre-school stage. Describing the 'pre-conceptual' phase of development (two to four years) Stones, for example, states that this is the phase where 'the child is beginning to develop concepts and before he is capable of dis-

---

*The authors would like to acknowledge the most generous help and co-operation they received from Mrs Robin Dowie, Mrs Barbara Best and the mothers and children at the St Stephen's Community Centre Play Group, in Canterbury.

† The tests may be obtained from the NFER (Guidance and Assessment Service) to whom inquiries should be addressed.

tinguishing between the specific concepts relating to an individual object and the generic concept relating to a class of objects'. He gives as a common example of this 'the tendency of children of this age to call men generally "daddy" '. Similarly, Beard claims that children's verbal concepts in the pre-conceptual phase 'lack the generality of true concepts'.

At a point even further removed from Piaget's own writing one finds students' interpretations of the interpreters. Witness, for example, the following comments which we have read in the answers of quite able students to questions on Piagetian researches (the comments having been selected from papers by BEd and Teachers' Certificate students from different colleges):

'Concepts can only be acquired from four onwards.'
'Pre-conceptual (two to four years) where everything on four legs is a dog and any man is "daddy".'
'Not until the age of four or five will the child distinguish between the characteristics which mark "dog" and those which mark other animals.'
'No distinction between generic and specific terms. Little point in teaching other than play.'

We believe that these extracts from the writing of 'authorities' and students are fairly typical examples of a widely held belief that children at the pre-school level are not capable of forming 'true concepts' and, in particular, that they cannot form generic concepts.

Piaget (1962) elaborates this belief in relation to the development of concrete operations. He states that hierarchical classification involving logical inclusion is not possible before about seven or eight years of age: 'the simplest operation is concerned with classifying objects according to their similarity and difference. This is accomplished by including sub-classes within larger and more general classes, a process which implies logical inclusion. Such a classification, which seems very simple at first is not acquired until around seven or eight years of age'. Other writers, however, such as Russell (1956) claim that normally children have been discriminating, abstracting and generalizing about environmental data from infancy and that by the age of three or four a child 'knows literally hundreds of concepts'. Welch (1940) also claims quite explicitly that pre-school children are capable of forming hierarchical concepts involving class inclusion.

Such apparently diverse views may be reconciled partly by reference to differences in the interpretation of the term 'concept'. There is a certain amount of confusion in the literature over the use of the term 'concept' in the sphere of intellectual development (see Blank, 1968) but one can also find a considerable degree of general agreement that the acquisition of a concept in its more usual connotation is concerned with abstracting the essential attributes of an object or idea, distinguishing this from other objects or ideas and generalizing to new situations. Brown (1967) put it this way: a concept is 'a way of grouping an array of objects or events in terms of those characteristics that distinguish this array from other objects or events in the universe . . . and a concept is considered to have been attained when a subject is able to identify new instances of it without further training'. If one accepts this meaning of the term 'concept' then the development of concepts is not, of course, concerned only with hierarchical classification. Thus statements which claim that children are capable of forming 'hundreds of concepts' by the age of three or four (Russell, 1956) may be partly reconcilable with the Piagetian viewpoint on the grounds that they are referring to concepts at a different hierarchical level.

Such an explanation, however, does not meet the claims put forward by Welch (1940) concerning the acquisition of *generic* concepts by pre-school children. He describes several hierarchical levels of concept acquisition. The first he calls the 'pre-abstract' stage at which the child learns the attributes of one class of objects (e.g. 'apples') – the concepts at this stage are specific and not generic. The child then learns that one class may include another, e.g. 'fruit/apple' (the first hierarchy) and, in turn, that this class may include other classes, e.g. 'food/fruit/apple' (the second hierarchy) and so on. Welch claimed that children are able to form concepts at the 'pre-abstract' level (e.g. 'chair', 'ball') before the age of two years and without the child using speech. The tests for the acquisition of such concepts involved the child responding appropriately to the test words by pointing out a chair or ball from among a group of other objects, and then generalizing to new situations (e.g. the presence of a differently shaped chair or a folded chair). Similarly, he suggests that by the age of about 26 months the children were able to understand some concepts involving the existence of a sub-class within a more general class (i.e. first hierarchy concepts). Thus, according to Welch, many children at this age understood that 'men' and 'women' are also 'people' and that 'potatoes' and 'apples' are both 'food'. Further, he suggested that children tend to acquire *second* hierarchy concepts rapidly at about four-and-a-half years of age.

There is a convincing relationship between many of Welch's conclusions and the straightforward observation of children's behaviour. Most parents would probably attest that children between the ages of two and four tend to have a fairly secure grasp of concepts such as 'cup', 'spoon', 'cot', 'dog', etc. These are specific concepts certainly and do not involve logical inclusion but they are nevertheless 'true concepts' on the definition which we have discussed above, i.e. the child has grasped the essential attributes of the object or idea, can distinguish this object or idea from others and can generalize to new situations. Similarly, parents and nursery teachers may well wonder at Piaget's assertion that children in the pre-school stage are not admitted to an understanding of some generic concepts involving class inclusion, when they find their children using generic terms such as 'clothes' and 'food' in an appropriate manner and responding appropriately to the adult's use of such terms. Thus there seem reasonable grounds for hypothesizing that many children in the age group usually taken to coincide with the pre-conceptual stage (*viz.* two to four years) are able to form generic concepts. For example, one might suggest with some confidence that pre-school children might be able to recognize and distinguish between a number of different kinds of food (e.g. ice-cream, apples, potatoes) and at the same time understand that these also constitute a further class of 'food'; and if they do have the capacity for such understanding then they have grasped something about hierarchical classification involving class inclusion.

Despite such considerations, Piaget and Inhelder (1964) dismiss the view that children are able to form hierarchical concepts at the pre-conceptual stage. They claim that Welch's work merely demonstrates that children in this phase are capable of forming 'non-graphic' collections although they do not appear to dispute Welch's argument that pre-school children can form concepts at the 'pre-abstract' level. In Piaget's view the child progresses towards full hierarchical classification in the following stages: from '*graphic collections*' where children place the objects together because they seem to 'belong', e.g. children might group a baby with a cot, instead of classifying the baby with people and the cot with furniture; through the second stage of '*non-graphic collections*' in which objects are assigned to one collection or another on the basis of similarity alone without any notion of hierarchical classification involving class inclusion; and finally to classification involving inclusion.

According to Piaget the understanding of class inclusion can be assessed most precisely by the use of certain questions, especially those involving the terms 'all' and 'some'. The 'all/some' questions are designed to elicit comments on the relationship between a sub-class ('some') and an enveloping class ('all'). A further set of questions relates to a situation in which one class, A (e.g. primroses), is included in another class, B (flowers), without being equal to the whole of B – the question is then asked, 'Are there more As than Bs or more Bs than As?' Although we have not set out specifically to examine this point, we would doubt the strength of Piaget's claim that these types of question are, in fact, adequate tests of a child's understanding of hierarchical classification.

It might be argued (and Piaget and Inhelder, 1964, do in fact discuss this point briefly) that an adequate understanding of these questions relates rather more closely to verbal facility and comprehension than to an understanding of hierarchical classification. Consider, for example, the question 'Are all the primroses some of the flowers?' For subjects of any age this is a distinctly odd question! Certainly in English it does not represent a linguistic structure with which children would be at all familiar and it does not seem entirely surprising that children find some difficulty in knowing how to answer. It is interesting that in Piaget's own experiments with children from six to eight years of age 'only 21 per cent of the subjects accepted statement (A) 'All the tulips are some of the flowers', while 81 per cent accepted the logically identical statement (B) 'Some of the flowers are tulips' (Piaget and Inhelder, 1964). One interpretation of this result on any commonsense basis would seem to be that the problem does not really make an ordinary sensible question when phrased as statement (A) whereas the second phrasing, statement (B), fits in quite sensibly to normal linguistic structures and is accepted and dealt with in a straightforward way. Piaget appears, however, to ignore such a straightforward explanation of the findings.

Similarly, if you give a child a bouquet having six daisies and six other flowers and then ask, 'Are there more daisies or more flowers?' this question again must appear rather surprising. It savours very much of the trick question and seems nearer to certain tests of reasoning ability than of concept acquisition. Moreover, the distinction drawn in the question between 'daisies' and 'flowers' tends to suggest that the questioner has created an artificial distinction between the daisies and the other flowers for the purpose of the question and may appear to indicate that he wishes the child to answer in the same vein.

It seems possible, therefore, that the type of tests Piaget has been using as the crucial criteria in determining the stage at which hierarchical classification emerges in children may in fact be less than adequate and may give a misleading impression of the stage at which children are capable of handling hierarchical classification. We incline to the view that many children in the pre-conceptual age range (two to four years) when tested by the more traditional tests of concept acquisition (such as those utilized by Welch, 1940, and described earlier) may show a reasonably certain grasp of class inclusion, as suggested by Welch. By 'traditional tests of concept acquisition' we refer to those tests which attempt to assess the degree to which the child has shown the capacity to abstract the essential attributes of a given generic class, to distinguish between this class of objects or ideas and other similar classes and to generalize to a new situation. Where a child demonstrates this capacity, it seems reasonable to argue that the concept has been acquired as adjudged by fairly rigorous and meaningful standards. It is still possible, of course, that some children who had attained this level of achievement might be unable to retain the stability of the concept in certain conditions, e.g. when subjected to the Piagetian line of test questions. It would suggest, however, that the standard textbook statement that children between the ages of two to four years are incapable of forming 'true concepts' is immensely misleading. Such statements may also have unfortunate consequences when one considers their effect upon the outlook which students (especially trainee teachers) may adopt in relation to their pupils (e.g. the possibility of seriously underestimating the capabilities of children at the nursery and infant school stages).

The present investigation was initiated in order to test our contention (supported by the work of Welch, 1940) that pre-school children can form both specific *and* generic concepts. We used as a basis for this study the definition of a 'concept' given by Brown (1967) and set out earlier in this paper. We also tested for concept acquisition by more traditional methods than those adopted by Piaget and his co-workers (Piaget and Inhelder, 1964) although we did use the series of Piagetian test questions in part of the investigation for comparison purposes. The study examines two main questions in relation to our sample comprising children of two, three and four years of age (i.e. at the age level usually taken to coincide with the pre-conceptual stage in intellectual development):

1 To what extent had the children acquired certain specific (i.e. non-generic) concepts?
2 Utilizing the specific concepts referred to in question 1, to what extent were these pre-school children capable of showing an understanding of generic or class concepts?

EXPERIMENTAL PROCEDURE

The subjects

Fifty-six British children in the 'pre-conceptual' age range (*viz.* two to four years). There were 32 boys and 24 girls. The youngest child tested was two years four months and the oldest four years ten months; the mean chronological age was three years nine months (SD = eight months). The children were attending a play group which drew upon a catchment area having a good representation from the different socioeconomic groupings. For example, at one extreme, there were children of unskilled manual workers living on a nearby council estate, whilst, at the other extreme, were children of university tutors. Using the criterion of 'father's occupation' as an indicator of the socioeconomic level of the home we categorized the sample into three broad groupings. Group I we termed 'Professional/Managerial', Group II 'Clerical/Skilled Manual' and Group III 'Semi- and Unskilled Manual'. Fourteen children (i.e. 25 per cent of the sample) were included in Group I, 28 (50 per cent) in Group II and 14 (25 per cent) in Group III. Again, the range of intellectual abilities seemed fairly representative of the normal distribution pattern. On the Peabody Picture Vocabulary Test, for example, the mean score was 103.9 with a SD of 16.99 points and a range of 66 to 141. The records of four children from the original 60 tested were excluded from the analysis of the results because of incomplete records and two were excluded because their parents were not British.

The tests

All the children were given two sets of test items, the Peabody Picture Vocabulary Test (PPVT) and the Hill and Povey Concept Acquisition Tests (HAPCAT). In addition 29 children were given some of the Piagetian test questions (Piaget and Inhelder, 1964).

The PPVT is a picture vocabulary test standardized in the USA giving norms for children from the age of two years three months to 18 years five months (Dunn, 1965). It has been found to be reasonably appropriate for use with British children (Moss and Edwards, 1960) and offers the advantage of providing a swift but at the same time fairly useful guideline to the level of verbal intelligence of very young children.

The Hill and Povey Concept Acquisition Tests (HAPCAT) were designed to assess the degree to which a child had acquired a certain concept – where 'level of concept acquisition' simply refers to the child's grasp or level of understanding of the concept. To assess the child's grasp of *specific* concepts he was asked to identify pictures of various objects (e.g. 'egg', 'girl', 'spoon'); and to assess the degree to which a child had acquired a *generic* concept he was asked to select the pictures which depicted a certain concept (e.g. 'food') from amongst a number of 'distractors'. As a further test of the child's level of understanding of the generic concept he was asked to say whether each of the various pictures was an example of the concept or not.

The 'generic tests' concerned 'food' and 'people'. Four pictures of specific items of 'food' were drawn in ink, each on a piece of 3½in. square white card. Most of the pictures contained some colour. The four pictures of items of food were: egg, bread, cake, apple. Similarly, four pictures of 'people' were drawn. These were of a man, lady, boy and girl. In addition to these pictures four 'distractors' were drawn in relation to each of the generic concepts tested. For 'food' the following items were chosen as distractors: a spoon and a cup, as examples of objects a child uses when eating or drinking and might be expected to group with food if the child is only producing a 'graphic collection'; a flower – something which grows out of the ground and can be picked but, unlike an apple, is not to be eaten; a crayon, which again looks to be something which might be eaten. As 'distractors' for 'people' the following items were selected: a teddy-bear, an inanimate object which often has the status of a 'person' within the child's family; and three examples of animate objects which a child might confuse with people – a cat, dog and bird.

The 16 pictures were presented to the child on a sheet of cardboard (13in. by 13in.) divided into 16 squares (3½in. by 3½in.). The pictures were displayed in a randomly determined sequence as shown below:

Egg	Girl	Spoon	Bird
Teddy-Bear	Man	Flower	Bread
Lady	Cake	Cat	Crayon
Apple	Boy	Cup	Dog

The children were tested individually by one of the two authors. First of all they were told that 'we're going to play a game with some pictures' and asked to identify each of the pictures in turn. Correct identification of these original drawings of objects was taken as evidence that the child had acquired certain specific concepts. We argued that this afforded reasonable evidence of concept acquisition since the child had generalized his knowledge of specific concepts to this novel situation and responded appropriately by identifying the particular object when asked to do so, and had successfully distinguished between one specific object, e.g. a cat, and similar but different objects, e.g. a dog and a bird. We allowed a limited amount of latitude in scoring this test, giving credit for children who gave close approximations to the correct identification, e.g. we allowed 'pencil' for 'crayon'. If the child was not able to identify a particular picture (usually because he mistook the actual drawing for something else) then he was told what it was meant to depict so that he would not be handicapped in his approach to the 'generic' test which followed.

The second part of the test concerned the acquisition of generic concepts. The tester said, 'Now I want you to give me all the pictures showing food.' The choices given by the child were noted and then all the pictures were replaced in their original positions. The tester then told the child, 'I am going to ask you some questions about each picture. Let's look at each one in turn.' Starting with the left hand side of the top row the tester said, 'Now this is a picture of an *egg*. Are eggs food?' The same procedure was repeated for each picture in sequence from left to right along each row. Finally, the child was asked if he could tell the tester 'What food is' (i.e. the child was asked for a definition). The same procedure was repeated for 'people'. If the child was able to pick out the instances of the generic concept, e.g. 'food' from the distractors then we argued that this provides evidence that the child has attained a reasonably certain grasp of the concept involved. If the child was also able to answer the follow-up 'positive/negative identification' questions concerning each picture then this would give further support to the contention that the child had achieved a fairly certain grasp of the concept. The additional ability to offer a verbal definition of the concept would offer further support at an even higher level of cognitive functioning (e.g. vocabulary definitions are not introduced until year six on the Stanford–Binet) that the child had, in fact, grasped the concept.

Just over half the sample (N = 29, age range two to four years) were also given some of the Piagetian questions designed to test the child's understanding of class inclusion (Piaget and Inhelder, 1964). These were the 'all/some' and the 'more than' questions described earlier. The questions were asked in relation to six pictures of people.
The pictures were placed on the table as shown below:

| 1 Girl | 3 Man | 5 Boy |
| 2 Lady | 4 Lady | 6 Lady |

and the subject was then asked to identify the pictures in the order indicated (one to six). This procedure was intended to assist the child in establishing that there were equivalent numbers of 'ladies' and 'non-ladies'. In this way we hoped to avoid the introduction of a numerical bias in favour of either 'ladies' or 'non-ladies' which might have led to some confusion in the interpretation of the results, particularly to Question Seven ('Are there more ladies or more people?'). For example, if we had used in our presentation two pictures of 'ladies' and four 'non-ladies' then we could not have been at all sure that the child who answered 'more people' to Question Seven did, in fact, mean the fully inclusive group of 'people' (i.e. 'ladies' plus 'non-ladies'). He might have been referring simply to the group of 'non-ladies' which would have been numerically larger than the group of 'ladies'. With equivalent numbers of 'ladies' and 'non-ladies' we could be more certain that an answer of 'more people' was meant to indicate the inclusive group of 'ladies' plus 'non-ladies'.

The pictures were then placed in a line in the order Man, Lady, Boy, Lady, Girl, Lady, and the child was asked the following seven questions: (1) Are all these people? (2) Are all the ladies people? (3) If you take all the ladies away, will there be any people left? (4) Are all the ladies some of the people? (5) Are all the people ladies, or are some of the people ladies? (6) If you take away all the people, will there be any ladies left? (7) Are there more ladies, or more people? With questions (3), (6) and (7) children who gave wrong answers were offered a practical demonstration with the pictures and then the question was repeated.

Test procedure

Every child took part in two testing sessions. On the first occasion the children were given the HAPCAT items and on the second, the PPVT. These test sessions were spaced one week apart. All the testing was carried out on an individual basis by the two authors during the normal play group sessions. In addition to this basic test programme we were able to test 29 children on the Piagetian questions four weeks after the first test session. After the same interval (i.e. four weeks after the first tests) 17 children were also given the HAPCAT items again in order to offer some indication of the reliability of the tests on a test/re-test basis. A few of the 're-test children' were also selected to take part in a very small-scale and rather 'raw' experiment. This consisted of an attempt to examine whether teaching these children the 'generic' concepts during an interval of four weeks from the pre- to post-test produced any discernible effect on the children's test performance.

RESULTS
PPVT scores

On the PPVT the distribution of scores showed a fairly close resemblance to the pattern of standardized scores given in the test manual, apart from the rather greater proportion of children in the above average range (see table 17.1).

HAPCAT scores

The results on the HAPCAT items will be presented in relation to the specific concepts first and then in relation to the generic concepts.

The *specific concepts* depicted by each of the 16 pictures were adjudged to have been acquired if the children were able to identify the pictures and respond to them appropriately by giving the name of the object. It was possible, therefore, for each child to score a maximum of 16 points on this test. Out of 56 children, 28, or 50 per cent, scored 16 points, i.e. they identified each picture correctly; 40 (or 71 per cent) were correct or made only one error and 47 (or 84 per cent) were correct or made one or two errors. There was a clear increase in capacity for correct identification with age although even with children below three-and-a-half years of age a high percentage of them (61 per cent) gained scores of 15 or 16. No child scored below ten points. It must be pointed out also that many of the errors appeared to be simply errors of recognition of the *drawings* rather than the objects themselves. We had, of course, taken measures to ensure that children of the age range being tested would recognize the pictures fairly readily, but some children still found other quite

Table 17.1   The proportion of children within each scoring range (a) in the present sample and (b) in the standardization results

PPVT standardized scores	N	Present sample %	Standardization %
125+	7	10.7	5
110–124	16	30.4	20
90–109	20	35.7	50
75–89	11	19.6	20
Below 75	2	3.6	5

reasonable interpretations of some of the drawings (e.g. one child thought the 'crayon' was a 'rocket').

As far as the *generic concepts* of 'food' and 'people' are concerned, about half the sample were able to select the pictures of food and people correctly from the group of 16 pictures, rather more children (59 per cent) choosing 'people' without error than 'food' (43 per cent), (see table 17.2). On the other hand, the children found it very much more difficult to answer the follow-up questions 'Are eggs food?', 'Are girls food?' etc. On this test only about one-third of the sample were able to give the correct answers, 30 per cent correct for 'people' and 36 per cent correct for 'food'. Taking correct performance on *both* the 'choice of pictures' test and the 'positive/negative identification' questions, then 30 per cent of the sample achieved full scores on 'people' and 25 on 'food'. Three to four times as many children over the age of four gained correct answers on both tests as did children under four. Comparing the ages of children giving correct responses on both tests for at least *one* of the concepts one finds a highly significant relationship between age (four years and over as compared with under four years of age) and accurate test performance ($P < 0.001$ on a χ^2 2 × 2 test of association).

Table 17.2   The proportion of children in each age range giving correct responses in the two HAPCAT tests

| | | People | | | | Food | | |
| | | Correct choice of pictures | | Correct pos./ neg. ident. | | Correct choice of pictures | | Correct pos./ neg. ident. |
Age group	Total N	N	%	N	%	N	%	N	%
Under 3 years	7	2	29	1	14	0	0	0	0
3–00 to 3–05	16	6	38	3	19	5	31	3	19
3–06 to 3–11	9	5	56	1	11	5	56	3	33
4–00 to 4–05	13	10	77	5	38	7	54	6	46
4–06 to 4–11	11	10	91	7	64	7	64	8	73
Total	56	33	59	17	30	24	43	20	36

There is also a significant though less pronounced association between performance on these tests and verbal ability as measured by the PPVT (above mean scores/below mean scores). The association was significant at the $P < 0.01$ level on the χ^2 test. There was no significant association between performance on the HAPCAT items and the socioeconomic background of the children. The PPVT scores showed a slight relationship with socioeconomic background (children from socioeconomic Groups I and II gaining a greater proportion of above mean scores on the PPVT than children from Group III) but the association was not statistically significant.

Some interesting tendencies are evident from the children's individual records. For example, over half the errors made by children in their selection of items representing 'people' concerned the inclusion of the 'teddy-bear' or the pictures of animals or both in the list of 'people'. Similarly, one-third of the errors in the selection of items of 'food' related to the inclusion of the article used for eating or drinking (*viz.* the pictures of 'cup' and 'spoon'). In Piagetian terms the children are forming 'graphic collections'. Another feature of some children's performance was their tendency to start off by making fairly accurate selections and then to 'clear the board' one by one with quite erroneous choices.

One further point of interest concerns the children's approach to the questions of 'positive/negative identification'. It seemed clear from the children's puzzled faces (and from some of the children's comments to their parents afterwards) that the questions we were asking were considered rather 'weird' or perhaps that they were not considered 'real questions' at all. This seems quite an understandable reaction when one looks at some of the questions, e.g. 'Are spoons people?', 'Are teddy-bears food?' About half the children who were unable to answer these questions on the first occasion simply answered 'Yes' to each question. Another common response, especially with the younger children, was to repeat the question as a question or to turn it into a statement, e.g. 'Eggs are people'. There is some indication also that the 'penny sometimes drops' suddenly and the children seem to see immediately that they are, in fact, being asked to answer a question which, though unusual, is also meaningful. Thus several children (14 per cent of the reliability sample) scored completely or almost completely correct records on the second testing session after having simply answered with a blanket 'Yes' on the first occasion.

It was also illuminating to watch the way in which some of the children were clearly striving to find the underlying basis for the generic concepts and vacillating in the certainty with which they approached the various tests of concept acquisition (cf. Piaget's discussion in Tanner and Inhelder, 1956, of 'equilibration' in the development of concrete operations). For example, one boy aged four years ten months making his selection of pictures of 'food' came to the 'cup' and asked himself aloud: 'This is food isn't it? We drink from it don't we?' He then proceeded to include it as 'food'. At the same time he rejected the 'cup' as 'food' on the 'positive/negative identification test'.

In relation to the concept definition test, not surprisingly few children were able to offer clearly articulated definitions of the concepts under consideration. One might hazard a guess that 'people' would be a difficult concept for many adults to define! Seven children gave an adequate definition of 'food' mentioning that 'we eat it', but three of these failed on both parts of the test in relation to 'food'! Only one child gave anything approaching an adequate definition of 'people': 'what talk', though two mentioned 'walk' and one 'watching tele'! The majority of children simply said they didn't know or they repeated their choices by pointing to the pictures or picking them out again. Most of the definitions were offered by children over the age of four years, though two children below four, one aged three years two months and the other three years three months, offered correct definitions of 'food'. Level of verbal ability, as adjudged by the P P V T, did not seem too relevant to ability to offer definitions. Thus the standardized scores of those children offering definitions for 'food' were : 140; 93; 108; 97; 82; 127; 106.

•   •   •

Teaching the generic concepts

The data were obtained from only five paired cases in which the matching process was only achieved at a very crude level and must, therefore, be treated with great circumspection. Nevertheless it was felt worth while to offer the results for consideration. The children's records were fairly evenly balanced, two of the 'taught' children showing an improvement over the records of the paired 'un-taught' children; two pairs of children in which the reverse situation applied and one pair in which the results showed fairly equivalent standards of performance on the two testing sessions. However, when the records of each individual child's performance were considered in detail the 'taught' children appeared to have done rather better. Thus the most dramatic improvements seen in the records related to 'taught' children. One child of three years one month on first testing, for example, simply picked up each of the pictures from the card when asked to show the pictures of 'food' and 'people'. When re-tested he selected the 'food' pictures entirely correctly and all the 'people' with the addition of a teddy-bear. None of the 'un-taught' children showed improvements of this magnitude.

Piaget's test questions

The responses to the Piagetian questions are summarized in table 17.3. The main observation which stands out from the table is that there is little correspondence between the proportion of children answering the questions accurately in Piaget's samples (ages five to nine) and the children in the present sample (ages two to four). This lack of correspondence will be discussed later. There was, similarly, very little apparent correspondence between the difficulty levels of the different questions. Again we will return to this point.

Over 80 per cent of the children tested in the present research answered the questions correctly either the first time or after a 'concrete' demonstration of the problem using the picture cards in front of them. The question which posed most problems for the older children in Piaget's research [viz. 'Are all the tulips (or roses) some of the flowers?'] formulated in the present research as 'Are all the ladies some of the people?', question (4), caused no problems at all to the children of two to four years of age in our sample. They all answered correctly 'Yes'. On the other hand, whereas 81 per cent of Piaget's sample answered correctly the logically identical question (5) only 69 of our sample did so. The question the children found most difficult to answer in our research was question (6): 'If you take away all the people will there be any ladies left?' After a concrete demonstration of the problem using the pictures, however, 86 per cent of the children also answered this correctly.

The individual records of the children also revealed some interesting data relevant to

Table 17.3 The proportion of children answering the Piagetian questions correctly (a) in the present research and (b) in the research of Piaget and Inhelder (1964)

| | (a) Present sample (N = 29, ages 2–4 yrs) | | | | (b) Piaget's sample [N = 32 for Qs (2), (4), (5), (7), ages 6–9 yrs; N = 20 for Qs (3) and (6), ages 5–6 yrs] |
| | On first testing | | After demonstration | | % answering correctly |
Q	No. answering correctly	%	No. answering correctly	%	
1	29	100	—	—	not asked
2	28	97	29	100	47
3	26	90	28	97	71
4	29	100	—	—	21
5	20	69	24	83	81
6	13	45	25	86	71
7	19	66	24	83	33

question (7): 'Are there more ladies or more people?' We have already argued that this seems rather like a trick question. It seems as if the child is led to suppose by the phrasing of the question that the questioner has created an artificial distinction between 'ladies' and 'people' for the purpose of the test. In answering, the child appears to accept the artificial dichotomy suggested to him by the authority figure of the tester. For example, one boy aged three years nine months having answered this question correctly by saying 'more people', then went on to give a spontaneous explanation of his reasoning. 'There are three ladies and three people' – here appearing to follow the lead given by the questioner. Then, as if dismissing the 'trick dichotomy' and adopting his own 'alternative' interpretation, he carried on: 'six people if you count them altogether . . . if they're all together there are more people'.

Seven out of the 29 children (or 24 per cent) answered *all* the questions correctly and a further seven children (i.e. a total of nearly half the sample altogether) having failed on *one* question – usually question (6) – answered all correctly after one demonstration. Four of the 29 children got all the Piagetian questions right but failed to complete the HAPCAT tests at all accurately. For example, one girl, aged three years ten months, scored 100 per cent on the questions but was unable to pick out the pictures of people from amongst the distractors. She chose the people together with 'dog', 'cat', 'bird' and 'teddy-bear', making similar errors in the 'positive/negative identification' test. Another illustration is of a boy aged four years ten months who selected the items correctly as representing 'people' but made errors in his 'positive/negative identification', including 'bird' and 'dog' as people. Some children also showed records in the opposite direction, i.e. they scored accurately on the HAPCAT items but did not complete all the Piagetian questions correctly. Five children, in fact, gave accurate selections of both 'food' and 'people' and were also able to answer the follow-up identification questions accurately but made one error on the Piagetian questions [question (6) in four out of five of the cases]. At the same time, with one exception, all these children were able to give a correct answer to the question after using the picture cards to work out the problem. Four children (i.e. 14 per cent of the sample of 29 given the Piagetian questions) gained full scores on all the HAPCAT items and also answered all the Piagetian questions correctly. All these children had PPVT scores in the 'above average' range (the lowest standardized score was 123). Their ages were three years two months, four years six months, four years seven months and four years seven months.

The children's responses to the Piagetian questions (unlike those to the HAPCAT items) appeared comparatively unrelated to chronological age, PPVT score and socio-economic background. Comparing the performance of children on the Piagetian tests (scores of five plus *versus* four or less) with chronological age ('four' *versus* 'under four') the chi-squared value was 0.02; the equivalent chi-squared result for comparison of the Piagetian tests with the PPVT scores was 0.02. Similarly, socioeconomic background appeared unrelated to performance on the Piagetian tests when tested by a 3 × 2 chi-squared analysis (socioeconomic Groups I, II and III, as opposed to scores of 5 + /4 or less on the Piagetian questions).

DISCUSSION

Although the research sample was not very large (N = 56) it was nevertheless reasonably representative of the characteristics normally found in much larger samples of children in relation to certain important variables (e.g. the socioeconomic backgrounds of the children and their verbal ability scores) though not in the proportion of the sexes (boys out-numbering girls in the present sample). It seems justifiable to postulate, therefore, that the results may well relate more generally to pre-school children in urban environments in England, though further corroborative work would be required to substantiate this claim.

As far as the first question is concerned ['To what extent had the children acquired certain specific (i.e. non-generic) concepts?'] the evidence suggests that these children had formed many specific concepts as adjudged by their ability to identify the pictures of certain objects from amongst a number of similar object concepts (e.g. 'dog' from 'cat', 'cup' from 'spoon') when presented in an entirely novel setting. Thus they appeared to have abstracted the common features of certain objects (e.g. 'cups') and to have demonstrated an ability to generalize their awareness of the concept to new situations in which it was necessary to recognize a novel presentation of the object and to distinguish one concept ('cup') from another similar concept ('spoon').

Similarly, with reference to our second question ('To what extent were these pre-school children capable of showing an understanding of generic or class concepts?') the evidence suggests that many children in this age group have formed some generic concepts and there is an indication that there may be something to be said for further experiments on the *teaching* of generic concepts at the pre-school level. Judged by very strict standards (correct answers to all the HAPCAT items and to all the Piagetian questions involving 'class inclusion') four out of 29 children (i.e. 14 per cent of the sub-sample of children given the Piagetian questions in addition to the HAPCAT items) showed what appeared to be an 'unshakeable' grasp of class inclusion. When one applies different test standards to the performance of the children, their grasp of class inclusion appears either more or less certain. For example, if one takes Piaget's test questions alone, 24 per cent of the sub-sample (seven out of 29 children) could be said to have attained an understanding of class inclusion, and this percentage rises to 80 per cent if one allows the scores of children who gained completely accurate answers after being allowed to work out the problem using the card pictures. On the other hand, if one takes only performance on the HAPCAT items as the criterion for the establishment of class inclusion, one finds rather different proportions.

The two HAPCAT items mainly relevant to the generic concept involved (a) the selection of pictures representative of the concept and (b) the positive/negative identification of the concept ('Are spoons food?' etc.). Between a quarter and a third of the pre-school children under consideration had attained an understanding of the generic concept if one takes as the criterion completely accurate performance on both these tests. On the other hand, if one takes accurate performance of the first test (a) only then the percentages rise to about half the sample of 56 children (59 per cent choosing the pictures of 'people' correctly and 43 per cent the pictures of 'food').

In general, therefore, the present results suggest that quite a substantial proportion of children in the age group two to four years (i.e. the age group normally taken to be in the pre-conceptual stage of development) are, in fact, quite capable of forming not only specific concepts but also, as Welch (1940) maintained, hierarchical classification involving class inclusion. The number of generic concepts which find a place in the vocabulary of the preschool child depends partly, of course, upon the language used by adults when talking to children, a point very clearly argued by Brown (1958). Thus 'cutlery' is probably a generic term which finds little usage whereas 'clothes' is frequently used in conversation between adults and children. Similarly, the extent to which a child is able to define the distinguishing attributes of any particular concept will vary with general experience, and intellectual maturity, just as adults constantly refine their own understanding of various concepts in the light of new experiences and increasing knowledge.

It seems clear from the results, however, that many pre-school children are able to understand the essential characteristics of a number of generic concepts. If these results are replicated in other studies they would suggest that some modification is required in the standard 'Piagetian texts' which claim that children between two and four years cannot form generic concepts.

The key point of dissension between these results and those of Piaget and Inhelder (1964) does not refer to the Piagetian thesis concerning the relationship between operational thinking and hierarchical classification (though it does cast doubt upon the suggested age level at which hierarchical classification can be achieved). The dissension rather relates to the *criterion tests* which are accepted as adequate for the demonstration of a child's acquisition of hierarchical classification involving class inclusion. Thus Piaget claims that his questions provide a sensitive and reliable test for the acquisition of class inclusion but on the evidence of the present research findings we would have to doubt this assertion.

The Piagetian questions, in fact, showed very little discriminatory power between the results of children of different age and ability levels. Unlike the HAPCAT items the Piagetian questions appeared unrelated to ability and also to chronological age at this level (two to four years), though the results of Piaget and Inhelder (1964) do show some age/concept development relationship with a sample of children between five and ten years. Similarly, the test question which Piaget's subjects found most difficult was answered correctly by each of the 29 children to whom we presented the item. This was the question 'Are all the ladies some of the people?' Further, whereas, in Piaget's sample, a *higher* proportion of children were able to answer the question containing a logically identical element (in our research 'Are all the people ladies or are some of the people ladies?') the present sample found this question *more* difficult. It seems probable that these discrepancies probably relate to the age ranges of the children involved. Thus the type of test questions used by Piaget to demonstrate the attainment of an understanding of generic concepts may, in fact, be quite inappropriate for use with children below the age of four years. For example, four of the children who answered all the Piagetian questions correctly were unable to answer the HAPCAT items on generic concepts accurately. Thus it may be that one is simply demonstrating that children at this age are not yet capable of appreciating the unusual linguistic structure of the question rather than that they have not attained an understanding of generic concepts. The 100 per cent 'Yes' to the question 'Are all the ladies some of the people?' in our sample of two- to four-year-old children may simply represent an 'uncomprehending affirmative' in the same way that children who did not understand the odd format of the HAPCAT 'positive/negative identification' questioning ('Are eggs people?' etc.) simply answered with a blanket 'Yes'.

It is possible that the Piagetian tests may show something about the level of linguistic comprehension when used with pre-school children but they do not appear to be useful guides to an understanding of hierarchical classification at this age. With older children they may perhaps help to demonstrate the degree of certainty with which the child has attained some generic concepts but it is also seemingly possible that they could be rather more closely related to the child's ability to answer questions concerning class inclusion which are phrased in the manner of verbal reasoning 'teasers'.

The HAPCAT items, on the other hand, do seem to provide a fairly meaningful measure of a child's understanding of generic concepts. The items appear, on this initial testing, to offer a reasonable degree of reliability (an aspect which would be interesting to check in relation to the Piagetian questions, though we did not do so on this occasion). They also showed a good discriminatory power in relation to the age and ability levels of the children, the higher the age and ability level the higher the scores on the items ($P < 0.01$ in relation to verbal ability and $P < 0.001$ in relation to age). There seems to be a substantial case, therefore, for arguing that children are able to respond appropriately to test items involving an understanding of generic concepts provided that the items are presented in a format which is meaningful to them. The HAPCAT items appear to satisfy such criteria.

ACKNOWLEDGEMENT

This article first appeared in *Educ. Res.* (1975), **17**, 180–192, and is published here with the kind permission of the authors and editor.

REFERENCES

Beard, R. M. (1969) *An Outline of Piaget's Developmental Psychology.* London: Routledge & Kegan Paul.

Blank, M. (1968) Experimental approaches to concept development in young children. In Lunzer, E. A. and Morris, J. F. (Eds.), *Development in Human Learning.* London: Staples.

Brown, R. W. (1958) How shall a thing be called? *Psychol. Rev.*, **65**, 1, 14–21.

Brown, R. W. (1967) Language and categories. In Bruner, J. S., Goodnow, J. J. & Austin, G. A., *A Study of Thinking*. New York: J. Wiley & Sons.

Dunn, L. M. (1965) *Expanded Manual for the Peabody Picture Vocabulary Test*, American Guidance Services Inc.

Moss, J. W. & Edwards, P. (1960) The PPVT with English children, *Brit. J. Educ. Psychol.*, **30**, 82.

Piaget, J. (1962) The stages of the intellectual development of the child. In Wason, P. C. & Johnson-Laird, P. N. (Eds.) (1968), *Thinking and Reasoning*. Harmondsworth: Penguin.

Piaget, J. & Inhelder, B. (1964) *The Early Growth of Logic in the Child: Classification and Seriation*. London: Routledge & Kegan Paul.

Russell, D. H. (1956) *Children's Thinking*. London: Ginn.

Stones, E. (1966) *An Introduction to Educational Psychology*. London: Methuen.

Tanner, J. M. & Inhelder, B. (Eds.) (1970), *Discussions on Child Development, Vol. 1*. London: Tavistock Publications Ltd.

Welch, L. (1940) A preliminary investigation of some aspects of the hierarchical development of concepts, *J. Gen. Psychol.*, **22**, 359–78.

18 Transitive inferences and memory in young children

P. E. BRYANT and T. TRABASSO

Contrary to the conclusions of Piaget, young children can make transitive inferences if precautions are taken to prevent deficits of memory from being confused with inferential deficits.

For some time, it has been believed that young children are unable to form transitive inferences about quantity until they pass the stage of logical preoperations at about seven years old (Piaget and Inhelder, 1956; Piaget, Inhelder and Szeminska, 1960). This argument has been very widely accepted (Flavell and Wohlwill, 1969; Smedslund, 1969). Piaget and his colleagues propose that the young child cannot infer, for example, that A > C from the information that A > B and B > C. They assert that the child is unable to coordinate the first two, separate items of information in order to reach the correct inferential conclusion about A and C. If true, this claim has important educational implications, for a child who cannot combine this information must also be unable to understand the most elementary principles of measurement.

We report two experiments which show that the claim is unjustified. The experiments demonstrate that four-year-old children can make transitive inferences about quantity, provided that they can remember the items of information which they are asked to combine.

One must ensure that the child has retained the comparisons which he has to combine, if one is to infer whether or not he can make transitive inferences. Otherwise, an error might simply be due to a failure in memory and have nothing to do with inferential ability. Yet experiments in which it is reported that children cannot make inferential judgements lack this elementary precaution. One can control for forgetting by taking two precautions. First, teach the child the initial comparisons (A > B and B > C) very thoroughly. Second, test for memory of these comparisons at the same time as one asks the inferential question about A and C. The first precaution ensures retention of the initial comparisons and the second checks for this retention during the inferential problem.

We found it necessary to introduce another control in our experiments. This was against the transfer of 'absolute' responses. The general procedure in prior experiments has been to use three quantities (A, B and C). If only three are used, the correct response to the two extreme quantities must be the same in both the inferential problem and in the initial direct comparisons. The quantity A is the 'larger' when compared with B, and C is the 'smaller' when compared with B, in the initial direct comparisons. Yet 'larger' is the correct response to A and 'smaller' is the correct response to C in the inferential AC comparisons. Thus a child who produces the correct response when asked the AC question may do so by parroting a verbal label picked up during the initial comparisons, and not, as has always been assumed, by making a genuine inference through the combination of two separate comparisons.

The correct control is to introduce more stimuli and thus more direct comparisons. If there are as many as five stimuli (in descending order of size they are A, B, C, D and E) four initial direct comparisons are possible, A > B, B > C, C > D and D > E. Note that B, C and D all feature in two of these comparisons and that each of them is the larger in one comparison and the smaller in the other. This means that no one absolute response can be transferred to any one of these three quantities, and it therefore follows that the crucial transitive comparison will be between B and D. This indirect comparison cannot be solved by transfer of absolute responses, since B and D were both larger and smaller in the initial direct comparisons.

Our experiments thus involved first a thorough training period with four direct comparisons, followed by a test period in which the children were tested for their ability to make transitive judgements *and* to remember the initial comparisons. In the first experiment, 60 children in three age groups of 20 each participated. The mean ages of the groups were 4.5, 5.6 and 6.7 years respectively. The youngest group came from a local nursery school and the older groups from two local infants' schools.

The training and testing materials were identical. Five coloured wooden rods, each of a different length and colour, were used. The lengths were coloured differently in order that they could be identified and remembered. Thus the child learned, for example, that blue was larger than red and red larger than green. The colours were red, white, yellow, blue and green, and the lengths were three, four, five, six and seven inches. The particular colour–length combinations differed from child to child and were counterbalanced within each age group.

The rods were presented in pairs throughout the experiment. The pairs were always presented in such a way that each rod protruded from the top of a container by one inch. The equal protrusion was achieved by sinking bores of different lengths in the container box. This kind of presentation forced the child to use the colour differences in making a choice between different lengths.

In the initial training, each trial consisted of showing the child a pair of rods of different colours, each rod protruding one inch from the top of the box. The child was asked to indicate which rod was the 'taller' or the 'shorter' ('big' and 'little' were the terms used with the youngest group, as they were more easily understood). When the child made his choice the experimenter drew out the rods and held them perpendicular to the table, so that the child could compare lengths directly. This was the feedback for the choices in the direct comparisons, which enabled him to learn to make the correct choice. The question asked (taller and shorter) and the positions of the rods (left and right) were varied in an irregular order from trial to trial.

The training was divided into two phases. In the first, the four comparisons, A > B, B > C, C > D and D > E, were trained separately and in order from either the tallest to the shortest or vice versa; half of the children in each group were trained with each order. Each of the pairs was learned to a criterion of eight out of ten successful choices. In the second phase which followed immediately, all four pairs were presented in a random order on different trials. This interweaving continued until each child responded correctly to six successive presentations of each pair.

Testing followed immediately after the completion of the second training phase. The testing procedure was the same except that no feedback at all was given, that is, the lengths were not shown after a choice. Each child was tested four times on every one of the 10 possible pairs of colours. These ten included the four, initial (direct) comparisons, and six, new, transitive (indirect) comparisons. The order in which the pairs were tested was random and varied between children. The type of questions and the position of the rods in each pair varied irregularly as in training.

All groups learned the initial (direct) comparisons rapidly. In the first phase of the training there seemed to be no age differences in speed of learning. In the second phase, however, the four-year-old children made more errors than the other two age groups who were not significantly different from each other.

The test results are summarized in table 18.1, which gives the average probability of a correct response on each pair of colours for each age group. The main diagonal cell entries (A, B: B, C: C, D: D, E) of each subtable in table 18.1 show the correct choice probabilities for the initial direct comparisons. The top row and the right column off-diagonal entries (A, C: A, D: A, E: B, E: and C, E) are those for transitive tests where one or both of the rods included one of the end points, which were always either larger (A) or smaller (B). (These transitive comparisons may have been susceptible to the transfer of absolute responses.) The critical entry is the off-diagonal B, D pair, in which each rod had been both larger and smaller in the initial comparisons. The importance of this cell is stressed.

The evidence for transitivity is impressive at all age levels. All the transitive comparisons (AC, AD, AE, BD, DE and CE) were well above chance level, since the upper 99 per cent confidence bound on the hypothesis of chance is 0.65 with a sample of $n = 20$. Turning back to the crucial BD comparison it should be noted that children at all three age levels were able to make genuine transitive inferences very well.

It should also be noted that the BD scores were consistently the lowest of all 10 comparisons. Of particular interest is the fact that the children seemed to perform at a lower level with the BD comparisons than with BC or CD comparisons, and yet these last two provide the information on which the transitive BD judgement must be based. This conclu-

Table 18.1 Probability of correct choices on tests for transitivity and retention (experiment 1)

Stimulus	B	C	D		E
4-yr-old children					
A	0.96	0.96	0.93		0.98
B	—	0.92	0.78[a]	(0.83)[b]	0.92
C	—	—	0.90		0.94
D	—	—	—		0.91
5-yr-old children					
A	1.00	0.96	1.00		0.98
B	—	0.86	0.88[a]	(0.80)[b]	1.00
C	—	—	0.92		1.00
D	—	—	—		1.00
6-yr-old children					
A	0.99	0.99	1.00		1.00
B	—	0.94	0.92[a]	(0.92)[b]	0.99
C	—	—	0.98		1.00
D	—	—	—		1.00

[a] Critical entry.
[b] Predicted.

sion is supported by an analysis of variance of the errors on these three comparisons, which produced a significant difference between pairs (F3.3 per cent, d.f.2,114, $P < 0.05$) and no interaction with age. Thus our conclusion from the first experiment was that young children can make genuine transitive inferences extremely effectively, but not perfectly. The reason for less than perfect inference is discussed later.

There is, however, one possible objection to our conclusion. In the training phase we showed the children the full length of the rods when we gave them feedback at the end of each trial. It is possible that the children solved the B D transitive question not by making a genuine transitive inference but simply by remembering that B was six inches and D was four inches. Such a solution to the problem is not an inferential one, and although we did not think that this kind of solution was likely, nevertheless we did not exclude its possibility in the first experiment.

We therefore carried out a second experiment on 25 four-year-old and 25 five-year-old children, in which our procedure was exactly the same as in the first experiment, except that we eliminated visual feedback during the training session. Instead of being shown which of the two rods was longer at the end of each training trial, the children were simply told which was the longer and which the shorter. The rods were never displayed completely until the whole experiment was finished.

The test results for this experiment are given in table 18.2, which shows that the removal of visual feedback had no effect on children's ability to make transitive comparisons. Once again performance on all transitive comparisons was well above chance. The performance of both age groups was as good in the B D comparison in this experiment as the performance of the equivalent age groups in the first experiment. Again, however, the B D scores were somewhat lower than the B C and C D scores. We analysed the scores of the four and five year olds on these three comparisons in the two experiments together, and again found a significant difference between pairs ($F3.89$, d.f.2,172, $P < 0.05$). There was no interaction with age or with experiments. Thus in both experiments, children's transitivity, though considerable, was not perfect.

We shall now argue that the lower performance on the crucial B D pairs is not due to a failure to make inferences but to a failure of retention of the information contained in the initial comparisons. Let $P_{b,c}$ and $P_{c,d}$ be the respective probabilities of recalling the information on the B C and C D pairs. Assume that the recall of these information units is independent. Then the probability of making a correct inference on the B D test ($P_{b,d}$) is the probability of jointly recalling the information for each of the training pairs. Since these events are independent, their probabilities multiply; that is, $P_{b,d} = P_{b,c} \times P_{c,d}$.

Table 18.2 Probability of correct choices on tests for transitivity and retention (experiment 2)

Stimulus	B	C	D		E
4-yr-old children					
A	0.98	0.98	0.93		0.97
B	—	0.89	0.82^a	$(0.77)^b$	0.90
C	—	—	0.87		0.88
D	—	—	—		0.94
5-yr-old children					
A	0.98	0.92	0.95		0.97
B	—	0.87	0.85^a	$(0.85)^b$	0.98
C	—	—	0.97		0.95
D	—	—	—		0.98

[a] Critical entry.
[b] Predicted.

These assumptions were tested by multiplying the observed probabilities for the B C and C D tests for each subtable of tables 18.1 and 18.2. The predicted $P_{b,d}$ is shown in parentheses. It can be seen that these predictions are reasonably close to the observed values. Hence, the lower performance on the B D tests may be attributed to a failure in memory rather than to inferential difficulty.

This last experiment conclusively demonstrates that very young children are able to make transitive inferences extremely effectively. They can combine separate quantity judgements very well and they can do so at a far younger age than has generally been assumed. This is a conclusion which has practical as well as theoretical importance.

ACKNOWLEDGEMENT

This article first appeared in *Nature* (1971), **232**, 456–458, and is published here with the kind permission of authors and editor.

REFERENCES

Flavell, J. H. & Wohlwill, J. F. (1969) In Elkind, D. & Flavell, J. H. (Eds.), *Studies in Cognitive Development*. New York: Oxford University Press.

Piaget, J. & Inhelder, B. (1956) *The Child's Conception of Space*. London: Routledge & Kegan Paul.

Piaget, J., Inhelder, B. & Szeminska, A. (1960) *The Child's Conception of Geometry*. London: Routledge & Kegan Paul.

Smedslund, J. (1969) In *Psychol. Bull.*, **71**, 237.

19   Piaget and the teaching of history

ROY HALLAM

In earlier articles (Hallam, 1967, 1969) it was explained that Piaget's work on logical thinking and moral judgements had been used as a basis for investigating children's thinking and judgements in history. Since only a hundred subjects from one school were tested, the application of the results might seem limited. Furthermore, the pupils lived in a rural or semi-rural environment and much of their teaching was conducted in a traditionally academic manner.

There does seem, however, to be some support for the view that the results may have a general application. Scalogram analysis (Hallam, op. cit.) indicated that the level of formal operations when subjects are able to reason by implication at an abstract level and to postulate hypotheses was reached after a chronological age of 16.2 to 16.6 years and a mental age of at least 16.8 years. Such seemingly advanced ages would evidently not surprise authors on methodology in history, nearly all of whom write without any overt reference to Piaget's work. These writers frequently stress that history is a particularly difficult subject below the level of the sixth form [Incorporated Association of Assistant Masters, (IAAM), 1952, p. 2]. Research work on thinking in history and related work on logical thinking (Hughes, 1965; Hallam, 1966; Booth, 1967; Reynolds, 1967; Alilunas, 1968; Schools Council, 1968) support the argument that formal thinking in history develops relatively late in the secondary school.

PLANNING THE HISTORY SYLLABUS

Scalogram analysis revealed that most of the pupils below the chronological age of 16.2 years were reasoning at the concrete operational level: they were able to use the evidence before them but were not able to postulate hypotheses. It must be remembered, however, that this method of analysis gives only general results. Certain pupils had reached the formal level at younger ages: the answers of a subject aged 14.8 years revealed great maturity of thought. Moreover, logical thinking was more positively correlated with mental age ($r =$

0.701) than chronological age ($r = 0.543$). It would seem that the more intelligent pupils, when measured by conventional intelligence tests, reached the formal level first. The easiest method for a teacher to discover the thinking skills of his pupils would seem to be to give the class a fairly simply worded historical passage and ask questions on it, some demanding no more than understanding of the material but others requiring inferential thought (Hallam, 1966, 1967 and ibid., p. 7).

Whatever stage might have been reached by a particular pupil, the majority of secondary school pupils up to a mental age of 16 years seem to be at the concrete operational level of thought. The syllabuses should therefore be organized to take account of the limitations in pupils' reasoning. Szeminska (1965, p. 56) reports from Poland, for example, that such a revision of school curricula is already in progress. Research work indicates that it is useless to present abstract material to pupils before they are ready to assimilate it. Wall (1955, p. 155) remarks that in all subject fields 'there appears to be a "maturational sequence" which we syncopate or violate at the risk of disturbing the child's subsequent capacity to learn'. Szeminska (op. cit.) also affirms that 'poorly assimilated information can become a mnemonic burden which is not only cumbersome but paralyses cognitive activity'.

The following suggestions are therefore made to try to prevent such a paralysis in thinking in history. They will have to be modified according to the ability of the form, whether that ability is measured by Piagetian methods or through conventional intelligence tests.

Younger pupils in the secondary school

The limitations revealed in the reasoning of nearly all the pupils under 14 means that the history taught in the early years of a secondary school should not be over-abstract in form, nor should it contain too many variables. Even such a sympathetic writer as Bryant (1967) seems to expect too high a level of thought among average children. Among topics which she recommends for a two-year course for pupils aged 11 to 13 years are 'parliamentary reform' and 'the business methods of trading companies'. If these were dealt with in the abstract, it is unlikely that average children would be able to understand them in any depth. Bryant (op. cit.) suggests 'themes' for the first two years at secondary school since the traditional chronological syllabus is a 'millstone'. A chronological syllabus need not, however, necessarily mean a wild rush through the ages. Used wisely, topics in such a syllabus can be arranged so that the younger children learn the less detailed history of early times, while the history of recent years, which contains important yet complex topics, can then be taught when the pupils are able to reason at a more mature level. Support for a type of chronological syllabus is given by Sturt and Oakden (1921) who discovered that younger children find it easier to distinguish the remote historical periods from their own age than other periods, since the far past affords such a complete contrast to their own lives. More recently, Musgrove (1963) discovered that children aged 10 to 15 years showed 'a consistent average preference for history remote in time . . . boys equally with girls, and in secondary modern as well as grammar streams' (op. cit., p. 42).

The way in which the syllabus is organized must obviously be left to the individual school. Dividing each year's work into a number of patches, as explained by Lewis (1960), allows time for thorough work, discussion, reflection and thereby a possible improvement in pupils' thinking skills. Bareham (1969) has selected certain vital periods in history and used these to give an imaginative introduction through a historically accurate story, followed by factual material and assignments which exercise the pupils' thinking skills. A term's work on pre-history, possibly based on Place's *Prehistoric Britain* (1959) can give pupils of all types of ability an insight into the work and methods of an archaeologist. For pupils mainly at the pre-operational – that is, illogical – stage the 'themes' (Bryant) or 'lines of development' (Jeffreys, 1939) have much to recommend them provided that the material is 'concrete' – for example, transport, clothing, homes.

Whatever plan is adopted, the material must be so selected that it 'matches' the pupils' schemata or thinking skills. Hughes (1965, p. 109) remarks that 'even more enlightened teaching methods cannot ensure success unless the existing schemata are sufficiently developed to deal with the situation'. The material should be of such a standard that it helps the pupils to improve their reasoning powers. A great deal of ancient history can be taught as a concrete subject: the homes, daily life, industries, agriculture and trade of the prehistoric period; the pyramids, calendar, writing and annual inundations of Ancient Egypt; the material achievements of the Greeks and Romans, and so on. With more intelligent children, in the early years of the secondary school, it is possible to include some abstract ideas in a simple manner, but it is preferable to link them with the pupils' everyday life. Democracy in Athens, for example, can be understood if the children have tried to discover how democracy works in their own country. Some of Plato's ideas can be grasped if they are connected, however crudely, with the educational system in Britain. In narrative work there should be constant attempts to give concrete examples of the events described verbally. Apart from the obvious use of diagrams, maps and illustrations, a few pupils defending the door against an imaginary Persian host at Thermopylae, or the collection of the names and denominations of neighbourhood churches before a lesson on Martin Luther, can help pupils to assimilate new ideas far more easily than through verbal exposition. McLaughlin's (1963) suggestion that the concrete operational stage could be equated with the ability to hold four concepts simultaneously has interesting implications for narrative work. Presumably no more than four variables of the same type should be used for any one story. If the story of Caesar's assassination and its aftermath is being told, for example, only four characters would be involved, such as Caesar, Brutus, Mark Antony and Octavian. If the characters are similar in name or type, then it would probably be wise to have fewer than four. It would be an intelligent class that could cope with Hamilcar, Hannibal, Hasdrubal and Scipio Africanus. Many children would confuse the names beginning with 'H', and after a while some would decide that it was Horatius who led the attack on Rome.

Following such a seemingly restricted course for the first two or three years, depending on the operational level of the pupils, need not mean that the traditional values of studying history are lost. The teaching of history is often recommended in the hope that children's imaginative fields will be widened. Pupils learn to contrast their present society with other civilizations and this should lead to the questioning of familiar values. Younger pupils will achieve this far more through the study of 'concrete' history than by trying to grapple with abstract topics. The study of Tudor houses, for example, could lead to a discussion of the differences between Roman, Tudor and modern houses, and might conclude with a realization of the rapid changes in the last four hundred years compared with the period from 410 A.D. to the sixteenth century.

Nor, if children are dealing with material that is largely concrete in nature, will they necessarily lose the intellectual values commonly associated with the study of history. Statements will still need to be queried and confirmed. Simple cause–effect relationships can be appreciated in studying such topics as the development of lake villages or the punishments meted out to sixteenth-century criminals. Relevant information still has to be gleaned from the textbook. The most worthwhile result of learning history, the cultivation of an inquiring spirit, is easier to stimulate in younger pupils through the study of concrete topics such as writing, houses, entertainments, clothing, transport and so on than in trying to force them to understand abstract political, constitutional and religious changes.

Older pupils

The thinking of some pupils, even after 14, may still show traces of illogical reasoning. For such children, probably the least intelligent in the third year, it will be necessary to concentrate on 'concrete' history. They will be happiest dealing with the everyday life of the past and will enjoy the type of imaginative work (see 'written work', below) done by the more able pupils in the earlier years of the secondary school. Such work may often show the limitations in their reasoning. Some pupils were taught by the writer about the Great Frost of 1683–1684 when the Thames was completely frozen. It was explained that a printer set up a booth on the River Thames and printed people's names on medallions in order to commemorate the occasion. When they were told to illustrate the type of inscription he would have sold, some pupils showed names printed on dripping blocks of ice. Few could appreciate the reasons why people wanted their names printing on such an occasion. When the more abstract type of religious or political history is taught to such pupils, it should always be linked, as far as possible, with some aspect of their lives. The story of John Wesley, for example, is best approached through a study of the present-day visible differences between the Anglican and Methodist Churches. Such topics as the right to vote, membership of a trade union, living conditions in the twentieth century, and local history, would seem the most suitable for such children. More abstract political, diplomatic and economic history should be strictly limited. With careful teaching, however, these pupils should be able to leave school at least with the ability to form rational judgements in relatively simple contexts. Whether they could attain the formal operational stage with continued education is impossible to estimate at the moment. When the school leaving age for all pupils is raised to 16 years – a necessary reform according to the results of this research – it may then be possible to begin to consider this problem.

Most children in the third year find no difficulty in dealing with the evidence before them, provided that the vocabulary is not too difficult. They should be ready to tackle the more abstract type of history presented in a simple form, seen, for example, in the changes of the Civil War and 'Glorious Revolution'. More variables can be introduced into narratives, but even then for all but the most intelligent there should not be more than six variables and usually only four. It is amazing how often textbook writers will give such a thorough and detailed account that they end in merely confusing the pupils. An admirable textbook, for example, included the following topics in a study of Clive in Bengal: Surajah Dowlah, the Black Hole of Calcutta, the French at Chandenagore, Mir Jaffir, the Battle of

Plassey, Omichund and Admiral Watson. A clear account of the following topics is all that most children of 14 years of age can readily understand:

> Clive in Bengal: Surajah Dowlah
> > The Black Hole of Calcutta
> > The East India Company
> > Mir Jaffir (for some pupils)
> > The Battle of Plassey.

A minority of secondary pupils may have reached the formal operational stage at 14-plus years. Such pupils should be able to use inductive and deductive thought and appreciate history at a fairly mature level, even though they will probably still enjoy concrete subjects, such as the social life of the period studied.

These pupils will often be sitting for external examinations. In the past the type of 'O' level questions set in history have seldom demanded more than the repetition of learnt facts and opinions and thus allowed teachers to rely on dictated or copied notes for successful results. Boards recently do seem to be setting questions which demand inferential thought, but their syllabuses are often over-crowded and so much ground has to be covered that little time is left for reflection or discussion during the lessons. A compulsory section on historical documents might give examination candidates the opportunity to exercise their historical judgement and thus avoid excessive dependence on memory work.

IMPROVING THINKING IN HISTORY

Whether it is possible to accelerate children's logical thinking is being strongly debated at present. How far does the development of thought depend on maturation and how far on interaction with the environment, both social and intellectual? (McV. Hunt, 1961; Sigel and Hooper, 1968; Pines, 1969). Do we have to accept that certain chronological or mental ages are essential before children can reach the concrete or formal levels, or is it possible to arrange the learning situation in such a way that the children's thought processes are so challenged that they have to adapt to the new, more complex material? The evidence is by no means complete or conclusive but a teacher's task is obviously to try to develop thinking skills as far as is practicable. Inhelder and Piaget (1958, p. 337) explain that the beginning of the formal stage 'may be, beyond the neurological factors, a product of a progressive acceleration of individual development under the influence of education and perhaps nothing stands in the way of a further reduction of the average age in a more or less distant future'. The suggestion that it may be possible to accelerate thought processes has been eagerly adopted in the USA – perhaps over-eagerly as far as Piaget is concerned. He has recently explained (Pines, 1969) that while it may be possible to accelerate these stages 'there is not much to be gained by doing it beyond a certain measure' (op. cit., p. 35). If the material is too advanced for the children they will either assimilate it without understanding, or will reject it with possible damage to their whole attitude to the subject.

In my research, scalogram analysis revealed that the subjects were able to answer at least one question at the concrete operational level from the chronological age of 11.6 years. The answers of the younger pupils were, however, frequently marred by pre-operational il-logicalities, and the concrete operational stage lasted in general until a chronological age of

16.2 years. The main intellectual aims in teaching history would therefore seem to be to eradicate as quickly as possible the pre-operational thinking and to help the older pupils to progress at least to the lower reaches of the formal stage before they leave school.

Both aims would possibly be realized if teachers consciously tried to make their pupils use reversibility in their thought by putting them in a conflict situation where they have to hold and balance seemingly contrasted facts or views. With the children who revert frequently to the pre-operational level, the teacher should pose only two variables on one particular topic, to avoid cognitive confusion. The two variables could be situated in the period being studied: thus, two contemporary opinions of an event or a person could be contrasted and compared. Two different types of variables could be posed, for example, by the teacher and class contrasting present-day attitudes to poverty or crime with those attitudes prevalent in the period studied. This policy of making a pupil move from one fact or idea to another and then return to the original fact or idea stems from Piaget's explanation for the attainment of the concept of conservation (Flavell, 1963, pp. 247–248). This process is called 'equilibration', meaning the temporary imbalance between the child's partially established thinking skills and the new demands of the environment (Sigel and Hooper, 1968, p. 430).

Progress towards the formal operational stage may be accelerated by a conscious effort to present at least four viewpoints in any historical topic. In order to help pupils to realize how many factors have to be balanced and compensated before any acceptable historical judgement is reached, the teacher could set the following problem situation for consideration:

(a) The overt reason(s) for any historical action compared with the inner motives deduced by contemporaries and/or historians.
(b) Two contemporary and opposed views of an event, for example, attitudes towards Elizabeth's ecclesiastical policy held by a Catholic and a Protestant compared with our approach towards religious conformity.
(c) Different opinions about an event or person held by people at the present time, for example, A. J. P. Taylor's views on the reasons for some of Bismarck's policies compared with the opinions of other historians and the opinions of his contemporaries.

Such methods would certainly lead to a state of 'cognitive conflict' advocated by Smedslund (Flavell, 1963, p. 374) as a means of improving pupils' thought processes, but there must be the right amount of discrepancy between the work and their current thinking skills.

Some of the more usual methods of teaching history will now be discussed in the light of this general approach to improving thinking in history.

Oral work

It may seem unnecessary to discuss the value of oral work in teaching history. A near-lecture and the dictating of notes still seem, however, to be used frequently in history lessons (Booth, 1967, pp. 122–123; Price, 1968). These methods can, and no doubt do, conceal serious inadequacies in the thinking processes of children. A class, for example, can write down many facts about Cardinal Wolsey but be unable to think of a single reason in reply to the question: 'Why was he not thrown out of the Church?'

Piaget recommends discussion, especially with one's peers, as the main educational method of improving thinking: 'When I say "active" I mean it in two senses. One is acting on material things. But the other means doing things in social collaboration, in a group effort. This leads to a critical frame of mind, where children must communicate with each other. Co-operation is indeed co-operation' (quoted by Sigel and Hooper, 1968, p. 431).

Elsewhere Piaget (1932, pp. 411–412) argues that we should 'try to create in the school a place where individual experimentation and reflection carried out in common come to each other's aid and balance one another'.

School or class debates in history would seem to offer the opportunity for 'contact with the judgements and evaluations of others' (op. cit., p. 408) but they can all too often simply consist of the more voluble and/or intelligent monopolizing the arguments while most pupils allow their minds to rest. The IAAM (1950, p. 60) points out, moreover, that many teachers 'find debates alien to the true spirit of historical study, which calls for balanced assessments rather than white-washing or denigration'. Class discussions could probably be educationally more valuable but are similarly prone to be controlled by a small number of children. Possibly the best way to allow discussions is to divide the class into small groups of four or five pupils. These can be formed spontaneously in any particular lesson or through sociograms (Evans, 1962). The groups then discuss the issues involved, for example, a third form has discussed some of Marx's ideas and the introduction of the Declaration of Independence in this way. A group leader then reports back to the whole class on the group's decision. Children seem to enjoy this as one method of learning history but they need the preliminary information and necessary cognitive skills with which to build constructive arguments. Inhelder and Piaget do realize the limitations placed on discussion through the inadequacy of the pupils' reasoning powers. They remark that for discussion to be successful the children need the appropriate group structure. This implies that they probably need to be near the formal operational level of thought.

Whether such group work improves the thinking levels of the class as a whole does not yet seem proved. Evans (op. cit., p. 74) states that while 'most workers seem to agree that there is little difference in the amount learned by students under the two methods' children enjoy their work more under group methods. The criteria of success for group work so far seems to be the amount learned. This would not seem to be such a worthwhile aim as the type of thought exercised on a problem.

Written work

To improve children's reasoning powers, teachers should give some written work which will make them deal with two or more different viewpoints. This means – at least for the younger secondary school pupils – that discreet use should be made of the method of copying notes from a textbook, since children often conceal misunderstanding by copying poorly assimilated concepts and ideas.

The following suggestions show how written work can be organized so that pupils have to use reflective thought. The pupils very often have to be warned, though, that these are historical exercises demanding the intelligent use of historical facts and not merely flights of fancy:

1 Making visits in time can help to provoke contrasts. Pupils can return to an historical period, for instance, and study a medieval town, or can re-create the reactions of an Athe-

nian visiting Sparta. Pupils can also be asked to contrast features of their life with those of a child in the past. At a simple level there could be contrasts in clothes and homes; at a more advanced level contrasts in work, unemployment, old age, and so on.

2 Dialogues can be re-created between people with different viewpoints, such as a Persian and Macedonian about Alexander the Great; Arthur Young and villagers over enclosures; a southerner and northerner in the USA over slavery; a Bolshevik and Tsarist in 1920.

3 Imaginative reconstructions can be made in which the children have to identify with some character. For example, in Bareham (1969), after reading a story about Akhenaten through the eyes of his daughter, Ankhesenpa-Aten, the children are asked to continue the story of what happened to Ankhesenpa-Aten after the death of her husband, Tutankhamen.

4 Contemporary 'newspaper' accounts can be used to make the children take an attitude towards some dramatic character or event in the past. Advertisements in the 'newspaper' frequently help them to understand how their minds are limited to the customs of the present day.

5 The titles of compositions should stimulate reflection; for example, instead of 'Describe the life of a medieval villein' the title could be 'Would you like to have been a medieval villein? Give reasons for your decision'.

6 A more difficult exercise which is possibly suitable only for older pupils is to give them two statements which they have to connect with a missing causal link. For example:

| More food produced through the Agrarian Revolution | Industries growing up in the new towns. |
| "Peace, land and Bread" | Bolsheviks in power in Petrograd, November, 1917 |

7 With younger pupils especially, passages can be set which contain absurdities. They can then be asked to explain why certain statements are incorrect.

8 Instead of asking pupils merely to discover facts about an event or person, questions can be set which need research and reflective thinking before they can be answered successfully. Thus, the following questions revealed different levels of reasoning among pupils of the same chronological age.
   (i) Why was Sir Thomas More executed?
   (ii) Would you have been prepared to face execution for the same reason as Sir Thomas More? Give reasons for your answer.
   (iii) What does the life and death of Sir Thomas More tell us about religious beliefs in the sixteenth century?

SOURCES

An important element in mature historical thinking is the ability to evaluate evidence in a logical manner. It therefore seems essential that school children should be introduced to some of the raw materials of history. Bruner (1960, p. 13) affirms that children should be made to work as historians, since he thinks that 'intellectual activity anywhere is the same, whether at the frontier of knowledge or in a third-grade classroom . . . The difference is in degree, not in mind'. While probably many historians would agree with such a contention, a careful selection of appropriate sources would certainly help the teacher to set work demanding inferential thought. Teachers at present would probably have to compile their own collections, as the results of the writer's work indicate that many secondary school pupils could be baffled by the length and obscurity of the extracts selected in some source books.

In a passage on the Norman Conquest of England (Hallam, 1967, pp. 198–199), for example, the following remark by a Norman soldier was included: 'It would have been just if wolves and vultures had devoured the flesh of the English'. Only 23 of the 100 subjects were able to give an adequate explanation of this remark. The normal approach was to change the phrase 'have been just if' into 'have been just *as* if'. Piaget warns about this tendency: 'the child often hears phrases, thinks he understands them, and assimilates them in his own way, distorting them' (quoted by Charlton, 1952, p. 20). Difficult words, Piaget explains, are given a meaning through their position in the general context 'owing to a syncretistic connection between all the terms of the context and owing to pseudo-logical justifications which are always ready to emerge' (quoted by Charlton, op. cit., p. 20).

The subjects, however, generally made sensible use of the following remarks on the devastation of the north by William: 'A man who lived at that time wrote: "Men, women and children died of hunger; they laid them down and died in the roads and fields; and there was no man to bury them . . . Between York and Durham every town stood empty, and in their streets lurked only robbers and wild beasts".' Hardly anyone accepted the passage uncritically while most children were rather sceptical in their attitude. One subject aged 12.9 years, for instance, decided that mistakes could have been made since stories were 'handed down from generation to generation'. He also thought that the passages sounded exaggerated with its emphasis on 'men, women *and* children. I think any kindly soul would have helped the women and children and maybe the men could have fended for themselves'. Even a subject as young as 11.9 years rejected implicit belief in such contemporary documents since 'both men seem to be favouring their own side'.

The last question on 'The Norman Conquest' (Hallam, 1967, op. cit.) was posed because it seemed to require some use of proportion. The subjects were told of the 'harrying of the North' and how villages in their district had depreciated in value. Their own township, on the other hand, increased in value. They were asked to suggest reasons for such a difference. Forty-seven of the 100 subjects could not hypothesize that their own township might have been spared. Through undue concentration on the general description of devastation in the North of England, they failed to realize that there might have been exceptional cases.

Answering questions on another passage about the Civil Wars, many children decided that Charles I was an admirable king simply because of the following extract: 'there was such a groan by the thousands then present as I have never heard before and desire I may never hear again'. In the same passage only 49 subjects were able to understand the implications of one of Cromwell's most famous remarks 'Trust in God and keep your powder dry', even though it was subsequently explained that Cromwell was referring to gunpowder which could not have exploded if it had been wet.

Such defects in understanding short historical statements show the difficulties involved in using original sources in teaching. Acceptable answers, however, were often given by young and not particularly intelligent children. If neither age nor intelligence handicapped certain pupils, with careful teaching it should be possible to use sources with nearly all children of secondary school age, provided that they are of the appropriate level of difficulty.

DISCOVERY METHODS

Some educational psychologists (Isaacs, 1955; Wall, 1955; Bruner, 1961) recommend that discovery methods should be used to improve children's thinking skills. Isaacs (p. 41), for example, suggests that 'finding out' is a most valuable educational method since, if any child is allowed to start 'along any readily pursuable' road the process will go on generating its own structure of knowledge and thought. Bruner (1961) argues that discovery methods have certain advantages over expository methods in that they lead to: (1) making information more readily viable in problem solving; (2) an intrinsic interest in the topic instead of the need for extrinsic rewards; (3) the learning of the techniques of discovery; (4) an improved memory of the material.

It would certainly be interesting to find out if discovery methods improve logical thinking in history. The pupils in my research had usually been taught in rather a formal manner. Hughes (1965, p. 109), in commenting on the generally low level of thinking of his subjects, explains that they had experienced 'a rather restricted "traditional" approach in their various junior schools and the atmosphere in the secondary modern school was somewhat rigid and authoritarian'. Recently, I discovered that highly intelligent children taught physics in a formal manner were able to quote the rule about equilibrium in the balance (Inhelder and Piaget, 1958, pp. 164–181) but were unable to operate successfully with the actual weights and balance. Somewhat less intelligent children of the same age who had 'found out' the law for themselves with the teacher's help were able to use proportion on the balance (Piaget's I N R C group).

Criticism can, however, be made against placing too great a reliance on discovery methods (Ausubel, 1968, pp. 473–504). In particular, Ausubel states that 'It appears that the various enthusiasts of the discovery method have been ... generalizing wildly from equivocal and even negative findings' (op. cit., p. 498). As far as history is concerned, Isaacs' phrase 'readily pursuable roads' would seem to imply that concrete subjects such as housing, costume and transport should be given as topics, at least to younger pupils. Possibly the time-consuming discovery methods can be most profitably used with such children who obviously need 'all the concrete-empirical experience' (Ausubel, p. 472) available in order to allow them to pass on to the more abstract stage of thinking. With the limited time usually allotted to history with adolescents, teachers may find that expository methods in which they consciously try to improve their pupils' level of understanding are more worth while than discovery methods.

Whatever the type of choice or age range, children's thinking skills will probably be more readily improved if the teacher sets specific questions to be answered with detailed page references rather than merely asks the pupils to 'find out'. All too frequently the latter request leads to the repetition of ill-digested facts. At the present date it is impossible to decide whether discovery methods can improve children's thinking in history; far more research is required.

Visual aids

The results of the writer's research work seem to indicate that any method by which the past can be made vivid and concrete should be employed in the teaching of history. Happold (1950) as early as 1928, emphasized that a boy of 12 years 'thinks concretely and he may learn best if he learns through concrete means . . . (To) the appeal through the brain . . . must be added the appeal through the eye and hand. The intellectual idea must be reduced to a concrete form' (op. cit., p. 22). Apart from the obvious necessity to use as many illustrations as possible, simple dramatic episodes can often quickly clarify abstract ideas or events. Visits to historical sites and buildings are invaluable as a means of introducing children to the reality of history. Making models in the children's own time can be educationally valuable but the limited time usually available for history in the school day could probably be spent in a more profitable manner. While these visual aids can often help to improve thinking skills, it is probably true that they are more useful as a means of clarification rather than as the chief method of teaching history since it is difficult to imagine how their constant use could lead pupils to the formal level of thought in history.

MORAL JUDGEMENTS IN HISTORY

The writer's research also dealt with the moral judgements made by children in history (Hallam, 1969). Although teaching can no doubt help to improve moral judgements, research work seems to show that the most potent influence on children is the family background, particularly when adults discuss moral issues with their children. Liu (Bloom, 1959, p. 7), for instance, found that native-born American children raised in America showed much greater severity of moral judgement and much less subtlety of analysis than Chinese-born Americans raised in America. He considers that the marked differences were due to the greater intimacy of the Chinese-American family and to the influence of Confucian philosophy which encourages the consideration of moral questions. Harrower and Lerner (Flugel, 1955, p. 256) found in England and the United States respectively that immature moral judgements were often more present in children from low social strata than in those who enjoyed greater cultural privileges.

Such research work does not seem to support Piaget's contentions (1932) that children's interaction with peers will lead to the development of individual moral judgements and that the exercise of constraint by adults impairs the development of children's morality. Piaget considers, for example, that democratic practices developed among children playing a game of marbles because there were no children present older than 14 years. Older children would have imposed rules, according to Piaget. He then suggests that most of the phenomena which characterize adult societies 'would be quite other than they are if the average length of human life were appreciably different from what it is' (op. cit., p. 69). Piaget adds that co-operation is necessary for intellectual and moral autonomy (op. cit., p. 103). He does explain that 'co-operation . . . presupposes intelligence' (op. cit., p. 168). Even with this qualification, however, the development of mature moral attitudes in history would seem to require more than peer-group interaction. Indeed, it might be considered that children left without adult control might regress to the level imagined by Golding in 'Lord of the Flies'. Certainly, the present results reveal that children need the guidance of a teacher in order to improve their moral judgements in history, especially if they lack the stimulus of discussion at home.

The children in general tended to make crass judgements on the historical characters considered. The history teacher evidently needs to help his pupils towards more subtlety in moral judgements. The IAAM (1965, p. 6) states that such a task 'will not necessarily be easy. The younger his pupils and the less able they may be, the harder it will be to establish . . . graduated differences'.

The moral judgements of less able children may be improved by their considering the motives behind a person's actions or contrasting the beliefs of different ages. Older pupils should be able to reflect on a number of factors which ought to lead to a balanced historical appraisal of an incident or action. With any age group topics such as slavery, heresy, 'entertainments', or the punishment of criminals can lead to valuable discussions. Bertrand Russell proposes that eloquent statements should be read, say, in favour of burning witches or slavery in order to provoke arguments. Children can also be presented, as A. J. P. Taylor suggests, with two violently different views of the same event. Taylor would then leave the pupils to make up their own minds: 'What we need is more chaos, more disagreement'. It is sadly probable that the minds of many of the subjects in the writer's research were indeed in a confused state when they were left to form their own conclusions. The types of moral judgement expressed confirm the general findings of the writer's research work. Most children below 16 years of age would seem to be far less sophisticated in their thought than is usually imagined. They need mature, sympathetic guidance in order to help them towards the advanced thinking skills desirable in such an abstract subject as history.

ACKNOWLEDGEMENT

This article appeared in *Educ. Res.* (1969), **12**, 3–12, and is published here with the kind permission of author and editor.

REFERENCES

Alilunas, L. J. (1967) The problem of children's historical mindedness. In Roucek, J. S. (Ed.), *The Teaching of History*. London: Peter Owen.

Ausubel, D. P. (1968) *Educational Psychology; A Cognitive View*. New York: Holt, Rinehart and Winston.

Bareham, J. (Ed.) (1969) *Changing World History*. Edinburgh: Holmes McDougall.

Bloom, L. (1967) A reappraisal of Piaget's theory of moral judgement. *J. Genet. Psychol.,* **95**, 3–11.

Booth, M. B. (1967) A critical analysis of the secondary school history curriculum. Unpublished M.A. (Ed.) thesis, University of Southampton.

Bruner, J. S. (1960) *The Process of Education*. Cambridge, Mass: Harvard University Press.

Bruner, J. S. (1961) The act of discovery. In DeCecco, J. P. (Ed.) (1967), *Human Learning in the School*.

Bryant, M. E. (1967) The history syllabus reconsidered. In *History in the Secondary School*. London: Historical Association.

Charlton, K. (1952) The comprehension of historical terms. Unpublished Ed. B. thesis, University of Glasgow.

Evans, K. M. (1962) *Sociometry and Education*. London: Routledge & Kegan Paul.

Flavell, J. H. (1963) *The Developmental Psychology of Jean Piaget*. Princeton: Van Nostrand.

Flugel, J. C. (1955) *Man, Morals and Society*. London: Duckworth.

Golding, W. (1960) *Lord of the Flies*. Harmondsworth: Penguin.

Hallam, R. N. (1966) An investigation into some aspects of the historical thinking of children and adolescents. Unpublished M.Ed. thesis, University of Leeds.

Hallam, R. N. (1967) Logical thinking in history. *Educ. Rev.*, **19**, 183–202.

Hallam, R. N. (1969) Piaget and moral judgements in history, *Educ. Res.*, **11**, 200–206.

Happold, R. C. (1950) *The Approach to History*. London: Christophers.

Hughes, M. M. (1965) A four-year longitudinal study of the growth of logical thinking. Unpublished M.Ed. thesis, University of Leeds.

Hunt, McV. (1961) *Intelligence and Experience*. New York: Ronald Press.

I.A.A.M. (1952) *The Teaching of History* (third ed.). Cambridge University Press.

I.A.A.M. (1965) *The Teaching of History*. Cambridge University Press.

Inhelder, B. & Piaget, J. (1958) *The Growth of Logical Thinking from Childhood to Adolescence*. London: Routledge & Kegan Paul.

Isaacs, N. (1955) *Some Aspects of Piaget's Work*. London: Nat. Froebel Foundation.

Jeffreys, M. V. C. (1939) *History in School*. London: Pitman.

Lewis, E. M. (1960) *Teaching History in Secondary Schools*. London: Evans Bros.

McLaughlin, G. H. (1963) Psycho-logic. *Brit. J. Educ. Psychol.*, **33**, 61–67.

Musgrove, F. (1963) Five scales of attitude to history. In *Studies in Education, III*. University of Hull Institute of Education.

Piaget, J. (1932) *The Moral Judgement of the Child*. London: Routledge & Kegan Paul.

Pines, M. (1969) *Revolution in Learning*. London: Allen Lane.

Place, R. (1959) *Prehistoric Britain*. London: Longmans.

Price, M. (1968) History in danger. *History*, liii, 342–347, London: Historical Association.

Reynolds, J. (1967) The development of the concept of mathematical proof in grammar school pupils. Unpublished Ph.D. thesis, University of Nottingham.

Schools Council (1968) The place of the personal topical history. *Exams. Bull.*, **18**, HMSO.

Sigel, I. E. & Hooper, F. H. (1968) *Logical Thinking in Children*. New York: Holt, Rinehart and Winston, Inc.

Sturt, M. & Oaken, E. C. (1921) The development of the knowledge of time in children. *Brit. J. Psychol.*, **12**, 303–336.

Szeminska (1965) The evolution of thought. In Mussen, P. H. (Ed.), *European Research in Cognitive Development*. University of Chicago Press.

Wall, W. D. (1955) Teaching Methods – psychological studies of the curriculum and of classroom teaching'. In *The Bearings of Recent Advances in Psychology on Educational Problems*. University of London Institute of Education Studies in Education, no. 7. London: Evans Bros.

20   Bruner's concept of strategy: an experiment and a critique

N. E. WETHERICK

INTRODUCTION

Bruner, Goodnow and Austin (1956) presented their subjects with an array of instances and pointed one out as a positive exemplar of a concept they had in mind. The subject had to find the concept by testing other instances; his 'strategy' determined which other instances he selected for test. Bruner distinguished four possible strategies, though the notion is capable of much greater theoretical refinement (e.g., six). The principal distinction is, however, between two broad classes of strategy – what Bruner called 'scanning' and 'focusing' strategies.

The subject using a scanning strategy selects instances that exemplify what he hypothesizes to be the concept the experimenter has in mind. This is clearly an unsatisfactory way to proceed. In Bruner's situation the initial positive instance exemplifies 15 concepts, any one of which may be correct. If a scanner happens to select two or three positive instances in succession, he often concludes that his hypothesis has been confirmed, although the instances may obviously have had more than one concept in common. If he selects a negative instance he has no choice but to start again with a new hypothesis based on his recollection of previous positive instances.

The subject using a focusing strategy has no hypothesis; he selects instances which test the relevance of particular dimensions. If a new instance turns out positive, any dimension that was varied cannot have formed part of the concept; if it turns out negative, at least one of the dimensions varied must be part of the concept. The concept may be identified unequivocally in as many trials as there are dimensions of variation.

Eifermann (1965) pointed out that the criteria by which Bruner characterized his subjects as 'focusers' or 'scanners' are unsatisfactory. In a footnote (Bruner, Goodnow and Austin, p. 95) Bruner suggests that any subject selecting an instance that varies in one dimension only from a previous positive instance is focusing. But an instance that varies in only one dimension will necessarily resemble the previous instance in the remaining three dimensions and they will therefore have seven concepts in common. The subject may have been scanning with one of these concepts as his hypothesis! It is in principle impossible to determine which strategy a subject is pursuing by reference to particular instances that he selects. There are, however, two methods by which the distinction can be made. In one of them the subject is asked to justify his selection verbally (this is the method adopted by Eifermann). The need to justify one's selections may, however, be thought to change the task; and it is pertinent here that, whereas the majority of Eifermann's subjects were focusers ('component-centred' in her terminology), other workers (Bruner, Goodnow and Austin, 1956; Wason, 1960) have usually found a majority of scanners ('concept-centred'). The other method requires the presentation to the subject of two instances that are likely to be equally attractive to a scanner (since they have the same number of concepts in common with the initial positive instance) but only one of which is attractive to a focuser (since only one permits the testing of a dimension whose relevance is still in doubt). Over a series of trials the scanner may select either instance, but the focuser should normally select the focusing instance. The second method was employed in the experiment to be reported here. The object was to distinguish focusers from scanners by showing that, in a series of trials, focusers choose a higher proportion of focusing instances than a scanner would be expected to choose by chance.

METHOD

The tasks

The type of problem employed was described in Wetherick (1966). Two or more instances (letter-groups) are presented and the subject's task is, normally, to find a subset of one or more letters present in the positive instances, but not in any negative instance. In this experiment, 12 of these problems were employed (three each of types 2, 4, 6 and 7). But the problems were presented minus the last instance and the subject's task was to select an instance which in conjunction with the instances already available enabled him to solve the problem. In effect the subject was in a position like that of a subject in Bruner's experiment who, having selected one instance in addition to the initial positive instance, which turned out positive (types 2 and 6) or negative (types 4 and 7), has now to select a second instance. The subjects in this experiment had to select their instance from a set of four, which included (a) the correct instance (which alone enabled the problem to be solved); (b) a dummy instance, which had at least as many concepts in common with the initial positive instance and was, therefore, likely to be at least as attractive to a scanner as the correct instance, but which did not permit the testing of any dimension whose relevance was still in doubt and was, therefore, not attractive to a focuser; and (c and d) two uninformative instances which could not be chosen on any rational ground. For example, in the first type 2 problem set the subject had the initial positive instance BFH and knew he was looking for a single-value concept. The second instance was BDH (also positive) which showed that F could not be the concept. He had now to select one from a set of four instances: ADG, AFH, CEI and BEH. A focuser will look at this stage for an instance which enables him to test the relevance of a dimension that is still in doubt (that is, either B or H) and the only one that does so is AFH; this turns out positive, eliminating B and showing that H must be the concept. A scanner will, however, have chosen a hypothesis – either B or H – and will look for an instance that exemplifies the hypothesis. If the hypothesis chosen was H, he may select AFH, but may also select BEH; if the hypothesis was B, he will have to select BEH. ADG and CEI are uninformative; they could not possibly help to solve the problem.

Procedure

Subjects were tested individually and were taken through a series of simpler problems (with the use of groups of two letters) with explanations at every stage before proceeding to the problems used here. Questions could be asked at any time, and were answered in full even if this meant a virtual repetition of the instructions. There were no time limits.

Subjects

Fifty adult male subjects were employed, ranging in age from 21 to 70. The subjects were drawn from a panel assembled by the MRC Unit for Research on Occupational Aspects of Ageing, Liverpool.

RESULTS

Table 20.1 shows the results obtained. The third column of the table shows the number of occasions on which uninformative instances were chosen. These account for only just over 5 per cent of the total. Any subject choosing at random would have been expected to choose about six instances out of 12 from the 'other' category, but in fact no subject chose more than three, and more than half chose none at all. If all the subjects had been scanners, the dummy would be expected to be chosen more frequently than the correct instance. As was seen in the example above of a type 2 problem, the dummy B E H could be chosen by a scanner whose hypothesis was either B or H, whereas the correct instance could only be chosen by a scanner if his hypothesis was H. If B and H are equally likely hypotheses, the

Table 20.1 Number of subjects choosing correct, dummy or other instances

Problem	Correct	Dummy	Other
Type 2	45	95	10
Type 4	60	74	16
Type 6	50	93	7
Type 7	89	59	2
Total	244	321	35

dummy will, therefore, be selected three times as frequently as the correct instance. By the same reasoning, in problems of type 6 scanners will select the dummy on average five times as frequently as the correct instance. In problems of type 4 and type 7, scanners will be equally likely to select either the dummy or the correct instance. It follows that in this experiment (with the use of three problems of each type) a scanner would be expected to select the correct instance and the dummy in the ratio 4.25/7.75. This may be treated as a binomial distribution with standard deviation 1.66, so that the lowest number of correct choices which is significantly greater than the number expected by chance from a scanner is $4.25 + (1.66 \times 1.64)$ at the 5 per cent level: that is, in effect, 7. Twelve of the 50 subjects scored 7 or more. These 12 made an average of 8.08 correct choices, 3.67 dummy choices and 0.25 other choices. The remaining 38 subjects made an average of 3.87 correct choices, 7.29 dummy choices and 0.84 other choices, which is very close to the calculated chance expectancy for scanners.

Since nonverbal intelligence scores were available for all the subjects, it was possible to hypothesize that there is an association between focusing behaviour and intelligence. The subjects achieved a range of scores on Raven's Progressive Matrices (1938) from 38 to 58. The 12 who could be classified as focusers had a mean score of 52.17, and the remaining 38 a mean score of 48.97. The difference between these means is not quite significant ($t = 1.91$, d.f. $= 48$, $0.10 > P > 0.05$). There appears to be at best only a low degree of association between focusing and nonverbal intelligence; many intelligent subjects are nevertheless scanners.

DISCUSSION

The results of this experiment are in accord with those obtained by Bruner, Goodnow and Austin (1956) and Wason (1960); a majority of intelligent subjects were found to be scanners rather than focusers. Eifermann obtained the opposite result, but this may have been because her subjects had to explain why they selected particular instances or because she used a much smaller array of instances (16 as against Brunner's 81). All these writers agree in thinking that focusing must be a more intelligent strategy to adopt than scanning because of its apparently superior efficiency, and are surprised to find that intelligent subjects do not invariably adopt it. Wickelgren (1964, p. 143) took as his object to find 'cues that elicit analytic-deductive methods in concept attainment' (his name for focusing strategies) and must obviously have been convinced that such cues were worth finding. It could, however, be argued that, if intelligent subjects do not adopt what appears to be the most efficient strategy, this is ground enough to question the representativeness of the experiment. There is a class of real problem situations which experiments in concept attainment purport to represent. Are they in fact truly representative? It is suggested here that they are not for the following reason. In the experimental situation the relevant dimensions of variation are specified either implicitly or explicitly; it is given that the solution to the problem will involve one or more of the specified dimensions. This is never the case with real problems (if we except textbook examples and the like from the class of real problems). In any real problem the problem solver himself has to decide which dimensions of variation to take account of. It can easily be shown that the efficiency of focusing as a strategy depends upon the fact that the relevant dimensions of variation are specified in advance. Suppose there are four specified dimensions, A, B, C and D. Focusing involves testing the relevance of these dimensions (preferably one at a time). The concept will consist of the subset of one or more dimensions that can be proved relevant. If, however, we suppose that A B C D . . . simply constitutes the set of dimensions that we propose to take account of without assuming that any of them necessarily forms part of the concept, and indicate by the dots . . . that there may be relevant dimensions that are not being taken into account, focusing ceases to be a useful procedure. All that we can hope to show by it is that a given dimension is not relevant; we can never show that a dimension is relevant. The consequence is that in real life we have no alternative but to scan. Nothing is to be gained by showing that particular dimensions are irrelevant when the set of dimensions that may be relevant is infinite. Admittedly, we can never be certain of the truth of the hypotheses we adopt as scanners, but it is a commonplace of philosophy that inductively derived concepts are never known to be true. It is always conceivable that nature may spring a surprise on us, apart from any errors of our own.

Whether a subject scans or focuses in the experimental situation will depend on how he sees the task rather than on his intelligence. If he sees the task as a model of real life, he may use the procedure he would have to use in real life: that is, he may scan. He may, however, see the task as a laboratory game in which the object is to play the game as efficiently as possible. If so he will be more likely to focus, since focusing is certainly the most efficient way to play the game in the laboratory.

SUMMARY

An experiment is reported in which subjects were classified as users of scanning or focusing strategies. Twelve out of 50 subjects were classified as focusers, but they did not differ significantly from the scanners in either age or nonverbal intelligence. The argument is advanced that it is a mistake to suppose that focusing is a more intelligent strategy to pursue than scanning. The efficiency of focusing in the laboratory derives from a respect in which the laboratory situation is not representative of real life. In real life persons usually have no choice but to scan.

ACKNOWLEDGEMENT

This article first appeared in *J. Gen Psychol.* (1969), 81, 53–58, and is published here with the kind permission of author and editor.

REFERENCES

Bruner, J. S., Goodnow, J. J. & Austin, G. A. (1956) *A Study of Thinking.* New York: Wiley.
Eifermann, R. R. (1965) Response patterns and strategies in the dynamics of concept attainment behaviour. *Brit. J. Psychol.*, 56, 217–222.
Raven, J. C. (1938) *Progressive Matrices, Sets A, B, C, D and E.* London, England: H. K. Lewis.
Wason, P. C. (1960) On the failure to eliminate hypotheses in a conceptual task. *Quart. J. Exper. Psychol.*, 12, 129–140.
Wetherick, N. E. (1966) The inferential basis of concept attainment. *Brit J. Psychol.*, 57, 61–69.
Wickelgren, W. A. (1964). Cues that elicit analytic-deductive methods in concept attainment. *Brit. J. Psychol.*, 55, 143–154.

PART 7

Learning, retention and recall

INTRODUCTION

Two papers dealing with the practical side of learning in the form of study methods have been included. Both Bassey's and my own articles emphasize study methods amongst higher education students, but the principles involved are not too far removed from studying at secondary level. Also, one way of discovering about learning difficulties is to inspect one's own. My work was a preliminary look at some factors which might influence study habits amongst sixth form, college of education and university students. There is still a great deal of groundwork to be done in exploring the effects of varying kinds of study in terms of general patterns, preparation for examinations, the influence of personal problems, attitudes to study and the impact of student culture. This area is still a comparatively virgin one particularly in regard to the link between study habits and performance.

Bassey's article 'Learning methods in tertiary education' was a deliberate attempt to guide students in their study performance using a number of psychological principles. Readers will doubtless want to read his article with their own problems in mind. Most students have had little, if any, tuition in study tactics; it has always been taken for granted in the British educational system that trial and error is the way to learn. It is important to note, and Bassey is the first to admit this, that study is an individual affair. There is no *one* method

164

suitable for all. One has to look at the advice given, become familiar with the variables involved, and attempt to tailor one's methods in the light of circumstances.

The Bullock Report, *A Language for Life*, arrived on the educational scene at a time when there was growing concern about standards of literacy and numeracy. It deserves to have an impact on the whole realm of learning to cope with reading, writing, oracy, comprehension and other language skills. Downing's paper is a splendid summary of that part of the Report dealing with reading and has some astute observations by him. This paper is not widely circulated, though it should be, and therefore provides another reason for including it. The paper could equally well have appeared in Part 8.

21   Some aspects of study habits in higher education

DENNIS CHILD

INTRODUCTION

It is taken as self-evident that study characteristics are crucial in determining the performance of individuals in all forms of conventional examinations. However, research into study methods has been singularly unhelpful in giving clear indications of the most efficient patterns of study best suited to individuals. This is not surprising, for the complexity of individual activities involved in studying, our inability to make accurate and objective observations (such as the amount of *productive* work ensuing in a study session) and the enormous task of accounting for contributory factors such as personality or the influence of the peer group make research in this field extremely taxing.

In a recent paper by Cooper and Foy (1969) a useful classification of four possible techniques for checking study habits is described. They are detailed interviews, keeping a log or diary of study events, inventories and questionnaires, and direct observation. Of these, the most widespread criterion has been the score from pencil and paper inventories such as the Brown–Holtzman Survey of Study Habits and Attitudes (1956) and the California Study Methods Survey. Basically, the questions attempt to assess, using rating scales, the methods and conditions of study available to the student and his attitudes to studying. Unfortunately, they tell us nothing about the origins of these mechanical or attitudinal characteristics or precise details of individual study styles which an interview profile might show. The questionnaire method has tended to throw light on the degree of study rather than the kind of strategies employed in particular circumstances.

Most American studies have shown a low positive correlation between what are generally accepted as good study procedures and examination results (see Lavin, 1965 for a recent summary). Ahmann, Smith and Glock (1958), on the other hand, concluded that scores taken from study habit inventories (Brown–Holtzman in their case) did not add significantly to a battery of intellectual measures in predicting college grades in the States. In this country, Gibbons and Savage (1965), at a college of education, found no correlation between scores on the Brown–Holtzman inventory and the final examination marks in Education. Similarly, Cooper and Foy (1969) using an inventory compiled from various sources found no relationship between study habits and attitudes and academic attainment for pharmacy students in a university. Their research, along with a number of others, showed conclusively that time spent on study was not a particularly important criterion. Possibly *method* of study is far more relevant than time spent on study.

The use of generalized inventory scores may also have obscured significant study habits which 'pay off' for particular types of examinations and particular academic requirements. It seems there is still a strong case for deriving detailed fundamental descriptive profiles of individual study methods using interviews along the same lines as Thoday (1957). The present enquiry was a field exercise for the 1968 entry to the Diploma in the Psychology and Sociology of Education in the Postgraduate School of Studies in Research in Education. It was devised to give experience in the formulation, administration and analysis of interview questionnaires whilst at the same time providing a pilot interview schedule on study habits which could be employed at a later date.

METHOD

Sample

Seventy-four students from second year sixth forms, 55 from colleges of education and 52 from a technological university were invited to attend an interview lasting about three-quarters of an hour. The sample size was not sufficiently large to allow a breakdown of years in the colleges of education and the university. Nevertheless, all years were interviewed to give the interviewers some experience at dealing with a variety of age groups.

Some account was taken of arts and science bias using 'A' Level subjects and main subject areas at college or university. Where residence in halls, digs etc. was a factor, roughly equal numbers of residents and non-residents were seen. The age range was limited to 25 years and less and married students were omitted (see table 21.1).

Table 21.1   The sample

| | Sixth form | | College of education | | University | |
	Arts	Science	Arts	Science	Arts	Science
Male	15	23	11	10	19	20
Female	23	13	25	9	13	0
Total	74		55		52	

Materials and procedure

Using various source materials such as the Brown–Holtzman inventory and personal judgement, an inventory was compiled in such a way as to explore the study patterns of students using an interview technique. Although specific items were put to the students, they were encouraged to elaborate whenever possible. Four broad aspects were selected for consideration. These involved an examination of the mechanical and attitudinal characteristics in: (a) general study during term time and not immediately before an examination; (b) preparation for examinations. The other areas of interest were the influence on study of: (c) personal problems and (d) the student peer group (see Appendix II for the interview schedule divided into four sections under the foregoing headings). Inevitably, some questions did not fit appropriately into any category and some overlap has occurred.

The interviewers, teachers in schools and colleges of education, saw between 10 and 20 students in their own school or college during the latter half of the Easter term, 1969. In some cases, particularly in the sixth form, the teacher would have taught the pupils, but in retrospect the interviewers were satisfied that the questions had been sufficiently harmless and familiarity with the interviewees had not produced undue distortion of the responses. A fixed preamble (Appendix I) was read to each student about the purposes of the study, the need for frankness and accuracy, and the confidential nature of any information they provided. Interviewers were advised to encourage students to elaborate on their responses where possible.

At this point in the enquiry it was hoped to test the usefulness of the questions and to establish some simple response profiles for the institutions in question. Consequently, the statistics are no more complicated than percentages and the occasional chi-square. Percentages have been rounded off to the nearest whole number since precision to the first decimal place was not appropriate. In most analyses of responses the sample was initially divided by institution, subject area and sex. However, where no significant difference resulted the responses were combined. Hence, in the instances where no distinction is made between institutions, subject areas or sex, it may be taken for granted that no significant difference existed.

RESULTS AND DISCUSSION

The results are treated under the headings indicated on the interview schedule (Appendix II) and items are taken in numerical order.

General study habits

Seventy-nine per cent of students in the sample preferred and used the weekday evenings for private study, particularly the early evening between six and ten o'clock. Evidently 21 per cent favour the late evening after 10 o'clock. Weekends were used more frequently by sixth formers than college and university students ($\chi^2 = 6.61$, d.f. $= 1$, 5 per cent – this percentage is the level of significance reached by the χ^2 value). At home, the sixth former comes under the scrutiny of parents who may insist on some work at weekends. They probably do not go out as much as college and university students. Amongst the latter there seems to have developed a concept of the working week – 'five days shalt thou labour'. Thoday (1957) found a similar low output at weekends for her university sample (25 per cent apparently did no work at all in the weekend prior to Thoday's interview). It has often been said that early morning is the best time for study because the mind is fresh and clear, but very few students (four per cent) found themselves able to take advantage of this suggestion.

Half the sample claim to spend, on average, between one and two hours at each study session, whilst 40 per cent spend more than two hours. The remaining 10 per cent spend less than one hour at a time. The amount of time devoted to each subject varies according to the amount and difficulty of the work set, the interest generated in the subject, the student's ability and the importance of the subject for future qualifications.

The most popular places for studying depend almost exclusively on where the student lives. Those in Halls claim that their studies are the best, those in the sixth form would rather study at home than anywhere else. Quietness (52 per cent), comfort (25 per cent) and convenience for books, materials and home comforts (coffee, cigarettes – 19 per cent) are the three commonest reasons for choosing their favourite place of study. One interesting difference in response rates occurred with reference to the use of libraries. Although a fair proportion of students profess to use the libraries (59 per cent), only 16 per cent actually prefer to study there – an appreciable reduction. When pressed to provide a reason for this, students implied that although libraries were essential for reference sources study was primarily a solitary, noiseless pursuit not deemed to be possible in a typical library. This ties in with the response to a question about revision (Question 24, Appendix II) in which very few (10 per cent) work in pairs, the majority preferring to work in solitary confinement when revising for examinations.

In general students do not take down the exact words of lectures even when given the opportunity (about 35 per cent do). Greater numbers in the sixth form and university take down the precise words of a lecture as compared with colleges of education ($\chi^2 = 13.6$, d.f. = 1, 1 per cent). Of particular note is the absence of any distinction between the arts and science students. It might have been thought that science students in their endeavour to obtain precise information would have preferred to record the exact terms used. However, sixth form scientists do prefer deliberately dictated notes compared with arts or science groups in other institutions ($\chi^2 = 27.6$, d.f. = 1, highly significant). These notes are preferred because the information provided can be taken as accurate, the limits of knowledge required for examination purposes is made clear and less work is required during revision. Alternatively, those students who do not like dictated notes prefer their own because they can follow their own style; in any case, they find dictated notes boring and occasionally difficult to understand at a later date.

A good majority of students (80 per cent) read beyond what is set, there being no difference between arts and science specialists. The main reasons are interest in particular subjects, to widen background knowledge and to exploit another point of view. Fifty-six per cent make notes from these additional readings – a surprisingly low proportion. Thirty-two per cent re-wrote their notes particularly in the university ($\chi^2 = 6.65$, d.f. = 1, 1 per cent when compared with the sixth form) presumably because material is presented and written in haste and needs to be deciphered fairly soon after recording.

When asked what use was made of practical notes, 55 per cent of science students claimed not to use them again; 43 per cent found them valuable for examination revision as supplementary notes. Sixth formers did not think they spent too much time writing up practicals whilst university students held the opposite view ($\chi^2 = 17.5$, d.f. = 1, 0.1 per cent). The reason becomes clear when one compares the average time devoted to practical notes in the sixth form (1.14 hrs/week) with that in the university (5.00 hrs/week).

Some difficulty was experienced in replying to the questions 'where did you first learn how to study?' and 'who taught you?' Students were diffident in their responses, but tended to suggest the secondary grammar school as the most likely place (67 per cent). Just over 20 per cent of the university sample did not think they had started to learn how to study until they had reached the university. Most claimed to be either self-taught (72 per cent) or indirectly assisted by their teachers (21 per cent) chiefly by a process of trial and error. Friends and family have very little direct influence in learning how to study (8 per cent). A substantial proportion of students in this sample (84 per cent) had never read a book about how to study and one wonders who buys these books! Most students recognize some difference between study in the sixth form and college or university, chiefly in having less guidance and direction from teachers and to a lesser extent the work at university is felt to be more interesting and to allow more opportunity for personal exploration. However, sixth formers as compared with college and university students feel secure in having more guidance in what to read and in the timing, planning and analysis of work set ($\chi^2 = 16.3$, d.f. = 1, 0.1 per cent).

The sample was asked if it knew of any current 'tales' prevalent amongst students about aids to improve learning; in a lighter vein it was thought that some of the student folk-lore of study habits might emerge. The outcome was a modest collection of familiar aids such as subliminal learning (particularly tape recorders under the pillow at night), memory 'training' by correspondence course, mnemonics, fact cards and drugs to drown the sorrows or calm the nerves at examination time. This aspect might repay further investigation perhaps in a more informal atmosphere with groups of students. In fact, as an alternative technique, it might prove valuable to tape record conversations between a participant observer and groups of students on the subject of study – often the students trigger each other to trains of thought which could add useful detail.

Examinations

Not surprisingly, very few students systematically revise for examinations (16 per cent) throughout the year and most of these are found in the upper sixth. There was close agreement between sixth formers, college and university students in the time spent in revision before examinations. On average they commence about five to six weeks before the first paper – Easter holidays being the usual landmark for starting revision.

Discovering the required standard for examinations can be quite an elusive affair for students. They appear to use a combination of marks obtained in exercises, comments from teachers and friends and backpapers by which to arrive at a hazy notion of the required standards. However, this particular problem of criteria in final examinations is filled with uncertainties and worries for examinees. Twenty-four per cent simply did not know how to arrive at a confident notion of examination standards. Collaboration between students in discussing examination tactics occurs in 44 per cent of the sample – significantly more so in colleges and university than in the sixth form ($\chi^2 = 7.04$, d.f. = 1, 1 per cent). Discussion centres on the likely questions, ways of revising, question timing and comparing standards.

Question 'spotting' (predicting in advance the subject of exam questions) is practised by 68 per cent of the sample. Teachers of sixth forms also indulge in speculations about possible 'A' Level questions (Arts 87 per cent, Science 69 per cent). Some teachers take this task very seriously and manoeuvre the questions from backpapers with great dexterity. Three-quarters of the sample prefer to select areas for detailed study in preparation for examinations. In the upper sixth, science specialists tend to revise the whole syllabus as compared with other specialists ($\chi^2 = 4.10$, d.f. = 1, 5 per cent). In selecting areas the students are guided mainly by question spotting, intuition or interest.

Prior to examinations about 64 per cent of the students felt nervous. Of these, 80 per cent were anxious during the week preceding the first paper. Once inside the examination room only 26 per cent of the sample experienced nervousness at some stage during the examination (surprisingly, half of these were still anxious at the end of the examination). It would be interesting to compare the examination results for those with and without anxiety during the exam.

Generally students do not admit to having difficulty expressing themselves on paper (65 per cent); only 22 per cent felt they had problems in comprehending questions. Almost 80 per cent managed to finish most papers, but 64 per cent were not satisfied with their timing of the answers. Three-quarters divide the time equally amongst the questions set. The remainder either allow for revision on each question (8 per cent) or time questions as they go (7 per cent).

Personal problems and attitudes

When asked if they felt that personal problems interfered with study, just under 70 per cent *did* experience such interference. The commonest sources of interference were emotional (44 per cent – family, boy or girl friends, feeling 'temperamental'), social (42 per cent – friendships, academic work competing with social activities), academic (9 per cent – feelings of inadequacy) and financial (4 per cent). Ninety-four per cent experienced periods when concentration was impossible primarily because of fatigue, outside attractions and feeling moody. Sixty per cent were disturbed by any kind of noise.

In response to the question 'do you feel that lectures/teachers allow personal prejudices to enter into their assessment', 42 per cent of the group thought they did. Compared with sixth form and university students, in the colleges of education the feeling was particularly strong, principally with respect to school practice assessment ($\chi^2 = 18.69$, d.f. = 1, 0.1 per cent).

During lectures nearly 45 per cent hesitate to ask questions. There is greater reluctance to ask questions in lectures on the part of both art and science specialists in colleges and the university when compared with the sixth formers ($\chi^2 = 7.85$, d.f. = 1, 1 per cent). The main reasons boil down to lack of confidence (40 per cent), fear of displaying ignorance (31 per cent), group too large – shyness (10 per cent), and actively discouraged by teachers (8 per cent). The relationship between the teacher and the student is held to influence the latter's attitude to study by 70 of the sample. The qualities most effective in influencing this relationship are respect for the lecturer (23 per cent of responses; this refers to respect for a teacher's or lecturer's ability both in his subject and in the presentation), sympathetic lecturer (24 per cent), ability to create an informal atmosphere (27 per cent), enthusiasm radiated by the lecturer (6 per cent) and on the debit side – if the lecturer is a perfectionist (12 per cent – sometimes a meticulous teacher can discourage pupils because the latter feel unable to live up to even the most modest expectations). Such expressions as 'friendly', 'friendly but authoritative', 'informal but able' occurred in response to a question about the kind of relationship which appealed to students.

We know precious little about the influence of teaching and lecturing techniques on the study methods and attitudes of the learner. It might repay someone to look at some characteristic teaching styles of a group of teachers and compare these with the patterns of study employed by the pupils [Joyce and Hudson (1968) present one possible, but limited, approach to the subject].

Student peer group

One neglected area of enquiry in this country is the extent to which study habits and strategies are influenced by one's friends. The Americans have gone much further in exploring the nature of agreements and understandings amongst students about their roles as students (Coleman, 1962; Sanford, 1962). The following brief analysis might suggest some possibilities for research.

Over 80 per cent of the sample discussed their marks and the comments made by teachers with their student friends. This collaboration consists essentially in comparing standards with others whilst trying to arrive at a notion of their position relative to the group. Two-thirds of the students are strongly influenced by the marks of their peers particularly if the mark is lower than the norm. In this case, most students (76 per cent) are stimulated by the rivalry and motivated to work harder; but some feel sufficiently dejected (10 per cent) for it to have an adverse effect on their efforts.

Amongst sixth formers about 32 per cent were persuaded by friends to go out. At college and university 55 per cent were persuaded – a higher proportion ($\chi^2 = 9.52$, d.f. $= 1$, 1 per cent). Moreover, 38 per cent of all students had feelings of guilt when they went out, primarily because they imagined they should be working. Very few (15 per cent) had arrangements with friends and neighbours about regular study times, i.e. when it was accepted that study was taking place.

Students nowadays are not particularly embarrassed at appearing enthusiastic about academic work in front of their fellows (only 11 per cent were disturbed). In fact, in only 25 per cent of cases was it frowned on to talk shop out of school or college time. The commonest topics of conversation outside lectures and relating to work appear to be lecture content (28 per cent), lecturers (20 per cent), current academic problems (19 per cent), assessments (16 per cent), lecture load (12 per cent) and personal prospects (3 per cent).

Thirty-seven per cent of the sample discuss between themselves the criteria for a reasonable stint of work in an attempt to arrive at a group norm. A similar percentage also discuss ways in which work can be presented in order to please particular teachers. This occurs with greater frequency in colleges of education and university than in the sixth form ($\chi^2 = 6.35$, d.f. $= 1$, 5 per cent). A quarter of the sample also discuss with friends how to avoid being rebuked by teachers or lecturers and how to discover their expectations.

Can students bring pressure to bear on teachers when the standard or content of lessons is not what the students anticipate to be good enough? Just over half the sample felt pressure could be applied by either direct means, using general classroom conversation or a spokesman (62 per cent), or indirect approaches (38 per cent). The latter include emphasizing a point jokingly (the 'many a true word spoken in jest' approach), adopting a policy of non-cooperation or non-attendance, systematic harassment or prompting if the atmosphere in the class will allow and by gestures and grimaces!

Clearly most of these questions require considerable elaboration and further research.

There are many more questions which could have been posed. However, longwinded interviews would not have fulfilled the function for which the inventory was devised. Biographical information was also collected and a future task will be to interrelate individual patterns of study to this information and the results of examinations.

APPENDIX I

Preamble which should be read to the student:

The questions which I am going to ask are part of an enquiry being carried out by the School of Education, University of Bradford into the study habits of students in sixth forms, colleges and universities. For the enquiry to be of any benefit, possibly in advising students on good study methods, it is *absolutely essential* that you answer the questions as accurately as you possibly can. Any information you supply will be treated in the strictest confidence and will only be used by the School of Education to give a general picture of the study habits of groups and *not* individuals.

APPENDIX II University of Bradford Postgraduate School of Studies in Research in Education

Students' study habits schedule

•   •   •

General study

1 When do you usually study?
2 Do you have a favourite time of day? Yes/No When?
3 In allocated study periods do you usually work (a) all the time (b) some of the time (c) hardly at all?
4 Do you, on average, spend at each study session outside school (or in your own time at college)

        a long (more than two hours)?

        a medium (between one and two hours)?

        or a short time (less than one hour)?
5 Do you spend the same time on each subject? Yes/No

        If No, why not?
6 Where do you usually study (note all places)?
7 Where do you most like to study?
8 If you get the chance do you generally take down the exact words of lessons/lectures? Yes/No
9 Do you prefer dictated notes? Yes/No

        Why?
10 Do you read in subjects beyond what is set? Yes/No

        If Yes, why?
11 Do you make notes from your reading? Yes/No

12 (Where applicable) What use do you make of your practical laboratory notes (or work with children)?

13 Do you think you spend a lot of time writing up practical work? Yes/No
How long would you estimate per week?   hrs.

14 Do you re-read notes taken in class (lecture)? Yes/No
Do you re-write notes taken in class (lecture)? Yes/No

15 Where did you first learn how to study?
Who taught you?

16 How do you think you developed your present study methods?

17 Have you ever read a book on how to study? Yes/No

18 How does study at university/college/in the sixth differ from the sixth/further down the school?

19 (Where applicable) What did you discover about study at college/university/sixth form, before you entered?

20 Do your teachers give you cues to study methods? Yes/No
If Yes, in what way?

21 Have you heard any 'tales' about how to improve study, e.g. unusual aids to passing exams or to help the memory?

Examinations

22 Do you revise for exams throughout the year? Yes/No
If not, how long before you begin?

23 Are some kinds of notes better than others from which to revise? Yes/No
What sort?

24 Do you revise with someone else? Yes/No

25 How do you discover what is the required standard for exams?

26 Do you discuss exam tactics with your friends? Yes/No
If Yes, what do you discuss?

27 Do you 'spot' questions? Yes/No
Do your teachers 'spot' questions? Yes/No

28 Do you select certain areas for detailed study rather than the whole syllabus? Yes/No
If Yes, how do you decide what to choose?

29 Are you nervous before exams? Yes/No
If Yes how long before?

30 Are you nervous during exams? Yes/No
If Yes how long for?

31 Do you have difficulty expressing yourself on paper? Yes/No

32 Do you have difficulty comprehending the questions? Yes/No

33 Do you usually manage to finish exam papers? Yes/No
Do you have difficulty in timing answers? Yes/No

34 How do you divide the time?

Personal problems and attitudes

35 Do you feel that personal problems interfere with study? Yes/No
If Yes, what kind of problems (family, girls, home study conditions, etc.)?

36 Do you feel that lecturers/teachers allow personal prejudices to enter into their assessment? Yes/No
  If Yes, what makes you feel this?
37 Do you have periods when concentration on study seems impossible? Yes/No
  If Yes, give examples
38 Are you easily upset by noise or other disturbances when you study? Yes/No
39 Do you hesitate to ask questions in lectures/lessons? Yes/No
  If Yes, why?
40 Do you think your relationship with the teacher affects your attitude to study? Yes/No
  If Yes, why?
41 What kind of relationship appeals to you?
42 Do you think that the subject matter of lessons/lectures is, by and large, a waste of time? Yes/No

Student culture

43 Do you discuss your marks with other students? Yes/No
44 Do you compare standards with others? Yes/No
  Do the marks of others in your group influence you? Yes/No
  If Yes how?
45 Do your friends persuade you to go out? Yes/No
46 Do you feel guilty about study when you go out? Yes/No
  If Yes, why?
47 What helps you to decide whether to go out?
48 Do you have arrangements with your friends about regular study times? Yes/No
49 Do you mind appearing to be enthusiastic about academic work? Yes/No
  or do you sometimes disguise the fact that you are enthusiastic in front of your friends? Yes/No
50 Is it frowned on to talk 'shop' out of university/college/school? Yes/No
51 If you talk about academic matters with friends, what are the most common topics of conversation?
52 Have you discussed with your friends what is a reasonable stint of work? Yes/No
  If Yes, how do you decide on a reasonable stint?
53 Do your friends' views about study or exam tactics influence you? Yes/No
54 Do you discuss ways in which you can please particular lecturers/teachers? Yes/No
55 How do you discover the expectations of particular lecturers/teachers?
56 Do you talk over with your friends how you can avoid being rebuked by lecturers/teachers? Yes/No
57 Do you find that you can bring pressure to bear on some lecturers/teachers to 'deliver the goods'? Yes/No
  If Yes, in what ways?

• • •

ACKNOWLEDGEMENT

This article first appeared in *Int. J. Educ. Sci.* (1970), **4**, 11–20, and is published here with the kind permission of the editor.

REFERENCES

Ahmann, J. S., Smith, W. L. & Glock, M. D. (1958) Predicting academic success in college by means of a study habits and attitudes inventory. *Educ. Psychol. Measur.*, **18**, 853–857.

Brown, W. F. & Holtzman, W. H. (1956) *Manual of the Brown–Holtzman Survey of Study Habits and Attitudes.* New York: The Psychological Corporation.

Coleman, J. S. (1961) *The Adolescent Society.* New York: The Free Press.

Cooper, B. & Foy, J. M. (1969) Students' study habits and academic attainment. *Univ. Qu.*, **24**, 203–212.

Gibbons, K. C. & Savage, R. D. (1965) Intelligence, study habits and personality factors in academic success – a preliminary report. *Durham Res. Rev.*, **16**, 8–12.

Joyce, C. R. B. & Hudson, L. (1968) Student style and teacher style: an experimental study. *Br. J. Med. Educ.*, **2**, 28–32.

Lavin, D. E. (1965) *The Prediction of Academic Performance.* New York: John Wiley.

Sanford, N. (1962) (Ed.) *The American College.* New York: John Wiley.

Thoday, D. (1957) How undergraduates work. *Univ. Qu.*, **11**, 172–181.

22 Learning methods in tertiary education

MICHAEL BASSEY

Teaching and learning are so intimately related that the competent teacher needs to be an expert on effective methods of learning as well as of teaching. It has often been said that where there is no learning there can be no teaching; it must also be true that where there is ineffective learning there can be only ineffective teaching.

The majority of students entering higher education are meeting lectures, seminars, tutorials and extensive periods of private study for the first time and the adjustment to these unfamiliar methods of learning is not easy, particularly for students coming from schools where their work was very closely organized by their school-teachers.

There is a number of identifiable study skills and useful habits, applicable to many different academic disciplines, and it is often helpful to students if these are discussed with their tutors early in their course. It must be stressed however that skills and habits are only acquired through practice and that in discussion students cannot be said to learn them, but to learn about them. (For example, nobody learns the skills of motor car driving by reading a manual; he only learns about the skills of driving).

In a simple analysis the aims of a student are to gain the maximum knowledge and experience in the minimum of time. Certain pointers to the achievement of these will now be described.

METHODS OF IMPROVING THE GAIN IN KNOWLEDGE

The first important point about academic learning is that this is dependent on the level of interest. The more one is motivated to learn, the more one is likely to learn. In a lecture the arousal of interest may seem to be largely the responsibility of the lecturer, but it is possible for the student to develop his own interest as a deliberate manoeuvre. This is done by asking unspoken questions. The student who attends a lecture after meditating on the title and thinking out some of the points that he hopes will be illuminated, is more likely to be attentive and receptive than his fellow who has arrived with an empty mind. This is even more valuable in reading; one of the most useful steps in the SQ3R approach, described later, is skimming through the headings of a chapter and formulating questions.

Note taking from lectures and books is a step in the learning process and these notes need to be both legible and intelligible, for subsequent learning, and adequate in their coverage of information. To achieve these during lectures is not easy and so students should be recommended to develop the habit of going over their lecture notes shortly after the lecture. This means that headings and sub-headings can be clearly marked, some omissions remedied and obscurities either clarified or obliterated, while the lecture is relatively fresh in the memory.

In personal copies of textbooks an alternative to writing a set of notes is to underline key phrases and to add sub-headings in margins.

Having made his notes a student needs to master them and it is fairly obvious that if the new knowledge is integrated with earlier material and has some kind of intelligible logical structure it is more easily remembered. For example ABEFIJOPUV is more easily remembered than FBEUJVAPIO because it integrates with previous knowledge of alphabetical order and of the vowels and it has a logical structure. These aspects may not be entirely in the hands of the student though he should both recognize the importance of, and feel that there is ample opportunity for, asking questions of clarification if he fails to comprehend the logical structure of a piece of teaching.

The practice of regularly following up lectures by making sure that the points have been thoroughly remembered is a valuable study habit, although few students seem to find the time or energy for doing this well. Too often it seems such revision occurs only shortly before the examination! Later the regular follow up of lectures is described as 'feedback learning'; the effect of the feedback, or re-learning, being to increase the intake of information.

Students often fail to appreciate the merit of recitation in the learning process. This does not mean the monotonous repetition of rote material, but the silent recall of the points in a section of notes or chapter, with the book closed. This active method of learning is much more effective than the passive method of re-reading notes.

METHODS OF MINIMIZING STUDY TIME

It was said earlier that the student seeks to gain the maximum knowledge in the minimum time. How can he reduce the time spent on study without losing in effectiveness?

In one respect, namely reading, there are well credited procedures whereby the speed of work can be increased, although considerable practice is required. There is a number of agencies through which this improvement can be achieved – books, films, special projectors, and machines-which-chase-you-down-the-page. Some are mentioned in the 'Further Study' list. Within limits, the increase in reading speed does not cause a loss in reception of information. (Although a cautionary tale is told of the man who, as a result of a quicker reading course, read *War and Peace* in twenty minutes. Questioned, he said, 'It's about Russia.')

In a more general sense students will conserve their study time if they learn to use Parkinson's Law of the Work–Time Relation: 'Work expands to fill the time available for its completion'. When first enunciated in 1957 this was seen as a witty criticism of the activity of certain civil servants; subsequently it has been recognized as a valid law of human behaviour. Parkinson's Law is used by deciding a time for the completion of a piece of work. For example a student may give himself two hours to write an essay, and may thus complete it in about that time, rather than, say, the three or four hours which it might have taken without a planned end-time.

Further to this students should be recommended to devise a regular weekly plan for their own study. In the notes for students which appear later in this paper, the keeping of a work diary is advocated in which the student keeps a record of the lectures he has attended and puts ticks when he has organized his notes, supplemented them by reading (if necessary), and learned them by active recall. He thus has a simple visual check on his study progress.

THE SQ3R METHOD OF READING

An elaborate research programme at the Ohio State University in the 1940s resulted in a method of study known as SQ3R. It consists of five stages – Survey, Question, Read, Recite, Review. It can be thoroughly recommended.

Before engaging in a piece of reading, *survey* the writing first. Try to construct in your mind a map of the route, based on the major landmarks which may be indicated by section headings, captions to charts and diagrams, and possibly the first lines of paragraphs, or words in italics or bold print. Get an idea of the ground to be covered before you become immersed in detail.

As you make this survey try to ask a *question* of each point on the route. Begin to wonder what this term means, how this point is relevant, why the author has used that example. This should help arouse your interest in the subject and promote learning when you read through the sections and (presumably) find answers to your questions.

The next step is the familiar one of reading, but try to *read* in an active way, sorting out the pieces which you want to remember (perhaps underlining words if it is your own book, or making separate notes if it isn't) and asking questions of the book as you move through it.

If it is very difficult material, due to the obtuseness of the author or your own unfamiliarity with the subject, try and find the main idea in each paragraph and put a precis of each on a notepad. Ignore everything except the points which seem to be the main idea – in well-written prose there should be only one per paragraph. By this paragraph analysis you should be able to get the gist of the work and a second or third reading should make the detail clearer. Don't be put off by paragraphs which you can't follow – skip these and come back to them, because later material may resolve their meaning.

After reading a section comes the step which is all important for remembering purposes. *Recite* the points which you want to remember. This means recreate them silently, in your mind, and in your own words, without prompting from the text. Then go back and see what you have missed. As your reading progresses, go back over earlier sections, from time to time, and ensure that you can still recite the selected points from these.

Finally, at the end of a chapter, say, comes the *review*. This is a second survey of the chapter, but instead of trying to draw a map of the route you are making sure that you can find your way blindfolded! The review is really a recitation of all the points that you intend to remember. It is useful to carry this out not only as soon as you have completed the chapter, but again in two or three days' time and perhaps again after a further interval. This helps to establish the material firmly in your mind.

The allocation of time to these five activities – survey, question, read, recite and review – should vary according to the material. If it is mainly concerned with developing a concept then most of your time will be spent on reading, in trying to grasp the underlying idea, for once you have achieved this you are likely to retain it. On the other hand factual material where there are numbers of points which you need to retain may require half of your time spent on recitation and review.

SELF ORGANIZED STUDY

Lecturing is like throwing mud at a wall: some never reaches it, some sticks, and some sticks but later drops off. This section aims to show how students can ensure that as much mud as possible sticks.

The basic hypothesis is illustrated in figure 22.1. It is supposed that of the many factors influencing the academic ability of a student, his intelligence and his study effectiveness will

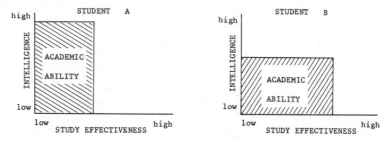

Figure 22.1   The hypothesis of instruction in effective study methods.

be the most significant and, for the sake of simplicity, it is supposed that the product of these two will correlate with his academic ability. Thus the two students of figure 22.1 have equal academic ability because the higher intelligence of A is compensated for by the higher study effectiveness of B.

(From a scientific view it is nonsense to talk of quantities such as 'study effectiveness', 'academic ability' and even 'intelligence' without defining them, but metaphoric nonsense can sometimes be useful.)

At the present time no method is known whereby a student may increase his intelligence, but there are methods which may help the average student to improve his study effectiveness and consequently to increase his academic ability. These methods are based partly on the results of psychological experiments and partly on the application of Parkinson's Law of the Work–Time Relation.

Psychological evidence points to the conclusion that the more information is *used* the more likely it is to be remembered, especially if it is applied in a different context to that in which it was first met. This is why you are set problems and exercises, but if you are to be really successful in your work as a *student*, i.e. one who studies, you should exercise your knowledge to a much wider extent than your set work requires.

Figure 22.2 shows the curve of forgetting. In an experiment five equally able groups of students were given some material to learn. Group 'A' was tested immediately after learning and was found to have remembered 52 per cent of the information. Group 'B' was tested one day later and remembered 28 per cent. Group 'C' at seven days had 20 per cent, Group 'D' at 14 days had 12 per cent and Group 'E' at 21 days had 9 per cent.

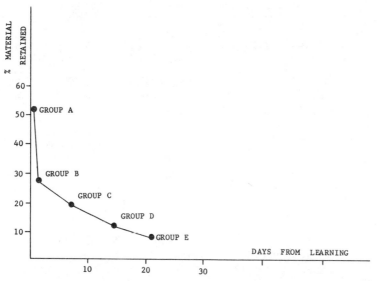

Figure 22.2   Experimental evidence 1: the curve of forgetting.

Each group was later tested again, and these additional results are shown with the earlier ones in figure 22.3. After seven days Group 'A' had remembered considerably more than Group 'B' had after one day, and this must have been due to the practice that they had gained, or, in other words, the re-learning, in their test on the same day of learning. Likewise after 63 days they still retained more than any other group. From this experiment, and many others in which these results have been confirmed, we draw conclusions about the importance of re-learning.

The processes of memory are illustrated in figure 22.4 and it will be noticed that there are three junctions: material is either learned or not learned, that which has been learned is either remembered or forgotten, and that which has been remembered is either recalled or

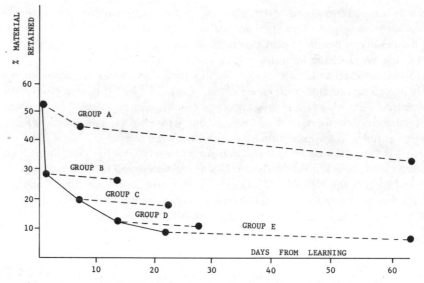

Figure 22.3   Experimental evidence 2: the value of feedback learning.

recognized. 'Recall' is retrieving material from the memory unaided; 'recognizing' is remembering with the aid of a prompt. The reason that most people find it easier to remember faces than names is that one involves recall and the other recognition. The latter is, of course, an easier method of remembering.

The ratio of material 'learned' to 'not learned' depends upon a number of factors including the interest of the learner and how awake or tired he is. Advice such as 'be interested in your subject' or 'go to bed early' is either obvious or unhelpful, and in general there is little that can be suggested to affect this ratio. (One book on study methods does recommend that the student should sit in the middle of the front row of the lecture room: it does not discuss the obvious difficulty!)

If we include all that is written down in lecture notes as 'learned', even if the retention time is sometimes as short as that between hearing information and writing it, then the most important junction is that which divides the 'lost' from the 'retained'. A method is available

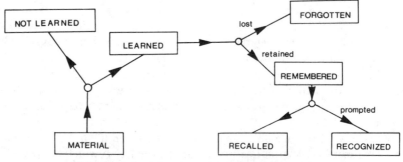

Figure 22.4   The three junctions of memory.

for increasing the amount retained, and likewise it may improve recall memory compared to recognition. The method is that of re-learning, or feedback learning, and can be induced from the experimental results described earlier.

Feedback learning is compared with straight learning in figure 22.5. Material that has been learned once is learned a second time, and in consequence a greater proportion is subsequently remembered.

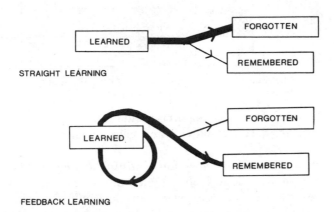

Figure 22.5   Comparison of feedback learning with straight learning.

But how can the method be applied? 'This method may be fine, but I haven't the time to use it', is a common view. First, define the problem: time for work is limited. Second, what relationship is there between work and time? The answer was given in 1957 by Professor Northcote Parkinson:

WORK EXPANDS TO FILL THE TIME AVAILABLE FOR ITS COMPLETION

Third, apply this relationship: limit the amount of time that is to be made available for each piece of work. Plan ahead.

PLAN AHEAD

Two levels of planning are suggested. Draw up a weekly Work Plan for the term of the form shown in figure 22.6 and enter on it your teaching engagements (lectures, tutorial, practicals, etc.) and your proposals for study time. Decide on regular hours during which you aim to work; be realistic, plan for as much as you can reasonably hope to cope with, but not more. Try to be as punctual with these private study times as you are (?) with lectures. This requires, of course, sufficient will-power to say to one's friends: 'I must go now. I am starting work at nine o'clock.' It needs the same certainty as saying: 'I must go now. I have a lecture at nine o'clock.'

The second level of planning work is deciding what to do during the time reserved for study. A few students keep written plans of what they intend to do at a given time, but most

MON	TUES	WED	THURS	FRI	SAT	SUN
INORGANIC LECTURE 9-10	STUDY 9-10	ORGANIC LECTURE 9-10	STUDY 9-10	PHYS-CHEM LECTURE 9-10	STUDY 11-1	STUDY 11-1
PHYSICS LECTURE 10-11	PHYSICS LECTURE 10-11	CHEMISTRY TUTORIAL 10-10.30	PHYSICS LECTURE 10-11	MATHS LECTURE 12-1		STUDY 7-10
MATHS LECTURE 12-1	INORGANIC PRACTICAL 11-1 2-5	MATHS EXER. CLASS 12-1	MATHS LECTURE 12-1	PHYSICS PRACTICAL 2-4		
STUDY 2-4		STUDY 2-4	STUDY 2-4			
STUDY 7-10			STUDY 7-10			

Figure 22.6   A work plan for a chemistry student.

carry out work on an *ad hoc* basis. The important thing is to have planned out in your mind what you are going to do during a study session before your allotted starting time. Plan ahead.

Sit down at nine o'clock with the intention of writing the required essay by ten o'clock, or of checking over yesterday's lecture notes by ten-thirty. Sometimes, perhaps usually at first, you need more time than you have given yourself. Don't just drift on, fix a new time limit and aim for that. This approach, of time budgetting, is to apply Parkinson's Law usefully.

There are two types of pressure acting on private study times, set and unset work. Unfortunately, and for obvious reasons, set work tends to oust unset work. Set work is the essays, exercises, reading, etc, which have to be prepared for handing in or for tutorials, while the unset work is the essential activity of assimilating material given in lectures. Because it is here that so many students are ineffective it is worth while preparing a system which keeps a check on progress.

In the follow-up of a lecture, three operations are recommended. Firstly, *organize* your notes: delete irrelevancies, underline headings, clarify obscurities, number pages. Secondly, *supplement*. From discussion, or reading, additional material may be worth inserting in the notes. (The need for supplementing depends very much on the subject and the teaching style of the lecturer.) Thirdly, *learn*. The material in your notes has been through your mind once in the lecture*; now, in accordance with the ideas of feedback learning, go through it again, perhaps twice. This last stage is an essential prerequisite of effective learning; the other two depend upon circumstances.

In order to ensure that this follow-up is carried out the keeping of a simple *work diary* is recommended as in figure 22.7. Day by day the main 'learning events' are entered in the boxes, and ticked when their notes have been organized, when (or if) supplemented, and when learned. The term 'learning events' for many students will mean just lectures, but where set reading is an important part of the course, the notes which you make on this need feedback learning in the same way as lecture notes. Likewise material to be learned may arise

---
* Notwithstanding the remark that 'a lecture is a process whereby material is transferred from the notes of the lecturer to the notes of the students without going through the minds of either.'

DAY	MON			TUES	WED	THURS		FRI	
LECTURE	INORGANIC	PHYSICS	MATHS	PHYSICS	ORGANIC	PHYSICS	MATHS	PHYS/CHEM	MATHS
DATE	14.10.68	"	"	15.10.68	16.10.68	17.10.68	"	18.10.68	"
Organized	✓	✓	✓	✓	✓	✓		✓	
Supplemented	✓				✓			✓	
Learned	✓	✓		✓	✓				

Figure 22.7   A work diary for a chemistry student. The chart shows that his 'lecture follow-up' for this week is about two-thirds complete.

from practical classes and tutorials, although usually these are a form of feedback learning that aims deliberately to use the material given previously in lectures.

A work diary of this form constantly reminds of the importance of keeping unset work up to date. (There is little need of a system to remind about set work.)

The most successful methods of learning are those that are *active* rather than *passive*. Reading is a passive method of learning; recalling the main ideas of a chapter after reading it is an active method. Some people are able to remember material having read it through once or twice, but the majority find that this is not nearly such an effective method as reading and then reciting the main ideas.

Every lecture and piece of reading contains a number of points which are worth being remembered precisely. Sometimes it is only one or two, other times a dozen or more. The postcard method is an effective way of learning these. These key points are written as brief notes on a postcard and are carried in pocket or handbag for a day or two. At odd moments in the day – while waiting for a bus, queueing for lunch, last thing at night – these points are recalled; the postcard being consulted if something is forgotten. This method can result in a considerable improvement in the retention of information. A variation is to use a very small pocket notebook for the same purpose.

Is it necessary to stress that while underwork may lead to the premature termination of your course the same may be true of overwork?

> If you can fill each unforgiving minute,
> With sixty seconds worth of time well run,
> Yours is the world and everything that's in it
> And a coronary at 51.

In summary, the following suggestions have been made, which should lead to more effective study:

1 Keep to a planned and regular schedule of study time (written).
2 Plan beforehand the work and time of each study session (unwritten).
3 Practise feedback learning of your lecture notes and keep a regular record of progress (written).

Figure 22.8 (a and b) contains a blank plan and a blank weekly work diary. You are recommended to draw up your own and to use them.

MON	TUES	WED	THURS	FRI	SAT	SUN

Figure 22.8a   Plan of work.

DAY									
LECTURE									
DATE									
Organized									
Supplemented									
Learned									

Figure 22.8b   Work diary.

ACKNOWLEDGEMENT

This paper is published with the kind permission of the author. Copyright, 1968, Michael Bassey.

FURTHER STUDY

(1) *Study methods*

Crow and Crow (1963) *How to Study*. Crowell-Collier.
Mace (1968) *The Psychology of Study*. Pelican.
Maddox (1963) *How to Study*. Pan.
Morgan and Deese (1957) *How to Study*. McGraw-Hill.

(2) *Faster reading*

Bayley (1957) *Quicker Reading*. Pitman.
de Leeuw and de Leeuw (1965) *Read Better, Read Faster*. Pelican.
Fry (1963) *Reading Faster* and *Teaching Faster Reading*. Cambridge U.P.

23   Psychology and the Bullock Report*

JOHN DOWNING

•   •   •

The Bullock Report's (Department of Education and Science, 1975) recommendations for improving the teaching of reading in England can be viewed as some of the phenomena of the education scene in England. Then they can be regarded as data for the psychological study of the behaviour of English educators. This was the approach followed in the *Comparative Reading* project (Downing, 1973).

The 'Comparative Reading' study was an international investigation of some of the factors which influence the experiences of children learning to read. Great Britain was one of the 14 countries selected to represent important cultural and linguistic differences. The aim was exploratory. It was hoped that this new research method would suggest hypotheses about the universal variables in learning to read. Because it was an initial exploration of a new area of research in reading, an open-ended approach was called for. One or two specialists in reading education were commissioned to write a descriptive account of teaching and learning to read in the country with which they were familiar. Each national contributor was given a great deal of freedom to allow him to stress spontaneously what were considered to be the chief characteristics of reading education in that country. In addition, three special studies were made: (1) methodological problems in cross-cultural research in education; (2) the attitudinal content of children's reading primers in different countries; and (3) a review of previous cross-cultural research on reading education. All the resulting data from the national reports and these three special studies were analysed for universal and idiosyncratic features of learning to read. As a scientific precaution, all the national reports and special studies were published verbatim in the volume, as well as their analysis.

The most important finding of the *Comparative Reading* report was that culture is an important variable in learning to read. The child's experiences in the task of literacy acquisition vary from country to country and some of these variations are extensive. The most outstanding example of this cultural variation was the differential prominence given to reading education in the several countries studied. At one extreme is the United States in which reading instruction has the highest priority, typified by the current 'Right to Read' programme. At the other are a number of countries in which less emphasis is placed on the teaching of reading. This is for a variety of reasons – economic, political, philosophical. But the important fact from the standpoint of psychology is that the child learning to read experiences widely differing degrees of pressure from parents and teachers according to the country in which he happens to go to school. Children in England do not appear to be under the most extreme pressure from the point of view of the cultural value of literacy, but

---

* Opening address for the Annual Conference of the British Psychological Society (Education Section), University of Sheffield, 6–8 September 1975.

two other factors in the English education system raise the pressure considerably so that many pupils cannot cope with the task. The first is the comparatively very early age of beginning school, and the second is the tradition that there is something wrong with the child who has not mastered the basic processes of reading by the age of seven. These two conventions create an artificial 'critical period' for learning to read. If English parents and educators were more flexible about the time for beginning and the necessary period for learning reading, it is likely that far fewer children would become disabled in reading.

However, the customs and institutions of a culture are well known to be very hard to change. Changes occur but they are usually within the grooves of custom. This seems to be the case with the recommendations of the Bullock Report. These were quite predictable from the national characteristics of English reading education detected in the 'Comparative Reading' study. Indeed, the Bullock Report provides new data to confirm the 'Comparative Reading' findings.

The phenomenon of change in educational practices is itself subject to cultural variation. When I was a visiting Professor at a university in the United States, I arranged for a group of my students to go to England to conduct their own research projects on English primary schools. One night they were being entertained to dinner by a famous Director of Education in the North East of England and he began the conversation by asking them why they had come to England. My student said 'to see for ourselves the revolution in English primary education'. The Director replied, 'in English education we have evolution, not revolution'. This is one of the chief differences between reading education in the United States and in England. In America there are rapid swings of the pendulum on the national scale in accordance with dramatic shifts in public fashion, and on the local scale with changes in the chief administrator who tends to have to act as a leader who has to maintain a distinctive and popular image. Strange to say, the outcome is not necessarily more rapid progress. American educational changes sometimes put the clock back, as happened when the Sputnik panic stampeded the schools into returning to formal alphabetic and phonic methods of teaching reading during the past decade.

One aspect of reading education treated in the Bullock Report quite unintentionally provides an interesting example of this characteristic evolutionary development in a consistent direction that contrasts so markedly with the treatment of the same aspect of reading in America. This is the question of the use of a comparatively recent innovation – the Initial Teaching Alphabet (i.t.a.). In America, i.t.a. has been subject to the usual swings of the pendulum both locally and nationally during the past 12 years. One school superintendent will adopt i.t.a. for every elementary school in his city. Then later, when he is replaced, i.t.a. goes with him. Nationally i.t.a. became the latest cure-all fad. But in many school districts *after a few months* it was rejected because it 'hadn't worked'. As a result, probably about 2 per cent of American elementary schools use i.t.a. today. In contrast, the Bullock Committee's survey in England found 10 per cent of schools with infants using i.t.a. If growth in the use of i.t.a. may be regarded as a measure of innovative change, it seems that the English evolutionary adaptation has produced five times as much change as the American's more dramatic pattern for innovation.

Of course, English education has not been free from exaggerated claims for the value of i.t.a., but these have tended to slow its adoption all along. The Bullock Report remarks that these overenthusiastic advocates for i.t.a. have annoyed teachers by their naive oversimplified view of the process of learning to read which is, in fact, highly complex. Thus, the Report states:

The experienced infant teacher can only be irritated by the suggestion that all that is needed to bring about general improvement in reading is the introduction of a simplified code [p. 110].

But the Bullock Committee's advice to teachers is to put these attitudes to one side. Then, the Report suggests that

... teachers should examine the question of i.t.a. on its merits. We hope they will make their own objective assessment of the various arguments for and against, and not accept the tendentious statements that are still made by some of its advocates and opponents [p. 112].

The Bullock Committee's own conclusions on the effectiveness of i.t.a. are based on the favourable findings of the Schools Council's report on i.t.a. (Warburton and Southgate, 1969). Therefore, the Bullock Report recommends that 'schools which choose to adopt it should be given every support' (p. 112).

As my American student was so properly, if tartly, informed, English education prefers a gradual evolutionary change. This characteristic is clearly discernible in other aspects of the Bullock Report. Its effect is particularly important in two ways: (1) the Bullock Committee's discussion of public accusations that literacy standards have fallen; and (2) their recognition and careful presentation of what they consider to be good in current principles and practices in the teaching of reading in English schools.

With regard to the alleged falling off in standards of literacy, the Bullock Committee coolly, calmly and with meticulous care examined all the evidence that could be brought to bear on this question. The evidence and its discussion are an outstanding contribution of the Report in the high quality of the objective reporting. It seems clear that the belief that standards have dropped is false. Typical also of the slow-but-sure feature of educational change in England is the Bullock Committee's refusal to feel complacent about the preservation of good standards of reading and writing. The Report recognizes that there has been, and there will continue to be a national need for higher and higher levels of skill in reading and expressive writing. Therefore, it calls for still better results than the good ones already being achieved.

Turning to the other effect of the cultural preference for evolutionary change – the careful conservation of what is considered to be good in the English education system – there are two established principles which are safeguarded throughout the Bullock Report: (1) the principle of child-centredness; and (2) the principle of school autonomy. As was shown in *Comparative Reading* the second of these principles is essential for the full implementation of the first.

Child-centred education was spelled out in the 1944 Education Act's demand that each child should be taught according to his age, ability and aptitude. The very title of the Plowden Report confirmed the same principle – that is, *Children and Their Primary Schools* (Central Advisory Council for Education, 1967). Now the Bullock Report gives a detailed account of the practical implications of child-centredness for the teaching of reading. Unlike the curriculum-centred approach found in many other countries, the emphasis on starting from the child's point of view, which is a feature of modern primary education in England, fixes the goal firmly on what the child is learning rather than on what the teacher believes he is teaching. When this principle is applied to best effect, it makes the best possible use of the pupil's time, because the teacher does not waste time teaching things which the child already knows, and because the teacher provides the appropriate stimulus at the most opportune moment for assimilation. An especially valuable contribution of the Bullock Report is its clear exposition of the psychological aim of reading and writing education to develop the child's *self-control* of the technical skills involved. Intrinsic motivation is regarded as the key to full self-control. The Report states:

The child should be brought up to see this technical control not as an abstraction imposed from without but as the means of communicating with his audience in the most satisfying manner [p. 8].

Some other examples of the Bullock Report's consistent attempt to approach reading from the point of the child's perceptions and conceptions of spoken and written language are the following:

To see letter shapes as adults see them is by no means a natural and automatic process. On the contrary, each child may have his own idiosyncratic ways of looking at letters . . . [p. 81].

They can see as well as any adult that b is p upside down, just as well as they can see that the doll or train is upside down. Where they have trouble is in learning to recognize these reflected and rotated forms as entirely different letters. They would regard it as very odd if a doll had to be called Betty instead of Susan according to which way it faced, or the train was called a motor car when it reversed [p. 81].

A learner needs to trace the steps from the familiar to the new, from the fact or idea he possesses to that which he is to acquire. In other words, the learner has to make a journey in thought for himself [p. 141].

The experience of individual children will vary, and this means that the teacher's appraisal of each child's needs and achievement is the key to success [p. 67].

Therefore:

. . . to expect a whole class to maintain a steady and uniform advance along a line of linguistic achievement is unrealistic [p. 173].

Furthermore:

Individual attention should not be confined to poor readers, for average and above average children also need it if they are to make optimal progress [p. 524].

The Bullock Committee's acceptance of the principle of child-centred education leaves them with only one possible conclusion to the question – which is the best teaching method for initiating children in reading? That is, that there is no royal road to success in learning to read. Because children differ in their aptitudes and ability they need many alternative paths to literacy. The Bullock Report's words are: 'There is no one method, medium, approach, device, or philosophy that holds the key to the process of learning to read' [p. 77].

For the psychologist who has not specialized in reading education it may seem that the Bullock Committee are contradicting themselves when the Report says some 25 pages after the above statement:

We described . . . how the good infant school develops the child's writing activities from small beginnings . . . Work of the kind discussed in those paragraphs is essential to *the language experience approach to reading we are advocating* [p. 103, italics added].

Whereas earlier the Report says there is no one key approach, now it advocates the language experience approach. That this is not contradictory, however, will be clear to those more familiar with the jargon of the pedagogy of reading. The 'language experience approach' is the technical name for the method of teaching reading which combines two principles: (1) an eclectic use of all available methods and materials according to the pupils' individual needs; and (2) the employment of the child's own individual language and experiences in the material he reads and writes – for example, the 'news', at first dictated and in later stages written by the children themselves. The following quotations from various parts of the Bullock Report show the consistent advocacy of this method by the Committee:

We must emphasize that we regard the reading scheme as an ancillary part of a school's reading programme, and nothing more ... and we welcome the enterprise of those schools which have successfully planned the teaching of reading without the use of a graded series [p. 109].

Our own view is that the kind of language development under discussion will be more likely to take effect the more it uses as its medium the daily experiences of the classroom and the home [pp. 66–67].

What we are suggesting is that children should learn about language by experiencing it and experimenting with its use [p. 173]. The surest means by which a child is enabled to master his mother tongue is by exploiting the process of discovery through language in all its uses [p. 519].

Competence in language comes above all through its purposeful use, not through the working of exercises divorced from context [p. 528].

The second principle that is carefully safeguarded in the Bullock Report and which is such an important feature of the English education system is the professional autonomy of the individual school and its teachers. This is linked with the belief that the teacher in this autonomous professional role is a prime factor in children's reading achievements. Every judgement and every recommendation in the Report is couched in terms of the individual school's and the individual teacher's right and duty to decide the what, how and when of teaching. But the Bullock Committee makes an important recommendation that this autonomy does require some voluntary limitation. The Report calls for each school to develop its own consistent policy for the teaching of reading, and it makes this call in forceful terms:

It cannot be emphasized too strongly that the teacher is the biggest single factor for success in learning to read and use language. The school with high standards of reading is the one where the teachers are knowledgeable about it and are united in ascribing to it a very high priority. A coherent strategy, understood and agreed by the staff, is the best instrument for improving standards of reading and language ... [p. 212].

In these ways the Bullock Report attempts to conserve current good principles in the teaching of reading in England. But it must not be thought that change is avoided altogether. A number of important changes are recommended, but they too are rooted in the characteristic features of reading education in England. Firstly, there is a continuation of certain trends which have been quite obvious in recent years. Secondly, there are some proposals for change which appear to be clearer breaks with the past.

One trend which is pushed further by the Bullock Committee is along the hard road to greater involvement of parents in the schools' work of helping children to learn to read. The Plowden initiative in breaking down the traditional attitude of 'no interference from parents' is carried further. The following are the main recommendations for change in this respect:

Parents should be helped to understand the process of language development in their children and to play their part in it [p. 519].

Authorities should introduce home visiting schemes to help the parents of pre-school children play an active part in the children's language growth [p. 519].

Schools should encourage the involvement of parents to provide additional conversation opportunities for young children. They should build on pre-school contacts where these have been established [p. 520].

Parents have an extremely important part to play in preparing the child for the early stages of reading [p. 522].

Measures should be taken to introduce children to books in their pre-school years and to help parents recognize the value of reading to their children [p. 522].

Schools should be enabled and encouraged to lend books to the parents of pre-school children and to provide book-buying facilities for them [p. 522].

There should be every effort to involve parents and help them to understand the nature of their children's difficulties [p. 540].

The 'Comparative Reading' study found that the actions and attitudes of parents constitute a very important variable in the child's development of reading and writing skills. The positive effect of parental involvement was particularly noticeable in Japan and Hong Kong, and among the 'old-timers' in Israel.

Another continuing trend which was predictable is the further effort to ameliorate the harmful effects of artificial groupings of pupils which arise from administrative convenience. The 1944 Education Act broke away from the old 'Standard' divisions and paved the way for true individualization of teaching. This is in marked contrast to education systems in many other countries where children are only allowed to learn what is proper for their 'grade'. If they cannot complete the work for the year in that grade, they must do it all again. If they finish the year's work several months ahead of time they are not permitted to use any more difficult materials because those are for the next grade. Nevertheless, although English children have escaped from the worst wastages and frustrations of the grade system, there has remained a number of artificial divisions which suit the convenience of administrators but do not fit the need for individual attention and continuity in teaching. As far as reading education is concerned, the break between infants and junior schools has been the chief problem here, and the Bullock Committee makes clear recommendations to overcome it. Specifically, their main proposal is:

The heads and staffs of infant and junior schools (and first and middle schools) should jointly plan the transition of the children between the two stages. Their planning should include such measures as:

(i)   regular inter-staff discussion;
(ii) an exchange of visits and teaching assignments;
(iii) an opportunity for small groups of infants to spend occasional days in the junior school in the term before transfer;
(iv) setting up common working and quiet areas where schools occupy the same building;
(v)   joint activities of various kinds.

Within this framework of co-operation, there should be special attention to language and reading development. There should be a common understanding of objectives in the teaching of reading. It should be recognized as a developmental process in which it is unrealistic to expect uniform levels of achievement for every child at a given age [p. 531].

This theme of learning to read as a developmental process is consistently maintained in the Bullock Report and leads quite logically to a number of proposals for maintaining this continuity at the stage of transfer to secondary schools, too.

The Bullock Committee's suggestions for improving the teaching of children from cultural and linguistic minorities are also quite predictable on the basis of known characteristics of the English education system. The child-centred principle necessarily calls for special educational provisions for the unusual needs of minority groups. Linguistic minority groups pose a particularly difficult problem for reading education. A number of studies have shown that teaching children to read in a second language or even a markedly different dialect from their own greatly increases the danger of failure (for example, Österberg, 1961; Macnamara, 1966; Modiano, 1968). The consensus of research is that the most efficient way of beginning initial literacy learning is in the child's vernacular (Downing, 1976). The practical difficulties of applying this research finding are sometimes very great, but the least that can be done is to make allowances for the minority group child with this linguistic problem and to adapt teaching to his special need, even if the medium of instruction has to be English. What makes the problem even more difficult is that these minority groups are different not only linguistically but also culturally. This causes two kinds of difficulty. One is the cognitive confusion which results from being instructed in initial literacy in a language which one does not know or knows only a little. The other difficulty is emotional. The child may perceive his own language as rejected by the teacher, and this may be equated with rejection of his family and friends.

It is a notable achievement of the Bullock Committee that they gave considerable attention to these problems of minority groups. The whole of chapter 20 is devoted to 'Children from Families of Overseas Origin' and there are many other references to minority cultures, sub-cultures, languages and dialects. A few quotations from the Report will illustrate this valuable step forward:

No child should be expected to cast off the language and culture of the home as he crosses the school threshold, nor to live and act as though school and home represent two totally separate and different cultures which have to be kept firmly apart [p. 286].

In assisting children to master Standard English, which in effect is the dialect of school, they should do so without making children feel marked out by the form of language they bring with them . . . [p. 287].

What we suggest is the central recommendation of this chapter: a sensitivity and openness to language in all its forms [p. 294].

Moving on to another trend pursued in the Bullock Report, teachers in England have long been aware of the educational inefficiency of over-large classes. Research has tended to show that class size is not an important variable in learning to read, but, as was pointed out in *Comparative Reading*, this may have been due to the fact that such research usually compared very large classes with slightly less large classes. There probably is a class size above which it makes rather little difference. That size is probably about 15 pupils. In Denmark it was found that changing the pupil/teacher ratio from 1 : 32 to 1 : 28 made no observable difference, but, when the classes of 28 were divided in half for part of the day producing a ratio of 1 : 14, more satisfactory results were obtained. This supports the teachers' consistent contention that they could achieve better results in reading if classes were smaller. Schools in England have had larger classes than in some other countries, but there has been a trend to reduce their size in England, too. In the present economic situation one does not feel optimistic about future improvements in pupil/teacher ratios, but the Bullock Report rightly underlines the potential improvement which could be effected if staffing could be increased. The following are some of the Bullock Report's comments on this issue:

The staffing of infant schools should be such as to allow a teacher to work with individuals and small groups as and when she believes it necessary [p. 104].

In our view there are still far too many classes which are larger than they should be . . . Many teachers told us that with large classes they were unable to give individual attention with sufficient frequency and in sufficient depth. This is of particular importance in the early stages of reading . . . [pp. 206–207].

An improvement in the staffing ratio should be related not simply to a reduction in average class size but to the opportunity to create very small groups as the occasion demands [p. 530].

One other trend in English education which is followed by the Bullock Committee is the persistent move away from streaming. Unfortunately, streaming has been made a political issue in England and this has slowed down the implementation of research findings which have shown the harmful effect of streaming on the development of reading and writing skills. The international consensus noted in *Comparative Reading* is that streamed classes influence teachers' expectations of pupils' aptitudes and abilities. The more homogeneous the class is believed to be the less the teacher expects to find individual differences and, correspondingly, the less he looks for them and allows for them. Thus, streaming works against the individualization of teaching. The Bullock Report notes:

However careful the process, classifying individuals in this way makes different pupils in the same group seem more similar than they are, and similar pupils in different groups seem more different than they are [p. 224].

Therefore:

The majority of the Committee have reservations about arrangements by which pupils are streamed or setted for English according to ability [p. 534].

Finally, let us turn to what appears to be the Bullock Committee's more dramatic breaks with past traditions of reading education in England. The most notable changes of direction are the Committee's recommendations: (1) for improving teacher training in reading education; and (2) for extending provisions for the teaching of reading into the junior and secondary levels (middle and third schools). But, although these proposed changes seem more radical than the others mentioned earlier in this address, they are quite predictably cast in the mould of conventional educational attitudes in England. Unfortunately, the practical effect of this conventional cultural context is likely to be an inadequate response to the needs of teachers and schools in coping with the demand for the higher standards of reading and writing which the Bullock Committee has recognized.

Mastery of any skill depends on learning a set of subskills and integrating these into the total skilled act. Mastery also depends on repeated practice over a long period, and retention of mastery only comes after the learner has passed beyond mastery into the area of 'overlearning'. Reading is one of the most complex skills and hence requires a long period for its full development. It is *par excellence* a developmental skill.

Unfortunately, this concept of reading as a developmental skill has been poorly understood in education in England, probably because reading has been seen as a part of the subject of 'English' and a low level part of 'English' at that. In England one of the most serious sources of difficulty in improving reading has been the traditional view that teaching reading is mainly the task of the infant school. In fact, research indicates that children are only just beginning to gain independence in work-attack skills when they transfer to the junior school, where, because of this conventional misconception, it has been generally believed, until quite recently, that the teachers needed no training in the teaching of reading. The result has been the failure of many children in developing mastery or retention of mastery of literacy skills. The majority of children have succeeded because they were able to overcome the shortcomings of their schooling in this respect. But a sizeable proportion of the population has not been able to escape the consequences of this flaw in the teaching of reading in England. Early failure or poor attainments for one reason or another have caused a distaste for reading which, in turn, causes lack of motivation to practise on one's own. Since the school makes no formal provision or plans for practice, mastery is never attained and overlearning does not occur. Then the skill is ready to atrophy as soon as the school's demands for literacy, minimal though they may be, are withdrawn.

The disastrous results of this past policy of confining reading education to the infant or first school is frankly admitted in the Bullock Report. Indeed, it would have been impossible to conclude otherwise when so much research from applied psychologists in education has confirmed Joyce Morris' (1959) original finding of this serious inadequacy in the English school system. It has taken 15 years for her very important research finding to be given appropriate official recognition. Some more insightful educators have been taking some steps here and there to correct this fault in the English education system, but the overall effect of this belated awakening seems likely to create something of a crisis.

The Bullock Report recommends that all teachers, including those in secondary education, no matter what their specialist subject may be, should have an understanding of their pupils' needs in developing reading skill. The Committee also calls for the creation of a force of specialist teachers and advisers well qualified in reading education as well as other aspects of language development. But where are these specialists to come from? And how are all teachers going to achieve this understanding of reading education? The Report asserts that

All teachers in training, irrespective of the age-range they intend to teach, should complete satisfactorily a substantial course in language and reading [p. 549].

But who will conduct these courses? The number of people specially qualified in reading education is pitifully small in this country. Six years ago at the Annual Conference of the British Psychological Society, I began my paper on teacher education with the statement:

There is growing research evidence of a serious gap in the teacher education system – a failure to provide teachers with adequate training in the teaching of reading and related language skills [Downing, 1969].

Since then there has been some improvement – and some deterioration in the situation. London University's Institute of Education's special option in the Psychology of Literacy was phased out for reasons known only to that institution. But Reading University's School of Education has continued and expanded its valuable pioneering work at its 'reading centre'. A number of colleges of education have succeeded in establishing diploma courses in reading. And the most substantial contribution to progress in this field has been Professor Merritt's post-experience course on Reading Development provided by the Open University.

The balance sheet clearly shows significant progress. Nevertheless, the needs for implementing the Bullock Committee's recommendations for teacher training and for creating a force of specialist advisers are so enormous that one must question how it can be done – if it is going to be done properly.

Unfortunately, there is a further important reason to doubt whether these recommendations will have the desired effect on reading education. This reason lies within the Bullock Report itself. In this case a traditional attitude among English educators seems likely to have a seriously weakening influence on the measures proposed for improving teachers' competence in reading education.

The *Comparative Reading* survey found that an educational status system exists in England and several other countries, and that this system is damaging to reading education. There is a teachers' 'pecking order' related more or less to the age of pupils they instruct. The rationale for this educational status hierarchy probably goes something like this, although one rarely hears it explicitly stated: The infants school teacher mostly plays games and reads stories to the children although she does teach reading. The junior school teacher does *teach*, but only very simple things. The secondary school teacher deals with more difficult concepts and specializes in a particular academic subject such as mathematics or history. The teacher trainer obviously must be superior because he's in charge of teachers and deals with these specialist subjects at an even higher level. The university professor is at the top of the hierarchy because he teaches these academic subjects at their most complex level. (The fact that special professional understandings are needed for each level in the educational system is ignored in this status hierarchy.) Also, literacy teaching traditionally is the work of the infants school teacher, and hence the very words 'reading' and 'writing' may have become tainted by their association with the low status of elementary teaching.

The effect on teacher training in reading education has been that, at the top of the educational hierarchy in the university, reading is rejected as too elementary a subject for its consideration. At the 'lower' level in teacher-training establishments, it has suffered low status because it is not included in university courses. Psychology, philosophy and sociology are 'good' in this regard. So are subjects that are shared by elementary schools and universities, such as mathematics and history. But reading is a non-university subject, and it suffers in contrast.

This state of affairs is not inevitable, as is shown by developments in Canada and the United States. In those two countries courses designed to prepare reading specialists are offered by colleges and universities most frequently at the master's degree (5th year) level either in reading *per se* or in other areas with a major in reading. Many universities give an Ed.D. and/or a Ph.D. in this subject, and there is a serious concern for the universities' responsibility for the postgraduate training of researchers in reading.

If the Bullock Committee had made proposals that Departments or Centres for Reading or Language Arts should be created at English universities, and if this proposal had been implemented, they could have been the spearheads for the rapid growth of a cadre of specialists in reading. These people, in turn, could have passed their training on to others in the teaching profession through in-service and pre-service courses. Thus, in a relatively short span of time, a much sounder basis of knowledge could have become generally available and the whole subject of reading education could have acquired the high status that its real importance deserves. But this was not recommended in the Bullock Report.

Instead, the laudable proposals for establishing specialist advisers and specialist teachers who will raise the general level among all teachers is shackled to the traditional concept, that reading is merely a part of the subject of 'English'. For example, the Bullock Report recommends that, 'Every authority should have an advisory team with the specific responsibility of supporting schools in all aspects of language in education. This would encompass English from language and reading in the early years to advanced reading and English studies at the highest level of the secondary school' (p. 536). Also, 'The advisory teachers should be appointed for their special interest in English and should be drawn from among those with responsibility for language in the primary schools and from English teachers in secondary schools' (p. 536). This advisory team is to have wide responsibilities including 'providing in-service training'. That this is likely to be a case of *the blind leading the blind* is clear not only from the past very bad record of 'English' teaching as regards reading education, but also from those parts of the Bullock Report that focus on 'English' teaching rather than reading.

They are not only pompous, dreary, inaccurate and out-of-date, but they also show a preference for subjective opinion and a disregard for published research which is in marked contrast to the objective research oriented approach in the sections devoted to reading education.

This is the most worrying defect in the Bullock Report. What should have been regarded as the province of the psychology of learning is removed even further from our discipline and tied firmly to 'English'. This must be contested because learning to read is a psychological process which occurs in all languages which have a written form. It is, therefore, a process which has universal characteristics irrespective of the specific language in which reading is learned. Furthermore, reading belongs to a category of behaviour about which psychological knowledge is rather advanced. Reading is *a skill*. Therefore, there are many psychological generalizations about skill acquisition which can be applied to learning the skill of reading. These psychological foundations of reading are repeatedly and explicitly recognized in the Bullock Report, yet, in the end, it is left firmly in the inept hands of the English Department.

*   *   *

ACKNOWLEDGEMENT

This extract is published with the kind permission of the author.

REFERENCES

Central Advisory Council for Education (1967), *Children and Their Primary Schools* (The Plowden Report). London: HMSO.

Department of Education and Science (1975), *A Language for Life* (The Bullock Report). London: HMSO.

Downing, J. (1969) Are current provisions for teacher training adequate for the effective teaching of reading and related skills? *Proceedings of Annual Conference of the British Psychological Society*, pp. 8–9.

Downing, J. (1973) *Comparative Reading*. London: Collier-Macmillan.

Downing, J. (1976) Bilingualism and learning to read. *Irish Journal of Education*.

Macnamara, J. (1966) *Bilingualism and Primary Education*. Edinburgh: Edinburgh University Press.

Modiano, N. (1968) National or mother language in beginning reading: a comparative study. *Res. Teach. English*, 2, 32–43.

Morris, J. M. (1959) *Reading in the Primary School*. London: Newnes.

Österberg, T. (1961) *Bilingualism and the First School Language*. Umeå, Sweden: Vasterbottens Tryckeri, AB.

Warburton, F. & Southgate, V. (1969) *i.t.a.: An Independent Evaluation* (Schools Council Report). London: Murray and Chambers.

PART 8

Language and thought

INTRODUCTION

The birth and growth of verbal behaviour in humans has fascinated psychologists. Factions have developed which are poles apart. Skinner has proposed a reinforcement theory of language development (see core text). Chomsky is totally committed to the central importance of inner mechanisms (which he believes are inherent) underpinning speech behaviour. The paper by McLeish and Martin is particularly helpful because it is introduced by a clear statement of the arguments existing between the extremists. Another part of the paper (not included in the Reader) also offers some evidence which meets some of the criticisms directed at Skinner by Chomsky.

'The course of cognitive growth' is a well-established résumé of Bruner's thinking on the subject. It will be valuable for those wanting a ready source of detail about Bruner's most fundamental work.

The paper by Thompson on self-concepts serves two purposes. First it gives an opportunity to show Osgood's Semantic Differential in action (see main text) and second, it

197

highlights an important area in the self-concepts of adjusted, maladjusted and delinquent children. More information also appears on this subject in Part 12.

Concept 7–9 is one of several programmes developed for children to improve their language skills. Language usage is not just a matter of speaking or learning to read. There are skills involving listening, understanding, concept formation and communication to be acquired. The extracts from *Concept 7–9* give an admirable introduction.

24　Verbal behavior: a review and experimental analysis [*]

JOHN McLEISH and JACK MARTIN

Summary　The aim of this study was to provide a test of B. F. Skinner's hypotheses about verbal behavior (Skinner, 1957) and reinforcement principles. An experiment was set up to test the criticisms of antibehaviorists, perhaps best epitomized by Noam Chomsky's attack (Chomsky, 1959; 1971). The main hypothesis to be tested was that reinforcement is not something specially contrived in laboratories with animal subjects (*pace* Chomsky), but the process under the constraints of which ordinary people behave in normal social situations.

With the use of a coding system based on the verbal operants defined by Skinner supplemented by affect categories from Bales' system (Bales, 1950; 1970), behaviors in four different kinds of 'live' groups, as well as verbal transcripts and videotape recordings of these 'live' sessions, were coded. These provided the basis for a functional analysis of the group interactions. A computer analysis of the codings was carried out through specially prepared computer programs. These analysed the ongoing interactions of group members in terms of the trimember sequence of (a) discriminative stimulus, (b) response, and (c) reinforcement. These and subsequent analyses determined whether or not fluctuations in the rates of emission of particular verbal operants were under the control of contingencies of reinforcement. The attempt was made to discover whether causal relationships could be specifically defined and charted in relation to the trimember sequences. Periods of increase for a total of 439 operants emitted by 31 individuals in four groups were analysed in this way.

It is concluded from the analysis that a *prima facie* case has been established for the following general principles:

(a) the verbal operant categories, as defined, satisfactorily describe *all* the communicative behavior we have observed. Our system, based on Skinner's analysis of behavior, supplemented by Bales' affect categories, is comprehensive, functional and operational;

(b) the basic principles of the experimental analysis of behavior, and in particular the concept of contingencies of reinforcement, satisfactorily account for all increases and decreases in the rates of emission of verbal operants in a group situation;

(c) the relatively 'spontaneous' behavior of human subjects in an interacting group is under the control of the principle of causality. This is revealed *only* by a systematic analysis of the behavior of *all* the participants in terms of some such complex and functional model as that provided by B. F. Skinner.

The project has shown that the conditioning paradigm of Skinner is not limited to a delineation of

---

[*] Dedicated to Robert Freed Bales who pointed the way.

subhuman motor behaviors in rigidly controlled laboratory environments; it has great explanatory power for higher forms of human behavior in relatively nonstructured situations.

•   •   •

CHOMSKY versus SKINNER

The publication of Skinner's *Verbal Behavior* in 1957 caused a violent reaction; many psychologists reacted strongly to the intrusion of behaviorism into the study of speech behavior. Linguistic philosophers, led by Noam Chomsky, were also very disturbed. The transfer of psychology from the study of motor behavior in laboratories to the study of everyday speech was regarded as illicit. The study of speech by science, a method which minimizes speculation, is unwarranted. So said the critics (Chomsky, 1959).

The attack goes to the root of the question of how we should study behavior. The critics say that behavioral science makes a great play, but merely mimics the surface features of science (Chomsky, 1959; 1971). The illusory scientific character depends on restricting the subject matter to the most trivial and peripheral issues – so it is said. This narrowing of content means that no significant results have been obtained – certainly nothing which can help us understand behavior as complex as speech and language.

Chomsky leads the attack. He is an unashamed dualist (Chomsky, 1966; 1968) who puts forward a mentalistic theory of linguistics as a counterweight to the oversimplified model of the behaviorists. He proclaims the need for a science of the mind (Chomsky, 1968). This will replace, or subsume, the science of behavior. Only such a mentalistic *revanchisme* can bring any insight into behavior. The slogan is 'Back to Descartes!' (Chomsky, 1966). For Chomsky, linguistics must be mentalistic. According to his view, 'competence' in a language is quite distinct from speech behavior. 'Competence' is a *mental* reality which exists in its own right quite independent of the way the language is actually spoken. Chomsky's criticisms of behaviorism (Chomsky, 1959; MacCorquodale, 1970) revolve around four main arguments:

1   To understand the behavior of a complex organism we must know its internal structures. Any attempt to ignore inner 'mechanisms' results in an unwarranted limiting of subject matter to externals. This leads to concentration on surface features and peripheral issues. No knowledge of any significance can be obtained from studies which deal only with overt behavior.

2   Behaviorists extrapolate from the 'thimbleful of knowledge', obtained in laboratory experiments with animals, to human issues of wide significance and social concern. In the study of language they have, at best, declared a program. There is no completed body of work on human verbal behavior.

3   With regard to verbal behavior, Skinner is incapable of accounting for the child's acquisition of grammar. His view of the development and function of language is marked by dogmatic and arbitrary claims. These are based on analogical reasoning from irrelevant experiments on animals. He has no method of dealing with 'linguistic creativity' which is the most important feature of human speech behavior.

4   The concepts of reinforcement theory do not survive the transition from the rigor of the animal laboratory to an analysis of human verbal behavior in a naturalistic environment. In particular, Skinner uses terms such as 'stimulus', 'response', and 'reinforcement' in such a way that they lose all meaning.

Before turning to an evaluation of these criticisms, it seems advisable to look, rather briefly, at the explanation of language acquisition and development which Chomsky proposes in place of the interpretations of Skinner (Chomsky, 1966; 1968).

The basic problem for linguistics, according to Chomsky, is the fact that speakers use sentences which have never been used before. With a relatively small stock of words, and a few general rules, the language user can produce and understand an infinite number of sentences. The question for Chomsky is: how can this 'linguistic creativity' be explained? Can we give a precise description of language as a step towards answering this question? What 'structures' underlie language? How are these represented in the bodily organization of the language user? What structures can we think of which will enable us to *deduce* the grammar of all possible human languages? Grammar enables the speaker (and listener) to understand new sentences and to produce appropriate sentences in reply. The question is: 'Where does the grammar come from in the verbal performance of the speaker?'

The most telling point he makes in this connection is that there is no algorithm known for computing or 'discovering' the grammar of a language – yet almost every infant successfully performs the task of language acquisition. The user *knows* the universal principles underlying the grammars of all languages without prior experience of human speech. At least so it seems. This points to an innate system, an innate ability, so thinks Chomsky (1966).

Chomsky's actual work consists in developing a method of analysing and synthesizing sentences. By this means, using logical procedures and intuitive analysis, he seeks to discover rules for 'transforming' and 'generating' sentences from 'kernel' sentences. The purpose of this work is to throw light on 'competence' which, in turn, will explain 'performance'. The rules – written in the form of a symbolic code resembling computer language – constitute a grammar.

For Chomsky, there is an interaction between the grammatical sentences which the child hears ('primary linguistic data') and the child's innate linguistic competence. The product of this interaction is grammar. The interplay between the data and the competence is accomplished by means of a 'language acquisition device'. The goal of Chomsky's linguistics is to describe and explain linguistic competence – i.e., that which underlies the actual use of language in normal communication.

Chomsky does not seem to be aware of it, but the basic model implicit in his thinking is that of the digital computer. The computer is constructed of a few simple and basic components which are repeated in thousands of units. These correspond to Chomsky's 'linguistic universals': that is, the universal principles underlying the grammars of all languages. In addition to the physical components, these basic elements (switches of various kinds simulating logical operations) are set out so that they generate instruction control units. These enable a particular program to be read in and retained. These units also interpret and carry out the sequence of operations in the program which is stored in the 'memory'. They control the whole series of operations according to the instructions built in at the most basic level. This represents what computer men call 'the hardware' – this comes ready-made to the 'user'. The program known as 'software' represents, so to speak, the grammar of a particular language. It is made up specially to suit the needs of the user. We could say that it describes the rules and specifies the categories of sentences, phrases and words available to the speaker. In addition to this 'hardware' and 'software' are the 'data'. The program works on the data fed in for analysis by the users. This results in an output.

The data fed into the computer represent the actual speech listened to and assimilated by the child. In ordinary life, dictionaries classify this input in terms of different categories of words – nouns, verbs, adjectives, etc. Grammars state the rules. The growing child performs the same functions as the dictionary and grammar. As speaker, he emits grammatical sentences. In principle, the computer can do the same provided we work out programs and feed in the rules of grammar. This must include syntax, semantics and, if we want spoken sentences, phonetics. The child is, in some unknown way, an analogue model of the computer, performing all these functions, without training, at a very early age.

Note that, working as he does with this electronic model, which really rules out 'creativity' in all normal senses of the word, Chomsky attacks Skinner for his alleged destruction of human freedom and human dignity. In fact, this is a basic inconsistency in Chomsky which leads him to do all the things he accuses Skinner of doing.

Chomsky maintains that a knowledge of linguistic competence is necessary for an understanding of verbal behavior (used in the traditional linguistic sense). The study of any finite sample of speech 'performance' (behavior) is inadequate, since we are compelled to use an *inductive* method with this kind of material. Linguistics must become a rationalistic science, based on deduction. This puts us back to Descartes (1596–1650), if not indeed to Plato. Behind the behavioral forms, Chomsky believes that there exist certain innate structures which generate inner states of consciousness. The way to obtain information about these 'inner states' can only be introspection and intuition. With their help, the speaker and linguist can discover the mental structures of the individual speaker. These inner structures will obviously be very different from the explanatory models which arise from study of overt speech behavior only.

Borrowing a concept from von Humboldt (Robins, 1967), Chomsky distinguishes the 'deep' and 'surface' structures of a language. Somewhere below the surface structures ('la parole' – the language as spoken) lie the deep structures ('la langue' – the language as it really is). The latter must be presented to the mind along with the surface structure, before language can be 'generated' by the speaker or interpreted by the listener. The deep structures relate directly to *meaning*. Meaning and speech are brought together by certain operations of the mind. These are what Chomsky calls 'transformational' operations. They are performed by the mind when a sentence is produced or understood.

For every language there is a fixed system of generative principles. This is called a grammar. The 'grammar' of a speaker evolves from his underlying linguistic competence. Creativity is the proof of competence. The ability to speak, another way of saying competence, points to hidden structures. These retain models, constraints and rules, in much the same way as the computer does.

Now Chomsky further assumes that the child is *innately* equipped with competence. This is in the form of a 'language-learning device' which is based on certain 'linguistic universals'. We must assume, says Chomsky, that the child is born with a knowledge of the principles of universal grammar, and with a predisposition to use them. It is because of this that he is able to analyse the utterances he hears and to produce grammatical sentences himself. The rules of universal grammar are part of the mind. This is what really separates man from the animals. Irrespective of the group in which he is reared, the child is able to speak the language. Not only does he speak the language, he does so grammatically. According to this theory, when the child is presented with samples of 'primary linguistic data' (the words and phrases of a particular language) he begins to build the grammar which belongs to his own language-group. It is this grammar which coordinates the deep and surface structures of the particular language. When this pairing of structures occurs, language can be produced by the speaker and understood by the listener (Chomsky, 1966).

From this brief sketch of Chomsky's theory, the first criticism aimed at Skinner becomes clear. This is to the effect that no valid knowledge of language behavior can be obtained from studies which deal only with behavior. Such knowledge can come only from an understanding of internal structures. It is clear that the criticism flows from Chomsky's acceptance of a rehabilitated mentalism and dualism. This clearly comes from Plato, as mediated by Descartes.

The notion of 'internal structures' is not necessarily unscientific. Internal structures are perfectly acceptable if the term refers to operationally defined and observable referents, including processes. These processes could even be inferred, if necessary, from measured correlates. For example, such overt indicators as records made by EEG machines, or brain processes indicated by drops of saliva as in Pavlov's method, or reading from electronic brain implants could be used as evidence, pointing to hypothesized processes. However, Chomsky offers us no guidance whatever as to how data could be obtained to back his contentions. His focus is on deep underlying and abstract mental structures which are inaccessible. His argument that these constitute the field of true science is difficult to accept. The existence of hypothetical entities such as these must be given some status in reality before Chomsky can be taken seriously.

Chomsky's definition of the nature of these inner mechanisms holds out no hope of any insight ever being attained into causal connections in this area of verbal behavior. In other words, we are talking of something other than science.

To support this charge, we would claim that the history of science testifies to the fact that the principle of economy rules out dualistic concepts in the scientific analysis of behavior. The argument that certain aspects of mental activity will forever remain unobservable (Chomsky) and yet that they must be postulated to account for human speech-behavior (Chomsky) seems arbitrary to a degree. In hypostatizing 'mental mechanisms' or 'devices' and speaking of innate abilities, Chomsky lays claim to a knowledge he does not have, and which must forever remain inaccessible to him or to anyone else.

Further, Chomsky's statement (Chomsky, 1959) that the science of behavior has given us no knowledge of any real significance is simply not true. One need only compare the writings of Pavlov, Thorndike and Skinner with those of Descartes, Plato and Chomsky to appreciate that nowadays we are in a different league, and indeed a different game altogether, in talking about behavior. It is a fact that the psychological model of the behaving organism is not only much more subtle than any provided by the dualistic philosophers. More importantly it has objective reference. We now compass the real organism, in all its complexity, and relate this to the environment in which it is functioning, in all its manifold diversity and dynamic changes (Pavlov, 1943). Even if this were not the case, it is impossible to appreciate (in the light of basic scientific principles) how Chomsky's theoretical stance can be accepted as giving promise of significant advances in our knowledge of human behavior.

The same arguments can be used to refute Chomsky's second main criticism that results obtained in the laboratory with subhuman species have no relevance to human behavior in a social context. The assumption behind this statement is that human beings are radically different from other animals (by virtue of their possession of a mind). This is taken to mean that the principles elucidated in the study of lower animals are quite divorced from the principles which account for human behavior. Chomsky says that, at best, the former apply only to trivial forms of behavior. To counter this argument, one need only refer to the many experiments and projects in which modification of human behavior has been achieved by the use of techniques developed in animal laboratories. Teaching machines represent one such advance due to reinforcement theory (Skinner, 1972). The supposed 'trivial' nature of these experiments refers to Chomsky's faith that, although overt behavior may change, the inner properties of the mind are not affected.

It is undeniable that many variables relevant to explaining human behavior remain to be discovered. But the experimental analysis of behavior offers the only sound scientific basis for such inquiry. In contrast, the 'mentalism' advocated by Chomsky offers no such foundation. This 'mentalism' is rooted in Cartesian dualism and Kantian agnosticism. Modern science has moved beyond these positions, since experience has shown that there has been no payoff in empirical research from this standpoint.

The attack on Skinnerian analysis as trivial is astonishing when one realizes that all of Chomsky's theorizing is based *not* on an analysis of the actual utterances of human beings as recorded by linguists – indeed, not upon empirical data at all – but upon manufactured sentences. These propositions, generated in the study and taken out of all context for analysis, can hardly be viewed as legitimate data to serve as the foundation stones for the construction of theories.

The third criticism levelled at Skinner relates to his alleged inability to account for the child's acquisition of grammar and the phenomenon of 'linguistic creativity'. As indicated by the brief description of Chomsky's theory of language, grammatical structures – or 'internalized strategies for speaking' – are basic constructs used in the study of transformational linguistics. This theory refers to the internalizing of complex sets of rules, or 'plans of speech'. Of course, it cannot be denied that this is a possible way to conceptualize the child's acquisition of verbal behavior. However, it is an *inference*, *not* a fact. There are numerous other ways of conceptualizing the problem. The concept of an internalized set of grammatical structures is of value *only* if it provides an aid to the thinking of the scientist. Skinner has pointed out that if verbal behavior itself shows regularity, such a theory is not required (Bales, 1970; Skinner, 1972). He attempts to deal with all of verbal behavior, including those regularities that lead the grammarian to infer grammatical rules (Skinner, 1957).

On the basis of the principle of parsimony, Chomsky's internalized structures become superfluous. Since the internalization of grammar is a theory *about* verbal behavior and not a fact, Skinner cannot properly be convicted of failing to account for significant facts because he fails to discuss this special theory of linguistics. In order to consider this a fact, we would need to have an empirical demonstration that a child has indeed learned the rules of grammar. This is quite different from being able to speak grammatically. The child would need to exhibit the verbal performance of 'uttering the rules of grammar'. This performance has never been manifested without special training.

'Uttering the rules of grammar' is a highly skilled verbal performance, requiring years of highly specialized training. Speaking grammatically is also a highly specialized performance: equally it can only be accounted for on the basis of the same principles of learning theory. The main difference is that we are usually quite well aware of our objectives in the former case. We deliberately *teach* the child the rules of grammar. On the other hand, in learning to speak grammatically the 'teaching' is makeshift and 'spontaneous'. There is no clear awareness of the final end, nor of the stages to be passed through. There is a 'shaping' process, usually by parents, operating on the basis of a felt need that their child should conform to the speech norms of their social group. It is surprising that Chomsky seems unable to understand the implications of this distinction.

The claim that Skinner fails to account for 'linguistic creativity' is true only if we accept Chomsky's definition of 'creativity'. For example, Chomsky's own manufactured phrase 'furiously sleep ideas green colorless' can be described as creative only because the words which constitute the phrase appear in a novel sequence. Incidentally, this is a sequence which Chomsky himself notes does not conform to the rules of English grammar. 'Creativity' depends on the size of the unit of language we choose to analyse. If we select the 'word' as unit, instead of the phrase, there is no reason to consider this utterance creative. Each of the words which occurs in the phrase is used commonly in the English language. Once decomposed into words, the phrase can be reconstituted. It can very readily be explained in terms of the associative process, as intraverbal connections, and in terms of the specialized 'verbal community' for which the sentence was produced. Chomsky's 'creativity' problem evaporates when we analyse the process and context of speech production along the lines suggested by Skinner.

As for the allegedly dogmatic and arbitrary nature of Skinner's views of language development, it is difficult to understand how Chomsky can make this criticism. The derivation of the properties of 'underlying' mechanisms from a paper-and-pencil analysis of made-up sentences exemplifies the qualities of dogmatism and arbitrariness to a remarkable degree.

The real problem for Chomsky, if his analysis of language acquisition is to be taken seriously, is to discover some connection between his proposed innate structures and the empirical realities of language behavior. A recent attempt by Lenneberg to provide a biological interpretation of Chomsky's views must be adjudged to be ineffective in accomplishing this end. The connection between the realities of behavior and the hypothetical structures is tenuous in the extreme.

The final criticism which Chomsky makes of Skinner is most relevant to the science of behavior. Chomsky claims that the terms and methods of reinforcement theory do not preserve the rigor of the experimental laboratory when applied to an analysis of verbal behavior in a naturalistic setting. This criticism completely fails to recognize Skinner's purpose in writing *Verbal Behavior*. The fact is that this contribution makes no promise of an account of laboratory experiments to account for development and production of verbal behavior. It is clear that what is proposed is an *interpretation* of speech behavior in the light of the learning principles established in the laboratory. It is a program of action, not a report of work accomplished. Skinner uses empirical data, in the form of literary sources, but this is merely to illustrate the principles of analysis of language behavior.

A misunderstanding arises from Skinner's definition of verbal behavior as 'behavior reinforced through the mediation of other persons'. In other words, Skinner is actually dealing with social behavior. This includes not only speech but also any *nonvocal* behavior which serves a communicative function. This is quite a different meaning of verbal behavior from that used by Chomsky to delimit the field of study. Chomsky is not concerned with *behavior* at all. He works with grammatical rules derived from an analysis of written sentences. For the purposes of his analysis, Chomsky need not, and never does consider the social context in which speech occurs. Nor is he concerned with the repercussions produced by such speech as it affects both speaker and listener. When he seeks to suggest that his abstract and restricted analysis accounts for speech behavior in a 'live' social situation, it is clear that Chomsky's sense of relevance must be questioned. His assumptions and working habits are an anachronistic 'throw-back' to the days of the Port Royal grammarians (Robins, 1967). In 1660 these scholars attempted to discover the enduring universal features characteristic of all languages by means of abstract dissections of the written phrase. In other words, it has to be said that Chomsky ignores the whole period of 'scientific linguistics' from about 1786 to 1925 (Katz, 1964; Esper, 1968; Herder, 1968; Marshall, 1970). This is a more serious charge than that he completely ignores the history of behavioral science from 1660 to 1957.

If one accepts Skinner's definition of verbal behavior, the emphasis must lie on the social nature and communicative function of language. The relevance of the behavioral principles discovered in the laboratory to this area of study should be obvious. One can hardly ignore the importance of social variables in the maintenance and development of spoken language. As we have just said, Skinner deals not only with spoken language, but with nonvocal behavior, such as gestures, which have social communicative value. Thus the problem presented by 'verbal behavior' is not the same for Skinner as it is for Chomsky.

The methods and techniques developed by Skinner in the laboratory obviously have little bearing on the Chomskyian analysis of written language, except insofar as this is a special case of linguistic usage. Chomsky deals only with what Skinner has called 'textual behavior'. Skinner can hardly be held responsible for this.

The ultimate value of Skinner's hypotheses concerning communicative behavior will depend upon whether or not it has objective reference. In other words, do things really happen the way he says they do? The scientific basis of Skinner's functional analysis must surely be attractive to the experimental psychologist. The fact that Chomsky seeks to blot out the achievements not only of psychology as it has developed thoughout the twentieth century, but the gains of linguistics over a much longer period, has a contrary effect.

However, the issue between Skinner and Chomsky cannot be settled by dialectics. The question is primarily an empirical one, to be settled by arbitrament of *experiment*, not by debate.

•   •   •

ACKNOWLEDGEMENT

This article first appeared in *J. Gen. Psychol.* (1975), **93**, 3–66. Extracts from it are published here with the kind permission of authors and editor. Copyright, 1975, by The Journal Press.

REFERENCES

Bales, R. F. (1950) *Interaction Process Analysis: A Method for the Study of Small Groups.* Reading, Mass.: Addison-Wesley.

Bales. R. F. (1970) *Personality and Interpersonal Behavior*. New York: Holt, Rinehart & Winston.

Chomsky, N. (1959) Review of Skinner's 'Verbal Behavior'. *Language*, **35**, 26–58.

Chomsky, N. (1966) *Cartesian Linguistics*. New York: Harper & Row.

Chomsky, N. (1968) *Language and Mind*. New York: Harcourt, Brace & World.

Chomsky, N. (1971) The case against B. F. Skinner: review of 'Beyond Freedom and Dignity'. *N.Y. Times Bk Rev. Sec.*, **17** (11), 18–24.

Esper, E. A. (1968) *Mentalism and Objectivism in Linguistics: The Sources of Leonard Bloomfield's Psychology of Language*. New York: Elsevier.

Herder, J. G. (1968 reprint) *Reflections on the Philosophy of the History of Mankind* (1772 ed. by L. Kreiger). Chicago: Univ. Chicago Press.

Katz, J. (1964) Mentalism in linguistics. *Language*, **40**, 124–137.

MacCorquodale, K. (1970) On Chomsky's review of Skinner's 'Verbal Behavior'. *J. Exper. An. Behav.*, **13**, 83–99.

Marshall, J. C. (1970) Review of E. A. Esper, 'Mentalism and objectivism in linguistics'. *Semiotica*, **2**, 277–293.

Pavlov, I. P. (1943) *Selected Works* (Ed. by Koshtoyants). Moscow: Foreign Languages Publishing.

Robins, R. H. (1967) *A Short History of Linguistics*. London: Longmans.

Skinner, B. F. (1957) *Verbal Behavior*. New York: Appleton-Century-Crofts.

Skinner, B. F. (1961, rev. ed.; 3rd ed., 1972) *Cumulative Record*. New York: Appleton-Century-Crofts.

Skinner, B. F. (1972) *Beyond Freedom and Dignity*. New York: Bantam Books.

25   The course of cognitive growth

JEROME S. BRUNER[*]

I shall take the view in what follows that the development of human intellectual functioning from infancy to such perfection as it may reach is shaped by a series of technological advances in the use of mind. Growth depends upon the mastery of techniques and cannot be understood without reference to such mastery. These techniques are not, in the main, inventions of the individuals who are 'growing up'; they are, rather, skills transmitted with varying efficiency and success by the culture – language being a prime example. Cognitive growth, then, is in a major way from the outside in as well as from the inside out.

Two matters will concern us. The first has to do with the techniques or technologies that aid growing human beings to represent in a manageable way the recurrent features of the complex environments in which they live. It is fruitful, I think, to distinguish three systems of processing information by which human beings construct models of their world: through

[*] The assistance of R. R. Olver and Mrs. Blythe Clinchy in the preparation of this paper is gratefully acknowledged.

action, through imagery and through language. A second concern is with integration, the means whereby acts are organized into higher-order ensembles, making possible the use of larger and larger units of information for the solution of particular problems.

Let me first elucidate these two theoretical matters, and then turn to an examination of the research upon which they are based, much of it from the Center for Cognitive Studies at Harvard.

On the occasion of the One Hundredth Anniversary of the publication of Darwin's *The Origin of Species*, Washburn and Howell (1960) presented a paper at the Chicago Centennial celebration containing the following passage:

> It would now appear . . . that the large size of the brain of certain hominids was a relatively late development and that the brain evolved due to new selection pressures *after* bipedalism and consequent upon the use of tools. The tool-using, ground-living, hunting way of life created the large human brain rather than a large brained man discovering certain new ways of life. [We] believe this conclusion is the most important result of the recent fossil hominid discoveries and is one which carries far-reaching implications for the interpretation of human behavior and its origins . . . The important point is that size of brain, insofar as it can be measured by cranial capacity, has increased some threefold subsequent to the use and manufacture of implements . . . The uniqueness of modern man is seen as the result of a technical–social life which tripled the size of the brain, reduced the face, and modified many other structures of the body [p. 49 f.].

This implies that the principal change in man over a long period of years – perhaps 500 000 thousand – has been alloplastic rather than autoplastic. That is to say, he has changed by linking himself with new, external implementation systems rather than by any conspicuous change in morphology – 'evolution-by-prosthesis', as Weston La Barre (1954) puts it. The implement systems seem to have been of three general kinds – *amplifiers of human motor capacities* ranging from the cutting tool through the lever and wheel to the wide variety of modern devices; *amplifiers of sensory capacities* that include primitive devices such as smoke signaling and modern ones such as magnification and radar sensing, but also likely to include such 'soft-ware' as those conventionalized perceptual shortcuts that can be applied to the redundant sensory environment; and finally *amplifiers of human ratiocinative capacities* of infinite variety ranging from language systems to myth and theory and explanation. All of these forms of amplification are in major or minor degree conventionalized and transmitted by the culture, the last of them probably the most since ratiocinative amplifiers involve symbol systems governed by rules that must, for effective use, be shared.

Any implement system, to be effective, must produce an appropriate internal counterpart, an appropriate skill necessary for organizing sensori-motor acts, for organizing percepts and for organizing our thoughts in a way that matches them to the requirements of implement systems. These internal skills, represented genetically as capacities, are slowly selected in evolution. In the deepest sense, then, man can be described as a species that has become specialized by the use of technological implements. His selection and survival have depended upon a morphology and set of capacities that could be linked with the alloplastic devices that have made his later evolution possible. We move, perceive and think in a fashion that depends upon techniques rather than upon wired-in arrangements in our nervous system.

Where representation of the environment is concerned, it too depends upon techniques that are learned – and these are precisely the techniques that serve to amplify our motor acts, our perceptions and our ratiocinative activities. We know and respond to recurrent regularities in our environment by skilled and patterned acts, by conventionalized spatioqualitative imagery and selective perceptual organization, and through linguistic encoding which, as so many writers have remarked, places a selective lattice between us and the physical environment. In short, the capacities that have been shaped by our evolution as tool users are the ones that we rely upon in the primary task of representation – the nature of which we shall consider in more detail directly.

As for integration, it is a truism that there are very few single or simple adult acts that cannot be performed by a young child. In short, any more highly skilled activity can be decomposed into simpler components, each of which can be carried out by a less skilled operator. What higher skills require is that the component operations be combined. Maturation consists of an orchestration of these components into an integrated sequence. The 'distractability', so-called, of much early behavior may reflect each act's lack of imbeddedness in what Miller, Galanter and Pribram (1960), speak of as 'plans'. These integrated plans, in turn, reflect the routines and subroutines that one learns in the course of mastering the patterned nature of a social environment. So that integration, too, depends upon patterns that come from the outside in – an internalization of what Roger Barker (1963) has called environmental 'behavior settings'.

If we are to benefit from contact with recurrent regularities in the environment, we must represent them in some manner. To dismiss this problem as 'mere memory' is to misunderstand it. For the most important thing about memory is not storage of past experience, but rather the retrieval of what is relevant in some usable form. This depends upon how past experience is coded and processed so that it may indeed be relevant and usable in the present when needed. The end product of such a system of coding and processing is what we may speak of as a representation.

I shall call the three modes of representation mentioned earlier enactive representation, iconic representation and symbolic representation. Their appearance in the life of the child is in that order, each depending upon the previous one for its development, yet all of them remaining more or less intact throughout life – barring such early accidents as blindness or deafness or cortical injury. By enactive representation I mean a mode of representing past events through appropriate motor response. We cannot, for example, give an adequate description of familiar sidewalks or floors over which we habitually walk, nor do we have much of an image of what they are like. Yet we get about them without tripping or even looking much. Such segments of our environment – bicycle riding, tying knots, aspects of driving – get represented in our muscles, so to speak. Iconic representation summarizes events by the selective organization of percepts and of images, by the spatial, temporal and qualitative structures of the perceptual field and their transformed images. Images 'stand for' perceptual events in the close but conventionally selective way that a picture stands for the object pictured. Finally, a symbol system represents things by design features that include remoteness and arbitrariness. A word neither points directly to its referent here and now, nor does it resemble it as a picture. The lexeme 'Philadelphia' looks no more like the city so designated than does a nonsense syllable. The other property of language that is crucial is its productiveness in combination, far beyond what can be done with images or acts. 'Philadelphia is a lavendar sachet in Grandmother's linen closet', or $(x + 2)^2 = x^2 + 4x + 4 = x(x + 4) + 4$.

An example or two of enactive representation underlines its importance in infancy and in disturbed functioning, while illustrating its limitations. Piaget (1954) provides us with an observation from the closing weeks of the first year of life. The child is playing with a rattle in his crib. The rattle drops over the side. The child moves his clenched hand before his face, opens it, looks for the rattle. Not finding it there, he moves his hand, closed again, back to the edge of the crib, shakes it with movements like those he uses in shaking the rattle. Thereupon he moves his closed hand back toward his face, opens it, and looks. Again no rattle; and so he tries again. In several months, the child has benefited from experience to the degree that the rattle and action become separated. Whereas earlier he would not show signs of missing the rattle when it was removed unless he had begun reaching for it, now he cries and searches when the rattle is presented for a moment and hidden by a cover. He no longer repeats a movement to restore the rattle. In place of representation by action alone – where 'existence' is defined by the compass of present action – it is now defined by an image that persists autonomously.

A second example is provided by the results of injury to the occipital and temporal cortex in man (Hanfmann, Rickers-Ovsiankina and Goldstein, 1944). A patient is presented with a hard-boiled egg intact in its shell, and asked what it is. Holding it in his hand, he is embarrassed, for he cannot name it. He makes a motion as if to throw it and halts himself. Then he brings it to his mouth as if to bite it and stops before he gets there. He brings it to his ear and shakes it gently. He is puzzled. The experimenter takes the egg from him and cracks it on the table, handing it back. The patient then begins to peel the egg and announces what it is. He cannot identify objects without reference to the action he directs toward them.

The disadvantages of such a system are illustrated by Emerson's (1931) experiment in which children are told to place a ring on a board with seven rows and six columns of pegs, copying the position of a ring put on an identical board by the experimenter. Children ranging from 3 to 12 were examined in this experiment and in an extension of it carried out by Werner (1948). The child's board could be placed in various positions relative to the experimenter's: right next to it, 90 degrees rotated away from it, 180 degrees rotated, placed face to face with it so that the child has to turn full around to make his placement, etc. The older the child, the better his performance. But the younger children could do about as well as the oldest so long as they did not have to change their own position vis-à-vis the experimenter's board in order to make a match on their own board. The more they had to turn, the more difficult the task. They were clearly depending upon their bodily orientation toward the experimenter's board to guide them. When this orientation is disturbed by having to turn, they lose the position on the board. Older children succeed even when they must turn, either by the use of imagery that is invariant across bodily displacements, or, later, by specifying column and row of the experimenter's ring and carrying the symbolized self-instruction back to their own board. It is a limited world, the world of enactive representation.

We know little about the conditions necessary for the growth of imagery and iconic representation, or to what extent parental or environmental intervention affects it during the earliest years. In ordinary adult learning a certain amount of motoric skill and practice seems to be a necessary precondition for the development of a simultaneous image to represent the sequence of acts involved. If an adult subject is made to choose a path through a complex bank of toggle switches, he does not form an image of the path, according to Mandler (1962), until he has mastered and overpractised the task by successive manipulation. Then, finally, he reports that an image of the path has developed and that he is now using it rather than groping his way through.

Our main concern in what follows is not with the growth of iconic representation, but with the transition from it to symbolic representation. For it is in the development of symbolic representation that one finds, perhaps, the greatest thicket of psychological problems. The puzzle begins when the child first achieves the use of productive grammar, usually late in the second year of life. Toward the end of the second year, the child is master of the single-word, agrammatical utterance, the so-called holophrase. In the months following, there occurs a profound change in the use of language. Two classes of words appear – a pivot class and an open class – and the child launches forth on his career in combinatorial talking and, perhaps, thinking. Whereas before, lexemes like *allgone* and *mummy* and *sticky* and *bye-bye* were used singly, now for example, *allgone* becomes a pivot word and is used in combination. Mother washes jam off the child's hands; he says *allgone sticky*. In the next days, if his speech is carefully followed (Braine, 1963), it will be apparent that he is trying out the limits of the pivot combinations, and one will even find constructions that have an extraordinary capacity for representing complex sequences – like *allgone bye-bye* after a visitor has departed. A recent and ingenious observation by Weir (1962) on her 2½-year-old son, recording his speech musings after he was in bed with lights out, indicates that at this stage there is a great deal of metalinguistic combinatorial play with words in which the child is exploring the limits of grammatical productiveness.

In effect, language provides a means, not only for representing experience, but also for transforming it. As Chomsky (1957) and Miller (1962) have both made clear in the last few years, the transformational rules of grammar provide a syntactic means of reworking the 'realities' one has encountered. Not only, if you will, did the dog bite the man, but the man was bitten by the dog and perhaps the man was not bitten by the dog or was the man not bitten by the dog. The range of reworking that is made possible even by the three transformations of the passive, the negative and the query is very striking indeed. Or the ordering device whereby the comparative mode makes it possible to connect what is *heavy* and what is *light* into the ordinal array of *heavy* and *less heavy* is again striking. Or, to take a final example, there is the discrimination that is made possible by the growth of attribute language such that the global dimension *big* and *little* can now be decomposed into *tall* and *short* on the one hand and *fat* and *skinny* on the other.

Once the child has succeeded in internalizing language as a cognitive instrument, it becomes possible for him to represent and systematically transform the regularities of experience with far greater flexibility and power than before. Interestingly enough, it is the recent Russian literature, particularly Vygotsky's (1962) book on language and thought, and the work of his disciple, Luria (1961), and his students (Abramyan, 1958; Martsinovskaya, undated) that has highlighted these phenomena by calling attention to the so-called second-signal system which replaces classical conditioning with an internalized linguistic system for shaping and transforming experience itself.

If all these matters were not of such complexity and human import, I would apologize for taking so much time in speculation. We turn now to some new experiments designed to shed some light on the nature of representation and particularly upon the transition from its iconic to its symbolic form.

Let me begin with an experiment by Bruner and Kenney (1966) on the manner in which children between five and seven handle a double classification matrix. The materials of the experiment are nine plastic glasses, arranged so that they vary in three degrees of diameter and three degrees of height. They are set before the child initially, as in figure 25.1, on a 3 × 3 grid marked on a large piece of cardboard. To acquaint the child with the matrix, we first remove one, then two, and then three glasses from the matrix, asking the child to replace them. We also ask the children to describe how the glasses in the columns and rows are alike and how they differ. Then the glasses are scrambled and we ask the child to make something like what was there before by placing the glasses on the same grid that was used when the

Matrix   Procedure

Scale in inches
0 1 2 3 4 5 6

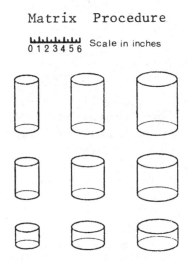

Figure 25.1   Array of glasses used in study of matrix ordering (Bruner and Kenney, 1966).

task was introduced. Now we scramble the glasses once more, but this time we place the glass that was formerly in the southwest corner of the grid in the southeast corner (it is the shortest, thinnest glass) and ask the child if he can make something like what was there before, leaving the one glass where we have just put it. That is the experiment.

The results can be quickly told. To begin with, there is no difference between ages five, six and seven either in terms of ability to replace glasses taken from the matrix or in building a matrix once it has been scrambled (but without the transposed glass). Virtually all the children succeed. Interestingly enough, *all* the children rebuild the matrix to match the original, almost as if they were copying what was there before. The only difference is that the older children are quicker.

Now compare the performance of the three ages in constructing the matrix with a single member transposed. Most of the seven-year-olds succeed in the transposed task, but hardly any of the youngest children. Figure 25.2 presents the results graphically. The youngest children seem to be dominated by an image of the original matrix. They try to put the transposed glass 'back where it belongs', to rotate the cardboard so that 'it will be like

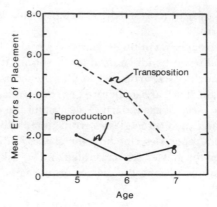

Reconstruction of Matrix

Figure 25.2   Mean number of errors made by children in reproducing and transposing a 3 × 3 matrix (Bruner and Kenney, 1966).

before', and sometimes they will start placing a few glasses neighboring the transposed glass correctly only to revert to the original arrangement. In several instances five- or six-year-olds will simply try to reconstitute the old matrix, building right over the transposed glass. The seven-year-old, on the other hand, is more likely to pause, to treat the transposition as a problem, to talk to himself about 'where this should go'. The relation of place and size is for him a problem that requires reckoning, not simply copying.

Now consider the language children use for describing the dimensions of the matrix (see figure 25.3). Recall that the children were asked how glasses in a row and in a column were alike and how they differed. Children answered in three distinctive linguistic modes. One was *dimensional*, singling out two ends of an attribute – for example, 'That one is higher, and that one is shorter.' A second was *global* in nature. Of glasses differing only in height the child says, 'That one is bigger and that one is little.' The same words could be used equally well for diameter or for nearly any other magnitude. Finally, there was *confounded* usage: 'That one is tall and that one is little', where a dimensional term is used for one end of the continuum and a global term for the other. The children who used confounded descriptions had the most difficulty with the transposed matrix. Lumping all ages together, the children who used confounded descriptions were twice as likely to fail on the transposition task as those who used either dimensional or global terms. *But the language the children used had no relation whatsoever to their performance in reproducing the first untransposed matrix.* Inhelder and Sinclair[*] in a recent communication also report that confounded language of this kind is associated with failure on conservation tasks in children of the same age, a subject to which we shall turn shortly.

The findings of this experiment suggest two things. First, that children who use iconic representation are more highly sensitized to the spatial–qualitative organization of experience and less to the ordering principles governing such organization. They can recognize and reproduce, but cannot produce new structures based on rule. And second,

---

[*] Bärbel Inhelder and Mimi Sinclair, personal communication, 1963.

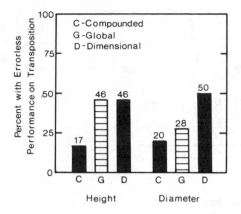

Descriptive Language Use

Figure 25.3   Percentage of children (aged five to seven) using different language patterns who reproduced transposed matrix errorlessly (Bruner and Kenney, 1966).

there is a suspicion that the language they bring to bear on the task is insufficient as a tool for ordering. If these notions are correct, then certain things should follow. For one thing, *improvement* in language should aid this type of problem solving. This remains to be investigated. But it is also reasonable to suppose that *activation* of language habits that the child has already mastered might improve performance as well – a hypothesis already suggested by the findings of Luria's students (e.g., Abramyan, 1958). Now, activation can be achieved by two means: one is by having the child 'say' the description of something before him that he must deal with symbolically. The other is to take advantage of the remoteness of reference that is a feature of language, and have the child 'say' his description in the absence of the things to be described. In this way, there would be less likelihood of a perceptual–iconic representation becoming dominant and inhibiting the operation of symbolic processes. An experiment by Françoise Frank (in press) illustrates this latter approach – the effects of saying before seeing.

Piaget and Inhelder (1962) (see figure 25.4) have shown that if children between ages four and seven are presented two identical beakers which they judge equally full of water, they will no longer consider the water equal if the contents of one of the beakers is now poured into a beaker that is either wider or thinner than the original. If the second beaker is thinner, they will say it has more to drink because the water is higher; if the second beaker is wider, they will say it has less because the water is lower. Comparable results can be obtained by pouring the contents of one glass into several smaller beakers. In Geneva terms, the child is not yet able to conserve liquid volume across transformations in its appearance. Consider how this behavior can be altered.

Françoise Frank (1966) first did the classic conservation tests to determine which children exhibited conservation and which did not. Her subjects were four, five, six and seven years old. See figure 25.5 for one procedure. She then went on to other procedures, among which was the following. Two standard beakers are partly filled so that the child judges them to contain equal amounts of water. A wider beaker of the same height is

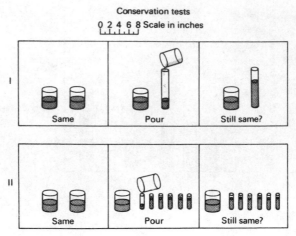

Figure 25.4   Two Geneva tests for conservation of liquid volume across transformations in its appearance (Piaget and Inhelder, 1962).

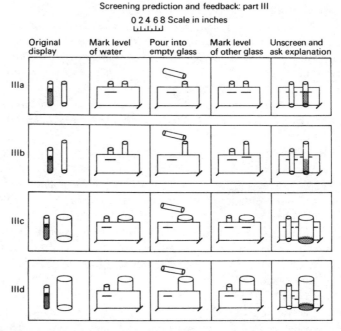

Figure 25.5   One procedure used in study of effect of language activation on conservation (Frank, 1966).

introduced and the three beakers are now, except for their tops, hidden by a screen. The experimenter pours from a standard beaker into the wider beaker. The child, without seeing the water, is asked which has more to drink, or do they have the same amount, the standard or the wider beaker. The results are in figure 25.6. In comparison with the unscreened pre-test, there is a striking increase in correct equality judgments. Correct responses jump from 0 per cent to 50 per cent among the fours, from 20 per cent to 90 per cent among the fives and from 50 per cent to 100 per cent among the sixes. With the screen present, most children justify their correct judgment by noting that 'It's the same water', or 'You only poured it.'

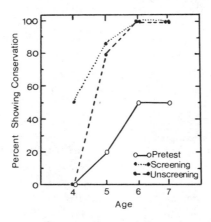

Conservation and Screening

Figure 25.6   Percentage of children showing conservation of liquid volume before and during screening and upon unscreening of the displays (Frank, 1966).

Now the screen is removed. All the four-year-olds change their minds. The perceptual display overwhelms them and they decide that the wider beaker has less water. But virtually all of the five-year-olds stick to their judgment, often invoking the difference between appearance and reality – 'It looks like more to drink, but it is only the same because it is the same water and it was only poured from there to there', to quote one typical five-year-old. And all of the sixes and all the sevens stick to their judgment. Now, some minutes later, Frank does a post-test on the children using a tall thin beaker along with the standard ones, and no screen, of course (figure 25.7). The fours are unaffected by their prior experience: none of them is able to grasp the idea of invariant quantity in the new task. With the fives, instead of 20 per cent showing conservation, as in the pre-test, 70 per cent do. With both sixes and sevens conservation increases from 50 per cent to 90 per cent. I should mention that control groups doing just a pre-test and post-test show no significant improvement in performance.

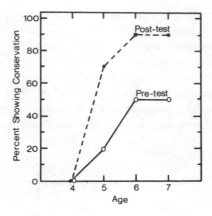

After-effects of Screening

Figure 25.7   Percentage of children showing conservation of liquid volume in identical pre-test and post-test run after completion of experiment (Frank, 1966).

CONCLUSIONS

My major concern has been to examine afresh the nature of intellectual growth. The account has surely done violence to the richness of the subject. It seems to me that growth depends upon the emergence of two forms of competence. Children, as they grow, must acquire ways of representing the recurrent regularities in their environment, and they must transcend the momentary by developing ways of linking past to present to future – representation and integration. I have suggested that we can conceive of growth in both of these domains as the emergence of new technologies for the unlocking and amplification of human intellectual powers. Like the growth of technology, the growth of intellect is not smoothly monotonic. Rather, it moves forward in spurts as innovations are adopted. Most of the innovations are transmitted to the child in some prototypic form by agents of the culture: ways of responding, ways of looking and imaging, and most important, ways of translating what one has encountered into language.

I have relied heavily in this account on the successive emergence of action, image and word as the vehicles of representation, a reliance based both upon our observations and upon modern readings of man's alloplastic evolution. Our attention has been directed largely to the transition between iconic and symbolic representation.

In children between 4 and 12 language comes to play an increasingly powerful role as an implement of knowing. Through simple experiments, I have tried to show how language shapes, augments and even supersedes the child's earlier modes of processing information. Translation of experience into symbolic form, with its attendant means of achieving remote reference, transformation and combination, opens up realms of intellectual possibility that are orders of magnitude beyond the most powerful image forming system.

What of the integration of intellectual activity into more coherent and interconnected acts? It has been the fashion, since Freud, to see delay of gratification as the principle dynamism behind this development – from primary process to secondary process, or from assimilation to accommodation, as Piaget would put it today. Without intending to question the depth of this insight, let me suggest that delay of immediate gratification, the ability to go beyond the moment, also depends upon techniques, and again they are techniques of representation. Perhaps representation exclusively by imagery and perceptual organization has built into it one basic operation that ties it to the immediate present. It is the operation of pointing – ostensiveness, as logicians call it. (This is not to say that highly evolved images do not go beyond immediate time and given place. Maps and flow charts are iconic in nature, but they are images that translate prior linguistic and mathematical renderings into a visual form.) Iconic representation, in the beginning, is built upon a perceptual organization that is tied to the 'point-at-able' spatioqualitative properties of events. I have suggested that, for all its limitations, such representation is an achievement beyond the earlier stage where percepts are not autonomous of action. But so long as perceptual representation dominates, it is difficult to develop higher-order techniques for processing information by consecutive inferential steps that take one beyond what can be pointed at.

Once language becomes a medium for the translation of experience, there is a progressive release from immediacy. For language, as we have commented, has the new and powerful features of remoteness and arbitrariness: it permits productive, combinatorial operations in the *absence* of what is represented. With this achievement, the child can delay gratification by virtue of representing to himself what lies beyond the present, what other possibilities exist beyond the clue that is under his nose. The child may be *ready* for delay of gratification, but he is no more able to bring it off than somebody ready to build a house, save that he has not yet heard of tools.

The discussion leaves two obvious questions begging. What of the integration of behavior in organisms without language? And how does language become internalized as a vehicle for organizing experience? The first question has to be answered briefly and somewhat cryptically. Wherever integrated behavior has been studied – as in Lehrman's (1955) careful work on integrated instinctive patterns in the ringdove, it has turned out that a sustaining external stimulus was needed to keep the highly integrated behavior going. The best way to control behavior in subhuman species is to control the stimulus situation. Surely this is the lesson of Lashley's (1938) classic account of instinctive behavior. Where animal learning is concerned, particularly in the primates, there is, to be sure, considerable plasticity. But it too depends upon the development of complex forms of stimulus substitution and organization – as in Klüver's (1933) work on equivalence reactions in monkeys. If it should seem that I am urging that the growth of symbolic functioning links a unique set of powers to man's capacity, the appearance is quite as it should be.

As for how language becomes internalized as a program for ordering experience, I join those who despair for an answer. My speculation, for whatever it is worth, is that the process of internalization depends upon interaction with others, upon the need to develop corresponding categories and transformations for communal action. It is the need for cognitive coin that can be exchanged with those on whom we depend. What Roger Brown (1958) has called the Original Word Game ends up by being the Human Thinking Game.

If I have seemed to underemphasize the importance of inner capacities – for example, the capacity *for* language or *for* imagery – it is because I believe that this part of the story is given by the nature of man's evolution. What is significant about the growth of mind in the child is to what degree it depends not upon capacity but upon the unlocking of capacity by techniques that come from exposure to the specialized environment of a culture. Romantic clichés, like 'the veneer of culture' or 'natural man', are as misleading if not as damaging as the view that the course of human development can be viewed independently of the educational process we arrange to make that development possible.

ACKNOWLEDGEMENT   ·

This article first appeared in *Am. Psychol.* (1964), **19**, 1–15. Extracts from it are published here with the kind permission of author and editor.

REFERENCES

Abramyan, L. A. (1958) Organization of the voluntary activity of the child with the help of verbal instruction. Unpublished diploma thesis, Moscow University. Cited by Luria, A. R. (1961) *The Role of Speech in the Regulation of Normal and Abnormal Behavior*. New York: Liveright.

Barker, R. G. (1963) On the nature of the environment. Kurt Lewin Memorial Address presented at American Psychological Association, Philadelphia.

Brown, R. (1958) *Words and Things*. Glencoe, Ill.: Free Press.

Bruner, J. S. & Kenney, Helen. (1966) The development of the concepts of order and proportion in children. In Bruner, J. S., *Studies in Cognitive Growth*. New York: Wiley.

Chomsky, N. (1957) *Syntactic Structures*. S'Gravenhage, Netherlands: Mouton.

Emerson, L. L. (1931) The effect of bodily orientation upon the young child's memory for position of objects. *Child Develpm.*, **2**, 125–142.

Frank, Françoise (1966) Perception and language in conservation. In Bruner, J. S., *Studies in Cognitive Growth*. New York: Wiley.

Hanfmann, Eugenia, Rickers-Ovsiankina, Maria & Goldstein, K. (1944) Case Lanuti: extreme concretization of behavior due to damage of the brain cortex. *Psychol. Monogr.*, **57** (4, Whole No. 264).

Klüver, H. (1933) *Behavior Mechanisms in Monkeys*. Chicago: Univer. Chicago Press.

la Barre, W. (1954) *The Human Animal*. Chicago: Univer. Chicago Press.

Lashley, K. S. (1938) Experimental analysis of instinctive behavior. *Psychol. Rev.*, **45**, 445–472.

Lehrman, D. S. (1955) The physiological basis of parental feeding behavior in the ring dove (*Streptopelia risoria*). *Behavior*, **7**, 241–286.

Luria, A. R. (1961) *The Role of Speech in the Regulation of Normal and Abnormal Behavior*. New York: Liveright.

Mandler, G. (1962) From association to structure. *Psychol. Rev.*, **69**, 415–427.

Martsinovskaya, E. N. (undated) Research into the reflective and regulatory role of the second signalling system of pre-school age. Collected papers of the Department of Psychology, Moscow University. Cited by Luria, A. R. (1961) *The Role of Speech in the Regulation of Normal and Abnormal Behavior*. New York: Liveright.

Miller, G. A. (1962) Some psychological studies of grammar. *Am. Psychol.*, **17**, 748–762.

Miller, G. A., Galanter, E. & Pribram, K. H. (1960) *Plans and the Structure of Behavior*. New York: Holt.

Piaget, J. (1954) *The Construction of Reality in the Child*. (Trans. by Margaret Cook) New York: Basic Books.

Piaget, J. & Inhelder, Bärbel (1962) *Le Développement des Quantités Physiques chez l'Enfant* (2nd rev. ed.). Neuchâtel, Switzerland: Delachaux & Niestlé.

Vygotsky, L. S. (1962) *Thought and Language* (Ed. & trans. by Eugenia Hanfmann & Gertrude Vakar). New York: Wiley.

Washburn, S. L. & Howell, F. C. (1960) Human evolution and culture. In Tax, S., *The Evolution of Man*. Vol. 2. Chicago: Univer. Chicago Press.

Weir, Ruth H. (1962) *Language in the Crib*. The Hague: Mouton.

Werner, H. (1948) *Comparative Psychology of Mental Development* (rev. ed.). Chicago: Follett.

26 Self-concepts among secondary school pupils

BARBARA THOMPSON

Summary Approximately 500 out of a sample of over 2000 first-year pupils in 20 secondary schools were identified by their teachers as being either particularly well-adjusted, maladjusted or as having appeared before a court. These pupils were asked to complete 'semantic differential' scales on which they rated for such concepts as 'myself', 'my mother thinks I am . . .', 'my father thinks I am . . .', 'my friends think I am . . .' and 'my teacher thinks I am . . .'. The investigation was repeated for most of the same pupils in the fourth year. There was little difference in the self-evaluations of the three groups, but interesting differences emerged between the groups as to how they believed others saw them.

The investigation was carried out in 1967 and 1970 as part of the NFER Constructive Education project, sponsored by the Home office and the Department of Education and Science.

INTRODUCTION

It is generally accepted that the way an individual perceives himself influences the way he behaves in interaction with his physical and social environment. It may also be assumed that school children who are perceived by their teachers to be particularly well-adjusted or maladjusted, or who have a record of delinquent behaviour, will have different concepts of themselves, and will also vary in the ways they believe significant people in their lives perceive them.

In an extensive study of the self-image of over 5000 New York adolescents, using a 10-item scale, Rosenberg (1965) found that those with low self-esteem were more likely to:

(a) display a number of psychosomatic symptoms;
(b) feel it necessary to present a false front to the external world;
(c) be sensitive to criticism or attack;
(d) feel isolated and lonely;
(e) have difficulty in making friends;
(f) have little faith in people;
(g) be shy and unwilling to initiate conversations.

Remarkably similar results were obtained by Coopersmith (1967) with a sample of 10-year-old boys. Thus low self-esteem would appear to be associated with the type of behaviour which is frequently assessed as maladjusted.

Reckless, Dinitz and Murray (1956) found that pupils with a positive self-concept were unlikely to become delinquent, and introduced the notion of the self-concept as an insulator against delinquency. The results of one of their studies are summarized by Schwartz and Tangri (1965) as follows:

The 'bad' boys see themselves as likely to get into trouble in the future; their mothers and teachers agree. The 'good' boys see themselves as unlikely to get into trouble; their mothers and teachers agree.

Their own study, using a 10-scale form of the 'Semantic Differential', confirmed that sixth grade boys designated as 'good' by their teachers had more positive self-concepts than those of their peers designated as 'bad'. When the self-concepts of the two groups of boys were correlated with their mothers', friends' and teachers' views of them, the 'good' boys' self-concept was only found to correlate significantly with the way their teachers saw them. The only significant correlation with the 'bad' boys' self-concept on the other hand, was with their mothers' view of them. This result can be interpreted in one of two ways:

(a) that the mothers of 'bad' boys fail to encourage independence, thus restricting the possibility that others can control the boys' behaviour by reflecting either negative or positive self-images;
(b) if the evaluations of the 'bad' boys made by their peers are not yet significant, and their teachers reject them (as they show by nominating them as 'bad') where but to their mothers can they turn for support?

Whichever interpretation is accepted the outcome remains the same; 12-year-old 'bad' boys are over-close to their mothers and therefore likely to have difficulty in developing appropriate masculine identifications. In addition, Hurlock (1967), reviewing some of the work on delinquency, reports that an unrealistic self-concept is likely to be associated with delinquency since it increases the probability that the child

will try to compensate for the feelings of inadequacy that come from falling short of an unrealistic self-image by behaviour that deviates from the socially accepted pattern [p. 485].

On the basis of the above findings, the following predictions can be made:

(a) *Well-adjusted pupils* will have positive and stable self-images;
(b) *Maladjusted pupils* will have less positive self-images, in particular they will feel themselves less 'good', 'reliable', 'successful', 'wise' and 'orderly' than well-adjusted pupils, and will be less certain of their sexual identification. As they are clearly having difficulties in school it will also be predicted that they will feel undervalued by their teachers;
(c) *Delinquent pupils* will also have less positive self-images than the well-adjusted pupils. However, unlike the other groups, their self-images are likely to be at variance with the images they believe others have of them. Where specific scales are concerned, it is predicted that delinquents will see themselves as less 'good' and 'reliable' and also have less clear sexual identification, but will see themselves as harder and stronger than other pupils;
(d) There will be a tendency for older pupils to have less positive self-concepts than younger

ones, and this will be particularly so in the case of the opinions they believe their teachers have of them.

METHOD

The data to be analysed here were collected as part of a study of attitudes of first- and fourth-year pupils in 20 secondary schools carried out as part of the NFER Constructive Education Project, sponsored by the Home Office and the Department of Education and Science.

(a) Subjects

The sample, in 1967, comprised 1310 boys and 1073 girls in their first year of secondary school; and, in 1970, any of these pupils remaining in the same schools in their fourth year (1170 boys and 949 girls).

Teachers were asked on each occasion to nominate pupils

(i)   who stood out in their age groups as stable and well-adjusted;
(ii)   'whose "maladjustment" is such that you would undoubtedly refer them for psychological or psychiatric guidance or treatment if such a service would readily cope with the demands to be made on it . . . ';
(iii) who had appeared before the court at any time.

Table 26.1 shows the numbers of boys and girls in each group in their first and fourth years.[*]

Table 26.1   Numbers of pupils nominated as well-adjusted, maladjusted and delinquent

	Boys			Girls		
	Well-adjusted	Maladjusted	Delinquent	Well-adjusted	Maladjusted	Delinquent
1st year	164	64	21	147	44	6
4th year	165	40	70	174	49	14

(b) The instrument

Osgood, Suci and Tannenbaum (1957) developed the 'Semantic Differential' as a measure of connotative meaning, i.e. that aspect of meaning concerned with the associations rather than the literal meaning of the word. Osgood's instrument attempts to register the connotations which a concept has for an individual on a number of bipolar scales such as 'bad' . . . 'good', 'unsuccessful' . . . 'successful'. The respondent has to place a mark in one of the intervals on each scale. Thus 'peace' might be rated as very good but relatively unsuccessful. Such an instrument was considered to be appropriate to explore how pupils saw themselves and how they thought others saw them.

Questions have been raised as to the validity of self-ratings as a measure of self-concept

---

[*] The data analysed in the paper refer to these pupils only.

(Coombes, Soper and Courson, 1963). Whereas it is agreed that a certain amount of distortion will inevitably occur when a person is asked to present a view of himself to outsiders, it is considered that:

(i)   an instrument such as the Semantic Differential, being less obvious in its intentions, will not be as subject to distortion as some of the instruments designed to measure self-concept more overtly;

(ii) a rating-scale of this type is the only way of getting comparable data on how a pupil views himself and how he believes others view him.

   All pupils were therefore asked to complete a 16-scale form of the Semantic Differential for 12 concepts including: 'Myself', 'My mother thinks I am . . .', 'My father thinks I am . . .', 'My friends think I am . . .', 'My teacher thinks I am . . .'.*

   In a number of factor analyses of semantic differential data, carried out by Osgood and others (Osgood, Suci and Tannenbaum, 1957; Warr and Knapper, 1968), the scales have generally been shown to fall into three main clusters identified as Evaluation, Activity and Potency. These are taken to represent three major dimensions of meaning. As the instrument on this occasion was to be used as a measure of attitudes, the majority of the scales (11 out of a total of 16) were selected to represent the evaluative dimension. This is the factor which accounts for the largest percentage of the variance and has been identified as the attitudinal component of meaning. The other five scales, three representing the potency dimension and two the activity dimension, were initially included in order to prevent pupils from identifying the purpose of the study too clearly.

   Financial limitations precluded carrying out a factor analysis of the scales on the data collected in this study. Hence it has not been possible to check directly the actual relation of scales to dimensions. Previous research has shown (Osgood, Suci and Tannenbaum, 1957) that the factors on which scales load vary according to the concept being rated. Evidence also exists that when judging particularly highly or lowly evaluated concepts all scores should tend to rotate towards a single dominant evaluative dimension. However, in the present analysis, the assumption has been made that the 11 scales selected to represent the evaluative dimension did indeed do so.

(c) Measures derived

Osgood suggests the use of two types of measures: (a) factor scores, and (b) 'D', or generalized distance, scores which indicate the overall distance between two profiles. A number of authors (Cronbach, 1958; Jackson, 1962; Warr and Knapper, 1968) have criticized the use of the D statistic, as the formula can result in the same score being derived from a number of different relationships between profiles. Warr and Knapper state their preferences for analysing differences between groups in greater detail, and adopt a procedure of testing for significant differences between sets of responses to each scale. This procedure has been followed in the current study. In addition, a Total Evaluation score obtained by summing the ratings on each concept over the 11 evaluative scales has been used, plus a difference score consisting of the sum of the differences on each evaluative scale between the ratings of 'myself' and of the views of mother, father, friends and teacher.

---

* Forms were completed for seven other concepts but these are not relevant to the current discussion.

(d) Analysis

The question as to whether it is appropriate to use parametric statistics for the analysis of semantic differential data has been discussed at length by Warr and Knapper (1968) who conclude that the three main requirements for the use of parametric statistics – similar variances, equal interval scales and normal distribution of responses – are normally met. All analyses quoted in this study therefore make use of the F and 't' statistics.

RESULTS

(a) Total evaluation scores

(i) *Myself* As predicted, well-adjusted boys and girls have very positive self-concepts. First year well-adjusted pupils have a total evaluation score of 61.35, giving an average position on the seven-point scale of 5.6; and fourth years, 59.88, with scale average 5.4.

First-year maladjusted pupils have significantly less positive self-concepts than their well-adjusted peers. However, by the time they reach their fourth years, the differences between the two groups no longer reach significance. Neither can their self-evaluation actually be considered low, as their average scale scores are still greater than 5.0, i.e. more than a point above the centre-point.

None of the delinquents' self-evaluations differ significantly from those of well-adjusted pupils.

There is a tendency, as predicted, for older pupils to have less positive self-concepts than younger ones, although the only comparison between first and fourth years to reach significance is that between all the well-adjusted pupils.

(ii) *Myself as others see me* In their first year at secondary school, pupils who are nominated by teachers as maladjusted rate themselves as seen by their mothers, fathers, friends and teachers less favourably than well-adjusted pupils, and the differences are more marked for girls than for boys. By the time they reach their fourth year, the maladjusted pupils see their mothers' and friends' views of them as being favourable, as do those who are well-adjusted. However, their fathers' and teachers' views are still rated as significantly less favourable than those of the well-adjusted group. As shown in table 26.1 only a very few first-year pupils (21 boys and six girls) were classified as delinquent. Having groups as small as this considerably reduces the probability of any of the comparisons leading to significant results. In fact, it is only when ratings for 'My teacher thinks I am' are compared for all delinquent and all well-adjusted pupils that a significant difference obtains, the delinquents perceiving their teachers' views of them as less favourable than the maladjusted pupils.

In the fourth year, the number of delinquent boys is 70, although there are still only 14 girls so classified. Delinquent boys rate their mothers', fathers' and teachers' views of them less favourably than do well-adjusted pupils, and these results also hold when ratings for boys and girls are combined.

Unlike the results for their ratings of themselves, there is a strong tendency for pupils' ratings of how others see them to decrease from their first to their fourth years. For well-adjusted pupils, it is their fathers and teachers who are now seen to value them less highly, while delinquent boys rate their teachers as well as both parents as having a less favourable view of them. No changes are found for maladjusted pupils.

When the change with age is looked at between the three groups of first- and fourth-year pupils of the same sex, it becomes clear that ways in which boys rate others as perceiving them deteriorates much more than those for girls. The older boys feel that their teacher and both parents value them less highly than when they were younger, whereas the change for the girls only reaches significance where their fathers' views are concerned.

(b) 'Myself' – other difference scores

It was predicted that well-adjusted pupils would have stable and realistic self-concepts. If this were the case, it would be assumed that they would not see themselves as under- or over-valued by parents, friends or teachers. This prediction holds to some extent for the well-adjusted girls, although in their first year they feel undervalued by their teachers, and in the fourth year by both teachers and their mothers. The picture for the boys, however, suggests that they feel undervalued by everyone except their fathers. This exception, however, is an important one, as Rosenberg (1965) found that a close relation with father was a crucial factor in high self-esteem.

The only prediction relevant to this section concerning maladjusted pupils was that they would feel undervalued by their teachers, who nominated them as in need of treatment. This is supported for all maladjusted groups except first-year girls.

There is little support from the results for first-year delinquents for the prediction that their self-images would be unrealistic, that is that they would feel generally undervalued. Like the maladjusted pupils, both boys and girls feel undervalued by their teachers, and girls feel this also of their fathers. The prediction is, however, strongly upheld for fourth-year delinquent boys. They feel undervalued by their teachers and by both parents. The group of girls is again too small for significant differences to be likely. The result which comes nearest to significance for them shows a tendency for them to perceive their friends as overvaluing them.

(c) Comparisons on individual scales

(i) *Myself* On the basis of previous work, predictions were made as to how particular groups of pupils would rate themselves on specific scales. As has already been stated, pupils did not vary greatly in their ratings of themselves. However, some significant scale differences were found when maladjusted and well-adjusted pupils were compared. The scale which best differentiated the two groups was 'unsuccessful–successful' (significant differences for first-year boys and boys and girls combined, as well as the combined fourth years). In addition, fourth-year girls rated themselves less 'good' than their well-adjusted peers, fourth-year boys less 'masculine' and the combined fourth years less 'reliable'. No significant differences were found on the other two scales for which predictions were made, 'foolish–wise' and 'muddled–orderly'.

Significant scale differences were even scarcer when delinquent pupils' self-concepts were compared with well-adjusted ones. The only scales to differentiate these were weak–strong (first-year delinquent boys seeing themselves stronger than their well-adjusted peers), and 'soft–hard' where again delinquent boys in the first year and all fourth-year delinquents rated themselves as 'harder' than comparable groups of well-adjusted pupils.

(ii) *Myself as others see me*   It is reasonable to argue that the way an individual believes others see him has even more influence on his behaviour than the way he sees himself. Comparisons between the ratings of how well-adjusted and deviant pupils believe others see them give considerably more information on the characteristics on which these pupils feel they differ.

Maladjusted first-year pupils are best differentiated from the equivalent well-adjusted group by the scales 'dirty–clean' and 'unreliable–reliable', rating others' views of them as less favourable on both scales. They also feel they are seen as less good generally by friends and teachers, and less successful by fathers and teachers. Finally, boys and girls see themselves as rated by both parents further from the ideal sex-type than the well-adjusted pupils do.

The scale 'unreliable–reliable' is also the one which best differentiates older maladjusted from well-adjusted pupils. Only their mothers are not perceived as rating them as less reliable than the mothers of the well-adjusted pupils are perceived as rating their offspring. Fathers, friends and teachers are also perceived as finding them less successful, and the boys believe everyone rates them as less masculine. The general tendency of older maladjusted pupils to devalue themselves is also shown in the lower rating of them attributed to father and teacher on the scales 'boring–interesting' and 'bad–good'.

When responses of first-year delinquent and well-adjusted pupils are considered, the situation is relatively unclear. In fact, there is a tendency for first-year delinquent pupils to rate others' views of them as more favourable than well-adjusted pupils of the same age. This becomes highly significant in the scale 'weak–strong', where ratings of themselves as mother, father and friends see them are more positive than the same ratings by well-adjusted boys.

The scales which most differentiate the fourth-year delinquent pupils from their well-adjusted peers are 'soft–hard', 'cruel–kind' and 'feminine–masculine', delinquents feeling harder and more cruel and less clearly identified with their own sex. They are also seen as less clean, good and successful from at least three other viewpoints. Perhaps the most important information to be gleaned from the analyses of these pupils' ratings is how undervalued they feel by fathers and teachers. Differences from well-adjusted pupils reach significance for perceived views of fathers and teachers on 12 out of the 16 scales.

DISCUSSION

Secondary school pupils generally evaluate themselves very favourably, as indicated by the high group averages for the Total Evaluation Scores. The average scale score of the group with the least favourable self-rating (first-year maladjusted pupils) is still over 5.0, i.e. more than a point above the centre of the scale.

Contrary to prediction, however, self-ratings vary very little from group to group, only first-year maladjusted pupils rating themselves sufficiently differently from the well-adjusted group for the result to reach significance. It seems possible that even an instrument which conceals its intent as well as the Semantic Differential does, inhibits pupils from displaying negative feelings about themselves; and that only when they are asked to rate themselves as others see them are these inhibitions released sufficiently to display those differences which have led teachers to classify them as deviant. A further possible interpretation of this finding would be that in fact it is the perceived views of others rather than the degree of self-esteem itself which affects people's behaviour, but this we cannot even attempt to explore here.

Certainly the results from comparisons between the way various groups of pupils feel others see them are far more revealing. Not only do first-year maladjusted pupils, as would be expected from the earlier finding, see themselves rated less favourably than their well-adjusted peers by parents, friends and teachers, but the results of comparisons are also significant for the older maladjusted pupils when their rating of themselves as fathers and teachers see them are compared with those of the well-adjusted group. Differences between delinquent and well-adjusted pupils now reach significance where teachers' views are concerned in their first year, and for teachers and both parents in the fourth.

As the original classification of deviancy was made by teachers, the pupils are clearly realistic in perceiving them as undervaluing them. Both older groups also attribute less favourable assessments to their fathers, suggesting that their problems are not confined to school. The low evaluation attributed to their mothers by older delinquents contradicts the findings of Schwartz and Tangri (1965) that delinquent boys, at least, are closely identified with their mothers. However, the delinquent boys in this study are three years older and would appear to have moved towards closer peer group identification. Their friends are the only people whose evaluations of them do not differ significantly from the ways in which they evaluate themselves.

The finding that fourth-year delinquents feel undervalued by teachers and parents appears to confirm the prediction that their self-images are at variance with the views they perceive others to have of them. An alternative interpretation, however, would be that these pupils are peer- rather than adult-orientated. This interpretation seems better to explain the difference from the well-adjusted boys, who feel undervalued by mothers, teachers and friends, but not by their fathers. This finding is not only further evidence for the importance of paternal support for adjustment and self-esteem, but also suggests that identification with an adult figure may be important for perceived success in school. The fact that well-adjusted girls do not feel under-valued by fathers or friends would indicate that the positive role played by father is the crucial factor in good adjustment.

A number of scales differentiate the two older deviant groups from their well-adjusted peers. Both deviant groups perceive themselves to be seen as less successful, good and masculine/feminine. However, the maladjusted pupils also feel themselves less reliable and interesting, scales which seem to indicate doubts about their acceptability as companions, while the other scales which differentiate the delinquents are part of the 'bad boy' stereotype – hard, cruel, dirty. The fact that they do not think they are perceived as masculine at the same time is a contradiction which gives rise to speculation as to the existence of some compensating mechanism.

MAIN POINTS

1 Secondary school pupils assessed as well-adjusted, maladjusted and delinquent do not vary greatly when evaluating 'myself' on a form of the semantic differential.
2 Their ratings of themselves as others see them indicate that both the maladjusted groups

and the older delinquents rate themselves as being perceived considerably less favourably than do the well-adjusted pupils.

3 Older delinquents appear to be peer rather than adult-orientated, in that only their friends are not seen to undervalue them.

4 The well-adjusted boys, on the other hand, feel that only their fathers do not undervalue them and this, combined with the fact that neither fathers nor friends are perceived as undervaluing the well-adjusted girls, underlines the importance of a positive adult identification.

5 The scales which appear to differentiate both deviant groups from the well-adjusted pupils are 'unsuccessful–successful', 'bad–good' and 'masculine–feminine'.

6 The scales on which maladjusted pupils also differ from well-adjusted pupils are 'boring–interesting' and 'unreliable–reliable', indicating doubts about personal value.

7 The scales differentiating delinquents on the other hand are 'soft–hard', 'cruel–kind' and 'dirty–clean', all part of the traditional tough 'bad boy' image.

ACKNOWLEDGEMENT

This article appeared in *Educ. Res.* (1974), **17**, 41–47, and is published here with the kind permission of author and editor.

REFERENCES

Coombes, A. W., Soper, D. W. & Courson, C. C. (1963) The measurement of self concept and self report. *Educ. and Psych. Measurement*, **xxiii** (3), 493–500.

Coopersmith, S. (1967) *The Antecedents of Self-Esteem*. San Francisco: Freeman.

Cronbach, L. J. (1958) Proposals leading to analytic treatment of social perception scores. In Taguisi, R. & Petrulle, L. (Eds.) *Person Perception and Interpersonal Behaviour*. Stanford University Press, Stanford.

Hurlock, E. B. (1967) *Adolescent Development*. Maidenhead: McGraw Hill.

Jackson, D. M. (1962) The measurement of perceived personality trait relationships. In Washburne, N. F. (Ed.) *Decisions, Values and Groups*, Vol. 2, Oxford: Pergamon Press.

Osgood, C. E., Suci, G. J. & Tannenbaum, P. M. (1957) *The Measurement of Meaning*. Urbana: University of Illinois Press.

Reckless, W. C., Dinitz, S. & Murray, E. (1956) Self concept as an insulation against delinquency. *Amer. Sociol. Rev.*, **21**, 740–746.

Rosenberg, M. (1965) *Society and the Adolescent Self-Image*. Princeton University Press.

Schwartz, M. & Tangri, S. S. (1965) A note on self concept as an insulator against delinquency, *Amer. Sociol. Rev.*, **30**, 6, 922–926.

Warr, P. B. & Knapper, C. (1968) *The Perception of People and Events*. New York: John Wiley.

27 Concept 7-9

Published by E. J. ARNOLD (for the Schools Council)

PREFACE

The Three Units of 'Concept Seven-Nine' have been designed to help children develop those skills which underlie success with language. The Units are closely interrelated. They direct attention on three critical aspects of oral language proficiency, and reflect the linguistic process which starts with the reception and decoding of sounds, involves the analysis of information and the development of concepts, and culminates in the production of efficient and explicit communication.

Unit One: listening with understanding The aim of this Unit is to increase the children's skills of aural comprehension. It focuses on attentiveness and concentration, memory, confidence and control, deduction, and the decoding of complex language.

Unit Two: concept building The aim of this Unit is to increase the children's skill and flexibility in classifying data. It focuses on perception of similarity and difference, essential attributes, conceptual sets and the language of classification.

Unit Three: communication The aim of this Unit is to increase the children's oral skills of description and inquiry. It focuses on selection of relevant detail, explicitness, sensitivity to audience, linguistic flexibility, confidence and control.

Although the numerical order of the Units reflects a logical sequence which requires understanding to precede active communication, the Units of 'Concept Seven-Nine' are not intended to be used one after the other. Initially teachers may find that Unit Two: Concept Building provides a useful way into the materials, introducing basic techniques which the other Units develop and draw upon. However, it is intended that the Units should be used concurrently, each one contributing to an expanding reservoir of language competence. The assumption has been made that short but frequent periods of practice with all three Units, spread over a whole school year, will have more lasting value than intensive work involving the completion of one of the Units each term.

The dialect kit In addition to the three Units, a Dialect Kit is available to help those children of West Indian origin who have difficulties resulting from the influence of West Indian language forms on the written production of Standard English.

About the development of Concept 7–9 (by P. H. Taylor)

The relationship between language and thought is close and the development of both is crucial if the primary school child is to profit from his education, enrich himself and play a full part in the social groups to which he belongs. This course aims to make a major contribution to these ends in interesting, exciting and practical ways.

The Units of the course are the result of five years of co-ordinated research and development work in which university staff and teachers have co-operated, and in which theory and practice have been closely matched. Detailed and reliable, interdisciplinary research informed the early stages of the work – see Schools Council Working Paper 29 (Evans/Methuen Educational, 1970). This research, drawing on up-to-date theories of language and teaching, set the framework for the development of classroom materials.

More than 200 teachers were involved either in the pilot development of the materials or in the national trials, and well over 100 schools have co-operated. In these trials under conditions which matter – in the hands of the children and under the direction of teachers – the Units have shown that they can each make an important contribution to the acquisition, command and production of language by children from widely differing social backgrounds.

The children are quickly involved in the work of the Units through the variety of learning strategies employed. Games, play activities, co-operative and individual learning each find a place, and the work is so ordered that steady achievement results, with all it means for interest in learning.

Throughout the development of the classroom materials a variety of teaching methods was explored both by the project team and by the teachers in the trial schools. The methods recommended are those which have seemed to work best – but no teacher using the materials, teaching one or more Units, should feel bound by them. Much of the material will lend itself to creative use and the whole range of its possibilities should be explored. What matters is the contribution which the materials make to the linguistic and cognitive growth of the child, and to his interest and involvement in what school has to offer.

About Unit 1 (by J. M. Sinclair)

This Unit is designed to help a child make the best use of his existing native language resources. Unlike the teaching of a foreign language, the emphasis in this material is on the development of abilities that are potential in the children. The vocabulary and structures are not very difficult, and there is no list of words or phrases that this Unit attempts to teach. Instead it concentrates on the probability that many children can make much better use of their language than their performance suggests, offering a carefully graded route towards considerable competence in listening with understanding.

The processes of listening and understanding are not separated. By conducting a sort of dialogue with the child, the materials pose a large number of small problems, each of which requires an immediate answer. The response-styles are designed to be simpler than the linguistic tasks, so wrong answers will indicate a failure of listening comprehension.

The Unit offers a novel style of teaching and is probably the first systematic course of its kind. The child's ability to control his own pace, to work the machine himself, to concentrate on doing a job which has a series of precise objectives and a clear end-product – these features all serve to increase interest and confidence.

The Unit is very popular with children, and the intensity of their concentration is often remarkable. Once the pupils become familiar with the use of the cassettes, the idea can be extended further: materials suitable for a local situation could be recorded on to spare cassettes, or one child could record a whole series of instructions for a complicated operation, and then see if this set would successfully guide another child. A teacher can diagnose from any recurrent difficulty those aspects of listening comprehension which need special treatment. He can, in effect, use the unit as an informal test.

This Unit is offered with the conviction that 'fluency' is a two-way concept, not only to do with production. Practice, speed and dexterity in the reception of the spoken language are fundamental to an individual's command of his language. These materials will provide useful practice, will draw attention to the importance of the skill, and help to diagnose difficulties.

•   •   •

About Unit 2 (by J. M. Sinclair)

The interrelationships between thought and language, concepts and words, mental and linguistic organization are the subject of perpetual discussion and research. Although the debate continues, practical language teaching must go on, and on the way must make some assumptions about the mental/verbal interaction. In this Unit it is assumed that there is a very close relationship between the language one uses to classify and refer precisely to objects, ideas and events, and the formation and manipulation of sophisticated concepts. Children are encouraged to form arguments based on the comparison of items. They must form criteria, test them against the features of the items, and note the similarities between different items and the differences between similar items.

The language of classification, then, goes along with acts of classification, each supporting the other, but we do not know exactly how. So this Unit concentrates on the production of suitable language. Classification is only one of many mental processes, but the language used in classification, for example the construction of complex nominal expressions, is of far-reaching importance in the language development of a child.

One feature of this unit worth mentioning is the stress on non-visual criteria for classification. Many of the conceptual demands on a child relate to ideas, social classifications and general logical and semantic ones. So even though pictures may be a large part of the stimulus, the intellectual processes involved take the child a long way from purely visual correlations, while giving him the interest and comfort of simple pictorial material.

The Unit has been designed to teach the language and the process of classification using multiple criteria. The subject matter is of fairly immediate interest to children and will provoke all sorts of supplementary questions, providing opportunities for extension of the teaching beyond the specific aims of the material. This is, of course, to be encouraged, and one can readily visualize opportunities for the teacher to continue using the same techniques at some removes from the original stimulus materials. There is always a risk that carefully planned materials may form a watertight compartment in one's teaching, not related to the other activities of the classroom, and it is hoped that such a fate will not befall this unit. The concerns of this material, the techniques and skills, are so basic to primary education that we may reasonably hope they will pervade the teaching.

•   •   •

About Unit 3 (by J. M. Sinclair)

Here is a novel approach to the language problems of young children. Instead of seeing sentences, messages, etc. as made in themselves, to be examined for such things as their structure, correctness and neatness, this unit explores how a child can *use* them, do things with them and cope effectively with his language in a range of situations.

It is important to be clear how these materials relate to conventional standards of language. Although not insisted upon, standards of linguistic correctness are in no way under attack in this unit, and it would be a pity if practice in language effectiveness were to be thought an erosion of standards. As a matter of general policy we have assumed that the speech of a native speaker is not open to lasting 'correction' by precept or analysis. A child's speech habits are the result of influence from round about (the family, friends, school teacher, radio and television) measured according to the child's transitory evaluations. Indeed, pressure to change speech habits for social or educational reasons may be inhibiting. We have assumed that confidence in command and control of his spoken language are the real goals, and that a child who feels this confidence will widen his linguistic horizons and have access to a greater range of modern speech. Writing is another matter. It is mainly learned at school, it is designed to carry a greater load of information than speech, and so it is fair to offer models for writing and teach the conventions straightforwardly. The writing conventions are partly dealt with elsewhere in Concept 7-9. This Unit is one of several making up a course, and at this point the concentration is upon the *effectiveness* of language behaviour. We are concerned with aims and goals and initiatives, with language for a purpose.

Successful communication involves sensitivity to whoever receives the communication. It is fairly clear that in the early stages of speech and writing children do not have the awareness of an audience that enables them to gain precision in producing language that does not rely heavily on the particular situation. This unit particularly teaches interaction.

Much of the unit can be practised with very little involvement of the teacher. It is depressing to reflect how little actual language practice one child gets in a class of normal size, and there is merit in any course which allows child to talk to child and get important language practice in the process.

In a child's development, his linguistic abilities and his general intellectual abilities develop in some sort of parallel relationship. Attention to the tactics and strategies of discourse will help a child to gain greater control over his environment. The ability to describe something with relevance to an aim is held to be very important in education, and the ability to direct inquiries in a dynamic situation is essential to learning.

ACKNOWLEDGEMENT

This article was first published for the Schools Council, London. Extracts are printed here with the kind permission of the publisher E. J. Arnold and the Schools Council.

PART 9

Human intelligence

INTRODUCTION

So much has been written and said about human intelligence that choosing a small collection of papers was a difficult task. In selecting the following, consideration has been given to definition (Miles, Pidgeon), recent attempts at measurement (Elliott), expansion of the argument for the partial inheritance of intelligence (Erlenmeyer-Kimling and Jarvik) and a contemporary theory attempting to explain the growth and decline of measured intelligence.

Miles' paper is a much quoted one with some difficult philosophy in it. But the germ of basic problems relating to the definition of intelligent behaviour, 'Intelligence: a changed view' by Pidgeon, is an attempt to put across in simple terms the direction in which views about the nature of intelligence have changed from a rigid belief in 'innate general ability' toward a greater concern for developmental aspects of intellect. Greater recognition is now given to the notion that intellectual potential is not fixed but something which can be worked on at home, school, etc.

Psychology and the Teacher makes brief mention of the British Intelligence Scale, a new concept in intelligence testing started at Manchester University by Professor Warburton in the 60s. The article by Elliott briefly, but clearly, elaborates the main features of the new test and the sub-scales to be used. Note the inclusion of divergent thinking tests, concrete and operational thinking scales and a tactile test.

Erlenmeyer-Kimling and Jarvik's paper has become well known. The figure in the main text (figure 31.1) is a summary of their investigations into many studies dealing with the relative magnitudes of correlations between intelligence test scores for people having varying degrees of relationship (from monozygotic twins to strangers). The full text of their paper is reproduced here.

The rise and fall of intelligence test scores through life has been (and still is) a taxing problem for psychologists. To begin with, how does the increase of wisdom with age counteract the ravages of physiological deterioration?

John Horn's article puts forward one view based on Cattell's theory of fluid (FI) and crystallized intelligence (CI). The charts he presents of change in FI and CI with age are appealing, largely because they seem to bear out the layman's day by day view of the development of intelligence.

28 Symposium: contributions to intelligence testing and the theory of intelligence

T. R. MILES

ON DEFINING INTELLIGENCE

'We have first raised a dust and then complain that we cannot see.'
BISHOP BERKELEY

Summary   In offering what purport to be definitions of intelligence, psychologists do not always seem to have worked out what sense of the word 'definition' they have in mind. Six possible senses of the word 'definition' are here distinguished. Each sense is then discussed with special reference to the problem of defining intelligence. In the light of the distinctions made, the definitions of intelligence offered by Wechsler and Burt are critically examined from the point of view of methodology.

Introduction

It is commonly thought to be a great scandal that psychologists cannot agree on a definition of intelligence. People then draw the conclusion that intelligence must be something very obscure and elusive to provoke such controversy. I do not dispute that there are many disagreements on matters of fundamental principle, but it seems to me that the issue has often been confused by *unnecessary* disputation and by argument at cross purposes.

I shall not, in this paper, offer any definition of intelligence of my own, nor shall I take sides on the question of whether a particular definition is a good or bad one. My task is the preliminary one of clearing the ground. The question towards which I wish to focus attention is: *By what arguments do we establish that one definition of intelligence is better than another?* I shall suggest in answer to this question that the word 'definition' is ambiguous, and that different arguments are appropriate according to the sense in which the word 'definition' is being used.*

Different senses of the word 'definition'

In distinguishing different senses of the word 'definition' I have relied largely on the work of Robinson (1950).† A distinction needs to be drawn in the first place between *nominal* and *real* definition.‡ Nominal definition is concerned in the main with the meaning of words rather than with the things for which the words appear to stand.§ Robinson subdivides nominal definition into two classes, (1) lexical definition and (2) stipulative definition. A lexical definition gives an account of how a word has in fact been used by a particular group of people; a stipulative definition states how the speaker proposes to use the word, irrespective of how that word has been used in the past.

In contrast, 'real definition' is commonly taken to be definition of *things*. A real definition is supposed to tell us the 'nature of the thing defined'. It is here that some of the biggest pitfalls in argument occur. Robinson distinguishes no less than 12 different activities, all of which have been bunched, very confusedly, under the general title 'real definition'. Of these 12 I shall mention three: (1) *The search for the essence or essential nature of a thing.* This notion Robinson regards as misleading, on the grounds that there are no such things as essences in the sense given to the word 'essence' by Aristotle. In Robinson's view, 'Is it part of the essence of a swan to be white?' is a disguised request for a nominal, not a real definition, and means no more than 'If I were to see a creature otherwise like a swan but black, should I continue to give it the label "swan"?' (2) *'Description plus naming.'* Robinson writes 'Many so-called "real definitions" of the form x is yz are equivalent to the statement that: 'The character yz occurs and I call this character (or it is commonly called) by the name "x".' Robinson regards this as a legitimate and useful activity, but suggests that 'real definition' is a misleading name for this activity. It suggests the hopeless search for real essences, and invites confusion with other activities also grouped under the heading of 'real definition'. (3) *The search for a key.* A definition of x, on this showing, involves a single short sentence from which follow all the things which we need to know about x. The stock example is geometry, where all the important things we know about triangles – so it was supposed – follow from the definition of a triangle as a plane figure bounded by three straight lines. This account of

---

* I have used throughout the phrase 'different *senses of the word* "definition"' in preference to the more familiar 'different *kinds* of definition'. Neither phrase is wholly satisfactory. The important point is that 'defining' is not the name of a single procedure, but refers to a group of procedures having a certain 'family-resemblance' (to use Wittgenstein's phrase) between them.

† This must not be taken as a suggestion that the work of earlier writers on the subject of definition can simply be dismissed. Many of the traditional 'rules', e.g., that a definition should be *per proximum genus et differentiam specificam* seem to me not so much wrong as in need of reformulation.

‡ Compare Burt (1947, p. 129).

§ This statement requires qualification, but is accurate enough for present purposes.

a triangle thus provides the key to understanding a wide range of other true sentences about triangles. Again Robinson is hesitant to call such procedure 'real definition', partly, once more, because it might be confused with his other 11 possible senses of 'real definition', and also because it tends to conceal from us the fact that in some cases no such key may be discoverable.

There is a further procedure, not discussed in any detail by Robinson, but playing quite a large part in modern psychology – the so-called 'operational' definition. This is an attempt to define the meaning of a word in terms of the observations, or scientific 'operations', necessary if that word is to form part of a true sentence. Thus it might be said that the word 'length' requires to be defined in terms of the operations involved in measuring length, and that 'This rod is 6-in. long' is meaningful in virtue of the possibility of specifying in detail the appropriate operations.*

This classification of definitions must not be regarded as exhaustive, nor need the different activities which I have distinguished be regarded as mutually exclusive. The important point which I wish to stress is that, until we know the sense in which the word 'definition' is being used, attempts to assess the merits or de-merits of a definition of intelligence are liable to lead to argument at cross-purposes.

Application to the study of intelligence

(i) *The 'real essence' of intelligence*   If we agree with Robinson that the notion of 'real essences' is a mistaken one,† then sentences which refer to 'the real essence of intelligence' are either illegitimate or in need of reformulation. Few, if any, writers at the present time speak in as many words of the 'essence' of intelligence.‡ But there are plenty of people who ask about its 'real nature' or 'real meaning', which comes to much the same thing. The presupposition underlying such questions is that there is one thing and one only which intelligence *is*, and that the task of psychologists is to discover it. Any sentence starting 'intelligence is . . .' justifiably arouses one's suspicions.

The assumption behind the mistake seems to be that every word has one settled and precise meaning, or, more strictly, that classifications of things in nature are somehow done *for* us. The truth is surely that *we* must classify as suits our purposes. For many purposes it is helpful to classify behaviour into 'intelligent' and 'unintelligent', but it does not follow that there is to be found in the universe one permanently existing 'thing' which intelligence *is*.

It is important in this connection to pay attention to inverted commas. One function of inverted commas – there are others – is to indicate that a word is being mentioned as opposed to used. Thus, when I say 'This table is brown', I am *using* the word 'table' not mentioning it, and no inverted commas are needed. On the other hand, if I say ' "Table" is the English equivalent of the Latin "mensa" ', I am *mentioning* the words 'table' and 'mensa' and both require inverted commas. In exactly the same way, if we are *using* the word

---

* For further discussion, see Bridgman (1927), esp. chapter 1.

† For the arguments which he gives in support of this view, see pp. 153–156. The relevant passage in Aristotle is *Metaphysics*, Z, 4–6.

‡ The word 'essence' does occur, however, in the earlier literature on the subject of intelligence. Thus, Spearman (1927, p. 15) quotes an earlier writer, Bobertag, as saying, 'The knowledge of the essence of intelligence is *naturally* a thing that merits profound research' (my italics).

'intelligence', as in 'Intelligence increases up to age 15', there are no inverted commas; but if we say, 'I recommend that the word "intelligence" be defined in a particular way,' we are mentioning the word 'intelligence', not using it, and the inverted commas are indispensable.

When Piaget (1950, p. 7), says, 'Intelligence is thus only a generic term to indicate the superior forms of organisation or equilibrium of cognitive structurings,' it seems fair to point out that the word 'intelligence' is being *mentioned* here, not *used*, and that inverted commas round the word 'intelligence' would make his formidable statement, if not crystal-clear, at least easier. In general, it may be said that the surest way of avoiding muddle about 'real essences' is to pay strict attention to inverted commas.

(ii) *Lexical definitions and the appeal to ordinary usage*   I propose to argue in this section that, as far as lexical definitions of intelligence are concerned, there need be no serious disputes among psychologists. It is implicit in the notion of a lexical definition that its merits should be decidable by an appeal to ordinary usage. This appeal presents certain problems which require discussion; but even if two psychologists did in fact disagree on what constituted ordinary usage, no important theoretical consequences would follow.

I shall begin by considering certain points about the way in which the word 'intelligence' normally functions, and I shall then attempt to remove some of the confusions and difficulties that are liable to arise in connection with discussions about the lexical definition of intelligence.

(a) The word 'intelligence' is the noun of the adjective 'intelligent'. This point seems obvious, but is nonetheless informative. If we are not careful, we are liable to suppose that all nouns refer to 'things', whereas it is by no means obvious that the word 'intelligence' can correctly be said to refer to a 'thing'. By using the adjective 'intelligent' any temptation towards misleading hypostatization (i.e., treating words as 'thing'-words when they are not) can be avoided. Instead of the unsatisfactory 'What is intelligence?' we can now ask 'What is the meaning of the word "intelligent"?' or, perhaps better, 'How does one test if a person is intelligent? i.e., what constitute samples of intelligent behaviour?'

(b) The word 'intelligent' may be labelled a *disposition-word*.[*] Here are further examples of disposition-words – 'lazy', 'bad-tempered', 'cheerful', 'kind-hearted', 'punctual'. In all these cases there is no necessary suggestion of a person's actually doing something here and now. 'X is very kind-hearted' may be true even though at this moment X happens to be asleep. The suggestion is rather that a person to whom any of these adjectives applies is *disposed* to act in certain ways, i.e., that if certain conditions are fulfilled, certain behaviour will follow. Thus 'X is lazy' is approximately equivalent to 'If X is given any hard tasks he usually tries to shirk them.' In general, sentences containing disposition-words can be replaced by sentences containing the words 'if . . . then'. Similarly, 'X is intelligent' can be taken as equivalent to 'If X is placed in particular circumstances he produces responses of a particular kind' – e.g., if he is present at a group discussion he makes appropriate remarks, if presented with a difficult crossword puzzle he can usually solve it, and so on.

I want now to introduce three further technical terms in addition to 'disposition-word'. The word ascribing the disposition, such as 'lazy' or 'punctual', I shall refer to as the *substrate*; the actual or possible manifestations of the disposition I shall refer to as the

[*] Compare Ryle (1949), chapter 5.

exemplaries. Thus the exemplaries of 'X is kind-hearted' are the particular occasions when he is kind to people, the exemplaries of 'X is lazy' are the particular occasions when he shirks tasks, and so on. Thirdly, I shall make use of the term *polymorphous*.* The concepts 'grocer' and 'solicitor' are, we might say, polymorphous as compared with the concept 'baker'. A baker, *qua* baker, does one thing only – he bakes. A grocer does all sorts of different things – he weighs out sugar, he sells butter, he cuts bacon, and so on. A solicitor draws up wills, advises clients, etc., etc. There is no one way to manifest being a grocer or a solicitor. Similarly, 'lazy' and 'bad-tempered' are polymorphous concepts as compared with 'punctual'. The exemplaries of being punctual are an unvaried series of arrivals on time, the exemplaries of being lazy or bad-tempered cover a wide range of different sorts of behaviour.

(c) Using this terminology we may say that 'intelligent' is a polymorphous concept. In other words there are many different exemplaries which the substrate 'intelligent' carries; intelligence may manifest itself altogether differently on different occasions.

(d) Finally, it should be stressed that the list of exemplaries carried by the word 'intelligent' is *open*. In other words, no one has ever made any precise legislation as to what shall or shall not count as exemplaries of the word 'intelligent'; nor is there any precise list laid up in heaven for the discerning to discover. Just now I mentioned two examples – making appropriate remarks in a discussion and being able to solve difficult crossword puzzles. But clearly these are only two exemplaries among many. By making stipulative definitions we can formulate a precise list of exemplaries if we wish, but 'intelligence', as it functions in ordinary speech, carries no such list.

Now the fact that the list of exemplaries carried by the word 'intelligent' is 'open' may give rise to disputes in the less straightforward type of case. Sometimes, of course, disputes may be genuinely factual. Thus, if it is known that X has an extraordinary facility for rapid calculation in his head, someone may still say, 'But he may not be intelligent', the suggestion being that other exemplaries carried by the word 'intelligent' will not be satisfied. In other cases the dispute is in a sense a verbal one – a matter for linguistic decision. Spearman (1927, p. 10) quotes an amusing example in this connection: 'Trabue . . . told of a woman who, although making a bad record with the tests, nevertheless became "the housekeeper at one of the finest Fifth Avenue hotels, where she successfully directed the work of a corps of approximately fifty maids, three carpenters, two decorators, and a plumber." He was moved to conclude as follows: "In spite of the evidence of the tests I insist that she is intelligent".' Perhaps there is *some* factual dispute here as to how the woman would behave in different circumstances, but Trabue's words suggest that the point at issue is not how the woman is likely to behave in different circumstances, but whether ability to supervise 50 maids, etc., constitutes exemplaries of the word 'intelligent'. To this question there is no uncontroversial answer, not because we are incompetent psychologists, but because the inexactness of ordinary language makes a conclusive answer impossible.†

Even, however, if a psychologist is accused in his definition of intelligence of doing extreme violence to ordinary usage, no important principle is at stake. All that he need do is

---

* This term, and the following examples, are due to Ryle. There is no reference to Freud's use of the word.

† Spearman seems to me to have shown himself extremely sensitive to this sort of problem. Compare his well-known dictum that 'intelligence' is 'a word with so many meanings that finally it has none' (1927, p. 14).

to leave the word 'intelligence' imprecise and invent a special technical term of his own. Thus, if we are sure in advance that it is informative to test a person's memory span for digits, and if, as a result, we include such an item in what we call an 'intelligence-test', we will not be seriously worried if someone says, 'But this is a test of memory, not intelligence.' All that is required is to invent a new technical term and to say that *that* is what we are measuring. The important point is not whether what we measure can appropriately be labelled 'intelligence', but whether we have discovered something worth measuring. And this is not a matter that can be settled by an appeal to what is or is not the correct use of the word 'intelligent'.

One final point should be made in connection with lexical definitions. When it is said that psychologists do not agree on the definitions of intelligence, the position may seem all the more absurd if we unwittingly assume that they disagree about its lexical definition. Psychologists in that case are guilty of using a word without explaining its meaning and perhaps without being able to do so. It is as though someone attempted to give a talk on armadillos when neither he nor his audience knew what the word 'armadillo' meant. Clearly, explanation of any new or unfamiliar word is obligatory as soon as that word is introduced.[*] In the case of the word 'intelligence', however, no one, surely, wants a definition in *this* sense. In the standard sense of 'know the meaning of', the great majority of English-speaking adults, including psychologists, know the meaning of the word 'intelligence' already. To put the matter somewhat more precisely, they can recognize particular pieces of behaviour as constituting exemplaries of the word 'intelligent'. No one thinks that, if the word 'intelligence' figured in the Terman–Merrill vocabulary test, most professional psychologists would fail to secure a pass. Psychologists may disagree as to what general formula, if any, will lead to significant advances in our understanding of intelligent behaviour; but, as far as lexical definitions are concerned, there is very little that they *could* disagree about, and certainly nothing of major importance.

(iii) *Stipulative definition*; (iv) *Description plus naming*; and (v) *The search for a key*   These three processes will be considered under the same heading since there is considerable overlap between them.

To frame a stipulative definition involves either coining a new word or announcing that one intends to use an existing word in a special way. Stipulative definitions of intelligence clearly involve the latter. In all uses the *purpose* of the stipulation needs to be considered. The need, in this case, is for concepts which help our understanding of intelligent behaviour.

'Description plus naming' is a helpful activity in psychology, provided what is named is something worth investigating. Similarly, to 'search for a key' is helpful, provided that the key, when we find it, really does unlock the requisite doors. Both these activities (which can legitimately be regarded as varieties of stipulative definition) involve, in effect, the commendation of a policy. Using our earlier terminology, we may say that to make a stipulative definition is to formulate a substrate – a substrate whose exemplaries are thereby assumed to be worth investigating. Differences of opinion on policy are *serious* differences, and give rise

---

[*] Compare Robinson (1950, p. 41). As Robinson in effect points out, the question whether definitions should come at the beginning or at the end of an inquiry cannot be answered unless we are told the sense in which the word 'definition' is being used.

to heated controversy. In the study of intelligence, as in any other study of personality, the crucial question is the choice of substrates. Thus, the substrates 'extraversion–introversion' are helpful if there is a suggestive association between people's scores on extraversion–introversion tests and their other independently observed behaviour. In the same way those who study intellectual differences need to produce substrates that are *worth while*. Disagreements over *stipulative* definitions of intelligence are far more fundamental and serious than disagreements over lexical definition.

It does not, of course, follow, because the substrate 'intelligent' is helpful for workaday purposes, that it necessarily holds the key to any great scientific advance. It may do so; but we have no right to assume it.*

(vi) *Operational definitions*   Those who insist on the importance of operational definitions for scientific method are in effect pointing out that a substrate has meaning only in relation to its exemplaries. The relation between exemplaries and substrate is not that of effects to an unknown cause, but of a series of occurrences to a general law under which they can be subsumed. It is pointless to assume the existence of an unknown entity lying behind or beyond the exemplaries.†

Applied to the notion of 'intelligence', this is, in effect, to say that the word 'intelligence' does not refer to a 'real thing' lying behind or beyond the manifestations of intelligence. Instead of '*What is* intelligence?' or even 'What does the word "intelligence" *really mean?*' we need to ask instead, 'How do you test – or what operations are involved in testing – whether a person is intelligent?'

This question can readily be answered. Psychologists have devised *standardized* tests. It is the items in these tests (or, more strictly, the person's behaviour in producing correct responses to these items) that are regarded as constituting the exemplaries of the word 'intelligent'. Intelligence, in other words, *is what intelligence tests measure*. This definition is a stipulative one. What is being said is, in effect, that correct responses to the test items *shall be deemed to constitute* exemplaries of the word 'intelligent'. To give a tidy list of exemplaries all that is needed is to specify what particular test we have in mind.

'Intelligence is what intelligence tests measure' does not, of course, tell us what test items are *good* ones, but this is not a ground for criticism since it does not set out to do this. Whether a list of exemplaries should be as tidy as this stipulation makes them is perhaps questionable. Some would say that a substrate should only *suggest* exemplaries, not specify them to the last detail, and that details of exemplaries can be worked out and modified in the course of future research. Despite this, however, the 'operational' approach to the study of intelligence seems to me fundamentally sound, and a great improvement on the traditional search for 'what intelligence really is'.

* • •

---

* Compare Heim (1954, p. 46): 'A majority of the factorists appear agreed that a clear-cut key to these problems exists and is in their hands.'
† Compare Berkeley's attack on the notion of *material substance*, passim.

ACKNOWLEDGEMENT

This article first appeared in *Br. J. Educ. Psychol.* (1957), **27**, 153–210. Extracts are published here with the kind permission of author and editor.

REFERENCES

Bridgman, P. W. (1927) *The Logic of Modern Physics*. Macmillan.
Burt, C. L. (1947) *Mental and Scholastic Tests*. Staples.
Heim, A. (1954) *The Appraisal of Intelligence*. Methuen.
Piaget, J. (1950) *The Psychology of Intelligence*. Routledge and Kegan Paul.
Robinson, R. (1950) *Definition*. Oxford University Press.
Ryle, G. (1949) *The Concept of Mind*. Hutchinson.
Spearman, C. (1927) *The Abilities of Man*. Macmillan.

29 Intelligence: a changed view

DOUGLAS PIDGEON

The use of intelligence tests has been dominated by the idea that intelligence was an inherited characteristic of the mind that could be reasonably accurately measured. The tests have been used to find out whether children were 'working up to capacity'. If the I.Q. was well above the attainment level, then clearly the fault lay with factors other than intelligence and, where possible, steps could be taken to remedy the situation. But if both I.Q. and attainment were low, then nothing could be done since it was assumed that the children were innately dull.

Intelligence was believed to be a fixed entity, some faculty of the mind that we all possess and which determines in some way the extent of our achievements. Since the I.Q. was relatively unaffected by bad teaching or a dull home environment, it remained constant, at least within the limits of measurement error. Its value, therefore, was as a predictor of children's future learning. If they differed markedly in their ability to learn complex tasks, then it was clearly necessary to educate them differently – and the need for different types of school and even different ability groups within schools was obvious. Intelligence tests could be used for streaming children according to ability at an early age; and at 11 these tests were superior to measures of attainment for selecting children for different types of secondary education.

Today, we are beginning to think differently. In the last few years, research has thrown doubt on the view that innate intelligence can ever be measured and on the very nature of intelligence itself. Perhaps most important, there is considerable evidence now which shows the great influence of environment both on achievement and intelligence. Children with poor home backgrounds not only do less well in their school work and in intelligence tests – a fact which could be explained on genetic grounds – but their performance tends to deteriorate gradually compared with that of their more fortunate classmates. Evidence like this lends support to the view, stressed by Sir Cyril Burt, that we have to distinguish between genetic intelligence and observed intelligence. Any deficiency in the appropriate genes will obviously restrict development, no matter how stimulating the environment. But we cannot observe or measure innate intelligence; whereas we can observe and measure the effects of the interaction of whatever is inherited with whatever stimulation has been received from the environment. Changes may occur in our observations or measurements if the environment is changed. In other words, the I.Q. is not constant.

Researchers over the past five or ten years, especially in the United States, have been investigating what happens in this interaction. Work in this country has shown that parental interest and encouragement are more important than the material circumstances of the home.

Two major findings have emerged from these studies. Firstly, that the greater part of the development of observed intelligence occurs in the earliest years of life. Professor Bloom in the University of Chicago has estimated that 50 per cent of measurable intelligence at age 17 is already predictable by the age of four. In other words, deprivation in the first four or five years of life can have greater consequences than any in the following 12 or so years. And the longer the early deprivation continues, the more difficult it is to remedy.

Secondly, the most important factors in the environment are language and psychological aspects of the parent–child relationship. Much of the difference in measured intelligence between 'privileged' and 'disadvantaged' children may be due to the latter's lack of appropriate verbal stimulation and the poverty of their perceptual experiences.

A SKILL TO BE LEARNED

These research findings have led to a revision in our understanding of the nature of intelligence. Instead of its being some largely inherited fixed power of the mind, we now see it as a set of developed skills with which a person copes with any environment. These skills have to be learned and, indeed, one of them – a fundamental one – is learning how to learn. From birth a baby learns *from* his environment, and how to *react* with it. He learns from one experience how to cope with other similar experiences and then with different ones.

It seems equally certain that any built-in mechanism for learning needs to be sustained and encouraged. As Piaget has said, a child must play an active part in regulating his own development; he must be allowed to do his own learning because full intellectual development will not occur if his role is a passive one. The more new things he has seen and heard, the more interested he is in seeing and hearing. The more different things he has coped with himself, the greater his capacity for coping. In this way the intellectual skills of intelligence are built up.

But some children are born into a world where there are few, if any, of the basic requirements for normal development. Jensen claims that while middle-class children with low I.Q. are indeed slow learners, disadvantaged children with low I.Q. show a wide range of learning ability. In other words, for them, low I.Q. is indeed a poor index of their ability to learn. It might be safest to assume that the I.Q. is an under estimate for *all* children, although clearly, the more a home is known to have provided appropriate cultural and educational stimulation, the more likely it is that the I.Q. does reflect innate potential.

Bloom suggests that most children will master any task or solve any problem provided they are given sufficient time. He admits that a few children, probably less than five per cent, may need an impossibly long time to learn some tasks. This fits in well with the changed view of intelligence. High intelligence is not the ability to learn complex tasks so much as the ability to learn rapidly. And a child of relatively low intelligence is not incapable of learning complex tasks but needs a longer time to learn them.

Although educationists have been aware of this idea – the term 'slow learner' is sometimes applied to a child of low I.Q. – the 'fixed potential' concept of intelligence has tended to dominate our education system. Teachers are being constantly assured through their classroom experiences that this concept is apparently sound, and that a system which separates children into groups according to their innate potential really works. This attitude towards the fixed potential concept of intelligence is likely to remain deeply ingrained, since the more successful teachers are at matching pupils' attainments to their apparent abilities, the more successful will any initial streaming or selection process appear to be. This is because the teacher who believes that observed intelligence largely determines the likely level of achievement *will strive to see that this happens*. Children themselves are obliging creatures and are very inclined to produce the standard of work that their elders regard as appropriate. Thus, streaming and selection procedures are, to some extent, self-fulfilling.

The modern ideas concerning the nature of intelligence put forward here are bound to have some effect on our school system. In one respect a change is already occurring. With the move towards comprehensive education and the development of unstreamed classes, fewer children will perhaps be given the label 'low I.Q.' which must inevitably condemn a child in his own, if not society's eyes. The idea that we can teach children to be intelligent in the same way that we can teach them reading or arithmetic may take some getting used to. But perhaps the greatest changes are still to come.

The greatest gains from this new view of intelligence must benefit the disadvantaged child, since there can be no doubt that we have in the past underestimated his potential. Not only must we train him in the skills of learning but if necessary we must make our education system more flexible to give him more time for learning if he needs it. Though all children may be to some extent disadvantaged, some are more so than others.

ACKNOWLEDGEMENT

This article is published with the kind permission of the author, of *Educ. Res.* (1969), **6** and of *The Sunday Times* (1969) in which it first appeared.

30   **British Intelligence Scale takes shape**

COLIN ELLIOTT

It should be said at the outset that there is some force in many of the arguments against intelligence testing. These arguments, however, are based to a large extent on the weaknesses of existing measuring techniques and upon their use (and, indeed, misuse). In particular, group-administered tests have been heavily criticized, especially for their use in secondary school selection procedures. Perhaps when any such technique becomes an instrument of social policy it is bound to become stigmatized by association if that policy becomes unpopular. The criticism of the use of so-called 'I.Q.' tests in school settings, particularly for the purpose of classifying or categorizing individuals, has led to a more general scepticism regarding the value of intelligence tests.

Nevertheless, the British Intelligence Scale is not a group-administered test, and its intended primary function is certainly not to classify or categorize children. So I feel I should not be too apologetic about reporting the work which is being conducted on it. Furthermore, the scale will not be an 'I.Q.' test as such, as the name of the project might misleadingly imply. The research project is still in the middle of its course, and the various tests which together form the BIS are still in various stages of development and analysis.

Consequently, many major questions are as yet unanswerable: the final form of the scale is undecided; the reliability and validity of the scale are unknown; and even the title of the scale may ultimately be altered. However, if the BIS even partially succeeds in its major aim of being a test of special abilities, it will represent a marked advance on any previously published test and hopefully will enable psychologists to define strengths and weaknesses in the abilities of a child with greater precision and with greater confidence and scientific rigour than is currently possible.

The research project was established in 1965 with the support and advice of a special committee of the British Psychological Society with the aim of replacing such tests as the Stanford–Binet and the various Wechsler scales which have been, and still are, extensively used in clinical work with children. The research was based at Manchester University, where a team led by the late Professor F. W. Warburton and consisting of Dr T. F. Fitzpatrick and Dr J. Ward, and, for one year, Miss M. Ritchie, conducted the initial stages of research on the BIS.

Warburton and his team stated that the problems which were likely to be encountered were concerned with two basic issues:

1 The construction of a scale of general mental capacity or 'educability' adapted to British intelligence and standardized on a British population.
2 The extension of the scale into a measure of special abilities.

They pointed out that the latter objective poses the main problem since most of the requirements for the construction of a test of general ability could be satisfied simply by the adaptation or re-standardization of one of the tests in current use.

From the start, therefore, the original research team had in mind the construction of an intelligence scale which would provide a profile of special abilities rather than merely produce an overall I.Q. figure. The early try-out version of the scale was written with the intention of measuring a wide range of abilities, such as verbal ability, verbal fluency, numerical ability, spatial ability, inductive reasoning and memory.

Additionally, the Number and Operational Thinking (i.e. verbal reasoning) subscales were structured in terms of developmental levels based on the main Piagetian stages of intellectual development, such as sensorimotor, pre-operational and operational, together with various subdivisions of these stages.

During the period 1965 to 1970, they succeeded in writing a large number of items and in supervising the administration of these items to a nationwide try-out sample of over 1 200 children in the age range of 2 to 17 years. The bulk of the test administration of the try-out scale was conducted by the educational psychologists employed by local education authorities.

The Department of Education and Science have agreed to finance the continuation of the project until December 1976, which is the estimated date for completion. During this period, the following stages of research will take place:

1 Completion of the analyses of the try-out data.
2 Further development work to fill gaps by devising new subscales and improving the existing subscales (see table 30.1).
3 The completion of the final standardization version of the scale and its production.
4 Identification of a national standardization sample of approximately 2800 children aged between 2 and 16 years.
5 Administration of the final version to the standardization sample.
6 Computation of norms and publication of the scale.

Table 30.1   Proposed profile of subscales in the BIS

Subscale	Age range		Description
	From	To	
Block Design	$3\frac{1}{2}$	16	Pattern production using cubes with different patterned sides; a form of spatial ability.
Comprehension	2	8	Early understanding of language.
Cubes	8	16	More advanced spatial reasoning.
Delayed memory for objects	5	16	Memory for pictures of objects after 20 minute delay. Similar to 'Kim's Game'.
Digit span	2	16	Memory for number sequences.
Formal operational thinking	8	16	Test based on Piagetian model, measuring formal logical reasoning.
Ideational fluency	5	16	General fluency in producing ideas. It is hoped in addition to obtain a rating on originality of ideas. Sometimes called 'creativity'.
Information	2	16	Knowledge of environment and a range of subject areas.
Matrices	5	16	Pattern completion, using progressions of varying complexity.
Number concepts	2	16	Understanding of numerical concepts covering conservation, seriation and reversibility. Piagetian basis.

Table 30.1—*continued*

Subscale	Age range		Description
	From	To	
Number computation	5	16	Orthodox skills of numerical calculation.
Picture vocabulary	2	8	Naming objects in coloured pictures.
Reading	5	13	Word recognition test, comprising words from the Vocabulary test.
Recall of designs	5	16	Drawing designs from memory.
Recognition	2	8	Recognition of toys, pictures and designs from memory.
Similarities	5	16	Similarities between pairs of objects or concepts.
Social reasoning	5	16	Reasoning about hypothetical social situations. May produce assessment of development in concrete operational and formal operational thinking, on Piagetian lines.
Speed of problem solving	5	16	Speed in arriving at correct solutions to problems.
Tactile testing	2	10	Ability to find, by touch, objects described verbally.
Visual–motor	2	8	Various manual tasks, such as pencil copying, brick building.
Visual–spatial	2	10	Tasks of varying complexity involving rotating and fitting templates on to rods of varying cross-section.
Vocabulary	5	16	Definitions of words.

The table lists the subscales which will probably be included in the standardization version of the BIS.

The BIS is the first individually administered test of general intelligence to be developed and standardized in Britain. More important than this, however, are the innovations in the scale itself. As stated earlier, the principal aim of the research team is to produce a test providing a profile of abilities rather than a more global I.Q. score. It should be emphasized that an approach involving the development of the maximum number of individual subtests would lend itself to more modern approaches to case work by psychologists. Such approaches, involving progressive hypothesis testing and the use of selected subtests or items in order to investigate the problems of an individual case, require a greater range of investigative resources than currently available intelligence tests can provide. It should, perhaps, be added that considerable flexibility in the use of assessment procedures is explicitly called for in the recent DES circular on the discovery and assessment of handicapped pupils.

It may appear at first sight as though the scale will take a considerable time to administer. However, it is *not* our intention that psychologists should give every subtest to every child. We intend to leave it open to the psychologist to decide, in his professional judgement, which tests are most appropriate to investigate the problem which faces him. Furthermore, we intend to leave it open to the psychologist to decide for himself how long he wishes each subtest to be.

In short, the old idea of an inflexible measuring instrument, which had to be given in full, and from which only one or two scores could be reliably obtained, has been abandoned. What we are attempting to produce is a range of test materials which can be selected by a psychologist according to the nature of the problem he is investigating. This is in accordance with current developments in professional practice. Indeed, there seems to be every likelihood that the BIS will give fresh impetus to such developments when it is finally published. The old Binet intelligence scale produced a profound effect upon investigations into individual children's learning. Indeed, this was one of the bases of practice in the new profession of educational psychology during the first half of this century. It must be said here that we would never wish the BIS to be used in such an all-purpose manner as was the Binet. Nevertheless we are confident that it will in its turn exert a major influence upon professional practice, helping psychologists to provide a better service to teachers, parents and children.

ACKNOWLEDGEMENT

This article first appeared in *Education* (1975), **25,** 460–461, and is published here with the kind permission of editor and author.

31   Genetics and intelligence : a review

L. ERLENMEYER-KIMLING and L. F. JARVIK

Abstract   A survey of the literature of the past 50 years reveals remarkable consistency in the accumulated data relating mental functioning to genetic potentials. Intragroup resemblance in intellectual abilities increases in proportion to the degree of genetic relationship.

Nomothetic psychological theories have been distinguished by the tendency to disregard the individual variability which is characteristic of all behavior. A parallel between genetic individuality and psychologic individuality has rarely been drawn because the usual assumption has been, as recently noted in these pages (Hirsch, 1963), that the organisms intervening between stimulus and response are equivalent 'black boxes', which react in uniform ways to given stimuli.

While behavior theory and its analytic methods as yet make few provisions for modern genetic concepts, the literature contains more information than is generally realized about the relationship between genotypic similarity and similarity of performance on mental tests. In a search for order among the published data on intellectual ability, we have recently summarized the work of the past half-century (Erlenmeyer-Kimling, Jarvik and Kallmann, 1963). By using the most commonly reported statistical measure, namely, the correlation coefficient, it has been possible to assemble comparative figures from the majority of the investigations.

Certain studies giving correlations had to be excluded from this compilation for one of the following reasons: (i) type of test used (for example, achievement tests, scholastic performance, or subjective rating of intelligence); (ii) type of subject used (for example, mental defectives); (iii) inadequate information about zygosity diagnosis in twin studies*; (iv) reports on too few special twin pairs.

The 52 studies (Erlenmeyer-Kimling, Jarvik and Kallmann, 1963) remaining after these exclusions yield over 30 000 correlational pairings† for the genetic relationship categories shown in figure 31.1. The data, in aggregate, provide a broad basis for the comparison of genotypic and phenotypic correlations. Considering only *ranges* of the observed measures, a marked trend is seen toward an increasing degree of intellectual resemblance in direct proportion to an increasing degree of genetic relationship, regardless of environmental communality.

Furthermore, for most relationship categories, the *median* of the empirical correlations closely approaches the theoretical value predicted on the basis of genetic relationship alone. The average genetic correlation between parent and child, as well as that between siblings (including dizygotic twins) is 0.50. The median correlations actually observed on tests of intellectual functioning are: 0.50 for parent–child, 0.49 for siblings reared together, and 0.53 for dizygotic twins, both the opposite-sex and like-sex pairs. Although twins are presumably exposed to more similar environmental conditions than are siblings spaced apart in age, the correlations for mental ability do not indicate a sizeable difference between the groups. Since only two studies dealt with siblings reared *apart*, it is possible to state only that the reported correlations for that group fall within the range of values obtained for siblings reared together and exceed those for unrelated children living *together*.

For unrelated persons in a large random-mating population, the theoretical genetic correlation is usually considered to be zero; for smaller populations, or those that deviate substantially from panmixia, however, the genetic correlation between presumably unrelated individuals in fact may be considerably higher. The observed median for unrelated persons reared apart is −0.01. Medians for unrelated individuals reared together (children reared in the same orphanage or foster home from an early age) and for the foster-parent–child group are 0.23 and 0.20, respectively. The relative contributions made by

---

* This survey does include reports on opposite-sex (hence dizygotic) twin pairs from these studies.
† Correlational pairings refer to the number of individual pairs used in deriving the correlation coefficients. Some investigators constructed a large number of pairings on the basis of a relatively small number of individuals. Altogether, we have been able to identify the following minimum numbers: twins, 3134 pairs (1082 monozygotic and 2052 dizygotic); sibs apart, 125 pairs plus 131 individuals; sibs together, 8288 pairs plus 7225 individuals; parent–child, 371 pairs plus 6812 individuals; foster-parent–child, 537 individuals; unrelated apart, 15 086 pairings; unrelated together, 195 pairings plus 287 individuals.

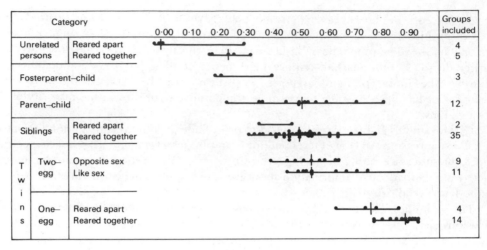

Figure 31.1 Correlation coefficients for 'intelligence' test scores from 52 studies. Some studies reported data for more than one relationship category; some included more than one sample per category, giving a total of 99 groups. Over two-thirds of the correlation coefficients were derived from I.Q.s, the remainder from special tests (for example, Primary Mental Abilities). Midparent–child correlation was used when available, otherwise mother–child correlation. Correlation coefficients obtained in each study are indicated by dark circles; medians are shown by vertical lines intersecting the horizontal lines which represent the ranges.

environmental similarity and sample selection to these deviations from zero are still to be analysed.

At the other end of the relationship scale, where monozygotic twins theoretically have 100 per cent genetic correlation, medians of the observed correlations in intellectual functioning are 0.87 for the twins brought up together, and 0.75 for those brought up apart.[*] The correlations obtained for monozygotic twins reared together are generally in line with the intra-individual reliabilities of the tests. The median for the separated twins is somewhat lower, but clearly exceeds those for all other relationship groups.

In further reference to twin studies, our survey (Erlenmeyer-Kimling, Jarvik and Kallmann, 1963) shows that mean intra-pair differences on tests of mental abilities for dizygotic twins generally are between 1½ to 2 times as great as those between monozygotic twins reared together. Such a relationship appears to hold also for the upper age groups, as suggested by a longitudinal study of senescent twins (Jarvik and Falek, 1963).

Taken individually, many of the 52 studies reviewed here are subject to various types of criticism (for example, methodological). Nevertheless, the overall orderliness of the results is particularly impressive if one considers that the investigators had different backgrounds and contrasting views regarding the importance of heredity. Not all of them used the same

---

[*] Correlational data are now available on 107 separated pairs of monozygotic twins from four series: Newman, Freeman and Holzinger, 1937; Conway, 1958; Juel-Nielsen and Mogensen, 1962; and Shields, 1962.

measures of intelligence (see caption, figure 31.1) and they derived their data from samples which were unequal in size, age structure, ethnic composition, and socio-economic stratification; the data were collected in eight countries on four continents during a time span covering more than two generations of individuals. Against this pronounced heterogeneity, which should have clouded the picture, and is reflected by the wide range of correlations, a clearly definitive consistency emerges from the data.

The composite data are compatible with the polygenic hypothesis which is generally favored in accounting for inherited differences in mental ability. Sex-linkage is not supported by these data (for example, under a hypothesis of sex-linkage the correlations for like-sex dizygotic twins should be higher than those for opposite-sex twins), although the possible effects of sex-linked genes are not precluded for some specific factors of ability.

We do not imply that environment is without effect upon intellectual functioning; the intellectual level is *not* unalterably fixed by the genetic constitution. Rather, its expression in the phenotype results from the patterns laid down by the genotype under given environmental conditions. Two illustrations of the 'norm of reaction' concept in relation to intellectual variability are seen in early total deafness and in phenylketonuria. Early deafness makes its stamp upon intellectual development, in that it lowers I.Q. by an estimated 20 score points (Salzberger and Jarvik, 1963). Phenylketonuria is ordinarily associated with an even greater degree of intellectual impairment. However, early alteration of the nutritional environment of the affected child changes the phenotypic expression of this genetic defect (Homer et al, 1962). Individual differences in behavioral *potential* reflect genotypic differences; individual differences in behavioral *performance* result from the non-uniform recording of environmental stimuli by intrinsically non-uniform organisms.

ACKNOWLEDGEMENT

This article first appeared in *Science* (1963), **142**, 1478–1479, and is published here with the kind permission of the authors and editor.

REFERENCES

Conway, J. (1958) Article in *Br. J. Stat. Psychol.*, **11**, 171.

Erlenmeyer-Kimling, L., Jarvik, L. F. & Kallmann, F. J. (1963) Report presented at XVII International Congress of Psychology, Washington, D.C. Now published.

Hirsch, J. (1963) Article in *Science* (1963), **142**.

Homer, F. A., Streamer, C. W., Alejandrino, L. L., Reed, L. H. & Ibbott, F. (1962) Article *New Engl. J. Med.*, **266**, 79.

Jarvik, L. F. & Falek, A. (1963) Article in *J. Gerontol.*, **18**, 173.

Juel-Nielsen, N. & Mogensen, A. (1962) Cited by Strömgren, E. in Kallmann, F. J. (Ed.), *Expanding Goals of Genetics in Psychiatry*. New York: Grune & Stratton.

Newman, H. H., Freeman, F. N. & Holzinger, K. J. (1937) *Twins: A study of Heredity and Environment*. Chicago: Univ. Chicago Press.

Salzberger, R. M. & Jarvik, L. F. (1963) In Rainer, J. D. et al (Eds.), *Family and Mental Health Problems in a Deaf Population*. New York: N.Y. State Psychiatric Institute.

Shields, J. (1962) *Monozygotic Twins Brought Up Apart and Brought Up Together*. London: Oxford Univ. Press.

32 Intelligence – why it grows, why it declines

JOHN L. HORN

There are two kinds of intelligence, a fact that helps solve some old riddles

One of the oldest and most thoroughly-studied concepts in psychology is the concept of intelligence. Yet the term 'intelligence' still escapes precise definition. There are so many different kinds of behavior that are indicative of intelligence that identifying the essence of them all has seemed virtually impossible. However, some recent research indicates that much of the diversity seen in expressions of intelligence can be understood in terms of a relatively small number of concepts. What's more, this research has also given us insight into understanding where intelligence originates; how it develops; and why and when it increases or decreases.

Studies of the interrelationships among human abilities indicate that there are two basic types of intelligence: *fluid* intelligence and *crystallized* intelligence. Fluid intelligence is rather formless; it is relatively independent of education and experience; and it can 'flow into' a wide variety of intellectual activities. Crystallized intelligence, on the other hand, is a precipitate out of experience. It results when fluid intelligence is 'mixed' with what can be called 'the intelligence of the culture'. Crystallized intelligence increases with a person's experience, and with the education that provides new methods and perspectives for dealing with that experience.

These two major kinds of intelligence are composed of more elementary abilities, called 'primary' mental abilities. The number of these primaries is small. Only about 30 can be accepted as really well-established. But with just these 30 primaries, we can explain much of the person-to-person variation commonly observed in reasoning, thinking, problem-solving, inventing and understanding. Since several thousand tests have been devised to measure various aspects of intelligence, this system of primaries represents a very considerable achievement in parsimony. In much the same way that the chemical elements are organized according to the Periodic Law, these primary mental abilities fall into the patterns labeled fluid and crystallized intelligence.

FLUID INTELLIGENCE

What follows are some examples of the kinds of abilities that define fluid intelligence – and some of the tests that measure this kind of intelligence.

Induction is the ability to discover a general rule from several particular incidents and then apply this rule to cover a new incident.

For example, if a person observes the characteristics of a number of people who are members of a particular club or lodge, he might discover the rule by which membership is determined (even when this rule is highly secret information). He might then apply this rule to obtain an invitation to membership!

Among the tests that measure induction ability is the letter series. Given some letters in a series like

A C F J O —

the task is to provide the next letter. Of course, the test can be used only with people who know the alphabet, and this rules out illiterates and most children. We can't eliminate the influence of accumulated learning from even the purest examples of fluid intelligence.

Figural relations refers to the ability to notice changes or differences in shapes and use this awareness to identify or produce one element missing from a pattern (as in figure 32.1).

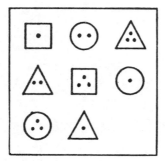

Figure 32.1   What figure fits into the lower right? (Answer: a square with two dots).

An everyday example of intelligence in figural relations is the ability to navigate cloverleaf and expressway turnoff patterns – an ability that may mean as much for adequate adjustment today as skill in finding one's way through a virgin forest had in the days of Daniel Boone. This ability also has ready application in interior decorating and in jobs where maps (or aerial views) must be compared a good deal – as by cartographers, navigators, pilots, meteorologists and tourists.

Span of apprehension is the ability to recognize and retain awareness of the immediate environment. A simple test is memory span: several digits or other symbols are presented briefly, and the task is to reproduce them later, perhaps in reverse order. Without this ability, remembering a telephone number long enough to dial it would be impossible.

Other primary abilities that help define fluid intelligence include:

General reasoning (example: estimating how long it would take to do several errands around town);

Semantic relations (example: enjoying a pun on common words);

Deductive reasoning, or the ability to reason from the general to the particular (example: noting that the wood of fallen trees rots and concluding that one should cover – for example, paint – wooden fence posts before inserting them into the ground);

Associative memory, or the ability to aid memory by observing the relationships between separate items (example: remembering the way to grandmother's house by associating various landmarks en route, or remembering the traits of different people by association with their faces).

CRYSTALLIZED INTELLIGENCE

Most of what we call intelligence – for example, the ability to make good use of language or to solve complex technical problems – is actually crystallized intelligence. Here are some of the primary abilities that demonstrate the nature of this kind of intelligence:

Verbal comprehension   This could also be called general information, since it represents a broad slice of knowledge. Vocabulary tests, current-events tests and reading-comprehension tests all measure verbal comprehension, as do other tests that require a person to recall information about his culture. The ability is rather fully exercised when one quickly reads an article like this one and grasps the essential ideas. Verbal comprehension is also called for when a person reads news items about foreign affairs, understands their implications, and relates them to one another and to their historical backgrounds.

Experiental evaluation is often called 'common sense' or 'social intelligence'. Experiental evaluation includes the ability to project oneself into situations, to feel as other people feel and thereby better understand interactions among people. Everyday examples include figuring out why a conscientious foreman is not getting good results from those under him, and why people disobey traffic laws more at some intersections than at others.

One test that measures experiental evaluation in married men is the following:

Your wife has just invested time, effort, and money in a new hairdo. But it doesn't help her appearance at all. She wants your opinion. You should:

1 try to pretend that the hairdo is great;
2 state your opinion bluntly;
3 compliment her on her hairdo, but add minor qualifications; or,
4 refuse to comment.

Answer 3 is considered judged correct – on the grounds that husbands can't get away with answers 1 and 4, and answer 2 is likely to provoke undue strife.

Formal reasoning is reasoning in ways that have become more or less formalized in Western cultures. An example is the syllogism, like this one:

> No Gox box when in purple socks.
> Jocks is a Gox wearing purple socks.
> Therefore: Jocks does not now box.

The task is to determine whether or not the conclusion is warranted. (It is.)

An everyday example of formal reasoning might be to produce a well-reasoned analysis of the pros and cons of an issue presented to the United Nations. Formal reasoning, to a much greater extent than experiental evaluation or verbal comprehension, depends upon dealing with abstractions and symbols in highly structured ways.

Number facility, the primary ability to do numerical calculations, also helps define crystallized intelligence, since to a considerable extent it reflects the quality of a person's education. In a somewhat less direct way, this quality is also represented in the primary abilities called mechanical knowledge, judgment and associational fluency.

Semantic relations and *general reasoning*, listed as primary aspects of fluid intelligence, are also – when carrying a burden of learning and culture – aspects of crystallized intelligence. This points up the fact that, although fluid and crystallized intelligence represent distinct patterns of abilities, there is some overlap. This is what is known as *alternative mechanisms* in intellectual performance. In other words, a given kind of problem can sometimes be solved by exercise of different abilities.

Consider the general-reasoning primary, for example. In this, typical problems have a slightly mathematical flavor:

There are 100 patients in a hospital. Some (an even number) are one-legged, but wearing shoes. One-half of the remainder are barefooted. How many shoes are being worn?

We may solve this by using a formal algebraic equation. Set x equal to the number of one-legged patients, with $100-x$ then being the number of two-legged patients, and $x+\frac{1}{2}(100-x)2$ being the number of shoes worn. We don't have to invent the algebraic techniques used here. They have been passed down to us over centuries. As Keith Hayes very nicely puts it, 'The culture relieves us of much of the burden of creativity by giving us access to the products of creative acts scattered thinly through the history of the species.' The use of such products is an important part of crystallized intelligence.

But this problem can also be solved by a young boy who has never heard of algebra! He may reason that, if half the two-legged people are without shoes, and all the rest (an even number) are one-legged, then the shoes must average one per person, and the answer must be 100. This response, too, represents learning – but it is not so much a product of education, or of the accumulated wisdom passed from one generation to the next, as is the typical product of crystallized intelligence. Fluid intelligence is composed of such relatively untutored skills.

Thus the same problem can be solved by exercise of *either* fluid intelligence *or* crystallized intelligence. We can also see the operation of such alternative mechanisms in these two problems.

ZEUS—JUPITER: ARTEMIS—?
    Answer: Phidias   Coria   <u>Diana</u>
HERE—NOW: THERE—?
    Answer: Thus   Sometimes   <u>Then</u>

The first problem is no harder to solve than the second, *provided* you have acquired a rather sophisticated knowledge of mythology. The second problem requires learning too, but no more than simply learning the language – a fact that puts native-born whites and Negroes on a relatively equal footing in dealing with problems of this sort, but places Spanish-speaking Puerto Ricans or Mexican-Americans at a disadvantage. As measures of fluid intelligence, both items are about equally good. But the first involves, to a much greater extent, crystallized intelligence gleaned from formal education or leisure reading.

Because the use of alternative mechanisms is natural in the play of human intelligence, most intelligence tests provide mixed rather than pure measures of fluid or crystallized abilities. This only reflects the way in which we usually go about solving problems – by a combination of natural wit and acquired strategies. But tests can be devised in which one type of intelligence predominates. For example, efforts to devise 'culture fair' intelligence tests that won't discriminate against people from deprived educational or cultural backgrounds usually focus on holding constant the effect of crystallized capabilities – so that fluid capabilities can be more fully represented.

Now that we have roughly defined what fluid and crystallized intelligence are, let us investigate how each of them develops over time.

The infant, whose reasoning powers extend little beyond the observation that a determined howl brings food, attention or a dry diaper, becomes the man who can solve legal problems all day, execute complicated detours to avoid the five o'clock traffic on his way home, and deliver a rousing speech to his political club in the evening. But how? To understand the intertwined development of the fluid and crystallized abilities that such activities require, we need to consider three processes essential to the development of intelligence: *anlage function*, the *acquisition of aids* and *concept formation*.

Anlage function, which includes the complex workings of the brain and other nervous tissue, provides the physical base for all of the infant's future mental growth. ('Anlage' is a German word meaning 'rudiment'.) The second two factors – the aids and concepts the child acquires as he grows up – represent the building blocks that, placed on the anlage base, form the structure of adult intelligence.

The anlage function depends crucially and directly upon physiology. Physiology, in turn, depends partly on heredity, but it can also be influenced by injury, disease, poisons, drugs and severe shock. Such influences can occur very early in life – often even in the womb. Hence it is quite possible that an individual's anlage functioning may have only a remote relationship to his hereditary potential. All we can say for sure is that the anlage process *is* closely tied to a physiological base.

A good everyday measure of a person's anlage functioning is his memory span (provided we can rule out the effects of anxiety, fatigue or mental disturbance). Given a series of letters or numbers, most adults can immediately reproduce only about six or seven of them in reverse order. Some people may be able to remember 11, others as few as four, but in no case is the capacity unlimited or even very great. Memory span increases through childhood – probably on account of the increasing size and complexity of the brain – but it is not much affected by learning. This is generally true of other examples of anlage functioning.

SHORT-CUTS TO LEARNING

Aids are techniques that enable us to go beyond the limitations imposed by anlage functioning. An aid can, for example, extend our memory span. For example, we break up a telephone or social-security number with dashes, transforming long numbers into short, more easily recalled sets, and this takes the strain off immediate memory.

Some aids, like the rules of algebra, are taught in school. But several psychologists (notably Jean Piaget) have demonstrated that infants and children also invent their own aids in their untutored explorations of the world. In development, this process probably continues for several years.

Concepts are categories we impose on the phenomena we experience. In forming concepts, we find that otherwise dissimilar things can be regarded as 'the same' in some sense because they have common properties. For instance, children learn to distinguish the features associated with 'bike' – two wheels, pedaling, riding outside, etc. – from those associated with 'car'. Very early in a child's development, these categories may be known and represented only in terms of his own internal symbols. In time, however, the child learns to associate his personal symbols with conventional signs – that is, he learns to use language to represent what he 'knows' from direct experience. Also, increased proficiency in the use of language affords opportunities to see new relations and acquire *new* concepts.

The concepts we possess at any time are a residue of previous intellectual functioning. Tests that indicate the extent of this residue may, therefore, predict the level of a person's future intellectual development. A large vocabulary indicates a large storehouse of previously acquired concepts, so verbal ability itself is often taken as a good indication of ability to conceptualize. Many well-known tests of intelligence, especially of crystallized intelligence, are based on this rationale.

However, language is really only an indirect measure of concept awareness. Thus verbally-oriented tests can be misleading. What about the child raised in an environment where language is seldom used, but which is otherwise rich in opportunity to perceive relationships and acquire concepts (the backwoods of Illinois, or by a pond in Massachusetts)? At the extreme, what about a person who never hears the spoken word or sees the written word? He does not necessarily lack the awareness that we so glibly represent in language. Nor does he necessarily lack intelligence. A child who doesn't know the spoken or written word 'key' surely understands the concept if he can distinguish a key from other small objects and use it to open a lock.

What is true of conventional language is also true of conventional aids. Lack of facility or familiarity with aids does not mean that a child has failed to develop intellectually, even though it may make him *appear* mentally slow on standard intelligence tests. Just as verbally-oriented tests penalize the child who has not had the formal schooling or proper environment to develop a large vocabulary, many tests of so-called mathematical aptitude rely heavily on the use of conventional aids taught in school – on algebraic formulas, for example. Someone who has learned few of these conventional aids will generally do poorly on such tests, but this does not mean that he lacks intelligence.

We cannot overlook the fact that an intelligent woodsman may be just as intelligent, in one sense of this term, as an intelligent college professor. The particular combination of primary abilities needed to perform well may differ in the two cases, but the basic wherewithal of intellectual competence can be the same – adequate anlage functioning, plus an awareness of the concepts and a facility with the aids relevant to dealing with the environment at hand. Daniel Boone surely needed as much intelligence to chart the unexplored forests of the frontier as today's professor needs to thread his way through the groves of academe.

EDUCATION AND INTELLIGENCE

It is obvious, then, that formal education is not essential to the development of important aspects of intelligence. Barring disruption of anlage functioning by accident or illness, the child will form concepts and devise aids to progressively expand his mental grasp as he grows up, and this will occur whether he goes to school or not.

Where formal instruction *is* significant is in making such development easier – and in passing along the concepts and aids that many people have deposited into the intelligence of a culture. The schools give children awareness of concepts that they may not have had the opportunity to gain from first-hand experience – the ability to recognize an Australian platypus, for example, without ever having seen one, or a knowledge of how the caste system works in India. Aids, too, are taught in school. A child well-armed with an array of mathematical formulas will likely be able to solve a problem faster and more accurately than one who must work it out completely on his own. Indeed, some problems simply cannot be solved without mathematical aids. Since the acquisition of both concepts and aids is cumulative, several years of formal education can put one child well ahead of another one, unschooled, who has roughly the same intellectual potential.

Education can thus play a powerful role in developing intelligence. Too often, however, it doesn't. Even in school, some children in perfectly good health and physical condition fail to develop, or develop slowly. Some even seem to be mentally stunted by their school experience. Why? What sorts of experiences can foster – or retard – the developmental processes of concept-formation and aid-formation in the school environment?

Even though we are only beginning to find answers in this area, it is already clear that learning can be speeded up, slowed down, or brought almost to a dead halt by a variety of school experiences. On the favorable side, abilities improve by *positive transfer*. Learning one skill makes it easier to learn a related one. A student who already knows Spanish, for example, will find it easier to learn Portuguese. And positive transfer also works in less obvious ways. There is even evidence to suggest that new learning is facilitated simply by having learned before – by a sort of learning how to learn.

But other factors too can affect the course of learning, and these factors are particularly prominent in the context of our formal educational system. For example, merely having the *opportunity* to learn may depend on both previous learning and previous opportunity to learn. Thus, even if his native potential and level of self-education are good, the person who has not had the opportunity to finish high school has a poor chance of going on to college.

Labeling operates in a similar way. If a person is labeled as lacking in ability, he may receive no further chance to develop. Kenneth B. Clark states this very well:

If a child scores low on an intelligence test because he cannot read and then is not taught to read because he has a low score, then such a child is being imprisoned in an *iron circle* and becomes the victim of an educational self-fulfilling prophecy.

Avoidance-learning is similar. This is learning not to learn. Punishment in a learning situation – being humiliated in school, for example – may make a child 'turn off'. Problem-solving may become such a threat that he will avoid all suggestion of it. Since an active, inquiring curiosity is at the root of mental growth, avoidance-learning can very seriously retard intellectual development. Moreover, since a child typically expresses avoidance by aggression, lack of attention, sullenness, and other behavior unacceptable to educators and parents, they – being human – may react by shutting the child out of further learning situations, and thus create another kind of iron circle.

Labeling, lack of opportunity, and avoidance-learning affect the development of both fluid and crystallized intelligence. Both depend upon acculturational influences – the various factors that provide, or block, chances for learning. And both depend upon anlage function and thus upon physiological influences as well. However, fluid intelligence depends more on physiological factors, and crystallized intelligence more on acculturational ones. It is the interplay of these factors throughout a child's development that produces the fact that fluid and crystallized intelligence can be separated in adult intellectual performances. But how does this separation arise?

A CLIMATE FOR GROWTH

In many respects, the opportunities to maintain good physiological health are the same for all in our society. The climate, air pollution, water, the chances of injury, and other hazards in the physical environment do not vary greatly. Even the social environments are similar in many ways. We acquire similar language skills, go to schools that have similar curricula, have a similar choice of television programs, and so on. In this sense, the most advantaged and the most disadvantaged child have some of the same opportunities to develop anlage functioning, and to acquire concepts and aids.

Moreover, we should be careful about how we use the term 'disadvantaged'. We do not yet know what is superior in all respects, at every age level, for the development of all the abilities that go into intelligence. At one stage, what seems a 'bad' home may give intelligence a greater impetus than an apparently 'good' home. It may be, for instance, that in early childhood 'lax' parents allow more scope for development. In later development, 'stimulating' and 'responsible' (but restrictive?) parents might be better. Some of the intellectual leaders of every period of history and of every culture have developed in environments that, according to many definitions, would have had to be classified as 'disadvantaged'.

It is clear, however, that favorable conditions for the development of intelligence are not the same for all. To avoid the iron circle, to gain opportunities to go on, children have to display the right abilities at the right times. To some extent, this depends on early and basic endowment. Intelligent parents may provide good heredity, good environmental conditions for learning, and good stimulation and encouragement. But the opportunities a child gets, and what he meets them with, can also be quite independent of his own characteristics. His opportunities depend on such haphazard factors as the neighborhood in which he lives, the kind of schooling available, his mother's interests and his father's income, the personality qualities of the teachers he happens to get, and the attitudes and actions of his playmates.

Thus, through a child's years of growth and education, societal influences can produce an effect that is largely independent of those produced by physiological influences. In an infant, cultural influences could not have accumulated independently of the physiological. But as children pass through preschool and school, their awareness of concepts and use of aids becomes more evident, and the influence of acculturation is felt and exhibited. The probable shape of future learning and opportunity becomes more clear. The child who has already moved ahead tends to be ready to move farther ahead, and to be accepted for such promotion. Crystallized intelligence feeds the growth of crystallized intelligence. By contrast, the child who has not moved ahead, for whatever reasons, tends to be less ready and to be viewed as such. His acquisition of the lore of the culture proceeds at a decelerating rate. This is how two children with roughly the same hereditary potential can grow apart in their acquisition of crystallized intelligence. Among adults, then, we should expect to find great variation in the crystallized pattern of abilities – and we do!

The cultural influences that can produce this kind of inequality operate almost independently of physiological factors, however. Thus, the child who fails to progress rapidly in learning the ever-more-abstruse concepts and aids of crystallized intelligence may still acquire many concepts and aids of a more common type. And if he is lucky in avoiding accidents and maintaining good health, this kind of development can be quite impressive. His intellectual growth may even surpass that of a seemingly more favored child who is slowed down by illness or injury. Thus, two children with about the same hereditary makeup can grow apart in fluid intelligence, too. The result is a wide range of variation in adult fluid intelligence – a range even wider than we would expect to be produced by differences in heredity alone.

THE DECLINING YEARS

Both fluid and crystallized intelligence, as we have just seen, develop with age. But intelligence also declines with age. This is especially true of the fluid kind. Looked at in terms of averages, fluid intelligence begins to decline before a person is out of his 20s. Crystallized intelligence fares better, however, and generally continues to increase throughout life. Because crystallized intelligence usually increases in this fashion, the decline in fluid abilities may not seriously undermine intellectual competence in people as they mature into middle age and even beyond. But let us look at these matters more analytically.

Figure 32.2 represents results from several studies, each involving several hundred people. Notice, first, that the curves representing fluid intelligence (FI) and crystallized intelligence (CI) are at first indistinguishable, but become separate as development proceeds. This represents the fact that both are products of development. It also illustrates the fact that it is easier to distinguish between fluid intelligence and crystallized intelligence in adults than in children.

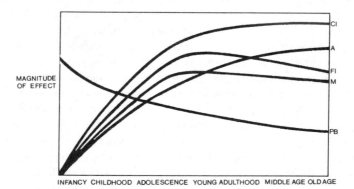

Figure 32.2 Development of fluid intelligence (FI) and crystallized intelligence (CI) in relation to effects produced by maturation (M), acculturation (A) and loss of physiological base (PB) due to injury.

The maturation curve (M) summarizes evidence that the physical structures and processes that support intellect (the brain, for instance) grow and increase in complexity until the late teens or the early 20s. Development is rapid but decelerating. Since both fluid and crystallized intelligence depend on maturation, their curves more or less follow it.

But maturation accounts for only part of the change in the physical structures that support intelligence. They are also affected by injuries, such as birth complications, blows to the head, carbon-monoxide poisoning, intoxication and high fever. Such injuries are irreversible and thus cumulative. In the short run, they are difficult to discern, and their effects are masked during childhood by the rising curves of learning and maturation. In the long run, however, injuries resulting from the exposures of living take their toll. The older the person, the greater the exposure. Thus, part of the physiological base for intellectual functioning will, on an average, decrease with age (curve PB).

The sum of the influences represented by M and PB form the physiological base for intellectual processes at any particular time. In the early years, the effects of one compensate for the effects of the other. But as the M curve levels off in young adulthood and the PB curve continues downward, the total physiological base drops. Those intellectual abilities that depend very directly upon physiology must then decline.

The effects of brain-tissue loss are variable, however. At the physiological level, an ability is a complex network of neurons that 'fire' together to produce observable patterns of behavior. Such networks are overdetermined – not all of the neurons in the network need to 'fire' to produce the behavior. And some networks are much more overdetermined than others. This means that when a loss of brain tissue (that is, a loss of neurons) occurs, some networks, and hence some abilities, will be only minimally affected. Networks that are not highly overdetermined, though, will become completely inoperative when a critical number of neurons cease to fire.

The crystallized abilities apparently correspond to highly overdetermined neural networks. Such abilities will not be greatly affected by moderate loss of neurons. The fluid abilities, on the other hand, depend much more significantly upon anlage functions, which are represented by very elementary neural networks. These abilities will thus 'fall off' with a loss of neurons.

Curve A in the graph shows how, potentially at least, the effects of acculturation and positive transfer may accumulate throughout a lifetime. On this basis alone, were it not for neural damage, we might expect intelligence to increase, not decline, in adulthood.

Whether intellectual decline occurs or not will depend upon the extent of neuron loss, and upon whether learning new aids and concepts can compensate for losing old skills. For example, the anlage capacity to keep six digits in immediate awareness may decline with loss of neurons. But the individual, sensing this loss, may develop new techniques to help him keep a number in mind. Thus the overall effect may be no loss of ability. What the evidence does indicate, however, is that, with increasing age beyond the teens, there is a steady, if gentle, decline in fluid intelligence. This suggests that learning new aids and concepts of the fluid kind does not quite compensate for the loss of anlage function and the loss of previously-learned aids and concepts.

On a happier note, and by way of contrast, the evidence also shows that crystallized intelligence *increases* throughout most of adulthood. Here alternative mechanisms come into play. Compensating for the loss of one ability with the surplus of another, the older person uses crystallized intelligence in place of fluid intelligence. He substitutes accumulated wisdom for brilliance, while the younger person does the opposite.

A word of caution about these results. They represent averages, and averages can be affected by a relatively few extreme cases. For example, if only a relatively few individuals experience brain damage, but the effect is rather pronounced in each case, this will show up in the averages. If such damage occurs more frequently with older people than with younger people, a corresponding decline of abilities with age will show up – even though such decline may not be an inevitable aspect of aging for everyone. But even though these cautions must be kept in mind, we should not lose track of the fact that the FI curve parallels the PB in adulthood.

Intelligence tests that measure mixtures of fluid and crystallized intelligence (and most popular ones do) show varying relationships between aging and intelligence in adulthood. If fluid tests predominate, decline is indicated. If crystallized intelligence is well represented, then there is no apparent decline.

Intellectual performance in important jobs in life will depend on both kinds of intelligence, and may be represented by a composite curve (FI and CI in figure 32.3).

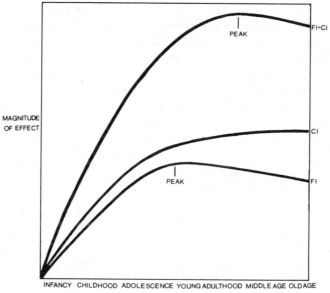

Figure 32.3   Fluid intelligence, crystallized intelligence and the effect of the two added together.

Notice that the peak of this curve occurs later than the peak of the FI curve below it. If fluid intelligence reaches its peak in the early 20s, intelligence in overall performance, influenced by the cultural accretion, may peak in the 30s. The evidence indicates that the greatest intellectual *productivity* tends to occur in the 30s or early 40s, although the most *creative* work often is accomplished earlier. For example, half of the 52 greatest discoveries in chemistry (as judged by chemists) were made before the innovator had reached age 29, and

62 per cent were made before he was 40. It would seem that creativity and productivity represent somewhat different combinations of fluid and crystallized intelligence, with productivity being relatively more affected by cultural factors.

The age at which the combined FI and CI function peaks varies from one person to another, depending on the development of new concepts and aids, the amount of brain damage, and other factors such as diet and general health.

Perhaps the most interesting result of all this recent work is the questions it provokes. What are the factors producing the apparent decline in fluid intelligence? Are they intrinsic to aging, or do they merely reflect the hazards of living? Are they associated with the hazards of different occupations? Do auto mechanics, for example, who are repeatedly exposed to carbon monoxide, show more decline in fluid intelligence than cement finishers, who work in the open air?

Most important of all, what experiences in infancy and childhood have favorable or unfavorable effects on the future growth of fluid intelligence? Of crystallized intelligence? Of both? Do experiences that affect fluid intelligence always affect crystallized intelligence, too? We are still far from finding firm and comprehensive answers to these questions, but they very clearly hold massive implications for our child-rearing practices, for our educational system, and for the whole complex of fields that bear on the development and management of human potential.

ACKNOWLEDGEMENT

This article first appeared in *Trans-action* (1967), **5**, 23–31, and is published here with the kind permission of the author and editor.

PART 10

Creative thinking

INTRODUCTION

The arguments for and against a separate but related identity for creative thinking as compared with intelligence as it is now measured have raged over the past 20 years or more, mainly from the time of Guilford's influential paper to the American Psychological Society on his model of the intellect (see basic text). One of the leading lights has been MacKinnon who undertook very detailed studies of famous scientists to discover if they had unusual, but distinctive, characteristics. The article in the Reader is not widely known but it gives both the accumulated findings of research into the characteristics of creative people and the implications.

Haddon and Lytton (1968 – see references in Lytton and Cotton for detail) looked at the divergent thinking scores of children in 'informal' and 'formal' primary schools to discover that the former obtained significantly higher divergent scores than the latter. The study reported here by Lytton and Cotton repeated the programme in secondary schools but failed to replicate the result. This interesting twist in the results should spark off a good debate as to why. Look closely at the concept of 'formal' and 'informal' schools.

The idea of a correlation between the student's learning style (convergent or divergent in this case) and the tutor's teaching style has been a tantalizing one for educationists. It seems an obvious candidate for research but has received surprisingly little attention. Joyce and Hudson's work is a start, but only a limited one. They took medical students in statistics classes (not merely a run-of-the-mill setting). Nevertheless, the outcome 'lends strong support to the view that academic learning is influenced by similarities in the intellectual styles of the student and the teacher'.

It is one thing to develop a theory about creative thinking, quite another to devise practical ways of stimulating it. Recently several programmes have been devised, chiefly in the U.S.A. (see Torrance reference in the basic text). Perhaps the best known in Britain comes from De Bono. In addition to several texts suggesting ways of inducing lateral thinking, he has devised a course for children, the CoRT method (Cognitive Research Trust), and the paper by Moore is a brief introduction to it.

33 Characteristics of the creative person: implications for the teaching–learning process

DONALD W. MacKINNON

Difficult as the task may be, it is far easier to describe the characteristics of the creative person than to indicate with any degree of certainty their implications for the processes of teaching and learning in higher education.

The difficulties are several. It is one thing to discover, as we have, the distinguishing characteristics of mature, creative, productive persons. It is quite another matter to conclude that the traits of creative persons observed several years after college characterized these same individuals when they were students. Our problem is further complicated by the fact that, though our creative subjects have told us about their experiences in school and college and the forces and persons and situations which as they see it nurtured their creativity, these are, after all, self-reports subject to misperceptions and self-deceptions. Even if we were to assume that their reports are essentially accurate we would still have no assurance that the conditions in society and in college, the qualities of interpersonal relations between instructor and student, and the aspects of the teaching–learning process which would appear to have contributed to creative development a generation ago would facilitate rather than inhibit creativity if these same factors were created in today's quite different world.

Creative persons are intelligent. But this is not the most important thing to say about them. There is no one-to-one relation between creativity and intelligence. The feeble-minded are not creative. Yet it is also true that the most intelligent persons are not always the most creative. In the various groups we have studied, intelligence, as measured by the Terman *Concept Mastery Test*, is not correlated with creativity. Among creative architects the correlation of the two variables is −0.08; in a group of research scientists, −0.07. Obviously this does not mean that over the whole range of creative endeavor there is no correlation between intelligence and creativity. It indicates rather that a certain amount of intelligence is required for creativity, but beyond that point being more or less intelligent does not crucially determine the level of a person's creativeness; and the level of intelligence required for creativity is sometimes surprisingly low. If we are to nurture creativity we shall have to disabuse ourselves of the idea that only the most intellectually gifted are creative.

Creative persons are original. This statement will strike you as a tautology, if, like many, you conceive creativity to be essentially novelty or originality of response. With such a notion I would strongly disagree. As I see it, creativity has at least three phases or aspects. It involves a response that is novel or at least statistically infrequent; but that is not sufficient. It must be adaptive to reality; it must serve to solve a problem or fit the requirements of a reality situation. And, finally, there must be an evaluation of the original insight, together with a sustaining and developing of it to the full.

In general, those who are most fluent in suggesting new solutions tend also to come up with the better, more adaptive ones. The quantity and quality of original responses correlate +0.53 in one test of creativity (Consequences) and +0.78 in another (Unusual Uses). These correlations suggest that some persons tend to make many original responses which are not very good, while others make fewer but generally better or more fitting ones; and this is our finding.

To nurture the fullest creativity, emphasis must be placed upon seeking the implications and deeper meanings and possibilities inherent in every idea. This involves pursuing ideas in depth and in scope. However fresh and clever they may be, insights do not enter the stream of creative solutions to urgent problems unless their consequences are tested in application and revised and extended to meet the requirements of the situation for which they were first devised.

Creative persons are independent in judgment and in thought and action, relatively free from the more conventional restraints and inhibitions, not preoccupied with the impression which they make on others and thus perhaps capable of greater independence and autonomy, inclined to recognize and admit self-views which are unusual and unconventional, and strongly motivated to achieve in situations which call for independence. Perhaps not unrelated to these dispositions is the fact that creative persons often report having been less than happy and satisfied at home, in school and in college. Such is the testimony of a group of research scientists, many of whom were honor students in high school whose academic performance, however, later worsened, most of them earning no better than a C plus or B minus average in college, in part due to their inclination to follow their own interests and to explore independently problems of their own setting. Creative architects whom we have studied performed somewhat better in college, averaging about a B. But in their college work they were no less independent than the research scientists. In work and courses which caught their interest they could turn in an A performance, but in courses that failed to strike their imagination, they were quite willing to do no work at all. In general, their attitude in college appears to have been one of profound skepticism. They were unwilling to accept anything on the mere say-so of their instructors. Nothing was to be accepted on faith or because it had behind it the voice of authority. Such matters might be accepted, but only after the student on his own had demonstrated to himself their validity. In a sense, they were rebellious, but they did not run counter to the standards out of sheer rebelliousness. Rather, they were spirited in their disagreement and one gets the impression that they learned most from those instructors who were not easy with them.

Creative students often chafe and rebel, not because they are lazy, or because their level of aspiration is low, or because they are 'rebels without a cause'. The problem, if we permit it to become one, derives from their high-level of energy channeled toward activities and goals which they set for themselves and which may well conflict with those we hold for them. How we respond to the creative student's need for independence, to what degree and under what conditions we grant this autonomy and even reward him for behaviors not entirely to our own liking, de-emphasizing group participation with its demands for conformity and providing him opportunity to work out his own interests are, I am sure, crucially determinative of the level of creative accomplishment which he will ultimately achieve.

Creative persons are perceptive, open to experience both of the inner self and of the outer world. The perceptive attitude expresses itself in interest and in curiosity. It is the hallmark of the inquiring mind and of the creative person. The open mind can, of course, become cluttered and may, until it orders the multiplicity of experiences which it admits, reveal a great deal of disorder. And such disorder can cause anxiety. Instead of seeking a rigid control of experience, repressing impulse and imagery, blinding oneself to great areas of experience, and never coming to know oneself, creative persons are able to recognize and give expression to varied aspects of inner experience and character, including the feminine in the case of the male and the masculine in the case of the female, admitting into consciousness and behavior much that others would deny, integrating reason and passion, and reconciling the rational and irrational.

Such richness of experience is not always easily or safely encompassed, and for that reason creative persons often show more than an average amount of tension and turmoil. But if creatives often reveal some measure of psychopathology, they also give evidence of ego strength and adequate mechanisms of control as the success with which they live their productive lives testifies.

Creative persons are intuitive, both in their perceptions and in their thought processes. In perceiving, one can focus upon what is yielded by the senses, emphasizing sense perception of things and facts; and in the extreme case one can remain stuck there, bound to the stimulus, the presented material, the situation; or one may, in his perceptions, be more sensitive and responsive to the deeper meanings, the implications and the possibilities for use or action of that which is experienced by way of the senses. The immediate apprehending of the real, as well as the symbolic bridges between what is and what can be, is intuitive perception, and it is the creative person's preferred mode of perceiving.

Similarly, in thinking, one can proceed slowly, cautiously, inductively, in step-wise fashion, reasoning analytically and logically, and sticking to formal methods of deduction and proof, or one can by making bold leaps in imagination and thought arrive at apprehensions of larger wholes and solutions of problems with little awareness, if any, of the process or of the steps by which the new insights are gained. Such immediate apprehension or cognition, which is characteristic of the creative person, may be called intuitive thinking. It stands in the same relation to logical and formal mediated thinking as intuitive perception does to sense perception.

We do not know the extent to which intuitive perception and intuitive thinking can be nurtured by appropriate educational methods. But I would venture to guess that rote learning, learning of facts for their own sake, repeated drill of material, too much emphasis upon facts unrelated to other facts, and excessive concern with memorizing can all strengthen and reinforce sense perception. On the other hand, emphasis upon the transfer of training from one subject to another, the searching for common principles in terms of which facts from quite different domains of knowledge can be related, the stressing of analogies and similes, and metaphors, a seeking for symbolic equivalents of experience in the widest possible number of sensory, imaginal and ideational modalities, exercises in imaginative play, training in retreating from the facts in order to see them in better perspective and in relation to more aspects of the larger context thus achieved; these and still other emphases in teaching and learning would, I believe, strengthen the disposition to perceive and to think intuitively.

If the widest possible set of relationships is to be established among facts, if the structure of knowledge is to be grasped, it is necessary that the student have a large body of facts which he has learned, as well as a large array of reasoning skills which he has mastered. I am not proposing any slighting of keen and accurate sense perception, but rather that we use it as something to build upon, leading the student whenever possible to an intuitive understanding of his experiences.

The creative person has strong theoretical and aesthetic interests. A prizing of theoretical values is congruent with a preference for intuitive perception and thought, for both orient the person to seek a deeper and more meaningful reality beneath or beyond that which is present to his senses. Both set one to seek truth, which resides not so much in things in themselves as in the relating of them one to another in terms of identities and differences and unifying principles of structure and function. Theoretical interests and values are carried largely in abstract and symbolic terms. In science, for example, they change the world of phenomenal appearances into a world of scientific constructs.

Although for some there may be a conflict between the theoretical value with its cognitive and rational concern for truth and the aesthetic value with its concern with form and beauty, these two values are the strongest values of creative persons. That they are both emphasized and reconciled suggests that for the truly creative person the solution of a problem is not sufficient; there is the further demand that it be elegant. The aesthetic viewpoint permeates all of the work of a creative person. I would call your attention to one more characteristic of creative persons – their preference for the unfinished, the disordered, the complex, the rich, which invokes in them an urge to discover unifying principles which order multiplicity and to carry to harmonious conclusion that which is unbalanced and incomplete.

ACKNOWLEDGEMENT

This article first appeared in *Current Issues in Higher Education* (1961), National Educational Association, 89–92, and is published here with the kind permission of author and editor.

34   Divergent thinking abilities in secondary schools

HUGH LYTTON and ALAN C. COTTON

Summary   In a previous study of primary schools, children in 'informal' schools scored higher on tests of divergent thinking than children in 'formal' schools. A parallel study of two 'informal' and two 'formal' secondary schools failed to yield a similar result. Some possible explanations of this finding are put forward.

Convergent ability was shown to be more closely related to social class than divergent ability.

INTRODUCTION

In an earlier experiment Haddon and Lytton (1968) found that children in two primary schools rated as 'informal' (stressing child-initiated learning) did better on five out of six divergent tests than children from two schools rated as 'formal' (stressing traditional learning). The present experiment, using the same tests, took the investigation from the primary field into the secondary, and there attempted to verify the hypothesis of a differential effect of differing school climates. In addition it investigated the interrelationships between divergent tests, verbal reasoning tests and social class.

Two secondary modern schools and two grammar schools were chosen; within each pair of schools socioeconomic background was very similar and the mean VRQ's showed no significant difference. The 143 children (97 boys and 46 girls) tested were 14 years old and in their third year in the school. By consensus among college or department of education lecturers, and local authority inspectors, one grammar school and one secondary modern were allotted to the 'formal' category, and the other pair to the 'informal' category. However, it was noted at the time the tests were given (and not only after the results were known) that the schools did not differ markedly in overall climate. The difficulty here is that teaching approach in a secondary school is uniform for a department rather than for the school; a department may be 'formal' or 'informal' without this permeating the whole school. The experiment was persevered with, as it was impossible to find better contrasted schools that were at the same time matched for socioeconomic background.

The tests used were those described in Haddon and Lytton (1968).

RESULTS

(*a*) *Types of school*   The results of the divergent thinking tests did not reproduce the sharp differentiation that was noted in the earlier investigation in primary schools (table 34.1). There were only two significant differences: the Imaginative Stories Test in the predicted direction and the Incomplete Circles Test in the opposite direction.

Since the tests (except for Test 2, which had been adapted from its previous version) were scored in exactly the same way as in the earlier study it is of interest to note the movement of raw scores from age 11 to 14. The only test for which a marked increase in scores occurred was Test 6 ('Imaginative Stories'); all the others showed only slight increases or decreases. It is possible that this reflects the drop in divergent productivity that Torrance (1965) noted around 13 years.

Table 34.1   Comparison of mean test scores (raw scores)

| | Formal schools | | | Informal schools | | | Differ. cf combined means | 't' for differ-ence |
| | | | | | | | Informal –formal | Combined means |
	A mean	C mean	Combined mean A and C	B mean	D mean	Combined mean B and D		
VRQ	118.4	103.8	111.13	118.8	105.3	112.05	0.82	N.S.
Test 1	12.97	11.89	12.35	10.41	10.97	10.78	−1.57	2.612[a]
Test 2	17.40	17.44	17.43	17.10	16.85	16.94	−0.49	N.S.
Test 3	7.96	6.67	7.20	6.86	8.07	7.65	0.45	N.S.
Test 4	12.21	10.38	11.13	10.68	10.09	10.29	−0.84	N.S.
Test 5	12.68	11.59	12.03	11.22	10.81	10.95	−1.08	N.S.
Test 6	15.22	15.72	15.52	21.45	16.40	18.14	2.62	2.72[a]
N	32	47	79	22	42	64		

[a] Significant at 1 per cent level.

Test 1: Incomplete Circles.   Test 4: Uses for shoe box.
Test 2: Vague shape of Dots.   Test 5: Problems in taking a bath.
Test 3: Block Printing.   Test 6: Imaginative Stories.

Table 34.2   Correlation of VRQ and divergent thinking tests

All schools. Sub-groups based on VRQ ranges		
	N	r
Full range of VRQ (87–137)	143	0.170
VRQ 116+	43	0.037
VRQ 101+[a]	114	0.141
VRQ 100 and below	29	−0.058

All schools. Sub-groups based on Divergent Test ranges		
	N	r
Full range	143	0.170
Divergent score 40.5+	72	0.207
Divergent score 40.4−	71	0.040

[a] This includes category VRQ 116+.

(*b*) *Relationships between divergent thinking tests, verbal reasoning tests and social class*   With the present population the overall VRQ/Divergent Test correlation over the full VRQ range was much lower (0.17) than in the earlier study, but far from increasing with the lower VRQ group, the correlation for this group practically vanished and, in actual fact, became negative (table 34.2). The correlation between the verbal and non-verbal divergent tests (0.43) was satisfactorily higher than the correlation between VRQ and divergent tests, thus providing some justification for considering divergent and convergent thinking as separable, though complementary aspects of intellectual functioning. But the study did not support the 'threshold theory' that convergent and divergent thinking become differentiated mainly at higher levels of general cognitive ability.

The correlation of social class (determined by father's occupation) with VRQ (0.58) was considerably higher than with total divergent test scores (0.26) suggesting that these latter tests are less dependent on environmental influences.

CONCLUSIONS

The negative result of the comparison between the 'types' of schools may be due to the lack of contrast between the schools, but it may also be that the effects of a more flexible approach to learning are not reflected in the performance of 14-year-olds in these divergent tests, perhaps because of the limitations of the tests (cf. Walker, 1967). The result should therefore not be interpreted as a negative verdict on 'informal' schools, but it illustrates the difficulty of this kind of investigation in the more complex secondary school organization.

The low correlations between VRQ and divergent tests suggests that these are two distinguishable aspects of intellectual ability. *Convergent* ability seems to be more subject to the influence of social class than divergent ability.

ACKNOWLEDGEMENT

This article first appeared in *Br. J. Educ. Psychol.* (1969), **39**, 188–190, and is published here with the kind permission of authors and editor.

REFERENCES

Haddon, F. A. & Lytton, H. (1968) Teaching approach and the development of divergent thinking abilities in primary schools. *Brit. J. Educ. Psychol.*, **38**, 171–180.

Torrance, E. B. (1962) *Guiding Creative Talent.* New York: Prentice-Hall.

Torrance, E. B. (1965) *Rewarding Creative Behavior.* New York: Prentice-Hall.

Walker, W. J. (1967) Creativity and high school climate. In Gowan, Demos and Torrance (Eds.), *Creativity: Its Educational Implications.* New York: Wiley.

35 Student style and teacher style: an experimental study

C. R. B. JOYCE and L. HUDSON

This paper is about the interaction of the personalities and intellectual styles of students with those of their teachers, based on observations made during an elementary statistics course taught to medical students.

Answers to two relatively simple questions were sought: (1) Do teachers and students recognize personal qualities readily and consistently in each other and in themselves? In particular, do they recognize the qualities of 'convergence' and 'divergence' which have recently been described in psychological research (Getzels and Jackson, 1962; Hudson, 1966)? (These qualities are defined in Appendix 2); (2) If so, does a teacher who is generally agreed to have either a convergent or divergent bias teach more successfully those students whose biases are similar to his own? Or, more generally, is there any significant interaction, favourable or unfavourable, between students and teachers of the same intellectual type?

The course in question is for first year preclinical students (aged between 17.5 and 20 years) at the London Hospital Medical College. The experiment extended over three successive classes. In Year 1, an attempt was made to relate success in learning about statistics to measures of pre-existing mathematical ability and of high grade intelligence. Detailed results will not be described, since they were largely negative in character and merely helped in forming opinions about what should be studied next. At the end of Year 1, it seemed likely that some personal qualities of students and teachers might prove of relevance to the amount of statistics learnt. Aptitude, as Cronbach (1967) has recently remarked, 'includes whatever promotes the pupil's survival in a particular educational environment, and it may have as much to do with styles of thought and personality variables as with the abilities covered in conventional tests'. The distinction between convergent and divergent intellectual types or 'styles' was thought to be a good starting point. So, during Years 2 and 3, the tests and questionnaires used were those relating directly to these dimensions (Hudson, 1966).

SUBJECTS

There were two kinds of subjects: the teachers and the students. The teachers throughout the experiment were the same: two (X and Y) were members of the Medical Research Council Social Medicine Unit, and two (W and Z) were members of the Department of Pharmacology. The students constituted three successive first year pre-clinical classes at the London Hospital Medical College, each from 60 to 80 in number. Each teacher was responsible for two groups per class of from eight to 10 students and usually taught these groups successively on any one day.

THE COURSE

The course consisted of from eight to 10 sessions, each lasting from one to two hours, with an average of one and a quarter hours. Each course was preceded by a session during which the whole class was given psychological tests and questionnaires, and ended with another whole class meeting for further tests and for the evaluation of the course. This included various kinds of examination questions. Each of the four teachers set a quarter of the examination questions used.

The formal material taught is to be found in the first few chapters of any elementary textbook on statistics (for example, Moroney, 1965): the teachers' common objectives were to produce students with sympathy for the purposes of scientific method and good experimental design, who would know when and how to consult a statistician, although not themselves becoming statistically sophisticated. The way in which these objectives were assailed varied with the individual teacher: some preferred a didactic method, while others resorted to various kinds of demonstration, or preferred to encourage their students to design and carry out experiments of their own.

Measures of cognitive style

A test of high-grade intelligence (AH5: Heim, 1956) was given to students at the pre-course meeting, as well as two open-ended tests ('Meanings of Words' and 'Uses of Objects': Hudson, 1966). At the end of the course, following the examination, a 'Convergence Divergence Questionnaire' was given (Appendix 1). Two rating scales of the 'thermometer' type (Joyce, 1966) were also completed by each student, one to estimate his own tendency towards convergence or divergence, and the other the convergence or divergence of his particular teacher. The extremes of the scale were labelled with descriptions of the typical converger and the typical diverger (Appendix 2). The four teachers each made thermometer estimates about themselves and about each other and answered the questionnaire about themselves; they also estimated the convergence or divergence of each of their pupils on a five-point scale. By an oversight, this was not done until six months had passed. During Year 3, one of the authors (L.H.), who was not concerned with the teaching, was a non-participant observer on at least one occasion for each tutorial group and estimated according to his own criteria the probable usefulness of each teacher to students of convergent or divergent type. The first analyses were performed on the results obtained in Year 3; hypotheses based on these results were then tested on those from Year 2, which until that time had not been analysed at all.

Allocation of students to tutors

The method of allocating students to tutors differed between Years 2 and 3. In Year 2, the composition of the tutorial groups was balanced with respect to the convergence–divergence measures; in Year 3, the groups were formed on the basis of academic interests (indicated in response to a pre-course questionnaire) and of 'A' level passes obtained, and assigned to tutors in accordance with tutors' preferences. The intention in Year 2 was that each tutor should teach a representative cross-section of the class as a whole, and in Year 3 that his groups should be composed of students with academic interests most resembling his own. In the outcome, the composition of all the groups, however each group in both years had been selected, was quite heterogeneous and the groups did not differ detectably from each other.

RESULTS

The first question posed in the introduction was answered in several ways:

1 the teachers themselves were consistently ranked as convergent or divergent by the students whom they taught. W and X were seen as convergent, Y and Z as divergent. These views coincided with the teachers' estimates of themselves and of each other. There was a remarkable degree of agreement between these and the other measures described (table 35.1): their own scores on the convergence–divergence questionnaire, students' views of them, and the non-participant observer's view of the classes that he attended;

2 students' estimates of their own convergence–divergence, made after the post-course examination, were compared with estimates made about them by their teachers. Even though only a little over 50 per cent of the class were considered by their teachers to be predominantly convergent or divergent, the relation between the two estimates was positive and significant ($P < 0.025$). The estimates by teachers Y and Z agreed significantly better ($P < 0.05$) with those of their students than did those by W and X. In answer to the first question, therefore, it seems that teachers and students alike indeed form consistent impressions of convergence and divergence, both in themselves and in each other.

Table 35.1   Ratings of teachers' convergence/divergence

Teacher	By each other				On themselves	By own students	By observer	Mean rank
	W	X	Y	Z				
W	—	2	4	4	3	4	4	2.5	3.4
X	2	—	3	3	4	3	3	4	3.1
Y	4	3	—	2	2	1.5	2	2.5	2.4
Z	1	1	1	—	1	1.5	1	1	1.1
Method	Th				Th	Q	Th	

1 = Most divergent; 4 = Most convergent. Th = Thermometer; Q = Questionnaire.
Overall significance of difference between tutors: $P < 0.02$.

Examination results

The second question, about the effects of student/teacher interaction, was studied in terms of examination results.

The results of the pre-course testing and of the post-course examination for Year 3 were subjected to a form of multivariate analysis (Harman, 1961), in which no *a priori* assumptions are made about the relationship between the observed variables and hypothetical underlying factors. All variation is attributed to as few components as possible, and their nature is subsequently determined by the associations of the variables with each component. The first component, but not the second, was found to be highly loaded on four measures derived from the intelligence test (AH 5), and the second component, but not the first, on the other measures of cognitive style: 'Meaning of Words', 'Uses of Objects', the questionnaire and the thermometer scale. The information about the first two components thus strongly suggests that coherent cognitive characteristics are estimated by the tests. The descriptive use of two categories appears to be appropriate and statistically justified, and we propose to use the labels convergence and divergence respectively for the purpose. Students whose scores were above the median on the first component and below the median on the second are labelled convergers; those with scores below on the first and above on the second, divergers; those with scores above the median on both, high all-rounders; and below the median on both, low all-rounders.

The mean marks gained in the statistics examination by students taught by different teachers were not significantly different from each other, nor were those in the sub-groups derived from the multivariate analysis ($P > 0.05$): the range of the group means was from 47 to 52, with a grand mean of 49. However, certain types of student gained better examination results if they were taught by particular teachers. For example, students taught by Y who had low convergence scores *or* high divergence scores tended to do poorly in the examination. With Z, however, exactly the reverse was true: such students if taught by him received particularly good marks. Specific patterns of scoring on the two components would be expected to favour students taught by each teacher. For example, Z should have been most successful with students low in convergence *and* high on divergence (divergers). When such predictions for all four teachers were taken together, the degree of agreement with the performance observed was found to be highly significant ($P < 0.01$).

But, most interestingly of all, teachers consistently gained similar degrees of success with the four sub-categories from one year to another (table 35.2). For example, X, whose style of teaching favoured convergers during Year 3, had also been relatively most successful with this group in Year 2. This agreement from Year 2 to Year 3 in the impact of each teacher's style of instruction was very unlikely to have been due to chance ($P < 0.01$).

Table 35.2 Consistency over two years of interaction between teacher and student

	Student cognitive style							
	High all-rounder		Converger		Diverger		Low all-rounder	
Year	2	3	2	3	2	3	2	3
Teacher								
W	2	1	3	1	1	2	2	1
X	3	3	1	2	4	3	3	4
Y	4	4	4	3	3	4	1	3
Z	1	2	2	4	2	1	4	2

Ranks represent mean standing of four types of student taught by each teacher in class examinations of two successive years.

High all-rounders = Students with scores above median on Components 1 and 2 in the multivariate analysis (see text).

Convergers = Students with scores above median on Component 1 and below on 2.

Divergers = Students with scores below median on Component 1 and above on 2.

Low all-rounders = Students with scores below median on Components 1 and 2.

DISCUSSION

This study lends strong support to the view that academic learning is influenced by similarities between the intellectual styles of the student and the teacher. On the other hand, it does not always seem to be true that like learns best from like: that convergent students learn best from convergent teachers, and similarly for the divergers. For example, the convergent W was almost equally successful with all four groups, and perhaps, even, least so (as Y certainly was) with those whose bias was similar to his own. Although similarity of temperament between teacher and student may have an important and predictable influence on the learning achieved, this influence sometimes seems to be distinctly harmful. So one divergent teacher may consistently get better results from divergent than from convergent students: while his colleague, also a diverger, may do quite the reverse. In other words, the influence of a teacher's convergence or divergence seems to be unpredictable before the interaction with his students has been studied at least once. Thereafter, the nature of the interaction was consistent in our study from one year to the next. Thus, convergence and divergence seem to be meaningful and relevant concepts for both teachers and students, and in some circumstances are stable over time (unpredictable changes have been reported despite an apparently suitable initial match in another study of a different kind: Thelen, 1967). We have at present no measure of the contribution that they make to the total variation in the teacher–taught relationship. They are not the only descriptive dimensions which could fruitfully be used in the study of student teacher interaction, nor is statistics the only subject matter worth studying in this way.

It should be emphasized that neither the convergent nor divergent style of problem-solving is necessarily better. Rather than expose students of any kind exclusively to one type of teacher in any subject, it seems preferable to give every student the opportunity to study the methods of teachers who provide appropriate convergent and divergent models for solving problems. The present study also suggests a way of making better use of those teachers who are available for a given course; even those whose overall performance is less successful than that of their colleagues will be more useful to some students than to others.

A final point: the study has the usual disadvantages of experiments in education (Joyce, 1962). The students may have learned in other ways than exclusively from the teacher and colleagues with whom they worked. (Indeed, it is to be hoped they did.) All the results reported have been conditioned by the fact that the examination took place immediately after the course, and was itself the only measure of 'successful' teaching. The extent to which the student retains information over longer periods of time and his ability to use it in situations when it actually matters have not been studied at all.

SUMMARY

One hundred and fifty medical students and four teachers consistently rated themselves and each other with respect to cognitive styles referred to here as 'convergence' and 'divergence'. Each teacher achieved characteristic and consistent success in teaching statistics to students of particular styles, as judged by the marks in end-of-course examinations held in two successive years. Although there was an indication that teachers and students of like style formed the most successful combination, the relationships were not entirely simple. Certain limitations and possible extensions of this work are pointed out.

APPENDIX 1: Convergence/divergence questionnaire*

1	I seem to do rather well at intelligence tests.	F
2	I prefer a problem to have one right answer.	F
3	I enjoy closely reasoned argument.	F
4	I find it easy to switch from one line of thought to another.	T
5	I think it desirable to be highly imaginative	T
6	I like to work very precisely.	F
7	I prefer to reason in terms of words rather than of numbers or symbols.	T
8	Faced with a new idea I would rather examine it in detail than offer a general comment.	F
9	I am more interested in literature than in any form of technology.	T
10	I would rather work with things than with people.	F
11	I prefer thinking about problems in terms of specific points rather than generalities.	F
12	I like to have human problems – psychology, medicine – discussed in relation to real people – patients, etc. – rather than imaginary or 'typical' cases.	T
13	I would rather make a speculation about human nature than learn a fact about a machine.	T
14	I enjoy discussing personal relationships.	T
15	I think that facts matter more than opinions.	F
16	I dislike revealing my feelings to other people.	F
17	I believe that 'falling in love' can be explained in physiological terms.	F
18	I dislike the idea that science will one day explain every aspect of human experience.	T
19	I was happy at school.	F
20	I like to feel that no one has quite the same thoughts as myself.	T

APPENDIX 2: Convergence/divergence thermometer

Among their other attributes, we believe, people may be classified along a continuum of a personality characteristic called 'convergence/divergence'. Definitions of these terms are as follows:

The converger enjoys thinking about technical, impersonal matters. He likes arguments to be clearly defined and logical, and to know when he is right and when wrong. He is not interested in probing into topics of a personal, emotional nature, or in controversy.

The diverger is the reverse. He likes discussion to be personal, and he enjoys controversy and uncertainty. On the other hand, he is not interested in the technical, or in argument which is purely a matter of impersonal logic.

Assuming that the left-hand end of the following scale represents maximum *convergence* and the right-hand end maximum *divergence*, mark a cross on the line at that point which represents your own assessment of where you personally stand in this dimension.

---

* Divergent answers indicated. F = False; T = True.

| Maximum | | Maximum |
| convergence | | divergence |

This dimension applies equally to teachers and to taught. So now do the same for the *tutor* who took charge of your discussion group through the course. (Honest opinions please: they will not be used against you, but are vital to our research.)

| Maximum | | Maximum |
| convergence | | divergence |

ACKNOWLEDGEMENTS

The authors are grateful to their colleagues Miles Weatherall, John Lee, and Martin Gardner for being three of the four teachers involved (the fourth was C.R.B.J.), as well as for criticizing drafts of this paper, and to 216 students of the London Hospital Medical College. Many other colleagues in addition to these have criticized the work, especially in the Departments of Pharmacology at Boston University, University of Cincinnati, and University of Stanford Medical Schools. Miss Jean Heard carried out the principal component analysis using the LS9 Programme on the London Hospital Elliott 803 computer, and Miss Jill Frances Bacon patiently typed many drafts.

This article first appeared in *Br. J. Med. Educ.* (1968), **2**, 28–32, and is published here with the kind permission of authors and editor.

REFERENCES

Cronbach, L. J. (1967) How can instruction be adapted to individual differences? In Gagné, R. M. (Ed.), *Learning and Individual Differences*. Columbus, Ohio: Merrill.

Getzels, J. W. & Jackson, P. W. (1962) *Creativity and Intelligence*. New York: Wiley.

Harman, H. H. (1961) *Modern Factor Analysis*. Chicago: Univ. Chicago Press.

Heim, A. W. (1956) *Manual for Test of High-Grade Intelligence AH5*. London: National Foundation for Educational Research.

Hudson, L. (1966) *Contrary Imaginations*. London: Methuen.

Joyce, C. R. B. (1962) The examination as an instrument of research in medical education. *Educ. Res., 5*, 29–36.

Joyce, C. R. B. (1966) The assessment of drugs with behavioural effects. In Trounce, J. R. (Ed.), *Second Symposium on Advanced Medicine,* pp. 370–378. London: Pitman Medical.

Moroney, M. J. (1965) *Facts from Figures*. Harmondsworth: Penguin.

Thelen, H. A. (1967) *Classroom Grouping for Teachability*. New York: Wiley.

36   Thinking for themselves

GORDON MOORE

That children should be taught to think for themselves is a proposition with which few teachers would wish to quarrel.

But how do you go about teaching children to think? To put it starkly, how do you teach thinking to a class of 30 pupils sitting in front of you on a Monday morning?

It is to this question that Dr Edward de Bono has been addressing himself for the past three years. The author of upwards of a dozen books on problem-solving and creativity (*The Use of Lateral Thinking, Beyond Yes and No, The Dog-Exercising Machine*), Dr de Bono is currently director of the Cambridge-based Cognitive Research Trust (CoRT) which has developed what is claimed to be a practical method of teaching thinking 'in as deliberate a manner as mathematics, or history, or French'.

Dr de Bono questions the validity of the traditional view that the ability to think can best be developed as a by-product of mastering the usual school subjects. He accepts that pupils learning history, science and so on have to do some thinking. But he points out that just how much thinking is required of them depends on the way the subject is taught, and that in most subjects it is all too easy for 'the sheer knowledge content' to become a substitute for thinking. He concludes that a place must be found for thinking to be taught directly, as a specific subject, to allow attention to be focused on the *process* rather than on its *content*.

Different

The materials* associated with the CoRT method are published as a series of six sets, each of 10 lessons. The lessons are intended to be used once a week and each set covers a term's work. Thus the six sets make up a course of 60 lessons, spread over two years.

The basic pack for each set costs £15 and comprises:

(a) 31 copies of each of the 10 lesson-notes for pupils; and
(b) a teacher's manual which provides information about the theory of the CoRT approach to the teaching of thinking, general practical advice about lesson structure, and detailed notes on each lesson.

The 'trigger' nature of these materials enables them to be used over a wide range of age and ability, and they have been introduced into a great variety of educational institutions from primary schools to colleges of further education.

The underlying rationale is that thinking is a broad practical skill made up of a number of identifiable and teachable component skills. The essence of the method is to pick out different aspects of the broad skill of thinking (as a cricket coach might focus attention on different aspects of batting) and provide practice in them, at first singly, and then in combination with one another.

First lessons

In the introductory set of lessons (the overall purpose of which is to broaden the way the pupils look at any situation) each of the skills dealt with is given a label – PMI, APC, FIP, AGO, CAF, C and S, OPV – which the pupils are expected to remember and use.

PMI involves looking at the plus (P), minus (M) and interesting (I) points in any idea one comes across. The APC lesson focuses on the operation of finding alternatives, possibilities and choices – beyond the obvious ones. FIP stands for first important priorities and has to do with deciding what is important and what should be considered first.

---

* Published by Direct Education Services, Blandford, Dorset.

A G O is concerned with identifying aims, goals and objectives, C A F with the deliberate switching of attention from the *importance* of the factors to considering *all* the factors, C and S with the consequences and sequels likely to flow from a decision, O P V with the other point of view someone else may hold.

It all seems rather contrived and unnecessary, to put it no more strongly, but de Bono defends the use of his labels on two grounds. Firstly, they help to crystallize the thinking processes into 'definite operations that can be looked at and used and practised and transferred'. Secondly, unless one can present an idea such as looking at the consequences of a decision in some new and striking way people will pay no more attention to it than they have always done. 'Obvious things get taken for granted and may have to be made unobvious in order to get the attention and deliberate practice they require.'

To see how a CoRT thinking lesson works let us imagine a class of 10-year-olds learning the skill of 'generating new alternatives and choices'. The lesson begins with the teacher explaining what this particular aspect of thinking involves.

'Every day,' she tells them, 'we have to make decisions about what we should do. Sometimes these decisions are not very important, sometimes they are. Often it may seem that the decision has been made for us because it looks as if there is only one thing we can do. But if we really look for them we may find that there are more ways open to us than we had thought. Similarly, for most situations there are usually obvious explanations. But again if we look hard we usually find that there are other possible explanations. That's what a good detective does, isn't it? He thinks twice about the obvious explanation of an event such as a murder or a robbery. He keeps looking and thinking. And quite often he comes up with another explanation which is better than the one everybody else was content with. Now that's what we're going to practise today – finding explanations other than those which occur straightaway to everybody, and finding other and perhaps better ways of behaving than the obvious ones in different situations.'

Dominated

After further explanation and discussion the pupils are divided into groups of four or five and settle down to the practice items on their A P C lesson-notes. For the next 15 minutes or so they wrestle with questions like these:

1 'You discover that your best friend is a thief. What alternatives do you have?'
2 'The brightest girl in the class starts making mistakes in her work on purpose. What possible explanations are there?'

De Bono sees the small working group as essential to the success of his thinking lessons. He dislikes class lessons because they tend to be dominated by the brighter and brasher pupils. By contrast, in the small group situation more pupils are more fully involved. The timid talk more freely, and the dull find it easier to follow the thinking of their more able classmates. He admits, however, that group work can be frustrating for 'high-achieving' pupils who find that they are hampered by the necessity to compromise and who dislike having their ideas credited to a group rather than to themselves. These pupils, he suggests, should be allowed to work on their own from time to time.

In the third phase of the lesson, one group, through a spokesman, presents its conclusions to the whole class. The other groups listen, comment, disagree, and add their own ideas where they are different.

The lesson concludes with the class discussing which of the APC principles listed in their notes is the most important. There is some disagreement, but when the teacher decides to close the discussion it is beginning to emerge that the balance of opinion favours the fourth principle, viz, 'You cannot know that the obvious explanation is best until you have looked at some others.' The whole lesson has taken about 35 minutes.

There is ample evidence, Dr de Bono claims, that the CoRT lessons have a marked effect on the thinking ability and attitudes of pupils. Asked to consider something, pupils who have had the lessons are unlikely to take refuge in personal anecdotes and stock answers, or to shrug the question off with embarrassed giggles. After even a few lessons pupils come to regard thinking as an acceptable activity.

For those who prefer 'hard' evidence, he provides data derived from experiments of various kinds. In one such experiment two classes (each with 32 pupils) in a secondary school were compared. One class had taken the first 10 CoRT lessons, the other had not. Both were asked to write an essay on the subject, 'Do you think there should be special week-end prisons for minor offenders?'

The CoRT class put forward a total of 200 arguments for and against the suggestion, while the non-CoRT class could manage only 105. The average number of arguments per person in the CoRT class was 6.2. In the non-CoRT class it was 3.3.

It may well be, of course, that high scores on such tests correlate no better with the ability to think (as judged by the criterion of everyday practical competence) than high scores on creativity tests correlate with the capacity to create anything.

One thing, however, is certain: Dr de Bono believes in the CoRT product. In a recent magazine article he expresses the conviction that the CoRT lessons 'may turn out to be the most significant innovation in education'.

Well, perhaps. He would be on safer ground, I feel, with another prediction – that three years from now there won't be many schools in Britain without a CoRT pack or two somewhere on the premises.

ACKNOWLEDGEMENT

This article first appeared in *Scot. Educ. J.* (April, 1975), 441–442, and is published here with the kind permission of author and editor.

PART 11

Personality

INTRODUCTION

The articles chosen from a vast literature on personality attempt to cover four major areas of interest in education. The humanist approach and studies of the self-concept have grown in significance and Bob Burns has summarized this work in relation to academic achievement in a paper specially written for the Reader. It's a thorough examination of the definition, measurement and development using an extensive literature review for those who want to dig deeper.

In the first edition of *Psychology and the Teacher* (1973) it was thought that Kelly's personal construct theory would prove to attract increasing attention. Ravenette's paper (1975) is a concise summary of grid technique providing a clear description of how the technique could be used with either normal or disturbed children.

In the psychometric realm, a mass of research exists using the current personality tests (usually the 16PF of Cattell or the EP1 of Eysenck) on the connection between personality and academic performance. The findings have been summarized elsewhere, but this paper endeavours to up-date the findings as well as to give a simplified version of some psychometric concepts frequently used in personality theory.

37   The self concept and its relevance to academic achievement

R. B. BURNS

The subject of this paper is the self concept, that individual and exceedingly private, dynamic and evaluative picture that each person develops in his transactions within his psychological environment and which he carries round with him on life's journey. The construct of the self concept is the psychologists' approach to the perennial philosophical question 'who am I?' and that ancient Delphic admonition 'know thyself'. Self concept theorists promote the concept as the most central and focal object within the life space of the individual because of its primacy, ubiquity and continuity. Once developed, it tends to mediate both stimulus and response. Although language has often been claimed to be the sole attribute that is unique to man, the self concept is possibly a stronger claimant for that role. Both Fromm (1964) and Dobzhansky (1967) were prompted to acknowledge that man transcends other forms of life since self awareness is the fundamental characteristic and evolutionary novelty of homo sapiens. The self concept has had a rather chequered history within the ambit of psychology. Controversies over definitions, theoretical standpoints and empirical measurement of such an apparently tenuous subjective and experimental element denied the self concept of its recognition as the *sine qua non* in the explanation of human behaviour until the last two decades.

DEFINITION OF THE SELF CONCEPT AND RELATED TERMS

In a field generally undistinguished by the precision of its terminology, self-referent constructs stand foremost in the ranks of confusion. A wide range of 'self' terms are employed by different psychologists in inconsistent and ambiguous ways. Primarily, these terms must be distinguished from the more inclusive concept of personality. Generally, definitions of the term personality do emphasize its all-inclusive nature, e.g., Allport (1961, p. 28) '. . . the dynamic organisation within the individual of all those psycho-physical systems . . .' But some authorities appear to imply that Self and personality are synonymous. For example, Jung's early writings designate Self as equivalent to total personality (Hall and Lindzey, 1957, p. 87), while Lecky states (1945, p. 188) that Self is the same as personality. The Self as consciously known must be distinguished from the more inclusive term personality, since both conscious and unconscious aspects are connoted by the latter.

The self concept needs to be clearly differentiated too from the concept of Self (figure 37.1). The latter relates to some non-physical function usually described in metaphysical terms as 'soul', 'spirit' or 'psyche'. During the last two centuries, writings of philosophers and latterly psychologists reveal a shift in emphasis from the Self as Knower or subjective 'I', to the Self as Known or objective 'Me'. This is a distinction stated most cogently by James (1890) between pure experience and the contents of experience. His thesis is that anything capable of being experienced whether Self or not-Self is objective, and he categorized two aspects of Self which were simultaneously Me and I. It does not, on the face of it, seem unreasonable to view the Self as 'I' or the experiencing subject. The Cartesian dictum 'cognito ergo sum' is both intellectually and emotionally compelling to the commitment of the existence of Self but such an approach restricts the Self to unscientific speculation in theological and philosophical terms. The concept of Self thus is that sense of continuity, or what James termed the 'stream of consciousness', which includes both the Self as Knower, or 'I', i.e., the process of active experiencing, and the Self as Known, or 'Me', i.e., the content of that experiencing. The concept of Self is a nomothetic concept (i.e., of universal application), since every individual is conscious, capable of self awareness and able to undertake active experiencing. However, this global concept includes so much that it ceases to have any value. The study of Self is no less than the study of the experiencing agent and all his mental processes. The Self as Known (Me) is the self concept, the individual's percepts, concepts and evaluations about himself, including the image he feels others have of him, and of the person he would like to be, i.e., an idiographic, or individualized element. In other words, while everybody has a Self, in Raimy's pithy phrase the self concept is, 'the individual as known to the individual' (1943, p. 18). The self concept, this conceptualization by the individual of his own Self, has very potent emotional evaluative components attached to it, since such beliefs are so personal and predispose the individual to behave in accord with the evaluated belief. This conceptualization of the self concept places it within the ambit of attitude study, since definitions of attitude tend to embody these three components of belief, evaluation and behavioural predisposition (Rokeach, 1968). This approach to the self concept facilitates the application of accepted attitude measurement techniques. The self concept is thus synonymous with self attitudes. Rosenberg (1965) demonstrates 'there is no qualitative difference in the characteristics of attitudes towards Self and attitudes towards soup, soap, cereals and suburbia' (p. 6). Such terms as self picture, self image or identity fail to portray in their static presentation such a dynamic emotionally charged concept. Both Staines (1954, p. 87) and Rogers (1951, p. 138) present extended definitions of the self concept which accord with an attitudinal approach. Another related concept, 'self esteem', is usually defined in terms of a positive or negative attitude towards a particular object – the Self (Rosenberg, 1965; Coopersmith, 1967). Thus, in the present state of self concept study, the positive and negative polarity of self attitudes suggest that a positive self concept can be equated with positive evaluation, self respect, self esteem, self acceptance; a negative self concept becomes equated with negative self evaluation, self hatred, inferiority, and a lack of feelings of personal worthiness and self acceptance. It could be objected that even negative attitudes may be accepted by an individual but how many individuals can hold negative self attitudes with equanimity and contentment?

Recent work on the factorial structure of motivation (Cattell and Child, 1975) demonstrates the consistent appearance of what the authors call the self sentiment. This pervading self sentiment they describe as a 'collection of attitudes all of which have to do with that self-concept which the human level of intelligent abstraction makes possible and which we all possess' (p. 97). Their analysis suggests that this dynamic self concept is composed of attitudes concerned with the preservation of the physical Self, the control of Self and the need for self esteem. This objective finding of a consistent and ubiquitous motivational and attitudinal structure is additional support for viewing the self concept as an attitude with all its evaluative and predisposing behavioural implications.

Thus, the writer promotes a conception of the self concept as a set of self attitudes which can be measured and subjected to hypothesis testing. Figure 37.1 demonstrates the writer's conceptualization of the relationships between various self-referent constructs.

THEORETICAL BACKGROUND

A major outcome of the encounter of the philosophy of science with the behavioural sciences has been the appreciation for observable fact. Events that can be observed and measured reliably and dispassionately are held to be better subjects for scientific investigation than those that cannot. From this point of view, the self concept is a poor candidate for scrutiny in a scientific sense, since it can only be known by the individual from his own frame of reference. The major rationale for the use of the self concept is that it has utility for understanding and predicting behaviour. The yardstick of validity is not whether there exists an actual mental entity. Rather, the construct is acceptable if it allows one to make better predictions, understand relationships between variables more thoroughly, and in any way increase one's comprehension of social behaviour. For example, if we observe that parents continuously attempt to convince a child that he is a failure and incompetent, and later find

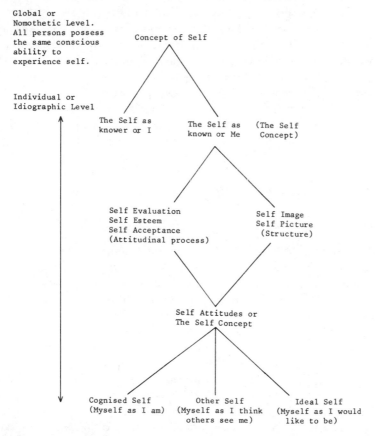

Figure 37.1   Hierarchical relationships between self referrent constructs.

that the child will take few risks or will attempt to achieve little, the concept may play an important role in explaining the relationship between the two observations. The child has learned a certain conception of himself as an ineffective person which causes him to behave as such. But Allport (1955, p. 54) warns against reifying the self concept, making it into a homunculus to solve all problems without in reality solving any. The fact that such a construct is the product of inference does not make it invalid.

The vagaries of ideological theory at first swamped the nascent concept during the 20s, 30s and 40s with the tide of the Behaviourist rationale for which the slightest hint of introspection and consciousness was an anathema. It was only when the rigorous Behaviourist emphasis on objectivity and the scientific method ebbed on the necessary inclusion of the hypothetical 'intervening variable' into the tenets of that faith by Hull (1943) and Tolman (1932) that the self concept could begin to attain respectability and with it a resurgence of interest in its investigation. But perhaps the relative decline in the study of self-referent constructs was also due in part to the failure of psychologists working in the area to adopt a sufficiently rigorous experimental approach as surveys by both Wylie (1961) and Diggory (1966) reveal.

Despite the decline in interest in self-referent constructs during the reign of Behaviourism a few psychologists, e.g., Cooley, Mead, Goldstein, Lecky, Hilgard, continued to emphasize their importance. The rise of phenomenological theory, as exemplified by Snygg and Combs (1949) and Rogers (1951), with its emphasis on the significance of the individual and his personal frame of reference, added impetus to the growing importance of the self concept as a means of understanding behaviour from the point of view of the behaving individual. Rogers (1951) made the self concept the core of his non-directive therapy. He saw the basic drive of the organism as the enhancement and maintenance of the self concept, with a tendency always towards self actualization. The phenomenal self concept is a learned perceptual system functioning as an object in the perceptual field and a complex organizing principle which schematizes on-going behaviour and experience. It 'includes those parts of the phenomenal field which the individual has differentiated as definite and fairly stable characteristics of himself' (Snygg and Combs, 1949, p. 112).

MEASUREMENT PROBLEMS

'You never really understand a person until you consider things from his point of view – until you climb into his skin and walk around in it' (*To Kill a Mockingbird*: Harper Lee).

This is an impossible counsel of perfection. Psychologists have to infer the self concept in other ways: (a) by self report, i.e., what a person is willing to reveal about himself on a questionnaire or in an interview; and (b) by observation of the individual's behaviour. In other words, we are faced with the inherent necessity of basing knowledge of the self concept on the vagaries of introspection and/or of unknown bias in the observation and interpretation of overt behaviour. Combs, Soper and Courson (1963) have argued that most of the studies purporting to measure the self concept are not studies of the self concept at all; they are studies of the self report. These terms are not synonymous; Combs and Soper (1957) differentiate them clearly by emphasizing that the self concept is how the individual sees himself while the self report is what an individual is willing to say about himself to an outsider. How closely they will approximate would seem to depend on such factors as degree of self knowledge, the availability of adequate symbols for expression, the distortion of responses by dishonesty, carelessness and ulterior motivation, social expectancy, response set, feelings of personal adequacy and freedom from threat.

The typical psychological experiment provides the subject with a stimulus whose properties can be agreed upon by a body of independent observers, followed by observation of the subsequent response to the stimulus. Since the experimenter's knowledge of the stimulus is independent of that of the subject, this provides an external criterion against which to measure the subject's response. If the subject gives an unexpected response then the experimenter may assume that the subject missed something or experienced something different from previous subjects. He might assume that the subject is withholding what he sees, or lacks the verbal skills to communicate his perceptions accurately. Those working in the field of the self concept do not have the advantage of an external criterion. Interest is located simply in the stimulus as the subject sees it. The researcher must infer the stimulus from the subject's report. He has no way of independently checking the report since there is often no immediate stimulus and no set of external observers can ever claim to pronounce on what the subject should presumably have experienced. This follows from the contemporary phenomenological approach adopted towards the self concept. Allport (1955) has argued that the individual has a right to be believed when he reports on himself.

The particular items included in a self-concept scale will affect the sort of score obtained. If the items concentrate on an area of life in which the individual displays little competence, e.g., academic pursuits, then his self concept may appear rather negative; if the items relate to athletic activities in which he has some success then the evaluations will be more positive. Therefore, a fairly broad range of items is necessary for the assessment of the general self concept though this is not to deny that a sample of items from a specific category of behaviour can provide valuable information about particular aspects of the individual's self concept. The use of questionnaire techniques to index self evaluation has provided an inaccurate impression that it can be viewed as global and fixed, i.e., that some people view themselves as negative and others see themselves as positive (or anywhere in between). It is clear from the earlier discussion that such a global conception is erroneous and individuals possess many self conceptions, e.g., academic, physical, social. Brookover's (1964) development of an academic self-concept scale is a notable advance in this respect.

As one reads the studies conducted on the self concept, it is obvious that measurement techniques used vary considerably, with great differences in theoretical orientation. Brookover, Erikson and Joiner (1967) make an important point when they note that sometimes the only similarity found in the literature between one study and another is the use of the term 'self concept'. Wylie's (1961) close examination of the studies reveals an amazing array of hypotheses, research designs and measuring instruments. Many researchers have developed their own instruments which have been poorly checked for reliability and validity; they are often inadequately described and impossible to locate. This prevents opportunities for replication and many of the instruments used in self-concept studies have been used only once. Cohen (1976) provides a comprehensive list of instruments indexing the self concept relevant to the needs of educationalists.

THE DEVELOPMENT OF THE INDIVIDUAL SELF CONCEPT

The self concept is learned and developed out of the plethora of 'I', 'Me' and 'Mine' experiences which bombard the individual. At first, the infant cannot differentiate between Self and not-Self, and for most of the first year of life his sense of Self suffers from over-extension encompassing even his caretakers so that to be separated from them is analogous to losing a part of his own physical body. Piaget emphasizes that a major achievement of the sensori-motor stage is the infant's gradual distinction of himself from the external world. The self concept, however rudimentary and diffuse, is born at that moment when the differentiation becomes a reality. As a corollary, the young child is able to view others as separate entities too, enabling him to attribute purpose and intention to them. According to Murphy (1947) such differentiations are facilitated by the child perceiving himself via the various sense modalities: visual, auditory, kinaesthetic, etc. But the process is accelerated by the advent of language. Gesell and Ilg (1949) record the emergence of certain pronouns in the child's vocabulary. At two years of age the pronouns 'mine', 'me', 'you' and 'I' come into use. Such pronouns serve as conceptualizations of the Self and others (Sherif and Cantril, 1947).

One of the first aspects which seriously affects the child's view of himself would appear to be body image. Mead (1934) indicates that adults frequently draw the attention of children to size, other physical attributes and sex role. Jourard and Secord (1955) also brought out the importance of body image in their study with size being the most important dimension. Males were most satisfied with their bodies when they were large; females were more satisfied with their bodies if they were smaller than normal. It suggests that people learn a cultural ideal of what a body should be like and this results in varying degrees of satisfaction with the Self via the body image. The re-evaluation of the body image is presumed to have potent effects on the self concepts and behaviour of adolescents.

During the pre-school period the child is greatly concerned with the view adults have of him and bases his self perception on this rather than on his own direct experience. Since for the young child few things are more relevant than how people react to him, it is not really surprising that the subjective reflections of himself in the eyes of significant others (Cooley's 'the looking glass self'), play a crucial role in the concepts the child acquires about himself. The 'cognised self concept' thus is very similar in content to the 'other self', the way a person thinks others see him (figure 37.1). Parents have the greatest impact on the developing self concept for pre-schoolers as they are the fount of authority. Snygg and Combs (1949) have emphasized the vital effects of construing how such significant others evaluate one:

As he is loved or rejected, praised or punished, fails or is able to compete, he comes gradually to regard himself as important or unimportant, adequate or inadequate, handsome or ugly, honest or dishonest . . . or even to describe himself in the terms of those who surround him. He is likely therefore to be affected by the labels which are applied to him by other people [p. 83].

This fairly direct feedback that parents, children, adolescents and students commonly convey to each other has been shown in several studies to affect the individual's self concept, e.g. Videbeck (1960). Guthrie (1938) describes how a dull, unattractive female student was treated by some male students for a time as though she was tremendously popular and attractive. Within a year she developed an easy manner, confidence and popularity, which increased the eliciting of positive reinforcing reactions from others.

As the child grows older, extension of his environment leads to increasing social interaction and more feedback of information that is subjectively evaluated and assimilated into the self concept. School is the major environmental extension and allows the development of new skills, providing the individual with more evaluative contexts in which to compare himself with others and perceive the others' evaluation of him. In- and out-group categories become available encouraging the labelling and categorizing of others and Self. School then continues and augments the processes that are involved in developing a self picture as Staines (1958) has shown so well in his study of the subtle influences of teachers and their verbalizations to pupils. How often have teachers said such things as, 'Peter, close the window please – no, sit down, you're not tall enough. John, could you close it please, you're the tallest.' Teachers' run-of-the-mill comments are fraught with evaluational, emotional and status content for pupils. During the Junior School period the process of identification with parents loses some of its force as peer groups, pop idols, sports stars, etc., are substituted as models to be emulated. From this period the self concept seems in most children to become fairly settled and stable, despite the supposed 'Sturm und Drang' of adolescence. Only as a result of extreme conditions does it alter drastically, e.g., after survival training (Clifford and Clifford, 1967).

The two major empirical works on the antecedents of the self concept are Rosenberg's (1965) investigation of social conditions associated with levels of self evaluation in adolescents and Coopersmith's (1967) study with younger school children. They both found that the broader social context may not play as important a role in interpreting one's own self concept as is often assumed. This finding was emphasized by the discovery that amount of parental attention and concern was the significant factor. In moving away from global societal variables to the more effective interpersonal environment, Coopersmith and Rosenberg focused research interest back to those 'significant others' the Self theorists had hypothesized were the source of data about Self. Day-to-day personal relationships provided the major source of self evaluation rather than external standards.

Those distortions in attachment generally studied under the aegis of maternal deprivation which appear to create defective social relationships are learning situations which teach the unfortunate offspring to interpret himself as rejected, or neglected, or unloved, or unacceptable, or incompetent or any combination of such debilitating attributes. It has been shown that those who harbour negative attitudes to themselves hold less favourable attitudes to others (Sheerer, 1949; Berger, 1952). That one of the causes of ethnic prejudice is the possession of negative self attitudes has been demonstrated by Burns (1976a). So it appears vital, not only for self happiness but social harmony too, that those concerned with the socialization of children facilitate the development of positive self concepts in their charges. A warm, accepting relationship with parents, teachers and peers seems essential to promote this desirable end. Jourard and Remy (1955) showed a significant relationship between the way their sample of students saw themselves and their subjective interpretation about the way their parents saw them, with the correlation being higher with the mother than with the father. Studies of the negro self concept in the USA summarized by Proshansky and Newton (1968) also illustrate the critical effect of the interpretation of the feedback from specific others and society in general.

From the self-report data of children, e.g. Jersild (1954); Strang (1957), it was shown that the younger children stressed mainly external criteria such as physical characteristics and grooming, while the older ones described themselves in terms of inner resources and the quality of relationships with other people. But generally speaking, categories of self description prominent at one age were prominent at other age levels also. Thomas (1974a) reports that 56 per cent of self comments by final year junior school children related to physical appearance, kindness and ability at sport. Livesley and Bromley (1973) analysed self-report data from 320 British children and found the categories manifesting a decrease with age were those relating to objective information about themselves, e.g. appearance, information and identity, possessions, family and friends. Categories demonstrating an increase with age were those concerned with personal attributes, interests, beliefs and values, relationships with and attitudes to others. This increased frequency of statements about beliefs and values made by the adolescents suggests an attempt to form a stable self concept incorporating a set of basic values. The information on the Self was better organized, consistent and coherent. They appear to be very socially aware; concerned with how others evaluate them and with their effect on the behaviour of others. The onset of adolescence with its physical, emotional and social-growth forces is claimed to be responsible for savage changes in self-conceptualization. The re-evaluation of the body image heightens concern with the reactions of others, and in the emotional and social competencies the adolescent manifests a need to establish himself as an individual with independence, balance and a unified consistent personality (as Livesley and Bromley show above). Erikson (1956) postulates an identity crisis at adolescence with the major developmental task being the resolution of the ultimate ego identity. But Engel (1959) and Carlson (1965) in longitudinal studies show that the self concept remains fairly stable in that period, while Coopersmith (1967) comes to the conclusion that by middle childhood the basic framework had been laid down and the general appraisal of worth on many fronts had been made and integrated into a relatively stable and consistent Self system.

Thus, by a slow process of differentiation the individual emerges into focus out of a totality of awareness and begins to define more clearly and progressively just who and what he is. The self concept is initially a percept with every sensory modality bringing information. It becomes conceptual as this raw data acts as the object of reflexive thought. As the individual grows older, the self concept is seen against more and more frames of reference and each conceptualized aspect becomes the occasion for a feeling response judged against the criterion, the frame of reference. This developmental emergence is organized in terms of constructs about reality that are generated by the particular social and non-social contents of repeated daily experience, and through comparison with standards and values inherent in individually significant elements of the culture.

THE SELF CONCEPT AND ACADEMIC ACHIEVEMENT

Academic performance has long been viewed as a function of such factors as I.Q., social class, parental interest, etc. However, it is now accepted that a major factor is the self concept which is particularly influenced in the educational context by the quality of the relationship between teacher and taught. Staines (1958) has indicated that the self concept is one of the major learning products of the classroom. It mediates all further learning, not only of itself, but of everything else. Thus, teacher's reactions and expectancies, cued in subtle ways to the pupil and the pupil's own feelings about his failures and successes, become integrated into the dynamically motivating set of self attitudes. Academic success is important in our social system hence such success provides pleasure for pupil, teacher and parent with concomitant feedback. Failure carries connotations of incompetency, unhappiness, anxiety, guilt and, in extremis, feelings of rejection. Perhaps William James (1890) was the first to show awareness of the reciprocal effects of performance level and self-concept level. As he wisely pointed out: 'With no attempt there can be no failure; with no failure no humiliation. So our self feeling in this world depends entirely on what we back ourselves to be and to do' (p. 313). Unfortunately, most pupils have little choice about the areas in which they must perform, and suffer evaluation, or in which they wish to make their mark on the world. In surveying American research Purkey (1970) concluded that 'overall the research evidence clearly shows a persistent and significant relationship between the self concept and academic achievement' (p. 15).

Children enter the school milieu with a self concept already forming but still susceptible to modification. Teachers and peer groups begin to replace parents as a major source of self information. With their aura of expertise, authority and evaluation, teachers are 'significant others' who feed the pupils' self concepts with a diet of positive, neutral and negative reinforcement, and create an ethos in the relationship which may enhance or debase academic performance.

While actual ability differences have an effect, because of the social origin of the self concept, the quality of the interpersonal environment within the classroom apparently monitors the self attitudes of many pupils. The teacher–pupil encounter is permeated on the teacher's side by his general outlook and philosophy of life. Three interrelated aspects of this general outlook which appear important in influencing the ethos in the classroom are the teacher's own self attitudes, his expectancies of others and his attitudes to teaching approaches.

(a) Teacher self attitudes

There is the well-documented relationship between the possession of positive self attitudes and the possession of positive attitudes to others (e.g., Sheerer, 1949; Burns, 1975). Secondly, Omwake (1954) and Fey (1954), amongst others, noted a strong relation too between self acceptance and perceiving others as more accepting. Hence the possession of positive self attitudes facilitates the construction of warm, supportive relations with others; this acts as a therapeutic mechanism to promote the development and continuity of positive self attitudes in those others. Davidson and Lang (1960) showed that pupils were well able to evaluate their teacher's feelings towards them and those who saw the teacher as one who presented favourable regard to them were the possessors of more positive self concepts, and higher scholastic performance. Staines (1958) was able to identify teachers whose verbal material and management of the teaching situation would enhance pupils' self concepts. Combs (1965) indicated that effective teachers have a more positive attitude to themselves than do ineffective teachers, and Burns (1976b) demonstrated that teachers who prefer child-centred methods rather than impersonal traditional approaches tend to possess significantly more positive self concepts than teachers who preferred the more formal methods. The conclusion of all this suggests that positive teacher self attitudes facilitate pupil performance perhaps because their accepting, rewarding approach to each child enhances the child's view of himself as someone of worth.

(b) Teacher expectation

Rosenthal and Jacobson (1968) were able to demonstrate that randomly-selected pupils revealed to their teachers by the researchers as high fliers did in fact produce significant I.Q. gains. Though this study has been severely criticized on technical grounds, later work substantiates the general finding of the effectiveness of teacher expectation. For example, Burstall (1970), in a study on Primary French, discovered that low-scoring children among slow learners were concentrated in particular schools where teachers had revealed negative attitudes to teaching French to low-ability pupils.

Palfrey (1973) noted a relationship between the headteachers' informal assessment of pupils and the pupils' self concepts. He claims that the informal segregation of children into good and bad academic prospects was determined by the headteachers' subjective beliefs about potential achievement. Hence, expectancy channelled through various verbal and non-verbal communications enhances some pupil self concepts and debases others, with consequent effects on performance. This study links teacher-expectation effects with the effect of teacher philosophy and attitudes.

(c) Teacher attitudes to teaching approaches

Burns' (1976b) study has been referred to already as indicating a relationship between teacher self concept and attitudes to teaching approaches. Since teachers with low self concepts favour a more traditional approach, with its evaluation and competition, and the possession of such low self concepts engenders a relative restriction in establishing warm personal relationships, then it is likely that many pupils under their aegis would be more liable to develop less positive self attitudes in this atmosphere of competition, impersonality and inflexibility of teaching style with consequent effects on performance. Acland's (1973) survey of research on streaming in primary schools suggests that 'non-streamers' base their stance on the enhancing effects of non-streaming on pupil self concepts. But earlier work by Lunn (1970), in an NFER comparative study of streaming and non-streaming, involving 5500 pupils, was able to show that school organization and teacher type only affected the self concepts of average and below-average ability pupils. Teacher type was a particular influence on average ability children in that those taught by a 'non-streamer' in an unstreamed school had more positive self concepts than their counterparts in streamed schools. The poorest self concepts in the average ability range were held by pupils in unstreamed schools, but taught by teachers who favoured streaming. Streaming had beneficial effects on the self concepts of boys of below average ability, but this effect was not so evident with girls. Non-streaming seemed to provide much opportunity for the low ability child to compare himself unfavourably with brighter and more successful classmates, and feel that teachers compared him with the latter too. This had debasing effects on his self concept. In a follow-up study, Ferri (1971) found, however, that in secondary school, both boy and girl slow learners had developed more favourable self concepts. Ferri claimed that this change arose from such pupils' no longer being in classes containing such wide ability ranges, i.e., a function of their relative position in class.

Lunn and Ferri appear to indicate that grouping procedures themselves have minimal effect on self concept in that high achievers tend to report more frequently the possession of positive self concepts than do low achievers. Also, it is apparent that teacher attitude and expectancy is vitally important, in that teachers who favour streaming but teach in an un-streamed school create a context similar to that in a streamed school replete with its evaluational and competitive overtones. As Wiseman (1973) saw, teachers are far more important in terms of their attitudes and expectations than organizational structures. Emmett (1959) and Thomas (1974b) concur in this importance of the teacher–taught relationship. In Thomas' study a similar level of self evaluation was revealed across three streams, a result of the teaching climate of the whole school which appeared to be democratic, and warmly supporting of every child *qua* child.

The effect on self attitudes of special placement of below average children has demonstrated some contradictory findings. American research, reviewed by Lawrence and Winschell (1973), suggests that special placement or segregation is not conducive to the development of positive self concepts. Andrews (1966) concurs, suggesting that below-average ability children have difficulty in gaining feelings of success and this has a debilitating effect on self-concept development.

Nash (1973) employed participant observation techniques and followed children from feeder primary schools into a comprehensive school, where some of the slow learners were placed in a remedial class. He found that the criterion for placement was behaviour, e.g., troublesome, as reported by the primary school teacher, not learning difficulties. Nash concluded that a self-fulfilling prophecy had been instituted with the likelihood of increasing negative self attitudes. In contrast, Lewis (1971) found higher mean self-concept scores for ESN day school boys than for a group of average ability comprehensive male pupils. Higgins too (1962) showed that the self concepts of slow learners in a special school (in New Zealand) were significantly higher than those of slow learners retained in a normal school. Perhaps these special arrangements can satisfy the emotional and social needs of such children but only when facilitated by interpersonal relationships with teachers who care in a supportive milieu. Musgrove (1966) noted the effect of remote and chilling staff–pupil relationships on the self concepts of sixth formers, which tended to be negative. He suggests that their developing critical faculties might partially account for the negative self appraisal in an ethos of required high academic attainment under competitive conditions.

Thus the thesis is that scholastic achievement can be determined in some measure by a pupil's self concept which in turn has been modified by the expectations, explicit or implicit, of teachers through verbal and non-verbal cues. Such expectations are based on the concept of fixed, measurable ability. This view of ability is most likely to be held by teachers who espouse more conservative traditional philosophies of life since such teachers are likely to be the unhappy bearers of negative self attitudes that demand emphasis on status and evaluation to reduce susceptibility to threat and anxiety.

This view that self attitudes influence school performance is only one simplified causal relationship in what is in reality a highly scrambled 'chicken and egg' situation. Actual ability and success differences may also create differences in self attitudes with subsequent feedback effects, for a small but positive and significant correlation is generally observed between

I.Q. and self concept (e.g., Piers and Harris, 1964; Coopersmith, 1967; Bledsoe, 1968). Hence self expectancy as well as expectancies of significant others fuel or dampen the fires of self regard. Jersild (1952) points out that when a person resists learning that would be beneficial to him, we may suspect that he is trying to safeguard his self image. It may be a false and inadequate image, but it is the only one he knows; this tends to ensure that scholastic performance is consistent with self concept. Coopersmith's (1967) high self-esteem group demonstrating poise, confidence, effectiveness, saw themselves as capable and expected to succeed academically. His low esteem group manifesting withdrawal, defensiveness and lack of motivation, anticipated failure in the learning situation. Coopersmith produced significant correlations between subjective self esteem and both academic performance (+0.30) and intelligence (+0.28). Everett too (1971) discerned meaningful and consistent differences between the self concept configurations of high, medium and low academic achievers at college level. High achievers saw themselves almost as ideal students with non-achievement orientated activities and clinical concepts such as anxiety and guilt being alien to them. The self concept of the average achiever contained some non-achievement elements, e.g., skipping lectures. The low achievers revealed a self concept containing anxiety, frustration, guilt and non-achievement activities, e.g., keeping irregular hours.

Research suggests that modification of self attitudes can be reflected in changes in academic achievement. Brookover, Patterson and Thomas (1965) attempted to discover whether enhancing the academic expectations of low-achieving adolescents would improve school attainment. The enhancement was undertaken:

1 by increasing parental evaluations of the student;
2 by having an 'expert' inform the student about his ability; and
3 by creating a significant 'other' (a counsellor) whose high academic expectancies and evaluations might be internalized by the student.

The first approach was the most successful. As parental perception changed in a positive direction, so too did the self perceptions of the students. However, improvement was not maintained when the treatment ceased. Lawrence (1971), using several counselling approaches with retarded readers, demonstrated a significant gain in reading attainment over control groups. Again, it would seem that modification to self perception has considerable effects on academic performance. Brookover and his co-workers (1964) found self concept of ability significantly related to academic performance even when measured intelligence was controlled. Additionally, specific self concepts of ability, which differed from the self concept of general ability, could be related to particular subject areas. This supports the view expressed earlier on multiple self conception and the regarding of the self concept as a constellation of attitudes.

There appears to be a sex difference in the self concept–achievement relationship. Purkey (1970) discerned a consistent and significant relationship between the self concept and academic achievement which was stronger for boys than girls. Shaw, Edson and Bell (1960) in studying the self perception of under- and over-achievers noted that male subjects in the latter group scored significantly higher than those in the former group, on an adjective check-list. Female achievers actually scored lower than female under-achievers on 'Ambition' and 'Responsibility'. Perhaps such sex differences are a result of the social expectations for males in Western society, especially in terms of academic progress and ambition.

Female self concepts may focus on different areas from male ones. Herman noted that girls are more concerned with personal appearance and social relationships than boys, who showed more concern with academic progress. The same trend had been found by Veness (1962). Fink (1962) noted that the girl achiever has a positive self concept, feels that others accept her and sees herself as capable. The under-achieving girl views herself as socially alienated, unhappy, misunderstood and impulsive. The boy achiever accepts himself un-critically, while the boy under-achiever is a most immature and inadequate person.

The implication from the small sample of research covered in this article is that there exists a highly complex interaction between levels of measured ability, levels of measured at-tainment, levels of self expectancy, levels of inferred teacher expectancy, two levels of sex, and levels of self attitudes. The design of a factorial analysis of variance study to take all these interactions and defined levels of variables into account almost defies comprehension. Yet in this lies the answer to the role of self attitudes in academic performance. At the present state of knowledge one general but vitally important conclusion which needs to be brought to the attention of all educators (including parents) is that it is the teacher who may make failure or success certain by emitting cues which ensure that the pupil is the first to be convinced of his own likely failure or success. Following Rogers' (1951) postulation derived from client-centred counselling, it would appear that teachers must alter their own self concepts before they can effect change for the better in those of their pupils. In accepting themselves, teachers would become more warm and accepting of others, and this supportive, en-couraging atmosphere should get the best out of all pupils. In other words, it is the quality of the relationship that seems most important and this depends, to a large extent, on what the teacher is like as a person. Personal encounter, not organizational form, matters.

ACKNOWLEDGEMENT

This paper is published with the kind permission of the author.

REFERENCES

Acland, H. (1973) Streaming in English primary schools. *Br. J. Educ. Psychol.,* **43,** 151–161.

Allport, G. W. (1955) *Becoming: Basic Considerations for a Psychology of Personality.* New Haven: Yale Univ. Press.

Allport, G. W. (1961) *Pattern and Growth in Personality.* New York: Holt.

Andrews, R. J. (1966) The self concepts of pupils with learning difficulties. *The Slow Learning Child,* **13,** 47–54.

Berger, E. M. (1952) The relation between expressed acceptance of self and expressed accep-tance of others. *J. Abn. Soc. Psychol.,* **47,** 4, 778–782.

Bledsoe, J. C. (1968) Self concepts of children and their intelligence, achievement and values. *J. Indiv. Psychol.,* **20,** 56–58.

Brookover, W. B., Thomas, S. & Patterson, A. (1964) Self concept of ability and school achievement. *Sociol. of Educ.,* **37,** 271–278.

Brookover, W. B., Patterson, A. & Thomas, S. (1965) *Self Concept of Ability and School Achievement: Improving Academic Achievement through Students' Self Concept Enhancement.* U.S. Office of Education, Research Project 1636. Michigan: Michigan State University.

Brookover, W. D., Erikson, E. L. & Joiner, L. M. (1967) *Self Concept in Ability and School Achievement*. U.S. Office of Education, Cooperative Research Project No. 2831. Michigan: Michigan State University.

Burns, R. B. (1975) Attitudes to self and to three categories of others in a student group. *Educ. Studies,* **1,** 181–189.

Burns, R. B. (1976a) The influence of various characteristics on social distance registered by a student group. Accepted for publication, *Irish J. Psychol.*

Burns, R. B. (1976b) Preferred teaching approach in relation to self and other attitudes. Accepted for Publication, *Durham Res. Rev.*

Burstall, C. (1970) *French in the Primary School: Attitudes and Achievement.* Slough: NFER.

Carlson, R. (1965) Stability and change in the adolescent self-image. *Child Dev.,* **35,** 659–666.

Cattell, R. B. & Child, D. (1975) *Motivation and Dynamic Structure.* London: Holt-Saunders.

Clifford, E. & Clifford, M. (1967) Self concepts before and after survival training. *Br. J. Soc. Clin. Psychol.,* **6,** 241–248.

Cohen, L. (1976) *Educational Research in Classrooms and Schools: A Manual of Materials and Methods.* London: Harper Row.

Combs, A. N. & Soper, D. N. (1957) The self, its derivative terms and research. *J. Indiv. Psychol.,* **13,** 134–145.

Combs, A. N., Soper, D. W. & Courson, C. C. (1963) The measurement of self concept and self report. *Educ. Psychol. Measurement,* **23,** 493–500.

Combs, A. W. (1965) *The Professional Education of Teachers.* Boston: Allyn and Bacon.

Coopersmith, S. (1967) *The Antecedents of Self Esteem.* San Francisco: Freeman.

Davidson, H. H. & Lang, G. (1960) Children's perceptions of their teachers' feelings towards them related to self perception, school achievement and behaviour. *J. Exp. Educ.,* **29,** 107–118.

Diggory, J. C. (1966) *Self-evaluation: Concepts and studies.* New York: Wiley.

Dobzhansky, T. (1967) *The Biology of Ultimate Concern.* New York: New American Library.

Emmett, R. G. (1959) Psychological study of the self concept in secondary modern school pupils. M.A. thesis, Univ. of London.

Engel, M. (1959) The stability of the self concept in adolescence. *J. Abn. Soc. Psychol.,* **58,** 211–215.

Erikson, E. H. (1956) The Problem of Ego Identity. *J. Amer. Psychoan. Assoc.,* **4,** 58–121.

Everett, A. V. (1971) The self concept of high, medium and low academic achievers. *Austral. J. Educ.,* **15,** 319–323.

Ferri, E. (1971) *Streaming: Two Years Later.* Slough: NFER.

Fey, W. F. (1954) Acceptance of self and others and its relation to therapy readiness. *J. Clin. Psychol.,* **10,** 266–269.

Fink, M. B. (1962) Self concept as it relates to academic underachievement. *Calif. J. Educ. Res.,* **13,** 57–62.

Fromm, E. (1964) *The Heart of Man.* New York: Harper Row.

Gesell, A. & Ilg, F. (1949) *Child Development.* New York: Harper.

Guthrie, E. R. (1938) *Psychology of Human Conflict.* New York: Harper.

Hall, C. S. & Lindzey, G. (1957) *Theories of Personality.* New York: Wiley.

Higgins, L. C. (1962) Self concepts of mentally retarded adolescents. Unpub. B. Litt., University of New England.

Hull, C. L. (1943) *Principles of Behaviour*. New York: Appleton-Century-Crofts.

James, W. (1890) *Principles of Psychology*. New York: Holt.

Jourard, S. M. & Remy, R. M. (1955) Perceived parental attitudes, the self, and security. *J. Consult. Psychol.*, **19**, 364–366.

Jourard, S. M. & Secord, P. F. (1955) Body cathexis and personality. *Br. J. Psychol.*, **46**, 130–138.

Jersild, A. T. (1952) *In Search of Self*. New York: Bureau of Publications, Teachers' College, Columbia University.

Jersild, A. T. (1954) *Child Psychology*. New Jersey: Prentice Hall.

Lawrence, E. A. & Winschell, J. F. (1973) Self concept and the retarded: research and issues. *Excep. Children*, **39**, 310–319.

Lecky, P. (1945) *Self Consistency*. New York: Island Press.

Lewis, A. R. J. (1971) Self concepts of adolescent E.S.N. Boys. *Br. J. Educ. Psychol.*, **41**, 222–223.

Livesley, W. J. & Bromley, D. B. (1973) *Person Perception in Childhood and Adolescence*. Wiley: London.

Lunn, J. C. B. (1970) *Streaming in the Primary School*. Slough: NFER.

Mead, G. (1934) *Mind, Self, and Society*. Chicago: Univ. of Chicago Press.

Murphy, G. (1947) *Personality, a Bio-Social Approach*. New York: Harper Bros.

Musgrove, F. (1966) The social needs and satisfactions of some young people. Part II at school. *Br. J. Educ. Psychol.*, **36**, 137–149.

Nash, R. (1973) *Classrooms Observed*. London: Routledge & Kegan Paul.

Omwake, K. (1954) The relation between acceptance of self and acceptance of others shown by three personality inventories. *J. Consult. Psychol.*, **18**, 6, 443–446.

Palfrey, C. F. (1973) Headteachers' expectations and their pupils' self concepts. *Educ. Res.*, **15**, 123–127.

Piers, E. V. & Harris, D. (1964) Age and other correlates of self concept in children. *J. Educ. Psychol.*, **55**, 91–95.

Proshansky, H. & Newton, P. (1968) The nature and meaning of negro self identity. In Deutsch, M., Katz, I. & Jensen, A. (Eds.), *Social Class, Race and Psychological Development*, ch. 5, New York: Holt.

Purkey, W. (1970) *Self Concept and School Achievement*. New Jersey: Prentice Hall.

Raimy, V. C. (1943) The self concept as a factor in counselling and personality organisation. Unpub. Ph.D. Thesis, Ohio State University.

Rogers, C. R. (1951) *Client Centred Therapy*. Boston: Houghton Mifflin.

Rokeach, M. (1968) The Nature of Attitudes. In *International Encyclopaedia of the Social Sciences, Vol. 1*. London: McMillan.

Rosenberg, M. J. (1965) *Society and the Adolescent Self Image*. Princetown: Princetown University Press.

Rosenthal, R. & Jacobson, L. (1968) *Pygmalion in the Classroom*. New York: Holt, Rinehart and Winston.

Shaw, M. C., Edson, K. & Bell, H. (1960) The self concept of bright underachieving high school students as revealed by an adjective check list. *Pers. Guid. J.*, **42**, 401–403.

Sheerer, E. T. (1949) An analysis of the relationship between acceptance of and respect for self and acceptance of and respect for others. *J. Consult. Psychol.*, **13**, 176–180.

Sherif, M. & Cantril, C. W. (1947) *The Psychology of Ego Involvements.* New York: Wiley.

Snygg, D. & Combs, A. W. (1949) *Individual Behaviour. A New Frame of Reference for Psychology.* New York: Harper.

Staines, J. W. (1954) A psychological and sociological investigation of the self as a significant factor in education. Unpub. Ph.D. Thesis, University of London.

Staines, J. W. (1958) The self picture as a factor in the classroom. *Brit. J. Psychol., 28,* 2, 97–111.

Strang, R. (1957) *The Adolescent Views Himself.* New York: McGraw Hill.

Thomas, J. B. (1974a) Self pictures of children. *Froebel J., 30,* 31–36.

Thomas, J. B. (1974b) Research notice. *Educ. for Devel., 3,* 50–51.

Tolman, E. C. (1932) *Purposive Behaviour in Animals and Man.* New York: Appleton Century.

Veness, T. (1962) *School leavers: their aspirations and expectations.* London: Methuen.

Videbeck, R. (1960) Self conceptions and the reaction of others. *Sociometry, 23,* 351–362.

Wiseman, S. (1973) The educational obstacle race: factors that hinder pupil progress. *Educ. Res., 15,* 87–93.

Wylie, R. (1961) *The Self Concept.* Lincoln: Univ. Nebraska Press.

38   Grid techniques for children

A. T. RAVENETTE

INTRODUCTION

As yet there exists no body of work on the clinical application of grid techniques for children. Livesley and Bromley (1973) however present a thoughtful and well documented account of the development of interpersonal perception through childhood to adolescence, which must be considered a standard reference to the subject, although its clinical relevance is less direct.

THE GRID

The grid was developed by Kelly (1955) as a technique whereby a client could be invited to disclose his ways (i.e. constructs) of discriminating his world of people (i.e. the elements) and to show in what ways they are in fact discriminated. His responses are entered into a grid which can then be analysed statistically to show the ways in which constructs are related and the ways in which people are perceived as alike or different. A full discussion of grid methodology is given by Bannister and Mair (1968) who also report important modifications of grid technique. These include the possibility of using photographs instead of real people and the provision of constructs by the investigator rather than the client. These modifications allow a wide range of statistical treatments to grid data and the possibility of standardizing the grid. These changes became an essential component in the development of grid techniques for children.

Constructs for clinical use

A construct represents one way in which two things are alike in contrast to a third. It provides, in relation to people, a basis for identifying most personal interactions. With adults, personal constructs can be verbalized to varying extents but in early studies with children it was not found profitable to attempt to elicit a child's own verbal constructs. In any case there was no established work to indicate how a child's system of personal constructs developed.

Kelly (1955) suggests a progression from states of the organism, through individual persons (e.g. parents) to constructs which can be verbalized, and experience suggests that a person's actions may also represent a stage of construct development. These ideas have led to the provision of constructs for children to use which have been based on people and affective states, e.g. 'would make mother angry/pleased', 'teacher angry/pleased', 'other children angry/pleased'. Constructs can also be provided which relate to the complaint about the child, e.g. 'doesn't like school'. Not infrequently children do provide their own constructs spontaneously (e.g. bigheaded) and these can be built into a grid. In essence the grid then becomes a means of investigating hypotheses about the child in relation to his world of significant people, with special reference to how they affect him and he affects them.

Elements

Any set of people, situations or objects may provide elements for a grid. There are difficulties, however, when a child is invited to construe real people in a systematic manner. Many children refuse to pass what they consider to be judgements about people. Many use different construct systems for adults than for their peers and many have different systems for contrasexual figures (see Livesley and Bromley, 1973, for confirmation of this). It is possible, however, to use sets of photographs of same sex, same age children as elements for a grid since these help to overcome such difficulties.

It is often more fruitful to use pictorial representations of situations as elements for a grid. The Pickford Projective Pictures (Pickford, 1968) offer a rich source of postcard size elements and the Family Relations Indicator (Howells and Lickorish, 1967) provides elements which are specifically family based. (Currently the author is using a set of school based situations specifically designed by Mr E. Jordan.) When situations are used the child is specifically invited to see himself as a person in the situation. In general the number of elements should be seven or eight when the child is asked to rank-order them. An alternative method uses 16/18 elements and the child is invited to place elements within two opposite categories (e.g. 'mother would be pleased', 'mother would be angry') or into a 'don't know' category (Ravenette, 1964; 1970).

Analysis of grids

For rank ordered grids Spearman's rank order correlation is used; for 'categories' grids, matching scores are used. The resulting correlation matrix can be analysed by principle components programmes (Slater, undated) or more easily by Hierarchical Linkage Analysis (McQuitty, 1966). The latter method can be carried out very simply 'by hand' and produces very similar results to those from the computer. The outcome of the analysis indicates how constructs go together and how elements are related within the construct system. A 'two-way' analysis for elements within clusters has recently been developed (Ravenette, 1972) which isolates the influence of specific elements within each cluster of constructs.

Further elaboration

The administration of a grid can act as a powerful technique for eliciting the child's own constructions of the elements with which he has been operating. To this end he is invited to talk fully about each element after he has completed the grid. In this way it is possible to link the use of the investigator's prescribed constructs to the child's spontaneous constructions of photographs or situations by means of the statistical analysis of the grid itself. The two-way analysis is based on this further elaboration.

An example

Matthew is ten years old. He chooses not to work at school, is aggressive to other children and sometimes defiant to teachers. He is the older of two adopted boys in a lower middle-class family. A school situations grid with eight elements and eight constructs was used and the constructs refer to self, teachers, other children and parents as the significant people and 'pleased' and 'different from' as affective states. Specifically M was invited to choose, in turn, the situations in which he would most likely be pleased with himself, and least likely to be pleased with himself, and the process was repeated until all situations were rank ordered. The same procedure was then used for each of the eight constructs. The rank-ordered data appear in table 38.1 and the resultant correlation matrix in table 38.2.

It can be seen in table 38.1 that the odd numbered constructs are in general the reverse of the even numbered constructs. In the correlational analysis the even numbered constructs have been reversed with a consequent reversal of the meaning of the constructs. Hierarchical Linkage Analysis showing how the constructs go together is presented in figure 38.1.

Two observations can be made from this analysis. In the first place it seems broadly the case that for Matthew to be pleased with himself and for others to be pleased with him he must see himself, and others must see him, as the same as other children. He is very aware however that he is, by virtue of his being adopted, different from other children. In the second place the two clusters separately suggest that he is sensitive to differences in the interpersonal contexts provided by teachers on the one hand and his parents on the other.

The results of a two-way analysis are indicated with the actual stories which M told. Situations labelled A and B respectively refer to Clusters A and B and the subscript + and − indicate the two ends of the Construct Cluster (i.e. most likely as opposed to least likely).

The situations as described by Matthew

1 Teacher is telling off one of the boys in class for not doing his work. (*Q.* I'm not the boy being told off. I'm helping the teacher get out of his seat in case the boy tries to run out of the classroom.) (Cluster $B-$.)
2 I like football. I seemed a lot peaceful [*sic*] when I'm playing football than at other times. (*Q.* I'm helping the other boy up, he may have tripped. Helping the boy is important.) (Cluster $A+$ $B+$.)
3 A whole school in the hall singing hymns together. (*Q.* I'm on the dais, I like to sing out. I would like to be called out.) (Cluster $A-$.)
4 A few people in the classroom doing the normal work doing some sums at the time. (*Q.* I'd like to be one of them really.)

Table 38.1   Rank orders for each situation by constructs

Constructs					Situations			
Most likely that/least likely that	1	2	3	4	5	6	7	8
1 You would be pleased with yourself	3	2	7	4	5	6	8	1
2 Teachers would think you are different from other children in class	5	7	2	6	3	4	1	8
3 Other children would be pleased with you	4	2	5	3	6	7	8	1
4 Parents would think you are different from other children in the class	2	7	4	3	5	6	1	8
5 Parents would be pleased with you	8	4	5	2	1	6	7	3
6 Other children would think you were different from them	2	7	5	3	6	4	1	8
7 Teachers would be pleased with you	5	2	6	3	4	7	8	1
8 You would feel different from other children in the class	1	6	5	3	8	4	2	7

5 If I was in that picture I'd like to be able to do some work on my own. (Cluster *B*+.)
6 Nice peaceful setting, not too far away from the house, a bike shed. (*Q*. I'd like to go to that school. He sees this as a different school.) (Cluster *A*−.)
7 Some of the people are mucking about in the class. (*Q*. I'm picking up the boy who's fallen and cut himself.) (Cluster *A*− *B*−.)
8 People playing in the playground, apparatus, ropes and slides. It would be good fun to play there. (*Q*. I would be climbing up the rope.) (Cluster *A*+ *B*+.)

This material suggests a wealth of observations from which in relation to the two-way cluster analysis, an understanding of Matthew might be inferred. The exercise, however, goes beyond the scope of this paper.

Table 38.2   Correlation matrix to show construct relationships

	1	2	3	4	5	6	7	8
1								
2	0.95							
3	0.90	0.90						
4	0.60	0.64	0.55					
5	0.31	0.33	0.38	0.48				
6	0.60	0.57	0.62	0.93	0.62			
7	0.90	0.88	0.93	0.64	0.64	0.74		
8	0.31	0.26	0.31	0.79	0.76	0.90	0.55	

CONCLUSIONS

Grid techniques provide flexible means whereby children can be invited to communicate various aspects of the ways in which they affect, and are affected by, their world of people.

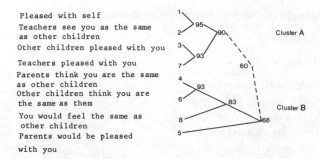

Figure 38.1   Hierarchical linkage analysis for constructs.

They are suitable for children from about the age of eight years and upwards. They are fairly quick to administer, and the statistical analysis is easily carried out by the psychologist himself. They have the special advantage of involving the child directly in looking at himself and others.

Two novel grid techniques in relation to the family are currently being developed and it is hoped to present these at a later date.

ACKNOWLEDGEMENT

This article first appeared in *J. Child. Psychol. Psychiat.* (1975), **16,** 79–83, and is published here with the kind permission of author and editor.

REFERENCES

Bannister, D. & Mair, J. M. M. (1968) *The Evaluation of Personal Constructs.* New York: Academic Press.

Howells, J. G. & Lickorish, J. R. (1967) *The Family Relations Indicator.* Edinburgh: Oliver & Boyd.

Kelly, G. A. (1955) *The Psychology of Personal Constructs.* New York: Norton.

Livesley, W. J. & Bromley, D. B. (1973) *Person Perception in Childhood and Adolescence.* New York: Wiley.

McQuitty, L. (1966) Single and multiple hierarchical classification by reciprocal pairs and rank order types. *Educ. Psychol. Meas.,* **26,** 253–265.

Pickford, P. W. (1968) *Pickford Projective Pictures.* London: Tavistock.

Slater, P. (undated) *The Principal Components of a Repertory Grid.* (Monograph) London: Vincent Andrews.

Ravenette, A. T. (1964) In Warren (Ed.), *Some Attempts at the Use of Developing Repertory Grid Techniques in a Child Guidance Clinic.* N.Y. Proc. Brunel Symposium.

Ravenette, A. T. (1966) The situation grid: a further development of grid techniques with children. Unpublished M.S. Thesis.

Ravenette, A. T. (1970) A further development of the situations grid: use of a certainty/ uncertainty dimension. Unpublished M.S.

Ravenette, A. T. (1972) The two-way analysis of one 8 × 8 grid. Unpublished M.S.

39   Psychometric measures of personality and achievement

DENNIS CHILD

It is common knowledge that there is more to human potential than can be predicted from measures of ability alone. The system of selection at 11+, for example, fell into disrepute because anomalies existed between predictions from standardized achievement tests and later performance in school work. Not least of the reasons for such anomalies was the almost complete absence of reliable knowledge regarding the temperamental, motivational and social factors so clearly affecting achievement. This chapter will examine some of the temperamental issues involved.

To say that temperament plays a crucial part in performance, whether in a formal classroom setting, or in the wider context of learning for living, would not surprise anyone. We are all well aware of being the victims of our emotions, and the impact of this on our achievements, either to advantage or disadvantage, need hardly be emphasized. Nevertheless, the attempts of psychologists to map out the prominent individual differences in personality which bear most directly and significantly on performance have not been too encouraging. Some trends are there as we shall see, but really convincing evidence is not as yet available. As most teachers will testify, the language of the staffroom abounds in expressions indicating a belief in the importance of personality to achievement. Such comments as 'persistent', 'anxious', 'lazy' or 'conscientious' are well-known examples. However, the process of converting these beliefs into hard evidence which can be of service to teachers has proved to be a difficult task.

There is, in fact, quite a folklore about the ideal traits required for success in various walks of life. The caricatures drawn up for those in particular occupations is an instance of this. The teaching profession has long been thought by some to attract those dedicated to the care and love of children, fond of imparting knowledge or needing to be in a position of authority (more easily satisfied if one has a captive, young audience). Medicine is said to attract those who feel great sympathy for the sick and who thereby would gain prestige from saving life. Whilst there may be germs of truth in these generalizations, the evidence is not yet persuasive. But it does raise the question as to whether there are particular temperamental characteristics which, all other things being equal (if that is ever possible), prove to be most beneficial to, or at least keep reappearing in, those pursuing particular activities. Do the demands, say, of a formal examination system – solitary study, reading difficult books, sitting examinations, writing long essays – appeal to some and not to others? Does a formal educational system, with its need for high achievement, conscientiousness, self-discipline and conformity attract those whose personalities are most compatible with the demands of the system and/or distort those who are most pliable? These and many other questions have not as yet been satisfactorily answered, but the present chapter attempts to introduce the student to some of the current ideas.

THE PSYCHOMETRIC STUDY OF PERSONALITY

Most general textbooks in psychology and education give an account of the major theories of personality (Vernon, 1953 and 1966; Cartwright, 1974) and we shall not elaborate them here. It will be assumed that readers who are considering the details of personality and achievement will already have some grasp of the various approaches to the study of personality. This chapter will concentrate on the findings gathered from psychometric measures devised by the two psychologists, Cattell and Eysenck. First, for those who wish, we shall look at some of the fundamental concepts needed for an understanding of the findings.

Source and surface traits

A central concept in personality study is the *trait*. Human behaviour is not random and because of this we can observe regularities in the way a person responds in given situations. Trait theory depends on the idea that an individual will, by and large, respond in a regular fashion given similar circumstances. Further, trait theory also depends upon variations between the ways in which different people respond to the same situation. If everyone reacted in precisely the same way to a given situation we would not be able to recognize traits. Traits, then, vary in magnitude from one individual to the next. The richness of everyday language used to describe personality is not only a recognition of the variability that exists between us, but also that regularities occur sufficient for us to label each other. Some have, in fact, argued (Cattell, 1946) that language is the basis for a study of human personality, because all the crucial observable aspects of social and personal behaviour have been captured in our language and all we need do is find a means of extracting the main components.

Of course, it is realized that no two people or situations are ever completely identical (not even identical twins), just as no two oak trees or pekinese dogs appear identical. Yet there are distinguishing features which enable the botanist or zoologist to arrive at criterion characteristics whose variation from one species to another enables classifications to be made. In a similar way, the psychometrician attempts to find criterion characteristics – personality traits – amongst human beings. However, there ought to be (and generally is) much greater humility in the use of these derived traits than in the classifications of the natural sciences because the 'instruments' we use are cruder and the nature of our observations more open to subjectivity.

Whilst several psychologists have helped to define the trait concept (Allport, 1937; McClelland, 1951; Guilford, 1959), perhaps the most prolific and far-reaching user of trait theory is Raymond Cattell (1965). His work started in the 1930s and has gathered momentum until the present day which sees the provision of several thoroughly designed personality inventories for different age groups. These were devised using factor analysis (Child, 1970; Gorsuch, 1974), a mathematical technique designed to discover underlying common factors amongst a large number of interrelated variables.

In order to search out the traits it is necessary to decide on the sources of information to be used. There are, in fact, many sources which Cattell has subsumed into three kinds, namely, L-data (L for Life), Q-data (Q for Questionnaire) and T-data (T for Test). Life data are collected from any of the numerous natural situations in which the overt behaviour of individuals can be systematically observed unnoticed. Questionnaire data are gathered largely from self-report and rating scales in which introspection on the part of the respondent forms the major source of information. Questionnaires and direct face-to-face consultation are clearly dependent on the honesty and awareness (that is, of motives or actions) of respondents and therefore the Q-data method, with its susceptibility to fake and fantasy, is the most suspect. T-data, which also depend on oral or written responses, are more subtly extracted because the purpose of the question is disguised; thus respondents, whilst they could sabotage with inconsequential answers, cannot intentionally 'fake good'. These designs are called 'objective' tests. Using these sources, Cattell has shown a compelling similarity between the structure of the traits obtained from each separately.

The structure emerging from these samplings in the domain of personality consists of several stable factors which Cattell refers to as *source traits*. A source trait is defined as a functional unity, that is a single behavioural influence occurring in all human beings in differing degrees and underpinning all temperamental behaviour. Their expression is a function partly of the individual's trait potential and partly of the specific circumstances in which the trait is being exposed. This variability in the extent to which a trait appears in a particular situation is referred to as the *state* aspect of the trait. It accounts for the fact that whilst everyone possesses traits, these latter are 'activated' to differing degrees from one situation to the next in any one individual. The full implication of this is brought home to us when we consider that in any testing situation both trait and state variability is operating.

In fact, Cattell (1973) and his associates have consistently found 16 firmly established primary source traits with a further seven less stable but distinguishable ones. These 16 form the core of his personality inventories designed for use with adults and children. They are the 16 PFQ (Sixteen Personality Factor Questionnaire – 'Sixteen PF' for short), the HSPQ (High School Personality Questionnaire) and CPQ (Child Personality Questionnaire). The primary source traits are shown in the columns of table 39.1. In finding the source traits, the factor analytic model adopted allowed for some correlation to exist between the factors whenever it enabled a more satisfactory solution to be obtained, as compared with another possible solution in which the factors are not related. As such, Cattell was recognizing that most if not all human traits are to some extent connected. We shall see later that not all psychologists choose to approach the study of personality in this way and consequently trait structures are derived which vary a little from Cattell's.

The primary source traits have been given special names by Cattell in an effort to avoid the confusion which often arises when everyday terms are used as if they were technical terms. Also, the unique and complex combination of trait elements which go to make up the source trait justifiably merit the creation of a new term. To simplify matters, each source trait is given a letter of the alphabet. Thus, source trait A (sometimes called Factor A), technically known as affectothymia-*v*.-sizothymia, covers the dimension from good-natured, easy going, co-operative, etc. (A+) to critical, grasping, reserved, etc. (A−). Source trait or Factor H (Parmia-*v*.-Threctia) runs from adventurous, likes meeting people, gregarious, genial, etc. (H+) at one pole to shy, timid, withdrawn, self-contained (H−) at the other. Notice how we have to replace the single technical term with a list of commonly used words in order to capture the essence of the trait. In our discussion of the traits we shall tend to use some of the common terms along with the Factor name in order to connect in the reader's mind the familiar with the unfamiliar (for more detail, see Cattell, 1965).

As explained above, the method of analysis used for detecting the source traits allowed of some small correlations between them where this gave a better solution. Consequently, it is possible to group or combine primary source traits, using factor analysis again, to give

Table 39.1 Cattell's primary personality source traits (adapted from the 16PF and HSPQ)

Primary source traits		
− Low score description	Factor	+ High score description
SIZOTHYMIA (Reserved, detached, critical, aloof, stiff)	A	AFFECTOTHYMIA (Warmhearted, outgoing, easygoing, participating)
LOW INTELLIGENCE	B	HIGH INTELLIGENCE
EGO WEAKNESS (Affected by feelings, emotionally less stable, easily upset, changeable)	C	EGO STRENGTH (Emotionally stable, mature, faces reality, calm)
PHLEGMATIC TEMPERAMENT (Undemonstrative, deliberate, inactive, stodgy)	D	EXCITABILITY (Excitable, impatient, demanding, overactive)
SUBMISSIVENESS (Obedient, mild, easily led, docile, accommodating)	E	DOMINANCE OR ASCENDANCE (Assertive, aggressive, competitive, stubborn)
DESURGENCY (Sober, taciturn, serious)	F	SURGENCY (Enthusiastic, heedless, happy-go-lucky)
LOW SUPEREGO STRENGTH (Disregards rules, expedient)	G	SUPEREGO STRENGTH (Conscientious, persistent, moralistic)
THRECTIA (Shy, timid, restrained, threat-sensitive)	H	PARMIA (Adventurous, thick-skinned, socially bold)
HARRIA (Tough-minded, rejects illusions)	I	PREMSIA (Tender-minded, sensitive, dependent, overprotected)
ZEPPIA (Zestful, liking group activity)	J	COASTHENIA Circumspect, individualist, reflective, internally restrained)
TRUSTING, accepting conditions	L	SUSPECTING, jealous
PRACTICAL, has 'down to earth' concerns	M	IMAGINATIVE, Bohemian, absent-minded
NAÏVETÉ (Forthright, unpretentious)	N	SHREWDNESS (Astute, worldly)
UNTROUBLED ADEQUACY (Self-assured, placid, secure, complacent)	O	GUILT PRONENESS (Apprehensive, self-reproaching, insecure, worrying, troubled)

Table 39.1—*continued*

Low score description	Factor	High score description
	Primary source traits	
—		+
CONSERVATISM OF TEMPERAMENT (Conservative, respecting established ideas, tolerant of traditional difficulties)	Q_1	RADICALISM (Experimenting, liberal, analytical, free-thinking)
GROUP DEPENDENCE (Sociably group dependent, a 'joiner' and sound follower)	Q_2	SELF-SUFFICIENCY (Self-sufficient, resourceful, prefers own decisions)
LOW SELF-SENTIMENT (Uncontrolled, lax, follows own urges, careless of social rules)	Q_3	HIGH SELF-SENTIMENT (Controlled, exacting will power, socially precise, compulsive)
LOW ERGIC TENSION (Relaxed, tranquil, torpid, unfrustrated, composed)	Q_4	HIGH ERGIC TENSION (Tense, frustrated, driven, overwrought, fretful)

second-order factors. Examples of these are Exvia–Invia (the now familiar extraversion–introversion mentioned later) which results from a compounding of Factors A+, E+, F+, H+ and Q_2–, and Anxiety (Factors C–, H–, L+, O+, Q_3– and Q_4+).

There are two further ways in which traits have been used to describe human behaviour. One is referred to as *surface traits* and the other as *types*. Surface traits, as the name implies, have a superficial conspicuousness about them because they arise from distinct combinations of particular source traits to give rise to pathological conditions. The classical *syndromes* of abnormal psychology, e.g., neurotic behaviour, conversion hysteria, psychotic conditions, fall into this category. The particular clusters of source traits involved in the abnormal behaviour are not, in fact, sufficient to define syndromes and a supplementary set of pathological dimensions has been designed by Cattell (the *Clinical Analysis Questionnaire*) to encompass the major source traits of abnormal behaviour.

The *type* is a most useful concept. Cattell defines it as 'a particular constellation of scores on factors or other variables which occur with high frequency in the population, relative to other possible combinations' (1965) but excluding the abnormal syndromes just described. One thing needs to be added to this definition. Types can originate as a matter of biological differentiation as in the case of characteristics associated with male and female, or as the outcome of environmental regularities shaping the development of personality. An example of the latter might be the typologies associated with occupational differentiation and the extent to which the demands of the job attract or shape the personality development of individuals or, alternatively, the idiosyncratic profiles which may arise from different cultural demands (Lynn, 1971). Of course, types may well arise as a result of both inherent and acquired sources of variance; thus whilst the distinction drawn at the beginning of this paragraph between these sources may be a descriptive convenience, it is probably not a practical reality.

Whatever the origins, there is no doubt that certain groups in all societies do evince unique combinations of traits in given circumstances.

Extraversion and neuroticism

A second psychometric line of approach, not too far removed from Cattell's, is that of Hans Eysenck, a well-known psychologist in Britain working at the Maudsley Hospital in London. It is important to our later discussion to have some idea of the ways in which the pathways cut by these two men in the personality domain converge or differ. In comparing the approaches there are two central questions, (a) what method has been used to give structure to the personality domain and (b) how extensively does the method actually sample the domain? There is an obvious geographical analogy here. In exploring a new land, not every square inch is covered. In fact, only the practical and significant features are attended to in the initial stages of discovery – and only where the explorers happen to go. When charting the territory, explorers will use different features as landmarks. Some may use a grid of longitude and latitude; others may use physical features as points of reference; yet others may use both. But whichever method is used, there will be cross-referencing and features common to both techniques.

Eysenck has chosen to apply the scientific principle of parsimony and as such his descriptive framework is pruned to the bare necessities. Three major dimensions, chosen so as not to be correlated, form the framework. These are neuroticism (emotional instability), extraversion/introversion and psychoticism. All human beings are said to be located somewhere in the domain and definable using these three dimensions. Cattell, on the other hand, has used a more extensive framework in which the dimensions (the 16 source traits and the clinical analysis Questionnaire mentioned above) are slightly correlated. The effect has been to encompass more of the personality domain in more detail. However, as they are in the same domain it is not surprising to find points of similarity. For instance, the second-order trait of exvia–invia in Cattell's scheme of things bears a close resemblance to Eysenck's extraversion/introversion. The second-order anxiety trait correlates to some extent with neuroticism because high anxiety can be part of the neurotic syndrome (although not all neurotics exhibit high anxiety, and high anxiety is not exclusive to the neurotic). Eysenck's social attitudes of tough/tender-mindedness and radicalism also possess a superficial similarity to Cattell's second-order source traits of Cortertia and independence (table 39.1). Psychoticism has no direct equivalent in the 16 factors, but a supplementary scale mentioned above, the *Clinical Analysis Questionnaire*, accounts for this and other clinical syndromes.

For our discussion later of the personality characteristics associated with achievement, it will help if we look at Eysenck's definitions of extraversion/introversion (E scale) and neuroticism (N scale). In figure 39.1 the model shows a build-up from simple behaviour – specific response habits displayed on a single occasion – through to more involved regularities in behaviour made manifest in the traits. These are related to Cattell's primary source traits. Traits give rise to personality dimensions (similar but not identical to second-order source traits) which can be combined to give personality types. More will be said of these later. Eysenck defines these major dimensions in the following way:

The typical extravert is sociable, likes parties, has many friends, needs to have people to talk to, and does not like reading or studying by himself. He craves excitement, takes chances, often sticks his

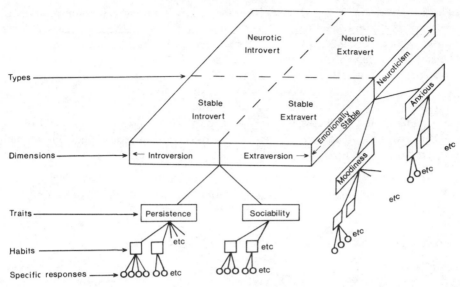

Figure 39.1   Eysenck's theoretical structure of personality (adapted from Cartwright, 1974, p. 397).

neck out, acts on the spur of the moment, and is generally an impulsive individual. He is fond of practical jokes, always has a ready answer, and generally likes a change; he is carefree, easy-going, optimistic, and likes to 'laugh and be merry'. He prefers to keep moving and doing things, tends to be aggressive and lose his temper quickly; altogether his feelings are not kept under control, and he is not always a reliable person.

The typical introvert is a quiet, retiring sort of person, introspective, fond of books rather than people; he is reserved and distant except to intimate friends. He tends to plan ahead, 'looks before he leaps', and distrusts the impulse of the moment. He does not like excitement, takes matters of everyday life with proper seriousness, and likes a well-ordered mode of life. He keeps his feelings under control, seldom behaves in an aggressive manner, and does not lose his temper easily. He is reliable, somewhat pessimistic, and places great value on ethical standards [Eysenck and Eysenck, 1963].

Highly neurotic people are likely to be nervous, moody, worrying, touchy, poorly organized, whilst stable people are emotionally well-adjusted, in control of their behaviour and not prone to undue moodiness.

Psychoticism is distinguished by an excess of solitariness, cruelty, insensitivity and sensation-seeking, but we shall not have need to refer to this dimension.

One of the bones of contention in comparing the Cattellian and Eysenckian approaches is that what Cattell gains in detail he loses in instability of the primary trait factors. This can to some extent be offset by completing several forms of the 16PF, compounding the scores and, in effect, increasing the length of the test; whereas Eysenck's dimensions, though they are robust, are too all-embracing and therefore less sensitive to nuances in the expression and analysis of personality. A simple illustration should suffice to show these points. Above we showed the exvia–invia second-order trait as a combination of primary factors A+, E+, F+, H+ and Q_2−. Two people may have exactly the same extraversion score from totalling the contributions of the primary factors, yet their profiles on A, E, F, H and Q_2 can be quite different. The illustration from the *Handbook for the 16PF* (Cattell, Eber and Tatsuoka, 1970) adds realism to the example, as the sten scores for each factor are taken from its table 12.2 in which groups 1 and 2 represent 'typical' accountants and artists respectively (see table 39.2).

Inspection of table 39.2 shows quite considerable differences in some factors (A, H). Even the smallest difference in factor F is just statistically significant, and yet the overall exvia/invia score is identical – both tending towards introversion. A test of profile similarity (*Handbook*, pp. 311–312) shows the two sets of sten scores to be profoundly dissimilar.

From the point of view of building up a knowledge of achievement styles for individuals, it is likely that we shall get more detailed information from the 16PF profile than from a single extraversion score; this is particularly so when an individual has provided a score derived from several parallel forms in order to overcome the problem of instability.

Table 39.2   Exvia profiles for typical accountants and artists

	A	E	F	H	Q_2	Exvia score
Group 1 (accountants)	7.1	5.2	4.5	4.7	6.2	4.8
Group 2 (artists)	3.1	6.8	3.9	7.0	7.0	4.8

Note: The exvia score is obtained by multiplying the sten score for each factor with the corresponding weights for converting primary-factor stens to the second-order exvia score (in the *Handbook for the 16PF*, pp. 128–129).

The method of profile measurement

But how can the theoretical structures elaborated above assist in the practical matter of defining the personality profiles of a given criterion group, and how do these profiles contribute to our knowledge of learning styles? What, if any, are the regularities or idiosyncracies of personality organization which can enhance or inhibit specific task performance?

One thing is certain, it takes all kinds to make a success of life. No two successful people are exactly alike and it would be foolish to pretend otherwise. Subtle blends of useful habits, special abilities and skills, motivation and environmental circumstances as well as temperamental traits are all likely to influence performance. Equally, it is clear that for certain tasks some qualities are more beneficial than others. Jockeys are more likely to be small than large; doctors are more likely to be recruited from the more rather than the less intelligent; the lazy or the carefree are less likely to do well than the hard-working or conscientious – the examples are legion. Thus, whilst recognizing the limitations of generalization, there does seem to be a case for looking systematically at human attributes for their likely effect on performance and seeing if certain combinations of these attributes are more advantageous than others. Both Cattell and Eysenck have provided us with a possible framework of descriptive personality variables which can be used to detect patterns, if such exist. Cattell, in discussing the definition of personality, believes that it is 'concerned with and deduced from all the behavior relations between the organism and its environment: it is that which predicts behavior, given the situation' (Cattell, 1946). Eysenck is more specific – 'the more or less stable and enduring organisation of a person's character, temperament, intellect and physique which determines his unique adjustment to the environment' (Eysenck, 1953). But both these definitions make it abundantly clear that what goes on in classrooms, libraries or private studies is a function of personality.

Passing from the haven of theoretical definitions to the troublesome waters of practical measurement raises two important questions. First, is the variability in achievement brought about by differences in personality sufficient to make a search worth while, and second, if so, what particular traits are involved? To answer the first question it is necessary to digress for a moment to indicate briefly a technique which has been used most frequently, that is *multiple regression analysis*. The title might be sufficient to put some people off, but the overall aim of the method is really not too difficult to follow. If we have a dependent variable, let us say school achievement, and several independent variables all thought to relate to the dependent variable (intelligence, social background, language competence and so forth), it is possible to find an overall correlation between achievement and the others. This is known as a multiple correlation coefficient. In effect, it gives the strength of relationship between the dependent variable and the other independent variables *taken together*. We can also find the cumulative or individual contribution of each independent variable (taken stepwise).

As the statistical measure is a correlation coefficient, there are several useful ways in which we can express the relationships. For example, if a correlation of 0.5 was found between school achievement and intelligence, the square of this value gives us the *variance* involved, that is 0.25. This can be converted to a percentage by simply multiplying by 100. Expressed in words, we are saying that 25 per cent of the variation in school achievement scores can be accounted for by variation in intelligence. We also know we have to look elsewhere in order to account for the remaining 75 per cent of the variance in achievement scores.

Researches so far have shown some intriguing possibilities in the distribution of variance. Cattell, Barton and Dielman (1972) attempted to predict achievement scores from intelligence, personality and motivation measures amongst 13- to 14-year-old pupils. Several school subjects were used to find achievement. In science, for instance, intelligence, personality and motivation correlated with achievement to give +0.54, +0.46 and +0.66 respectively. By squaring and converting to percentages as described above the percentage variance would be 29 per cent, 21 per cent and 43 per cent respectively. The multiple correlation (giving the effect of all three variables taken together) was +0.74 (55 per cent of the variance).

Multiple correlations of the order shown above have not shown up to quite the same extent in relating Eysenck's E and N scales to achievement. The multiple influence of these scales, using two major studies (Entwistle and Cunningham, 1968; Eysenck and Cookson, 1969) was only 2.6 per cent and 5 per cent respectively (derived from multiple correlations of +0.16 in Entwistle and Cunningham and +0.22 in Eysenck and Cookson).

Having established a broad link between personality and achievement in terms of variance, the second question to which we must now turn concerns the detection of those particular traits associated with achievement. For this we need to look at the derivation of profiles, or sets of trait scores for a person or well-defined group (*criterion group*). These are most fruitfully compared with population means for the trait being considered. Thus the population becomes the basic criterion group from which deviations of other more specific criterion groups are calculated. Of course, profiles are only feasible where we have a sufficient number of traits to consider. The 16PF is especially suited to this purpose and its wide usage has enabled population norms to be well grounded. These are near normal distributions of scores for each personality factor which for convenience are standardized to a mean of 5.5 and standard deviation of 2.0. This gives a range, deliberately, from 0.5 to 10.5 covering 2.5 standard deviations on each side of the mean, and the scale is referred to as a *sten* scale (sten = standard ten). Any criterion group, be they doctors, teachers, high achievers, truants, could be tested against this scale for significant deviations from the norm.

There are two basic ways of approaching the criterion. One, called by Cattell the *Adjustment (or Type Placement) Method*, rests on the assumption that members of a well-defined group (doctors, teachers, shop stewards) who remain in the group will do so because they are well adjusted to, and satisfied with, the criterion activity. The mean score for each factor is found for the adjustment criterion group and this is taken to represent the optimum for membership. The longer individuals stay in the group, the greater, it is supposed, will be their satisfaction with membership. In other words, they become adjusted to group membership. There is no question of whether the individuals in the group have been successful; persistence of membership alone decides.

A second basic method of determining the criterion is by success – referred to by Cattell as the *Effectiveness (or Fitness by Performance) Method* (this is where the well-known 'specification equation' is also used). The criterion group is depicted using 'success' in given activities such as occupations, leadership, school achievement (or maladaptive circumstances as in clinical syndromes).

The Effectiveness criterion is particularly useful and relevant in building profiles for such groups as high or low achievers. Achievement is most often found from standardized tests, 'O' or 'A' levels or teacher assessments suitably standardized.

To illustrate the use of profiles, some results worked out by the author (from basic data in Spelman, 1975) are shown in figure 39.2. There are two profiles derived from HSPQ scores (using British norms in Saville and Finlayson, 1973) for 15–16 year olds taking 'O' levels and CSE examinations. The sten mean score for each factor is plotted on the scale. The darker band down the centre of the figure between approximately 4.5 and 6.5 gives the range within which we would expect average scores (half a standard deviation on either side of the mean of 5.5). With the extensive samples used by Cattell, it has been possible to show that scores outside this range are 'departing from the average'.

The British sample was divided according to performance in 'O' levels and CSE to give three groups of high, medium and low performances. Only the high (N = 115) and low performances (N = 117) are shown. One important point to note is that not a single significant difference appeared for any of the factors between high and low achievers when the sample was divided into boys and girls; thus the sample was considered as a whole.

To interpret the profiles, we may look at the sten scores in comparison first with the norms. Clearly the high achievers are above average in ability (B). Other factors are not really too different from the average (shaded zone) except marginally high on E, Q_2 and Q_3 (assertive, self-sufficient and high self-concept control) and low on D and O (phlegmatic and self-assured). The low achievers only deviate on factors E+, F+ and I– (assertive, happy-go-lucky and tough-minded). Perhaps more significant is a direct comparison between high and low achievers' profiles. This will, to some extent, control for any idiosyncracies of the group as a whole. The sten scores for each factor have been tested for significant differences (t-test) and the following emerged: high achievers were more intelligent (B+), conscientious (G+),

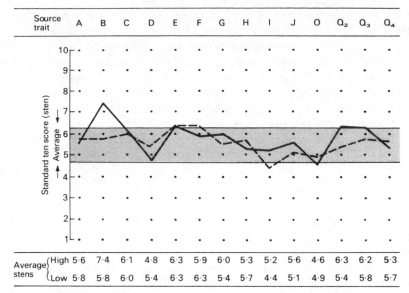

| Source trait | A | B | C | D | E | F | G | H | I | J | O | Q₂ | Q₃ | Q₄ |

| Average stens {High | 5·6 | 7·4 | 6·1 | 4·8 | 6·3 | 5·9 | 6·0 | 5·3 | 5·2 | 5·6 | 4·6 | 6·3 | 6·2 | 5·3 |
| {Low | 5·8 | 5·8 | 6·0 | 5·4 | 6·3 | 6·3 | 5·4 | 5·7 | 4·4 | 5·1 | 4·9 | 5·4 | 5·8 | 5·7 |

Figure 39.2   HSPQ profile for high and low achievers in secondary schools taking 'O' and CSE examinations (high N = 115, low N = 117). From Spelman, 1975.

tender-minded (I+), self-sufficient (Q₂+) and phlegmatic (D−). In our summary of various researches later in the chapter, it will be seen that all these factors figure quite markedly amongst high achievers. A minute's thought will soon reveal the logic of this particular combination of qualities as beneficial to effective performance at school.

Zone analysis

Whilst this technique is not referred to in this chapter it is mentioned here for completeness should it appear in the literature. The E and N scales have been the focus of much research activity in Great Britain particularly related to achievement. The two commonest ways of using scores from these dimensions with other measures are (1) by calculating means, correlations and so forth and (2) by creating a typology using *zone analysis*.

Zone analysis is illustrated at the top of figure 39.1. On dividing the E and N dimensions either at the mean or median for the sample (suitably large and representative) four 'zones' are generated within which all the sample will fall. The *personality* or *zonal types* of neurotic introvert, neurotic extravert, stable introvert and stable extravert are shown at the top of the figure. The zonal types should not be confused with Cattell's types mentioned above. In the latter, the types are defined by a particular score combination of several factors and these scores can be at any point along the scale of each factor. On the contrary, the zonal analysis of Eysenck's dimensions is most effective when the sample is limited to those having significantly high or low scores on the two dimensions (see Cattell, 1965, pp. 254–256 for more detail).

In fact, zone analysis suffers from all the dangers inherent in using a continuous variable as if it were basically a dichotomous arrangement with most individuals at the poles. As the distribution should be normal, most individuals will be located at or near the norm of the range of scores and zone analysis therefore tends to eliminate a large proportion of the sample (ambiverts). Another disadvantage in using dichotomous descriptions is that we tend to grow lax in their use and become snared into thinking of personality qualities in all-or-nothing terms. We talk of introverts or convergers as if they possessed only those qualities associated with introversion and convergence, but even those high on introversion or convergence will display some extravert or divergent qualities.

PERSONALITY AND ACHIEVEMENT

Cattell's traits and achievement

Perhaps the most comprehensive survey of researches into the correlates of scholastic attainment and personality traits was undertaken by the late Professor Frank Warburton (1968). He gathered most of the research in this area up to 1968 and the following summary brings together his work plus some of the more recent findings recorded in the manuals of the HSPQ and 16PF along with a replication study by Cattell, Barton and Dielman (1972). The measure of school or college attainment is in most cases terminal marks, grade point averages, degree results or standardized tests in mathematics and English. Few of the studies took account of possible sex or cultural differences (HSPQ scores for example were largely derived using American norms). Most of Warburton's reported researches were British. Table 39.3 is, therefore, given in very broad terms. Some factors are excluded which make little contribution to achievement variance.

Warburton's original analysis (1968; table 39.3) used age groups of 5–11, 12–14, 15–17 and 18 upwards so as to correspond roughly with primary, secondary, sixth form and university age ranges. It could be argued that age is largely an 'effect' variable between individual personality, achievement and learning environment, so that using age ranges comparable with particular educational institutions, as in Warburton's case, is likely to be more profitable than looking at ages year by year. Because of the paucity of researches using the CPQ and the uncertainties surrounding year by year analyses, table 39.3 is divided into two major age ranges – pre- and post-fifteen. Warburton chose this as a major transition age and the results support his hypothesis.

Out of the confusion of findings, there do emerge certain tendencies which have wide confirmation in the literature. Common to most high achievers is the likelihood of their being more intelligent, serious, conscientious, circumspect, imaginative, self-assured, self-sufficient and self-controlled. Nevertheless, one prominent point is the inconsistency in the relationship of achievement to certain factors as one progresses from younger to older students. Successful younger students of primary and early secondary age tend to be outgoing, stable, phlegmatic, conforming, socially bold, tough-minded (amongst American students essentially) and tense. Older students who attain well appear to be more reserved, emotional, excitable, competitive, shy, tender-minded and unfrustrated than other students.

Insufficient detailed research has been done which accounts for differences arising from sex, subjects of study, method of measuring attainment, and cultural influences. The little we do know (see for instance the manuals of the questionnaires) points to some minor

Table 39.3 Summary of results from studies using Cattell's Inventories: signs indicate direction of association with scholastic achievement.

Factor			Age range	
−		+	14 and under	15 and over
Consistent				
Low intelligence	B	High intelligence	B+	B+
Sober, serious	F	Happy-go-lucky	F− (low)	F− (low)
Expedient	G	Conscientious	G+	G+
Zestful	J	Circumspect	J+ (low)	(not present on 16PF)
Practical	M	Imaginative	(not present in HSPQ)	M+
Self-assured	O	Apprehensive	O−	O−
Group-dependent	Q₂	Self-sufficient	Q₂+	Q₂+
Low self-sentiment	Q₃	High self-senti-ment	Q₃+	Q₃+
Inconsistent				
Reserved	A	Outgoing	A+	A− (low)
Emotional	C	Stable	C+ (low)	C−
Phlegmatic	D	Excitable	D−	D+ (not present on 16PF)
Submissive, conforming	E	Assertive, competitive	E−	E+
Shy	H	Socially bold	H+	H−
Tough-minded	I	Tender-minded	I− (except British samples which tend to be I+)	I+
Low ergic tension	Q₄	High ergic tension	most inconsistent findings – the manuals give:	
			Q₄+	Q₄−

Sources: Warburton (1968); Manual of the HSPQ (Cattell and Cattell, 1969); Manual of the 16PF (Cattell, Eber and Tatsuoka, 1970); Cattel, Barton and Dielman (1972).

variations in profiles of achieving British and American students and certain broad subject differences especially between science and non-science students. The latter has been much more searchingly explored using Eysenckian dimensions.

Extraversion and achievement

At the second-order level, using mainly the E and N dimensions of Eysenck, another crop of results has been harvested. Like the previous section, we will have to show that whilst possible trends can be seen in the research, we have found few certainties. Some results already discussed are mirrored in the present findings, as would be expected from the connection between first- and second-stratum measures. Again, the trends are confounded by intervening variables of sex, age, institutional expectations, state as well as trait factors, etc. Unfortunately it may be that the broader and more complex second-order factors, especially neuroticism, obscure rather than clarify the influence of traits – the 'flat-iron' of generalization in the form of the principle of parsimony not only irons out some statistical wrinkles but removes the colour as well.

Several researchers, particularly Entwistle (1974), have attempted to summarize the findings so far. Again, as with Warburton's work, one major result has been the age inversion. Once more we find support for a transition in extraversion–achievement relationships somewhere in the early to middle secondary age group. Table 39.4 shows a number of correlational studies. The introversion–extraversion correlation with attainment changes from a positive to a negative value in early adolescence as we progress up the age range. It would seem that certain extravert qualities are advantageous in primary and early secondary school, whereas introvert qualities come into prominence more and more as one proceeds through the educational system. One serious criticism of the overall correlations in table 39.4 is their magnitude. As shown earlier, the variance (square of correlation values) is generally quite low and this point is taken up in recent work by Kline (1976).

What detail is being obscured in using the broad Eysenckian second-order factor of extraversion–introversion? First let us return to table 39.2 and extract from this the primary factors A, E, F, H and Q_2 found to give the second-order exvia–invia factor. A–, E–, F–, H– and Q_2+ contribute in some degree to introvert tendencies. The *actual* direction of the best correlations to date with achievement are:

young students (14 and under)   A+,   E–,   F– (low),   H+, Q_2+
older students (15 and over)   A– (low),   E+,   F– (low),   H–, Q_2+

With younger pupils such extravert traits as outgoing – participating (A+), adventurous and friendly (H+) – are beneficial. When one recalls the attainment criteria one is likely to see in almost any primary or junior secondary school, in addition to conventional performance skills, teachers are highly likely to be impressed by willingness to participate, by exploratory and adventure-loving children and, of course, by friendly ones – in spite of the fact that their performance may be moderate or even poor. The A+, H+ child who is also intelligent would be an outright winner! But these are both *extravert* qualities. The remaining factors are in the direction of introversion in being conforming (E–), a decided advantage in formal classroom settings, serious (F–) and self-sufficient (Q_2), all self-evident attributes for the would-be scholar.

Older high attaining students are similarly serious and self-sufficient, but they differ from younger students in displaying the introvert qualities of being aloof (A–) and socially withdrawn – helpful for the studious. The anomaly in terms of the pattern of introvert qualities just described is the E+ factor of aggressive competitiveness. But who could survive our public examination system with its highly developed grading without also having a strong sense of academic competitive 'aggro'? The thoroughly introverted character who is also timid and docile would hardly stand a chance in the competitive world of universities.

Nobody knows the answer to the question as to why the basic pattern of invia–exvia attributes concomitant with academic success gradually shift in emphasis with age. Speculations are rife. Could it be the changing demands of the institutions we attend (primary schools contrast markedly with universities)? Maybe it is the development from concrete to abstract cognitive skills occurring about this time which is having an effect on attitudes. Could it be that the junior forms of personality inventories are not quite measuring the same thing as the adult forms? But perhaps the most teasing question of all is whether it is the same people who succeed in all these institutions and are thus playing the system as required, or is there a genuine change in personnel – i.e., does the successful extravert child in primary schools sink into obscurity in later academic years, whilst the backroom boys and girls in primary schools find their feet in secondary schools? This in turn raises the unanswered question of the adaptability of human personality and the effects of state changes in traits. Anthony (1973) presents a developmental argument in which he suggests, from large-scale studies of ten variations of E scores with age, that there is an increase of E scores from 7 to 13 years, and a decline in E scores from 15 years onwards. Could it be that this dimension is a developmental one with some, possibly the intellectually bright, passing through an 'inverted U' developmental phase more rapidly? Thus, in early years the brighter would be more extraverted and subsequently (because of quicker development) more introverted. Does the educational system with its emphasis on examinations (and all that these demand of individual enterprise) tend to filter out those with particular temperamental and motivational (as well as intellectual) profiles? Or does the system encourage the development of certain traits in advantageous directions in those capable of adapting to the demands (trait deformation by a repeated state condition)? Any answer will doubtless contain something of all these possibilities.

Anxiety and achievement

The role of anxiety in performance is another essential consideration. We shall use the term anxiety rather than neuroticism for reasons already explained, but when referring to Eysenck's N dimension it will be recalled that a correlation does exist between it and measured anxiety. The picture here is much cloudier than for extraversion. The results in table 39.4 using largely Eysenck's N are sufficiently diverse as to be almost random. The irresistable logic of low anxiety—low drive—poor performance; moderate anxiety—healthy drive—good performance; high anxiety—disruption—poor performance (the now famous Yerkes–Dodson effect) does not work out, or at least is not borne out for a task as difficult as academic achievement. As mentioned above, in state and trait theory we may have an explanation for the rag-bag of relationships in table 39.4. Anxiety levels, whilst depending to some degree on the trait potential of an individual, are so task and situation specific (Gaudry and Spielberger, 1971) as to make a clear relationship between anxiety and performance difficult to find and one between N (a more complex concept) and performance highly unlikely. The tasks we require of the student are quite complex and if anything the research indicates, in line with Yerkes–Dodson, that complex tasks generate high anxiety. Thus the level of variability possible is greatly increased. The competence (self-perceived) of an individual, for instance, is likely to play a part in raising or lowering anxiety levels (a person who thinks or knows he is able to cope with an examination may tend to generate less anxiety). Therefore, the anxiety provoked in an individual by a given situation is more subtle than our testing procedures would allow and should account for differences in trait-level, task difficulty (e.g., open book or essay v. three-hour unseen examination paper), the situation (e.g., streamed *v.* unstreamed), the teacher (e.g., ogre *v.* soft-touch), personal competence and intelligence (Denny, 1966).

The usual research tools in anxiety measurement have been such scales as the Children's Manifest Anxiety Scale (Castaneda, McCandless and Palermo, 1956), the Test Anxiety Scale for Children (Sarason et al, 1960), Achievement Anxiety Test (Alpert and Haber, 1960), more recently the State–Trait Anxiety Inventory (Spielberger, Gorsuch and Lushene, 1970) and the IPAT anxiety scales derived from Cattell's 16PF and HSPQ. The results from all but the last of these have been much less equivocal than for the N scale of Eysenck in showing, almost without exception, that high anxiety at any age is associated with low academic achievement (Gaudry and Spielberger, 1971, ch. 5).

The second-order anxiety factor of Cattell gives the following specifications for high achievement:

factor and direction of high anxiety	C−	D+	H−	L+	O+	Q_3-	Q_4+
young students (14 and under)	+ (low)	−	+		−	+	+
older students (15 and over)	−	+	−	−	−	+	−

(there is no L factor on the HSPQ and the D factor for older students is derived only from the HSPQ). These two alongside the summary work of Warburton (1968, p. 45) give strong

Table 39.4   Correlations between Extraversion (E), Neuroticism (N) and Attainment (A) at various ages in some British studies.

Study (see below)		Mean C.A.		r E–A	r N–A	Attainment measure
1	Univ.	21+	males	−0.30[b]	n.s.	} Final
	Univ.	21+	females	n.s.	−0.37[b]	} degree
2	Univ.	21+		−	+	Final degree
3	Univ.	18–23		−0.27[a]	+0.36[a]	Mill Hill Vocab.
4	Univ.	18–19		−0.30[b]	−0.03	⎫
				+0.10	+0.23[b]	⎪
				+0.04	−0.07	⎬ 1st year exams
				+0.02	−0.03	⎪
				+0.01	−0.09	⎭
5	Univ.	18–19	males	−0.33[a]	−0.13	⎫
	Univ.	18–19	females	−0.14	+0.04	⎬ 1st year exams
	College	18–19	males	−0.21[a]	−0.10	⎪
	College	18–19	females	−0.01	−0.07	⎭
6	Tech. college	18–19		−0.04	0.00	ONC exams
7		14	males	−0.02	+0.05	⎫
		14	females	−0.15	−0.20	⎬ School marks
8		13		−0.18[a]	−	School marks
9		13		+0.16	−0.04	English quotient
		13		+0.28[a]	−0.11	Arithmetic quotient

Table 39.4—*continued*

Study (see below)	Mean C.A.		r E–A	r N–A	Attainment measure
10	13		+0.02	−0.16[b]	Teacher's estimate
11	12		+0.04	−0.14[b]	Teacher's estimate
12	11.25	males	+0.23[b]	−0.06[a]	Reading test
	11.25	females	+0.22[b]	−0.06[a]	
	11.25	males	+0.20[b]	−0.11[a]	Maths quotient
	11.25	females	+0.19[b]	−0.11[a]	
	11.25	males	+0.19[b]	−0.10[a]	English quotient
	11.25	females	+0.19[b]	−0.10[a]	
13	10.5		+0.15	−0.16	School record
14	8.9		+0.60	−0.59	Reading quotient
15	7.9		+0.19	−0.22	Reading quotient
	7.9		+0.24	+0.08	Arithmetic quotient

[a] = significant at 5 per cent level; [b] = significant at 1 per cent level; n.s. = not significant; (where no figure available, + = positive relationship; − = negative relationship).

1	Wankowski and Cox (1973)	9	Frazer (1967)
2	Kelvin, Lucas and Ojha (1965)	10	Entwistle and Cunningham (1968)
3	Lynn and Gordon (1961)	11	See 10
4	Kline and Gale (1971)	12	Eysenck and Cookson (1969)
5	Entwistle and Entwistle (1970)	13	Rushton (1966)
6	Cowell and Entwistle (1971)	14	Elliott (1972)
7	Entwistle and Welsh (1969)	15	Savage (1966)
8	Child (1964)		

support to the conclusion that with younger students high anxiety is not an advantage in scholastic endeavours. All factors but Q_4, for which the evidence is very scant and inconsistent anyway, are in the direction of emotional stability. The younger pupil who is stable (C+), phlegmatic (D−), emotionally responsive (H+), self-assured (O−) and high on self-sentiment (Q_3) has the edge on his contemporaries. With older students the pattern is very confused. It seems that some factors may veer towards the emotionally unstable (C−, D+, H−), but the successful student still needs to be compliant and trusting (L−), self-assured (O−), high on self-sentiment (Q_3+) and moderate in ergic tension (Q_4+ low). In other words, he can feel to have all the symptoms of emotional instability but he still has to have faith in himself to succeed. This observation fits well with the research of Lipsitt (1958) and Rosenberg (1953) who found highly anxious students who held themselves in low esteem were decidedly poor performers at school (see also Part 3, chapter 6 in this Reader, 'Motivation and dynamic structure').

SUMMARY

There is a tendency for academic success to be linked by age to certain introversion–extraversion traits. Younger students, whilst showing social interest [participating (A+) and friendly (H+)], have introvert qualities of conformity (E–), seriousness (F–) and self-sufficiency (Q$_2$+). Older successful students, apart from the extravert characteristic of aggressiveness and competitiveness (E+), are thoroughgoing introverts. Custom-made anxiety scales (test, achievement, state and trait anxiety) almost invariably show that high anxiety is correlated with low achievement at any age. On looking at the primary factors which go to make up the second-order anxiety trait, we find one or two age differences again. Successful younger students show a remarkably consistent first-order profile of low anxiety. But older students deviate on factors C, D and H in the direction of high anxiety. Nevertheless, the achieving student still needs the emotional-stability qualities of compliance, self-assuredness and high self-sentiment to survive. Notional values of the age band through which the transition in beneficial traits seems to occur have been put between 10 and 15 years. This may be linked to institutional changes, changes in method of assessment, cognitive or affective developmental changes (or all three) which occur at this time in a pupil's life.

REFERENCES

Allport, G. W. (1937) *Personality: a Psychological Interpretation.* New York: Holt.
Alpert, R. & Haber, R. N. (1960) Anxiety in academic achievement situations. *J. Abnorm. Soc. Psychol.*, **61,** 207–215.
Anthony, W.S. (1973) The development of extraversion, of ability, and of the relation between them. *Br. J. Educ. Psychol.*, **43,** 223–227.
Butcher, H. J., Ainsworth, M. & Nesbitt, J. E. (1963) Personality factors and school achievement. *Br. J. Educ. Psychol.*, **33,** 276–285.
Callard, M. P. & Goodfellow, C. L. (1962) Neuroticism and Extraversion in school boys as measured by the JMPI. *Br. J. Educ. Psychol.*, **32,** 241–250.
Cartwright, D. S. (1974) *Introduction to Personality.* Chicago: Rand McNally.
Castaneda, A., McCandless, B. R. & Palermo, D. S. (1956) The children's form of the Manifest Anxiety Scale. *Child Dev.*, **27,** 317–326.
Cattell, R. B. (1946) *Description and Measurement of Personality.* New York: Yonkers-on-Hudson.
Cattell, R. B. (1965) *The Scientific Analysis of Personality.* Chicago: Aldine Publishing.
Cattell, R. B. (1973) *Personality and Mood by Questionnaire.* San Francisco: Jossey-Bass.
Cattell, R. B., Barton, K. & Dielman, J. E. (1972) Prediction of school achievement from motivation, personality and ability measures. *Psychol., Rep.*, **30,** 35–43.
Cattell, R. B. & Cattell, M. D. L. (1969) *Handbook for the Jr–Sr High School Personality Questionnaire (HSPQ).* NFER Publishing, with permission of IPAT, Illinois.
Cattell, R. B., Eber, H. W. & Tatsuoka, M. M. (1970) *Handbook for the Sixteen Personality Factor Questionnaire (16PF).* NFER Publishing, with permission of IPAT, Illinois.
Child, D. (1964) The relationships between introversion–extraversion, neuroticism and performance in school examinations. *Br. J. Educ. Psychol.*, **34,** 187–196.
Child, D. (1970) *The Essentials of Factor Analysis.* London: Holt, Rinehart and Winston.

Cowell, M. D. & Entwistle, N. J. (1971) Personality, study attitudes and academic performance in a technical college. *Br. J. Educ. Psychol.*, **41**, 85–89.

Denny, J. P. (1966) Effects of anxiety and intelligence on concept formation. *J. Exp. Psychol.*, **72**, 596–602.

Elliott, C. D. (1972) Personality factors and scholastic attainment. *Br. J. Educ. Psychol.*, **42**, 23–32.

Entwistle, N. J. (1974) Personality and academic attainment. In Butcher, H. J. & Pont, H. B. (Eds.), *Educational Research in Britain: Vol. 3*. London: University of London Press.

Entwistle, N. J. & Cunningham, S. (1968) Neuroticism and school attainment – a linear relationship? *Br. J. Educ. Psychol.*, **38**, 123–132.

Entwistle, N. J. & Entwistle, D. M. (1970) The relationships between personality, study methods and academic performance. *Br. J. Educ. Psychol.*, **40**, 132–143.

Entwistle, N. J. & Welsh, J. (1969) Correlates of school attainment at different ability levels. *Br. J. Educ. Psychol.*, **39**, 57–63.

Eysenck, H. J. (1953) *Uses and Abuses of Psychology*. Harmondsworth: Penguin.

Eysenck, H. J. & Cookson, D. (1969) Personality in primary school children: 1 – ability and achievement. *Br. J. Educ. Psychol.*, **39**, 109–122.

Eysenck, S. B. G. & Eysenck, H. J. (1963) The validity of questionnaires and rating assessments of extraversion and neuroticism and factorial validity. *Br. J. Psychol.*, **54**, 51–62.

Frazer, B. (1967) An investigation into the relationship between personality variables and attainment in a secondary modern school. (Facts from Warburton 1968.)

Gaudry, E. & Spielberger, C. D. (1971) *Anxiety and Educational Achievement*. Sydney: Wiley.

Gorsuch, R. L. (1974) *Factor Analysis*. Philadelphia: Saunders.

Guilford, J. P. (1959) *Personality*. New York: McGraw-Hill.

Kelvin, R. P., Lucas, C. & Ojha, A. (1965) The relation between personality, mental health and academic performance of university students. *Br. J. Soc. Clin. Psychol.*, **4**, 244–253.

Kline, P. (1976) *Personality Theories and Dimensions*. Open University, E201, block 2.

Kline, P. & Gale, A. (1971) Extraversion, neuroticism and performance in a psychology examination. *Br. J. Educ. Psychol.*, **41**, 90–93.

Lipsitt, L. P. (1958) A self-concept scale for children and its relationship to the children's form of the MAS. *Child Dev.*, **29**, 463–472.

Lynn, R. (1971) *Personality and National Character*. Oxford: Pergamon.

Lynn, R. & Gordon, I. E. (1961) The relation of neuroticism and extraversion to educational attainment. *Br. J. Educ. Psychol.*, **31**, 194–203.

McClelland, D. C. (1951) *Personality*. New York: Dryden.

Naylor, F. D. (1972) *Personality and Educational Achievement*. Sydney: Wiley.

Rosenberg, M. (1953) The association between self-esteem and anxiety. *J. Psychol.*, **48**, 285–290.

Rushton, J. R. (1966) The relationship between personality characteristics and scholastic success in 11-year-old children. *Br. J. Educ. Psychol.*, **36**, 178–184.

Sarason, S. B., Davidson, K. S., Lighthall, F. F., Waite, R. R. & Ruebush, B. K. (1960) *Anxiety in Elementary School Children*. New York: John Wiley.

Savage, R. D. (1962) Personality factors and academic performance. *Br. J. Educ. Psychol.*, **32**, 251–253.

Savage, R. D. (1966) Personality factors in academic attainment in Junior School children. *Br. J. Educ. Psychol.*, **36,** 91–94.

Saville, P. & Finlayson, L. (1973) *British Supplement to the High School Personality Questionnaire (Form A) Anglicised 1968/69 Edition.* London: NFER Publishing.

Spelman, J. (1975) The relationships between study habits, personality and academic attainment of fifth form students. Unpublished M.Sc. (Education) dissertation, University of Bradford.

Spielberger, C. D., Gorsuch, R. L. & Lushene, R. E. (1970) *The State-Trait Anxiety (STAI) Test Manual for Form X.* Palo Alto: Consulting Psychologists Press.

Vernon, P. E. (1953) *Personality Tests and Assessments.* London: Methuen.

Vernon, P. E. (1966) *Personality Assessment: A Critical Survey.* London: Methuen.

Wankowski, J. A. & Cox, J. B. (1973) *Temperament, Motivation and Academic Achievement.* Birmingham: University of Birmingham Educational Survey.

Warburton, F. W. (1968) The relationship between personality factors and scholastic attainment. Unpublished survey, Department of Education, University of Manchester.

PART 12

Educational handicap

INTRODUCTION

Successive governments have generally been vigilant about the provision of special educational facilities for those less fortunate. Extracts from two HMSO pamphlets bear witness to this, and these are only two of several reports prepared on the subject. *Slow Learners at School* and *Educating Mentally Handicapped Children* are well worth reading. These short extracts give an idea of concern for these children and an attempt to understand and provide for them. In *Slow Learners at School*, the second chapter on some characteristics of slow-learning children has been chosen because it gives a sound basis for more detailed study of the problem. In the other pamphlet the chapter on educating the severely handicapped is most instructive about the methods and materials being used.

Wilkins' review of juvenile delinquency up to 1962 is so full of basic information that it readily finds a place in the Reader. The topic has moved on since it was written but this does not detract from the sound nature of the content.

40   Some characteristics of slow-learning children

HMSO

The wide variety of terms used to denote children who are not succeeding in their school work indicates in some measure the complexity of the problem: they are now variously known as 'educationally subnormal', 'backward', 'retarded' and, more recently 'slow learning'. The only characteristic common to all these children is that they are in some way failing in school, though their backwardness may well differ in degree and in kind. As 'educationally subnormal' has become associated with pronounced educational backwardness, so the term 'slow learning' has come to be widely applied to all children who are, to a greater or lesser degree, failing in school.

From the early days of universal education the presence of many children who were unable to learn quickly raised controversy over the reason for their failure. The controversy over the relative importance of heredity and environment has lasted long and has, in its time, been pursued with vigour and even acrimony; recent research, however, has served to make some of the earlier arguments look artificial. Though few people would now dispute that heredity plays an important part in determining the upper limits of intellectual growth, research which has taken place during the last 15 or 20 years and has greatly increased our knowledge of the intellectual and temperamental characteristics of backward children leads us to believe that the various influences combining to form the child's environment exercise a wider and more potent effect on his development than had once been assumed. The psychological and material conditions in which a child grows up play a very vital part in determining the equipment that he brings to learning. Only when environmental conditions are ideal will a child's hereditary endowment determine the upper limit of his development.

The importance of a mother's love, in the early years of a child's life, for his future emotional well-being is now well known, but its significance for his intellectual development may prove to be no less vital. Recent observations made in the course of training guide dogs for the blind may be significant. These have revealed that if they are not handled by human beings early enough to form a satisfactory attachment their capacity for future training is so seriously impaired that they later prove unable to take responsibility or exercise judgement when confronted with unusual situations. They are, in effect, less able to learn. Of course there are obvious dangers in drawing too close an analogy between the experimental learning of animals and the far more complex learning process of young children; nevertheless an inadequate mother–child relationship may also result in impaired intellectual development in the child. Some recent researches into the intellectual growth of foundling children tend to corroborate this belief. Physical deprivation – malnutrition, poor physical care, neglect or cruelty – may also materially affect the growth of the ability to learn.

Greater insight has been gained in recent years into the connection between a child's capacity to learn and his physical maturity. Just as there must be maturation of the nerve cells and fibres before he can see and hear and move, so too must there be maturation of the neurological network of the brain before a child can effectively learn. And not only does the rate of maturation vary considerably from child to child; for full growth of his powers of mind and body he needs stimulus to use them; this is no less true of his mental than of his physical powers. The theory has recently been advanced that there is a critical period in this pattern of development when the child is best fitted to develop certain skills – the second year of his life for beginning to talk, the third and fourth for developing mature speech. It has been suggested that if the relevant skill is not learned during this critical period it is far harder to acquire later, either because the brain has developed beyond the critical point, or because the child has acquired the ability to do without the skill. Nor are the child's emotional relationships and his physical development the only important factors in intellectual growth. Some recent work has drawn attention to the importance of adequate language development if children are to profit from education. Children from homes which use a limited vocabulary and where conversation and discussion are rare are at a disadvantage in school. If the young child therefore has failed to enjoy experiences which give him opportunities to develop – interesting things to see and touch, encouragement to talk and to listen – then his latent abilities may remain unrealized.

Investigations such as these, though still in their infancy, must make the layman more cautious in thinking of limited ability as simply innate or irremediable. Some children brought up in very adverse circumstances have shown considerable improvement in their effective ability when transferred to a stimulating and satisfying environment. Some children do in fact show significant increases in intelligence test scores as the result of special education. Some teachers are convinced that the mental development of their pupils is still incomplete when they leave school at 16. Though it may be fruitless for teachers to speculate on the relative effects of heredity and environment in determining a child's present ability, yet it is important to distinguish between the needs of those children who are likely to be more or less permanently backward and those whose backwardness may be remediable. The latter will include those whose backwardness has been caused by frequent short absences, or by a longer illness that may have kept them away from school just when they were ready to acquire a new skill; sometimes by changes of school, a not unusual occurrence with children whose parents' occupation involves frequent changes of home; sometimes by unsatisfactory home conditions leading to a degree of emotional disturbance, a very stubborn obstacle to learning.

Two other contributory factors to backwardness remain to be mentioned – the presence of some physical defect in the child or unsatisfactory conditions in the school itself. Even today, when tests of sight and hearing are given to most children in the course of medical examinations, a child's backwardness can be caused at least in part by his inability to see or hear clearly in class. It is, therefore, still important that teachers, especially teachers of younger children, should be alert to detect signs of such disabilities if any child is unaccountably failing in his lessons.

Shortcomings in the schools themselves can lead to backwardness, and there are many children, backward children among them, who could achieve more were conditions more favourable. Teachers, however capable, cannot give all the individual help they would wish to slow learners if their classes are large. Although efforts are made in many schools to give special help to the slowest by some form of grouping within the class or school, the pace may still be too fast for them, the matter too difficult, the lessons too abstract, and formal work introduced before they are ready for it. Moreover backward children are more than usually vulnerable to an inexperienced or unsympathetic teacher and frequent changes of staff.

An attempt has been made, in the foregoing paragraphs, to outline some of the main factors which contribute to a child's failure to learn. One can distinguish between those children who have apparently limited potential and those who seem to have ability which they cannot use effectively. One can also distinguish between children whose difficulties appear to need long-term help and those who may be expected to respond fairly quickly to remedial measures. And while it is sensible to assume that children with limited potential need prolonged help, it must be recognized that the reverse is not necessarily true, namely, that the intelligent child will always respond quickly. Children are not easily classified and an overemphasis on any single characteristic such as I.Q. or attainment age may result in problems being oversimplified and categories being defined too rigidly. For the purpose of this pamphlet it is proposed to use the term 'backward' or 'slow-learning' for children of any degree of ability who are unable to do work commonly done by children of their age. The word 'dull' will be used for those who have limited mental potential and the word 'retarded' for children whose poor educational achievements appear to result from factors other than limited general ability. In the context of this pamphlet 'retardation' is used to convey a general notion of underfunctioning without specifying whether such a condition is necessarily remediable or implying that an assessment of general ability is closely related to the extent and rate of progress possible in a specific field.

These distinctions are important to enable the practising teacher to adopt suitable aims and methods. For dull children there will always be limited intellectual objectives even with the most skilful teaching; for the retarded the aim will be to seek and to remove the causes of their backwardness. In chapter 4 of this pamphlet reference is made to remedial education, but elsewhere the emphasis is mainly on the needs of those children of limited ability found in special schools or in the lowest classes of ordinary schools.

In discussions about backwardness it sometimes happens that backward children are spoken of as if they were a special type, and even today there are some teachers who assume that every backward child is a potential candidate for a special school. In fact dull children are not in a sharply defined category, but merely form the lower end of a far larger group with limited ability. Just as there are some who are strong and others who are weak, some tall and others short, through every gradation of strength and size, so there are the brilliant and the dull, with every imperceptible gradation in between. The brilliant merge gradually into the clever, the clever into the average, the average into the slow, and the slow into the dull. Some gifted children may, however, lack some of the talents of others less gifted; some of only average ability may have particular gifts of a specific kind; all have many fundamental needs and characteristics in common, irrespective of ability. And just as geniuses are comparatively rare, so are people with a severe mental defect; those of rather more than average ability are counterbalanced by those who have rather less. These conclusions are hypothetical, but substance is given to them not merely by common experience but by the results of research. The distinguishing feature of all backward children is that they are slow to learn, but just as they share many of the characteristics of the normal, so do they share the characteristic of differing considerably one from another. For a human being does not consist solely of an intellect: what he is and what he does depend on the interaction of many forces of which the mind is only one. Backward children differ one from another in their abilities, in outlook, in temperament, in their likes and dislikes and in their interests. If the teacher is to make a success of teaching them, it is even more important than with abler children to know as much about them as possible.

Before the end of their first year at school some children attract the teacher's attention by their lack of interest in toys or picture books or by their clumsiness in handling them, by the slow development of their power to talk and the paucity of their vocabulary, by their seeming inability to join in other children's play, or possibly by disturbing other children's work. These characteristics single out those children who may need special education; many of them may be dull. Other children may not show their limitations until more formal work is reached; unusual slowness in learning to read is a common characteristic of dull children. Inability to read may, of course, not be indicative of general backwardness, but be caused by factors other than limited intellectual powers. But a failure to acquire the rudiments of reading is often the symptom that first draws attention to dull children, and is usually accompanied by poor command of language and a poverty of vocabulary.

Dull children are unable to develop a fluent command of language. This is symptomatic of a more fundamental limitation, a difficulty in forming clear concepts. They find it difficult to formulate the similarities and differences between objects and between situations, and to generalize from these experiences. Normal children early acquire the power to distinguish for example a ball from an orange. They learn by direct experience, by observing and handling these objects, to identify sufficient characteristics of both in order to recognize and name them. Similarly an orange is distinguished from an apple, two from three and long from short. They begin to understand words, to have an idea of their meaning. The development of language involves children in this activity to an increasing degree until they are capable of forming abstract concepts such as goodness, equality and freedom. Normal children, as Terman and Piaget have shown, develop this power from the age of 11 years onwards. Dull children developing their concepts and language in a much slower and more concrete way may never acquire many abstract ideas at all. They tend to be tied to the particular experience or familiar example. The inability of dull children to generalize from experience is evident in fields other than language development. Normal children, after some preliminary experience of pairs of objects, quickly realize that two of them put with two others make four, and from this and similar experiences derive an understanding of the concept of $2 + 2 = 4$. Once this has been understood it is a simple matter for them to realize that, conversely, if they have four and give two away, they will have two left; in fact that $4 - 2 = 2$. This concept they are able to utilize not only with the number four but with other numbers, and will later deduce the generalization that $a + b = c$ implies $a = c - b$. They have, in fact, learned to use their experience in other situations, or to reason. Dull children will always find the process difficult; the dullest may have to learn everything new from the beginning, while others will need far more experience on which to base their generalizations than do more gifted children. This is to say no more than that they learn slowly, and learn more readily by doing than by reasoning, by dealing with things rather than with ideas. But it would be wholly mistaken to assume that dull children cannot think and that they learn only by the thoughtless execution of manual tasks. Rather is the power to think to be developed by learning in practical situations. Every task needs to be designed to develop the intellect. The child is helped to analyse the situation and derive from it the experience which enables him to undertake a comparable task more confidently. For dull children learning that evokes no thought and develops no insight is of limited value; they need to learn intelligently, not by rote.

The implications of this are of the greatest importance. Backward children learn primarily by doing and need experience of actual situations before they can generalize. They therefore proceed by slower steps and need more repetition of a kind that demands new thought and arouses fresh interest. This demands from teachers patience and resourcefulness in providing repetition without boredom.

Limited ability to utilize previous experience in new situations leaves dull children far less able than others to learn spontaneously from their environment. Bright children, with their eager interest in everything around them, derive a great deal of knowledge incidentally, but the dull have to be taught much that others learn for themselves. Though it is unlikely that many of the children in special schools today have quite such a restricted experience of life as those Sir Cyril Burt investigated over 40 years ago, many dull pupils are without that knowledge of everyday things on which so much of their learning, and not least their language, will depend. The significance of much of what they see passes them by, and they remain surprisingly lacking in the kind of general knowledge that a brighter child intuitively gathers – what ordinary things cost, how costs vary with weight, the miscellaneous stock of information gained from reading notices, signs and advertisements. Many of these will need to be taught later, and the knowledge of one fact will not, with the dull child, lead spontaneously to a perception of others directly related to it. A bright child can with little difficulty apply abstract knowledge to real-life situations, yet older backward children are found who are able to work pages of accurate calculations but cannot tell the length of the interval of time between 9.15 and 9.45 or the change from five shillings after 2/11 has been spent. Knowledge must not only be based on experience; its value is limited unless it can be readily used.

These intellectual limitations must be recognized if teaching is to be effective; it must also be remembered that each child is likely to differ from others in interests and in temperament as well as in level of ability. The backward, like any cross section of the population, contain the stolid and the fickle, the talkative and the silent, the clumsy and the dexterous; a teacher of dull children, though he needs to be aware of their limitations, is more likely to be successful if he is unfailing in his search for their many positive qualities. A curriculum based purely on seeking to remedy weaknesses is likely to be arid and unsuccessful; it needs rather to be based firmly on those things they can do best, to develop their talents, interests and personal qualities to the fullest extent, and be associated with teaching methods that take full account of individual differences.

It is often truly asserted that dull children have poor concentration and poor memories, but the generalization is too sweeping without modification. Children of similar ability show wide variation in their capacity to remember and to concentrate, but their powers depend very much on what they are asked to remember and on what they are asked to concentrate. Confronted with a purely academic task which seems to them meaningless and boring, their concentration may well be brief and their memory short-lived; if the task is interesting and is seen to have point and purpose, they will persist for remarkably long periods and show a surprising memory for detail. One incident at a special school serves to illustrate the point. The school includes animal husbandry in its curriculum, and two senior boys had responsibility for the care of a sow about to farrow. Throughout the night when the litter was being born they watched over her devotedly and obeyed instructions to the letter without adult supervision. Other boys showed a similar concentration and reliability over the care of newly incubated chicks. If dull children are called upon to memorize facts which, however important, do not for them have meaning and relevance, they find the task insuperably difficult; if the same facts are presented in a meaningful situation, they may well achieve success. Witness their memory for sporting details or for the events on the last school journey.

The dull, like any other children, need the security of a good home and loving parents. To be loved and wanted is necessary to any human being, old or young; the traumatic effects of early deprivation are now generally familiar. Not all dull children are deprived; many indeed come from homes where material conditions are poor, but if there is love and security they are likely to achieve as much as their limited capacities will allow. In other cases a dull child may be less acceptable to the social group in which he finds himself. His parents, especially if they are intelligent themselves, may be unable to conceal their disappointment at his inferiority, or suffer from unjustified feelings of guilt at having a child of poor capacity. His brothers and sisters, friends and playfellows may be intolerant of his clumsiness and his obvious failure to grasp things quickly. In such circumstances the dull child may rapidly lose confidence and the desire to try anything that may lead to further failure and unfavourable comparisons. He may well seek solace by withdrawing into himself or by being defiant or mischievous to conceal feelings of inadequacy. Added failure at school can only aggravate this unhappy state of mind.

Given love, understanding and security, and enabled to achieve some measure of success, dull children have it within them to grow up happy and self-respecting. Sometimes little can be done to improve a child's relations with his parents, even though many schools are doing excellent work in helping parents to accept him and to see the good in him. What is important is that what he does in school shall give him self-confidence. It is still unfortunately true that some slow-learning children are allowed to go too long without special education and are allowed to fail until failure has eaten into their souls. 'Nothing succeeds like success' carries with it the equally valid corollary that 'Nothing fails like failure'. It is therefore important that they should be discovered and given help as early as possible, whether it be in their own schools or in a special school or class.

It is an illusion to think that the dull are unaware of their limitations. Everyday life, bringing with it encounters with others more gifted, must inevitably show that in some things they cannot hope to excel. But this is no reason to think that they must always feel inadequate and sorry for themselves. One feels a failure only when one's failings are so extensive as to undermine confidence and self-respect. Everyone knows there are some things he cannot do: one man cannot paint, another has no ear for music; many people admit to being 'hopeless at mathematics'. But these deficiencies cause little anxiety in those who know that they have other positive qualities that win them respect. Dull children too can enjoy a good measure of happiness and achievement if they are first given a chance to succeed in whatever ways they can. In this way they gain confidence, feel a pride of achievement and the approval of others and so are ready for greater efforts. They come to realize that they are not total failures, but have, on the contrary, a useful contribution to make to school, home and society. This will not be achieved if there are unhealthy or even wounding comparisons made at school. Self-respect and confidence developed at school are likely to continue in later life.

There must naturally come a time when each has to face his limitations, and know clearly that there are some things he will never be able to do – when the hopes of the boy who wants to be a pilot or the girl who sets her heart on becoming a ballerina must finally be dispelled. But if confidence based on achievement of some kind has been developed, then they can be dispelled without injury to self-respect. Indeed, the education of dull children cannot be considered complete unless they have also come to know their limitations and to bear failure. They are not necessarily any more or less sensitive than others but their limitations do increase the chance of failure. It is continuous lack of success that may lead either to anti-social behaviour or to withdrawal; both responses show that the child is protecting himself from failure.

Slower intellectual development carries with it the likelihood of slower or possibly distorted emotional growth, in fact a slower general development, notably in the earlier years. Dull children often take longer to reach the stage of playing and co-operating with their fellows, longer to become acceptable group members, and tend to be solitary unless encouraged to join in. Their physical development may proceed as fast as that of abler children, yet they are apt to feel inadequate when playing with other children of their own age, sometimes taking refuge in the company of younger children or withdrawing into themselves for protection. If the teacher can draw them into the social groupings of the classroom they enjoy sharing in the songs and rhymes and poems and the games that the rest enjoy. But they will show little imagination or leadership, usually being content to follow the example of others – a characteristic that can be a cause of danger later on, when ready suggestibility can lead a boy into mischief or a girl into being exploited. Not least among the advantages of education in a special school is that the dull can there enjoy the company of others who are at the same stage of intellectual and emotional maturity. They are more readily accepted as members of the group and less exposed to unfavourable comparisons.

If their earlier years can be passed in an emotionally satisfying atmosphere most dull children follow a fairly normal pattern of development. They can become acceptable at home, in the club or at work and show the same desire for independence and responsibility as ordinary children. But throughout their lives many remain conscious of their limitations; fear of failure frequently makes them diffident in accepting responsibility or in entering a new field of activity or a new social grouping, though once they have overcome their diffidence they may adjust happily. Many older backward boys are, for example, very shy of making new acquaintances, of joining a youth club, of entering a café or of using a telephone, but gain confidence rapidly once they have been helped to take the plunge. Sometimes they fail, and the resulting feeling of inadequacy can lead to quarrelsome behaviour or excessive timidity. The influence at this period of the school as a good society cannot be over-emphasized; its well ordered routine, good aesthetic standards, good personal relationships and its expectation of good work, play and behaviour are of the greatest value.

In the past probably the majority of children who were dull were also subnormal in physical development, suffering more frequently than other children from malnutrition, bodily defects, and minor physical ailments. With the great improvement in conditions since the war, with better housing, higher standards of nutrition and medical care, this is no longer so evident. However, the fact remains that most of the educationally subnormal children who need education in a special school come from poorer homes, and the incidence of minor physical disabilities is higher than among children in the ordinary school. It is important that backward children receive all the benefits from the social and medical services since physical difficulties, in themselves not severe, are an added impediment to learning when they occur in conjunction with limited ability. The dull child needs every possible advantage so that his total development may not be hindered.

ACKNOWLEDGEMENT

This paper is an extract from *Slow Learners at School* (1964), Education Pamphlet No. 46, pp. 7–17, HMSO, London, and is published here with the kind permission of the Controller of Her Majesty's Stationery Office.

41 Educating the most severely handicapped children

HMSO

THE CHILDREN CONCERNED

In the day schools there has been a tradition that one part of the school should be designed for children whose behaviour or associated physical handicaps make them difficult to educate with other class groups. Similarly in hospitals some children attend school while others remain in the wards or receive some treatment elsewhere. It is now the duty of local education authorities to provide education for all children irrespective of the degree of their handicap. The education programme must provide for the most severely handicapped, whether in school or hospital, and this presents a challenge to ingenuity and inventiveness.

The children concerned tend to form two sub-groups: those who may be hyperactive, aggressive, self-destructive and who have psychotic features in their behaviour; and those with multiple physical handicaps. Both groups may be incontinent, unable to feed themselves and unable to communicate.

In the past, social and educational improvement was not expected of these children. But more recently the work of pioneers in a number of different professions has led to an acceptance that there are approaches which can bring change and development even in the most seriously handicapped. Many programmes devised by nurses, psychologists and teachers have had limited but encouraging success. It is no longer right to assume that any child should be deprived of planned programmes without first a very prolonged and systematic trial period of stimulation. Such efforts may not immediately lead to the child moving through recognized stages of development, but they do increase the range of responses he is able to make in a variety of activities; which in turn may improve his general alertness, attention and satisfaction, so that both adults and children feel that real progress is being made.

MULTIDISCIPLINARY APPROACHES

The essence of successful programmes is often the co-operation of workers from a number of different fields. In the day school, the medical officer, the psychologist, speech therapists and physiotherapists, together with teachers, school nurses and non-teaching assistants, all have a part to play. In hospitals these workers join consultants in mental sub-normality, and nurses, in forming the group from which teamwork may develop.

Such teamwork has developed in one residential unit where a programme is planned for each child. Initially the child's behaviour is recorded by all the adults in contact with him and testing may take place. This information is analysed to highlight strengths and a programme is devised which builds on these, at the same time specifying aspects of development which require training. All concerned know each child's programme and their part in it. Parents are included and may stay overnight if necessary while learning how to continue the programme when the child is at home. The same phrases, words and gestures are consistently used by all adults and attempts are made to use a consistent level and tone of voice. Mime is used with non-speaking children. Regular staff discussion is organized in turn by nurses and teachers, and progress is continuously assessed.

The Department of Education and Science, education authorities, regional hospital boards and hospital authorities, as well as voluntary associations, are all aware of the importance to a child's development of co-ordinated programming; most of them are arranging conferences to bring workers together. The Department's Conference on Co-operation and Care and Education of Children in Hospitals, and the Leeds Regional Hospital Board Training Division multidisciplinary management courses are examples. However it is at the personal level in working situations that most successful co-operation is developed. Because of the complex nature of mental disability a multidisciplinary approach can bring about the greatest success in living and learning for these children.

SOME SUCCESSFUL METHODS

Children are still excluded from school or placed in a special unit because of difficult behaviour, for example outbursts of screaming, temper tantrums, constant pinching and biting, self-mutilation, and head banging. Although attempts at helping these children are not always successful, improved staff/pupil ratios may allow regular periods of individual training based on skilled observation. It is still sometimes the practice to apply forms of restraint – for example restraining children in chairs, stiffly bandaging their arms, or putting heavy gloves on their hands. A more positive approach is to offer periods of purposeful activity, avoiding periods of inactivity when the child falls back into bad habits.

When June came to school for the first time at the age of eleven she was wearing a leather strap around her wrists and waist restraining both hands. Despite this she still managed to disfigure her face and legs. The teacher began a programme of releasing her hands for five minutes in every hour during which time she gave June undivided attention and made her use her hands in a positive way such as holding on to a rail, or the side of a slide, or a swinging rope. She gave her clay and dough to feel and squeeze. Gradually the time was extended to 10 minutes in the hour, then one hand was freed for the whole day and so on. Over a two-year period her self-destructive tendencies steadily decreased, although she could still be aggressive if she became jealous or felt neglected by her teacher. In another case severe self-biting was prevented by one teacher and her assistant who were persistently on hand to direct the child's attention to squeezing a sponge in water, or thumping a desk bell as the situation demanded.

Mary, aged six and a half, came to day school with the reputation of being unmanageable. She was disruptive, she bit and kicked, but she was able to talk. Unfortunately her behaviour precluded her admission to the nursery group and she was placed in the special care unit where most of the other children were unable to speak. Mary refused to speak and spent her time shaking and attacking the other children in turn. Although this behaviour was violent and hurtful to the children the teacher correctly interpreted it as Mary's attempt to make them talk. After a time she managed to shift Mary's violent attention to a large heavy toy bear, and at the same time she introduced a talking doll, puppets and a tape recorder. No child in the school could persuade Mary to speak, although as her behaviour improved she was placed part-time with other groups, but after several months she was heard to say 'No' to the doll. About the same time she learned to make her voice come out of the tape recorder. Slowly she began to talk to the other children.

Programmes can be devised for individuals or for groups with particular needs. The two examples which follow illustrate different approaches found effective by those working with the profoundly handicapped.

Example I

This programme was prepared for children described as 'immobile, severely physically and mentally handicapped with no speech but some hearing and sight'. Each lesson was divided into three parts, Part 2 being the work developed over a period of time.

Part 1
Come to the child greeting him by name looking into his eyes. Pick him up and take him to the room to be used, or to another place. (It is important that his environment should be changed.) In the new situation talk and sing to him, rocking him on the lap until he is relaxed.

Part 2
(i)   Touch, stroke and tap the child's right hand, separating the fingers, turning the hand over and using other movements of this kind. Take the child's right hand and make it feel the teacher's. From all angles repeat the movements, tapping sometimes rhythmically accompanied by singing and humming, then silently and talking quietly. Move to different positions round the child and place him on a sofa or at a table as well as having him on the lap. Make a definite break with the child in a different position on the mat, so that he can see the teacher's movements. Go to a box and take out a balloon. Touch his hand with it, pat it, etc., see if his fingers curl to squeeze it. Fix a piece of string across supports in front of the child and hang the balloon from it. Move the balloon as it hangs with the child's right hand. Return the balloon to the box in the child's vision.
(ii) Speed up activities in (i) and add similar work with right arm up to the elbow.
(iii) As (ii), adding work with the top part of the arm to the shoulder with the balloon sometimes on the shoulder touching the face.

Part 3
(iv) As (iii) plus stroking the sides of the face and neck. Take the child's hand. Take a small

bright piece of material from the box and repeat movements over the hand, arm, neck and face. Return the child to his ward or bed, calmly talking, making a definite goodbye and touching his hand and looking into his face.

Other programmes may be designed to meet individual needs. They may be strictly organized, leading to precise objectives, and be based on systematic rewards. The rewards can only be determined by knowing the child – some may not like sweets. One teacher chose a child's favourite toy as a reward; often it is a smile and cuddle from the teacher. Some research workers recommend allowing the child to indulge in what has been observed to be his most frequent response.

Example II

Another programme was described by the teacher as follows:

We decided to concentrate first on the teaching of crawling and walking as this appeared to be Jim's main handicap. Training sessions took place each school day, the first 30 were of 30 minutes' duration after which each session lasted 1 hour. It was necessary to analyse the unit 'crawling' into smaller units. The first five sessions were used to find out if he would start to move about in some way *of his own*. He began to pull himself up into a standing position by holding on to the clothes of a person, anticipating being picked up and carried on the arm for some minutes. As soon as the person moved out of his reach he discontinued any further movement.

The next eight sessions were used for exercises which would keep his body in a crawling position by the use of his own strength. When he was able to hold himself safely in a crawling position, the teacher started to tap at first one hand, later with both hands alternately against the floor. Jim began to copy this and the tapping became a movement of the arms similar to that required for crawling. In order to get his legs moving as well they were pushed and a biscuit held at a yard's distance in front of him. About five weeks after his first attempts at crawling he discovered that crawling enabled him to overcome distance in order to reach a desired object, and the movement became rewarding in itself. From this point on, the crawling exercise as such, with food reward, was discontinued, as he now maintained this behaviour permanently.

It may be difficult for the teacher to recognize an appropriate starting point with the result that the very disabled child may make no progress. It is important to select an existing response to stimulation and build on it. Equally important is the need to make clear to the child what the teacher wishes him to do. Phrases such as 'look', 'sit down', 'stand up' and 'swing' need constant repetition and demonstration.

Feeding is particularly difficult for the profoundly handicapped child. He may be unable to chew or to swallow or to feed himself because of difficulties of control and co-ordination. But for some children an appropriate starting point can be discerned.

Susie, aged nine, had always refused to eat from a plate, drink from a cup or use a spoon. After watching her play in sand, with a scoop, it was decided to offer her a large cup and a very small spoon. After playing with food for one week she began to shovel the food into her mouth. By gradually increasing the size of the spoons and decreasing the size of the cup she was, within one month, eating with a normal spoon from a plate.

Many successful practices are based on theories of operant conditioning, in essence the systematic application of reward to reinforce selected items of behaviour. The attention span of the profoundly handicapped child may be short but it can be increased and controlled by the manipulation of rewards. If noisy behaviour has in the past gained attention improvement may be brought about by ignoring noise and giving attention at the point when such behaviour stops. Carefully monitored programmes of this kind, although carried out by teachers in the classroom, should normally be part of an integrated approach also adopted by parents, helpers and anyone else involved.

A good deal of pioneer work with these children has been carried out by psychologists rather than teachers. Increasingly, however, teachers are becoming responsible for developing individual programmes for the children they teach and are depending on psychologists for advice rather than direction. Local education authorities are, as a result, considering the child/adult ratios necessary and the flexible timing of teaching arrangements, especially in hospitals. Some of the children may be ready to profit from a full day's educational stimulation while others may only respond to part-time teaching. A ratio of one adult to four children is accepted as reasonable, although groups may vary in size depending on the age of the children, their disabilities, and the teaching conditions.

MATERIALS AND EQUIPMENT

Toys, materials and equipment are tools which enable the child to investigate his environment; in choosing them it is necessary to have a clear idea of their purpose. Often conventional toys are provided because adults think children should have them and not because children are known to play with them. With the most profoundly handicapped it is an adult's presence which provides the greatest stimulus. Her movement, her language and her play with the child and his toys and materials provide the best opportunities for assessment, for responding to the child's actions and for selecting those things which may give continued satisfaction for him. Much traditional apparatus requires activity from the child and with the most heavily handicapped its presence creates a static situation. Greater stimulation can come from specially designed equipment which enables the child to gain some control over his surroundings. If at the same time the child's position is planned so that he can sit or lie at the right angle, have materials in the best position for handling, and be in a good position to see other people and the events in his immediate environment, a more positive response may be expected. Children need to explore objects, to prod and poke at them. They need to explore the sources of sounds and to follow visually the movements of people and objects.

In schools and hospitals teachers are bringing fresh and imaginative approaches to the provision of suitable toys and equipment for the profoundly handicapped. The sensory stimulation provided by lights, sounds and moving objects increase awareness and attention, and promote movement, self-help and confidence. In one school a piano offers opportunities to make sounds; the mechanism is exposed and the keys are painted bright colours. In another a piano has been cut down so that the key board is at floor level. A play pen has been securely mounted on the bottom of an office stool so that it can revolve at a height which provides the child with a safe observation post and which encourages eye to eye contact with adults. Suspended pram bodies have become swing boats to provide movement for those who are immobile. Mirrors, both plain and curved, may help to encourage self-awareness and a developing body image.

One teacher mounted a variety of wheels, brightly painted, from bicycles and mangles so that they could be revolved with minimum effort. A bicycle pedal was used to spin a colour board, self operating lights were arranged to display different colours and different beams to interest children with poor sight. Liquid light, shadow patterns and changing light displays, as long as the periodicity of the light changes are watched for their possible effects on epileptic children, may all play their part in providing valuable stimulation. One school uses special lighting on the paddling pool to help children develop awareness of their bodies and to encourage movement. Lighting has been found to be particularly valuable in stimulating vocalization. Mobiles of different sizes, placed at different heights, springing or swinging by touch of hand or foot or by blowing, all excite interest, often to the point of vocalization. A mirror on the ceiling and the decoration of the undersides of tables can provide interest for children who look upwards. Different textures displayed on magnetic boards may produce tactile awareness for immobile children.

Some children respond to loud noises which can be disturbing to the whole group. A device connecting headphones to a tape recorder operated by the child can solve this problem. In one unit this operation is taken one stage further. The signal strength of speech is increased and the pattern of sound waves reproduced on old TV tubes. As a result some of the least able children have produced sounds and words. In another school a child showing no apparent response up to that time became interested in an outsize sand clock. The 'click' from the two plastic bottles as they were turned inspired the child first to reach out and later to turn the clock herself. In another example a gently running shower was fixed up for children who enjoyed water but who could not safely sit in it, so making water play possible. Clumsy children were helped to control their movements by using very large form boards, a controlled hanging punchball and an enlarged Morganstein threading apparatus. Large balls to push, and foam rubber wedges and inflatable mattresses of all sizes were also found effective in promoting movement and confidence.

Teachers have continually to ask themselves how much movement 'immobile' children make; whether they roll or change position. Moving them to new positions and new outlooks may be an important part of their education. In several schools classrooms have been adapted to provide 'hide-outs', which are shallow insets in the floor which prove satisfying to some crawlers, who gain self-assurance by rolling in and out of them and so progress to self-initiated movement. Sand and water play at floor level gives children the satisfying experience of playing in the materials rather than with them.

A difficult problem may be moving a child from one activity to another; for example the child who finds almost obsessive satisfaction in manipulating one object. There is no general answer to this, but for the teacher there is always an awareness of the difference between satisfying a child's desires and providing a programme aimed at developing new patterns of behaviour. Carefully planned objectives and activities may make it easier for a child to move from one thing to the next, whereas changing a situation in a general and un-specified way may reinforce the need for the security of the obsessive behaviour.

INTRODUCING THE MOST SEVERELY HANDICAPPED INTO OTHER GROUPS

The children with whom this chapter is concerned are often placed in special groups, but it is important to recognize that such arrangements should not necessarily be considered permanent. A number of schools are experimenting with alternatives. In one the part-time integration into the main school of children with severe multiple handicaps was arranged. It was agreed that the children should return to their own base for feeding, toileting and dressing, but that they should spend one to two hours each day with another class group. The most noticeable thing that emerged was the protective attitude developed by the other children, who appeared to gain confidence from the need to care. One child, imitating the teacher, helped to prevent his more handicapped friend from continually scratching his face by giving a sharp handclap each time it happened. For one severely handicapped child the first indication of response was a fleeting change of facial expression. Later he smiled when he was allowed to join the music group, and cried when the session was over. After one term he could make his own whistling sounds and his hands moved in a rhythm. This is a very small gain judged by the standards of less severely handicapped children but for this profoundly handicapped child it was a great step forward.

The teachers in one school decided to try and integrate one hyperactive, disruptive child into each group of ten, taught by one teacher and one class helper. The policy was to be pursued for six months so that conclusions might be drawn. It was generally expected that the ten children would copy the unacceptable behaviour and that there would be damage to equipment, and some neglect of the other children, as the teacher concentrated on the disruptive one. After the first month many of the children in the class had become less stable and the teachers felt that they were losing control of the class. They were spending a great deal of time in modifying the behaviour of the problem child: equipment was smashed; one classroom was flooded during water play; another room had its electrical system put out of action; and some toilets were blocked. After this initial shock there was a gradual improvement and the teachers were encouraged to continue. At the end of the six months it was found that classes no longer copied the disruptive behaviour, teachers felt in control of their groups, the behaviour of the difficult children had improved and they were speaking better, and in a few instances, also, warm relationships had been established between the children and their teachers.

Both examples illustrate that progress can be made if the school team is convinced of the value of experiment and is prepared to persist in the face of initial difficulties.

In hospitals the situation is more complex. In some the most disturbed children are taught for all or part of the day on the ward or in day rooms. In others school classes include some children who may not apparently benefit from being in a group and others who require close adult supervision because of bizarre and disturbed behaviour. A number of patterns of organization have emerged in the last few years which show more flexibility in the grouping of children and the use of staff.

In one hospital the children concerned had never attended school because of the severity of their disabilities even though the school was not highly selective. The head teacher at first arranged for these children to have individual teaching in a small room with one teacher. It became apparent that some of the children were difficult to transfer from the 'one to one' situation into a class of ten. There were others who could share an adult's attention but could not tolerate the larger class. This experience led the head to establish a unit for the profoundly handicapped consisting of four different groupings:

Group 1 consisted of eight children who attended in pairs for one hour a day;
Group 2 consisted of 12 children who attended in groups of three for one hour a day;
Group 3 consisted of 12 children in three groups of four, one of which attended morning sessions and two of which were taught for one hour every afternoon;

Group 4 consisted of 12 children in groups of six who attended for either the morning or afternoon session.

Some children passed through the different groups fairly rapidly, and after a period in Group 4 were able to join other classes in the school. Others remained in special groups for much longer periods. The unit was sited in a suite of small classrooms and a large adjoining hall. At appropriate times teachers could move from their group rooms to join with other groups in the hall, where large equipment could be used and where physical activities were possible. In addition to a teacher in charge of each group welfare assistants were employed. The whole team was supervised by a teacher in charge who visited and assessed children on the ward, arranged for their admission to the unit and maintained links between the school and the wards. She also helped teachers to plan work with individual children.

The school building in another hospital had inadequate facilities for the most severely handicapped and so provided a ward service. Alterations were carried out to provide small side rooms and a large playroom. Two teachers and two assistants, who staggered their holidays, provided education throughout the year for 16 children. Each member of staff was responsible for up to six children with whom she worked on individual programmes devised with the teacher in charge. A non-ambulant child could be taught in either a small room or the large room, but each mobile child normally completed his more precisely programmed session with his special teacher in a side room and then moved into the playroom for at least half an hour to work with larger equipment. A group of up to five children could be together in the playroom with one or two adults, but if only one adult was present there would only be one mobile child. One child's programme indicates the type of equipment in the playroom:

1 Throwing a ball into large boxes.
2 Catching a ball.
3 Stepping in and out of boxes.
4 Walking quietly – stamping feet.
5 Going through hoops.
6 Carrying heavy and big objects.
7 Stepping over a bench and other obstacles.
8 Climbing over a gap between benches.
9 Climbing over a horse.
10 Building a tower of foam bricks.
11 Stepping over a long foam brick.
12 Stepping over two long foam bricks.
13 Walking through a gate without knocking it down.

THE FUTURE FOR THE MOST SEVERELY HANDICAPPED

These children present the greatest challenge to education but at the same time they provide the opportunity to learn a great deal about early stages of learning and effective methods of teaching. By a careful assessment of existing behaviour and responses, by imaginative use of familiar things, and by exploiting a wide range of different stimuli, much may be accomplished. Above all, such children, like all others, need sustained personal relationships within which to grow and develop as far as they can. There is evidence that all children can acquire some enjoyment and satisfaction through learning if situations are carefully planned and if different professional skills are mobilized to common ends.

In a hospital where a nursery environment had proved beneficial only to moderately and fairly severely handicapped children, an alternative approach was tried with the profoundly handicapped. Behaviour modification techniques were used. At first nursing staff agreed to follow a programme as far as their normal duties permitted, but it became apparent that everyone on the ward had to be willingly involved if the programme was to be effective. A more ambitious project over two years was set up for 20 profoundly handicapped children, with a medical officer, a psychologist, a team of nurses and research workers. Techniques were developed which provided for rewards and the withdrawal of rewards for acceptable and unacceptable behaviour. Rewards had to be re-appraised periodically and suited to the individual. The withdrawal of reward involved taking the child from what it was doing to a neutral 'time-out' area. Training was designed to promote communication, socialization and occupation.

Particular attention was given to toilet training and dressing but a play programme which included water play, music sessions, painting, outdoor activities and formal toy play was carried out. Each nurse had a personal programme for a group of children. Opportunities were also provided for individual play in a small cubicle. Small toys were specially devised by the staff – for example chains to swing and cotton reels on springs to bounce up a rod. There were 17 training sessions daily, 12 run by nursing staff and five by research workers. At the end of the first year a teacher joined the team. In addition the research workers devised and carried out other work related to the application of operant conditioning techniques – the development of an effective method of training children to imitate and to apply skills acquired in one situation to others. During the whole period in-service training was available to ward staff, including 16 half-hour lectures and discussions over a four-week period as well as ward meetings twice a week.

At the beginning and end of the two years the progress of this special group of children was compared with a similar group of children in the hospital. They had made obvious gains in one or more of the areas, those in socialization being greater than in self help. Maladaptive behaviour had decreased. The control group too had shown small steady gains. Results have been sufficiently encouraging to ensure the continuation of the project but have shown a need for improved staffing ratios if better results are to be obtained.

This project and others of a similar nature are beginning to provide evidence of what can be done and what might be attempted with these children. They endorse the value of continued effort over extended periods with the most profoundly handicapped and indicate possible future developments.

ACKNOWLEDGEMENT

This paper is an extract from *Educating Mentally Handicapped Children* (1975), Education Pamphlet No. 60, pp. 31–43, H M S O, London, and is published here with the kind permission of the Controller of Her Majesty's Stationery Office.

42   Juvenile delinquency: a critical review of research and theory

L. T. WILKINS

So many people have written so much about juvenile delinquency that it is not surprising that this area of criminology is characterized by confusion and disagreement. This paper will not put forward any new theories or facts, but will present a selective critical review of a number of important contributions to this problem.

SOME THEORIES

Since juvenile delinquency became a phrase in common usage, there have been attempts to blame one factor or another as its cause. Social scientists are, however, in agreement that there is no single 'cause' by which the criminality or pre-criminal behaviour of juveniles can be explained. Indeed, criminal behaviour is itself a multiple concept. This does not mean that the so-called theory of 'multiple causation' can be accepted. As was discussed in an earlier article in this journal, the theory of 'multiple causation' is not even a theory.

It is interesting to consider some of the factors which from time to time have been blamed for juvenile delinquency or for rises in the juvenile delinquency rate. Poverty and high standards of living, both broken homes and the spoiling of children, both bad companions and loneliness, biological factors and social circumstances, in fact almost all features of life itself have been mentioned by some writers, either singly or conjointly, as supposed explanations.

The explanations of juvenile delinquency have varied geographically and chronologically, often in fairly systematic ways. It is possible to trace fashions in the types of explanations put forward or preferred at different times and in different national cultures. For a long time poverty and poor living conditions were believed to be the most important factors. But it has been shown that in countries where national and average family income, educational levels, housing conditions and other social indices have been steadily improving, juvenile delinquency is not necessarily decreasing. Indeed, as a recent U.N. Survey indicates, in more cases than expected the opposite is taking place. It would appear, at least superficially, that the better the living conditions, the greater the amount of crime. It should not be forgotten, however, that increased technical competence may lead both to the improvement in living conditions and to a more stringent expectation of behaviour coupled with a more efficient detection of deviations from the stricter norms.

THE FAMILY BACKGROUND

It is, perhaps, the family setting or features in the upbringing of children which have been most commonly blamed for juvenile deviance. The family is supposed to provide the moral integrating background for the child, and from time to time various defects or deficiencies in the family life have been selected and emphasized. In 1889, Colajanni discussed the connection between the family and crime and expressed the conviction that an integrated family life would prevent criminality. In the same year the French criminologist, Joly, also supported the idea that family life was a factor in preventing criminality. Mischler considered the situation regarding juvenile delinquency in several European countries, and arrived at the conclusion that family life and criminality were closely correlated. These are instances of only a few of the very early supporters of this type of theory. Since the beginning of this century, hardly any criminologist has failed to refer to the family as a fundamental factor in juvenile delinquency. It must be agreed that this seems logical since the family is the first social group to which the child belongs and to which he nominally remains attached as long as he is regarded as a juvenile. Lundberg and others (1954) make the forthright statement, 'the family is the most persistent factor in the child's life. Friends, teachers and other associates are comparatively temporary influences'.

Sutherland and Cressey (1960) list six types of home and family relationships which it is claimed are associated with juvenile delinquency. These are families where: (1) immoral, alcoholic or criminal members exist; (2) one or both parents are absent; (3) parental control is lacking; (4) uncongenial home conditions, such as favouritism, over-severity, neglect, etc., prevail; (5) racial or religious differences exist; (6) severe economic pressures are apparent. According to Cavan (1957) children cannot get adequate personality training where the parents experience personal and emotional difficulties, or where the parents' own cultural defects prevent them from resisting pressures from a deviant community, or where the parents are themselves criminal.

For the last 50 years the most commonly quoted 'cause' of juvenile delinquency has been the 'broken home'. This term is usually applied to homes where the family is incomplete due to death, desertion, separation or divorce. Breckinridge and Abbott, in 1912, make one of the first references of significance to this factor.

It seems that if the child of any family became delinquent, it would be possible to find some things in the home conditions of that child which have been proposed, by some writers at least, as causes of delinquency. For example, not only over-severity on the one hand and leniency on the other are blamed, but even the middle course in the bringing up of children could be considered as revealing some traces of indifference or inactivity in respect of the parental duty of socialization.

There is empirical evidence to support the connection between the probability of delinquency and some of the factors in home conditions. The Gluecks claim in their *Five Hundred Delinquent Women* (1934) that 81 per cent came from homes characterized by 'criminal or deviant parents'. In this country Burt (1944) showed a frequency of such homes against non-deviant homes for delinquent children of five to one.

THE ENVIRONMENT

In some ways in contrast to the theories centred on the family, a number of writers have pointed out that in many countries juveniles, particularly adolescents, show rebellion against the family and distrust and protest against prevailing mores and principles. But these two theories are not necessarily in conflict. Nye (1958) suggested that similar or greater effects upon the socialization of the child may be experienced if the home is not 'broken' but is subject to internal conflict. He suggested that unbroken but unhappy families produced more juvenile delinquency. It may be that if the child or adolescent cannot find the satisfactions he needs within the home he will be driven, or at least become more susceptible, to influences outside the home. If the home is situated in an environment where an anti-authority adolescent sub-culture exists, the child is likely to be drawn into it, and to learn delinquent behaviour outside the home. The lack of integration, affection, or other desirable features in the home situation may result in a failure to offset the subcultural values external to the home. Modification of Cohen's (1955) theory proposed by Kitsuse and Dietrich fits this type of explanation. They postulate that:

1 the individual learns the values of the delinquent sub-culture through his participation in gangs which embody that sub-culture;
2 the malicious, non-utilitarian and negativistic behaviour which is learned through participation in the sub-culture, is met by formal negative sanctions, rejection and limitation of access to prestigeful status within middle-class society;
3 the motivation of individuals for participation in such gangs is varied;
4 participation in the delinquent sub-culture creates similar problems for *all* its participants;
5 the participants' response to the barriers raised to exclude them from status in the middle-class system is a hostile rejection of the standards of respectability and an emphasis on status *within* the sub-culture (gang);
6 the hostile rejection response reinforces the malicious non-utilitarian and negativistic norms of the sub-culture.

Attractive as it is to theorize, it is essential for any real understanding of the problem of juvenile delinquency upon which social action might be based, to have sound, rigorous evidence which can only be derived from empirical research studies.

PROBLEM OF DEFINITION

The main problem to be faced by persons attempting empirical studies of juvenile delinquency is that juvenile delinquency is not itself a satisfactory concept for the application of scientific methods. Different nations and different cultures at different times define it in different ways. Yet, clearly, before it is possible to discuss the causes of juvenile delinquency it is necessary to be able to say what it is. Such definitions have to be specific. It is not possible to find a definition which fits all cultures at all times which is not so wide in scope that it is valueless.

Since the problem of definitions is central to empirical research, it might be useful if this point were elaborated. Certain sexual behaviour may be regarded in one culture as a necessary sign of manhood or womanhood, but within a different culture the same behaviour would attract extreme public disapprobation – indeed, almost all degrees on a scale from approval to disapproval may be shown towards the same act. Persons who migrate from one culture to another and who carry with them to their new environment the norms of behaviour socially acceptable in their previous country, may be defined as delinquent by the laws of their new home. Within a country and even within the same culture, the same behaviour may be defined as delinquent before a certain birthday and not after that birthday. What is delinquent in terms of the legal definition one day, becomes only morally reprehensible the next. Legal definitions of delinquency follow the national boundaries of the law, whereas what is regarded as rebellion against or non-compliance with the norms of a culture may not. Culture patterns may be materially the same across national boundaries; or, within a national boundary, there may be different cultures and thus different expectations of types of behaviour. Thus, by reasonable inference, it is unlikely that the same form of behaviour in different countries or at different times, which in the one case is defined as delinquent and in the other case not, will have different causes according to how it is defined. It is probable that what may cause one form of maladjustment to one society may not cause the same maladjustment in a different society. It is probable, for example, that the causes of criminal gang activity are different in different countries, and the causes of gang activity are different from the causes of the criminality of the maladjusted isolate. But juvenile delinquency is usually defined to include the anti-social activities of the gang as well as the anti-social activities of the neurotic, maladjusted, isolated, individual offender.

It may be represented that it is possible to define juvenile delinquency within the limits of a national boundary or a culture pattern. Perhaps the best statement that can be made along these lines is that serious deviation from the norms of any culture on the part of the juvenile or adolescent members is likely to be defined as delinquent. But there is more than an element of circularity in this type of definition because the boundaries of the 'culture' define the expectations of behaviour. Where the cultures have common expectations of juvenile behaviour it is highly probable that other norms of behaviour will also be similar. It does not seem very satisfactory to define juvenile delinquency as *any behaviour on the part of the younger age groups of the population such that the senior age groups object to it*. None the less, it does not seem possible to find any other definition which will fit. Failure to comply with the cultural expectations seems to be the only common ground defining delinquency. The problem of finding the causes of juvenile delinquency thus seems to reduce to finding the answer to the question, 'Why don't young people conform to the standards desired by their elders?' For example, if children are expected to go to school and they play truant, such truancy is often classified as 'delinquency'. Clearly, there can be no such delinquency if there is no expectation in the culture that children should attend school – indeed, if they should choose to do so rather than work in the parents' paddy field, this might be defined instead as delinquent behaviour. It is necessary to stress, therefore, that any research studies of juvenile delinquency must be referred to the culture in which they are carried out. Although the collective term 'juvenile delinquency' is both sweeping and variable, it is possible to postulate that different acts within a culture will receive different degrees of social approbation or disapprobation. That is, different acts of conformity with or rebellion against the norms of a culture will be viewed differently by that culture. Thus, the reference standard which may be used to describe juvenile delinquency in research projects seems to be as follows:

1 degrees of delinquency are related to the intensity of public disapprobation and the extent to which the offender against the cultural norms persists in this behaviour;
2 the cultural norms are defined by the encoded law applicable within the national boundaries of which the culture forms a part.

The second part of the definition is necessary because an individual may conform to the norms of his culture or sub-culture, and the norm may be in conflict with the criminal law. Indeed, it has been shown by some workers that conforming approved behaviour in the sub-culture is defined as delinquent according to the norms of the larger society. In particular, conformity with the norms of the delinquent sub-culture is by definition juvenile delinquency. This is the point discussed earlier with respect to criminal gang activities. Perhaps this analysis adds point to the argument that it is unlikely that the same causes will lead to behaviour conforming to norms (even where these norms are sub-cultural) and at the same time explain non-conforming behaviour. One of the major tasks for research in juvenile delinquency is that of breaking down the total aggregate concept into meaningful subdivisions.

RESEARCH METHODS

Despite the difficulties of research briefly indicated in the preceding paragraphs, a variety of research methods has been applied to the problem. None the less, is it true that little or nothing is known about 'causes' or even about pre-disposing factors with any substantial degrees of certainty? Recently there has been a convergence among some of the research findings, but all research designs suffer from deficiencies of one kind or another.

The difficulties in defining delinquency are not solved by adopting arbitrary definitions. Even if arbitrary definitions are adopted for purposes of counting and measuring delinquency, many problems remain. Clearly, a deviant act cannot be said to be 'juvenile delinquency' without it first being established that the action was carried out by a juvenile. Not all juvenile delinquency is detected, but until it is detected there is no way of knowing that it is juvenile delinquency: there is no characteristic in the event itself that marks it out as being performed by a person defined within the age limits of 'juvenile'. Juvenile delinquent acts cannot be differentiated from the general body of crime, no matter how that is defined, unless and until the crime is cleared up. Thus, there can be no 'juvenile delinquency known to the police'. Figures relating to juvenile delinquency relate only to detected crimes. Clearly, research can concern itself with the manifestations of juvenile delinquency and there are many and various levels of manifestations.

The different research methods which have been applied to juvenile delinquency divide into two broad groups according to whether only proved delinquents were studied or whether the delinquent population was compared with some control population. Certainly, inferences derived from differences between the delinquent group and the matched non-delinquent group depend upon the adequacy of the matching method. The majority of studies falling into this category suffer from gross deficiencies in the matched sample. Indeed, it might not be unfair to say that no adequate matched control sample design has yet been carried out. In the main this is due to the difficulty of obtaining information from individuals who have not been marked out as delinquent in some acceptable way. Usually, when something has gone wrong in the life of a child, the parents are prepared to reveal and discuss those intimate details which may have led to the breakdown. But parents are very resistent to providing similarly 'deep' information in respect of children whom they regard as completely normal. Attempts to obtain information from similar delinquent and non-delinquent groups have always resulted in a very large proportion of refusals to co-operate by or on behalf of the control sample. It is to be regretted that the majority of research workers who select this method for the study of delinquency are content to compare their delinquent sample with other samples equally as accessible, such as those referred to child guidance clinics. Others have been content to seek much less 'deep' information from the control sample which has meant that the two samples could be identified by those making assessments of the data, and this in turn reduced the power of the data and induced the probability of bias.

Another research method is based on the techniques of ecology. This method compares geographical areas which produce a large amount of juvenile delinquency with areas which produce little. This method also presents many technical problems, although it is more acceptable to the general public on ethical grounds. Correlations which are derived from ecological factors do not hold for individuals; indeed, it is possible to find a positive association in ecological variables but a significant negative correlation for the same variables on an individual basis.

The methods of anthropological research and the case study approach (both individual and group) have also been applied. In this category fall some excellent studies of the criminal gang.

Some examples from each of these different types of research design will be given and their weaknesses discussed.

MATCHING STUDIES

One of the best matching design studies in the field of delinquency is that of McCord, McCord and Zola (1959). This study was a re-evaluation of the Cambridge–Somerville Youth Study. Cases appearing before the Boston Massachusetts Court were matched with non-delinquent cases. These data were read and coded without previous knowledge of the criminal record. None the less, the 'control' cases were normally less well documented and apart from the loss of information, the persons undertaking the ratings and codings might have been able to identify the 'control' individuals. It is unlikely that any conscious bias would have been introduced, but research designs which allow even for unconscious bias to appear are not completely satisfactory. The following summary of generalizations may be drawn from the reported work. Intelligence and physical well-being did not appear to be related to delinquency. Social environment was also not strongly associated – a slum area would be expected to leave its impression on a child's personality, but, say the authors, it did not appear that he was likely to become delinquent or accept the sub-cultural norms of his surroundings unless other factors were also applicable. There must, however, remain some doubt as to whether this finding might not have resulted in some indirect way from the nature of the matching design. Family cohesiveness (no quarrels), consistent discipline (whether strict or lax), and affection from parents seemed to have the effect of inoculation against sub-cultural influences. Children who live in good class areas although they might show disturbances in various ways seldom tended towards delinquency. The McCords identified pre-disposing factors for different types of delinquency. The most concise summary of their findings is provided by them and reproduced in table 42.1.

It is interesting to compare the McCords' findings with those of Nye (1958). Nye studied all students in Grades 9–12 in their regular classrooms on an unselected day. Three small cities in Washington State were concerned. He obtained a sample of 3158 children who may be regarded as typical of the child population of the area. He compared the information obtained from these children with a group of children in the State Institutions. His work is

Table 42.1   Summary of casual syndromes

	Property crimes	Crimes against the person	Sex crimes	Drunkenness	Traffic violation
Maternal background	Neglect P 0.001	Overprotection neglect P 0.005	Passivity neglect P 0.01	Neglect P 0.001	Overprotection passivity P 0.001
Paternal background	Neglect P 0.005 Criminal role model P 0.01	Cruelty, neglect P 0.005 Criminal role model P 0.02	Neglect P 0.05	Absence neglect P 0.025	——
Disciplinary background	Absence of consistency; erratic – punitiveness, laxity P 0.005	Absence of love; erratic punitiveness laxity (P 0.02)	Absence of consistency erratic – punitiveness laxity P 0.05	Absence of consistency and love; erratic – punitiveness P 0.01	——
Home atmosphere	Quarrelsome neglecting P 0.001	Broken quarrelsome neglecting P 0.005	Quarrelsome – neglecting P 0.001	Broken quarrelsome neglecting P 0.001	Broken quarrelsome neglecting P 0.05
Intelligence	Average P 0.05	——	——	——	——
Neighbourhood	——	——	——	——	——

Reproduced from McCord, McCord & Zola (1959), table 74, p. 150, ref. 13.

notable in that he did not rely upon the court convictions for his delinquency scale, but rather used the information supplied by the children themselves. He included certain items in his questionnaire to identify children who did not reply accurately, and he discarded 32 cases on this evidence. It may be regarded as odd that only 1 per cent of the questionnaires were rejected as false, although there is no evidence to suggest that is too small a proportion. The technique of using internal evidence to identify false replies is most commendable and is worthy of further attention and development. Nye reported that he found little social effect in the delinquency rates as scaled by means of his questionnaire. Among children who fell into his most delinquent category and who came from broken homes, 48 per cent were in the institution sample, and only 24 per cent in the school group. He suggests that this might be due to differential treatment by the police, parents and other social agencies, rather than to real differences in behaviour. Interesting and challenging as Nye's work is, it is not beyond criticism. In particular a number of the definitions he used, such as 'happiness' of the home, are not clearly made. His findings are reported in a very general form, and it is difficult to identify his operational definitions. In addition to his finding that social class is not related in any great measure with his scale for delinquency, he claims that the rejection of the child by the parent is less significant than the rejection of the parent by the child, and no significant differences were found between the rejection of the mother or father. In many ways the value of this work rests on the assumption that self-ratings are a better measure of delinquency than detection and court adjudication. Without more evidence from comparative studies, using a cross-over between the different definitions, it is difficult to comment on this point.

Healy and Bronner (1936) compared delinquents and non-delinquents in the same families. The matching may be seriously criticized. For example it is difficult to see how boys can be compared with girls, if only because the crime rate for detected delinquency is nearly 10 times greater for boys. Matching boys with girls seems to be completely unjustified. In these circumstances the findings are suspect.

Another attempt to discuss the problem of delinquency without reference to adjudication by the courts is that by Kagan. He was concerned with aggression in children, and he used as his criterion teachers' ratings. Beginning with a sample of 118 boys aged between 6 and 10 years, he selected the 21 most and the 21 least aggressive. He compared these in terms of fantasy stories told by them in response to pictures and answers obtained in the initial interviews. More of the aggressive boys told stories involving anger between parent and child. More of the non-aggressive boys reported themes of dependency on adults and regarded the mother as the punitive agent. From the interview data, a significant difference was found in that more of the non-aggressive boys in answer to the question, 'who is the boss in your home?', replied, 'mother'.

It may be doubted whether teachers' ratings are a very good criterion. It is probable that children tend to behave differently in school from other social settings. Whether the criterion was sound or not, the study must be criticized on the grounds that the sample was very small, and was drawn from one school. It is to be expected that social class and other factors will be somewhat similar in a restricted area, such as that from which the pupils of one school may come, and accordingly social factors might not be expected to appear. Indeed social factors were not sought in this study. The findings of the mother as the punitive agent in non-aggressive homes does not fit in with other results. But perhaps this is not surprising in view of the limitations of the research design.

Bowlby (1946) studied 44 juvenile thieves. Both the thieves and their controls were referrals to a child guidance clinic. Only nine of the thieves were sent to the clinic by a court, and half were under 11 years of age. The controls were similar in age range and in intelligence. The history of mental family illness was about equal for both samples, but seems to be rather high – 18 of the thieves had such a family history. No data are given regarding the socio-economic status of either group. This may be one of the major weaknesses of the study, since it seems reasonable to suppose that voluntary attendance at a child guidance clinic is more likely to occur in middle- and upper-class families.

Bowlby claims that affectionless children were significantly more delinquent. The majority were truants. Eighteen of the thieves had suffered complete and prolonged separation from their mothers or established foster-mothers during the first five years of life, whereas only two of the controls had had similar deprivation experience. Maternal deprivation in the first five years of life was believed to be a foremost cause of delinquency and persistent misbehaviour. It is easy to criticize this important piece of work. It is probable that some of the controls had committed offences, and there is a number of points on which it is impossible to compare the two samples. Whatever the merits of this study it has greatly influenced thinking about the causes of delinquency in the past decade. It represents one of the few attempts by psychiatrists to test their theories by observation. It is of course doubtful whether the categories which seemed to discriminate fairly well between the two samples could be reproduced by other clinicians or workers trained in other disciplines.

Perhaps the most ambitious, most costly and most criticized research into the problem of juvenile delinquency is that of Sheldon and Eleanor Glueck. This study was limited to Boston (USA). Comparisons were made between 500 'persistent delinquents' and 500 'proven non-delinquents' in Boston schools. Samples were matched for age, intelligence, ethnic–racial factors, residence in under-privileged areas. Matching was done by first taking the delinquents and then trying to find non-delinquents with similar backgrounds. It appears that matching was done by sub-groups although some individual matching was also carried out. Most of the generalizations given by the Gluecks are based on tests of significance – but it is not at all certain that the tests were appropriate to the inference drawn from the results of the tests. The following were the main conclusions regarding differences between delinquent and non-delinquents:

1 home conditions: delinquents are more mobile; the homes are more often over-crowded; their families are more often dependent on social welfare services; few are living with their own parents;
2 family life: families of delinquents show more mental backwardness; more emotional disturbance, drunkenness and criminality;
3 home life: domestic routine in delinquent households is more disorganized; there are lower standards of conduct [sic!];
4 physique: certain biological differences were identified, in particular the adolescent development spurt was delayed;
5 delinquents were more extroverted, impulsive and showed less self-control [sic!].

It will be seen that a number of the descriptions of delinquency factors appears to be no more than different words for the same basic characteristic. This is known as 'overlapping', a feature which the Gluecks did not attempt to deal with until their work had attracted much criticism on this point. Indeed, much of their work attempts to justify the fact that they took no account of this. A number of the factors were used to obtain weighted scores for prediction of likely delinquency before it had manifested itself. Fifteen factors were selected to distinguish delinquents from non-delinquents by three separate tables. One table which has become known as the 'social prediction table' used:

discipline of the boy by the father;
supervision by the mother;
affection of the father;
affection of the mother;
cohesiveness of family.

Another table used character assessments derived from a Rorschach Test; social assertion, defiance, suspicion, destructiveness and emotional liability. The third table used factors relating to temperament as determined by psychiatric interview – adventurousness, extroversion, suggestibility, stubbornness and emotional instability. Of the 500 delinquents and 500 controls with which the study began, there was full information in these areas only for 205 delinquents and 219 controls. These were used as the basis for the tables.

It was the five social factors alone which provided the best prediction of delinquency. But 'prediction' was not forward prediction, but rather specification of the cases in the sample used to derive the tables. No forward validation of the tables has yet been satisfactorily carried out. It should also be noted that the failure to obtain information in respect of all cases may give rise to serious bias. It may be that just those factors which cause information to be lost may be those which are most important in separating delinquent from non-delinquent. Although the tables seemed likely to be able to predict delinquency fairly well in the actual sample, this sample consisted of about equal numbers of delinquents and non-delinquents and these were matched according to certain important factors. It is impossible, therefore, for the tables to predict with equal efficiency in a realistic state where it is expected that the proportion of delinquents will be very much less, and where they cannot be supposed to be matched with non-delinquents.

In 1961 an attempt was made in New York by the Youth Authority to test the validity of the social prediction table on an unselected sample of children. No results are yet available, but Professor Jackson Toby in a private communication to the author of this paper pointed out that although the prediction table was of some value in prognosis, an equally good prognosis could have been obtained merely by noting those families who were receiving poor relief. Whether this will remain true as more data become available cannot be known for some years.

Apart from the practical aspects of the lack of validation of the Gluecks' prediction tables, perhaps the most serious criticism that can be made is, again, the failure to define their terms and concepts in a satisfactory manner. Too many categories are far too vague. For example, what exactly is 'emotional disturbance', and do psychiatrists agree among themselves about it or with others of different disciplines? What is meant by 'immorality of parents'? It seems that the authors were using 'middle-class norms' as though they formed a realistic value structure.

There is nothing inherently wrong with the method of matching in research designs in the study of delinquency, but few social scientists who have used the methods seem to be fully aware of the difficulties of drawing valid inferences from their results. It is often not realized that factors which are initially matched cannot appear in any subsequent analysis, unless the matching had not been properly carried out. The matching method provides correlations and partial correlations mixed together, and in interpretations of the data it is not easy to keep in mind exactly which is which, and what the implications are. It has certainly proved too difficult for many writers, but it does not follow that what has not been done well cannot be well done and is not worth doing well.*

ECOLOGICAL METHODS

Ecological studies make use of data regarding small geographical areas such as census tracts,

---

* It would simplify matters a lot if research workers realized the difference between stratification of samples on the one hand (which is a satisfactory procedure), and matching which, on the other hand, is seldom satisfactory.

polling sectors, local authority areas, wards, or other convenient areas for which demographic and social data are available. Areas having widely different rates of criminality are examined in respect of variables relating to socio-economic factors, health data and other demographic information. Inferences are drawn from the way in which the variables relating to crime vary with each other in respect of the areas studied.

There are, of course, many logical difficulties in deriving information which is valid for inference regarding persons from data relating to clusters of persons living in a specific geographical area. Indeed, it has been shown that a high correlation between indices from ecological data can be very misleading if they are assumed to apply to individuals. Nevertheless, the methods of ecological analysis provide a powerful tool for the investigation of delinquency. Moreover, it should not be assumed that all useful information about delinquents must relate to individuals; quite often decisions are taken regarding administrative districts and special areas.

Lander (1954) studied census tracts in Baltimore using information taken from the 1940 census. He based his delinquency rates on court records covering 8464 cases representing the total for the years 1939–1942. These rates for the different census tracts were related to age of completion of education, estimated rental of houses, overcrowding, houses without separate bath or in gross disrepair, and percentages of foreign born and non-white persons. Lander's work has been criticized on two grounds. First it is argued that measurement of factors relating to delinquency cannot be made adequately on census tract data and that such measurements might obscure individual differences and the effect of the culture upon individual persons. Second, that Lander's claim that the best summary of his findings is provided by the theory of anomie is regarded by some as bordering on tautology. It is argued that anomie does not explain why certain individuals in the anomic culture chose delinquency rather than some other solution to their anomic situation.

Shaw and McKay did not use census tracts or other administrative divisions but divided their urban area into concentric zones by uniform distances. Delinquency rates were calculated by taking for each zone a ratio of official juvenile delinquency to the population of juvenile court age. They found the highest rates of delinquency were in the central areas and the lowest rates in the outer zones. The rates tended to decline with distance from the inner to the outer areas. They found also that juvenile delinquency rates were highly correlated with such factors as population change, bad housing, poverty, foreign born and negroes, the tuberculosis rate, adult crime and mental disorder. Juvenile delinquency they claim follows the pattern of the physical and social structure of the city, being concentrated in the slum and the deteriorating areas and in areas of general social disorganization. The variations in the juvenile delinquency rate in the areas of the city also correlated highly with economic status.

There has been a number of other studies utilizing ecological methods. Some have been fairly sound and others have not been very well designed. One further example will be given.

Reckless, Dinitz and Kay used sixteen census tracts with the highest delinquency rates in Columbus (Ohio). Teachers in the sixth grade of the schools concerned were asked to predict boys who would, in their view, in future commit some crime, and those who in their view were likely to remain crime free. One hundred and ninety-two boys were predicted as non-delinquent and 108 as potentially delinquent. Twenty-three per cent were not categorized and there was a very wide variation between teachers in the ratio placed in the two categories. It was found that just over 8 per cent of the boys who were predicted as being non-delinquent had, in fact, records of offences, and 23 per cent of those predicted to be delinquent had records of prior offences. Reckless, Dinitz and Kay rejected boys who were found to have a previous record of crime from the predicted non-delinquent group.

It will be realized that by commencing the selection of cases with the restriction to census tracts with the highest delinquency rates, the authors were restricted in the variables which they were likely to find from their analysis to be significant discriminating factors. To some extent they were achieving a stratification by a number of unspecified variables. Moreover, the subsequent rejection of cases initially nominated as non-delinquent, where the subjective judgement was found to be incorrect, further modified the nature of the inferences that could logically be drawn from their data. It is perhaps not surprising that they found nothing to support Lander's correlation between home ownership and delinquency and that they did not find any relationship with father's occupation, mother's employment or length of residence. Certainly race and socio-economic status factors must have been considerably reduced or eliminated by the sampling procedure they used. The authors found, however, that the potentially delinquent group more often came from broken homes. Among the delinquents there were more family conflicts, there was less family participation in social activities, parents punished more often, and the friends of delinquents were more often delinquent also. It is difficult to see what may be deduced from this piece of research, because it may be that the factors in the subjective evaluation of 'potentially delinquent' children were just those factors which were finally drawn out by the analysis. The rabbit which was produced from the hat was perhaps placed there in the first instance by the unwitting teachers acting as assessors. This is probably a very important point, and worth some emphasis. Suppose, for example, the teachers who made the ratings had the belief that one of the factors leading to delinquency was that of a broken home. Then, when they were asked by Reckless to nominate children likely to become delinquent, it is probable that they directed their attention to children who were known to have broken homes. The fact that only high delinquency areas were chosen ensured that factors related to the area of residence (socio-economic status, living conditions and the like) would not appear when subsequently the two groups were compared. Thus the analysis would 'hand back' to the research workers those particular items which were believed to be related to delinquency by the teachers who were responsible in the first instance for the classification into the groups used in the analysis.

There have been very few pieces of research utilizing control group techniques which are equal to that of Sir Cyril Burt's study in pre-war London.

ANTHROPOLOGICAL METHODS AND CASE STUDIES

It has long been noted in Western countries that Jewish children are less frequently delinquent than others. Robinson (1958) made an intensive study of 226 Jewish families who had had children referred to the Childrens' Court. His work relates to four of the five New York city boroughs in 1952. It was found that if Jewish children were delinquent in proportion to the population size, there would have been 10 times as many as were in fact noted. Robinson found that 60 per cent of the children were living with parents and another 2 per cent were living with their mothers. The size of the family was generally small, and only 2 per cent were apparently illegitimate. Unfortunately Robinson does not compare the sample of

Jewish children with other delinquents in any detail, and there is no comparison with non-delinquent Jewish children. Although Robinson emphasizes the probable influence of the occupation of the father, this was recorded in only 59 cases, and even then it was described in subjective terms. However, the author claims that no menial occupations were found among fathers of the sampled children. It should be noted that this study claims a ratio of ten to one for the delinquency of American nationals' children against the Jewish sample. This is a very favourable ratio. It is usually claimed to be somewhat lower. In Holland, where the Jewish families are integrated into the culture, no distinction has been reported between the delinquency rates of Jewish and other Dutch children.

Wood made an intensive study of three groups: one, a group of American Indians living in a small community; another, a group of Bohemians; and a group of citizens of Kentucky living in a town in Wisconsin. Wood was interested in the criminality of minority groups. He claims that with strong social integration low economic status strengthens the cultural ties within the group and crime is minimal. Low status with persecution by the majority with a high degree of integration, he says, leads to low crime rates.

Perhaps the most interesting feature of Wood's work is that it provides a very reasonable hypothesis explaining low delinquency rates among lower classes and perhaps persecuted Jews and Orientals. It may also explain the divergence between the results for the integrated Jewish families in Holland and those in New York. Wood also noted strong family and group loyalties and the many mutual help associations found in such societies as being important in the prevention of delinquency.

Perhaps the best examples of the application of anthropological methods are the studies of delinquent gangs. One of the more important studies of gangs is that by Cohen (1955). He sought to explain the origins of delinquency among middle-class children and the phenomenon of delinquent sub-cultures. The characteristics of delinquent sub-culture were reported by him to be:

1 non-utilitarian ('just for the fun of it');
2 malicious (floating, rather than merely avoiding social norms);
3 negativistic (the norms of the sub-culture are diametrically opposed to middle-class cultural values);
4 versatility (no tendency to specialize in any form of delinquent behaviour);
5 short-term hedonism (there is very little interest in long-term objectives);
6 group autonomy (a tendency to be intolerant of all rules, except those imposed by the sub-culture).

Another central theme of Cohen is that sex identification plays an important part in delinquency. Children of both sexes tend to form earlier in life feminine identifications. A boy comes under strong social pressures outside the home to establish his masculinity. Because his mother is the 'object of his feminine identification' and it is the mother who is normally the chief agent of training in conforming behaviour, he gradually seeks to give up his identification with the mother. Delinquency which is characterized as bad behaviour serves to offset the early identification and the *good* standards associated with the 'feminine identification'. Bad behaviour is thus seen to be serving a function (for the delinquent) in demonstrating his masculinity.

Another thesis of Cohen is that of status frustration. This is perhaps the most questionable, particularly in attempts to generalize findings regarding delinquency to Western cultures. He postulates that the working-class boy is orientated towards middle-class values. Reviewers of Cohen's work have also pointed out that his emphasis on the non-utilitarian criminality among gangs is doubtful in that there are varieties of delinquent groups some of which are certainly utilitarian.

Cohen and Short (1960) took the earlier work somewhat further. They describe different delinquent sub-cultures – a conflict-orientated sub-culture, a drug-addict sub-culture, a semi-professional criminal sub-culture and a middle-class delinquent sub-culture. The conflict-orientated sub-culture is typified by the New York street gang. These groups are often large gangs which appear to have a formal structure emphasizing their rights on their own territory ('turf') and their reputation ('rep') for toughness. A gang's status is determined mainly by its prowess and toughness in fighting. A number of New York adolescent gangs have committed murders in the course of demonstrating their toughness.

The drug-addict sub-culture appears to recruit mainly from the population which is already delinquent. The drug-addict sub-culture, according to Cohen and Short, is non-violent.

The semi-professional sub-culture does not need any further description.

The middle-class delinquent sub-culture is perhaps akin to the 'playboy type' with the desire to seek danger. In some countries this sub-culture has been identified with motoring offences of joy-riding and car theft.

Salisbury (1958) has obviously penetrated some of the defences of the gang and has described his experiences vividly. He postulates that early parental neglect and failure to achieve status and self-esteem are among the causes of delinquency. Because of the lack of self-esteem the delinquent directs his efforts towards achieving status in the peer group, proving himself by outdoing the others in toughness and daring. Some boys are coerced into joining gangs; they are afraid of being called 'chicken' (cowards) and for that reason are detained within the orbit of the gang from which they would prefer to escape. Others join gangs freely as a means of obtaining status among their peers. Salisbury says that he did not meet a single gang leader who did not want to get away from the pattern of street life. He believed they were sincere in this.

A number of persons has studied delinquent and non-delinquent children referred to Child Guidance Clinics. Usually the absence of adequate controls makes these studies un-satisfactory as has already been noted. Reference should, however, be made to the work of Bach and Bremer because they showed considerable ingenuity in utilizing standardized play with dolls to evaluate aggressive anti-social tendencies. Twelve delinquent and 20 normal boys were compared. Both groups came from families of the lower middle class and were of average intelligence. The delinquents, however, were from broken homes and had been committed to the care of a home for psychopathic and neurotic children. They were between the ages of seven and ten years. Bach and Bremer observed that delinquents showed more indifference to their fathers and were not so able to anticipate punishment. The design of the study, apart from the use of standardized projective play situations is not outstanding. The sample was not only extremely small, it was also biased. It seems odd to make comparisons between attitudes of delinquents from broken homes with those of non-delinquents whose homes were not broken. Some of the findings of this study, not discussed here, were in direct conflict with other research findings.

EVALUATION OF EMPIRICAL STUDIES

The examples of research given here are, of course, only a selection of those reported in the literature. Perhaps the criticism levelled at these studies may give the impression that they have been selected as examples of how research should not be done. This is not so. Views will doubtless differ as to whether the selection has shown a bias. The principle of selection used was that of frequency of reference in some of the current literature.

The purpose in discussing these research studies was not to suggest that these or any other provide irrefutable evidence regarding the causes of delinquency. Some concordance may be noted among a number of the studies, and such findings may be more soundly based than others not replicated in different studies using different methods.

Causation is a concept which has little meaning except in terms of something which, if changed, changes the outcome. By this standard, none of the factors discovered in any of the studies to date has been demonstrated to be a cause of delinquency. To this extent it is true to say that the causes of delinquency remain unknown, and will remain unknown until there is rigorous experimentation along the lines of the medical clinical trial and other similarly valid experimental social action.

ACKNOWLEDGEMENT

This paper first appeared in *Educ. Res.* (1963), **5**, 104–119, and is published here with the kind permission of editor and author.

REFERENCES

Bach, G. & Bremer, G. Projective father fantasies of pre-adolescent delinquent children. *J. Psychol.*, **24**, 3–17.

Bowlby, J. (1946) *Forty-four Juvenile Thieves*. London.

Breckinridge, S. P. & Abbott, E. (1912) *The Delinquent Child and the Home*. New York.

Burt, C. (1944) *The Young Delinquent* (4th edn.). London.

Cavan, R. S. (1957) *Criminology* (2nd edn.), pp. 107–108. New York.

Cohen, A. K. (1955) *Delinquent Boys: The Culture of the Gang*. Glencoe.

Cohen, A. K. & Short, J. (1960) Research in delinquent sub-cultures. *J. Soc. Issues*.

Colijanni, N. N. (1889) *La Sociologia Criminale*. Catania.

Glueck, S. & Glueck, E. (1934) *Five Hundred Delinquent Women*. New York.

Glueck, S. & Glueck, E. (1950) *Unravelling Juvenile Delinquency*. New York.

Healy, W. & Bronner, A. (1936) *New Light on Delinquency and its Treatment*. Newhaven.

Joly, H. (1889) *La France Criminelle*. Paris.

Kagan, J. Socialisation of aggression and the perception of parents in phantasy. *Child Devel.*, **29**, 311–320.

Kitsuse, J. I. & Dietrich, D. C. Delinquent boys – a critique. *Amer. Soc. Rev.*, **24**(2), 207.

Lander, B. (1954) *Towards an Understanding of Juvenile Delinquency*. New York.

Lundberg, G. A., Schragg, C. C. & Larsen, O. N. (1954) *Sociology*, p. 531. New York.

McCord, W., McCord, J. & Zola, I. (1959) *Origins of Crime*. New York: Columbia Univ. Press.

Mischler, E. (1893) *International Statische*. Tubingen.

New forms of juvenile delinquency (1960) *Second United Nations Congress on Crime and the Treatment of Offenders*, p. 41, London. Report prepared by the Secretariat of the United Nations Department of Social and Economic Affairs (1960). New York.

Nye, F. (1958) *Family Relationships and Delinquent Behaviour*. New York.

Reckless, W., Dinitz, S. & Kay, B. The self-component in potential delinquency. *Amer. Soc. Rev.*, **22**, 566.

Robinson, S. (1958) A study of delinquency among Jewish children. In Sklare, Marshall (Ed.), *The Jews*. Glencoe.

Salisbury, H. (1958) *The Shook-up Generation*. New York.

Shaw, C. R. & McKay, H. D. (1942) *Juvenile Delinquency and Urban Areas*. Chicago.

Sutherland, E. H. & Cressey, D. R. (1960) *Principles of Criminology* (6th edn.), p. 172. Chicago.

Wood, A. L. Minority group criminality and cultural integration. *J. Crim. Law Crim.*, **37**, 498–510.

PART 13

Educational assessment

INTRODUCTION

The articles and papers in this Part all relate, not surprisingly, to aspects of our various examination systems. Some are critical, others favourable, and one, the extract from the Schools Council's pamphlet, is descriptive.

Boyall's article on CSE Mode III in English will be of interest to those who will teach in schools operating the CSE examination. Mode III was a valiant attempt to hand on much more responsibility to teachers for the design and evaluation of their subjects. It has not caught on as widely as hoped. Nevertheless, the idea of more control by the participants (teachers and taught) in curriculum matters is inevitable. This article gives a few ideas about how Mode III might operate.

The extract from Fawthrop's pamphlet is a useful counterbalance for those who believe that examinations are more or less faultless. He attacks many of the assumptions held by protagonists and these should be carefully considered alongside arguments for the retention of formal examinations.

The Schools Council Examination Bulletin 3 (and 4), *An Introduction to Some Techniques of Examining*, is well worth reading in its entirety. The short extract chosen covers the difficult area of teachers' assessments, course work and practical and oral exams.

43 Teachers' assessments, the practical examination and other forms of examining

HMSO (Schools Council)

The written paper is only one way of making an assessment of a candidate's achievement. In the past it has been to some extent a maid-of-all-work. It is certainly suitable for many purposes but not for all. There is a wide range of educational objectives – using a skill appropriately, speaking, working with material and tools – which cannot be assessed directly by a written paper. If these ways of working or behaving are considered to be valid objectives of a course of study, they should be examined by the appropriate form of examination.

Once again, however, it is clarity about the objectives of a course of study which will suggest the most appropriate action to take, and therefore the form of examination most likely to provide a valid estimate of the candidate's achievement.

TEACHERS' ASSESSMENTS

There is a number of good reasons for suggesting that teachers' assessments are the best means of estimating the level of attainment of pupils:

(a) assessments can be based on the pupil's work over a period of time rather than on his performance on one day;
(b) assessments reflect the normal work of the pupil under everyday conditions;
(c) assessments do not have a harmful backwash effect on the curriculum and on teaching. Each teacher is teaching what he considers appropriate and in the way he considers right, and without reference to what may be in the mind of the examiner;
(d) assessments can take into account the performance of the pupil in many dimensions; his written work, his oral work, his practical work, his contribution to group work, his interest and enthusiasm as well as his creative and imaginative flair can all be given weight;
(e) assessments do not cause revision and the memorization of facts to be stressed more than is necessary for the development of the pupil's understanding.

The freedom of the teacher to teach what he considers appropriate in the best way he knows is thus assured where the criterion of the pupil's performance is assessment by the teacher. In so far as the teacher appreciates the individual differences of his pupils, the freedom of the pupil to pursue his work in his own way is preserved and so is his means of relating himself to the subject of study.

There are, however, a number of defects in this process of assessment. They arise from the acknowledged unreliability of many human judgements, especially when judging the ability of others:

(a) In making an assessment about a pupil's performance it is not always possible for the teacher to set aside his personal reactions to the pupil, or his judgement about the pupil's personal qualities and values, even though they may be irrelevant to the judgement of performance.

(b) There is evidence that assessments by teachers can be unreliable. That is to say, they can be variable, and the more so over the range of average pupils than at the extremes of high and low performance.

(c) There is the major difficulty that many teachers do not at any one time teach pupils exhibiting the full range of performance in a field of study, and will generally have to rely on memory of past experience in judging the attainment of their pupils relative to the whole range of pupils who may be appropriately entered for the examination.

To some extent these defects can be overcome by applying as rigorously as possible certain procedures:

(a) the scholastic performance to be assessed should be as clearly defined as possible. This part of the procedure should provide clear statements about a number of distinguishable elements of scholastic performance. These are those items of behaviour which the pupil exhibits in his work which are known to make for success within a particular field of study. The elements should be listed. An assessment of a pupil should be given for each element independently of the assessment he has been given on the others. For example, in geography, the appropriate use of sketch maps may be one such element;

(b) assessment should be made by ranking the pupils in order of merit on each of the items of performance. This is sometimes not easy at the middle ranges of ranking, and where the group is large it may be necessary to give two or more pupils the same rank;

(c) wherever possible assessment should be made by more than one teacher and the assessments totalled to give a final assessment;

(d) assessments of items of performances should be made wherever possible on separate occasions and without reference to previous assessments. This is not, as it may seem, just making difficulties. Evidence shows that it can reduce 'halo' effect.

The problem of comparability of teachers' assessments within and between schools cannot be dealt with simply. If a number of schools take a common-core paper, then teachers' assessments can be scaled against it. If they do not, some form of moderation is needed: more will be said about this later in this *Bulletin*.

There is no reason, however, why teachers' assessments should not play an important part in the CSE examinations. It can be argued that the most *valid* information obtainable about a candidate's level of attainment comes from his teachers. The results of an external examination are not likely to increase the validity of these judgements very significantly, provided that they are related to the whole range of candidates and are not relevant simply to the teacher's own pupils. It is in the area of *reliability* that teachers' estimates are weaker. Some form of rigorous continuous assessment over a long period may increase their reliability, and so make it unnecessary for external examinations to be used save for the limited purpose of establishing criteria of comparability between schools. This kind of technique has been used in secondary school selection, and has led in some areas to the abolition of external examinations. Moreover, as will be suggested later in this *Bulletin*, moderation does not necessarily depend upon the existence of an external examination in order to provide a means of improving the reliability of teachers' assessments.

THE ASSESSMENT OF COURSE WORK

Course work may be a special exercise set during the course of study, a folder of work done by the pupil, an individual pupil's project, a personal study, or a range of other appropriate activities on which the pupil is engaged during the course. What is considered to be appropriate course work will depend on the nature of the subject being studied, and on the judgement of the teacher about whether it sets the pupil the correct level of tasks in relation to the objectives of the course.

Whatever form it takes the assessment of course work should be carried out with the same attention to valid objectives as any other method of examining. The method of marking course work, whether by using a rating form which states the qualities to be marked or by the overall impression of a number of competent judges, should similarly be related to valid objectives within a course of study. For example, field work in geography might be assessed using the following method of rating by impression.

Geography: The assessment of field work

The candidate's field work should be marked by impression on a scale of 0–20 marks. Take special care to use as much of the scale as possible. The following are the qualities that should be looked for in assessing the candidate's work: accuracy of observation; clarity and precision in recording the observation by maps, photographs, models, drawings and in writing; accuracy of generalizations from these observations; correlations and explanations of observed facts – including use of reference material in arriving at explanations; touches of initiative and originality shown in the work; organization and presentation of the work as a whole. Look for excellencies to reward rather than errors and omission to penalize.

Course work may call upon the pupil to employ skill in the use of books and reference material, and to seek out methods of working appropriate to the material being studied. Because it calls on a range of skills and involves the pupil in continuous work, it may provide a highly valid estimate of a pupil's level of attainment in a field of study. On the face of it, it is a means of examining which, if reliable, may prove more valid than methods which are less close to the situation in which attainment is acquired. It is certainly a method which should be vigorously explored.

PRACTICAL EXAMINATIONS

A practical examination can, and ought to be, as rigorous as other forms of examining with the same attention paid to reliability and validity. However, as the range of practical work is so wide and the conditions under which it may take place so various, it is perhaps wise to suggest that rigour may need to be tempered by other considerations.

Nevertheless, the qualities of performance to be exhibited by candidates need to be identified very carefully and to be described with equal care. It may also be that a finished job is not necessarily the only valid, or even the most valid, statement about a candidate's practical ability in a particular field. The planning, the organization and the methods of working may prove to be at least equally valid and reliable indices of performance. There is need for research in this field before firm guidance can be given.

The most common form of practical examination in some subjects is the 'set piece'. The examiner decides that the production of one item, say, a piece of furniture, a family meal, or a tool, will call into play a sufficient range of skills to sample effectively the practical abilities of the candidates in a reasonable time. The 'set piece' may indeed sample a wide range of skills but it does so, very often, within a narrow area of the content of the course. It may well prove that greater reliability and validity can be achieved by ranging not only over skills, but also over areas of the course even if no single job is carried through from beginning to end in the course of the examination.

Trade tests in the forces during the war employed this last method. The objectives of the trade course were broken down to provide a picture of skills and relevant areas of their application. The examination then required the candidate to start a job, to complete a job, to continue a job up to a certain point, to correct what had gone wrong, to select tools for a job, to plan a job and to appraise a finished article. Candidates moved from one item in the practical test to another after a given time, handing in their work or whatever was required for marking purposes as they went round.

A procedure along these lines is common practice in science practical examinations, and might well be relevant in other practical subjects. For example, a practical examination in housecraft might take the following form:

A practical examination in housecraft

The candidates are given a booklet containing the following questions and instructions. The booklet provides ample space for the answers and tells the candidates how much time they have for each practical activity.

Practical Examination

Test A   Time 30 minutes

Scotch eggs
Tomato
Roll and butter
Fruit salad

(a) Make a time plan to show how you would set about preparing this meal.
(b) What is the approximate cost of the meal?
(c) Of what value is this food to the body?

Test B   Time 10 minutes

Look at these six examples and state *what* is wrong and *why*.
(1) Cake
(2) Pastry
(3) Scones
(4) Nylon
(5) Table linen
(6) Tea towel

Test C   Time 15 minutes

Connect the most suitable flex for an electric iron to the plug provided.
State here what kind of flex was connected.

Test D   Time 5 minutes

The detergent displayed here can be bought in three package sizes – note the price of each.
How would you prove to mother which is the most economical size to buy?
Answer in one sentence.

Test E   Time 30 minutes

Using some or all these ingredients *make* a simple mid-day meal for one.
Remember you only have half an hour in which to do this.
State here what you have made.

Test F   Time 30 minutes

(1) In the test tubes there are three samples of water. They are labelled A, B and C.
(2) Take test tube A, add soap flakes *one* at a time and shake well. Note how many you have to add
before a lather remains for approximately $\frac{1}{2}$ a minute. (Count slowly up to 30.) Record the number
under 3A. Do the same for test tubes B and C.
(3) How many flakes did you add to
    (A)   (B)   (C)
(4) What do you learn from this experiment about the different samples of water?

Test G   Time 20 minutes

Here there are a number of stain removers, including water.
Using the most suitable stain remover take out the stains from materials A, B and C.
Write your examination number clearly on each piece of material. What did you use to remove stain
    (A)   (B)   (C)

It may be that teachers' assessments will prove to be a more valid estimate of a candidate's achievement in practical subjects than any form of practical examination. This may be so because the teacher knows more about the candidate's ability both to plan and carry out a practical task and, if the pupil has needed help, the teacher knows precisely what help has been given. On the other hand some form of pictorial test may prove more reliable than teachers' assessments and only marginally less valid. Again, the need for experiment and research is clear.

ORAL EXAMINATIONS

Much of the evidence available about oral examinations suggests that it is a method of examining which has low reliability and validity unless it is used by a skilled examiner for a quite precise purpose.

As with all other methods of examining, the oral examination should attempt to measure valid outcomes of all or part of a course of study. It is important to be quite clear what is to be assessed. Is it reading the language, speaking the language, understanding the language, using the language for a specific purpose such as carrying on a conversation, communicating with an audience, or giving an interview? Once this has been decided, it may then be necessary to specify what qualities of voice, style, stress and so on the examination is to measure, and to provide a marking scheme or rating form which will enable the examiners to do this.

It may not be possible to isolate aspects of the spoken language, whether it is the mother tongue or a foreign language, for precise marking. It may be that, as with English composition, a number of independent judgements of the candidate's performance as a whole would provide a more reliable and valid estimate of a candidate's level of achievement.

Possibly a combination of marking of specific areas, or for specific qualities, and the combined judgements of a number of markers within the areas would serve the purpose. The independent judgements of specific qualities or areas of performance could then be added to give a final assessment.

A number of researches into ways of oral examining are being undertaken. But there is no doubt that more work will be required before reliable and valid methods to serve a variety of purposes are developed.

THE STYLE OF EXAMINING

The form or style of the examination is a factor in the examination situation. This is so whether the examination is a written paper, a practical examination or an oral.

With a new form or style of examination the candidate is set the problem of appreciating the form or style as well as communicating his merits in a particular field of study. It is, therefore, advisable to give candidates appropriate pre-examination experience of the form or style of an examination.

It is not uncommon with the objective type of paper to provide some preliminary practice testing, lasting about 10 to 15 minutes. Here, for example, is a preliminary practice test from a multiple choice mathematics paper:

To make sure that you know what to do, please try the following specimen example, which will *not* count in the test.
Do not hesitate to ask your teacher for help or further information when you are doing this.
Your teacher will provide you with paper on which to do rough working if you wish. This paper will *not* be handed in with your test answers.

Here is the specimen example:

Situation   A boy, asked to multiply 37.5 by 2.5, proceeds first to multiply 375 by 25. He obtains the result 9375.

Questions   (4 possible answers are given for each question. Only *one* of these is correct. When you have decided which is the correct answer, place a tick ($\sqrt{}$) alongside it.)
(A) How many times as great or as small is the boy's result as that of the sum he was asked to do?
(B) What is the answer to the sum he was asked to do?
(C) How much would a Frenchman pay for $2\frac{1}{2}$ railway tickets for which the full fare is 75 francs each?
(D) What is the area of a rectangular strip of paper $2\frac{1}{2}$ cm wide and $37\frac{1}{2}$ cm long?
(E) How long would a car take to do a journey of 93.75 Km at an average speed of 37.5 Km per hour?

A	10 times as great	10 times as small	100 times as great	1000 times as great $\sqrt{}$
B	937.5	93.75 $\sqrt{}$	93,750	9.375
C	187.50 francs	300 francs $\sqrt{}$	1875 francs	93.75 francs
D	93.75 sq. cm.	937.5 sq. cm. $\sqrt{}$	150 sq. cm.	1875 sq. cm.
E	3 hours	25 hours	5 hours	$2\frac{1}{2}$ hours $\sqrt{}$

The right answers are ticked.

The aim of any examination should be to offer the candidate conditions in which he, equally with other candidates, can demonstrate his abilities. Candidates cannot be expected to give of their best if their task is surrounded by uncertainty.

ACKNOWLEDGEMENT

This extract from *An Introduction to Some Techniques of Examining* (1964), Schools Council Examinations Bulletin No. 3, is published here with the kind permission of the Schools Council and the Controller of Her Majesty's Stationery Office.

44 CSE Mode III in English

DON BOYALL

'More demands should be made on the pupils, both in the nature and in the amount of work required. There is a need to stimulate intellectual and imaginative effort, and to extend the pupil's range of ideas in order to promote a fuller literacy.'

NEWSOM REPORT, CH. 4

'Real communication begins when the words are about experience, ideas and interests which are worth putting into language.'

NEWSOM REPORT, CH. 19

Following the introduction of the CSE examination in 1966, greater opportunities were provided and formalized for the participation of teachers in the content and scope of an external examination. Subject–teacher discussion meetings were crowded and enthusiastic. Here was a chance for class and teacher to become involved in what they considered to be the important aspects of their subject for them. It seemed futile at the time to avoid the tyranny of one syllabus, only to accept another (however more civilized) offered by the Mode I scheme. The half-way house of Mode II seemed coy and maidenly so we plunged like libertines into the virgin pastures of Mode III. I do not wish to write in a negative fashion about Modes I and II but rather to stress the positive virtues of Mode III.

The areas of English study which we regarded as important would obviously be so regarded by any teacher of English. Furthermore these values are, for the most part, reflected in the content of the examination papers set by most examining boards. Children should be able to write with fluency, maturity and imagination. They should be able to read with discrimination and understand what they read. They should be able to listen and to speak. There is nothing remarkable or innovatory in these suggestions. Most O-level *English Language* examinations test the first two qualities and the Mode I scheme tests the third. There are probably other external examination forms that test all three. Why then Mode III?

Paramount in our minds was the desire to erode the magnitude of the single day of judgement. Course work had to be an important feature of the scheme and this was duly included and heavily weighted. In the event most of our interest has developed out of this part of the work as I shall indicate later. At its introduction Mode I did not include written comprehension and we felt that this should play a part in any English course. A further quibble with the then offered Mode I scheme involved group situation oral work about which we had several misgivings. We replaced this with an aural test as we believed that the ability to listen was just as important as the ability to speak. We retained the oral work (speech) then included in the Mode I scheme. Our scheme, as to 95 per cent, is shown in table 44.1.

Table 44.1   Mode III scheme

Course work	{ Language 25%
	{ Literature 25%
Aural test	15%
Oral test	15%
Written comprehension	20%

The development of course work as part of the examination has meant freedom for the teacher and freedom for the pupil. At the end of a two-year course students present for assessment a folder of work containing their language and literature studies. This simple device has enriched, liberated and complicated the teacher's work. This is most clearly seen in the teacher's handling of the literature content of the syllabus. We have a simple, basic requirement that each student's folder will include work on poetry, prose and drama. There are no set texts and each individual teacher can choose material to suit the tastes of the class and himself. A concrete example will best reveal the expansive nature of a Mode III course.

During last term one of the English staff set in motion a piece of work by introducing in class a selection of poetry from the First World War which included poems by Brooke, Sassoon, Owen, Gerald Cumberland and Lawrence Binyon. Study of these poems naturally involved discussion of the period and one of the history staff was invited in to talk about the war from a historical point of view. The class was then introduced to *Goodbye to All That* and *All Quiet on the Western Front* (note that under Mode III we can use relevant foreign literature) which they finished reading on their own. Some of the class were involved (on a voluntary basis after school, of course) in a school production of *Oh! What a Lovely War* and most of the class went to see a professional production of *Journey's End*. Other members of the class developed their interest by contacting men who had survived the First World War and using portable tape-recorders to record their reminiscences. These recordings were later used as the basis for written work. A mass of written material was accumulated which included letters, postcards, newspaper cuttings, pamphlets and official war documents. Much useful 'precis' work was done on these. Written work resulted from all of these activities and found its place in all sections of the course-work folder.

The visits to the theatre and the work with tape-recorders have revealed the enormous interest that can be derived from English field studies. The freedom offered to the student in this area is obvious. At a simple, private level each student can add a further dimension to his studies by making careful use of radio, television and the cinema. In a controlled way there is much the teacher can do outside the classroom. We, for example, make extensive use of the theatres in Manchester, Stoke, Bolton, Derby and Liverpool. In addition we have developed friendly and mutually profitable links with the Department of Drama at the University of Manchester. One group of drama department students did a fascinating series of 'lessons' on *Macbeth* in school and on other occasions groups of CSE candidates have worked with students in the University's drama studio. A new theatre, the Forum Theatre, Wythenshawe, run by the Library Theatre Company, has recently opened right on our doorstep. We have naturally made full use of this. A group of candidates saw their production of *Waiting for Godot* which we later discussed in school with the director of the play. This kind of work can be done under any scheme but as part of a Mode III course it contributes directly to the examination result.

After six years of experience with Mode III it has become clear to us that one of its most vital aspects has been the scope it affords the individual student fully to develop a relevant interest. Many of our CSE candidates are members of the school's Brontë Society and take full advantage of the library facilities and lecture programme which it offers. The Society also runs a one-week residential course in Haworth every Easter which many CSE candidates attend. The written work which the candidates produce during the week can be included in their course-work folder. During our annual residential course we take an interest in several aspects of local history. In this connection we have gradually been accumulating information about Jonas Bradley, who was headmaster of the Stanbury Day School from the 1880s to the early 1920s and had a reputation as a teacher with remarkable gifts. One of our candidates has taken a particular interest in this topic and has done a great deal of imaginative biographical research. His inquiries have caused him to place letters requesting information in Yorkshire papers, to make inquiries at Somerset House, to seek out and interview men and women who were pupils of Jonas Bradley, to get information from Moray House where Bradley trained as a teacher and to consult Parish Registers. In other words he has been following the basic procedures which any biographer must follow, working as far as possible from primary sources. The work is so extensive that this candidate will not complete it before his CSE course is over but eventually he will be in a position to write a reasonable biography of his subject as his interest will undoubtedly continue beyond the termination of his examination course. We still have ex-CSE candidates returning to school for literary society meetings. All candidates are encouraged to write about their interests and experiences for the language section of their folder, and each folder should then reflect the personality and developing tastes of its author rather than the requirements of an external examining board.

Our other main departure from the Mode I scheme has been in the area of the spoken word. On one occasion we pre-rehearsed sixth formers who were not involved with the examination in the parts of Antony and Brutus in the funeral oration scene in *Julius Caesar*. We then conducted a rehearsal of the scene using the candidates as the crowd. The rehearsal lasted about 40 minutes and was mainly concerned with the crowd's fluctuating reactions to the two main speakers. The examination questions were based on the rehearsal. For the 1971 examination we took advantage of a matter of local interest – the proposed Manchester Lottery which received a good deal of TV exposure – to base the examination on a debate. We persuaded the two leading TV protagonists to meet each other in debate on the topic in school. The candidates formed the audience and joined in the debate as speakers from the floor. On this occasion, with the Board's permission, we actually wrote the examination questions as the debate proceeded. These were then rapidly typed on a stencil as the candidates left the debating hall for the examination room and were duplicated on the Board's headed, blank examination papers. By the time the candidates were at their desks the papers were ready for distribution.

Such a scheme involves the teacher in much more work than a more conventional scheme. The marking load is heavier – so heavy, in fact, that some form of selective marking, or sample marking, has to be employed. Interested students write at much greater length than bored ones! The liberation has to be paid for. Once the field is wide open, the imaginative teacher will take full advantage of it. He will be involved in the duplication of starter extracts, the acquisition of film, tape and slide material, the recording of radio material; the weekly scanning of TV, radio, cinema and theatre programmes, the organization of theatre visits and work outside the classroom.

On the pupils' side the fact that the course requires sustained effort and an enormous amount of reading and interested involvement will inevitably mean that the lazy or indifferent candidate is penalized in the course-work section. Such a candidate might perhaps achieve a higher grade under Mode I than under our Mode III. On this aspect however I will refrain from comment.

ACKNOWLEDGEMENT

This paper first appeared in *Dialogue* (1972), **11**, 8–9, and is published here with the kind permission of editor and author.

45 An examination of examinations

T. FAWTHROP

A significant fact in analysing examinations is that great importance is attached to them by modern society, and yet though they matter so much to so many people, little sustained research has been carried out on them.

Meanwhile the staffs of universities have carried on in their own sweet way, largely in 'ignorance of the pitfalls that surround the examiner' (Dale, 1959). Dale asserted that 'the biggest obstacle to reform is the calm assurance with which lecturers and professors alike believe that they can carry around in their heads an unfailing correct assumption of an absolute standard of 40 per cent as the pass line', and further that this assumption 'is incomprehensible to anyone who has studied research on the reliability of examinations'.

Other research sustains this viewpoint, but first let us investigate the possible purposes and assumptions of examinations at college level. Examinations must be judged according to their aims, assumptions, functions and results/effects. Only an overall assessment of these four facts can provide one with a comprehensive view of the workings of the whole system, and each aspect of examinations should be related both to the purpose of higher education, and the more specific aims of the course.

Any measure of educational achievement should be *reliable*, *objective* and *relevant* (to the aims of education). The assumptions of examinations are both explicit and implicit. In the next section it is the explicit ones that are dealt with, i.e. the aims of examinations, which assume that existing methods of assessment do and should fulfil certain tasks. The last section considers the other assumptions.

THE AIMS OF EXAMINATIONS

These aims are generally expounded by the staff of universities, whose intellectual task it is to justify to the students and to a wider public the type of examinations that they set, asserting that their own system is a valid test of intellectual achievement. Clearly, there is a considerable area of overlap between the aims and assumptions of the existing system.

Their aims (of an academic nature) include:

  (i) to measure the intellectual ability of the student;
 (ii) to maintain and demonstrate a consistent standard of performance;
(iii) the selection and categorization of different levels of ability;
 (iv) to feed back information concerning the effectiveness of the teaching;
  (v) consolidation of learning;
 (vi) selection for jobs;
(vii) stimulus for students to work.

These are some of the more explicit assumptions underlying the use of examinations, which can be listed (as above) as deliberate aims.

We may question the validity of the examination system on three levels:

(*1*) *Reliability* of examinations, which accepts the assumptions of the present system, but challenges the accuracy of the results.

The other two challenge the assumptions of the system:

(*2*) *Objectivity* in that they do *not* test what they purport to test (i.e. intellectual ability), thus they are not relevant to the stated aims (above).
(*3*) *Relevance* that what they do test conflicts with the 'liberal' aims of education (community of scholars, etc.), thus they are not relevant to the real aims of education.

(1) Reliability

The present system is above all designed to be an efficient selection mechanism. In order for this general purpose to be fulfilled, examinations must be marked with great accuracy, and also the performance of the student should similarly be standardized. All the aims listed above depend for their fulfilment on this criterion of the *reliability of the examinations as a fair measure* of intellectual ability.

Evidence – markers and standards
One must differentiate at this point between those examinations used in natural sciences as opposed to the typical essay-examination, upon which our attention is mainly focused.

The essay-examination has been regarded as suspect since the research work of the 1930s, when these main types of error in marking were exposed:

(a) differences in the standard of marking between different examiners, i.e. the number of marks awarded for individual points, and the overall essay;

(b) differences in the range or dispersion of marks awarded;

(c) differences in criteria used for awarding marks (one aspect of the unreliability of examinations is that of the incredible secrecy about the examination results themselves, and about how the paper has been marked. The students are largely forced to guess the expectations made of them, and certainly they have no way of checking whether even their bad handwriting may have lost them a few vital marks);

(d) artificial fixing of standards to maintain approximately the same number of degree awards each year (e.g. about the same number with first class honours) in spite of the increase in standards of entrance requirements;

(e) differences between departments in most universities (natural sciences tend to gain a larger number of firsts. The Robbins Report found that in 1959 in Britain 12 per cent of students graduating in technology gained firsts compared with 10 per cent in science and 5 per cent in arts);

(f) differences between universities in examination results, suggesting that each university has its own standards, in spite of external examiners;

(g) the personal bias of the examiner. Clearly the individual examiner has considerable power and responsibility for the paper he is marking, yet at the same time he is human (we hope!). The examinee's chances of a good mark may well depend on a 'personal' interaction between the way in which the student presents his arguments and the predispositions and biases of the examiner. Other ephemeral factors such as the mood and health of the examiner, and the order in which the papers are marked, may all enter – subconsciously or otherwise – into the final calculation. One must emphasize that in the final analysis the university examination is an extremely subjective test involving *those who have taught the examinees as their examiners: thus the expectations* of the teacher are almost certain to impinge on and influence the judgement of the examiner.

Now listen to the cry of 'external examiners' in response to the previous indictment! Doubtless they modify the situation in some way, though their capacity to fundamentally change the inherent subjectivity of the university examination system is very doubtful in view of the small number of papers that they usually check themselves. Further, if their judgement involves them in a clash with their colleagues at another university their position might become somewhat difficult, especially if they were challenging the marking of an undisputed authority on the subject. The academic pressure to suppress doubts is clearly greater than that to follow them up and risk conflict and antagonism with the colleagues:

(h) ability of the examiner – experience of an examiner, the degree of precision in his marking, his strictness/latitude, knowledge of the subject;

(i) range of subject matter (the range of subject matter present in an examination represents only a fragment of the whole syllabus, and tests have shown that a second set of questions on the same syllabus with the same students has produced marks often widely at variance with the first examination).

These nine variables combining both errors of marking and fluctuation/stability of standards pose grave 'doubts' concerning the reliability of the system. The research that has been done shows that the range of error can be considerable, and that apart from the factors (g) and (h) dealing with the psychology of the individual examiner, all the other variables have been investigated with the conclusion that the existing system most definitely is unreliable, and unquestionably unfair, to the individual examinee.

In 1963 Pieron summed it up as follows: 'All the experimental data has shown that for a particular performance expressed in terms of an examination script, assessment by different examiners produces marks with considerable variability such that in the *determination of these marks the part played by the examiner can be greater than that of the performance of the examinee.*'

So far we have considered the reliability of the traditional examination in terms of the role of the marker and the standards themselves. What other factors may upset the aspirations of the system (i.e. the *accurate assessment of intellectual ability*)?

Individual performance

'It isn't a matter of knowing all about your subject, it's a matter of knowing all about examinations' (Dennis B. Jackson, Educationalist).

The role of the examinee, and his attitude towards, and performance in, the examination, affect both the immediate issue of *aims-reliability*, but are also intimately related to the other criteria of (2) *objectivity* and (3) *relevance*.

A list of 17 variables below are among the more important factors that determine the performance of the examinee, and these are all *irrelevant to the individual's intellectual capability* (i.e. intellectual capacity may or may not coincide with them – there is no necessary correlation).

These influences are:

(a) examination technique, i.e. proficiency at examinations, ability to adapt to examination requirements;
(b) speed – both in thinking and writing;
(c) timing – ability to conform to the time allowed for each question (the student who knows too much may be penalized!);
(d) 'question spotting' or 'exam-telepathy', perhaps the most important factor of all!
(e) luck – the right question(s) just happening to come up;
(f) normal variance of performance;
(g) quality of teaching, i.e. good 'examination teaching';
(h) ability to persuade/deceive the marker of your intellectual worth;
(i) ability to 'cram' huge 'chunks' of knowledge into one's mind just long enough for an examination;
(j) individual capacity to indulge in a 'memory-orgy';
(k) individual's skill at 'cheating';
(l) the degree of motivation for success, fear of failure, etc.;
(m) the strength of motivation to conform – 'give examiners what they want' attitude – a form of examination strategy designed specifically not to offend the personal views of one's tutor;
(n) ability to make the correct choice of examination questions (inside the hall);

(o) capacity to undergo psychological pressures – stress and strain;
(p) specific social or emotional problems occurring near examination time;
(q) students' ignorance of requirements of the examiner, criteria for marking, etc. ·

All these factors may affect the final result of the examination. Some may be regarded as only marginally significant, e.g. 'cheating', but most of the others are constant variables operating as endemic features of the formal essay-type examination. These factors are largely inconsistent with the basic educational aim, i.e. measuring intellectual ability. How can one measure the latter, when intellect becomes entangled with this formidable array of imponderables, which have no correlation with intellectual ability? Perhaps the outstanding variable is that of examination technique. One exponent of this viewpoint is Dennis B. Jackson ('The Examination Secret') who claims that students, by using his techniques, can achieve and *have* gained exceptional marks whilst only covering 25 per cent of the work set (on average).

Conclusions
How far, then, are the apparent aims of examinations fulfilled? Of the aims enumerated at the beginning of this section, only (i) and (ii) are under consideration at this point, i.e. to measure the intellectual ability of the student; and to maintain and demonstrate a consistent standard of performance. Clearly examinations do not maintain academic standards as such, except arbitrary ones, which have no rational justification. Neither are they successful in providing accurate data on intellectual ability because they fail to fulfil the criteria of reliability, relevance and objectivity. The marker is confronted by a dilemma; his explicit objective is to assess academic ability as such, but in reality he is marking a complex of unknown factors, among which somewhere, submerged beneath the examination debris he may find some *clues* to intellectual ability.

The fact that as students our future is being determined on the basis of such slender, tendentious evidence should be a matter of alarm for all concerned.

These variables, which every examination tests to a lesser or greater extent leads one to draw the following conclusions – that the *present examination system does not so much test intellectual ability as a combination of the errors of the markers, the distortions of accepted standards of 'intellectual attainment' per department per university per year* plus the *seventeen variables* which, fused together with the particular combination of knowledge and understanding of a specific subject, go to make up the individual performance. Any analysis of examination papers, then, uncovers so many variables which affect the final mark, that any attempt to isolate and assess the intellectual component within the traditional system is doomed to failure. We may suspect that the system does a grave injustice to many individuals, but it is so amorphous that its magnitude cannot be determined with any precision.

THE OTHER ASSUMPTIONS OF THE PRESENT SYSTEM

(2) Objectivity, (3) Relevance

The present system clearly defies any attempt to specify what it measures except for a 'hotchpotch' of imponderables. New analysis is required of the validity of testing such variables and, more important, the overall relevance of the basic assumptions and orientations. [The figures in brackets indicate where the specific assumptions are given more detailed consideration, the first figure indicating which part of the book (I) or (II), (III) or (IV).]

Vis-à-vis the student, it is assumed that the present system motivates him/her to work [II(2)], and that the examination results will be an accurate reflection of his academic endeavour and intellectual powers combined together. But the fact remains that some students who prefer not to indulge in too much study during their three years may yet do exceptionally well in their finals through the careful perusal of past examination papers and highly selective methods of learning.

The present system is only valid if society desires to test such capacities as one's ability under pressure [I(7)], the individual's grasp of examination technique, the willingness of the student to enter into the spirit of a glorified memory-orgy. What valid argument can be used to justify on educational grounds the adoption of a time limit on examinations?

More fundamental assumptions may be challenged – *one may doubt*:

whether intellectual ability can be objectively measured [II(4)].
that grading is a necessary process [II(2)].
whether it is wise to attempt to isolate the work of the individual [II(2),(6)].
that examination results have much significance for employers [Part II(5)].

similar assumptions that:

each examinee has individual responsibility for his own performance [I(6)].
the merits of selection [II(2)].
that the quality of academic performance is rateable on a single continuum, or that examination results are predictive of future performance.

It is these assumptions which form the basis of this critique rather than questions of reliability, because even if (unlikely) the existing system was academically fair to the student (i.e. reliable), and the marking system standardized, the deeper education problems remain, which are:

1. *What are you really testing?* and
2. *What qualities should one test? and why?*
3. *How far can these be tested at all?*

(all relating to the relevance of examinations).

Conclusion

'It is not the best student or the best scholar who gains the highest marks in examinations, it is the student with the greatest knowledge of examination technique' (G. E. Grace).

It is a strange system that penalizes the best scholars, those who know too much for examinations, and thus are forced to leave unfinished answers. Is the primary purpose of education to develop examination technique? This is the only basis on which examinations could be justified, in which case one might suggest that education has deteriorated into a form of academic gambling, i.e. play your cards right and you will end up with a good degree!

However, the real problem is that the poverty of academic thinking on the aims of higher education leads to a parallel uncertainty concerning the aims of an assessment system. The educationalists pontificate, the professors can't agree, the junior staff are seen but not heard, and the students are told to accept it – so nobody knows! Until we decide on what higher education is trying to achieve, examinations cannot be justified – a de facto justification is symptomatic of the present intellectual degeneracy.

Further, our empirical 'examination' of the 'de facto' system demonstrated that:

(a) it is notoriously unreliable in awarding marks;
(b) it is an educational fraud, in that it does *not* test what it purports to test but a proliferation of intellectually irrelevant factors; and
(c) that finally its assumptions, explicit and implicit, are ill-founded, conflicting with the objectives of the 'liberal' education. (See Part 2, Sections 1 and 2.)

ACKNOWLEDGEMENT

This paper is an extract from *Education or Examination* (1968), published by The Radical Student Alliance, London.

PART 14

Vocational development and guidance

INTRODUCTION

Of all the theories of vocational development, Super's is one of the best known and most quoted. For this reason an article by him is included. Since writing the paper in 1955, Super has made a massive contribution to the subject and his books should be consulted by those wishing to probe deeper.

A recent paper by Daws presents a widely held view of the function of counselling in schools and provides a thought-provoking summary of the central issues involved.

McKenzie gets down to the 'classificatory dimensions' for the identification of occupational characteristics. He has taken the work of Rodger (seven point plan mentioned in the core text), Bingham and Super from which to compound the dimensions. The paper may now be regarded as too 'quantitative' without offering much in the way of prediction, but it covers most of the significant considerations which are the same today as when the paper was written in the 50s.

46   A theory of vocational development *

DONALD E. SUPER

Two and one-half years ago a colleague of mine at Columbia, Dr Eli Ginzberg, an economist, shocked and even unintentionally annoyed many members of the National Vocational Guidance Association by stating, at the annual convention, that vocational counselors attempt to counsel concerning vocational choice without any theory as to how vocational choices are made. A year later Dr Ginzberg published his monograph on *Occupational Choice*, in which he stated:

> Vocational counselors are busy practitioners anxious to improve their counseling techniques . . . the research-minded among them devote what time they can to devising better techniques. They are not theoreticians working on the problem of how individuals make their occupational choices, for, though they have no bias against theory, they have little time to invest in developing one [Ginzberg et al, 1951, p. 7].

Ginzberg continues, apropos of the fields of psychology and economics:

> . . . there are good reasons why the problem [of how occupational choices are made] has not been a focus of investigation for psychology or economics. . . . The process has roots in the interplay of the individual and reality, and this field is only now beginning to be included in the boundaries of psychological inquiry. The obverse formulation applies to economics, which as a discipline concentrates on a detailed analysis of reality forces and satisfies itself with a few simplified assumptions about individual behavior [Ginzberg et al, 1951, p. 7].

These conclusions were based partly on a review of the research literature which I did at his request, and partly on a number of discussions in which he, his research team, and I participated. Consequently, I have a feeling of responsibility, not for the conclusions which he drew, but for drawing my own conclusions and for sharing them with my colleagues in psychology and guidance.

Basis of Ginzberg's criticisms It may help to point out that Ginzberg's conclusions were based on a review of the research literature which was designed to provide answers to specific questions asked by his research team in order to help them plan their own research project. What synthesizing of results I did was undertaken to answer these questions. I did not attempt to answer the question 'What theories underlie the principles of vocational guidance now generally accepted by practitioners?'

But I do agree with his analysis of the situation with regard to theory construction: we have done relatively little of it, and for the reasons he has suggested. However, this does not mean that we have operated without theory. It is the principal purpose of this paper to set forth a theory of vocational development, a theory inherent in and emergent from the research and philosophy of psychologists and counselors during the past two decades. But first I should like, as a help in formulating a more adequate theory, briefly to present the theory of occupational choice put forth by Ginzberg and his associates, to show how each of

---

* Presidential address at the annual meeting of the Division of Counseling and Guidance, American Psychological Association, Washington, D.C., September 1, 1952.

its elements had already been set forth by psychologists doing research in this field, and to point out some of its limitations.

THE GINZBERG THEORY

As Ginzberg et al (1951) summarize their theory of occupational choice, it contains four elements:

1 *Occupational choice is a developmental process which typically takes place over a period of some ten years.* This theory of Ginzberg's, it should be noted, is one of the points made by the official statement of the *Principles and Practices of Vocational Guidance* (1927), first formulated by the National Vocational Guidance Association 25 years ago; it is a point stressed by Kitson in his *Psychology of Vocational Adjustment* (1925) and in my own *Dynamics of Vocational Adjustment* (Super, 1942) several pages are devoted to a discussion of the fact that 'choosing an occupation . . . is a process which . . . may go on over a long period.'

2 *The process is largely irreversible:* experience cannot be undone, for it results in investments of time, of money, and of ego; it produces changes in the individual. This second theory of Ginzberg's is clearly implied in Charlotte Buhler's 20-year-old theory of life stages (1933), in Lehman and Witty's equally old studies of play interests (1927), in Pressey, Janney and Kuhlen's 13-year-old discussion of adolescent and adult development (1939) and in my own 10-year-old text on vocational adjustment (Super, 1942).

3 *The process of occupational choice ends in a compromise between interests, capacities, values and opportunities.* This third theory of Ginzberg's is well illustrated in the practices of individual diagnosis developed by the Minnesota Employment Stabilization Research Institute 20 years ago and described by Paterson and Darley (1936); it was further demonstrated and described by the Adjustment Service experiment 17 years ago (Bentley, 1935); and it is basic to presentations of the use of diagnostic techniques in texts such as Bingham's (1937) and mine (Super, 1949), both of which appeared before the completion of Ginzberg's study. In fact, Frank Parsons, in 1909, discussed vocational counseling as a process of helping the individual to study both himself and possible occupational opportunities, and to work out a compromise between his abilities, interests and opportunities. He called this last process 'true reasoning'.

4 Ginzberg's final theoretical formulation is that *there are three periods of occupational choice*: the period of *fantasy* choice, governed largely by the wish to be an adult; the period of *tentative* choices beginning at about age 11 and determined largely by interests, then by capacities, and then by values; and the period of *realistic* choices, beginning at about age 17, in which exploratory, crystallization and specification phases succeed each other. Those who are acquainted and Lehman and Witty's early research in the change of interest with age (1927), with Strong's more searching work (1931) in the same area, with Sisson's research in the increasing realism of choice with increasing age (1938), with Charlotte Buhler's research in life stages (1933), and with the use made of these data by Pressey (1939) or by me (Super, 1942), will find these three choice periods familiar. The special contribution of Ginzberg and his associates is the postulation of the successive dominance of interests, capacities and values as determinants of choice before reality begins to play a major role.

It is easy, and perhaps even rather petty, thus to take a theoretical contribution and demonstrate its ancestry, showing that there is nothing particularly original about it. This is, undoubtedly, the normal reaction to claims of originality. But originality is more generally the result of a rearrangement of the old than the actual creation of something new: the rearrangement is original because it brings out details or relationships which have been missed or points up new applications. Ginzberg's theory is indeed an important contribution: this seems clear to me, at least, as I recollect the struggle I had in writing parts of my *Dynamics of Vocational Adjustment* (a struggle which resulted from the lack of a theoretical structure and from inadequate research), and as I work on its revision in the light, among other things, of Ginzberg's theoretical formulation and the thinking which it has stimulated. I have used this critical approach to Ginzberg's work in order to demonstrate that we have not entirely lacked a theoretical basis for our work in vocational guidance, and to show that the elements of theory on which we have based our practice have been sound, at least in that they have foreshadowed the elements which one group of theorists used when they went about constructing a theory of occupational choice.

Limitations of Ginzberg's theory

But this is not the whole story. Ginzberg's theory is likely to be harmful because of its limitations, limitations other than those of research design and numbers in his basic study.

First, it does not build adequately on previous work: for example, the extensive literature on the nature, development and predictive value of inventoried interests is rather lightly dismissed.

Second, 'choice' is defined as preference rather than as entry or some other implementation of choice, and hence means different things at different age levels. To the 14-year-old it means nothing more than preference, because at that age the need for realism is minimized by the fact that the preference does not need to be acted upon until the remote future. To the 21-year-old student of engineering, on the other hand, 'choice' means a preference which has already been acted upon in entering engineering school, although the final action will come only with graduation and entry into a job. No wonder that reality plays a larger part in choice at age 21, when, unlike choice at age 14, it is by definition a reality-tested choice!

A third defect in Ginzberg's theory emerges from these different meanings of the term 'choice' at different ages: it is the falseness of the distinction between 'choice' and 'adjustment' which he and his research team make. The very fact that choice is a continuous process going on over a period of time, a process rather far removed from reality in early youth but involving reality in increasing degrees with increasing age, should make it clear that there is no sharp distinction between choice and adjustment. Instead, they blend in adolescence, with now the need to make a choice and now the need to make an adjustment predominating in the occupational or life situation.

Finally, a fourth limitation in the work of the Ginzberg team lies in the fact that, although they set out to study the process of occupational choice, and although they properly concluded that it is one of compromise between interests, capacities, values and opportunities, they did not study or describe the compromise process. Surely this is the crux of the problem of occupational choice and adjustment: the nature of the compromise between self and reality, the degree to which and the conditions under which one yields to the other, and the way in which this compromise is effected. For the counseling psychologist's function is to help the individual to effect this compromise. He must not only know the factors which must be compromised and how these have been compromised in the experience of others, but also the dynamics of the compromising process, so that he may facilitate this process in his counselee with constructive results.

ELEMENTS OF AN ADEQUATE THEORY OF VOCATIONAL DEVELOPMENT

An adequate theory of vocational choice and adjustment would synthesize the results of previous research insofar as they lend themselves to synthesis; it would take into account the continuity of the development of preferences and of the differences in the stages, choices, entry and adjustment; it would explain the process through which interest, capacities, values and opportunities are compromised. The second part of this paper will be devoted to a sketch of the main elements of such a theory of vocational development as they appear in the literature, and the third and final part will consist of an attempt to synthesize these elements in an adequate theory. The term 'development' is used rather than 'choice', because it comprehends the concepts of preference, choice, entry and adjustment. There seems to be a dozen elements to a theory of vocational development: they are taken up in sequence.

Individual differences   One of the basic elements of a theory of vocational development has been the theory of individual differences, a cornerstone of modern educational and vocational psychology. Kitson based much of his early *Psychology of Vocational Adjustment* (1925) on this theory and on the findings on which it was based. It was essential to the work of the Minnesota Employment Stabilization Research Institute (Paterson and Darley, 1936). It is surely unnecessary to document the fact of individual differences in aptitudes, interests and values, or the significance of these differences for vocational development.

Multipotentiality   A second basic element of theory has been the concept of the occupational multipotentiality of the individual. It was first documented for intelligence by Army psychologists in World War I, and was stressed by Kitson in his early textbook. It was documented for interests by Strong's work on the classification of occupational interests (1943). It is a well-established fact and a basic assumption of vocational counseling that each person has the potential for success and satisfaction in a number of occupations.

Occupational ability patterns   The existence of occupational ability patterns, that is, the fact that abilities and interests fall into patterns which distinguish one occupation from another, was established by the Minnesota Employment Stabilization Research Institute (Paterson and Darley, 1936) and has been confirmed in other studies, particularly those of the United States Employment Service (Dvorak, 1947). People have been found to prefer, enter, remain in, like and succeed most consistently in occupations for which they have appropriate patterns of traits. The theory of the patterning of aptitudes and interests within individuals and within occupational families and the significance of this patterning for choice, entry and adjustment are widely accepted and applied by counselors and psychologists today.

Identification and the role of models   Much has been made of the importance of identification with parents and other adults in individual development by psychoanalytically oriented writers, and this concept is widely used by counseling psychologists regardless of orientation. It has been little documented, however, in psychological research in the vocational choice and adjustment process. The work of Friend and Haggard (1948) and a study by Stewart (Barnett et al, 1952) do, however, provide some objective basis for the theory that the childhood and adolescent identifications play a part in shaping vocational interests, and also provide role models which facilitate the development and implementation of a self-concept, provided that the required abilities and opportunities are present.

Continuity of adjustment   The continuity of the adjustment process was stressed by Kitson in his 1925 textbook as a result of his analysis of the careers of men whose success was attested to by being listed in *Who's Who in America*. The fact that adolescents and adults face a succession of emerging problems as they go through life, and that some of these problems are peculiar to the various life stages, was brought out by the studies of life stages made by Charlotte Buhler (1933) and by those of occupational mobility conducted by Davidson and Anderson (1937), Strong (1943) and Miller and Form (1951). And theories of the development of interests have been formulated by Carter (1944) and by Bordin (1943), theories which I modified slightly in my book on testing and upon which I drew in describing the process of vocational choice and adjustment in a speech first made at Ft Collins, Colorado, in 1949, revised several times, and later published in the journal *Occupations* under the title of 'Vocational Adjustment: Implementing a Self-Concept' (Super, 1951). These formulations are drawn on again as the cement for the various elements which need to be brought together in a theory of vocational development and as an explanation of the process of compromise between self and reality.

Life stages   The work of psychologists and sociologists in describing the stages through which growth and development proceed, and in showing how these stages bear on the process of vocational choice and adjustment, has already been referred to. It was drawn on heavily in the text by Pressey, Janney and Kuhlen (1939), in my own first text (Super, 1942), in Ginzberg's research (1951) and in a recent text on *Industrial Sociology* by Miller and Form (1951) which is as important for its original contribution and synthesis as it is annoying for its bias against anything that does not conform to sociology as they conceive of it. Buhler's theory of development through the exploratory, establishment, maintenance and decline stages is translated into occupational terminology by Miller and Form, who also documented the theory for American careers, while Ginzberg et al (1951) have developed in more detail the phases of the exploratory stage. This latter theory needs confirmation with a larger sample and more objective procedures, in view of Small's (1952) recent failure to confirm it with a somewhat different adolescent sample, but the general theory of life stages is basic to vocational guidance and will be drawn on heavily in my attempt at synthesis.

Career patterns   The formulation of a theory of career patterns resulted from the occupational manifestations of life stages first documented by Davidson and Anderson (1937), added to for a select group by Terman's genetic studies of gifted persons (1947), and then pointed up by Ginzberg and his associates (1951) and by Miller and Form (1951). Career pattern theory appears to be a key element in the theoretical basis of vocational guidance, for it gives the counselor basic assumptions concerning the social, educational and occupational mobility of his counselees, and it enables him to foresee types of problems which a given client is likely to encounter in establishing a career.

Development can be guided   Another basic element in a theory of vocational development is the theory that development through the life stages can be guided. Although there is ample evidence that ability is to some extent inherited, and that personality too has its roots in inherited neural and endocrine make-up, there is also good evidence that manifested aptitudes and functioning personality are the result of the interaction of the organism and the environment. It is a basic theory of guidance as we know it today that the development of the individual can be aided and guided by the provision of adequate opportunities for the utilization of aptitudes and for the development of interests and personality traits.

Development the result of interaction   That the nature of the interaction between the individual and his environment is by no means simple has been brought out by a variety of investigations ranging from studies of the effects of foster homes and of education on intelligence (National Society for the Study of Education, 1940) to evaluations of the effects of occupational information and of test interpretation on vocational plans and on self-understanding (Johnson, 1951). The realization of this fact and the acceptance of this principle have led to a greater humility in our claims for counseling and to a greater degree of sophistication in our use of guidance techniques.

The dynamics of career patterns   The interaction of the individual and his environment during the growth and early exploratory stages, little understood though the process actually is, has been much more adequately investigated than has this same process during the later exploratory, establishment and maintenance stages. We still know relatively little about the dynamics of career patterns. Terman's work (1947) tells us something about the role of intelligence, Strong's (1943) about interests, and Hollingshead's (1949) about social status, but no adequate studies have been made of the interaction of these and other factors in determining whether the individual in question will have a career pattern which is typical or atypical of his parental socioeconomic group. It was partly with this objective that an investigation known as the Career Pattern Study was launched in Middletown, New York, last year.

Job satisfaction: individual differences, status and role   Early theories of job satisfaction stressed the role of intelligence and interest in adjustment to the occupation or to the job, building on studies of the relationships between these traits and occupational stability such as those made by Scott, Clothier and Mathewson (1931, ch. 26) and by Strong (1943). More recently other investigations such as the Hawthorne (Roethlisberger and Dickson, 1939) and Yankee City studies (Warner and Low, 1947), anticipated in this respect by Hoppock's work (1935) and by a minor study of mine (Super, 1939) in job satisfaction, have played up the importance of the status given to the worker by his job, status both in the sense of group membership or belongingness and of prestige.

While researchers interested in the role of one kind of factor or another have tended to emphasize the signal importance of that type of factor, there is nothing inherently contradictory or mutually exclusive in these findings. They can all be included in a comprehensive theory of job satisfaction or work adjustment. This is the theory that satisfaction in one's work and on one's job depends on the extent to which the work, the job and the way of life that goes with them, enable one to play the kind of role that one wants to play. It is, again, the theory that vocational development is the development of a self concept, that the process of vocational adjustment is the process of implementing a self concept, and that the degree of satisfaction attained is proportionate to the degree to which the self concept has been implemented.

Work is a way of life   This leads to a final theory, one that has been more widely accepted and stressed by sociologists than by psychologists, but familiar to most counselors and considered basic by some writers in the field. This is the theory that work is a way of life, and that adequate vocational and personal adjustment are most likely to result when both the nature of the work itself and the way of life that goes with it (this is, the kind of community, home, leisure-time activities, friends, etc.) are congenial to the aptitudes, interests and values of the person in question. In the estimation of many, this is a basic element in a theory of vocational development.

A THEORY OF VOCATIONAL DEVELOPMENT

Now that we have surveyed the diverse elements of a theory of vocational development, there remains the final task of organizing them into a summary statement of a comprehensive theory. The theory can be stated in a series of ten propositions:

1 People differ in their abilities, interests, and personalities.

2 They are qualified, by virtue of these characteristics, each for a number of occupations.

3 Each of these occupations requires a characteristic pattern of abilities, interests and personality traits, with tolerances wide enough, however, to allow both some variety of occupations for each individual and some variety of individuals in each occupation.

4 Vocational preferences and competencies, the situations in which people live and work, and hence their self concepts, change with time and experience (although self concepts are generally fairly stable from late adolescence until late maturity), making choice and adjustment a continuous process.

5 This process may be summed up in a series of life stages characterized as those of growth, exploration, establishment, maintenance and decline, and these stages may in turn be subdivided into (a) the fantasy, tentative and realistic phases of the exploratory stage, and (b) the trial and stable phases of the establishment stage.

6 The nature of the career pattern (that is, the occupational level attained and the sequence, frequency and duration of trial and stable jobs) is determined by the individual's parental socioeconomic level, mental ability and personality characteristics, and by the opportunities to which he is exposed.

7 Development through the life stages can be guided, partly by facilitating the process of maturation of abilities and interests and partly by aiding in reality testing and in the development of the self concept.

8 The process of vocational development is essentially that of developing and implementing a self concept: it is a compromise process in which the self concept is a product

of the interaction of inherited aptitudes, neural and endocrine make-up, opportunity to play various roles and evaluations of the extent to which the results of role playing meet with the approval of superiors and fellows.

9 The process of compromise between individual and social factors, between self concept and reality, is one of role playing, whether the role is played in fantasy, in the counseling interview, or in real life activities such as school classes, clubs, part-time work and entry jobs.

10 Work satisfactions and life satisfactions depend upon the extent to which the individual finds adequate outlets for his abilities, interests, personality traits and values; they depend upon his establishment in a type of work, a work situation and a way of life in which he can play the kind of role which his growth and exploratory experiences have led him to consider congenial and appropriate.

ACKNOWLEDGEMENT

This paper first appeared in *Am. Psychol.* (1955), **8,** 185–190, and is published here with the kind permission of editor and author.

REFERENCES

Barnett, G., Handelsman, I., Stewart, L. H. & Super, D. E. (1952) The occupational level scale as a measure of drive. *Psychol. Monogr.*, **65,** No. 10 (Whole No. 342).

Bentley, J. H. (1935) *The Adjustment Service.* New York: American Association for Adult Education.

Bingham, W. V. (1937) *Aptitudes and Aptitude Testing.* New York: Harper.

Bordin, E. S. (1943) A theory of vocational interests as dynamic phenomena. *Educ. Psychol. Measmt*, **3,** 49–66.

Buhler, Charlotte (1933) *Der menschliche Lebenslauf als psychologisches Problem.* Leipzig: Hirzel.

Carter, H. D. (1944) Vocational interests and job orientation. *Appl. Psychol. Monogr.*, No. 2.

Davidson, P. E. & Anderson, H. D. (1937) *Occupational Mobility.* Stanford: Stanford Univer. Press.

Dvorak, Beatrice (1947) The new U.S.E.S. General Aptitude Test Battery. *Occupations*, **25,** 42–49.

Friend, J. G. & Haggard, E. A. (1948) Work adjustment in relation to family background. *Appl. Psychol. Monogr.*, No. 16.

Ginzberg, E., Ginsburg, J. W., Axelrod, S. & Herma, J. L. (1951) *Occupational Choice.* New York: Columbia Univer. Press.

Hollingshead, A. B. (1949) *Elmtown's Youth.* New York: Wiley.

Hoppock, R. (1935) *Job Satisfaction.* New York: Harper.

Johnson, D. G. (1951) The effect of vocational counseling on self-knowledge. Unpublished doctor's dissertation, Teachers College, Columbia University.

Kitson, H. D. (1925) *Psychology of Vocational Adjustment.* Philadelphia: Lippincott.

Lehman, H. C. & Witty, P. A. (1927) *Psychology of Play Activities.* New York: Barnes.

Miller, D. & Form, W. (1951) *Industrial Sociology.* New York: Harper.

National Society for the Study of Education (1940) In Whipple, G. M. (Ed.), *Intelligence: its Nature and Nurture.* Bloomington, Ill.: Public School Publishing Co.

Parsons, F. (1909) *Choosing a Vocation*. Boston: Houghton-Mifflin.

Paterson, D. G. & Darley, J. G. (1936) *Men, Women and Jobs*. Minneapolis: Univer. of Minnesota Press.

Pressey, S. L., Janney, J. E. & Kuhlen, R. G. (1939) *Life: a Psychological Survey*. New York: Harper.

Principles and Practices of Vocational Guidance. (1927) Cambridge, Mass.: National Vocational Guidance Association.

Roethlisberger, F. J. & Dickson, W. J. (1939) *Management and the Worker*. Cambridge: Harvard Univer. Press.

Scott, W. D., Clothier, R. C. & Mathewson, S. B. (1931) *Personnel Management*. New York: McGraw-Hill.

Sisson, E. D. (1938) An analysis of the occupational aims of college students. *Occupations*, **17**, 211–215.

Small, L. (1952) A theory of vocational choice. *Vocat. Guid. Quart.*, **1**, 29.

Strong, E. K., Jr (1931) *Change of Interest with Age*. Stanford: Stanford Univer. Press.

Strong, E. K., Jr (1943) *The Vocational Interests of Men and Women*. Stanford: Stanford Univer. Press.

Super, D. E. (1939) Occupational level and job satisfaction. *J. Appl. Psychol.*, **23**, 547–564.

Super, D. E. (1942) *Dynamics of Vocational Adjustment*. New York: Harper.

Super, D. E. (1949) *Appraising Vocational Fitness by Means of Psychological Tests*. New York: Harper.

Super, D. E. (1951) Vocational adjustment: implementing a self-concept. *Occupations*, **30**, 88–92.

Terman, L. M. & Oden, M. H. (1947) *The Gifted Child Grows Up*. Stanford: Stanford Univer. Press.

Warner, W. L. & Low, J. D. (1947) *The Social System of the Modern Factory*. New Haven: Yale Univer. Press.

47　Mental health and education: counselling as prophylaxis

PETER P. DAWS

Though school counselling is concerned primarily with prevention rather than cure, in practice the urgent needs of the wayward and the sick leave little time for genuinely preventive work. Furthermore, effective prophylaxis in the strong sense of laying foundations of robust mental health, competence and well-being in *all* children must involve the whole school to some degree, and particularly a team of willing and able teachers working along with the school counsellor on curriculum development in personal and social education. Though the needs of the few can be met by one-to-one counselling, the needs of the many will be answered only through group work. Trained counsellors must take the initiative in such work. They will retard the mental health movement if they permit their colleagues to feel complacently that the appointment of a school counsellor is an ample school contribution to the objectives of preventive psychiatry. Mental health is *every* teacher's business.

It has been repeatedly emphasized since the beginning of the school counselling movement in the mid-sixties that its purpose is prevention of breakdown rather than the rescue of those who are already casualties, and that it is intended to serve the normally occurring needs of all children and not the psychotherapeutic needs of a disturbed, unhappy few. A number of factors has been responsible for this prophylactic conception. One important factor was the initiative of the National Association for Mental Health, which was then preoccupied with finding an appropriate form of expression for its concern with the preventive rather than therapeutic aspects of its work. Seminars were held in Bristol (1963) and in York (1966) under the chairmanship of Lord James of Rusholme, attended by a small but varied group of professional workers in the fields of medicine, education, psychology and social work, to consider the school's responsibility for protecting and promoting the mental health and well-being of children. They recommended that school counselling be considered as one potentially valuable contribution to the protection of the mental health of children (NAMH, 1970).

In addition to the NAMH's concerns, there were other reasons for the emphasis on the problems of *normal* children. It was for instance necessary to allay the anxieties of some psychiatrists and psychologists who feared that counsellors in their enthusiasm might undertake psychotherapeutic tasks with very disturbed children and perhaps also delay the referral of such children to specialist psychomedical services. It is also clear that those who began the training programmes at the Universities of Keele and Reading in 1965 had an essentially educational rather than clinical view of the purposes to which trained counsellors would address themselves, all rather neatly and simply summed up in those days as *educational*, *vocational* and *personal*. Today, there are approximately ten courses claiming to be school or college counsellor training programmes to some extent. They are very varied in their content. Some claim to prepare counsellors 'to do something' for disturbed pupils; none of course prepares counsellors to 'treat' such pupils. All would claim to be concerned with preventive work in the field of mental health.

DEVELOPMENTAL COUNSELLING AS PROPHYLAXIS

Of the theoretical models available at the time when the first British courses in school counselling were set up, that of developmental counselling seemed to fit best the preventive and protective spirit. The writings of Wrenn (1962) and Tyler (1961) have particularly familiarized us with this model. In the course of their development all children are confronted with a series of challenges and transition points which they must adjust to, master, or come to terms with in some way. In Tyler's descriptive phrase, these are opportunities to progress or regress. All children experience the rapid physical changes of puberty and must come to terms with their dawning sexuality. All must work through a changing relationship with adults and authority, including parents, as they move through adolescence, and all must find an identity, if only to face and accept what the world has imposed upon them. All must feel their own way into the adult, post-school world that will be much less considerate and forgiving than school. Furthermore, each child confronts these common challenges and stresses from his own unique standpoint and must therefore find the answers that best suit him. Instruction in universal remedies and solutions is not enough; there is need also for individual counselling if young people are to extract the maximum profit in personal growth from these challenges and not be at times overwhelmed by them. Where there is readily available to young people a counsellor who has considerable understanding of the developmental hurdles that lie before them, including the less certain or predictable ones like bereavement, it is assumed that such young people are enabled to grow into strong, mature personalities better able to withstand life's pressures. They have been protected from the crippling consequences of suffering overwhelming stress unaided.

Such briefly is the theoretical viewpoint of developmental counselling. It has the appearance of idealized and professionalized *parenting* in its purposes, though the counselling relationship through which these objectives are achieved is much more like *befriending*. Basically, the intention is to encourage and protect the child's development not by excluding the pressures of life but by helping him to cope with them and the potential impediments to his development. One would hardly quarrel with the theory. But in practice, one is unlikely ever to achieve the numbers of counsellors that such an ambitious conception implies. They are not likely to in the United States either. In Britain, the transition from school to work or to higher education is the only common developmental hurdle that we have recognized as requiring the guiding help of professional expertise, and even here there are not yet many schools where educational and vocational guidance aspires to – let alone achieves – a very lofty ambition.

COMMON COUNSELLOR ROLES AND THE PREVENTIVE PRINCIPLE

The reality of the counsellor's current position is that he commonly finds he is the only trained person to serve 800 or more pupils, and is given only a part-time counselling brief anyway. In such circumstances, what expression can be reasonably given to the notion of counselling as preventive work? More often than not, crisis-counselling occupies most of his time. He may be asked to 'deal with' the most disturbed children in the school on the grounds that this is where the greatest need lies and that his training fits him better than anyone else in the school to understand them and help them. Most counsellors see the fatuity of attitudes that proscribe them from attempting to do anything for disturbed pupils – on the grounds that their training is inadequate – but which exhort them as teachers to do what they can for such pupils in the classroom. The counsellor may therefore undertake supportive work with such children, working in close collaboration with the specialist psychomedical services and perhaps also with parents. Certainly a strong case could be made for such a therapeutic counsellor (*vide* Maguire, 1971), but such work can only be termed preventive on the grounds that terrible situations should at least be prevented from becoming unendurable.

Another kind of role that the counsellor may find himself pushed into, though he will resist it strenuously, is dealing with all the school's misfits: that is, those whose behaviour is institutionally and perhaps even socially unacceptable – the truants, the persistently violent, the anti-authority nonconformists, the underachievers and poorly motivated, and so on. Most counsellors will resist such a brief partly because they see themselves as identifying and responding primarily to children's needs and problems and only secondarily to those of the school, and partly also because the counsellor's task is made difficult if not impossible if he is perceived by pupils as another arm of the school's disciplinary process. Again, it is straining the notion of prevention to apply it to remedial work with the deviant, the delinquent and the maladjusted, even though it is evident that disapproved behaviour is often a symptom of excessive strain and disturbance.

Perhaps the commonest role that is given the counsellor – and which he fashions for himself – does qualify as prophylaxis, but only in the weakest sense of that term. The counsellor attempts to identify, with the help of colleagues, all cases of distress and distur-bance. The more serious cases are referred to the specialist agencies; the walking wounded are helped in school, either by himself or by a colleague to whom the pupil has preferred to take his problem. The preventive element here lies in the assumption that most psychiatric disturbance begins in small remediable ways and can be prevented by vigilant early detection and helpful intervention. It is a role that only weakly expresses the preventive principle, because an attempt is made to identify the needs not of all children, but only of those who are already flying distress signals. It is always crisis-counselling. Its image is clinical rather than educational.

Of course, prophylactic mental health services in education need not focus upon pupils. They can choose instead to focus upon environmental inadequacies and stresses, intending to remedy the former and alleviate the latter. Much pupil disturbance for example originates in the home, in the inadequacies and hostilities of parents. Some school counsellors prefer to become school-based home-visiting social workers, feeling that in doing so they are get-ting at the roots of a pupil's disturbance. Others, with a taste for diplomacy and with a sense of compassion for a faltering and ailing colleague, attempt to do what they can for those teachers who are producing more than their fair share of unhappy and hostile pupils. Such milieu therapy, such environmental manipulation and rectification, is again prophylactic only in the weakest sense. It derives from responding to those children who are already in the process of breaking down.

Another common counsellor role is centred upon careers work (educational and vocational guidance) and provides a very partial and fragmentary expression of the purposes of developmental counselling. To have helped pupils to make wise educational and oc-cupational choices is to have prevented some potentially serious cases of maladjustment and personal misery. Because of the narrowness of its focus of concern, however, it too cannot be said to be a very strong expression of the preventive principle, however generally useful it undoubtedly is.

Thus despite the emphasis that has been consistently put upon the preventive as distinct from the remedial character of school counselling by originators, theoreticians, trainers and practitioners, one finds only secondary attentiveness to the processes and objectives of prevention in the common counselling roles that have emerged. This is partly the result of counsellors being a scarce resource. To identify and respond to *all* the personal developmen-tal needs of children would require thousands of counsellors. We have, perhaps, 300. Furthermore, it is predictable and perhaps justifiable that in the competition for benefit from a scarce resource the needs of the disturbed and unhappy should have priority over the less pressing ones of the competent and the confident. But perhaps we should question the view that individual counselling is the main or the most appropriate vehicle for the achieve-ment of mental health objectives in schools. In the end counselling must restrict itself to attempting only what it most appropriately can, and we must desist from claiming for counselling more than this. What is left undone should at least be very evidently so, and counsellors should be prepared in co-operation with other staff to seek more appropriate ways of achieving those prophylactic purposes for which one-to-one counselling proves to be less suited or too costly.

LEVELS OF PREVENTIVE WORK

The counselling movement with its emphasis on preventive work in the mental health field has followed by little more than half a century the inauguration of the School Health Service, whose concern has been to protect the physical health of children. The pioneering example of that service provides a useful guide for the development of sound prophylactic measures by those concerned with protecting and enhancing the mental health of children. The provision of school meals, milk and health education has added significantly to the benefits obtained from routine medical inspection of all pupils. By the same token, mental health provision must do more than merely screen the total school population regularly for signs of distress and maladjustment (a modest level of provision that we are still far from achieving). It must make positive steps to provide healthy children with insight and skills so that their vulnerability to breakdown is reduced. To change the medical analogy: a mental health equivalent of inoculation is needed, providing whatever will increase the child's protection against the adverse effects of stress. Of late, there have been visionary moves to bring mental health more explicitly within the prophylactic purposes of the School Health Service (Francis, 1966). The coincidence of such progressive thinking and the development of school counselling services makes it doubly ironic that the School Health Service is to be disbanded in 1974 and its medical and social work components relocated within hospitals and social service departments. If preventive mental health is to be taken seriously by schools, the starting-point is to recognize especially *vulnerable* children – those who are particularly *at risk* in some sense or other. There are three main classes of vulnerable child: (a) those who will be subject to some special form of stress or risk, such as immigrant and coloured children, the handicapped, the sexually active, children in care, the immature school leaver, the bereaved, etc.; (b) those whose capacity for coping with normal stresses is atypically low – that is, delicate children and dull children; and (c) those whose deviant and delinquent behaviour will bring down upon them the wrath and the censure of the rest of us. If children within these categories can be identified before they are showing evidence of adaptive stress (though of course deviance and delinquence are often themselves distress signals) some genuinely preventive work can be undertaken. They can be helped to understand in advance the kinds of challenge and stress that lie ahead for them, and can be given the insights and competences they specifically need to deal with them effectively. Such work will require a teaching or group guidance approach rather than individual counselling, though counselling will be an invaluable support service.

But the strongest expression of the preventive principle in secondary school work is that devoted to the personal and social education of *all* pupils, for such work genuinely attempts to anticipate the developmental needs of all children, or at least those needs that are universal. It is an economically sensible alternative way of meeting the objectives of developmental counselling outlined at the beginning of this paper. It lacks only the sensitivity that counselling would have of responding to the unique individual needs of children. It implies such areas as health and sex education, moral education and personal relationships, social education, careers education (including self-awareness work, decision making and uses of leisure), and so on. It implies that time will be found on the timetable, that competent and willing staff will be available for the innovative curriculum planning that is required as well as for doing the work. It also implies a considerable opportunity and responsibility for the counsellor, who can help his colleagues appreciate the mental health objective of such work and the ways in which they are most effectively achieved in group work. This requires of the trained counsellor a co-ordinative function and an educative one as far as his colleagues are concerned.

Finally, it must not be overlooked that environment-focused (as distinct from pupil-focused) preventive work is possible and desirable. If all children were wanted children, welcomed by emotionally secure and loving parents, mental health casualties in our society would be more than halved. This implies a very ambitious conception of parental education far beyond the counsellor's or even the social worker's insinuation into a disturbed home on behalf of a reactively disturbed child. Similarly, great benefits would accrue to the mental health of children if schools were purged of unnecessarily stressful values, customs and practices, and staffed by caring and vigilant teachers. This, too, implies a degree of institutional change and of attitude change in many teachers that goes far beyond the friendly quiet word with the harassed and fractious teacher. Though one cannot ask counsellors to involve themselves in the emotional education of parents-to-be, except as part of the upper school's personal and social education programme, it is legitimate to ask them to find acceptable ways of introducing their insights and their values to colleagues for their consideration. After all, counsellors are in the best position to evaluate the impact of the school and of individual teachers on pupils. They can say where the shoe is pinching. It is long-term work and should only be undertaken with modesty and humility, but the counsellor's potential value as an agent of change on the educational scene may prove to be his most important long-term contribution to preventive psychiatry.

CONCLUSIONS

Let us summarize the observations, the arguments and the recommendations:

1 Pupil-focused preventive work has three levels which in increasing order of strength are (a) the deviant and the distressed, (b) vulnerable children, and (c) *all* children. Few counsellors go beyond the first stage except to be involved in educational and vocational guidance.
2 Contextual or environment-focused preventive work has two main areas: the school and the home. Here, too, what is done by counsellors is frequently remedial rather than preventive: help for an irascible teacher or intervention in a disturbed family. Counsellors should find opportunities to acquaint their colleagues with their philosophy, their values and their insights so that mental health objectives may become more explicitly evident in the ethos of the school.
3 The pressure of coping with the immediate and the urgent is likely to keep counsellors crisis-orientated and therefore only weakly involved in prophylactic work, the major contribution to which is more likely to be personal and social education programmes and not

individual counselling. It follows that if the counsellor is to put his training to serve prophylactic purposes in a stronger way he must take the initiative in guiding teams of colleagues – a pastoral care team and a personal and social education team – and in co-ordinating their endeavours. The counsellor should also try to make time to be personally involved in the personal and social education programme. It will serve to introduce him to his possible clients and it will refresh him for the more emotionally draining work of counselling the distressed.

There is a real danger that the prophylactic role of the counsellor has been so widely emphasized and disseminated that the minimal sense in which most counsellors serve preventive ends (a situation unlikely to change very much) will go unrecognized. Heads of school may then feel that the mental health needs of their school are being adequately met by the trained counsellor. In fact, a strong prophylactic programme is not so cheaply achieved. It requires a team of suitable teachers, curriculum planning and a share of the timetable for all children. It would be a pity if the gap between the counsellor's prophylactic image and the realities of his work was allowed to retard rather than enhance the rate of progress in developing a positive educational programme to give all children sound foundations to their mental health.

Finally, a postscript. A paper on counselling and the implications for education of preventive psychiatry must at least question the assumption that the secondary school is the most appropriate place to start making special provision for the protection and enhancement of the mental health of children. Quite evidently, many cases of serious adolescent disturbance could have been identified during the primary school years and more effective help given. If suitable primary school teachers were offered something analogous to the counselling training now available to secondary school teachers, the mental health movement in education could be helped to spread effectively down to the youngest pupils. Three purposes could be considered: (a) the prompt identification of disturbed children; (b) the early involvement of parents in any work that is undertaken; and (c) the development of suitable personal and social education programmes. This way it may be possible to bring help to those parents who cannot readily admit their own inadequacies or their children's disturbance and who resist their children's referral to a child guidance clinic. The coming dismemberment of the School Health Service gives an added urgency to the development of a primary-school-based mental health movement.

ACKNOWLEDGEMENT

This paper first appeared in *Br. J. Guid. Counsel.* (1973), 1 (2), and is published here with the kind permission of editor and author.

REFERENCES

Francis, H. W. S. (1966) The medical examination of children in relation to the prevention of mental ill-health. *Med. Officer*, **116**, 209–214.

Maguire, U. (1971) *The Effectiveness of Short-Term Counselling on Secondary School Pupils*. Ph.D. thesis, University of Keele.

National Association for Mental Health (1970) *School Counselling*. London: NAMH.

Tyler, L. (1961) *The Work of the Counsellor*. New York: Appleton-Century-Crofts.

Wrenn, C. G. (1962) *The Counsellor in a Changing World*. Washington: American Personnel and Guidance Association.

48   An occupational classification for use in vocational guidance

R. M. McKENZIE

INTRODUCTORY

Theoretically, in giving vocational guidance one could assess the characteristics of a 'client' and then match them one by one or as a pattern against those needed in various jobs to find the best fit. But jobs are so many, the characteristics of people so diverse, that this is impracticable. Our approach, on which a preliminary note has appeared elsewhere (McKenzie, 1952), is to select certain important characteristics of people actually in jobs, and on these base our grouping of jobs. Assessing the client in similar terms leads one to the relevant area of classification, so reducing choice to jobs that are definitely feasible for him. Within this range, choice will then depend on other factors, including such local considerations as which jobs are actually available in the district, what kind of workmates he will meet, idiosyncrasies of firms, and even of foremen, and so on.

Thus the first aim is to make a 'Search List' which provides worthwhile job suggestions all within the client's range. It must be easy to use, it must narrow the search without blinkering the user, it must be psychologically sound. It must aim not at solutions, but suggestions. At the same time it should fit into or be easily adapted to existing vocational guidance methods so as to make the fullest use of all the material available.

CHOOSING CLASSIFICATORY 'DIMENSIONS'

There is some agreement on characteristics that differentiate people in a way useful in guidance. Thus Rodger's seven main points (1939, p. 259; 1952), Bingham's nine points (1942, p. 94), and Super's 'psychological' facts and 'social' facts (1949, pp. 6–7), all cover much the same ground. The headings are roughly: intelligence, educational attainments, aptitudes, interests, personality traits and attitudes, general 'circumstances' (resources, responsibilities, ambitions, family and cultural background, etc.), and physique. In selecting 'dimensions' from these for our basic grouping of jobs, six criteria are suggested. Each 'dimension' should:

1 have a precise, easily communicable definition;
2 be reliably and economically measurable in clients;

3 be similarly measurable in people in various jobs. If a test is used, it must (a) be easily administered to groups of people in different jobs, often under primitive conditions, and (b) be comparable with tests of the same dimensions used elsewhere, so as to build up occupational norms;
4 differentiate people in different jobs or groups of jobs;
5 be relevant to satisfactory job performance or stipulated for entry;
6 persist in the client, unless needed only for entry.

These criteria raise problems we have space only to mention, such as the familiar one of criterion of 'satisfactory' performance; and the possibility that success depends on similar basic qualities in many different jobs; or that it may depend less on the man than on his relationship with his workmates, or his supervisor, for perhaps in peace, as in war, there are no bad regiments, only bad officers. Leaving these on one side, however, we may now go on to check possible dimensions, somewhat summarily perhaps, against our criteria. (See table 48.1, below.)

General intelligence

1 This can be suitably defined and forms a continuum.
2 It can for our purpose be reliably and cheaply measured in clients.
3 It can be measured in the field, too; some occupational scores are already available.
4 Intelligence test scores differentiate between groups or levels of jobs, less well between individual jobs. Mean scores of occupational samples do fall into a hierarchy (e.g., Cattell, 1934; Super, 1949), but may differ from one another by very little. Thus 15 points of raw score (test maximum 60) can cover the means of 17 occupational samples (Lingwood, 1952). Also, scores in a single job may range as widely as from the 20th to the 90th percentile (Vernon, 1949), so that ranges, even inter-quartiles, overlap considerably (Cattell, 1934). These wide ranges might be due to grouping scores of people who nominally do the same job, but actually have different scope, responsibilities, or degrees of skill. They occur so regularly, however, that the hypothesis is doubtful. At the moment, certainly, intelligence test scores do not differentiate jobs so precisely that a client's score can do more than point to a fairly wide area of jobs.
5 Correlations between intelligence and training criteria are often high (Vernon and Parry, 1949). Sometimes this simply shows how much theoretical or abstract material is included in the training (Jenkins, 1946); relevance of intelligence to the actual work is hard to prove. Thus, although Wyatt (1929) showed that while the more intelligent girls of his group disliked certain repetitive work and the less intelligent liked the same work, yet output of the brighter stayed above the average, that of the duller stayed below. It can be argued that if a person's score is much higher than the job requires he will need other incentives like promotion prospects, high pay, etc., to prevent his becoming so dissatisfied that he leaves. The argument for 'streams' in schools has some similarities. This consideration would imply a relevant upper limit of intelligence, not so much for doing the job as for staying in it. On the other hand, as Super (1949, p. 103) points out, a score above a certain minimum for the job does not necessarily pay corresponding dividends in the form of better performance.

It may be supposed too that a person will 'adjust' best where the mean score of fellows resembles that of his own, but evidence outside school is scarce. If the score is far below the

Table 48.1 Characteristics of people checked against six criteria to select dimensions for a basic classification of occupations for vocational guidance purposes

	Intelli-gence	Attain-ments	Aptitudes	Interests	Person-ality	Circum-stances	Physique
1. Precise definition	Yes	Yes	Yes, as factors	Only by inventory	A few traits have	Cumbrous	Negatively
2. Assess-ed relia-bly, cheaply, in clients	Yes	Yes	Reliably; not cheap	Yes, by inventory. Not cheap	Not yet	Some aspects, others difficult	Negatively
3. Assess-ed relia-bly, cheaply, in the field	Yes	Yes	Reliably; not cheap	Yes, by inventory. Not cheap	Not yet	Some aspects, others difficult	Negatively
4. Differ-entiate jobs	Broad levels only	Broad levels only	Most too specific	*A priori* exc. by inventory	Not yet	Broad groups only	A few
5. Rele-vant to success	In some jobs, especially to training	In some especially to entry	Hard to validate	*A priori* mainly	Not yet	Relevant to guidance	Some-times
6. Persists	Yes	'Nominal' yes; 'residual' may	Yes	Inventory yes, over 17 years	Aspects do	Some aspects only	Yes
Useful later	Possibly	Yes, e.g. specific subjects	Yes	As 'leads'	Yes	Yes, in detail	Yes, bars may be critical

occupational mean he may find it hard to compete for promotion, perhaps even to do the job. But the occupational mean found is not necessarily the optimal nor the minimal score for the job. Unger and Burr (1931) showed that many jobs can come within the reach of girls of the lowest intelligence. If they are suitably trained and have no personality difficulties, girls with a mental age of six years, for instance, can successfully do light factory or domestic work. In any case the range of intelligence found in many jobs is so wide, and often reaches so low that clearly intelligence is at best only one factor in success. Super (1949, p. 103), commenting on the lack of research into the relation between intelligence and success in higher professions, in skilled trades and in unskilled occupations, suggests there would be a positive relation in the first two and none in the last, but says 'this is still an unverified hypothesis'.

6 Tested intelligence is relatively constant over the ages involved, i.e., from 15 years onwards.

Summing up, intelligence can be suitably defined, and assessed reliably and cheaply. It differentiates groups of jobs; a certain minimum for the job may be a factor in success, especially in intellectual work, or where training is intensive; intelligence persists. Some occupational data already exist; they show intelligence found. Minimum intelligence *required* is usually a function of the time available for training. Fuller validation is possible. General intelligence, then, is a possible basic dimension, if used cautiously and along with others.

Educational attainments

1 The general level of attainment can be usefully defined by certificates won, type of curriculum, duration of schooling, consistency of progress, scores on attainment tests, or by combinations of these, and can be made into some kind of continuum.

2 and 3 In such terms it can be assessed in clients and in the field.

4 Attainments required differentiate between groups of jobs, less well between individual jobs. Use of standardized tests can improve this (e.g., Lingwood, 1952).

5 Attainments are believed relevant in many jobs, subjects or groups of them being quoted as important; relevance to the actual work of scores on standardized tests can be validated (Vernon and Parry, 1949). What is critical in guidance, however, is quite often the entry level stipulated or accepted, even if this serves simply to raise the status of the job, or to limit entry, without being related to the actual work at all.

6 A certificate gained is gained for ever, but 'residual ability' in terms of attainment test scores may change considerably after leaving school (Wall, 1944). With reference, then, to jobs where 'nominal level' only is involved, attainment level persists; where 'residual ability' is involved it may not persist.

Summing up, general level of attainments seems useful as a basic dimension; it is already used as a main criterion in many fields of selection.

Special aptitudes

1 'Aptitudes' can be clearly defined only as test scores.

2 'Tested' aptitudes can be reliably assessed. Being so specific, however, several tests may be needed, adding to time and cost.

3 Assessment in the field is costly; few useful data are ready to hand.

4 Some, especially the *v:ed* and *k:m* groups, do differentiate jobs usefully (Vernon, 1950). As Vernon remarks, others are too specific for vocational guidance, though useful in selection.

5 Some are known to be associated with success in jobs, but wider validation is needed. Apparent relevance suggested through 'naming' may be spurious.

6 'Aptitudes' persist well enough for our purpose.

Summing up, many aptitudes are very specific; occupational validation in this country is scarce. Aptitudes cannot yet offer a basic classification, but may be useful within classes or levels, or to confirm eventual choice.

Interests

This word is used to mean so many different things, and the notion in general is so closely connected with such factors as abilities, environment, education and emotional needs, that any full discussion would be lengthy.

1 'Interest' as a psychological concept is hard to define (Berlyne, 1949; Vernon, 1953). We may perhaps confine ourselves to 'interests' as usually spoken of in vocational guidance. Here interests in the sense of 'specific interests' can simply be indicated – woodwork, cycling, etc. Taken singly, however, these rarely have direct counterparts in jobs; moreover a person's specific interests are often limited by experience and opportunity, while their actual content may mean less to him than the friends, status, etc., involved. Specific interests, in short, may not show 'what he is really after'. As a result stress is usually laid instead on his underlying pattern or type of interests. Such 'types' can be identified on *a priori* grounds. Various 'interest factors' have also been statistically isolated, e.g., 'scientific', 'system', etc. (Super, 1949, p. 381; Eysenck, 1953), but naming of these has to be very tentative. In any case, the interest 'type', 'pattern', etc., of a client, and also the 'types' of interest involved in jobs, are difficult to identify except in terms of an agreed test. Strong (1943) makes his approach to this by showing that people in different jobs make characteristically different patterns of responses to items on his Vocational Interest Blank. A particular client's pattern of responses may then be typified as resembling that of dentists, bankers, etc.; the actual 'interests' or 'types of interest' need not be named at all.

2 and 3 One may assess interests (Super, 1949) as *Expressed* – 'he likes, dislikes, or is indifferent to' a given activity; as *Manifest* – inferred from how he actually spends his time; as *Tested* – achievement in, or knowledge about, various activities; as *Inventoried* – the pattern found from a standardized and validated questionnaire (Strong, 1943; Kuder, 1949). (Sometimes, too, Expressed, Manifest and Tested aspects are taken as a continuum of *degree* of interest.) Expressed specific interests tend to be unstable, although giving interview leads, while it is hard to tell how far a Manifest interest is a function of opportunity, parents' income, etc., i.e., how far it shows what a person would be interested in if he had a wider choice. Similarly Tested interest is a function of intelligence, education and opportunity. 'Inventoried interests', however, can be reliably assessed. Unfortunately some Inventories are laborious to score, except by machine; material is expensive; no such Inventory has been validated in Britain.

4 'Inventoried interests' do differentiate jobs, in that responses of people in different jobs differ. Interests assessed in other terms look as if they *must* differentiate, but validation is hard to find. In differentiating jobs by the type of activity involved (rather than by the interests of people in them) so as to link with the type of interests the client has, various difficulties arise. One is how to limit the number of possible groups; another is how to decide – 'from the outside' – what the main activity is in jobs which involve several. Some jobs, too, seem to call for different interests at different stages; an engineer may at first do practical work, advance to drawing office and technical studies, graduate to costing and estimating, and finally, as a manager, handle many human problems. Thus the Committee on Education for Management (1947, p. 20) found in one survey of professional associations that 70 per cent of men who originally qualified as engineers or accountants engage later in some managerial function. Another difficulty in *a priori* grouping is seen in a study by

Thurstone (1932) who analysed 18 of Strong's occupational scales (each built on the responses of people in the given occupation). He found four factors which he named interest in science, language, people and business. Taking only three of the scales the loadings were: Doctors: science +0.71, language +0.33, people −0.26, business −0.09. Teachers: +0.36, +0.15, +0.68, −0.22. Psychologists: +0.77, +0.47, −0.04, −0.28. *Prima facie*, all these jobs involve a marked interest in people, but evidently not in the same terms.

5 As for relevance of interests to jobs, it would have to be shown that entrants with certain interests do the work better and/or enjoy it more than entrants with other interests, and also that they do certain jobs better than they do other jobs. Evidence of this kind is obviously scarce. Strong, however, finds a relation between inventoried interests and success (1943). There are signs too (Strong, 1952) that the more closely a person's pattern of responses resembles that of a given occupation, the more likely he is eventually to be engaged in it.

6 Specific interests may be unstable, especially in adolescence. Inventoried interests too may be unreliable below the age of 17 (Strong, 1943). From that age onwards, however, inventoried interests do seem to persist. Thus the correlation between scores on Strong's 'engineer' scale, taken at the university, with scores one year later is 0.91, with re-test nine years later 0.77, and 19 years later 0.76 (Strong, 1952). Even so, the older a person is at first test, the more likely are test and re-test to agree (Strong, 1951).

Summing up, interests are hard to define and objective measures in this country few. Even when using occupationally validated inventories extrapolation beyond validated jobs must be cautious. Interest in the sense of drives and emotional needs is clearly important, but just as hard to validate occupationally. Lacking validated instruments interests cannot be used for basic classification, though offering useful leads later on.

'Personality'

1 This can be variously defined. To exclude aspects like cognitive abilities, physical characteristics, etc., is artificial but useful, but to separate, say, 'Interests' from 'Personality' is barely possible. Even so, what remains has many dimensions. Operational definition of some is possible, e.g., Eysenck's two 'main dimensions' of general neuroticism and 'introversion–extraversion' (1947), or Vernon's 'dependability' and 'extraversion–introversion' (1953). Some traits discussed in guidance are in line with these, e.g., 'steadiness or reliability'. Others are less easy to define, e.g., 'influence over others', 'initiative'.

2 As for assessment in a client, even the agreed important dimensions involve using several tests, few of which are yet in general use in Britain. Other methods of assessing traits tend to be unreliable. A group of people can be reliably compared with each other, but it is less easy to rate a single client reliably unless against an actual job.

3 Measuring personality dimensions of good and bad workers in jobs is even harder.

4 It may be that people in certain jobs differ characteristically from those in others in respect to some dimensions of personality, e.g., on the face of things, extraversion–introversion, but this awaits validation. One feels too that some of the subjectively defined and assessed traits *must* differentiate jobs, but again validation is needed.

5 Aspects of personality (as in 1 above) are believed to be relevant to success in many jobs, e.g., as accounting for some variance beyond intelligence, etc., but it is not clear how much of which aspect is needed in which jobs. Certain traits do appear relevant to success.

Some unfortunately seem relevant to all jobs, i.e., do not differentiate; Vernon's 'dependability' would *sound* like an example. Behaviour too depends partly on the context; e.g., on group pressure to arbitrary norms of output; the impact of the group in shaping attitudes and motivations; the type of supervision; lack of definition of one's role or status; implications for behaviour of the technological process; and so on. Performance in any job depends not only on the person's traits, and of course his intelligence, aptitudes, etc., but on the interaction of these with the characteristics of the situation, the role he is given, etc. Considering how unreliable is the assessment of many traits, validation of their differential relevance to jobs is bound to be especially difficult.

6 Aspects of personality do persist. Since, however, behaviour is partly determined by actual job conditions, the range of prediction is clearly limited.

Summing up, personality, even in our restricted use here, has in itself many dimensions. Objective measurement of some is possible, and occupational studies have started (e.g., Heron, 1951). At present, however, we cannot make a basic classification of occupations in terms of personality traits.

Circumstances

This refers to a person's 'general context'; points that arise include: How long a training, or even delay in picking a job, can he afford? How important will his wages be? Will his family back him up? Encourage him through his apprenticeship or classes? Will they worry about status? Will tensions in the family upset his work? What are the jobs of relatives and friends and their attitudes towards them? What are their ambitions, values, standards? It is clear that many factors are involved, acting upon one another, counter-balancing one another in complex ways.

1 For our purpose these factors are important in so far as they affect choice of jobs. It may be possible to consider them as a single complex 'dimension', in such terms as 'Background Support' – how much, or how little, he can rely on outside of himself. Points on a scale may be sufficiently clearly indicated by general statements combined with examples.

2 Some aspects of the 'dimension' can be reliably assessed, e.g., economic ones. Others, like stability of the family group, parents' values and standards, involve difficulties, yet are familiar and in fact regularly assessed for various purposes. The more time available, however, the more chance there is of reliable assessment.

3 Similarly this 'dimension' is hard to measure in people in jobs, although certain aspects can be reliably assessed.

4 The 'dimension' does differentiate broad groups of occupations. The economic aspect is often critical, though losing its importance in many jobs. It remains true, however, that entrants need better Background Support in some jobs than in others.

5 'Background Support' is often relevant to satisfactory work, to judge from statements by foremen and others; its importance, in one form or another, is stressed by various authorities (e.g., Wilson, 1945). In guidance it is certainly relevant; often a single aspect may make it critical, e.g., cash for living costs while training. On the whole it is most often relevant to entry into, or during training for, a job.

6 Some aspects persist or can be predicted; others are unpredictable.

Summing up, the 'dimension' Background Support is difficult to validate occupationally, but seems to differentiate broad groups of jobs, and is usually persistent enough for our purpose. In our society its relevance to guidance, if not to performance, is hard to dispute; this alone probably makes it an essential dimension.

Physique

1 Physical measurements can be precise (height, weight), but are rarely relevant. Operational definitions of 'physique' are unwieldy and often impracticable – e.g., 'can lift x lbs. through y feet z times a day'. 'General health' too is hard to define except as lack of apparent disabilities. 'Unfitness' can be defined by specific disabilities; these may exclude or 'bar' particular jobs, e.g., 'not fit to stand all day', rather than lead to positive suggestions.

2 A general estimate of a client's health can be made and disabilities noted as 'bars'.

3 Similarly workers in jobs can be assessed physically in rather general terms and disabilities associated with low success noted. Emphasis is usually on negative statements.

4 Physique sometimes differentiates jobs, but most need moderately active, healthy people. Some 'bars' do differentiate; e.g., colour blindness does not debar from all jobs.

5 In a few jobs general physique is relevant; single elements may be critical, e.g., height for a policeman. Some disabilities too are critical, but 'bars' must be carefully validated; a bus conductor would seem to need all his fingers, yet one with a total of five missing is known to be doing well.

6 Physique in general terms persists; disabilities may be temporary.

On the whole, physique is not a convenient 'dimension' for basic classification. On occasion, of course, even a single aspect of it may be critical in guidance. Because stress is so often on negative statements – on 'ruling out' – it is simpler to consider physical characteristics after reaching a 'short list' of jobs.

SUMMING UP

Our list probably includes those dimensions about which most is at present known for vocational guidance. Of these, Intelligence, Attainments and Background Support most nearly meet the criteria, as table 48.1 shows. With fuller occupational validation Aptitudes might come higher on the list; already the $v{:}ed$ and $k{:}m$ dichotomy, used cautiously, is valuable. Interests and Personality come some way behind, while Physique, however important, does not give *positive* leads. All through, however, relevance to actual job requirements is still in question, even for instance in the case of intelligence. The danger lies in stressing characteristics, less because they are essentially relevant, than because they are conveniently measurable. With these provisos in mind, however, it seems possible to use Intelligence, Attainments and Background Support, or a combination of them, to make a basic classification fit for our purpose, i.e., to produce in a limited time reasonably sound job suggestions. Though these three measures probably correlate with one another over large samples, in individual cases (our main concern here) each is likely to add something new to the assessment of the client.

It is not our aim, however, simply to say how jobs *might* be classified. We must go on to the next step, which is to find the Intelligence, Attainments and Background Support actually required in different jobs. We can then rate each job, by rating people in it, in terms of these. Jobs of similar ratings can then be grouped together. Rating a client in corresponding terms leads us to a group of jobs all needing basic abilities at his level. To decide which of the jobs *of his general level* should be further considered, we must turn to other characteristics including aptitudes, interests, traits, and to our local knowledge. Such considerations need differentiate only within that level. Eventual choice thus demands more detailed study both of the client and of the job suggestions that arise. Our present discussion suggests a definite order of priority in collecting information for job descriptions and the limits of weight that can safely be put on the information thus obtained. It is hoped in a later article to describe the actual construction of a Search List in these terms, and to outline its use.

ACKNOWLEDGEMENT

This paper first appeared in *Occup. Psychol.* (1954), **28**, 108–117, and is published here with the kind permission of editor and author.

REFERENCES

Bingham, W. V. (1942) *Aptitudes and Aptitude Testing.* London: Harper.

Berlyne, D. E. (1949) Interest as a psychological concept. *Br. J. Psychol.* (*General Section*), **39**, 184–195.

Cattell, R. B. (1934) Occupational norms of intelligence and standardisation of an adult intelligence test. *Br. J. Psychol.* (*General Section*), **25**, 1–28.

Committee on Education for Management (1947) *Education for Management.* Report of a special Committee; Ministry of Education. London: H M S O.

Eysenck, H. J. (1947) *Dimensions of Personality.* London: Routledge & Kegan Paul.

Eysenck, H. J. (1953) *The Structure of Human Personality.* London: Methuen.

Heron, A. (1951) *A Psychological Study of Occupational Adjustment.* Ph.D. Thesis London: University of London Library.

Jenkins, J. G. (1946) Validity for what? *J. Cons. Psychol.*, **10**, 93–98.

Kuder, G. F. (1949) *Examiner Manual for the Kuder Preference Record.* Chicago: Science Research Associates.

Lingwood, Joan (1952) Test performances of A.T.S. recruits from certain civilian occupations. *Occup. Psychol.*, **26**, 35–46.

McKenzie, R. M. (1952) Occupational classification in vocational guidance. *Br. Psychol. Soc. Qu. Bull.*, **3**, 88–90.

Rodger, A. (1939) The work of the vocational adviser. In Bartlett, F. C. et al (Eds.), *The Study of Society.* London: Routledge & Kegan Paul.

Rodger, A. (1952) *The Seven-Point Plan.* Paper Number One. London: National Institute of Industrial Psychology.

Strong, E. K. (1943) *Vocational Interests of Men and Women.* London: Oxford University Press.

Strong, E. K. (1951) Permanence of interest scores over 22 years. *J. Appl. Psychol.*, **35**, 89–91.

Strong, E. K. (1952) Nineteen-year follow-up of engineer interests. *J. Appl. Psychol.*, **36**, 64–74.

Super, D. E. (1949) *Appraising Vocational Fitness.* New York: Harper.

Thurstone, L. L. (1932) A multiple factor study of vocational interests. *Person. J.*, **10,** 198–205.

Unger, Edna W. & Burr, Emily T. (1931) *Minimum Mental Age Levels of Achievement.* Albany: New York State Department of Education.

Vernon, P. E. (1949) Occupational norms for the 20-minute progressive matrices test. *Occup. Psychol.*, **23,** 58–59.

Vernon, P. E. (1950) *The Structure of Human Abilities.* London: Methuen.

Vernon, P. E. (1953) *Personality Tests and Assessments.* London: Methuen.

Vernon, P. E. & Parry, J. B. (1949) *Personnel Selection in the British Forces.* London: University of London Press.

Wall, W. D. (1944) The decay of educational attainments among adolescents after leaving school. *Br. J. Educ. Psychol.*, **14,** 19–34.

Wilson, N. A. B. (1945) Interviewing candidates for technical appointments or training. *Occup. Psychol.*, **19,** 161–179.

Wyatt, S., Frazer, D. A. & Stock, F. G. L. (1929) *The Effects of Monotony in Work.* Industrial Health Research Board Report 56. London: HMSO.

PART 15

The curriculum process

INTRODUCTION

Philip Taylor was able to say in 1967 that our thinking about the curriculum had not got very far. Perhaps we could not say quite the same now largely as an outcome of vast research and resources of the Schools Council's programmes. But the issues are similar. We are still contemplating models of curriculum processes, debating curriculum evaluation, arguing about social and educational goals and turning all these upon ourselves to see in what ways we can improve our own contribution given the kinds of pupils, the subject(s), our own strengths and weaknesses and the climate of educational opinion of the day. Taylor's paper attempts to summarize this process from a psychologist's point of view.

The most recent major structural change, middle schools, deserves special consideration from the point of view of curriculum aims and content. Ross, Razzell and Badcock have put together a Schools Council pamphlet *The Curriculum in the Middle Years* which should be read by all those concerned to know more about the challenges and problems of this innovation. For the Reader, I have extracted the section discussing aims. The fact that it is written with middle schools in mind should not prevent other specialist teachers from reading it.

The research paper by Musgrove and Taylor quantifies what many teachers had suspected – that teachers in general see their work in intellectual and moral terms. Grammar schools were more so than secondary modern and the latter more so than primary schools. Further, teachers seemed 'comparatively indifferent to the more specifically social aims of education'.

Parents of students at any level of education have a share in expressing an opinion about the system as they see it and as they would like to see it. Very little systematic study has been made of parental views on curriculum aims. The Musgrove and Taylor paper looked at parents' conception of the teacher's role – which came out close to that held by the teachers. At university level this agreement was not upheld. The more abstract, remote nature of university aims (such as 'learning for its own sake') were not high on the parents' list of priorities. What did come out in Child's paper as the ideal was personal service to the students both in terms of applicability of their studies to improving career life-chances and in the counselling role of universities. The instrumental attitude of parents came through strongly.

49   Purpose and structure in the curriculum *

PHILIP H. TAYLOR

INTRODUCTION

In this lecture I shall attempt to do four things: I shall attempt to explore where our thinking about the curriculum of the school has got to, propose a model for it, illustrate how this and other models can be used, and discuss the nature and determinants of curriculum objectives. I shall also touch on some issues which are currently of general interest.

First, then, where has our thinking about the curriculum got to? Not very far I'm afraid. Educational thinkers in this country have been caught napping over much that has been taken for granted about the curriculum. In the last decade only one book, and that by a Scot (Nisbet, 1957), has appeared which has attempted in any formal way to analyse the meaning we give to the term curriculum and to relate this to the way in which the curriculum functions in the school. Similarly, there have been few articles of note. The most important have been by a psychologist with a keen interest in both the theory of knowledge and education (Meredith, 1946). This is not to say there hasn't been a welter of books about the curriculum. There has. But they have invariably had their starting-point in purely practical considerations. Formal analysis and theory have not raised their heads in them nor has research been called into service. They are like much other literature in education, statements of good intentions and gospels of personal practice.

Given this state of affairs, I feel I must start at the beginning, sketching out as I go what

---

* Professor Taylor's Inaugural Lecture in the Chair of Curriculum and Method, 3rd November 1966.

has been latent in our thinking about the curriculum of the school and ending up by suggesting ways in which our thinking about the curriculum may become of increasing value in planning the changes that lie ahead as well as informing them by research.

THE LEARNING EXPERIENCES MODEL

The curriculum is usually thought of as a subject or a grouping of subjects for study which are to be treated in a way that will promote learning in pupils. In order for learning to take place certain things must follow. Pupils need to have their attention drawn to relevant subject matter and teachers have to create experiences for them out of which their learning can arise. The kind of learning which it is hoped to promote in the classroom is preferred to other possible learning and it is, therefore, valued. It is that learning, the elements of which as they build up over time have a 'structure', a structure which belongs to one or other body of knowledge: to history, science, mathematics and so on. It is this structured nature which distinguishes it from the learning arising from everyday experiences, and for which, among other reasons, it is valued.

Learning, as psychologists have made us aware, brings about a change in behaviour. This being so it would seem that the purpose of the curriculum is to seek to bring about valued changes in pupil behaviour. These changes can be specified as the intended outcomes or the objectives of the pupil's curricular experiences.

Moreover, as Bruner (1963) has pointed out, in order to achieve these objectives the pupil must submit to a number of rather peculiar demands. 'He must regulate his learning and his attention by reference to external requirements. He must eschew what is vividly right under his nose for what is dimly in the future and is often incomprehensible to him, and he must do so in a strange setting where words and diagrams and abstractions suddenly become very important . . . And often it puts the learner in a spot where he does not know whether he knows, sometimes for minutes, sometimes for hours on end. He has no indication as to whether he is on the right track or the wrong track.' And, one might add that many pupils never know whether or not they have been on the right track or what their curricular experience has been about. Studies of school leavers have been sharply salutory in this respect. For some pupils their learning experiences seem to have had little or no point, except as Musgrove has suggested, in writing themselves off (1966).

It is possible to know this because considerable attention has been given to the part learning plays in curricular experiences. This attention has given rise to a model for our thinking about the curriculum. Schematically it looks like this:

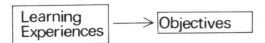

The larger part of the model is learning experiences. It is these experiences, the events associated with them, which give rise to desired learning which are the objectives, the intended ends of the activities associated with the curriculum.

It is such a model as this which has been latent in much of other thinking about the curriculum over the past thirty years or more. Attention was drawn away from considerations of subject matter, and the aims of education which dominated educational thinking until then, to the domain of child psychology, to the how and why of intellectual, social and moral development, and to the problems of human learning; to questions of motivation and stimulus and response. Insight, concept formation, reinforcement and readiness as well as intelligence operationally defined in terms of I.Q. became familiar in the education of teachers. Masters of Method departed from the training colleges to be replaced by lecturers in educational psychology and child development. A knowledge of statistics and the design of psychological experiments became for an increasing number of students the means to a higher degree in education. Teachers in the classroom acting as stimuli concentrated on arousing interest. Their attention was focused to a greater extent than before on their pupils. 'We teach children not subjects' gained currency as a rallying cry for action. Action which resulted in the recasting of the methods of teaching for many subjects and in a new ordering of criteria against which to assess teaching capabilities. Robertson (1957), for example, in a research conducted about a decade ago, found that 'attitude and insight in dealing with others . . . represented the most important aspects of teaching ability as judged by supervisors of student teachers'.

More centrally, the *learning experience* model for the curriculum drew attention to the modes of thinking used by pupils in particular subject areas: to their reasoning in mathematics, science and history, and to their thinking strategies. Recent work of this kind in the area of children's thinking about religious concepts promises a quite new approach to religious education in the schools (Goldman, 1964). Moreover, this work has impinged striking on the function of language in teaching, and a new formulation of the role of language in the classroom is emerging.

Much of this work gave a new gloss to the concept of teaching. Its function was to provide relevant learning experiences which would facilitate the development of concepts and the emergence of productive thinking. Teaching methods came as a consequence to be described in terms of understanding, problem solving and discovery, and much current curriculum development work is well salted with these terms.

The effect on the way in which many teachers now behave in the classroom is witness to the potency of these terms. Engaged in discovery or problem solving with their pupils, they are not so often to be found formally addressing the class. More frequently they are to be found in an intimate give and take with the individual pupil or with small groups. New relationships between teacher and taught have also arisen under the impress of the *learning experience* model for the curriculum. The child psychologists' assertion that children need 'love' has not gone unnoticed by teachers nor has the idea of personality as self-directing and purposive. The development in the pupil of a realistic and stable self-concept cast the teacher to some extent in the role of a therapist and some studies have suggested that the important part played by the pupil's self concept in curricular achievement depends on how he is treated by the teacher (Staines, 1958). Other studies have explored the relationship between certain personality dispositions, extroversion and introversion, for example, and academic attainment (Lynn and Gordon, 1961). The introvert may have an anxious time but does well.

Teaching methods have also been studied in terms of the kind of learning which they promote and it is fairly clear from many of these studies that the method of teaching used and the learning promoted are intimately related, though not in any simple and direct way.

Both the teacher's and the pupil's personality are also important factors as is the extent to which the subject matter is structured for learning.

A considerable step forward in our understanding of the problems to be faced in elaborating teaching methods has been made possible by developments in the field of programmed learning, particularly in analysing the 'task' to be presented to the pupil and in determining the most effective sequencing of subject matter. This work has been greatly influenced by the 'behaviourist' school of psychology, especially by J. B. Skinner, one of its most inventive practitioners.

The *learning experience* model for the curriculum is grounded in psychology, one of the social sciences. As a science psychology has developed an appropriate form of measurement and in so doing has given to many ostensive definitions an operational meaning. A good example, and a fine hare to chase, is the measurement of intelligence: a human quality which teachers want to use and to expand. From the psychological interest in, and development of techniques for measurement, there has sprung an educational counterpart. Thus, measures of educational achievement have been developed and used in the evaluation of different methods of teaching the same material, in the allocation of pupils to different kinds of curricular treatment and in assessing the relative contribution to curricular attainments of home and school.

It is a rule of educational measurement that the operational definition to be employed has to have meaning in terms of specified pupil behaviour. The definition has to say what the pupil will be doing when measurement is taking place: whether he will be recalling something taught, solving a problem in a familiar or unfamiliar setting, comprehending a prose passage, a graph or diagram, or recording an interest, an attitude or a value. Moreover, the pupil behaviour has to be judged as to its educational worthwhileness, i.e. it has to be valid educational or curriculum objective: the intended end point of valued learning.

Work in the field of educational measurement has made it possible to assess the outcome of the *learning experience* model for the curriculum provided these outcomes or objectives are stated in operational terms, i.e. in terms which make the intended pupil behaviour clear. The objectives of curricular learning experiences are to encourage pupils to acquire knowledge, understanding and skills, to develop values, interests and beliefs. History, for example, is taught, it is claimed by teachers of history, so that pupils will acquire historical knowledge, understand historical concepts, develop insight into the nature of historical judgement and so that they will become interested in and curious about things historical as well as develop practical skills in using source materials. All these objectives can be given an operational definition in terms of how the pupil will behave when he has achieved them.

Of course history is also taught for reasons less easily defined in operational terms: to exercise a general influence on character, to develop freedom from prejudice and to encourage a sense of our national heritage. In fact most subjects of the curriculum carry a burden of objectives which go well beyond the subject matter and over into the realms of character and social conscience. These, in many cases, are the subject's 'ring of confidence' and make it an acceptable member of the club. Teachers themselves no longer take such claims as these as seriously as they once did. Empirical studies of the 'transfer of training', of the extent to which learning in one subject carries over to a much more generalized area, have cast very considerable doubts in this direction. It can no longer be claimed as strongly as once it was that mathematics for instance gives rise to a sense of beauty through the experience of order and symmetry which it affords or that the study of literature makes pupils sensitive to the suffering of others. The claims made by a Newman or a Whitehead for the curricula which they advocated now seem extravagant and unlikely to be substantiated.

Such broad claims apart, educational objectives operationally defined in terms of pupil behaviour cover the whole range of human achievements. Some attempts have been made to classify them. These attempts, all American, had their origins in the construction of objective-type achievement tests. The most noteworthy is the *Taxonomy of Educational Objectives*. In the two handbooks of objectives which have so far been published Bloom and his co-workers (1956) have made a systematic attempt to classify them according to distinct logical types. They have so far used two main headings for their work: the Cognitive Domain and the Affective Domain. The first might very generally be thought of as intellectual objectives: knowledge of facts and principles, of theories and structures and the ability to interpret various types of data; and the second, as objectives related to attitudes, interests, value and beliefs.

This scientific, tough-minded approach of Bloom's, which incidentally owes much to the pioneering work of Tyler in the late 30s, to insist on the precise formulation of curriculum objectives is beginning to have a marked effect on our thinking about the extent to which the curricula we use are successful. Successful, that is, in terms of their own intentions. Thus, like any other respectable field of study, that of the curriculum may in time come to elaborate for itself its own criteria and its own tests. But Bloom's work has too strong a psychological bias for many educationists. It takes, they say, too little account of the 'unique educational yield' of particular fields of study. Nevertheless, it represents the best disciplined approach to the formulation of objectives so far undertaken and may well force educationists to develop their own thinking more rapidly.

Psychology then would seem to have provided a very fruitful model for thinking about the curriculum and for practice in relation to it. A model which takes into account all its significant characteristics-content for teaching, methods of teaching and valued objectives. This University (Birmingham) through the work of Professors Valentine, Schonnell and Peel has made and is continuing to make a distinguished contribution to this model. It is a model which remains fruitful, in that through the researches and enquiries which it continues to generate we come to a more comprehensive understanding of what makes an effective method of teaching, what sequencing of material is necessary for learning to take place and what contribution to learning, the interests, personality and general ability of the pupil makes.

But for all that psychology has been and remains a powerful stimulus to educational thinking and practice there has remained the constant concern with why we teach what we teach: the role of subject matter and its purpose in the curriculum. No one has been more concerned about this than the teacher in the classroom. This concern is reflected in the 'trade press' which finds its way into every staff room, in the constant stream of books on the teaching of this or that subject, and in the pages of national reports. The Newsom Report, for example, devotes some 70 per cent of its discussion of the curriculum to subject matter.

Much of this writing is aimed to provide reassurance, to give a new basis for beliefs in the worthwhileness of this or that subject for teaching, and to pass on ways of teaching which have proved, at least for some teachers, effective. It is, of course, not surprising that teachers should be interested in this kind of writing. Knowledge in subject form is what they daily traffic in with their pupils. It is more their bread and butter than is psychology. They can, and do, get along without a formal knowledge of instrumental conditioning, motivation and personality structure. They know what works if not why it works and are certainly greatly expert in much that they do.

Related to the teacher's concern about knowledge, and their role and function in transmitting it, is a much wider issue: that of our cultural heritage. 'The funded capital of social experience' (Brubacher, 1956), as it has been described; those 'realms of meaning' (Phenix, 1964) which we have come to know as subject disciplines and which include the systems of moral beliefs which men have elaborated for their own good. Studies in the role of the teacher suggest that most teachers place first in importance moral training with instruction in subjects a close second. This tends to be true whether they are teachers of sixth formers or of infants.

Now the teacher of infants knows, as anyone who visits an infant class can see, that the beginnings of knowing both about morals and about subjects is 'artless' (Rhyle, 1949). This 'artless' experience is given form and shape by the ways in which the teacher progressively directs the attention of her pupils by the methods and matter which she uses toward more formal modes of meaning. No less than the teacher of sixth formers, the teacher of infants is opening windows on domains of knowledge and understanding. In the sixth form the structure of the subject matter is more clearly discernible as history, mathematics, or science. But in both situations subject knowledge, its meaning and teaching methods have to be brought together for a purpose. It is out of this bringing together that pupils learn though not in many cases without encouragement.

A PROPOSED MODEL

This description of the curriculum as a bringing together of knowledge, methods and objectives may be much more acceptable to the teacher than the *learning experiences* model. It is perhaps a better representation of the interplay of forces associated with the curriculum in action. It is a better analogue and it is easier to locate the pupil as someone undergoing a purposeful experience created for him in terms of matter and method as a consequence of which he is encouraged to know those things which the adult community considers worth while. Perhaps figure 49.1 illustrates more clearly what the curriculum seems to be.

The three axes of the cube are knowledge (K), teaching methods (T) and objectives (O). It is described as the *total intended curriculum* because at no one moment is the pupil experiencing more than part of it though during his educational career he may experience much of it.

The knowledge axis (K) ranging from K_E to K_F embraces knowledge arising from simple elements of experience to formal knowledge or knowledge of the disciplines including those of aesthetics and morals. The teaching methods axis (T) ranges from direct teaching (T_D) or the didactic method to (T_P), the point at which the pupil is his own teacher. It is somewhere toward this point on the teaching method axis that the pupil is when he is engaged on a project or thesis of his own choice.

Where curricular materials – books, charts, diagrams, learning programmes, and the like – replace the teacher in immediacy of contact with the pupil you still have the range of teaching methods. Books can be used as directed by the teacher or as directed by the pupil.

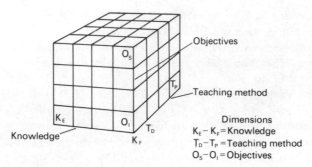

Figure 49.1   The total intended curriculum.

Similarly where the teacher employs a 'discovery' method there is more for the pupil to do for himself than where the didactic method is employed.

The objectives dimension, O_I to O_S, ranges from intellectual objectives such as the knowledge of some specific facts, the names of things, from simple intellectual skills such as reading, to self-knowledge including knowing what one knows and how it is known both about oneself and about the world around one.

In terms of the diagram the curriculum of the infant school would look like figure 49.2.

It is narrow in terms of knowledge, concentrating on experiences and some pre-formal knowledge in number and reading. It is so because the pupils have reached only an early stage in their development. On the other hand it is broad in terms of objectives because the pupils need both to begin to make meaning out of their experiences and to begin to develop self-awareness in relation to it. And it is broad in terms of teaching methods because the teaching has to be adapted to the needs of the pupils.

Similar abstractions from the main diagram can be made to demonstrate other curricula or, for that matter, curricula which we know to be in operation and about which we want to say something.

Frequently we want to say that a curriculum is too *narrow* or is *lacking in depth* or is too *specialized* and we want to *broaden* it. To what are we referring? To which dimension — knowledge, teaching methods or objectives or to all three? Each dimension can be broad or narrow and it might be of great help in discourse about the curriculum to be clearer about

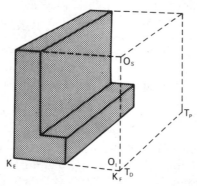

Figure 49.2   The curriculum of the infant school in diagrammatic terms.

what it is to which we refer. Similarly, the term *balance* used about the curriculum can refer to knowledge, teaching methods or to objectives. Thus an elementary model of this kind may be of use in helping us to talk about the curriculum.

There is also another way in which this model of the curriculum can be used. It can be used to distinguish between the motivation of pupils which is extrinsic to the curriculum, outside the cube, and that which is intrinsic, inside the cube. In this way we can see, for example, more clearly what a philosopher of education means when he writes:

'The aim of the educator is to get others on the *inside* of worthwhile activities and forms of awareness so that they will explore them for ends which are intrinsic to them. But in the early stages he may have to use extrinsic motivation both to get children started on them and to sustain their interest when the stage of precision begins to exert an irksome discipline' (Peters, 1966).

MODELS FOR PLANNING

•   •   •

The notion of curriculum planning in the minds of many educationists, 'payment by results' apart, is depressed by three factors. One I have already touched on: the proposition that to know one's subject is largely to know how to teach it. The second is bound up in the word 'syllabus'. When one looks at most syllabuses and listens to the talk about them one is immediately struck by how much ends and means are inextricably compounded. As Lamm says, 'The syllabus is a translation of aims into a language of subjects, a translation which does not explain at all the aims . . . just the opposite it adds non-clarity by the use of symbols of many meanings' (Lamm, 1966). A syllabus is a statement not only about the subject matter or content of teaching for a particular group but also about the objectives for that group stated in subject terms. This we should begin to recognize in the way we use the term.

The third factor is in the meaning of the word plan. Many people use the word to convey hopes, dreams, expectations and wishes rather than to convey the reality of an object having special characteristics which can be constructed to serve a purpose, and which calls for the employment of a range of techniques. This implies technology *in* an educational process which all too readily leads to the conclusion that the claim being made is that education *is* a technology.

No such claim is being made. All that is being suggested is that the intuitive judgements made about the curricula should be given as far as is possible an objective and verifiable form. What we seek to know in this respect is whether the plan works, how well and why. This is its technology. The worthwhileness of the plan is not a question of technology. It is a matter of values.

Such factors as these make one doubt whether the curriculum development work being sponsored at the moment in this country will leave us at the end of the day with any more worthwhile knowledge than we now have of the effectiveness of the new curricula or with any better techniques than we now have for planning curriculum changes. Certainly many pupils will be familiar with more up-to-date knowledge of science, mathematics, history and language than they are today, but will they make either better scientists, mathematicians and

English scholars or understand better what science and mathematics is about than the pupil of today? Much will accrue in terms of motivation both of teachers and pupils from these changes and in that they are founded on a syllabus approach to curriculum planning, some old objectives for teaching will give way to newer ones. More teaching may be directed away from knowing what and towards knowing how. But what will account for whatever desirable changes in the pupil do occur? Will it be in the new content, the new objectives, the new teaching methods which may arise or the motivation of the pupil and teacher? If the last, will the drive arising from it have a long or short 'cooling-out' period? After all the much celebrated Hawthorne effect on industrial productivity disappeared when the psychologists packed their bags and left for factories new. In the long run, questions such as these will have to be tackled if curriculum development is to get away from the stop–go policies of the past. As in the economic field, curriculum changes arising from market forces alone may have to be subject to planning if they are to be cumulatively beneficial.

But my strictures are too severe. Apart from the fact that the Schools Council is as yet a young organization which has shown remarkable energy in its first two years of life despite its complex representative committee structure, it has already shown itself willing to tackle this problem by setting up a Working Party to produce recommendations about methods for evaluating curricula. Nevertheless it remains the case that if we in this country are to initiate worthwhile curriculum changes we may need to recognize not only the value of techniques for planning and evaluation but also the value of a theory for planning. More than this we must begin to rely on evidence of effective implementation. In short we may need to learn about, and not be frightened by *praxiology* which is the science of efficient action.

There is also much in the fields of operational research and systems analysis which may prove useful. I am, myself, struck by how much 'path analysis' may have to offer the curriculum planners. After all it is about 'the right order of things' and this is what is called for in planning curricula.

CURRICULUM EVALUATION

One of the salient issues which arises again and again where curriculum change is planned and initiated comes in the form of a general question: 'Is curriculum A better than curriculum B?' Now this question can refer to any one of the three dimensions of curriculum or to all three at once. Much depends on who is asking it. Furthermore, there are quite distinct criteria for evaluating each of the dimensions separately and for judging them as a functioning whole. If the questioner is concerned with curriculum objectives, evaluation is a matter of judging the worthwhileness of desired pupil behaviour. Up to a point this is an empirical question though in the end it is not. If the concern is with teaching method, this is an empirical question though whether it is a *scientific* one is a matter of contention. If the concern is with knowledge or subject matter, this is a question about what is, for example, science, mathematics, history and so on *for teaching*, with all this implies in the selection of content from a larger body of knowledge. Moreover this last question cannot be answered adequately unless it is placed in the context of the wider question. What is science, history, mathematics? Unfortunately most educationists are not able to answer such questions. Their training has not fitted them to do so nor does what they read encourage them to think such questions important. However, in science and mathematics scholars are coming forward with help and there is some evidence that this is having a considerable effect on the quality of thinking which is going into the reform of mathematics and science curricula. But it is not happening to anything like the same degree in the humanities. If it does not, then questions about the relative merits of humanities curricula may be answered on a totally wrong basis.

Now none of the foregoing questions about the comparative merits of different curricula is a small one but each, I suspect, can be answered. The trouble is that most of the questions about the curriculum have, up to now, been lacking in clarity of direction. It has not been made plain to what they refer. But if it is clear that the question refers to the functioning complex of all three dimensions together and to whether curriculum A is better than curriculum B then the answer will be, of necessity, a complex one. It will be a matter of curriculum evaluation, of something which has only very recently been invented and is, as yet, little understood. It will certainly be necessary to write in extremely clearly the clause *other things being equal* and just as necessary to specify whether the evaluation relates to long- or short-term effects. Even then it will be as well to advise people as a general rule that even where the evaluation suggests that curriculum A is better than curriculum B, or B than A, neither may be as good as another curriculum which could be invented from what has been discovered in studying the comparative merits of A and B.

In a period of radical curriculum change new curricula are likely to be different in more than one major respect from old curricula, in which case things are likely to be very unequal indeed and there is not much to be gained from comparisons. This is the situation that exists at the present and resources would, it seems to me, be better employed in the efficient planning of new curricula rather than in attempting to demonstrate the irrelevant. But there may come a time when comparative studies are worth while and could provide a base for the continued inventing of improved curricula.

•   •   •

ACKNOWLEDGEMENT

This lecture was first published by *Educ. Rev.* (1967 and 1968). An extract is published here with the kind permission of editor and author.

REFERENCES

Bloom, B. S. (1956) *Taxonomy of Educational Objectives.* David McKay.

Brubacher, M. (1956) *Modern Philosophies of Education.* World Books.

Bruner, J. S. (1963) *Motives for Learning,* in Jenning Scholar Lectures, 1963. Cleveland, U.S.A.: Educational Research Council of Greater Cleveland.

Bruner, J. S. (1963) *The Process of Education.* Harvard U.P.

Goldman, R. (1964) *Religious Thinking from Childhood to Adolescence.* Routledge & Kegan Paul.

Lynn, R. & Gordon, I. E. (1961) The relation of neuroticism and extraversion to intelligence and educational attainment, *Br. J. Educ. Psychol.,* Vol. xxxi, Pt II.

Meredith, G. P. (1946) *The Method of Topic Analysis.* Educ. Devel. Assn.

Musgrove, F. (1966) *Faith and Scepticism in English Education,* Inaugural Lecture, Univ. of Bradford.

Newsom Report (1963) *Half our Future*. HMSO.

Nisbet, S. D. (1957) *Purpose in the Curriculum*. Univ. of London Press.

Peters, R. S. (1966) *Ethics and Education*. London: George Allen & Unwin.

Phenix, P. (1964) *Realms of Meaning*. London: McGraw-Hill.

Rhyle, G. (1949) *The Concept of Mind*. London: Hutchinson.

Robertson, J. D. C. (1957) An analysis of the views of supervisors on the attitudes of successful graduate student teachers, *Br. J. Educ. Psychol.*, Vol. xxvii, Pt II.

Staines, J. W. (1958) The self-picture as a factor in the classroom, *Br. J. Educ. Psychol.*, Vol. xxviii, Pt II.

50   The whole curriculum – aims and content

A. M. ROSS, A. G. RAZZELL and E. H. BADCOCK

There are so many different things that *could* be done in school; there are so many different things that *are* done. How are we to decide what *should* be done? It is particularly important for British teachers to ask this question, for our system is noteworthy for its relative lack of central direction. In many countries the teacher is able to say: 'I teach this and I teach that because the official curriculum requires me to do so.' A British teacher (or perhaps more accurately a head) can say: 'I teach this and I teach that because in my professional judgement it is the right thing to do.' Our first report, *Education in the Middle Years* (1972), emphasized the fact that value judgements are constantly being made in deciding what shall and shall not be done with the children. The considerable freedom possessed by British teachers makes it all the more important to consider the criteria for choosing the elements which go to make up a whole curriculum. It is perhaps even more important for middle-years teachers to give careful thought to this. At the first-school stage, though methods may vary in detail, there is a wide measure of agreement about the main emphasis of the work. At the upper-secondary-school stage, external public examinations and the task of easing the school-leaver into the world of everyday work act as constraints. Teachers of middle-years children are more free from outside pressures, especially when transfer is achieved without an external assessment. Unlike the first-school and upper-secondary-school teacher, the middle-years teacher receives the child from a school and sends him out to a school. A greater measure of freedom brings with it greater responsibility for decisions about the curriculum.

There are many questions to be asked. Why do we do what we do and why do we not do the other things we could do? Is there an overall shape to the curriculum? Has it coherence? Cynics have suggested that the curriculum of many schools is the result of unexamined tradition warped by the excesses of enthusiasts. Teachers should respect tradition and should listen to the enthusiast, but the thinking teacher will seek criteria by which the various claims may be judged. The point of view taken in this chapter is firstly that any curriculum should be the result of conscious planning as well as intuition, and secondly that planning is of particular importance in middle-years education since these years are so important in the development of the child as a thinking person. This viewpoint may well be resisted by those teachers – perhaps primary-school teachers in particular – who regard planning as the enemy of freedom. The writers can vividly recall visiting a primary school in which each day ended with the only timetabled session of the day – a discussion of what to do tomorrow. There can be no doubt that it is possible for highly gifted teachers to develop, over a period of weeks and without formal planning, a programme of work which, though it seems to be derived solely from the children's declared interests, is, in an acceptable sense, balanced, rewarding and full of rich learning experiences. From time to time the children's interests may have to be nudged in the direction considered by the teacher to be desirable, but the whole programme could nevertheless be seen to flow entirely from what appeared to be the children's spontaneous interests. However, it would not be realistic to assume that all teachers could, or indeed should, be expected to organize their work in this way. There is also room for doubt about the extent to which short-term day-to-day planning, even in skilled hands, can be relied on to provide a properly articulated programme of work for older junior- and lower secondary-school children. Careful planning of the curriculum need not exclude the possibility of pursuing fruitful lines of inquiry further than originally intended or of encouraging those unusual turns of thought and action which often attract the term 'creativity'. Indeed all plans should encompass and even plan for unplanned developments. Much that is lasting and valuable in learning is the result of the happy accident, and good planning will always recognize this. Whether the curriculum is planned in detail or not there can be no doubt that the children themselves will leave their mark on it. The curriculum is nothing more than the back-cloth and the lighting for the action of children actively learning and there will be as many ad lib or forgotten lines as there will be scripted passages.

In this chapter we look at the curriculum as a whole. There is a sense in which the curriculum may be regarded as the sum of its parts, the parts being various activities, subjects or whatever sub-category the commentator prefers. There is also a sense in which it is more than the sum of those parts. A common reaction when asked to draw up a curriculum, whether it be for 8-year-olds or 13-year-olds, is to draw up a list of subjects and then to begin to give 'weightings' to these – two periods a week of this, an hour of that, and so forth. Even when the initial assumptions are not in 'subject' form the process is similar. The weightings given usually reflect the tradition for these activities and any specialist can mount convincing arguments for a significant part of the resources available to be given to his or her specialism. Indeed, those who try to look at the curriculum as a whole rapidly reach the conclusion that any one aspect of the curriculum can be shown to be capable of providing almost every conceivable learning outcome. It may be taken for granted that all subjects that are in the usual curriculum (and a good many more that are not) are essential to an understanding of the world and for future survival, provide unique opportunities for the development of cognitive, affective and psychomotor skills, are almost a full education in themselves, require specially trained teachers and specialist facilities, are undervalued in the schools and require more time on the timetable. It is easy to see how cynical the whole-curriculum thinker becomes after a series of such 'unanswerable' cases has been heard. Clearly the only solution is a 40-hour teaching week! With little more than half that number of teaching hours available, each subject (or activity) must justify itself in a highly competitive situation. The approach used here is to begin not with the list and all the assumptions already implicit in the acceptance of these sub-categories but with three major and interrelated dimensions of the problem. These are the aims of education in the middle years, the activities through which those aims might be achieved and the content of the activities. The three are interdependent and provide a model to help the thinking teacher in making decisions.

AIMS OF EDUCATION

Education in the Middle Years argued the case for giving attention to this first significant step in the task of reasoning a way through to a curriculum (pp. 11–24). The aims which teachers have in their minds are an amalgam of ideas (articulate or not) about the individual and his development, with other ideas about society and its evolution. It is perhaps misleading to differentiate aims in this way, for the interdependence of the individual and the society he shapes, and which in turn shapes him, is so great as to defy complete separation. It should also be pointed out that the aims an individual teacher may have, even if described as 'purely educational', have political implications in the sense of making judgements about what kind of life, what kind of society is 'best', what kind of ideas are 'worth' passing on and which individual skills are 'desirable'. All the quoted words imply a scale of values against which the judgement is made and it is possible to argue that scales of value of this kind are as much political as educational. (For a development of this point see Young, 1972).

For present purposes attention is directed first at the aims which, in so far as they can be separated out, could be called societal. Schools seek to pass on to each new generation of children the knowledge, skill, ideas and feelings which are judged necessary to make it possible to live – and live well – in our society. This calls for an understanding of the process by which the norms of our society have been evolved and in this sense the school stands for tradition and for conformity. Societies change, however, and in modern times they change quickly. Indeed it is now a truism to say that the one permanent feature of our society is change. It follows then that the societal view will be forward as well as back and schools will seek to provide not only experiences which enable a child to grasp the essentials of our world as it is but also experiences which will make him ready to fulfil himself in a world which will be very different from the world of today. In this sense the school stands not only for tradition and conformity but also for the future and a willingness to accept – even to provoke – change. It is here that the teacher realizes that political questions are not far away and the professional task of the teacher is to make the nice judgements called for while transmitting the culture as it is and at the same time developing in the young the capacity to adapt that culture to the changed world of tomorrow. Some schools catering for middle-years children have already decided that problems such as race relations, population policies and environmental pollution are significant enough to merit attention in the formative period of 8 to 13. But the future makes its impact on method as well as content and it can be argued that since we cannot know with certainty what knowledge will be most relevant to the needs of the year 2000 we should concentrate upon the development of attitudes needed to cope with a rapidly changing world. Attitudes which accept change, which tolerate the differences to be found in an increasingly pluralist society, and which arrive at a view after open discussion, are seen by some teachers as desirable and have their impact upon the ways of learning practised in the schools.

The problem may, however, be seen from the point of view of trying to provide the opportunities each child needs to develop and fulfil himself as a person; in fact to provide for that child the experiences which will enable him to become the best kind of person he is capable of becoming. Even if the value-laden word 'best' is allowed, it is clear that fulfilment of this kind is only possible in a social setting. The approach which takes the child's personal development as its starting point could also be regarded as the culmination of the approach which begins with a view of society. However strongly personal development and self-fulfilment is held as an aim, it cannot be followed through without reference to wider social aims. Those who take personal development and self-fulfilment to its extreme produce schools (sometimes called 'progressive') in which the pupils decide on their own curriculum. In many schools catering for middle-years children opportunities are created for children to choose particular activities which interest them but there can be few schools which can provide anything like the range of activities which could, quite reasonably, be asked for today. If a middle-years child can fulfil himself in the study of science, mathematics, or on the football field, he is more likely to find what he needs in school than the child whose development as a person would be enhanced with coaching in diving, instruction in a less usual musical instrument or by learning Greek. If the range of activities which can be provided is to be extended it will be necessary to think of extending the school day and of making all the educational facilities of the area available to all the children. Clearly the means as well as the end must be willed, but if middle-years children are to be allowed to seek out and pursue their special interests it will be necessary to move away from the concept of the single school as the provider of all that is needed. It is important too to develop this idea not merely as the means of providing 'enrichment' for the gifted. If the point has validity at all it has validity for all children.

At this point a further extension of the argument is possible. It could be said that the personal development of the child cannot be planned or even provided for without involvement with many people and institutions which exist outside the educational system as narrowly defined. Schools are increasingly seeing themselves as part of the community they serve and it is therefore legitimate to think of the curriculum being as much community-based and involved as school-based. The strongest links with the community are the parents and their participation in the work of education is likely to increase.

The broad aim of providing opportunities for self-development and self-fulfilment is capable of taking the curriculum deviser a considerable way, possibly in directions away from those which are traditional. The middle-years teacher has a particular responsibility here because the years 8 to 13 are those in which children begin to decide how best they may develop and fulfil themselves. Ideas about what they would like to do and what they find rewarding emerge. If the educational system is to develop the potential of each child, it is important for middle-years teachers to keep the range of activities and experiences as broad as possible. Our system has long been successful at seeking out, reinforcing and developing potential for success when it is clothed in the academic form which teachers themselves display. Today we realize that talent may display itself in other ways and it is important for our curricula to reflect this realization.

•   •   •

ACKNOWLEDGEMENT

These extracts are from *The Curriculum in the Middle Years* (1975), Schools Council Working Paper 55. They are published here with the kind permission of Evans/Methuen Educational and the authors.

REFERENCES

Bloom, B. S. (Ed.) (1956) *Taxonomy of Educational Objectives: the Classification of Educational Goals*, Handbook I: Cognitive Domain. Longmans Green.
Schools Council Working Paper 42 (1972) *Education in the Middle Years* by E. H. Badcock, P. B. Daniels, J. Islip, A. G. Razzell and A. M. Ross. Evans/Methuen Educational.
Young, M. D. F. (1972) On the politics of educational knowledge, *Econ. Soc.*, **1**, 194–215.

51   Teachers' and parents' conception of the teacher's role

F. MUSGROVE and PHILIP H. TAYLOR

Summary   An inquiry was carried out among 470 teachers in grammar, modern, junior and infant schools to establish how widely or narrowly they conceived their role and what elements they gave greatest weight to within it. Grammar school teachers had a more constricted view of their role than their modern school colleagues, and junior school teachers working in middle-class areas than their colleagues in working-class districts. Married women junior school teachers had a more restricted view of their role than single teachers.

In all types of school teachers saw their work primarily in intellectual and moral terms and were comparatively indifferent to more general social training, although modern school teachers gave more emphasis to social training than grammar school teachers. All saw parents as comparatively indifferent to moral objectives in the education of their children, primarily concerned with 'instruction' but also attaching great importance to 'social advancement.' A sample of 237 parents, in fact, gave a list of educational priorities which agreed in substance with the ratings made by teachers.

INTRODUCTION

Changes which are taking place or thought to be imminent in the contemporary teacher's role have been discussed in rather general terms by sociologists. Actual investigators of the teacher's role, the professional behaviour in which he engages and which is expected of him, have been few. Taylor (1962) reported an inquiry into pupils' expectations of teachers in different types of school; Musgrove (1961) reported an inquiry into parents' expectations of teachers in different types of urban area and at different social levels. The teacher works within a framework of expectations. He may respond to some of these expectations and reject others; he may misjudge the pressures brought to bear upon him and defend himself against demands which have not, in fact, been made. This paper reports an empirical inquiry into the way he sees his role in relation to the perceived and the actual expectations of parents.

Wilson (1962) has argued that the teacher's role must become more 'diffuse' at a time when most professional roles are becoming more specialized and specific. 'The diffuse role means diffuse involvement.' Mays (1962) has similarly argued that a teacher's role must broaden in scope, embracing ever more 'parental' functions and calling for the skills and interests of the social worker. 'The argument then is between the ideas of the teacher as a pure inculcator of knowledge and the teacher as a welfare worker. It is not so much that the two interpretations of the teacher's role need be mutually exclusive. The disagreement concerns the degree of emphasis and the amount of time and energy to be devoted to these related aspects of the job.'

PLAN OF INVESTIGATION

The purpose of the inquiry reported below was to estimate to what extent teachers in different types of school and circumstances saw their roles as 'diffuse' or 'restricted'; what weight they attached to different aspects of their work; what weight they thought parents expected them to give to different educational objectives; and what weight parents did, in fact, attach to these objectives.

The instrument used was a questionnaire which listed six commonly accepted educational aims. These aims which teachers are seen as pursuing were those most frequently mentioned by parents in the author's earlier inquiry (Musgrove, 1961). The aims were: (1) Moral Training (the inculcation of values and attitudes, e.g., honesty, kindliness, tolerance, courage); (2) Instruction in Subjects (imparting information and promoting understanding of a body of knowledge); (3) Social Training (encouraging politeness, good manners, decency in speech and dress, etc.); (4) Education for Family Life (training in human relationships with special reference to attitudes to the opposite sex); (5) Social Advancement (preparing children to 'get on in life'); and (6) Education for Citizenship (developing an understanding of the modern world, etc.).

The teachers involved in this research were asked to rank these objectives as they valued them and also as their experience led them to believe that parents in general valued them. They were also asked to indicate any objective which they regarded as no concern of theirs and none of their business as teachers. The parents who took part in the inquiry – a sample of 108 parents of primary school children and 129 parents of children at the secondary stage in one of the local authority areas selected for research – were asked to rank these objectives as they thought they should weigh with the teachers in charge of their children, and to indicate any of the listed objectives which they regarded as none of the teacher's business.

Grammar, modern, junior and infant schools were approached in three randomly selected local education authority areas. Four grammar schools cooperated (two mixed, one boys' and one girls'), and 14 secondary modern schools (nine mixed, three boys' and two girls'). The schedule was completed by 50 men teaching in the grammar schools and by 37 women; and by 103 men and 91 women in the modern schools.

Ten infant schools co-operated in the inquiry and 17 junior (mixed) schools. One-hundred-and-eighty-nine teachers completed the questionnaire, 51 (all women) in infant schools, and 138 (48 men and 90 women) in junior schools.

The primary schools were classified as denominational and non-denominational; and also according to the type of social area they served. (Scattered catchment areas made this classification impossible or unrealistic in the case of secondary schools.) Areas were classified as 'middle class' if some two-thirds of the parents were in white-collar occupations, as 'working class' if two-thirds were manual workers; as 'mixed' if the proportions of white-collar and manual workers were approximately equal.

RESULTS

(1) Diffuseness of role conception and expectation (tables 51.1 and 51.2)

An individual teacher's diffuse or restricted conception of his role was measured by the number of educational objectives he regarded as none of his business. On this estimation grammar school teachers had a more restricted notion of their role than secondary modern school teachers: 9 per cent of the ratings of male grammar school teachers indicated 'no concern of mine', only 3.2 per cent of the ratings by men teaching in modern schools (C.R. = 3.7, $P < 0.01$). The corresponding ratings by women in the two types of school were 11 per cent and 4 per cent (C.R. = 3.6, $P < 0.01$). The objectives which were rejected were exclusively social, as opposed to moral and intellectual aims.

Primary school teachers stood between grammar and modern school teachers in their restricted view of their role: 8 per cent of their ratings indicated 'no concern'. Like teachers at the secondary stage, the aims they rejected were all social in nature.

Infant school teachers, whether married or single, old or young, with or without much teaching experience, and irrespective of whether they worked in schools serving predominantly upper- or lower-class social areas, rejected around the same percentage of all objectives.

Married women teachers in junior schools rejected a significantly higher percentage of objectives than men teachers, single women teachers, and teachers in infant schools (C.R. =

Table 51.1 Restricted or diffuse role conception of junior and infant school teachers according to sex and marital status

Teachers' sex and marital status	Junior teachers				Infant teachers			
	N	Max. ranks	'No con- cern'	%	N	Max. ranks	'No con- cern'	%
Men	51	306	19	6.2				
Single women	51	306	23	7.5	25	150	12	8.0
Married women	35	210	46	12.4	22	132	11	8.3
All women	86	516	49	9.5				
Total	138	328	68	8.2	47	282	23	8.2

Table 51.2   Teachers' restricted or diffuse role conception according to social-class area and denominational status of school

Type of area and denominational status of school	Junior teachers				Infant teachers			
	N	Max. ranks	'No con-cern'	%	N	Max. ranks	'No con-cern'	%
Middle class and mixed	66	396	42	10.6	32	192	16	8.3
Working class	72	432	26	6.1	15	90	7	7.8
Denominational	40	240	23	9.6	14	84	6	7.7
Non-denominational	98	588	45	7.6	33	198	17	8.6

2.47, $P < 0.02$, 1.99, $P < 0.05$ and 2.35, $P < 0.02$, respectively). (See table 51.1.) Junior school teachers working in schools serving a predominantly middle-class catchment area have a significantly more restricted role conception than their colleagues in schools serving working-class districts. They rejected over 10 per cent, as against 6 per cent of the objectives (C.R. = 2.3, $P < 0.02$). Married women junior school teachers and junior school teachers working in middle-class areas thus exhibited about the same degree of role restriction as teachers in grammar schools.

The 108 parents of primary school children who completed the questionnaire ascribed a significantly wider range of educational objectives to teachers if they were working class than if they were middle class. The opposite was the case with the 129 parents with children in secondary schools: working-class parents ascribed to teachers a comparatively restricted role, particularly with regard to social objectives; middle-class parents now expected a significantly wider range of services from teachers (see table 51.3).

(2) Teachers' role conception, perceived expectations of parents, and actual expectations of parents

Teachers in all types of school saw their work primarily in intellectual and moral terms, placing greatest weight on instruction in subjects and moral training. They placed comparatively little emphasis on social objectives in general, and least of all on 'social advancement' in particular. In no type of school were teachers prepared to see themselves primarily as agents of social mobility. They saw parents as being comparatively indifferent to moral and social training, but placing great weight on instruction and on social advancement. In fact, the parents in general emphasized the same objectives as teachers: moral training and instruction in subjects; and, like teachers, gave comparatively little weight to 'social advancement' (although there were significant social-class differences in this regard).

There were no significant differences between the emphases of junior and infant teachers. Both gave greatest weight to moral training and least to social advancement; instruction in subjects and social training were given roughly equal weight after moral training.

Table 51.3   Ascription of diffuse or restricted role to teachers by parents

| | Percentage of ratings indicating objectives of no concern to teachers | | | |
| | 'Social class' (Registrar-General) | | | |
	I–II	III Non-manual	III Manual	IV–V
Parents of primary children. N: 108	11.8	9.7	6.3	2.8
Parents of secondary children. N: 129	1.6	5.2	10.6	9.2

Among teachers at the secondary stage, as at the primary, moral training took pride of place over 'instruction' for all except men teaching in grammar schools, who seem to perceive their job primarily in intellectual terms. As with primary school teachers, 'social advancement' came last except for women teachers in modern schools who, rather curiously, gave least emphasis to 'education for family life' (see table 51.4).

Some statistically significant differences emerged between the order of priorities found among modern school and grammar school teachers. Forty-two per cent of men teaching in modern schools ranked 'social training' first or second, only 20 per cent of men teaching in grammar schools did so ($\chi^2 = 7.03$, $P < 0.01$). Similarly, with regard to moral training: 74 per cent of modern school teachers gave it a high rating, only 60 per cent of male grammar school teachers did so ($\chi^2 = 12.88$, $P < 0.001$). Eighty-six per cent of male grammar school teachers rated 'instruction' first or second compared with 63 per cent in the modern schools.

Male grammar school teachers of non-academic subjects – woodwork, metalwork, religious instruction, art and music – gave no less weight to 'instruction' as their primary goal than teachers of academic subjects. Women teachers in the two types of school differed significantly in only one respect – in the greater emphasis which secondary modern school

Table 51.4   Median rank order of teachers' aims (in brackets, order ascribed to parents by teachers)

	Moral training	Instruction	Social training	Family life	Social advance	Citizenship
Grammar school men	2 (3)	1 (1)	4 (4)	5 (6)	6 (2)	3 (5)
Grammar school women	1 (5)	2 (1)	5 (3)	4 (4)	6 (2)	3 (6)
Modern school men	1 (3)	2 (1)	3 (4)	5 (6)	6 (2)	4 (5)
Modern school women	1 (3)	1 (1)	3 (4)	6 (5)	5 (2)	4 (5)
Actual parents' ranks	1	2	4	6	5	3
Junior teachers	1 (4)	2 (1)	3 (3)	5 (6)	5 (2)	4 (5)
Infant teachers	1 (3)	2 (1)	2 (4)	4 (6)	5 (2)	3 (5)
Actual parents' ranks	2	1	4	6	5	3

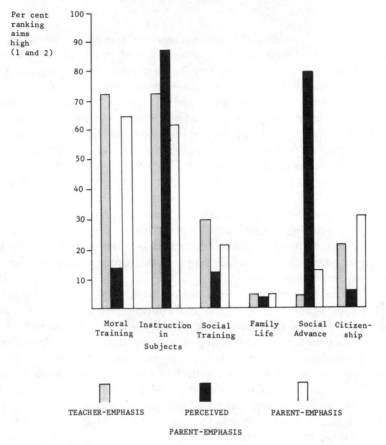

Figure 51.1 Teacher-evaluation, perceived parent-evaluation and actual parent-evaluation.

teachers placed on social training as an educational aim. Only 5.6 per cent of women teaching in grammar schools ranked this objective high, but a third of the women teachers in modern schools did so ($\chi^2 = 9.31$, $P < 0.01$).

Figure 51.1 shows the educational priorities of all the teachers at the secondary stage compared with the priorities they ascribed to parents and with the priorities which were, in fact, found among the sample of parents of secondary school children. (There were 281 teachers and 129 parents.)

Parents, like teachers, in fact, gave greatest weight to moral training and instruction and comparatively little to social advancement. Working-class parents, however, gave significantly more weight to social advancement than did middle-class parents: 18 per cent of the former ranked it high, only 2 per cent of the latter (C.R. = 3.1, $P < 0.01$). There were no other significant differences between parents of different occupational standing. There was a trend for middle-class parents to rank 'instruction' high (72 per cent did so compared with 59 per cent of working-class parents) but this difference falls short of statistical significance.

DISCUSSION

According to the measures used in this inquiry, teachers in grammar schools appear to have a more restricted notion of their role than teachers in modern schools: they see their work in moral and intellectual terms and to a marked degree reject social training as any part of their business. The more diffuse role conception of modern school teachers is not surprising in view of the short history and more uncertain and perhaps wider objectives of modern schools, and the grammar school's traditional concern with intellect and 'character'.

Junior school teachers working in predominantly middle-class areas have a more restricted view of their role than teachers in working-class districts. This probably reflects a realistic response to the social environment in which they find themselves, an acceptance of the need to provide social training which in socially better districts can safely be left to the home.

Married women teachers in junior schools seem less prepared to accept a diffuse role than their single colleagues, whatever kind of social district they serve. This was not the case with married women teachers in infant schools; and we might speculate that infant teaching in any case attracts women who are more prepared to accept a general 'mothering' function as a necessary aspect of their work.

Parents' 'diffuse' or 'restricted' expectations of teachers appear to be related both to their social class and to their children's stage of education. In a previous inquiry Musgrove (1961) found that working-class parents of primary school children wished to place far greater responsibility for behaviour-training on teachers than middle-class parents, who felt that this was the responsibility of the home. The responses of parents of primary school children in the present inquiry are in line with these earlier findings. At the secondary school stage it seems to be middle-class parents who would make the widest and most general demands on teachers (except that working-class parents have stronger expectations with regard to 'social advancement'). Working-class parents perhaps look particularly to the school as an ally when their children are young, vulnerable and exposed to an inauspicious local social environment.

Teachers in all types of school see their role in moral and intellectual terms and are comparatively indifferent to the more specifically social aims of education. Secondary modern school teachers placed more weight on social objectives than their grammar school colleagues, but nevertheless placed much greater emphasis on 'instruction in school subjects'. In emphasizing 'instruction' teachers were in line with what they thought parents expected and with what parents in fact expected.

But the area of discrepancy between teachers' aims and what they imagine to be parents' is still very large. On the whole, teachers take an unflattering view of parents (and their own aims are remarkably idealistic), seeing them as indifferent to moral training but very concerned with social advancement. In fact, parents were substantially in agreement with teachers. The area of (unnecessary) tension might be considerably reduced if parents and teachers established more effective means of communication.

ACKNOWLEDGEMENT

This paper first appeared in *Br. J. Educ. Psychol.* (1965), **35**, 171–179, and is published here with the kind permission of editor and authors.

REFERENCES

Mays, J. B. (1962) *Education and the Urban Child.* Liverpool: Liverpool University Press.
Musgrove, F. (1961) Parents' expectations of the junior school. *Soc. Rev.*, **9**, 167–180.
Taylor, P. H. (1962) Children's evaluations of the characteristics of the good teacher. *Br. J. Educ. Psychol.*, **32**, 258–266.
Wilson, B. R. (1962) The teacher's role – a sociological analysis. *Brit. J. Soc.*, **13**, 15–32.

52 Parents' expectations of a university

DENNIS CHILD, H. J. COOPER, C. G. I. HUSSELL and P. WEBB

At a time when there is widespread curiosity as to what goes on in universities and a growing public consciousness of its stake in education, it comes as a surprise to discover that there is little empirical knowledge of the public's views on the major functions of universities. Judging from press comment, conflicts between students and institutions have left many people with distorted attitudes toward universities. A full-scale investigation involving all sections of the community would probably reveal a confused picture of dissatisfaction and suspicion. But there is one group, the parents of undergraduates, with a special case and the research reported below has concentrated on their opinions.

Parents were chosen for a variety of reasons. Their claim to an active interest in universities is obvious. They have the best opportunity for becoming informed (or misinformed) by direct feedback from their offspring. There was also a belief amongst some of the authors that parents have some place in the arena of university affairs, however remote. Another consideration was the ease with which a willing and representative sample could be mustered. But basically we wanted to know the priorities and posteriorities about university life from those closest to the students.

Most previous researches have started with the student and what he perceives to be his (or her) parents' views. Malleson, for example, in the *Universities Quarterly* (1959), touches on the subject of parental attitudes and their relationship to the success of students at university. His information about their attitudes was obtained indirectly from the students. Musgrove (1967) showed that parents figured prominently in the lives of university freshmen, much more so than friends and lecturers, as the most important people who were concerned with the students' university performance. He also drew attention to the sparseness of information on the relationship between parental attitudes and the life-chances of university students. In a follow-up study of this sample two years later (Child, 1970), it transpired that parents remained the most important reference group. What, then, does this important reference group anticipate will be the attributes of an 'ideal' university? To what extent does it think these attributes are realized in existing universities?

To enlist the help of parents, 102 students at the University of Bradford were approached. They all proved willing to volunteer their home addresses. Names and addresses of ex-sixth formers from a nearby school provided an additional 39 homes having students in a variety of universities. A complete set of questionnaires was provided for *each* parent. 76 mothers and 74 fathers (more fathers had died than mothers) returned completed forms in time for the analysis giving a 53 per cent response rate. We were still receiving completed forms six months later and the response rate to date is 70 per cent. To allow for possible differences between responses relating to male and female students, year of entry and subject areas, roughly equal numbers of each sex were chosen from 2nd and 3rd year under-graduates covering arts, social science and science subjects. Second and 3rd years were chosen because it was felt that parents would have had more opportunity for feedback than might have been possible with first year students.

Each parent was invited to complete two questionnaires containing identical sets of 20 items. Table 52.1 illustrates these. One set, referred to as the 'ideal' questionnaire, enabled respondents to rate each of the 20 attributes on a six-point scale reflecting how essential they would be to an ideal university. The other set, the 'real' questionnaire, required respondents to use a five-point scale to show the extent to which they were satisfied that universities possessed these attributes.

In the first place, Trow's (1960) typology of academic, vocational, collegiate and non-conformist college sub-cultures was considered as a basis for deciding on the scope of the questions. The items displayed in table 52.1 will be seen to relate to all but the non-conformist sub-culture. The questionnaire also includes items which might be broadly classified as 'social' and 'personal' elements of university life. One main intention was to explore as widely as possible with a minimum of questions so as not to frighten off the sample.

Appropriate statistical tests showed no significant distinction between responses to the 20 items by subject areas of undergraduates or the sex of either the student or the parent. The results were therefore combined. The similarity in the patterns of response for both parents was not altogether unexpected. There could well have been collaboration between them. On the other hand, we could conclude at face value that parental opinion about universities is uniform, and this conclusion is supported by the distribution of the responses displayed in table 52.1. The similarity in expectations for men and women students was un-foreseen. We had expected some diversity in the response patterns.

Table 52.1 contains the response rate for the 'ideal' questionnaire arranged in rank order of the means from most to least essential. The six-point scale offered parents the choice of writing a number from 1 to 6 against an item where 1 would indicate that the cor-responding item was 'absolutely essential', 2 – 'important but not essential', 3 – 'of only moderate importance', 4 – 'of very little importance', 5 – 'of no importance at all' and 6 – 'totally opposed to the suggestion'. For clarity these have been condensed in the table so that 1 and 2 were put together to represent 'very important', 3 – 'moderately important', 4 and 5 – 'unimportant' and 6 – 'totally opposed'.

The first 13 attributes in rank order were thought to be very important by over 60 per cent of the sample.* The first seven items are conspicuously well endorsed. They seem to

---

* If we assumed there was a fifty-fifty chance of parents rating an item as very important as compared with other points on the scale, any value greater than 58 per cent (or less than 42 per cent) for this size of sample would be significantly better than chance.

Table 52.1   Universities as you would ideally like them (N = 150)

Attribute	Mean	Expressed as a percentage			
		Very important	Moderately important	Unimpor-tant	Totally opposed
Provides a counselling service for students with academic problems	1.22	96.0	3.2	0.8	0.0
Provides a counselling service to help students in their choice of career	1.23	100.0	0.0	0.0	0.0
Encourages tolerance of other people's opinions	1.32	93.8	5.3	0.9	0.0
Makes the students work hard at their studies	1.33	94.6	4.1	1.3	0.0
Gives opportunities for improving students' skill at dealing with people	1.34	96.5	3.5	0.0	0.0
Is primarily concerned with preparing students for a career	1.43	91.2	4.0	4.8	0.0
Offers a degree with one or two subjects in great factual detail	1.59	90.3	6.9	2.1	0.7
Has distinguished scholars on the staff who are well known for their research	1.82	78.8	15.6	5.6	0.0
Should enable students to secure a 'top' job after graduation	1.88	78.8	14.3	4.8	2.1
Discourages sexual freedom between unmarried students	1.94	76.1	9.5	9.5	4.9
Provides plenty of opportunity for cultural activities (music, drama, etc.)	2.04	72.3	27.0	0.7	0.0
Encourages independence from parental influence	2.24	70.0	12.0	14.7	3.3
Encourages student membership on Committees dealing with the curriculum and examinations	2.41	64.5	19.5	10.8	5.2
Provides plenty of opportunity for sports and athletics	2.44	55.1	32.3	12.6	0.0
Provides plenty of opportunity to meet members of the opposite sex	2.72	44.6	34.0	21.4	0.0

Table 52.1—*continued*

		Expressed as a percentage			
Attribute	Mean	Very important	Moderately important	Unimpor- tant	Totally opposed
Offers a degree with a wide range of subjects in moderate detail	2.83	53.8	20.0	13.8	12.4
Offers a counselling service for students on sexual matters	3.09	39.6	26.2	26.2	8.0
Encourages the student to be active in politics	3.24	32.9	26.9	37.0	3.2
Gives students plenty of free time to use as they (the students) see fit	3.25	34.4	31.1	20.3	14.2
Is concerned about learning for its own sake without regard for its practical applications	3.93	23.9	18.5	30.1	27.5

concentrate on three aspects of university life: (a) students should be worked hard in a few specialized subjects with a supporting cast of academic counsellors; (b) the University should be primarily concerned with preparing and guiding students for a career; (c) the University should help in developing students' skills for dealing with other people. These appear to be a highly business-like and instrumental order of priorities.

At the other end of the rank we find 'learning for its own sake *without regard for its practical applications*' and 'gives students plenty of free time to use as they (the students) see fit'. Parents certainly have no time for the idealistic notion of university dons and students indulging themselves in the pursuit of knowledge 'for the kicks'. This order of preference brings to mind a crisp observation by Walsh (1968) that

In the modern world a third note was to be added to the research–teaching concept of the university, that of public service. The university was to break out of that decorative universe in which claret-coloured dons lolled among the lotuses, occasionally dipping an idle finger into the waters of knowledge, to become a Balliol-minded, Beveridge-inspired citizens' advice bureau.

Predictably, 'activity in politics' and 'counselling on sex matters' were also at the bottom of the list. The relative positions of the two items referring to subject specialization (rank 7 – 'offers one or two subjects in great factual detail' and rank 16 – 'offers a degree with a wide range of subjects in moderate detail') suggests that parents are still in favour of concentrated and highly specialized degrees.

What do parents think of existing arrangements in universities? The second questionnaire containing the identical items to the first gave parents the chance to rate their level of satisfaction using a five-point scale. These were condensed in the final analysis to three reflecting 'satisfaction' (scale points 1 and 2), 'no opinion' (point 3) and 'dissatisfaction' (scale points 4 and 5). Table 52.2 portrays the response distributions. The first 14 attributes listed on the table attracted over 60 per cent of responses showing some degree of satisfac-

Table 52.2   Universities as you really think they are (N = 150)

Attribute	Mean	Expressed as a percentage		
		Satisfied	No opinion	Dis-satisfied
Provides plenty of opportunity to meet members of the opposite sex	1.82	83.4	15.3	1.3
Provides plenty of opportunity for cultural activities (music, drama, etc.)	1.84	84.4	10.0	5.6
Offers a degree with one or two subjects in great factual detail	1.85	80.4	16.7	2.9
Encourages independence from parental influence	1.87	81.3	16.7	2.0
Provides plenty of opportunity for sports and athletics	1.93	84.5	11.5	4.0
Is primarily concerned with preparing students for a career	2.05	79.7	8.7	11.6
Gives students plenty of free time to use as they (the students) see fit	2.08	81.1	8.8	10.1
Gives opportunities for improving students' skill at dealing with people	2.12	72.3	21.0	6.7
Provides a counselling service for students with academic problems	2.15	72.2	18.6	9.2
Has distinguished scholars on the staff who are well known for their research	2.21	60.0	40.0	0.0
Encourages tolerance of other people's opinions	2.22	71.6	15.5	12.9
Makes the students work hard at their studies	2.30	67.6	14.2	18.2
Encourages the student to be active in politics	2.33	54.2	39.6	6.2
Should enable students to secure a 'top' job after graduation	2.34	62.0	26.0	12.0
Provides a counselling service to help students in their choice of career	2.37	60.6	22.7	16.7
Encourages student membership on Committees dealing with the curriculum and examinations	2.50	50.9	35.5	13.6
Is concerned about learning for its own sake without regard for its practical application	2.54	52.7	33.8	13.5
Offers a degree with a wide range of subjects in moderate detail	2.59	42.9	46.2	10.9
Offers a counselling service for students on sexual matters	2.61	29.7	67.0	3.3
Discourages sexual freedom between unmarried students	2.89	28.1	48.3	23.6

tion (the first column). The highest levels of satisfaction related to sport and cultural activities (items ranking 1, 2 and 5), the existence of a specialized degree (rank 3) and a recognition that students were being encouraged to become independent of parental influence (rank 4). At the other extreme, 24 per cent were not satisfied that universities were discouraging sexual freedom between unmarried students, although it will be noticed that 48 per cent held no opinion. The 'no opinion' category could well represent ignorance on the part of parents as to what goes on. The last three items in rank order of satisfaction have also the highest 'no opinion' response rate. Consequently, it would be unwise to read much significance into the position of these items at the end of the rank.

Finally, the highest values of response rates in the column headed 'dissatisfied' show some interesting tendencies particularly in relation to the results from table 52.1. In the latter, the attributes of providing a career counselling service, encouraging tolerance and making students work hard come right at the top of the list. However, they also attract high levels of dissatisfaction (ringed in column 4). In other words, parents are least satisfied that universities are catering for their highest priorities.

From this gross fragment of information one thing is clear; parents emerge with definite opinions about the functions of a university. Biographical details relating to parental occupation and education, still to be explored, may reveal some specific differences. But the overall picture confirms the parents as down-to-earth investors concerned about the occupational prospects and personal development of their sons and daughters.

ACKNOWLEDGEMENT

This paper first appeared in *Univ. Qu.* (1971), **25,** 484–490, and is published here with the kind permission of the editor and authors.

REFERENCES

Child, D. (1970) Some reference groups of university students. *Educ. Res.*, **12,** 145–149.
Malleson, N. (1959) University student 1953, II. Schooling. *Univ. Qu.*, **14,** 42–56.
Musgrove, F. (1967) University freshmen and their parents' attitudes. *Educ. Res.*, **10,** 78–80.
Trow, M. (1960) The campus viewed as a culture. In Sprague, H. T. (Ed.), *Research on College Students*. Univ. California.
Walsh, W. (1968) *Fight for Education: a black paper*. Dialogue and the Idea, p. 68.

PART 16

Psychological research and education

INTRODUCTION

Some of the content in this section could be read alongside the papers in Part 1. The purpose of choosing these three papers is to highlight the criticisms levelled at the methods and findings of psychology applied to education and to make suggestions for an improvement. Medawar's well-known swipe at 'scientific method' is interesting reading. It jolts the mind out of so many acts of faith we may hold about the sanctity of scientific method. The number of writers taking this line has increased markedly in the past few years, so much so that we shall have to guard against losing the baby of systematic observation and analysis with the bath water of antiscience.

Ausubel rightly questions the relevance of laboratory findings in psychology to the practical problems in classrooms. His plea is for more 'chalk-face' research. There are in existence and on the horizon a number of alternative frames of reference. Until these newer methodologies have taken root and begin to bear fruit, we shall have to continue to get what nourishment we can from the findings of established methods.

The paper by Parlett presents one of these newer methods (or rather an old one revived and extended). Illuminative evaluation attempts to meet several obligations. One is that the method should account for the situations (in classrooms in this case) as they actually exist (no control groups); second, reality-based research must be conducted in all its multivariate 'glory' with allowance for irregularities; third, the research should lead to results which are useful and interesting. The paper goes on to show how these are met in the practice of illuminative evaluation.

53   Is the scientific paper a fraud?

P. B. MEDAWAR

I have chosen for my title a question: is the scientific paper a fraud?[*] I ought to explain that a scientific 'paper' is a printed communication to a learned journal, and scientists make their work known almost wholly through papers and not through books, so papers are very important in scientific communication. As to what I mean by asking 'is the scientific paper a fraud?' – I don't of course mean 'does the scientific paper misrepresent facts', and I don't mean that the interpretations you find in a scientific paper are wrong or deliberately mistaken. I mean the scientific paper may be a fraud because it misrepresents the processes of thought that accompanied or gave rise to the work that is described in the paper. That is the question, and I'll say right away that my answer to it is 'yes'. The scientific paper in its orthodox form *does* embody a totally mistaken conception, even a travesty, of the nature of scientific thought.

THE TRADITIONAL FORM

Just consider for a moment that traditional form of a scientific paper (incidentally, it's a form which editors themselves often insist upon). The structure of a scientific paper in the biological sciences is something like this. First, there's a section called the 'introduction' in which you merely describe the general field in which your scientific talents are going to be exercised, followed by a section called 'previous work' in which you concede, more or less graciously, that others have dimly groped towards the fundamental truths that you are now about to expound. Then a section on 'methods' – that's O.K. Then comes the section called 'results'. The section called 'results' consists of a stream of factual information in which it's considered extremely bad form to discuss the significance of the results you're getting. You have to pretend that your mind is, so to speak, a virgin receptacle, an empty vessel, for information which floods into it from the external world for no reason which you yourself have revealed. You reserve all appraisal of the scientific evidence until the 'discussion' section, and in the discussion you adopt the ludicrous pretence of asking yourself if the information

[*] Dr Medawar's article is a revised version of a broadcast talk delivered unscripted; the broadcast form and style have been preserved.

you've collected actually means anything; of asking yourself if any general truths are going to emerge from the contemplation of all the evidence you brandished in the section called 'results'.

Of course, what I'm saying is rather an exaggeration, but there's more than a mere element of truth in it. The conception underlying this style of scientific writing is that scientific discovery is an *inductive* process. What induction implies in its cruder form is roughly speaking this: scientific discovery, or the formulation of scientific theory, starts with the unvarnished and unembroidered evidence of the senses. It starts with simple observation – simple, unbiased, unprejudiced, naive, or innocent observation – and out of this sensory evidence, embodied in the form of simple propositions or declarations of fact, generalizations will grow up and take shape, almost as if some process of crystallization or condensation were taking place. Out of a disorderly array of facts, an orderly theory, an orderly general statement, will somehow emerge. This conception of scientific discovery in which the initiative comes from the unembroidered evidence of the senses was mainly the work of a great and wise, but in this context, I think, very mistaken man – John Stuart Mill.

John Stuart Mill saw, as of course a great many others had seen before him, including Bacon, that deduction in itself is quite powerless as a method of scientific discovery – and for this simple reason: that the process of deduction as such only uncovers, brings out into the open, makes explicit, information that is already present in the axioms or premises from which the process of deduction started. The process of deduction reveals nothing to us except what the infirmity of our own minds has so far concealed. It was Mill's belief that induction was the method of science – 'that great mental operation', he called it, 'the operation of discovering and proving general propositions'. And round this conception there grew up an inductive logic, of which the business was 'to provide rules to which, if inductive arguments conform, those arguments are conclusive'. Now, John Stuart Mill's deeper motive in working out what he conceived to be the essential method of science was to apply that method to the solution of sociological problems: he wanted to apply to sociology the methods which the practice of science had shown to be immensely powerful and exact.

MASS OBSERVATION

It is ironical that the application to sociology of the inductive method, more or less in the form in which Mill himself conceived it, should have been an almost entirely fruitless one. The simplest application of the Millsian process of induction to sociology came in a rather strange movement (which for all I know is still in progress) called Mass Observation. The belief underlying Mass Observation was apparently this: that if one could only record and set down the actual raw facts about what people do and what people say in pubs, in trains, when they make love to each other, when they're playing games, and so on, then somehow, from this wealth of information, a great generalization would inevitably emerge. Well, in point of fact, nothing emerged from this approach, unless somebody's been holding out on me. I believe the pioneers of Mass Observation were ornithologists. Certainly they were man-watching – were applying to sociology the very methods which had done so much to bring ornithology into disrepute.

The theory underlying the inductive method cannot be sustained. Let me give three good reasons why not. In the first place, the starting point of induction, naive observation, innocent observation, is a mere philosophic fiction. There is no such thing as unprejudiced observation. Every act of observation we make is biased. What we see or otherwise sense is a function of what we have seen or sensed in the past.

TWO NOTIONS CONFUSED BY J. S. MILL

The second point is this: scientific discovery or the formulation of a scientific idea on the one hand, and demonstration or proof on the other hand, are two entirely different notions, and Mill confused them. Mill said that induction was the 'operation of discovering and proving general propositions', as if one act of mind would do for both. Now discovery and proof *could* depend on the same act of mind, and in deduction they do. When we indulge in the process of deduction – as in deducing a theorem from Euclidian axioms or postulates – the theorem contains the discovery (or, more exactly, the uncovery of something which was there in the axioms and postulates, though it wasn't actually evident) and the process of deduction itself, if it has been carried out correctly, is also the proof that the 'discovery' is valid, is logically correct. So in the process of deduction, discovery and proof can depend on the same process. But in scientific activity they are not the same thing – they are, in fact, totally separate acts of mind.

But the most fundamental objection is this. It simply is not logically possible to arrive *with certainty* at any generalization containing more information than the sum of the particular statements upon which that generalization was founded, out of which it was woven. How could a mere act of mind lead to the discovery of new information? It would violate a law as fundamental as the law of conservation of matter: it would violate the law of conservation of information.

In view of all these objections, it is hardly surprising that Bertrand Russell in a famous footnote that occurs in his *Principles of Mathematics* of 1903 should have said that, so far as he could see, induction was a mere method of making plausible guesses. And our greatest modern authority on the nature of scientific method, Professor Karl Popper, has no use for induction at all: he regards the inductive process of thought as a myth. 'There is no need to mention induction', he says in his great treatise on *The Logic of Scientific Discovery* – though of course he does.

Now let me go back to scientific papers. What's wrong with the traditional form of scientific paper is simply this: that all scientific work of an experimental or exploratory character starts with some expectation about the outcome of the inquiry. This expectation one starts with, this hypothesis one formulates, provides the initiative and incentive for the inquiry and governs its actual form. It's in the light of this expectation that some observations are held relevant and others not; that some methods are chosen, others discarded; that some experiments are done rather than others. It's only in the light of this prior expectation that the activities the scientist reports in his scientific papers really have any meaning at all.

Hypotheses arise by guesswork. That's to put it in its crudest form. I should say rather that they arise by inspiration; but in any event they arise by processes that form part of the subject matter of psychology and certainly not of logic, for there is no logically rigorous method for devising hypotheses. It is a vulgar error, often committed, to speak of 'deducing' hypotheses. Indeed one does not deduce hypotheses: hypotheses are what one deduces things from. So the actual formulation of a hypothesis is – let's say a guess; is inspirational in character. But hypotheses can be *tested* rigorously – they are tested by experiment, using the word 'experiment' in a rather general sense to mean an act performed to test the deductive consequences of a hypothesis. If one formulates a hypothesis, one can deduce from it certain consequences which are predictions or declarations about what will, or will not, be the case. If these predictions and declarations are mistaken, then the hypothesis must be discarded, or at least modified. If, on the other hand, the predictions turn out correct, then the hypothesis has stood up to trial, and remains on probation as before. This formulation illustrates very well, I think, the distinction between on the one hand the discovery or formulation of a scientific idea or generalization, which is to a greater or lesser degree an imaginative or inspirational act, and on the other hand the proof, or rather the testing of a hypothesis, which is indeed a strictly logical and rigorous process, depending upon deductive arguments.

This alternative interpretation of the nature of the scientific process, of the nature of scientific method, is sometimes called the 'hypothetico-deductive' interpretation, and this is the view which Professor Karl Popper in the *Logic of Scientific Discovery* has persuaded us is the correct one. To give credit where credit is surely due, it is proper to say that the first professional scientist to express a fully reasoned opinion upon the way scientists actually think when they come upon their scientific discoveries – namely William Whewell, a geologist and, incidentally, the Master of Trinity College, Cambridge – was also the first person to formulate a hypothetico-deductive interpretation of scientific activity. Whewell, like his contemporary Mill, wrote at great length – unnecessarily great length, one is nowadays inclined to think – and I cannot recapitulate his argument, but one or two quotations will make the gist of his thought clear. He said: 'An art of discovery is not possible. We can give no rules for the pursuit of truth which should be universally and peremptorily applicable'. And of hypotheses, he said, with great daring – why it was daring I'll explain in just a second – 'a facility in devising hypotheses, so far from being a fault in the intellectual character of a discoverer, is a faculty indispensable to his task'. I said this was daring because the word 'hypothesis' and the conception it stood for was still in Whewell's day a rather discreditable one. Hypotheses had a flavour about them of the wanton and irresponsible. The great Newton, you remember, had frowned upon hypotheses. *'Hypotheses non fingo'*, he said, and there is another version in which he says *'hypotheses non sequor'* – I don't pursue hypotheses.

So to go back once again to the scientific paper: the scientific paper is a fraud in the sense that it does give a totally misleading narrative of the processes of thought that go into the making of scientific discoveries. The inductive format of the scientific paper should be discarded. The discussion which in the traditional scientific paper goes last should surely come at the beginning. The scientific facts and scientific acts should follow the discussion, and scientists should not be ashamed to admit, as many of them apparently *are* ashamed to admit, that hypotheses appear in their minds along uncharted by-ways of thought; that they are imaginative and inspirational in character; that they are indeed adventures of the mind. What after all is the good of scientists reproaching others for their neglect of, or indifference to, the scientific style of thinking they set such great store by, if their own writings show that they themselves have no clear understanding of it?

Anyhow, I am practising what I preach. What I've said about the nature of scientific discovery you can regard as being itself a hypothesis, and the hypothesis comes where I think it should be, namely, it comes at the beginning of the series. Later speakers will provide the facts which will enable you to test and appraise this hypothesis, and I think you'll find — I hope you'll find — that the evidence they will produce about the nature of scientific discovery will bear me out. *(Third Programme: This is the first of a series of broadcasts by different speakers to be given under the heading 'Experiment'.)*

ACKNOWLEDGEMENT

This broadcast was first published in *The Listener* (1963), **70,** 377–378, and is reproduced here with the kind permission of the editor and author.

54   The nature of educational research

DAVID P. AUSUBEL

The author points out that educational research, as a field in its own right, is immature and characterized by dilemmas which confusedly oscillate between 'basic science' research, 'extrapolated' research, and 'applied' research. Drawing on his training and experience in medical research, he points towards a possible development of research methodology in pedagogy which may give education status as a scientific discipline.

Few persons would take issue with the proposition that education is an applied or engineering science. It is an applied* science because it is concerned with the realization of certain practical ends which have social value. The precise nature of these ends is highly controversial, in terms of both substance and relative emphasis. To some individuals the function of education is to transmit the ideology of the culture and a core body of knowledge and intellectual skills. To others, education is primarily concerned with the optimal development of potentiality for growth and achievement — not only with respect to cognitive abilities, but also with respect to personality organization and adjustment. Disagreement with respect to ends, however, neither removes education from the category of science nor makes it any less of an applied branch of knowledge. It might be mentioned in passing that automobile engineers are also not entirely agreed as to the characteristics of the 'ideal' car; and physicians disagree violently in formulating a definition of health.

Regardless of the ends it chooses to adopt, an applied discipline only becomes a science when it seeks to ground proposed means to ends on empirically validatable propositions. The operations involved in such an undertaking are commonly subsumed under the term 'research'. The question under discussion relates to the nature of search in applied science, or, more specifically, in education. Is educational research a field in its own right with

---

* The term 'applied' is used here to distinguish between sciences which are oriented toward practical ends as opposed to 'basic' sciences which do not serve this function. *Applied* does not imply that the content of the practical disciplines consists of applications from the 'basic' disciplines. The problems rather than the knowledge of applied sciences are 'applied'.

theoretical problems and a methodology of its own, or does it merely involve the operation of applying knowledge from 'pure' scientific disciplines to practical problems of pedagogy?

RESISTANCE TO EDUCATIONAL RESEARCH

It should be noted at the outset that there is both little general acceptance of the need for educational research and little appreciation of the relevance of such research for the improvement of education. A tradition of research does not exist in education as it does, for example, in medicine or in engineering, where both professionals and consumers commonly agree that research and progress are almost synonymous. This much is clearly evident from the marked resistance which educational researchers encounter from school boards, school administrators, teachers and parents.

Generally speaking, educational research institutions and public school systems have not succeeded in working out orderly and systematic procedural machinery providing for long-term research programs in the schools. In most cases, each individual researcher is obligated to conduct his own separate negotiations with school authorities every time he wishes to work on a problem; and more often than not he meets with indifference or outright resistance. He has learned that it is more effective to carry on research activities through personal 'contacts' in the schools than to obtain the necessary permission through official channels. This chaotic situation is in marked contrast to the well established working agreements which all medical schools have with hospitals relative to the conducting of clinical research.

In addition to, or perhaps reflective of the lack of, perceived relevance of educational research to educational progress are other frequently encountered resistances to the performance of research in the public schools. It is alleged, for example, that research utilizes time urgently needed for subject matter or other purposes, that children are 'exploited' by being cast in the role of 'guinea pigs', and that irreparable psychological or educational damage is inflicted on some children to further 'experiments' of questionable value. Furthermore, some educators demand to know how such research is going to help them solve their immediate problems.

Satisfactory answers to such questions can easily be given once the importance of educational research itself is accepted. It can be pointed out that research projects are not so demanding of pupil or teacher time that they interfere with the curricular program of the school; that the school spends time on many things of less intrinsic value; that the ethical standards of educational researchers are generally high enough to preclude harmful or dangerous experimentation; that many research programs are educational in themselves and can be made enjoyable to children. Finally it can be shown that the criterion of *immediate* value and utility is unreasonable and is not applied in other engineering sciences.

NON-RESEARCH APPROACHES TO THE IMPROVEMENT OF PEDAGOGY

If so much resistance to educational research exists, how do educators and others commonly propose to further pedagogical methodology? A time-honored method employed by many 'successful' teachers is to examine their own practices, to abstract what seems to them the basis for their success, and to advocate that these practices be universally emulated. The weaknesses of this approach are obvious. The claimed success of these teachers is rarely verified by objective means, the factors to which success is attributed are merely subjective impressions which have not been objectively identified or measured, and no control data are available as a basis for comparison. Often such teachers are successful for entirely different reasons than those of alleged superior methodology. Some have good teaching personalities, others have unusually good students, and still others teach under atypically favorable conditions. To remedy these shortcomings, some teachers have conducted crude classroom experiments. But since the vast majority of these experiments fail to control relevant variables (i.e., significant characteristics of the experimental population, of the proposed method, of the teacher, of the school environment), do not utilize reliable measuring instruments, and do not subject results to tests of statistical significance, they contribute little to the science of pedagogy.

Another less rational approach merely relies on the authority of presumed expert opinion. Some educators are convinced that after 25 years of experience in the profession they are entitled to make dogmatic pronouncements on pedagogic method which require no rationalization whatsoever and are valid by fiat alone, i.e., because of the wisdom which extended experience or high status in an administrative or university hierarchy presumably confers.

A third approach places greater weight on logic than on experience. Method A is inferred to be superior to Method B because it is more compatible (a) with certain theoretical considerations that have logical or face validity or (b) with indirectly related empirical findings. Such thinking is obviously necessary as a preliminary step in the formulation of hypotheses to be tested, and is probably the only approach possible in deciding upon the ends that education should pursue. Clearly, however, it cannot constitute an adequate approach in itself with respect to providing a scientific basis for the means employed toward such ends.

EMPIRICAL (RESEARCH) APPROACHES TO PEDAGOGIC METHODOLOGY

Three different kinds of research orientations have been adopted by those who are concerned with scientific progress in applied disciplines such as education: (a) basic science research,* (b) extrapolated research in the basic sciences, and (c) research at an applied level.

The 'basic science' research approach is predicated on the very defensible notion that applied sciences are ultimately related to knowledge in the underlying sciences on which they are based. It can be convincingly demonstrated, for example, that progress in clinical medicine is intimately related to progress in biochemistry and bacteriology; that progress in engineering is intimately related to progress in physics and chemistry; and that progress in education is similarly dependent upon advances in psychology, statistics, sociology and philosophy. However, two important kinds of qualifications have to be placed on the value of basic science research for the applied sciences: qualifications of purpose or orientation, and qualifications of level of applicability.

---

*The term 'basic' refers to the distinction between 'basic' and applied sciences made earlier. It does not mean 'fundamental'. In the latter sense applied research is just as 'basic' as research in the pure sciences.

By definition, basic science research is concerned with the discovery of general laws of physical, biological, psychological and sociological phenomenology as an end in itself. Researchers in these fields have no objection, of course, if their findings are applied to practical problems which have social value; in fact there is reason to believe that they are motivated to some extent by this consideration. But the design of basic science research bears no *intended* relation whatsoever to problems in the applied disciplines, the aim being solely to advance knowledge. Ultimately, of course, such knowledge is applicable in a very broad sense to practical problems; but since the research design is not oriented to the solution of these problems, this applicability is apt to be quite indirect and unsystematic, and relevant only over a time period which is too long to be meaningful in terms of the short-range needs of the applied disciplines.

The second qualification has to do with the level at which findings in the basic sciences can be applied once their relevancy has been established. It should be self-evident that such findings enjoy a much higher level of generality than the problems to which they can be applied. At the applied level, specific ends and conditions are added which demand additional research to make manifest the precise way in which the general law operates in the specific case. That is, the applicability of general principles to specific problems is *not given* in the statement of the general principle, but must be specifically worked out for each individual problem. Knowledge about nuclear fission for example does not tell us how to make an atomic bomb or an atomic-powered airplane.

In fields such as education the problem of generality is further complicated by the fact that the practical problems often exist at higher levels of complexity with respect to the order of phenomenology involved than the basic science findings requiring application. That is, new variables are added which may qualitatively alter the general principles from the basic science to such an extent that at the applied level they only have substrate validity but no explanatory or predictive value. For example, antibiotic reactions that take place in test tubes do not necessarily take place in living systems, methods of learning employed by animals in mazes do not necessarily correspond to methods of learning children use in grappling with verbal materials in classrooms.

The basic science approach in educational research, therefore, is subject to many serious disadvantages. Its relevancy is too remote and indirect because it is not oriented toward solving educational problems, and its findings, if relevant, are applicable only if much additional research is performed to translate general principles into the more specific form they have to assume in the task-specialized and more complex contexts of pedagogy.

These limitations would not be so serious if they were perceived. If the limitations of this approach were perceived, it would be defensible for educational institutions to set aside a *small* portion of their research funds for basic science research as a long-term investment. But since these limitations are *not* perceived, some bureaus of educational research confidently invest their major resources in such programs, and then complacently expect that the research findings which emerge will be both relevant and applicable in their original form to the problems of education.

Naivete with respect to the second premise, i.e., of immediate applicability, is especially rampant and has led to very serious distortions in our knowledge of the psychology of learning that is relevant for pedagogy. The psychology of learning that teachers study is based on findings in general psychology which have been borrowed wholesale without much attempt to test their applicability to the kinds of learning situations that exist in classrooms. It would be a shocking situation indeed if a comparable procedure were practised in medicine, i.e., if physicians employed therapeutic techniques validated only *in vitro* or by animal experimentation.

The second general research approach in the applied disciplines is 'extrapolated basic science research'. Unlike pure basic science research it is oriented toward the solution of practical or applied problems. It starts out by identifying significant problems in the applied field, and designs experiments pointed toward their solution on an analogous but highly simplified basic science level. In this way it satisfies the important criterion of relevance, but must still contend with the problem of level of applicability. The rationale of this approach is that many practical problems are so complex that before one can develop fruitful hypotheses leading to their solution they must first be reduced to simpler terms and patterned after simpler models. Thus simplified, problems of control and measurement are rendered more manageable.

Depending on the nature of the problem under investigation, this approach may have genuine merit providing that the resulting research findings are only regarded as 'leads' or hypotheses to be tested in the applied situation rather than as definitive answers *per se* to problems in pedagogy. As already noted, however, educational researchers have a tendency to extrapolate basic science findings to pedagogical problems without conducting the additional research necessary to bridge the gap between the two levels of generality involved. Also, when it is necessary to cross levels of phenomenological complexity in extrapolating, this approach has very limited usefulness for the reasons already given above.

The third approach to educational research, research at the applied level, is the most relevant and direct of the three, yet paradoxically is utilized least by professional research workers in the field. When research is performed in relation to the actual problems of education, at the level of complexity in which they exist, that is, *in situ* (under the conditions in which they are to be found in practice), the problems of relevance and extrapolation do not arise.* Most rigorous research in applied disciplines other than education is conducted at this level. The research program of a hospital or medical school would be regarded as seriously unbalanced if most of its funds and efforts went into biochemical or bacteriological research instead of into clinical research. The major responsibility for furthering research in the former areas belongs to graduate departments of chemistry and bacteriology. On the other hand, unless medical schools undertake to solve their own clinical problems who else will? And the same analogy obviously holds for education as well.

Although applied research presents greater difficulties with respect to research design, control and measurements, the rewards are correspondingly greater when these problems are solved. Certainly such problems cannot be solved when they are avoided. If other applied disciplines have been able to evolve satisfactory research methodologies, there is no reason why education cannot also do so. In fact, if any applied discipline with unique and distinctive problems of its own is to survive as a science it has no choice in the matter – it is obliged to do so.

---

* Applied research is also directed toward the discovery of general laws within the framework of its applied ends. The generalizations it discovers, therefore, exist at a different plane of generality than those of 'basic' science research.

DIFFERENTIATION BETWEEN PSYCHOLOGICAL AND EDUCATIONAL RESEARCH PROBLEMS

Since both psychology and education deal with the problem of learning, how can we distinguish between the special research interests of each discipline in this area? As an applied science, education is not concerned with the general laws of learning *per se*, but only with those properties of learning that can be related to efficacious ways of deliberately effecting stable changes in individuals which have social value. Education, therefore, refers to guided or manipulated learning deliberately directed toward specific practical ends. These ends may be defined as the long-term acquisition of a stable body of knowledge (ideas, concepts, facts), values, habits, skills, ways of perceiving, adjusting and aspiring, and of the capacities needed for acquiring them.

The psychologist's interest in learning, on the other hand, is much more general. Many other aspects of learning apart from the efficient achievement of designated competencies and capacities for growth in a directed context concern him. More typically, he investigates the nature of current, fragmentary or short-term learning experiences rather than the kinds of long-term learning involved in assimilating extensive and organized bodies of knowledge, values, habits and skills.

The following kinds of learning problems, therefore, are particularly indigenous to educational research: (a) discovery of the nature of those aspects of the learning process affecting the long-range stability and meaningfulness of organized bodies of knowledge, skills, etc. in the learner; (b) long-range modification (improvement) of learning capacities; (c) discovery of those personality and cognitive aspects of the learner and of the interpersonal and social aspects of the learning environment that affect motivation for learning and characteristic ways of assimilating material; and (d) discovery of appropriate and maximally efficient practices and ways of organizing and presenting learning materials, of deliberately motivating and directing learning toward specified goals.

CONCLUSION

The failure of education to acquire status as an applied scientific discipline can be largely ascribed to two contrasting approaches to the discovery of pedagogical knowledge. One approach has relied on empirically untested theoretical propositions, on dogmatic assertion, or on the unwarranted generalization of subjective impressions from personal teaching experience. The other approach, going to the opposite extreme, has avoided coming to grips with the fundamental research problem of education as an applied science, i.e., the discovery of how pupils assimilate and grow in ability to assimilate symbolical materials in a social and interpersonal environment, and what the optimal conditions for these processes are. Instead it has become preoccupied with basic science research, failing to recognize important limitations of this approach with respect to relevancy and level of generality and complexity, and uncritically extrapolating findings from one level to another without performing the intervening research operations that are necessary.

If the profession of education is open to attack, it is vulnerable on the grounds of failing to make the progress it could reasonably have been expected to make in providing a scientific basis for pedagogy. It is vulnerable because of its complacency, its resistiveness to applied educational research, its tendency to spend more time and effort on dogmatically disseminating unvalidated hypotheses than on endeavoring to secure validation through painstaking research activity. Unfortunately, criticism of professional education is not directed along these lines, but is usually based on the fallacious notions that a science of pedagogy is unnecessary for teaching, that children are not learning as much as they used to, and that the only proper aim of education is the acquisition of factual knowledge and of intellectual skills.

The best defence that education could make to these latter baseless charges is to admit that a science of pedagogy does not yet exist, and to direct its attention toward formulating a research methodology in pedagogy at the applied level of operations at which it functions.

ACKNOWLEDGEMENT

This paper first appeared in *Educ. Theory* (1953), **3,** 314–320, and is published here with the kind permission of the editor and author.

55 The new evaluation

MALCOLM PARLETT

THE CRITERIA TO BE MET?

Evaluation is on the move. Not only is there a steady expansion in the amount going on, but as a field of education research it is coming under increased critical scrutiny. The level of interest and discussion is high. Curriculum evaluators have met; committees have been formed and funds set aside. Arguments centre in what evaluation aims to do and how best to go about doing it. What has precipitated this rapid spate of activity?

There seem at least three major factors. First, there is the official enthusiasm, both at government and at other levels, for increased accountability and attention to cost-effectiveness. Second, there is an abundance of innovations and alternative curricular schemes in circulation. Increasingly it is troublesome to choose between them: it is like choosing a new refrigerator before the days of *Which?* Both factors encourage and promote evaluation: how do you 'measure benefits' to weigh against the costs? How can you decide on a 'best buy'? The third, and major reason for the new initiatives and questioning stems from a worrying realization about evaluation studies in the past: namely, that they have often been hopelessly inadequate as aids to practical decision-making of any sort. In other words, a situation exists in which there is both demand for the services of evaluators, and scepticism about what they have done in the past.

THE CHURCHILL COLLEGE CONFERENCE

This is precisely the climate in which new ideas can germinate and grow rapidly. And this is what is happening. One of the most significant recent developments was a Nuffield-supported conference at Churchill College, Cambridge, in December 1972 at which a small group of 'non-traditional' evaluators, from Britain, the USA and Sweden, sat down and pooled their experiences. Each was sharply critical of traditional, orthodox evaluation. Each had tried to develop radical alternatives. But before the Churchill meeting, each had worked in isolation. It had been a case, we discovered, of multiple simultaneous discovery.

The conference (organized jointly by Barry MacDonald – evaluator of the Schools Council Humanities Curriculum Project – and by the author) concentrated both on new developments in research method and theory, and also on how evaluation relates to educational policy. 'Decision-makers' were there in force: representatives from the Centre for Research and Innovation in Education of OECD, from the DES, and from the Nuffield Foundation took an active part. They addressed the problems of evaluation as seen from their perspectives, and intervened whenever the evaluators' constructions began to look too well-oiled and smooth-running.

What characterized the Churchill discussions? What is 'non-traditional' evaluation? What was wrong with 'traditional'? And what sort of evaluation is, in fact, useful for educational decisions, varied and complicated and politically sensitive as so often they are? There were many differences in detail and a lot of constructive argument at the conference. But there was a strong agreement about the basic issues.

THE NEED FOR CHANGE

First, we agreed that conventional styles need to be radically changed: that the predominant evaluation model is inappropriate. It has centred on the idea of 'testing educational effects under controlled conditions': a laudable ambition perhaps, but one that is probably impossible ever to achieve technically, given the nature of educational practice. So many random, unpredicted and human factors intervene that neat experimental designs cannot contain them all. For this reason, results from such studies rarely carry conviction: they present an emaciated and artificial picture of real-world educational life. The results are usually numerical in form, difficult to mesh with the 'qualitative' view of the world held by most of us. Moreover, differences are often negligible or hedged about with statistical qualifications. To interpret such findings sensibly often means going beyond the formally reported data – using the very type of information that was excluded from the design (because it 'could not be tested scientifically' or because it 'cropped up too late for inclusion in the study').

This basic, experimental model I have referred to elsewhere as the 'agricultural-botany paradigm': appropriate for testing fertilizers on carefully tended fields of crops at agricultural research stations, but inapplicable and incongruous for monitoring how innovations become absorbed and adapted in a diversity of school settings, by teachers with different perspectives, teaching separate and distinctive groups of children.

Second, we found ourselves in substantial agreement about what an alternative model or paradigm should look like. The first obligation upon it was that it should be applicable to situations as they actually exist; and that no artificial arrangements (such as 'balanced control groups') should have to be incorporated. The second obligation was that it should be reality-based: that it should do justice to the complex and to the atypical, review the curriculum or innovation not in isolation but as it interacts with its context, and study unexpected and unintended consequences as well as those that were planned. The third, and most severe obligation, was that the new model or paradigm should lead to studies that are useful and interesting – what's the good of research reports that are never read?

The view of evaluation we settled on, therefore, had certain characteristics. It should set out not to 'test' so much as to 'understand and document' an innovation – examining its background, its organization, its practices and its problems, in addition to its outcomes. It should constitute a thoroughgoing and detailed exploration of the innovation-in-action. It should provide, for all concerned with the curriculum or programme, as well as for outsiders, an informed and accurate description of the operation of the scheme, summaries of the various points of view expressed by those associated with it, and a detailed historical-type account of the development of the innovation over time – its teething troubles, success stories and the improvements devised.

Studies along these lines, we considered, were likely to provide a far more effective and realistic means of helping decision-makers than did evaluation of the old type. They could assist, for instance, in deciding whether a particular innovation is what they want; whether it has done what it set out to do and what aspects of it could be improved, curtailed, modified or reassessed.

'ILLUMINATIVE' EVALUATION

What exactly is entailed in such a type of study? Perhaps this can best be portrayed by referring in greater detail to one of the particular approaches discussed at the Churchill meeting: 'illuminative' evaluation. To quote from a paper describing the mode,[*] the aims of illuminative evaluation are to study an innovatory programme: how it operates; how it is influenced by the various school situations in which it is applied; what those directly concerned regard as its advantages and disadvantages; and how students' intellectual tasks and academic experience are most affected. It aims to discover and document what it is like to be participating in the scheme, whether as teacher or pupil, and, in addition, to discern and discuss the innovation's most significant features, recurring concomitants and critical processes. Generally speaking, there are five different phrases of an illuminative evaluation study:

Stage 1: setting up the evaluation   Illuminative evaluation constitutes a general strategy, not a detailed research blueprint. Each study evolves separately, uses a different combination of techniques, and serves different functions. The evaluator has to clarify, at the outset, what type of study is being commissioned, and what type of report is envisaged. He has to ensure that there is no ambiguity in the range, scope, character and status of the study; that those who will be most directly concerned (e.g. head teachers, LEA officials) are properly consulted and informed of the plans; and that the message is got across clearly that the illuminative evaluator is not going to 'inspect' or 'pass judgement on' the scheme, but study it with a view to understanding it as a working system, its processes and its impact. Decisions

---

[*] Parlett, M. R. and D. F. Hamilton. Evaluation as illumination: a new approach to the study of innovatory programs. Occasional Paper 9, Centre for Research in the Educational Services (University of Edinburgh).

are made about the size, duration and overall plan of the study. But there is no detailed pre-specification of 'variables to be included': no closing of research doors before discovering what lies behind them.

Stage 2: open-ended exploration   This phase is usually one of the longest and most significant. The researcher must familiarize himself thoroughly with the day-to-day reality of the scheme in schools. He gets his feet well and truly wet. He spends a lot of time visiting the participating schools, observing what is going on, listening to teachers and pupils, getting to know each school's particular circumstances, and generally behaving somewhat like a social anthropologist on location – though here he is studying not a village community but a group of schools. During this phase the researcher is receptive to a mass of different information: he listens and observes and becomes 'knowledgeable' about the total scheme. He notes, for instance, how teachers use it, how it fits into long-term departmental curriculum plans, what resources and hidden costs are involved, and what activities and intellectual tasks pupils are asked to perform. His inquiries are not confined to the schools themselves: he will also trace the background, rationale and history of the curriculum or innovation, how it was set up, accepted by the LEA and introduced into the schools. He will meet not only teachers and pupils, but advisors, LEA officials and the originators of the scheme. He will want to know how they see the innovation from their respective points of view. In short, he tries to build as comprehensive a picture as possible.

Stage 3: focused inquiries   There is no sharp cut-off between Stages 2 and 3. During Stage 2 the researcher is constantly sifting through his experiences, spotting the similarities and differences between view-points expressed (by participating teachers, say, about the suitability of resource materials provided), noting the issues and problems most frequently raised (e.g. possible time-tabling difficulties arising from adopting the innovation on a greater scale), and observing recurring classroom events and trends (e.g. the evident enthusiasm of pupils for a particular type of instructional material). Stage 3 begins when these phenomena, occurrences, or groups of opinions become topics for more sustained and intensive inquiry. The study takes on a more directed and systematic look. Interviews become more focused, observation in classes more selective. Certain forms of pencil-and-paper inquiry may also be introduced. Questionnaires have many faults (e.g. they are impersonal, expensive and difficult to produce, and most people find them a frustrating and trivializing medium for communicating their views); but on occasion they can be useful – e.g. to provide an independent check on findings from interviews. Useful sometimes, too, are conventional tests of achievement and attitude – but, if used, they occupy no privileged position; they represent merely another source of data.

Stage 4: interpretation   Illuminative evaluation sets out to clarify and interpret: in short, to 'illuminate'. Detailed, accurate and sensitive reporting is an essential component. But extensive description is not enough. The investigator must organize and order his description, adding interpretative and explanatory comment. By Stage 4 of an illuminative evaluation, the researcher is busy organizing and arranging his data, going back to fill in gaps in his knowledge, weighing alternative interpretations, and already structuring his report. To quote from the same paper: 'The transition from stage to stage, as the investigation unfolds, occurs as problem areas become progressively clarified and redefined. The course of the study cannot be charted in advance. Beginning with an extensive data base, the researchers systematically reduce the breadth of their enquiry to give more concentrated attention to the emerging issues. This "progressive focusing" permits unique and unpredicted phenomena to be given new weight. It reduces the problem of data overload, and prevents the accumulation of a mass of unanalysed material.'

Stage 5: reporting the study   The outcome of an evaluation study is usually a report. A weak, dull, over-technical, or sloppily written report can sabotage what has gone before, however skilfully the study was conducted. The illuminative evaluator is conscious, throughout his investigation, of his audience or readership. He will ensure that he provides the information that they want to have at their fingertips, that he addresses the issues that concern them, and that he presents his findings in an appropriate format and style. This sensitivity to the needs of the audience must not undermine his autonomy, of course, nor cause him to censor what he has discovered. A safeguard against doing so is that rarely is there a single constituency or audience: the report is likely to be read and to be used by widely different groups, e.g. by administrators, teachers and the public at large. What is 'uncomfortable' for one group is likely to be a happy vindication for another, and vice versa. It is important to remember, however, that while straight reporting is certainly called for, so is tact and humanity.

First encounters with illuminative evaluation prompt several different types of question. Some refer to the 'lack of objectivity' and the possibility of research bias. These, of course, are hazards in all social research, however numerical and statistical: take, for instance, how statistical findings are selected for public presentation. The illuminative evaluator finds himself in a similar position methodologically to the anthropologist, historian or psychiatrist. There is the same necessity for the careful exercise of intelligent human judgement in handling the complex material and evidence encountered. Like them, he makes no apology for doing so. But counter-checking his findings (against the opinions of others or with data accumulated from other sources) for accuracy and consistency, is a crucial part of his activity. If his readers can spot factual errors, he is unlikely to retain their confidence.

A second question is whether such an intensive style of research is suitable for evaluating large-scale curricula or programmes. It certainly can be so adapted, though a good part of any larger sample research will still compromise close-up study of specific school situations. Appropriate inquiry methods and shorter visits can be used for studies in the remainder of the schools.

Third, there is often concern at the supposed lack of emphasis on finding out about 'educational effects'. This is a mis-reading. In fact, finding out the innovation's effects on pupils necessarily lies at the very centre of an illuminative evaluation of a curriculum scheme. It is important to remember that 'learning' is a highly complicated set of experiences, of which 'assimilating content' is only part. People develop habits of study which may become habits of mind; they acquire 'experience'; they are introduced to 'legitimate' knowledge, to conceptions of 'what is stupid' or 'bright' and what constitutes 'good work'. In short, they respond to a total 'learning milieu'. An innovatory scheme does not exist in abstract. Its adoption entails its being absorbed into a pre-existing milieu or context. The scheme and the milieu interact together: pupils respond to both together. Illuminative evaluation aims to elucidate the interaction, and to demonstrate how pupils' educational experiences – widely conceived – are affected by the total learning milieu. It is for this reason that a major portion of the research effort is directed towards exploring the milieu.

The foregoing constitutes a brief, summary introduction to one particular model discussed at the Churchill conference. Like others proposed there, it is still evolving rapidly. There is no shortage of ideas, research opportunities, or problems to grapple with. Before such models can be widely applied we need more experience and more skilled research workers. But as a new direction for curriculum evaluation the portents are good. Not only is the new evaluation likely to contribute to increased understanding of educational innovations – it can also serve as a signpost towards a more pertinent and intellectually exciting educational research.

ACKNOWLEDGEMENT

This paper first appeared in *Trends Educ.* (1974), **34,** 13–18, and is published here with the kind permission of the editor and author.